GENERALS IN THE MAKING

How Marshall, Eisenhower, Patton, and Their Peers

Became the Commanders Who Won World War II

BENJAMIN RUNKLE

STACKPOLE
BOOKS

Guilford, Connecticut

STACKPOLE BOOKS

Published by Stackpole Books
An imprint of The Rowman & Littlefield Publishing Group, Inc.
4501 Forbes Blvd., Ste. 200
Lanham, MD 20706
www.rowman.com

Distributed by NATIONAL BOOK NETWORK

British Library Cataloguing in Publication Information available

Library of Congress Cataloging-in-Publication Data

Names: Runkle, Benjamin, author.
Title: Generals in the making : how Marshall, Eisenhower, Patton, and their
 peers became the commanders who won World War II / Benjamin Runkle.
Description: Guilford, Connecticut : Stackpole Books, [2019] | Includes
 bibliographical references and index.
Identifiers: LCCN 2019004667 (print) | LCCN 2019005859 (ebook) | ISBN
 9780811768498 (e-book) | ISBN 9780811738507 (hardback : alk. paper)
Subjects: LCSH: Generals—United States—History—20th century. | United
 States—Armed Forces—History—20th century. | World War,
 1939-1945—United States.
Classification: LCC E745 (ebook) | LCC E745 .R86 2019 (print) | DDC
 355.0092/2 [B]—dc23
LC record available at https://lccn.loc.gov/2019004667

♾️™ The paper used in this publication meets the minimum requirements of American National Standard for Information Sciences—Permanence of Paper for Printed Library Materials, ANSI/ NISO Z39.48-1992.

Printed in the United States of America

Contents

Introduction

Homecoming

STANDING TEN STORIES HIGH, STRETCHING THE LENGTH OF THREE FOOT-ball fields, and weighing over 54,000 tons, the German-built SS *Vaterland* was the world's largest passenger ship upon her completion in 1913. The ship had the bad luck to be in New York City when World War I erupted in Europe a year later, and was prevented from returning to its home port of Hamburg by the threat of interdiction by the British navy. Consequently, the *Vaterland* suffered the ignominy of spending the next three years laid up in Hoboken, New Jersey. When the United States entered the war in April 1917, the U.S. Shipping Board seized her for conversion into a troop-ship, and in September 1917 President Woodrow Wilson aptly renamed her USS *Leviathan*. Over the next fourteen months the *Leviathan* transported 119,000 doughboys to France, and when the war ended with the November 11, 1918 armistice she began to reverse the flow of men, making nine western crossings of the Atlantic.

Although she could carry up to 14,000 personnel per trip, on her final voyage one passenger towered above the others as the *Leviathan* approached the Eastern Seaboard. At 0700 on September 8, 1919, Gen. John J. Pershing was awakened by a cacophony of whistles and sirens emanating from the motley flotilla of boats streaming out from New York harbor to welcome home the conquering hero who had led the two million soldiers of the American Expeditionary Force (AEF) to victory in "the war to end all wars." From the *Leviathan*'s deck, Pershing, his ten-year-old son Warren, and his staff officers watched in amazement at the mass of ships and people. An honor guard of tugboats circled the great ship, escorting the *Leviathan* toward Hoboken, tooting their horns, and wildly spraying jets of water into the air. At 0800 a U.S. Navy destroyer maneuvered alongside, bearing Secretary of War Newton Baker, Army Chief of Staff Gen. Peyton March, chairman of the Senate Military Affairs Committee James Wadsworth, amongst other congressmen and former AEF staff officers. Another vessel carried the mayor of New York City, Pershing's two sisters, his nephew, and the families of his officers. As the *Leviathan* sailed past Ambrose Light, planes flew overhead, guns fired, and sirens screamed the news of Pershing's arrival to the awaiting city. Pershing was "frankly overwhelmed" at the size and the enthusiasm of the welcome, and modestly replied that the raucous reception was not for him alone, but "for all those Americans whom I had the honor to command."[1] When the ship docked, floods of newsmen and photographers crowded aboard and "some hundred" pictures were taken. In the pictures, the tall, broad, and deep-chested general with white hair and "steely eyes" is beaming and gesticulating at the pandemonium around him.[2]

Garnering little attention that day was the reserved colonel with deep-set blue eyes and sandy hair standing behind Pershing. The officer had only become an aide to the general a few months earlier, and had not served in the trenches nor performed any conspicuous acts of bravery under fire to attract the attention of military correspondents eager to promote heroes to the American public. Yet it would be hard to disagree with the assertion that Pershing's quiet aide was, in fact, the most important officer standing on Pier 4 in Hoboken that day. For in twenty years George Catlett Marshall would be asked to recruit, train, and deploy an army more than twice as large as the force Pershing had just commanded against enemies that had already conquered most of Europe and East Asia. President Harry S. Truman would say of Marshall's role as U.S. Army chief of staff during World War II: "Millions of Americans gave their country outstanding service.... George C. Marshall gave it victory," and British prime minister Winston Churchill would describe Marshall as "the Organizer of Victory."

Marshall's achievement is all the more impressive given the travails the Army and its officers would endure over the next two decades. Indeed, that sunny September morning and the celebrations in the days that followed represented something of a high-water mark for the U.S. Army. Although Pershing and the AEF's veterans were held in high esteem and feted upon their return from France in 1919, the traditional American distrust of foreign entanglements and large military establishments would quickly reassert themselves. In the ten months since the Armistice, the Army had already discharged some 3.28 million officers and men from duty. This exodus included talented younger officers who had served with temporary officers during the war possessing good connections in civilian life and offering salaries that dwarfed the Army's miserly compensations. For those officers able to resist such temptations, the wartime Army's decline into a small peacetime establishment meant demotion on a mass scale with little hope for future advancement. Promotions in the interwar army came at such a glacial pace that Dwight D. Eisenhower was a major for sixteen years, Joseph Lawton Collins spent thirteen years as a captain, and Maxwell Taylor served as a lieutenant for thirteen years. This stagnation led many promising young officers to resign and seek their fortune in civilian life.

With their reduced rank, these officers who remained commanded units that either existed merely on paper or, at best, possessed skeleton strength. In the interwar period, the Regular Army's nine infantry divisions possessed the actual combined strength of just three full divisions. As late as 1939 when Marshall became chief of staff, the United States only possessed the world's nineteenth-largest army, finishing just ahead of Bulgaria. Because of the lack of funding with which to build proper housing, these skeleton units were scattered across the country in small, nineteenth-century posts, many of which were relics of the Indian Wars. This dispersion prevented serious training, and almost completely isolated the Army from the society it was sworn to defend. As one historian has noted, "Veterans who months earlier had been wined and dined as national heroes suddenly found themselves shunned," and that "During these dismal years it was not uncommon in communities where military men were stationed to find signs ordering dogs and soldiers to keep off the grass."[3] Whereas today the U.S. military consistently rates as the American institution "most respected" by the public, when *Fortune* magazine ran two feature stories on the Army in September 1935, the authors were bemused by the alien culture of the professional officer, whom they described as: "A queer mixture of the clergy, the college professor, and the small boy playing Indian . . . The Sam Browne belts, the brief, unqualified commands, the perpetual acknowledgment of salutes, the blind worship of rank, are manifestations of the primitive that lies hidden in almost every one of us."[4]

Although the travails of the U.S. Army in the 1920s and 1930s may seem a remote epoch to our modern sensibilities, in reality it is in many ways analogous to the situation America faces today. Just as the return of the two-million-man AEF represented the largest redeployment and demobilization in U.S. history to that point, America's "Forever Wars" in Iraq and Afghanistan have produced more than 2.9 million veterans.

Following World War I, Americans were disturbed by the horror and waste of the conflict and profoundly disappointed by the vindictiveness of the subsequent peace. Consequently, they turned to isolation and the false assumption that the interwar disarmament treaties rendered war "a vanished art and a dead monstrosity."[5] Similarly, after the longest period of continuous war in U.S. history, 74 percent of Americans told a September 2013 NBC/ *Wall Street Journal* poll that "it's time for the United States to do less around the world and focus on domestic problems," up from 54 percent in 2005.[6] In December 2013 Pew Research found that 80 percent of respondents wanted to "concentrate more on our own national problems" while focusing less on international troubles, representing a high in the fifty years that Pew has periodically asked this question.[7] Despite their initial support for the war, Americans have come to view Operation *Iraqi Freedom* as a mistake in numbers reminiscent of post-Versailles perceptions of World War I. In April 2016 57 percent of those Pew surveyed said that the United States should "deal with its own problems [and] let others deal with theirs as best they can." And although his administration has not retreated into isolationism as many feared, Donald Trump's 2016 campaign successfully exploited Americans' growing disinterest in the rest of the world, often threatening to withdraw from NATO and various free trade agreements, promising significant cuts in foreign aid and military assistance, and even adopting the name of the leading pre–World War II isolationist movement—"America First"— as the branding label for these policies.[8]

Just as World War I was touted as "the war to end all wars" to be followed by a "Return to Normalcy" expressed by strict economy on military spending, during his second inaugural address President Barack Obama proclaimed that "a decade of war is now ending" and vowed to focus on a variety of domestic issues. In response to America's massive structural debt, Congress passed the 2011 Budget Control Act, which required automatic budget cuts reducing planned defense spending by $487 billion over a decade. In March 2016 the Army's end strength fell to 479,172, its smallest force since 1940.

Beyond personnel reductions, these budgetary pressures on the Army echo those of the interwar period. In 1924 Secretary of War John Weeks warned in his report to the president that the Army could not meet its missions of providing overseas garrisons, maintaining a combat-ready emergency force, and training civilian components due to its budget-driven manpower shortages.[9] In October 1927 Army chief of staff Maj. Gen. Charles P. Summerall likened the Army to "a mere skeleton of defense." The question, he said, was "one of money, and until the United States is willing to support an army of sufficient size . . . nothing can be done, and we shall, as an armed force, continue to perish by fast degrees."[10] By 1934 George Marshall ironically noted that the entire combat force available in the United States could be comfortably seated in the stadium at Chicago's Soldier Field.

Similarly, recent budgetary pressures have forced the Army to raid its "readiness" accounts to produce immediate savings. General Odierno told reporters in 2013: "While I really don't want to leave a hollow Army, that's the road we're headed down."[11] In its 2014 Quadrennial Defense Review, the Pentagon admitted: "We will continue to experience gaps in training and maintenance over the near term and will have a reduced margin of error in dealing with risks of uncertainty in a dynamic and shifting security environment over the long term."[12] In 2016 the secretary of the army and chief of staff reported that only one-third of the service's active duty units were rated as "ready" for war, and that of those twenty brigade combat teams considered ready, more than half were already deployed. And when former Marine general James Mattis joined the Trump Administration as secretary of defense in 2017, he was "shocked by what I've seen with our readiness to fight."[13]

Moreover, in the wake of the controversies surrounding the wars in Afghanistan and Iraq, the quality of American generalship has been called into question. In May 2007, Lt. Col. Paul Yingling wrote in the *Armed Forces Journal* that the "debacles" in the Iraq war "are not attributable to individual failures, but rather to a crisis in an entire institution: America's general officers corps," who "failed to prepare our armed forces for war."[14] In 2012 journalist Thomas Ricks argued that "To a shocking degree, the Army's leadership ranks have become populated by mediocre officers placed in positions where they are likely to fail. Success goes unrewarded, and everything but the most extreme failure goes unpunished."[15] In a 2013 *Armed Forces Journal* essay, Lt. Col. Dale Davis charged:

> *Over the past 20 years, our senior leaders have amassed a record of failure in major organizational, acquisition and strategic efforts. These failures have been accompanied by the hallmarks of an organization unable and unwilling to fix itself: aggressive resistance to the reporting of problems, suppression of failed test results, public declaration of success where none was justified, and the absence of accountability.*[16]

In a January 2015 *Atlantic* essay, "The Tragedy of the American Military," Congressman Seth Moulton—who served four tours in Iraq as a U.S. Marine Corps officer—was quoted asserting that the military's highest ranks have become populated "by careerists, people who have gotten where they are by checking all the boxes and not taking risks."[17] And Lt. Gen. (ret.) Daniel Bolger, who served two tours in Iraq and one in Afghanistan, was even more blunt when he wrote: "I am a United States Army general, and I lost the Global War on Terrorism."[18] Regardless of the merits or shortcomings of these critiques, the retention and development of junior officers for future strategic leadership remains an issue of vital importance to U.S. national security, and continues to be hotly debated topic amongst current generals, former commanders, and academics.[19] The *2018 Army Strategy*, for example, states that "The Army will prioritize development and promotion of smart, thoughtful, and innovative leaders of character who are comfortable with complexity and capable of operating from the tactical to strategic level," and chief of staff Gen. Mark Milley has described leadership development as a key component of Army readiness.[20]

As U.S. military commanders and defense analysts debate the best way to prepare officers to be combat commanders for the conflicts America will face in the future, it is perhaps instructive to look backwards. No less an authority than Winston Churchill remarked:

> *To create great armies is one thing; to lead them and to handle them is another. It remains to me a mystery as yet unexplained how the very small staffs which the United States kept during the years of peace were able not only to build up the Armies and the Air Force units, but also to find the leaders and vast staffs capable of handling enormous masses and of moving them faster and farther than masses have ever been moved in war before.*[21]

Similarly, Secretary of War Henry L. Stimson reminisced:

> *[I]n 1945 we captured [Field Marshal Gerd von Rundstedt], one of the Commanders of the German forces, who said to one of his captors something like this: 'We cannot understand the difference in your leadership in the last war and in this. We could understand it if you had produced one superior corps commander, but now we find all of your corps commanders good and of equal superiority."*[22]

Despite the budgetary and organizational obstacles noted above, the impoverished, shrunken force of the interwar Army was nevertheless the incubator for future leaders such as Eisenhower, MacArthur, Bradley, and Patton, and also proved the cradle for brilliant army and corps commanders such as

Lucian Truscott, Joseph "Lightning Joe" Collins, Troy Middleton, and Matthew Ridgway, amongst others.

Shakespeare famously asserted that some men are born great, some achieve greatness, and others have greatness thrust upon them. The U.S. Army has modified this equation to suggest factors in three broad domains shape leadership development: the *Institutional Domain*, to include variables such as professional military education experiences and processes for the promotion/retention of officers; *Operational Domain* variables, to include specific service assignments; and the *Self-Development Domain*, i.e., the influence of mentors, peers, and personal self-development.[23] This equation can be adapted to serve as the framework for asking how America's World War II generals developed into leaders between the wars: Were their victories the product of specific institutions—such as the United States Military Academy at West Point or the professional military schools? Was their talent the result of specific staff assignments or service abroad? Was there something innate to these men that made them effective operational commanders, or were they shaped by specific personal experiences in the interwar years? Given the frequent accusations that the U.S. Army is failing to develop effective strategic and operational leaders, the question of how arguably the greatest generation of senior commanders in American military history emerged from the ashes of the resource-starved interwar Army is of vital importance to our national security today.

These leaders' experiences during the interwar period are a particularly fruitful subject for inquiry given the degree to which these men's lives and careers overlapped. It is commonplace for today's officer corps to joke about it being a "small Army" when unexpectedly reuniting with a former brother in arms. Yet given that the officer corps shrunk to just 12,000 men between the wars, the interwar Army *was* a remarkably small force, one in which many of the officers who would become household names in World War II served in multiple units together or were classmates at Army schools. During occupation duty in Germany after World War I, Joseph Collins served alongside Wade Haislip, thirty years before they served together again as Army chief of staff and vice chief of staff, respectively. Eisenhower and Patton were next door neighbors at Camp Meade in 1920. Omar Bradley and Matthew Ridgway were frequent hunting and golf companions while instructors at West Point during the years MacArthur served as superintendent, when Collins, Jacob Devers, Courtney Hodges, and Ernest Harmon were also on the faculty. Marshall accumulated an equally impressive stable of instructors during his tenure at the Infantry School that included Joseph Stilwell, Hodges, Bradley, Collins, Ridgway, and Walter Bedell Smith. The link analysis diagram in Figure 1 illustrating the interwar connections between the World War II Army and Corps commanders demonstrates how tightly knit the officer corps was.

Although in retrospect history often appears to have unfolded in a straight line, reality is almost always more chaotic and uncertain. It is easy to view the photographs of Marshall standing behind Pershing on the Hoboken

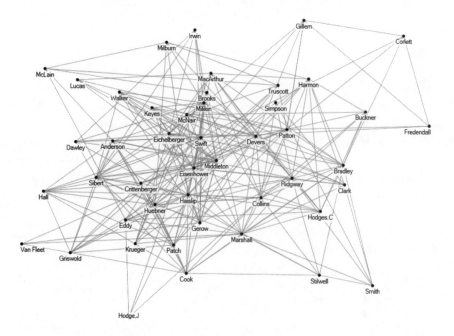

docks, or of George Patton standing next to a tank in 1918, know what they achieved in building and leading the U.S. Army in World War II, and therefore perceive their rise as inevitable. But that generation of officers' eventual triumphs were anything but predetermined.

In a sense, then, this is the story of a group of middle-aged men toiling in a profession that most Americans viewed with distrust. They earned lower salaries than their civilian counterparts, and despite being motivated and driven, often went more than a decade without receiving a promotion. Indeed, at one point they had to take pay cuts and forfeit earned vacation time merely to save their positions. In addition to these professional frustrations, most of these men endured some form of personal tragedy in these years: the sudden death of a child or a spouse; divorce, alcoholism, depression; in some cases legal difficulties that threatened to erase everything they had achieved in their careers. Yet when the world faced possibly its darkest hour, as fascism and barbarism were on the march across four continents, they stood ready to lead America's young men in the fight for civilization.

Beyond the institutional lessons to be learned, how these men persevered in the face of professional and personal adversities is a worthy tale in and of itself.

CHAPTER ONE

The General's Apprentice: Marshall's Years with Pershing

ALTHOUGH IN 1916 PRESIDENT WOODROW WILSON CAMPAIGNED ON THE slogan "He kept us out of war," events quickly rendered the former university professor's best intentions obsolete. On February 1, 1917, Germany announced it would resume unrestricted submarine warfare such as the attack that had sunk the *Lusitania*, dismissing American warnings that it considered the policy a violation of the principle of freedom of the seas upon which U.S. trade—and therefore the American economy—depended. Later that month British cryptographers informed the American embassy in London that they had intercepted a coded telegram from the German foreign secretary, Arthur Zimmermann, to the German embassy in Mexico offering that government an alliance if America entered the war after the submarine attacks resumed. While the vast majority of Americans had wished to avoid the conflict in Europe, together these developments shifted public opinion on the question of intervention.

As America inexorably slid toward war with Germany, President Wilson planned to give command of an American Expeditionary Force (AEF) to Maj. Gen. Frederick Funston. The fifty-one-year-old Funston was one of the most unconventional officers ever to serve his country. Five-foot-four, 120 pounds, Funston had not begun his military career through a traditional route such as an appointment to West Point or graduation from another military institution. Instead, the thirty-year-old son of a Union artilleryman-turned-U.S. congressman volunteered to fight with the Cuban insurgents against Spain in 1896. When the Spanish-American War began he agreed to serve as the colonel of the 20th Kansas Volunteer Infantry, which deployed to the Philippines. The bantam officer was awarded the Congressional Medal of

Honor for leading an assault against Filipino entrenchments in April 1899, and two years later Funston gained national prominence by leading a daring raid 100 miles behind enemy lines to capture the Philippine Insurrection's leader, Gen. Emilio Aguinaldo. Funston went on to further distinguish himself by leading the relief effort after the 1906 San Francisco earthquake and commanding the forces that seized and occupied Vera Cruz, Mexico, in 1914. He was subsequently promoted to major general and given command of the Army's Southern Department, in which position he oversaw the 1916 Punitive Expedition into Mexico. Consequently, as pressure increased for America to enter World War I, Funston emerged as the leading candidate to command the AEF.

On February 19, 1917, Secretary of War Newton Baker threw a dinner party at his home with President Wilson as guest of honor. Late in the evening the "gay party" was interrupted when an officer from the General Staff pushed by the butler and tried to attract Baker's attention to deliver an important telegram. President Wilson saw the officer and called out, "Come in, Major, and tell all of us the news. There are no secrets here."

The guests clapped their hands. Reluctantly, Maj. Douglas MacArthur clicked his heels together and saluted the president. "Sir," he barked like a drill sergeant, "I regret to report that General Funston has just died."

The room fell under a silence that MacArthur later recalled was "like that of death itself."[1]

Funston had survived five wounds by enemy fire and repeated bouts of tropical diseases. While sitting in the lobby of the Saint Anthony Hotel in San Antonio that evening, the general heard an orchestra playing and commented, "How beautiful it all is," when his heart finally failed him. His body was the first to ever lie in state at the Alamo, before eventually being buried at the Presidio in San Francisco.

With Funston's passing, the question immediately arose as to who would succeed him. "Newton," President Wilson asked, "who will take over the Army now?" Baker evaded the question that evening, but in reality there was only one choice. Although five other major generals were senior to John J. Pershing, all but Leonard Wood were too old for the physical and mental rigors of a combat command. And Wood—despite winning the Medal of Honor during the Geronimo Campaign and having commanded in both Cuba and the Philippines—was *persona non grata* in the Wilson Administration for having publicly criticized the president's reluctance to enter the war. Using the severe limp Wood had acquired in a previous accident as a pretext for keeping him stateside, Wilson appointed the fifty-six-year-old Pershing to organize and lead the AEF.

Pershing was a rugged veteran of the Indian Wars who had earned a Silver Star for gallantry during the 1898 charge up San Juan Hill in Cuba. As a major in the Philippines, Pershing's success at fighting the Moros led President Theodore Roosevelt to promote him to general over 862 officers with more seniority. During his second tour in the Philippines, Pershing's men were so impressed with his personal courage during the 1913 attack on Mount Bagsak that they gathered testimonials and affidavits and sent them to the adjutant general in Washington seeking the Medal of Honor for their commander. When the Mexican bandit Pancho Villa led a raid on Columbus, New Mexico, in March 1916 that killed seventeen Americans, Pershing was given command of the 11,000-man Punitive Expedition to pursue him. Although Villa was never captured, within three months more than three-quarters of his 485-man raiding force had been killed, captured, or wounded.

Pershing did not inspire warm, personal enthusiasm in his troops, but was respected for his competence and toughness. One veteran referred to Pershing as an "S.O.B." and said he hated his guts, but added: "As a soldier, the ones then and now could not polish his boots."[2] As a tactical officer at West Point, Pershing's excessive strictness led cadets to derisively nickname him "Nigger Jack," a reference to his prior service in one of the Army's four black regiments. The name stuck, although it was later sanitized as "Black Jack." Pershing was hardworking, direct, and honest. He disliked wasting time in pointless talk or digressions, and resented being interrupted. He demanded his subordinates match his drive, discipline, and determination, and he had little patience for those who blamed their failures on circumstances beyond their control. He was "a no-nonsense disciplinarian whose glacial stare when he was angry could instantly instill fear into even the most veteran trooper."[3]

When Pershing assumed command of the AEF in the spring of 1917, no U.S. divisions existed anywhere but on paper. He therefore had to create and organize an army essentially from scratch. The first American unit to arrive in France, the 1st Infantry Division, did not exist as an organic unit until 1917, and thus was sent to Lorraine for training rather than to the front lines. At the same time, upon arriving in France Pershing immediately faced pressure from British political and military leaders to relinquish his troops and integrate them into the British army. The possession of combat-ready forces would help stave off these British demands, and with few other units to visit that summer and fall, Pershing took a disproportionate interest in the 1st Division's training, frequently visiting the division headquarters to review their progress.

On September 6 Pershing inspected the 1st Division with French president Raymond Poincare. Scattered over 20–30 miles of countryside, some units did not learn of the inspection until the previous afternoon. After marching all night, these units were exhausted by the time they arrived at the parade grounds. They were training for combat rather than parades, and with most of the officers and the troops new recruits who had only been in uniform a few months, they were inexperienced at close order drill. Moreover, the field for the review had been selected late the previous evening in failing light, so the division wound up marching over churned up, muddy ground unsuitable for precision marching. Unsurprisingly, the review was ragged, and Pershing took out his frustration on the division's commander, Maj. Gen. William L. Sibert.[4]

Pershing inspected the 1st Division again on October 3, this time at Gondrecourt to watch a demonstration by Maj. Theodore Roosevelt Jr.—the former president's son and a battalion commander in the 26th Infantry—of a new method for attacking enemy trenches. After the demonstration Pershing called upon Sibert for a critique. Sibert possessed a brilliant record as an engineer, but had little experience with infantry tactics. Having only witnessed the demonstration for the first time alongside Pershing, his comments were halting and confused. Pershing then called upon a junior officer whose presentation was also inadequate. Pershing erupted and "just gave everybody hell." *The division showed little for the time it had spent in training*, Pershing snapped. They had not made good use of the time, and had not followed instructions from AEF headquarters at Chaumont regarding open warfare formations. Pershing excoriated Sibert, questioning his leadership, his attention to details in training, and his acceptance of such poor professionalism. He turned to Sibert's chief of staff, who had only arrived two days before, and grilled him as well. Once again, receiving nothing but faltering replies, Pershing sneeringly dismissed the officer and turned to leave.[5]

The 1st Division staff felt a possessive affection for Sibert, and as Pershing began to leave, the tall major who had been serving as acting chief of staff spoke up, talking rapidly and with anger rising in his voice at Pershing's unfairness. Pershing was in no mood to listen. He shrugged his shoulders and turned back to the door to walk away. Suddenly, he felt the major grabbing his arm.

"General Pershing," the major said, "there's something to be said here and I think I should say it because I've been here the longest."

Pershing turned back and gave the impertinent young officer a cold, appraising glance. "What have you got to say?"

"Well," the major began, "to start with, we have never received anything from your Headquarters. When I was down there two months ago, as a matter of fact, three months ago I think, I was told about this Platoon Chiefs' Manual that was coming up. It's never come out yet."

Pershing turned to one of his staff officers: "What about this?"

"Well, General, we've had trouble with the French printers," the staff officer replied. "You know they are very difficult to deal with."

Pershing then looked at the major and calmly said: "You must appreciate the troubles we have."

The major replied, "Yes, I know you do, General, I know you do. But ours are immediate and every day and have to be solved before night. Now we have never gotten the Platoon Manual. We have made the best we can of this thing. The only thing you've gotten out was to change the names . . . and now you are criticizing us for using the names you changed."

Pershing offered to "look into it," but the major replied there was no need. "It's right here in the orders," he said, "It's a fact. It's here. That's the only thing we've gotten from you and now we are being harassed for that."[6]

A torrent of facts poured forth: the inadequate supplies that left men walking around with gunnysacks on their feet because the quartermaster did not have enough large shoe sizes; the inadequate quarters that had troops sleeping in barns; the lack of motor transport that forced troops to walk miles to the training grounds. Finally, the deluge subsided.[7]

Pershing eyed the major narrowly before leaving, the 1st Division staff looking nervously at the ground in stunned silence. After a while, General Sibert gratefully told Maj. George C. Marshall that he should not have stuck his neck out on his account, and the rest of the staff predicted that Marshall's military career was finished.

That George Catlett Marshall would have *any* military career at all—much less one so important and prestigious—once seemed improbable at best. He was born in 1880 in Uniontown, Pennsylvania, to a small businessman from a family descended from legendary Supreme Court chief justice John Marshall. Although his father regaled him with stories of the American Revolution and the Civil War, and his older brother Stuart attended the Virginia Military Institute in Lexington, Virginia, he was a mediocre student. In fact, when he expressed his interest in following in his brother's footsteps, Stuart urged their mother to prevent George's matriculation at VMI lest his awkward younger brother disgrace the family name.

"That made more impression on me than all the instructors, parental pressure, or anything else," Marshall recalled. "I decided right then that I was going to wipe his face, or wipe his eye."[8]

Indeed, Marshall blossomed at VMI. Although he arrived as an academically undistinguished boy from a modest family—and worse, a Yankee from Pennsylvania—he was immediately drawn to the Institute's southern traditions. While still a middling student, Marshall's peers admired his self-control, his leadership, and his ability to manage men. In 1899, the summer between his sophomore and junior years, he saw the local company of volunteers return from service in the Philippines and was so moved that he later considered it "the determining effect on my choice of a profession." He made VMI's football team that fall, and for his senior year was the unanimous choice as first captain, the school's highest ranking cadet officer. As one biographer noted, this selection was a tribute "not to his brains but to his prowess as a precision machine."[9] Marshall's record in military discipline was unequaled—in four years as a cadet he did not receive a single demerit.

One day, however, he was walking through Lexington when he heard a piano emanating from a cottage just outside VMI's gate playing "some of the airs my mother had played to which I had become devoted."[10] Marshall frequently returned to the cottage to listen to the music, but it took some time before he summoned the courage to approach the house and introduce himself to the young lady whose music had surprised him. Yet when Ms. Lily Coles invited him in, it was love at first sight. Lily was an auburn-haired beauty, considered the belle of Lexington. At twenty-six, she remained unmarried due to her "condition," a vaguely diagnosed heart problem that limited her physical activities. In order to visit Lily more frequently, the disciplined Marshall risked his rank and his dream of becoming an army officer by sneaking out at night from VMI. "I was very much in love," he recalled years later, "and I was willing to take the chance."[11]

Even if he managed to get away with his secret romantic excursions, Marshall's goal of obtaining a commission was far from guaranteed. When he matriculated in 1897, VMI had fewer than a dozen graduates in the U.S. Army. Marshall's timing was fortuitous, however, as he was graduating just as the Regular Army was expanding from 25,000 to 100,000 to deal with the Philippine Insurrection, and thus needed an additional 1,200 commissioned officers. Still, priority for these commissions would be given first to West Point graduates, then to successful applicants from the ranks, then to former officers of volunteers, and *only then* to qualified civilians such as Marshall. Even then, all but the West Pointers were to be selected by competitive examination, and Marshall had to spend months of petitioning politicians—including a personal visit to President William McKinley—merely to be allowed to go before an examining board.[12] By then, there were 10,000 applications for the new commissions and only 142 positions left. Marshall, however, achieved one of the highest scores on the three-day exam, and on January 4, 1902, received his commission as a second lieutenant in the U.S. Army. With orders to report to Fort Myer, Virginia, on February 13, Marshall and Lily were married February 11 in a hastily arranged ceremony at the Coles' cottage. A week later, he said goodbye to his new bride to report for a two-year tour in the Philippines.[13]

Over the next fifteen years Marshall held nearly every significant staff job in the U.S. Army, establishing a reputation for brilliance. In 1906, as a second lieutenant, Marshall was assigned to the General Services and Staff School at Fort Leavenworth. Although all other fifty-three officers in his course were senior to him in rank and experience, Marshall graduated first in his class. The faculty board unanimously selected him as one of five student officers to remain as an instructor even though he would be outranked by all of his students. In January 1914, despite being a junior lieutenant, Marshall effectively commanded nearly 5,000 men during maneuvers in the Philippines. During the exercise, Lt. Henry "Hap" Arnold—future chief of U.S. Air Forces in World War II—saw Marshall examining a map and dictating orders under the shade of a bamboo grove. Arnold was so impressed that he wrote his wife to tell her he had just seen a future chief of staff in action. In 1916, when asked on Marshall's performance evaluation whether he would like to have the junior officer serve under his command, Lt. Col. Johnson Hagood (a future major general) replied: "Yes, but I would prefer to serve *under his command.*"[14] Regardless of his drive to succeed, stories abound of Marshall racing home after completing each day's tasks to be with Lily, and of their quiet evenings together at home because her heart condition precluded heavy social engagements.

The deep respect and praise from his peers notwithstanding, Marshall grew increasingly frustrated with the Army. The pace of advancement within the officer corps was so glacial that Marshall was not promoted to captain until August 1916—nine years after he became a first lieutenant, fourteen years after being commissioned—at the age of thirty-five. The lack of opportunities for advancement despite his obvious talents had Marshall considering leaving the Army. Fortune intervened, however, and in June 1917 he was assigned as the assistant chief of staff for the 1st Division. Marshall stepped off the transport onto French soil just behind Major General Sibert, the second man ashore in the first convoy of American troops. In the ensuing months, Marshall's curiosity frequently led him into the trenches, and as the division's chief of operations, he often rode on horseback through areas being shelled. He was commended for bravery under fire, and multiple commanders recommended Marshall for promotion and a battlefield command.

After his confrontation with Pershing, however, the 1st Division's staff officers assumed Marshall's career was finished. He shrugged off their condolences, saying: "All I can see is that I may get troop duty instead of staff duty, and certainly that would be a great success."[15] Surprisingly, no retribution for the incident ever came. Pershing had finally found someone who would tell him the unvarnished truth rather than gloss over inadequacies. Consequently, whenever the AEF commander visited 1st Division from his Chaumont headquarters, he would find a moment to pull Marshall aside to ask how things were *really* going.

In July 1918 Marshall received orders transferring him to the AEF General Staff. He was placed under the supervision of Col. Fox Conner, the "towering, imperturbable, concise" Mississippi-born West Pointer who headed Pershing's Operations section, and who would become known as the brains of the AEF.[16] Forty-two years old, fluent in French, straight talking, and completely loyal, Pershing said of Conner: "I could have spared any other man in the AEF better than he."[17] Marshall and Conner clicked immediately, becoming so close they were referred to as a "mutual admiration society." They worked together continuously, with Conner deferring to Marshall's sharper intelligence, and Marshall heeding Conner's superior wisdom.[18] Together, they formed the core of the group that planned the two great U.S. offensives of the war—Saint Mihiel and the Meuse-Argonne.

While the Saint Mihiel operation was being planned and operationalized, Marshall was assigned to simultaneously plan and deploy forces for the Meuse-Argonne operation. His task was to determine how to withdraw eleven French and Italian divisions with two corps headquarters from the front and replace them with fifteen American divisions and three corps headquarters, a movement of 220,000 troops out of the front line and 600,000 troops into it, along with 3,000 guns and 900,000 tons of supplies and ammunition. By comparison, the total *combined* Union and Confederate forces at Gettysburg totaled 164,000 troops and 655 guns for both armies. To move all these men and equipment, Marshall had only three rail lines and three roads at his disposal, and all movements had to be conducted at night to maintain secrecy. All movements had to be coordinated with similar French army redeployments to the east and west, thereby requiring a crash course in diplomacy beyond the already daunting logistical challenges.[19]

Experienced army staffs normally required two to three months to develop a comprehensive battle plan with all its technical annexes. Marshall had about three weeks. Moreover, he never knew more than twenty-four hours in advance which units would be ready to move. Yet through a combination of intelligence and improvisation, drive and dedication, patience and preparation, he pulled off the impossible. Every unit reached its destination in time, the Germans were caught completely by surprise, and the attack was successful. Marshall was soon being called "the Wizard" for his accomplishment. Even the profoundly skeptical British were impressed. The *London Times*'s influential military correspondent, Col. Charles Repington, wrote: "Few people in England know that this operation was preceded by one of the most interesting and difficult Staff operations of the war. . . . It was a fine piece of Staff work and no other Staff could have done it better."[20] Marshall was awarded the Distinguished Service Medal for his "untiring, painstaking, and energetic efforts," and became one of the most highly respected officers in the U.S. Army. Before the war ended, Pershing recommended Marshall for promotion to brigadier general and made him chief of operations for the First Army.

Yet providence would play almost as important a role as industry in Marshall's rise. At around 1030, November 11, 1918, Marshall was in the mess for a late breakfast. As the officers debated what should be done to Germany after the Armistice set to begin in half an hour, a bomb unexpectedly exploded in the garden ten yards from where they sat. Marshall was thrown against the wall, stunned. "I thought I had been killed," he recalled. He ended up on the floor, a nasty bump on his head. Moments later a young aviator rushed in, apologizing profusely. A last bomb stuck in its rack had shaken loose just as he was about to land on the other side of the headquarters building. As one historian observes, "Had the walls of the old house been less sturdy, a different chief of staff would have led the American armies against the Germans in the next war."[21]

After the Armistice, American troops began the march toward Germany. At Fox Conner's suggestion, Marshall returned to General Headquarters (GHQ) to help plan troop movements into Germany. By February 1919 there were more than 262,000 forces on occupation duty in the Rhineland around Coblenz. Marshall and the other AEF staff officers subsequently drafted contingency plans for a movement beyond the Rhineland if Germany failed to sign a peace treaty. As months passed and it became clear the fighting was over for good, Pershing's staff faced the task of redeploying almost two million soldiers and their equipment to the United States. They also prepared various after-action reports on the war, including special reports on the Saint Mihiel and Meuse-Argonne offensives.[22]

When slighting references to these victories appeared in the French press, Pershing was convinced the French were attempting to downplay the American contribution to the Allied victory. To counter this, and to instill pride in the U.S. soldier, Pershing selected 900 doughboys who were writers, editors, and publishers in civilian life, and sent them on a two-week tour of U.S. forces so they could disseminate the narrative of the AEF's accomplishments in the war when they returned home. Pershing also deployed Marshall, Hugh Drum, and Willey Howell on a lecture tour of divisional camps to tell the American version of events, with Marshall proving to be the most effective spokesman. On April 20, during a lecture at Chaumont to visiting members of the House Military Affairs Committee, he was so fluent in the AEF's accomplishments and spoke so rapidly that stenographers assigned to take notes could not keep up with him.[23]

Pershing was impressed. Ten days later, Marshall travelled to Metz with other members of Pershing's command to receive the French Legion of Honor. Before the ceremony, one of Pershing's staff members, Col. James L. Collins, walked beside Marshall and—timing his words to the cadence of the step—asked in a low voice: "How would you like to be the General's aide?" Marshall said yes and the next day joined Pershing's other two aides, Col. John G. Quekemeyer and Maj. John C. Hughes. Again, fate played a role in Marshall's ascent, as he was asked to fill the position vacated in February when Col. Carl Boyd—a close friend and aide to Pershing—died of pneumonia in Paris.[24]

The social demands on Pershing's time in the spring and summer of 1919 were extensive, filled with victory parades, ceremonies, parties, and receptions. Since Pershing already had an aide to handle his crowded social calendar, Marshall served more as an adviser or personal chief of staff. Pershing and his staff stayed in the luxurious Paris home of American lawyer-financier Ogden Mills, and Marshall accompanied the general on a triumphal tour of Allied capitals and old battlefields, including a trip to Waterloo.

On Bastille Day, July 14, Paris held what Marshall called the greatest victory parade he ever saw. It began early in the morning on a solemn note, as 1,000 blind, lame, and mutilated veterans walked in procession. They were followed by pure military pageantry, as row upon row of troops from every Allied nation marched to the martial music. Field Marshals Ferdinand Foch and Joseph Joffre led off, carrying their marshal's batons. Then came contingents of up to 1,500 men from the principal Allied nations, marching alphabetically: the Americans, Belgians, British, Czechs, Greeks, Italians, Japanese, Portuguese, Serbs—with the host French ending the procession. Pershing led the American contingent, the old cavalryman casting a stunning figure on horseback. Behind him rode an officer bearing the large, silk, four-starred flag, followed by Maj. Gen. James Harbord, Pershing's chief of staff. Ten yards behind Harbord, Pershing's three aides—Marshall, Quekemeyer, and Hughes—rode abreast. Then, eight abreast at 10-yard intervals, rode thirty American generals. Next came the AEF band, "Pershing's Own," leading the Composite Regiment, a select group of Regular Army officers and men, all 6 feet or taller, chosen from the best U.S. troops in Europe. They conveyed a strong impression with their manliness, precision, and sheer physical power, and Pershing called them "the finest body of troops I have ever seen in my life."[25]

With at least ninety American and regimental flags in their ranks, the blaze of color was breathtaking as they marched through the Arc de Triomphe and down the Champs-Élysées. The two million people who lined the parade route cheered wildly, wave after wave of sound breaking over the boulevards along the 7-mile route. Years later, Marshall recalled it as "a magnificent affair," and told a young American friend: "As long as I live I will never forget the faces I saw that day. . . . Because France was the battlefield, I don't suppose there was a single person there who had not lost someone dear."[26]

Five days later Pershing, his aides, and the Composite Regiment marched again in London's victory parade. Marshall intentionally selected a docile horse from the string furnished by the British army, but at the last minute had to swap mounts with Gen. Andre Brewster, whose horse was more fractious. "For eight miles I had the ride of my life," he recalled, as the horse tried to kick spectators, reared and pranced sideways while Marshall struggled to keep his place in the formation. Just as they entered the Admiralty Arch, the horse reared, slipped, and fell over backwards. Marshall was able to tumble clear, rolled three times to escape the flailing hooves, and remounted with the animal still on the ground. Although he broke his hand in the accident, Marshall would long savor it as a moment of exquisite equestrianship.[27] The rest of the trip was a weeklong social whirl in which he accompanied Pershing to numerous formal events, meeting the king and queen of England and even managing to step on the king of Portugal's foot at one reception. Marshall also met a man who would figure prominently in his life two decades later, Britain's secretary of state for war, Winston Churchill. Acknowledging the ratification of the Eighteenth Amendment, Churchill ruefully lamented of the American troops: "What a magnificent body of men never to take another drink."[28]

On September 1, Pershing, his staff, and selected members of the 1st Division finally boarded the *Leviathan* in Brest bound for New York. Upon docking, they were met by Secretary Baker, who led Pershing to a small stand where he made a formal welcoming address and presented the AEF commander with a commission as a permanent four-star general. Pershing and his staff were honored guests of New York City and enjoyed free lodging at the Waldorf-Astoria. There, Marshall reported to Pershing that he had received 2,000 telegrams—mostly social invites—and hundreds of letters.

New York's victory parade took place on September 10, a three-hour procession of the 1st Division and the Composite Regiment from 110th Street to Washington Square. The city had prepared for the occasion with lavish care, erecting a full-sized replica of the Arc de Triomphe over Fifth Avenue, through which Pershing and his men passed. Pershing walked his mount gracefully at the head of the column, followed by his standard bearers, staff, officers, and men, downtown through dense crowds beside themselves with excitement.[29]

The party entrained on the morning of September 12 for Washington, DC, arriving that evening. Five days later, on the 17th, the nation's capital held the last great victory parade. Hundreds of thousands lined the route from the Peace Monument down Pennsylvania Avenue to the White House to watch 25,000 troops march. Secretary of the Navy Josephus Daniels described the occasion as a tribute "such as the capital had never seen."[30] Marshall, however, wryly recalled that "the people were most impressed of all by one mule licking the soup that was coming out the back of a rolling kitchen."[31]

Almost as soon as the guns fell silent along the Western Front, the Army's leaders began considering what a future war would look like and how the nation and the Army could be better prepared than they had been for the Great War. World War I provided a shocking example of the costs of unpreparedness. It took a year from the declaration of war in April 1917 before an American division was ready for battle. When U.S. troops finally joined the fray, casualties were higher than necessary because of the lack of peacetime training. Moreover, American war production never achieved its potential during the conflict, and the AEF had to rely on Britain and France for materiel such as guns, ammunition, and airplanes.

Developing a viable military policy at war's end provided its own set of unique challenges. Congress was intent on contracting the Army from 3.7 million men back to its peacetime strength of 98,000. Representative George Huddleston of Alabama disparaged the Regular Army, saying: "Many of the officers are engaged in the business merely as a profession, which is a loafing job in time of peace, as it might be considered, not doing anything useful, except perhaps giving a little of their time to fitting themselves for a duty that may never come."[32] Representative Harold Knutson of Minnesota framed the issue in economic terms: "The time has arrived to democratize the American Army—better still, replace it with the National Guard, so far as possible. If we do that we will make an important step in the retrenchment of our expenditures."[33] Woodrow Wilson ignored military matters as he planned a League of Nations he believed would make armies largely obsolete. And those Americans who opposed the League sought to avoid the foreign entanglements that necessitated an expeditionary capability. As King Swope, the first World War I veteran elected to Congress, observed: "Everybody had a bellyful of the damn Army."[34]

Thus, as the wartime Army disintegrated and the American public focused on the Paris Peace Conference, Congress began to consider the legislative foundations of future military policy. By the time Pershing and Marshall returned home in September 1919, the debate over the reorganization of the Army was reaching its apogee, with the size and function of the Regular Army, the power of the General Staff, and the role of the National Guard and universal military training at the center of the argument.

The man responsible for making the Army's case in these debates was the chief of staff, Gen. Peyton March. March was "tall and formal," standing over 6 feet tall, with sharp, piercing blue eyes and a gray goatee. The son of a famous professor, March eschewed academia for the United States Military Academy, graduating in 1888, two years after Pershing. March distinguished himself in the Philippines as a major commanding the 33rd Volunteer Infantry, nearly capturing Aguinaldo at the Battle of Tirad Pass fifteen months before Funston's successful mission. In June 1917 March was promoted to brigadier general and given command of the 1st Division artillery. Three months later he received another star and became the AEF's chief of artillery.

In September 1917 Secretary Baker informed Pershing that he was considering selecting March as chief of staff to replace Gen. Tasker Bliss, who was due to retire at the end of the year. Pershing suggested Maj. Gen. John Biddle instead, a former superintendent of West Point who was commanding an engineering brigade in the AEF. Baker accepted Pershing's recommendation and brought Biddle back stateside as acting chief of staff in October. The enormous problems of mobilization quickly overwhelmed Biddle, however, and on March 4, 1918, March replaced him as acting chief of staff.[35]

March brought qualities to the position that his predecessors lacked—a clear sense of the proper role and power of his office, and the dynamism and ruthlessness necessary to galvanize the Army's effort. The aggressive March quickly pushed men and materiel overseas in quantities inconceivable just a few months earlier. During the eight months from March's arrival at the War Department to the end of the war, more men—almost 1.8 million—deployed to France than were in the entire army on March 1. Brig. Gen. Charles Dawes noted that during the last five months before the Armistice nearly twice as much tonnage was shipped as had been in the preceding year. The *New York Times* praised March, saying: "It is undeniable that in a surprisingly short time he brought order out of confusion and achieved success which probably will cause discriminating critics to rank him as an organizer and executive without a superior in our military history."[36] Similarly, the chairman of the War Industries Board, Bernard Baruch, said that as wartime chief of staff, March was simply "the right man in the right place."[37]

On Armistice Day March ordered the War Department's War Plans Branch to begin planning for the Regular Army's organization around a field army of 500,000 men. He discussed the project with Secretary Baker and secured both his and President Wilson's approval for the half-million-man force. March eventually rejected the War Plans draft and devised his own design for the postwar Army, virtually dictating the bill according to one staff officer. On January 16, 1919, the War Department's bill was introduced to the House Military Affairs Committee. "The general idea of the bill was to put into legal form what the present organization of the army is," March testified. "[I]t embodies the experience of the war."[38] March proposed a permanent Regular Army of 500,000 organized into division cadres that would train raw recruits in time of war. In August Secretary Baker sent an updated bill to Congress, which was the same as January's version but with three months universal military training added to fill out the Regular Army cadres in war. It provided for a strong General Staff, promotion by selection, and for the retention of new services created during the war such as the Air Service, the Tank Corps, and the Motor Transport Corps.[39]

Yet in proposing a force five times larger than America's prewar Army, March misjudged the nation's temperament. Reverting to their traditional distrust of foreign alliances and large standing armies, the American people were unwilling to support a force larger than that required to defend the continental United States and its overseas territories. The bill immediately aroused strong congressional opposition. On the first day of Senate hearings on the bill, Hiram Johnson asked March: "[W]hat is the necessity ... for a permanent army of 576,000 officers and men? ... I can not quite fathom why at this particular time, when we are facing an era of universal peace, we should have an army many times larger than we have ever had in our history before."[40] Senator James W. Wadsworth, chairman of the Senate Military Affairs Committee and no enemy of military preparedness, thought it inappropriate that the Army should be offering a military program that with its large Regular cadres and conscript reserves so closely resembled Germany's. Senator Henry S. New of Indiana concurred: "It smacks too much of that very militarism which is righteously abhorrent to our national ideals and which we have denounced from every stump and housetop in the country." Senator George E. Chamberlain simply denounced the bill as "militarism run mad."[41] In an outburst on the House floor, a member of the Military Affairs Committee expressed the dominant mood: "They propose that outrage in time of peace. My goodness think of it."[42] Consequently, March wrote his Intelligence chief—the wonderfully named Marlborough Churchill—that "Conditions in America with reference to the Army are very bad."[43]

Even within the Army there was opposition to March's plan. On August 7, 1919, the Senate began hearings on future military policy, followed four weeks later by the House. Despite the chief of staff's adamant stand for the large Army, many officers who appeared before the committees contradicted him. The most convincing of these was Col. John McAuley Palmer. The son of a Civil War general of volunteers, Palmer was "a little fellow of the school-professor type," and had been a student of Marshall's at Leavenworth. He was one of the principal authors of the secretary of war's "Report on the Organization of the Land Forces" in 1912, and was acknowledged throughout the Army as an expert on organization and policy. An infantry officer, Palmer had gone to France with Pershing as his chief of operations until illness forced him to give way to Fox Conner in November 1917. He returned to duty in time to command the 58th Infantry Brigade of the 29th Division in action east of the Meuse. Shortly after the Armistice he was recalled to the War Department to analyze the military's future requirements. Although he arrived after the General Staff had already formulated its plan, the protracted congressional hearings allowed younger officers who found Palmer persuasive to urge Senator Wadsworth to have him testify.[44]

On October 9, Palmer entered the Senate Military Affairs Committee Room carrying "a stack of papers a foot high." The colonel dismissed March's plan, stating: "In my opinion, the War Department bill proposes incomplete preparedness at excessive cost, and under forms that are not in harmony with the genius of American institutions."[45] Palmer believed the effective work of American citizen-soldiers in France had refuted the conventional wisdom that it took at least a year, preferably two, to make a soldier. Given this, Palmer asked, why must there be so much emphasis on the Regular Army that the General Staff should insist upon a force well beyond what Congress would accept, while proposing to skeletonize the Regular organization so it would not be ready to fight in an emergency? Although Palmer's plan included a Regular Army of 275,000–300,000 men, it also provided for a substantial National Guard and an organized reserve based on universal military training. Such a Regular Army could be ready to serve immediately in any military emergency short of one requiring mass mobilization, while its peacetime energy would be devoted to training the citizen army America would rely upon in a major war. Palmer's companies, regiments, and divisions would be organized in peace to prepare for war, but they would be mostly citizen-army formations, not half-strength Regular Army units into which citizen soldiers would be absorbed and submerged as in March's conception. In sum, Palmer explained, his plan made the citizen army "the foundation of national defense."[46]

"In half an hour he had us fascinated," Wadsworth recalled. "In an hour, he had torn Peyton C. March's bill into scraps—figuratively speaking—and thrown it in the wastebasket."[47] Following his testimony, the committee conferred and "in about two minutes by unanimous vote" directed Wadsworth to request Palmer's assignment as its military adviser to aid in drafting legislation. Reluctantly, and disclaiming responsibility for his view, the War Department agreed. General March, however, was less than delighted, and Palmer would be denied promotion as long as March remained chief of staff.[48]

Despite opposition to his bill, March remained optimistic, as the military committees of both houses had endorsed the large Army on a one-year basis earlier in 1919. Moreover, the committees had yet to hear from the most influential man in uniform, General Pershing. Although Palmer's testimony had weakened the bill's chances of passage—in part because many perceived him as representing Pershing's views—if the victorious AEF commander supported the 500,000-man force it would be difficult for Congress to oppose him. Such was Pershing's prestige that, when Secretary Baker submitted the Army bill in August 1919, he refrained from formally endorsing it since Pershing had not yet been consulted. Yet as the Senate and House reorganization hearings proceeded through September and October, nobody actually knew where Pershing stood on the issue. Although congressional leaders had expected AEF input in postwar planning, March wanted immediate action and did not send Pershing a copy of his proposal until March 7, 1919—two months after it had been submitted to the House. Thus, the reorganization bill's fate seemed to rest on the outcome of Pershing's eventual testimony.

The drama surrounding the AEF commander's testimony was heightened by a burgeoning rivalry between March and Pershing, who in 1903 had shared an office together as junior officers on the Army's first General Staff. Although March's logistical acumen enabled the AEF to commit large numbers of troops to battle in the summer and fall of 1918, his relationship with Pershing was often fraught with tension. President Wilson and Secretary Baker had intended for Pershing to be supreme in France, an independent commander answering directly to the president and secretary of war. Whereas Generals Bliss and Biddle accepted their supporting roles, March felt that having a chief of staff supreme in the United States but charged with supporting a field commander dominant overseas was an inefficient way to fight a war. He believed his position should include supervisory power over the line as well as the staff. The friction created by these differing interpretations of roles and responsibilities was compounded by his autocratic temperament. Marshall recalled that March "was a master administrator . . . with a great weakness of antagonizing everybody."[49] Even Secretary Baker, March's strongest supporter in the Wilson Administration, described the chief of staff as "arrogant, harsh, dictatorial and opinionated," and noted that March ruled by a reign of terror, "riding rough-shod over everyone."[50]

When March began issuing orders to Pershing that spring, hostilities quickly ensued. Pershing treated March as merely the head of the AEF's logistical system. He either ignored or disdained the chief of staff's strategic and military advice, to which March could only fume in rage. Pershing was put off by what he considered "a very curt tone" in March's cables, and complained forcefully in letters about March's manner.[51] In August 1918 March issued General Order #80, which stated that the chief of staff "takes rank and precedence over all officers of the Army." Accustomed to a large degree of independence, Pershing rejected March's assertion of superiority.[52] These personality clashes were exacerbated by persistent—but wholly unconfirmed—rumors that March wanted to succeed Pershing as commander of the AEF.

Sometimes the tension between the two generals sprang from relatively trivial issues, such as their disagreement over the Sam Browne belt. The Sam Browne was a leather over-the-shoulder strap adopted by the British army in India to hold up an officer's waist belt when it was weighed down by a sword, revolver, binoculars, canteen, and other items. As few of these items were used in the trenches, it no longer served its original functional purpose. Pershing thought it "set off" the uniform, however, and soon after arriving in France in June 1917 he ordered it worn at AEF headquarters, and subsequently prescribed it for all AEF officers. Conversely, March considered the belt a waste of good leather, banned its use in the United States, and in May 1918 suggested that Pershing do away with it, advice Pershing declined.

One day shortly before returning to France in 1918, Colonel Palmer was in Washington, DC, walking down Connecticut Avenue in uniform when he saw General March striding toward him. Palmer rendered the chief of staff a crisp salute and a pleasant greeting. March, however, seeing that Palmer was wearing a Sam Browne belt, coldly replied: "Palmer, you're out of uniform."

Palmer, who while on convalescent leave was unaware of the spat over the belt, said: "I am wearing the uniform prescribed for a member of General Pershing's command."

March stalked off in silence.[53]

Their growing rivalry came to the fore most prominently in the matter of promotions. In May 1918 the War Department asked for Pershing's recommendations for six major generals and thirty-three brigadier generals. To Pershing's dismay, when the promotions were made in July, men whom he had *not* recommended were promoted over scores of others who had served longer and, in his opinion, were more efficient. Pershing and Harbord believed the recommended AEF colonels denied promotion to brigadier general were those who had clashed with March when he was the AEF's artillery chief. "The question of promotions involves some transactions on the part of the Chief of Staff in Washington which I am afraid would not look well in the light of an honest investigation," Pershing noted in his diary.[54] When a new list of promotions was published in October, once again AEF officers whom he had not recommended were promoted while others he had were not, and this time half the promotions went to men still stationed stateside. Again, Pershing was furious with March.

Pershing continued sending recommendations in the weeks before the Armistice, but the day after the war ended March announced it had been decided not to promote any more general officers. This seemed to Pershing to be a grave injustice, as during the Meuse-Argonne campaign many division commanders were heavily engaged in battle and did not have time to make recommendations for promotions. Pershing asked that he be authorized to make such promotions as he considered merited. But March, who was in the process of reducing the Army from 3.7 million to a few hundred thousand, would not budge. He believed the necessary promotions could be issued for men to have the proper rank in the new peacetime force once the Army was demobilized. Until then, he suggested Pershing reward deserving officers by awarding them the Distinguished Service Cross or Distinguished Service Medal, or with a promotion in the Reserve Corps. Secretary Baker backed March on this issue, and Pershing and some of his subordinates retained a strong sense of grievance against March.[55]

As one historian notes, "Service journals were full of news about the continuing rivalry" between March and Pershing, and in June 1919, Harbord warned Pershing: "Everything indicates that the higher officers of the Regular army are lining up in two general groups. A) Those who are in step with General March and whom he is using the great power of his position to place.... b) The group who look to you as Chief, who have served you with the best they had, and who, wearing your AEF brand, have no hope except through you."[56] In a special message to Congress in July 1919, President Wilson recommended that March, Pershing, and Admirals William S. Benson and William S. Sims be awarded permanent four-star rank.

When Pershing's name was read before the House, the entire chamber rose to its feet, applauding and cheering. When March's name was announced, a number of congressmen groaned, hurriedly took their seats, and hooted, "No. No. Sit down, sit down."[57] Although Baker lobbied vigorously for March, the chief of staff had antagonized members of Congress with his brusqueness and refusal to do favors. Congress subsequently voted permanent rank for Pershing, with only four congressmen voting against the measure, and refused it for March. Consequently, March only held four-star rank while serving as chief of staff and would eventually revert back to major general. Even worse from March's perspective, Pershing had become a four-star general first and thus had seniority, leading to the awkward situation of him outranking the chief of staff. Thus, even if their relationship during the war had been—a few disagreements aside—generally cordial and productive, the situation in the fall of 1919 was ripe for a clash of sizable egos just as the fate of the postwar army was being determined.

General Pershing dropped out of the public eye after the Washington, DC, festivities for his first real rest in four years. He decamped to William Cameron Forbes's estate on Naushon Island off Cape Cod. Marshall joined him there after spending a few days with Lily, and three weeks later they traveled to the Adirondack wilderness where Fox Conner's father-in-law owned a 27,000-acre hunting camp. The Brandreth compound lacked any utilities, was 7 1/2 miles from the nearest train station, and was accessible only by buckboard over a mountain road. Yet upon arriving at the old log house, Pershing threw his hat and coat on a chair and declared: "I'm never going back!" For the next three weeks the general and his aides filled their days with hunting, with sufficient whiskey on hand in the cabin to warm anyone chilled from the autumn cold.[58]

The Brandreth retreat was not a simple stag getaway, however. Pershing knew he would be called upon to testify before Congress, and realized his prestige would determine the reorganization bill's fate. Thus, Marshall obtained the galley proofs of the testimony of various witnesses before the committees. "I would sit up until about midnight every night," Marshall recalled, "going over the congressional hearings with General Pershing in preparation for his hearing."[59]

Pershing returned to Washington in late October and spent two days interviewing bureau chiefs and General Staff officers to prepare for his testimony. The day before Pershing was to appear at the hearing, General March came to his office at the Old Land Office Building to give his opinion of the reorganization bill. March leaned forward, his elbow on Pershing's desk, and pointed his finger at the general of the armies to emphasize his views. Pershing simply leaned back in his chair and listened as March spoke so rapidly that the poor stenographer had difficulty getting the flood of words on paper.[60]

On October 31, 1919, General Pershing began three days of testimony before a joint session of the House and Senate Military Affairs Committees. Although today it is rare to see a majority of a House committee show up for a hearing, much less stay beyond opening statements or their turn to ask a question on C-Span, the House Office Building Caucus Room that day was packed as representatives skipped other meetings to hear the general of the armies' testimony. With Marshall and Conner sitting on either side of him, Pershing read a prepared statement declaring his opposition to the Baker-March bill. "In discussing preparedness," Pershing stated, "it is to be remembered that our traditions are opposed to the maintenance of a large standing army." Arguing that a 500,000-man force would cost too much, he proposed an army of 275,000–300,000 troops. Like Palmer, he envisaged a small professional force whose task would be to train a large civilian reserve force. "Our wars have practically all been fought by citizen soldiers," he said. Consequently, he proposed six months' universal military training.[61]

Over three days of testimony, the legislators displayed deference to Pershing that suggests they would have had difficulty opposing the half-million-man force had he thrown his prestige behind it. Pershing made his points, but if pressed, would shift to a compromise position. "My experiences in War Department affairs as such has been very limited," he conceded. "I am only viewing it from the side of the Army, from the point of view of the Army as to its effectiveness in the field."[62] While his testimony was not as intellectually impressive as Palmer's, on November 4 the *Washington Post* pronounced the March/Baker plan dead. The *Stars and Stripes* headline that week concluded: "Pershing Gives Finishing Blow To Baker's Bill."[63]

The result of the committee hearings was the National Defense Act (NDA) of 1920, which set the postwar army's strength at 280,000 men as per Pershing's recommendation. America's principal military reliance was placed upon citizen soldiers, and the NDA created the machinery for an expansion to 2.3 million by the National Guard and an organized reserve force in time of emergency. Training the National Guard and Organized Reserves would become a major peacetime task of the Regular Army, and to fulfill that mission, Congress authorized the Regular Army 17,726 officers, more than three times the prewar number. The act also required that officer promotions—except for doctors and chaplains—be made from a single list, thereby equalizing opportunities for advancement throughout most of the Army.[64]

The new law abandoned the traditional territorial division of the United States into military administrative departments, replacing them with nine geographic corps areas of approximately equal population that assumed command and administrative responsibilities for the field forces in the continental United States. These nine corps areas would be assigned to the headquarters of three armies, and each corps area was allocated six infantry divisions: one Regular Army, two National Guard, and three Organized Reserve divisions. Unlike March's expansible army plan, the Regular divisions would be full strength rather than skeletonized. Thus, the division became the basic unit of the interwar Army, particularly for mobilization planning. Reflecting the new combat innovations of the war, Congress confirmed the separation of the Air Service from the Signal Corps, and authorized the addition of a Chemical Warfare Service to the previously existing branches.[65]

Many contemporary observers viewed the 1920 NDA as one of the most constructive pieces of military legislation in American history. "The new law," Pershing enthusiastically pronounced, "simply provides that our traditional citizen army be organized in time of peace instead of being extemporized, as in the past, after danger has actually come."[66] William A. Ganoe, an Army major turned historian, judged this legislation "by all odds the greatest provision for prolonging peace and the efficient control of war ever enacted by the Congress."[67] Yet the NDA contained a fatal flaw. Although both March and Pershing had called for universal military training, congressmen were bombarded with letters objecting to the cost, the threat that it would "prussianize" America, and the interference in people's lives at a time when war had seemingly been abolished. Southern Democrats further opposed the measure out of fear of training Negroes. Consequently, universal military training was dropped from the House Military Affairs Committee's bill before it was brought to the floor, and Republicans abandoned the provision lest Democrats make an issue of it in the 1920 elections. With universal military training out of the way, the bills passed both houses, with the conferenced bill largely following the House version. President Wilson signed the measure on June 4, 1920.[68]

By eliminating the universal military training provision, however, Congress had emasculated the policy advocated by Palmer and Pershing. By accepting one part of their scheme (a small Regular Army whose main purpose would be the training of a citizen reserve) and rejecting the other (universal military training to provide the reserve), Congress created an impracticable hybrid—a military structure resting on a body of trained citizens, but eliminating the means of providing that body. Although the War Department authorized the establishment of training centers where "volunteers" might come and be instructed by Regular Army cadre, the volunteers were not forthcoming. Thus, by compromising rather than choosing between two irreconcilable systems, Congress ended up making matters worse.[69]

Moreover, as anyone familiar with Congress understands, the authorizing committees are impotent without the necessary appropriations. As Representative Daniel R. Anthony, a powerful Republican congressman, told his colleagues: "We are going to try to put an end to some of the waste and extravagance which has characterized the conduct of the Military Establishment in recent years."[70] In December 1920, Henry Cabot Lodge Sr., Republican chairman of the Senate Foreign Relations Committee, began blocking Senate consideration of the War Department's nominations for promotion as part of his effort to reduce military spending. In its rush to return to normalcy, Marshall noted, Congress was dominated by concern for "the war debt, high taxes, and their reduction. Economy is demanded by public opinion; everybody loathes war; and a reduction of the military establishment is the easiest political makeshift for immediate retrenchment."[71]

Congress gave an ominous portent in the appropriations bill it passed in the closing hours of the 1920 session. Although the NDA authorized a force of 298,000 officers and men, Congress appropriated funds for less than 200,000 for the coming year. In the last two years of the Wilson Administration, Congress appropriated just over a third of the War Department's requested budget for Fiscal Year (FY) 1921 and less than half the request for FY22. In January 1921 Congress directed a reduction in enlisted strength to 175,000, and that June decreased the figure to 150,000. After the successful conclusion of the Washington Naval Conference in February 1922, the House passed an Army Appropriations Act reducing the number of enlisted men to 115,000—less than half the strength authorized in 1920. This application of the congressional budgetary axe prevented the completion of the nine Regular divisions planned under the 1920 NDA. Financial pressure was also offered as justification for eliminating the nine corps training detachments who were to oversee the citizen-soldiers' training. Moreover, given that the National Guard depended on federal drill pay to fill its ranks, paltry appropriations ensured that its formations rarely reached half the 435,000-man strength authorized in 1920. Unable to carry out the 1920 organization plans, the War Department decided to skeletonize the existing establishment and abolish the training centers altogether.[72]

Despite the high hopes of Palmer, Pershing, and others for effective army reorganization, historian D. Clayton James notes that by 1922 the military establishment was "almost worthless even as a nucleus for mobilization."[73] After Congress's cuts, the Army was forced to discharge men, and future World War II corps commander Charles Corlett recalled that "Our regiment seemed to melt away overnight."[74] Marshall recalled: "We just had nobody. You couldn't even train a battalion—didn't have any communications people. You didn't have your special platoons. When the Headquarters Company was supposed to be . . . 318 men, it had gotten down to about 18. You couldn't train."[75] General March later noted that America had willingly rendered itself more impotent than Germany under the Treaty of Versailles's military limitations.

Once Pershing finished his vacation and testimony, Secretary Baker confessed to Harbord: "I do not exactly know what to do with General Pershing. There does not seem to be anything in the United States for a [four-star] General." It was inconceivable that Pershing should serve under March in the War Department. Besides the thorny issue of Pershing outranking the chief of staff, the temperamentally incompatible officers would inevitably clash if both were serving in Washington. Baker temporarily solved the problem by assigning Pershing special projects, such as writing the AEF's final report. Pershing was given office space and clerical assistance at the Old Land Office Building at 7th and E Streets, ten long blocks away from the War Department's office in the State, War, and Navy Building. Pershing was also permitted to retain key staff officers such as Marshall and Conner, who helped in the writing.[76]

After the AEF report's release in December 1919, Baker sent Pershing on a national tour of army camps and war plants to recommend those to be retained in the postwar drawdown. Pershing picked Marshall—along with other AEF standbys such as Conner, George Van Horn Moseley, and Malin Craig—to accompany him on the inspection trip. On December 3 they departed from Washington in two special rail cars put at Pershing's disposal. They visited eleven states before Christmas, and by mid-February had visited thirty-two. At each post the local commander held a briefing on the post's facilities, troops on station, and administrative procedures, and with his staff was prepared to answer questions on morale, recreation, training capacity, land available for maneuvers, buildings, supply, hospital, sanitation, and health. Pershing divided the inspection duties amongst his staff, and the length of stops varied from minutes to several days depending on the size of the installation, the size of the town, and the local arrangements.

The trip also served as a triumphal tour for America's conquering hero, with parades, receptions, and speeches in major cities, in which Pershing advocated preparedness. Because each community wanted to roll out the red carpet for him, Pershing and his staff were subjected to repeatedly eating the same banquet meal: chicken and Thousand Island dressing, served at a head table presided over by local VIPs and their often rotund wives. When one community wrote ahead to ask if Pershing had any special requests, Marshall wired back an emphatic YES: "Do not have chicken or thousand island dressing and go fifty-fifty with pretty girls at speakers table." Moseley later recalled: "They had steak, and every other girl at the speakers table was a knockout."[77]

In the election year of 1920, the parades and receptions accompanying the inspections inevitably generated a "Pershing for President" buzz that the general chose not to squelch. Viewed as the man who won the war, consideration of Pershing as a potential candidate started in 1919, when Democratic representative Guy E. Campbell declared to applause on the House floor: "I would like to see the people of this country and this House put aside our partisanship . . . and make him the unanimous choice of the conventions that assemble next year and elect him President of the United States."[78] Throughout the first months of 1920 unofficial delegations urged the general into the race, and despite public disclaimers, deep down Pershing felt the same attraction to the presidency as Generals Andrew Jackson, Zachary Taylor, and Ulysses S. Grant had before him. On the eve of the Republican convention in June 1920, he applied for retirement with an eye toward a presidential bid and indicated he would accept the nomination if offered. Among Pershing's staff and advisers, Marshall was one of the few who disapproved of his entry into the campaign. "I thought it was a shame that he might in some way cut down his prestige by being involved in that sort of a thing unless it was almost by acclamation," Marshall recalled.[79] When one political delegation visited from Tennessee, Marshall sent them packing, thereby drawing Pershing's anger.

In June, however, backroom maneuvering propelled Senator Warren Harding past Gen. Leonard Wood and Illinois governor Frank Lowden to the Republican nomination. His political foray over, Pershing decided to stay in the Army, and the dilemma of what to do with him remained. During the reorganization debate some legislators proposed making Pershing the permanent chief of staff. Baker's solution for the remainder of Wilson's presidency was to keep Pershing on active duty status, available to advise the president or the secretary of war, with most of his time free to write "the final history" of the war and thus "preserve the experience of this war for our future generations."[80] Following Harding's election and inauguration, in April 1921 the new secretary of war John Weeks proposed Pershing should have a General Headquarters that would perform many of the General Staff's functions, thereby making him a virtual co–chief of staff. This was quickly realized to be unworkable, however, and rather than trying to create the job for the man, on May 13 Secretary Weeks took the obvious step of naming Pershing chief of staff.

Pershing's accession as chief of staff further enhanced the power and prestige of the office—and of the General Staff—as he began instituting the reforms embodied in the NDA. With Harbord as his executive assistant and Marshall as his aide, Pershing promptly remade the Army in the AEF's image. Within a week he ordered all officers to wear the Sam Browne belt, symbol of the overseas officer. He replaced March's General Staff organization with the AEF system: G-1 (Personnel), G-2 (Intelligence), G-3 (Operations), G-4 (Training), and a War Plans Division charged with preparing plans in peace and executing them as a field army headquarters in war. The division heads each received the title of assistant chief of staff, and Pershing made it clear that in any future wars the commander-in-chief in the field would be superior, *not* the chief of staff in Washington. Pershing also rectified the disservice done to Colonel Palmer for his opposition to March's reorganization bill, bringing him out of exile and back to the War Department to study and advise on policy matters.[81]

Pershing's primary task as chief of staff quickly devolved into defending the Army as Congress descended into a mood of fiscal austerity amidst a rising tide of pacifism. Senator William Borah warned in 1921 that "The Secretary of the Treasury states that the only way in which relief can be had which the President says must be granted is through the reduction of the Army and the Navy."[82] In the appropriations debate that spring, talk of reduction to 100,000 began to circulate, and one representative suggested 50,000 as the proper size for the army. By June 1921, less than two years after Pershing received near-unanimous acclaim on the House floor and hundreds of thousands cheered the conquering heroes of the AEF, Harbord wrote: "There is hardly a committee meeting in either house of Congress on matters touching the Army that there is not hostility expressed toward the service and particularly toward the General Staff."[83] Another General Staff officer noted the same month, "The Army is like a yellow dog running down the street with a tin can tied on it, and everybody on the sidewalk is throwing rocks."[84]

In personal correspondence, in magazine articles, in testimony before congressional committees, and in speeches to private groups across the country, Pershing labored to stave off further manpower cuts. He was fighting a losing battle, however. Although Pershing enjoyed better personal relations with Congress than March had, he could not alter the reality that with the "war to end all wars" won and the world supposedly made safe for democracy, many congressmen thought the Army superfluous except for riot duty. By 1925 military appropriations stood at one-quarter of their 1920 levels. Despite Pershing's personal popularity, Marshall recalled: "I saw the Army ... start rapidly on the downgrade to almost extinction.... His views didn't count at all."[85]

As the staff officers who served under Pershing in France moved on to other assignments, Marshall's importance increased. He was installed in an office near his chief in the State, War, and Navy Building. Pershing sent proposed letters, draft reports, and staff recommendations to Marshall for comment.

"General Pershing," Marshall explained, "had a way of sending most all of these things into me and nobody knew about it, and all he would put on the paper was 'Colonel M.' Then it was up to me to take a look at it and tell him what I thought. But that was never betrayed outside of the office, that I was put into this position of maybe criticizing my superiors."[86] Marshall wrote Pershing's speeches and assisted in preparing the general's memoirs. One Pershing biographer summarized the relationship, writing: "Knowing the keen intelligence of Marshall, his thoroughly professional view, Pershing seldom acted without the younger man's opinion."[87]

Marshall's opinion in peacetime Washington was offered as frankly as at Gondrecourt years earlier. Once, Marshall suspected that Pershing had changed a War Department procedure primarily because Peyton March had initiated it. When Marshall wrote a memorandum criticizing the change, Pershing sent for him. "I don't take to this at all," he said. "I don't agree with you."

Thinking he had not articulated his objections clearly, Marshall went back and wrote another, more detailed memorandum. When Pershing read the second memo, he again said, "I don't accept this."

Marshall rewrote his criticism a third time, explaining why the old procedure was superior to Pershing's proposed change. This time Pershing slammed his hand on his desk and roared, "No, by God, we will do it this way!"

"Now General," Marshall coolly said, "just because you hate the guts of General March, you're setting yourself up . . . to do something you know damn well is wrong."

Pershing looked narrowly at Marshall. He handed back the memorandum and said, "Well, have it your own way."[88]

Marshall became the individual Pershing could trust with any assignment and a virtual amanuensis. In 1923, Congress created the American Battle Monuments Commission, and during the winter of 1923–1924 Pershing left America for six months to work in Paris, turning the War Department over to his deputy, Maj. Gen. John L. Hines. From October 23 to March 24 Marshall virtually ran the chief of staff's office. He sent Pershing at least one private memorandum or letter per week to keep him apprised of developments in Washington, to supply him with information for his memoirs, and to keep him posted on personal matters such as Warren Pershing's schooling and the rental of Pershing's Washington apartment. Marshall also prepared reports—including writing the 1923 chief of staff's annual report—carried out special assignments, and served on numerous boards.[89]

Despite his central role in the War Department, Marshall was still able to pick favorite mounts from the stable at Fort Myer and ride before work each day from 0700 to 0830, often taking a quick swim in the Tidal Basin. He and Lily settled down to the longest period of shared domesticity in their nearly two decades of marriage. They slipped easily into the ceremonial round of courtesy visits in official Washington and less formal parties among close friends on post. Rose Page, a young neighbor whom Marshall had befriended, recalled years later how he lavished attention on Lily: "He fetched and carried. He planned little surprises. He was ever solicitous of her health and comfort. He relieved her of mundane financial budgeting and any like chores and decisions. . . . He gave her unremitting consideration, smoothed the path before his queen and led her by the hand."[90]

Marshall's five years with Pershing enabled him to broaden his horizons immensely. Reading the flow of paper in and out of Pershing's office, Marshall could observe the entire Army establishment. While still in France after the war, Pershing had attempted to lay the foundation for fighting a future war by establishing boards to evaluate the lessons learned by the AEF's various branches. After the stateside celebrations were completed, Marshall was put to work sifting through these board's reports and the AEF's records. Marshall reviewed the tragic wastefulness of the American effort in the war, as green recruits were thrown into combat with insufficient training. Gas casualties among untrained troops were twice as great as among trained troops. Tanks would rumble ahead and get lost deep in enemy territory because the tankers were not trained to maintain communications. Marshall summarized these lessons in the January 1921 issue of the *Infantry Journal*, warning of the dangers of divided command, of reliance upon textbook tactics, and of assuming the next war would be the same tactically. "It is possible," he wrote, "that officers who participated only in the last phase of the war may draw somewhat erroneous conclusions from their battle experiences." He also noted that quick thinking and quick action were more important than proper formats: "Many orders, models in their form, failed to reach the troops in time to affect their actions, and many apparently crude and fragmentary instructions did reach front-line commanders in time to enable the purpose of the higher command to be carried out on the battlefield."[91]

By the end of the 1920 inspection tour, Pershing knew more about the Army than anyone else, knowledge that was almost completely shared by Marshall. In the fall of 1921, Marshall served as recorder to a board investigating the alleged inequities of the Army's single-list promotion system. His work examining the service records of hundreds of officers gave him detailed background on the careers of many men who would later serve under him. The time in Washington also gave him essential experience interacting with civilian leaders. He met with congressmen on the Military Affairs Committees, rubbed shoulders with the secretary of war, and briefed Presidents Harding and Calvin Coolidge. Regardless of his personal aloofness from partisan politics, he came to understand politics and politicians far better than most military men, a skill that would prove critical two decades later. By 1923 Marshall was one of the most knowledgeable officers in the Army, and his function as the unofficial deputy chief of staff enhanced his wartime reputation as a wizard of military efficiency.

Perhaps equally important to Marshall's life and career, in ways unperceivable at the time, was the close personal bond he formed with Pershing. Marshall came to admire his boss tremendously, especially his common sense, his backbone, and his ability to receive criticism dispassionately. His relationship with Pershing went beyond the professional to the mentor-student and father-son level. Despite their mirrored austerity, Marshall was able to see Pershing's joyous, relaxed after-hours spirit, which he strictly separated from his official demeanor. Once Pershing left the office, he enjoyed staying up late, talking about his youth, laughing, drinking, and joking. In the early 1920s, when both were traveling on a train together and enjoying a bottle of scotch, Pershing suggested they offer some to Senator George Moses in the next car. Pouring a little into a glass, they proceeded to where Pershing thought Moses was sleeping in a Pullman. "Senator Moses," whispered Pershing as he scratched the closed green curtain of a berth.

When there was no answer, Pershing raised the curtain, only to discover not Senator Moses, but an angry woman who cried: "What do you want?"

Pershing dropped the curtain and bolted down the aisle like a frightened schoolboy, pushing Marshall ahead of him and spilling the scotch.

"I had a hard time keeping out of his way," Marshall said, "because he was running up my back. But we got to the stateroom and got the door shut. Then he just sat down and laughed until he cried." Finally, wiping his eyes, Pershing noticed a little scotch remained in the glass and mischievously suggested Marshall return and try it again. "Not on your life," Marshall replied. "Get another aide."[92]

Marshall's respect for the chief of staff was reciprocated. Pershing called his aide "a very exceptional man" and urged that he should be made a general officer "as soon as eligible."[93] Pershing repaid Marshall's loyalty by visiting his aide's beloved alma mater, VMI, in June 1920. While in Lexington, Pershing delivered remarks at Robert E. Lee's tomb at Washington and Lee, which prompted a clamor of criticism for having visited the Confederate monument. "You got me to go there," Pershing chided his assistant, "now you attend to the letter objecting to my having gone."[94] When Marshall's bedridden mother moved into a Washington hotel, Marshall visited her almost every day, sometimes twice a day, with Pershing occasionally accompanying him.

Finally promoted to the permanent rank of lieutenant colonel and confronted with Pershing's imminent retirement, in the spring of 1924 Marshall applied for the troop command he had put off for the past five years. Pershing threw the Marshalls a farewell luncheon at the Shoreham Hotel on June 8, 1924. On July 12, after a farewell lunch in New York City with Pershing, Marshall, Lily, and her mother boarded an army transport—appropriately named the *St. Mihiel*—in New York Harbor, bound for Tientsin, China. From his next duty station Marshall wrote his mentor and friend: "No words can express the regret and loss I feel at the termination of my service with you. Few men in life have such opportunities and almost none, I believe, such a delightful association as was mine with you. May all good things be yours—Goodbye."[95]

Summarizing the fortuitous timing of Euric, king of the Visigoths' death, and the subsequent ascension of Clovis that enabled fractured Frankish tribes to unify in the fifth century into the country that would become modern France, Edward Gibbon observed, "The fortune of nations has often depended on accidents." A similar string of accidents and coincidences were vital to the Allied victory in World War II. Although success in war is the product of countless variables, seen and unseen, it can plausibly be argued that without Dwight Eisenhower, Omar Bradley, George Patton, Joe Collins, Matthew Ridgway, and a handful of other key army and corps commanders, America and its allies would not have been able to defeat Nazi Germany and Imperial Japan. If so, then it could also be argued that since none of these men would have held their commands if not for George Marshall, either due to his direct intervention or because of his herculean efforts to expand, train, and equip the army on the eve of that conflict, victory would not have been possible without Marshall. It follows that victory in World War II would have been less likely had Frederick Funston survived to lead the AEF, had Pershing not accepted Marshall's courageous rebuttal at Gondrecourt and taken him under his wing, or had the bomb accidentally released over the First Army's officer mess on November 11, 1918, fallen 15 feet to the left.

If America owed an incalculable debt to Marshall for the leadership he would provide in the next world war, a significant portion of the interest would deservedly go to Gen. John J. Pershing. As Bradley later observed of Marshall's apprenticeship under Pershing: "Few junior officers in the history of the U.S. Army had ever had . . . so much high-level exposure and responsibility for so long a period. Few gained so much in terms of personal and professional growth."[96] Marshall's relationship with Pershing marked him for high command, and Pershing's loyalty to, and support for, his former aide on both a professional and personal level would prove critical in the years to come. This relationship was itself only possible due to the unpredictable vicissitudes of fortune that put them in the right place at the right time on that cold day in France in October 1917. Although Marshall's apprenticeship under Pershing in France and in Washington was not as glamorous as the battlefield exploits of some of his contemporaries, the experience gained during this period would prove more significant for the greater conflagration that lay a generation over the horizon.

CHAPTER TWO

MacArthur at West Point

NOT EVERY SOLDIER ENJOYED THE TRIUMPHANT HOMECOMING THAT greeted Pershing and Marshall. More than four months earlier, on April 25, 1919, the *Leviathan* deposited a tranche of 12,000 doughboys back on their home soil via the Hoboken pier. The first man down the gangplank that blustery spring morning wore a huge raccoon coat and knitted scarf over his soldier's tunic. He had a sharp, aquiline nose and soft brown eyes. He tilted his head back as he walked, producing an erect posture that invariably made him appear taller than his 5 foot 10 inches.

Brig. Gen. Douglas MacArthur, commander of the 42nd "Rainbow" Division and the most highly decorated American officer of World War I, was home.

Whereas MacArthur had expected a "howling mob to proclaim us monarchs of all we surveyed," the only spectator on the pier was an urchin at the foot of the gangplank who asked who the troops were.

"We are the famous 42nd!" MacArthur proudly announced.

Apparently unimpressed, the young boy asked whether they had been in France.

"Amid a silence that hurt—with no one, not even the children to see us," MacArthur lamented, "we marched off the dock, to be scattered to the four winds—a sad, gloomy end of the Rainbow."[1]

MacArthur's disappointment did not end there. Later that evening, the division's senior officers were honored at a ball at the Waldorf-Astoria in New York City. MacArthur wore a full dress uniform that included seven silver stars, two Distinguished Service Crosses, and a traditional pair of cavalry spurs. When MacArthur stepped onto the dance floor with a young woman, his waltzing was quickly interrupted as the maître d'hotel rushed onto the dance floor. "Sir," he protested, "you may not dance in spurs. You might injure the dance floor."

MacArthur glared at the man, and said, "Do you know who I am?"

"Yes, sir. I do. But I must request you leave the dance floor and remove your spurs."

MacArthur took his date by the arm and, without a word, walked off the dance floor and out of the hotel, silently swearing never to set foot in the Waldorf again.[2]

MacArthur did not have time to stew on these petty humiliations, however. Two days later the chief of staff summoned the young hero to his office in Washington, DC. Peyton March had known MacArthur since the latter was a boy, and had served under his father Gen. Arthur MacArthur during the Philippine Insurrection. When Arthur MacArthur's brigade unexpectedly ran into serious resistance in the battle of Manila on August 13, 1898, then-Lieutenant March distinguished himself by leading a charge, followed by a successful reconnaissance mission, for which MacArthur recommended March for the Medal of Honor. Although the nomination was denied, during March's second deployment to the Philippines he served as MacArthur's aide and formed what would become a close association with the MacArthur family.[3]

When the younger MacArthur entered March's office on April 27th, the chief of staff abruptly said: "Douglas, things are in great confusion at West Point. . . . [Secretary] Baker and I have talked this over and we want you to go up there and revitalize and revamp the Academy. It has been too parochial in the past. I want to broaden it and graduate more cadets into the Army."

March felt the Academy's curriculum and leadership development system needed a complete overhaul, but realized that the professors and traditionalist alumni would fight any change to the revered institution. The previous winter he had tried to convince West Point's Academic Board of the need for reforms, but the board and the current superintendent adamantly rejected his suggestions. Secretary Baker enthusiastically supported March, however, so the chief of staff sought a young, progressive officer with an unimpeachable record and the intelligence, persuasiveness, and tenacity needed to enact a complete reform. Moreover, because of his rivalry with Pershing, March wanted a superintendent not drawn from the general's Chaumont clique.[4]

MacArthur was stunned. "I'm not an educator. I'm a field soldier," he protested. "Besides, there are so many of my old professors there. I can't do it."[5]

March responded to the young general's doubts by simply saying, "Yes . . . you can do it," and ordered MacArthur to assume the superintendency in June.

The United States Military Academy at West Point sits on a small plateau of roughly 40 acres jutting into the Hudson about 50 miles north of New York City. Sitting high above the river's western bank, the Academy's Gothic buildings of gray granite resemble a medieval fortress, an architectural style intended to evoke a sense of strength and permanence amidst the natural beauty of the forested heights surrounding West Point's plain. In 1919 West Point remained an isolated bastion tenuously linked to the outside world by the West Shore Railway, excursion boats on the Hudson, and a winding road leading into New Jersey.

West Point was America's largest fort during the Revolutionary War— one which Benedict Arnold had infamously attempted to betray to the British—and it remained a garrison and training area after the war. After independence was won, and for the next two decades, the U.S. Army lacked a sufficiently educated professional officers corps, particularly with regard to the engineers critical to early-nineteenth-century warfare. Consequently, on March 16, 1802, President Thomas Jefferson signed legislation creating a separate Corps of Engineers which "shall be stationed at West Point, in the State of New York, and shall constitute a military academy."[6]

The Academy languished in its first decade until Col. Sylvanus Thayer was appointed superintendent in 1817. Thayer gathered an elite faculty to West Point, and the textbooks written by the Academy's professors soon dominated American mathematics, chemistry, and engineering fields. West Point became the nation's premier civil engineering school, and as Stephen Ambrose notes, "The importance of the Academy to the early development of American roads, canals, and railroads cannot be overstated."[7] The railroads that connected Boston with the interior, the harbors in Rhode Island and Connecticut, the Susquehanna and Baltimore and the Baltimore and Ohio Railroads, new roads in Michigan and Arkansas, harbor improvements on the Gulf Coast and Mississippi River—all were the products of civil engineers trained at West Point. In 1860 a Senate commission concluded: "Nearly all the great public works of the country, the river and harbor works, the lighthouses, and even the public buildings have been directed by its graduates; they were the pioneers in the construction of railroads, and among the teachers of that art; and the great scientific works of government have been chiefly conducted by them."[8]

West Point's reputation was further enhanced by the critical role its alumni played in the Civil War. Beyond legendary commanders such as Ulysses S. Grant and Robert E. Lee, 294 West Pointers became generals in the Union army. Of the 269 graduates who served the Confederacy, 151 became general officers. Of the sixty most important battles, all but five were commanded on both sides by Academy graduates; of those five, one side in each battle was commanded by a West Pointer.[9] Thus, when the Academy celebrated its centennial in 1902, President Theodore Roosevelt lavished praise on West Point and its graduates, proclaiming: "This institution has completed its first hundred years of life. During that century no other educational institution in the land has contributed as many names as West Point has contributed to the honor roll of the nation's greatest citizens."[10]

Less than two decades later, however, the American entry into World War I nearly destroyed the traditions to which Roosevelt had paid tribute. Two weeks after President Wilson's declaration of war, the Class of 1917 was graduated early in April. In May the Class of 1918 began an abbreviated version of the First Class course of studies: intensive military training was added the next month, and ten weeks later they were graduated as the Class of August 1917. As the need for officers intensified, the cadets who should have been the Class of 1919 were graduated on June 12, 1918, and almost immediately deployed to France.

The war's outcome remained in doubt in October 1918, and the War Department panicked when U.S. casualties began to mount in the Meuse-Argonne offensive. As Superintendent Samuel Tillman recalled: "On the 3d [sic] of October I got a telephone message from the Adjutant General at half past 10 o'clock at night telling me we were to graduate [the classes of 1920 and 1921] on the 1st of November."[11] On November 1, both classes graduated, bringing the total to five classes graduated in just over eighteen months, leaving only fourth classmen on West Point's plain. Even those plebes would not be at the Academy for long. The War Department further ordered the course of study reduced to one year for the duration of the war, so that the plebes would graduate in June 1919. A special plebe class of 800 new cadets, exempted from the normal entrance requirements, would be matriculated in November 1918 and graduated in June 1919 with the plebe class already on post. Thus, the Academy had been transformed into little more than yet another camp for providing young men a quick commission. Tillman, who had served on West Point's faculty for over thirty years before coming out of retirement to serve as wartime superintendent, lamented that "The regime and traditions, which have taken a century to develop, can never be restored."[12]

Although the war ended ten days after the hasty graduation of the Classes of 1920 and 1921, the Academy remained in turmoil. The sole class remaining at West Point after the November graduation wore the traditional gray uniform with bell-buttoned dress coats and black-striped trousers. Yet due to a lack of provisions, the 360 new plebes who arrived on November 2nd were issued olive drab AEF privates' uniforms with leggings and campaign hats circled with orange bands, causing them to be derisively nicknamed "Orioles" by the cadets. Because there would only be other plebes to haze and train them, the Academy administration decided it would be unfair to put them through the regular Fourth Class program, and kept the two classes strictly segregated. The Class of 1921 (285 "high school pupils with one year's training at West Point") was reassembled and brought back to the Academy on December 3rd, for an additional six months' instruction—not as cadets as Tillman had requested—but as student officers. Since they already had commissions they were uniformed and paid as officers, yet they were still treated, drilled, and instructed as cadets by the administration. This paradoxical status understandably infuriated them, and they made no attempt to hide their resentment.[13]

The hodgepodge of uniforms caused confusion (a member of the Class of 1920 described the mess formations as the "weirdest thing that was ever seen") as three distinct sets of young men marched about the Plain, and the Cadet Corps degenerated into disunity and low morale. Within a week of the Armistice General March determined that the 425 cadets who entered in June 1918 would complete a two-year course and graduate in 1920, while the 360 November entrants would not be given diplomas until 1921. Many cadets had entered the Academy in pursuit of short-term goals, however, and when this three-year program was announced over one hundred cadets resigned because they had anticipated graduating in one year.[14]

Moreover, the Academy had always depended upon its upperclassmen to carry on its honor code and traditions, and to instill these in new cadets. Yet because of the early graduations there *were no* upperclassmen for cadets to emulate. The winter and spring of 1918–1919 were marked by fights among the cadets and often brutal, excessive hazing. On January 1, 1919, an "Oriole" named Stephen M. Bird committed suicide due to the hazing he received, prompting a congressional inquiry. Consequently, as Maj. Jacob L. Devers, then a tactical officer at the Academy noted, the new superintendent would inherit "an old institution with a great heritage of success and tradition, but now reduced to a pitiable state as a result of actions of the War Department."[15]

Yet perhaps the biggest threat in 1919 to West Point's mission of preparing young men* for service as commissioned officers in the U.S. Army was not the chaos of the last two years, but rather the stagnation of several decades. Because of the Academy's success in the Civil War, West Point's traditions became sacrosanct. Whenever critics or reformers suggested a change, the response both within and outside the Academy was outrage at the suggestion that the system which had produced Grant and Sherman, Lee and Jackson, might require alteration. Judging the educational system to be near perfect, these traditionalists resisted any and all changes that might have upended the carefully constructed curriculum. By the end of the nineteenth century, West Point was badly behind the times as it clung to outdated assumptions about education, military training, leadership, and other developmental activities.[16]

The cadets still followed a curriculum dominated by mathematics and engineering, even though most would become infantrymen, cavalrymen, or artillerists rather than engineers. The Academy's leadership believed the quantitative disciplines the best tools for instilling mental discipline. As the Academic Board wrote in December 1918: "The power and habit of clear, exact and logical thought engendered by the proper study of mathematics and in the application of mathematical principles and processes to Mechanics, Engineering, Electricity, Ordnance and other practical sciences are the best assets that can be provided our graduates. . . ."[17] Even if one accepted this assertion, the majority of instructors learned all their mathematics, history, English, and other subjects at the Academy, and thus were almost completely oblivious to innovations in higher education.

Moreover, the instructional methods at West Point were out of date and varied little from discipline to discipline. The cadets were expected to memorize a daily assignment, and most class time was spent in monotonous recitation by memory either orally or at the blackboard. The instructor rarely lectured or explained the material. Instead, his main function was to grade the cadets' performance on the basis of preparation and presentation, with little if any discussion, intellectual stimulus, or experimentation.[18]

Diversions from the tedium of academics were rare. Academy leaders regulated the cadets' every activity, and cadets enjoyed few privileges. In order

---

* It would still be fifty-seven years before the first female cadets were admitted in 1976.

to insulate them from the perceived corrupting influences of the outside world, cadets could not leave the Academy except for athletic competitions and on furlough after their second year. Virtually all military training took place at West Point, and consisted of an updated version of the demonstrations and parade-ground exercises of the past. Thus, as Oriole cadet—and future commander of the 101st Airborne and Chairman of the Joint Chiefs of Staff—Maxwell Taylor observed, West Point in 1919 remained a perfect "military cloister."[19]

This prewar stagnation was actually perpetuated by the Great War, as traditionalists believed that West Pointers' performance on France's battlefields had validated the design of the Academy's technical curriculum. General Pershing said the Academy had "justified itself a hundred times over in furnishing to this great American Army . . . the splendid men who have served . . . in the old West Point spirit."[20] In addition to Pershing and March, twenty-four of the thirty-eight American corps and division commanders on the Western Front, and 74 percent of the 480 general officers were West Pointers.[21] Consequently, the Academy's all-powerful Academic Board believed the only change needed in 1919 was an immediate return to pre–World War I conditions, and that in these turbulent times, more than ever, they were the guardians of a sacred trust in defending the Academy's traditional values and methods.

"West Point is forty years behind the times," March had warned MacArthur, a fact that was apparent to observers from both within the War Department and beyond. After serving on a board appointed by Secretary Baker to investigate the Academy's course of instruction, Major General Bliss wrote in March 1917: "We will all be in error if we do not take serious account of the fact that there seems to be a general consensus of opinion that some change ought to be made" to West Point's curriculum.[22] In 1919 Dr. Charles R. Mann of the General Staff's Committee on Education and Special Training recorded his doubts about the Academy's exclusive attention to "character and logical power" as ends in education, suggesting that during the war "difficulties" had been experienced with respect to West Pointers' "resourcefulness, initiative, and adaptability to new ideas."[23] Marshal Henri-Philippe Pétain, the hero of Verdun, was shocked when he visited West Point after the war:

I do not think that young men who are being prepared for the duties of an officer should be required to repeat the same gestures every day during four years. This seems to be too long, and I fear that this monotony must result in fixing the graduate's mind into a groove so rigid that elasticity becomes impaired.

He comes out a well-instructed and obedient subaltern and a first rate drill-master, but outside of a small category that have exceptional force of character, he has got to pass considerable time before he can break the rigid forms into which his nature has become crystallized and regain his mental vigor."[24]

The killing of initiative inherent in the Academy's disciplinary system led Army surgeon Dr. Charles Woodruff to conclude that "The best way to extinguish a man is to send him to West Point."[25]

"West Point is an example of just what an educational institution should not be," declared the president emeritus of Harvard University, Charles W. Eliot, in perhaps the most far-reaching critique of the Academy.

In my opinion, no American school or college intended for youth of between 18 and 22 years of age should accept such ill-prepared material as West Point accepts. Secondly, no school or college should have a completely pre-scribed curriculum. Thirdly, no school or college should have its teaching done almost exclusively by recent graduates of the same school or college who are not teachers and who serve short terms. West Point, so far as its teachers are concerned, breeds in and in, a very bad practice for any educational institution.[26]

Or as Winston Churchill had observed years earlier in registering his horror at Academy regulations: "The cadets enter from nineteen to twenty-two and stay four years. . . . They are not allowed to smoke. . . . In fact they have far less liberty than any public school boys in our country. . . . Young men of 24 or 25 who would resign their personal liberty to such an extent can never make good citizens or fine soldiers."[27]

The combination of short-term turmoil and long-term stagnation would have posed a formidable challenge for whoever was appointed as the first postwar superintendent, much less a thirty-nine-year-old soldier with no pedagogical experience. But in many ways, Douglas MacArthur had liter-ally been born and bred for West Point. His father Arthur was the son of a prominent Wisconsin judge, and had planned on attending the Academy himself until the Civil War's outbreak and the subsequent call for volunteers proved irresistible. In August 1862, at age seventeen, Arthur joined the 24th

Wisconsin, and because of his education and intelligence (and his father's political connections) was appointed as regimental adjutant with the rank of first lieutenant. Under intense enemy fire, on November 25, 1863, he rallied a faltering Union charge up Missionary Ridge outside Chattanooga. He was awarded the Medal of Honor for his heroism, and was eventually brevetted to full colonel at the age of nineteen, the youngest to hold that rank in the Union army.

Nearly forty years later he again led a brigade in combat during the Philippine Insurrection, eventually rising to command the Eighth Army Corps in May 1900, overseeing all operations in the archipelago. Major General MacArthur initiated a vigorous—and ultimately successful—counterinsurgency campaign, as in 1901 more than 20,000 *insurrectos* surrendered and sought amnesty. MacArthur had a reputation for bluntness and flamboyance, however, and could not refrain from speaking out of turn. His inability to work with the Civilian Commission overseeing the islands' political and economic development—especially his overt hostility to the commission's head, William Howard Taft—led him to be relieved of command in 1901. When Taft later became secretary of war and then president, MacArthur's career was effectively ended. Despite his rank and outstanding record, he spent his final years deeply embittered with no official position or command.[28]

Whereas today a high proportion of military officers are themselves military "brats," the milieu in which Douglas MacArthur was raised was relatively unusual for the officers of his generation. He was born on Fort Dodge, Arkansas (now a part of the capital, Little Rock) on January 26, 1880. "My first recollection is that of a bugle call," MacArthur was fond of saying, and his earliest memories were of growing up on remote frontier posts. As his biographer D. Clayton James notes, "The color, excitement, and romance of the military had cast a spell on . . . MacArthur which would last his entire life."[29] Before he could even walk, MacArthur's father had him headed for West Point to complete his unfulfilled dream. According to Peyton March, "He told me that he started Douglas towards West Point the day he was born."[30]

The young MacArthur entered West Point in 1899. Although he was scrutinized—and sadistically hazed—from the start because of his father's command in the Philippines, he possessed several distinct advantages over his classmates. During his plebe year he was allowed to room with an upperclassman, thereby gaining an extra hour of study time each night thanks to his roommate's privileges. While her husband was deployed to the Philippines,

MacArthur's mother, "Pinky" MacArthur, moved to West Point when her son enrolled at the Academy. This provided him with critical relief from the crushing isolation most other cadets suffered. Moreover, it was Pinky who had sharpened his competitive instincts to a razor's edge in his youth, so her proximity helped spur his already prodigious will to win. From her room in Cramer's Hotel just off post she could see the lamp in her son's room and tell whether or not he was studying. Beyond this incentive, he still sometimes studied through the night, covering his windows with blankets to avoid detection.

MacArthur's biggest advantage at West Point, however, was his near-photographic memory, which was tailor made for the daily recitations upon which the cadets' grades were based. MacArthur finished first in his class of 94 cadets, earning 98.14 of 100 possible points, surpassed only by an 1884 graduate with 99.78 and by Robert E. Lee's 98.33 in 1829. Moreover, as classmate Robert E. Wood noted, other members of the Corps "recognized intuitively that MacArthur was born to be a real leader of men." Each year at the Academy he achieved the highest rank available to him—senior corporal as a sophomore, and senior first sergeant as a junior. During his final year at West Point—like Lee and Pershing before him—MacArthur held the position of first captain, the highest military honor a cadet could receive. On June 11, 1903, MacArthur graduated and was commissioned as a second lieutenant, with his classmates voting him "most likely to succeed."[31]

The reputation for brilliance MacArthur earned at West Point—and his father's connections—opened doors to him unavailable to other junior officers. Like George Marshall, his first duty station was in the Philippines, after which he served as an aide on his father's military tour of the Far East. He served as a social aide to President Theodore Roosevelt in the winter of 1906–1907, and from late 1912 to April 1913 served as an aide to Chief of Staff Leonard Wood before joining the General Staff. At General Wood's request, in 1914 MacArthur undertook a dangerous reconnaissance mission behind enemy lines during the occupation of Vera Cruz. He killed two bandits in a firefight and was nominated for the Medal of Honor. Yet because there were no other Americans present to corroborate his account of events—and because it was feared that decorating an officer for a mission undertaken outside the normal chain of command would encourage a dangerous entrepreneurism amongst ambitious officers—the recommendation was rejected.

MacArthur returned to the General Staff, and in 1915–1916 worked on the drafting of national defense legislation. After the passage of the National

Defense Act of 1916, Secretary of War Baker appointed MacArthur as his military assistant. Thus, in the spring of 1917, responsibility for selling the Selective Service Act fell squarely on Major MacArthur's shoulders. He had spent the past two years carefully cultivating the press, however, and consequently the country's newspapers published editorials overwhelmingly in favor of the draft.[32]

MacArthur was subsequently chosen to be the chief of staff of the 42nd Infantry Division—nicknamed the "Rainbow Division"—because it had been his idea to create a composite division from multiple states to avoid the political minefield of determining which National Guard units would be first to deploy. The division commander, Maj. Gen. Charles Menoher, was competent albeit colorless. Consequently, the Rainbow developed a distinct sense of its uniqueness and derived much of its personality from MacArthur. His soldiers idolized him. At thirty-seven he was closer to their age than the division's other senior officers, and he shared their discomforts and danger as one of the few senior officers who accompanied his troops into battle.

MacArthur was daring, repeatedly exposing himself to enemy fire. On February 26, 1918, now-Colonel MacArthur volunteered to go on a French raid across no man's land without notifying Menoher and earned his first Silver Star. He received the Distinguished Service Cross less than a month later for his "coolness and conspicuous courage" while leading a raid by a battalion of Iowans that captured a German trench.[33] On September 12, Lt. Col. George S. Patton and thirty of his Renault tanks advanced with the Rainbow Division during the St. Mihiel offensive. In the morning, Patton wrote, "I walked along the firing line of one brigade. They were all in shell holes except [General MacArthur] who was standing on a little hill. . . . I joined him and the creeping barrage came along toward us, but it was very thin and not dangerous. I think each one wanted to leave but each hated to say so, so we let it come over us."[34] MacArthur earned his fifth Silver Star and Patton's enduring respect. He told his family that MacArthur was "the bravest man I ever met."[35]

When MacArthur was given command of one of the 42nd's brigades, the Rainbow headquarters staff presented him with a gold cigarette case to mark his departure as chief of staff. It was inscribed "To the bravest of the brave," a rare tribute for a staff officer. When Menoher was promoted to corps commander, MacArthur was designated his successor, and at age thirty-eight became the youngest division commander in the AEF. As historian Robert Cowley notes: "For all the controversies that his later career would arouse, there is one fact about his life that is indisputable: He was one of the genuine heroes of World War I."[36]

The petty humiliations of his homecoming notwithstanding, MacArthur was a war hero renowned throughout the country, an inspiring soldier-leader who West Point's cadets could be proud of and hope to emulate. Yet as his biographer William Manchester observed, MacArthur "was a great thundering paradox of a man, noble and ignoble, inspiring and outrageous, arrogant and shy, the best of men and the worst of men, the most protean, most ridiculous, and most sublime. No more baffling, exasperating soldier ever wore a uniform."[37] The journalist William Allen White recalled of MacArthur: "I had never met so vivid, so captivating, so magnetic a man."[38] Yet even early in his career, before he had achieved fame on the battlefields of France, MacArthur behaved as if the Army's rules did not apply to him. As a junior officer he argued with superior officers if given an assignment that inconvenienced him. While in France he refused to wear the standard uniform worn by countless other officers. MacArthur took the grommet out of his cap so that it looked shapeless and jaunty. He wore a thick turtleneck sweater and a 7-foot-long purple muffler his mother had knitted for him. He justified his distinctive garb by claiming it made him easier for couriers and scouts to find, although in theory a divisional chief of staff could be found by anyone in a hurry at the division headquarters.[39]

MacArthur also demonstrated a disturbing paranoid streak. He fervently believed a coterie of officers at Pershing's headquarters were personally out to get him because he opposed a plan—quickly aborted—to use the 42nd's men as replacements for other divisions. Although Pershing personally pinned on his first star as a brigadier general, MacArthur nevertheless believed GHQ was comprised of enemies conspiring against him. When an awards board decided in January 1919 that he was ineligible for the Medal of Honor, MacArthur blamed the decision on "enmity" against him "on the part of certain senior members of Pershing's GHQ staff," a resentment that stayed with him throughout his career.[40]

Despite his flair for the dramatic, MacArthur declined the customary ceremonial review by the Corps of Cadets when he assumed command of West Point on June 12, 1919. The thirty-nine-year-old bachelor and his now-widowed mother Pinky quietly slipped into the superintendent's historic brick and iron grill mansion. "If memory serves me," MacArthur explained to his new adjutant, Maj. William A. Ganoe, "we didn't lack for ceremonies as cadets. There was a constant excuse for turning out the Corps for a show. What possible benefit can be found in an extra one for me? They'll see me soon and often enough."[41] Earl "Red" Blaik, then a cadet and later a legendary football coach at West Point recalled: "We soon learned he was not one to soiree the Corps with unnecessary pomp and ceremony." Several days passed before cadets saw "this tall, striding officer of casual dignity on Diagonal Walk." Even then MacArthur looked unlike any general the faculty or cadets had ever seen or imagined. They knew MacArthur had returned from France with more decorations for gallantry than any other soldier in the AEF, yet he did not wear a single ribbon on his chest.[42]

MacArthur arrived at West Point with "an Army-wide reputation for brilliance" and a fresh outlook on the Academy's mission. The new superintendent believed that future wars would require a different type of West Pointer than those from the age of small, professional armies, when officers employed rigid discipline and harsh punishments to control men in battle. World War I had shown that twentieth-century conflicts would be massive struggles necessitating the mobilization of entire nations. These armies would consist of young men fresh from the factory or farm, the classroom or office, amateurs who bore little resemblance to the cannon fodder that comprised the armies of centuries past. In MacArthur's experience, too many Academy graduates emerged from the cloistered confines on the Hudson poorly prepared to cope with volunteers and draftees straight from civilian life. Moreover, some West Pointers he observed during the occupation of the Rhineland evinced little knowledge of any fields beyond the military even though they were required to deal with political, economic, and social problems.[43] Consequently, MacArthur envisioned developing an entirely new breed of officer to meet these future challenges. "The rule of this war can but apply to that of the future," he wrote.

> *Such changed conditions will require a modification in type of the officer, a type possessing all of the cardinal military virtues as of yore, but possessing an intimate understanding of the mechanics of human feelings, a comprehensive grasp of world and national affairs, and a liberalization of conception which amounts to a change in his psychology of command.*[44]

Arriving at West Point, however, MacArthur found "the entire institution was in a state of disorder and confusion." In the postwar turmoil, "The Old

West Point could not be recognized. . . . It had gone; it had to be replaced."[45] In private, he called conditions "chaotic" and believed his mission was "to fight for the very life" of the Academy.[46]

It is difficult to overstate how ambitious MacArthur's vision was for his beloved alma mater, as he sought to revolutionize the Academy's academics, military training, and athletics. His initial efforts, however, were intended to "introduce a new atmosphere of liberalization in doing away with provincialism, a substitute of subjective for objective discipline, a progressive increase of cadet responsibility tending to develop initiative and force of character rather than automatic performance of stereotyped functions."[47] He began with the system for indoctrinating plebes. The report on Cadet Stephen Bird's suicide established that harsh and even sadistic treatment of plebes was being condoned by upperclassmen. MacArthur had been a cadet during one of the Academy's worst periods of hazing, and speaking with his commandant Robert Danford, recalled cadets "who seemed to take delight in being cruel" in 1899.[48] MacArthur had witnessed officers bullying their men in the war, and saw the seeds of this behavior in the upperclassmen's treatment of West Point plebes.

Although previous superintendents had tried to eradicate hazing, each Third Class felt compelled to make life hellish for the next class, and few cadets were suspended or expelled for hazing. Cadets were generally proud that enduring the ordeal of plebe life carried a badge of distinction for "being able to take it."[49] As one West Point graduate justified the custom, hazing:

> *Accustoms a man to panic, to having to do things that require a lot of coordination, to remember a great many details and to do it under great time pressure. Cadets learn by this to be familiar with the feeling of panic, to control it. They learn to do things at a very fast pace, but calmly so as not to forget any details. It doesn't take much imagination to see the utility of this for a war situation. I never once saw the significance and purpose of the clothing formation when I was a cadet, but I had occasion to remember it in the war and my understanding of the significance of it came after I was actually in combat.*[50]

Whereas historian Jorg Muth argues "A collection of potential hazing techniques reads like a supplement to the Marquis the Sade's writings," even officers such as Omar Bradley thought hazing was a great "leveler," removing preconceived notions of merit and replacing them with military discipline and recognition of the command structure and privileges of rank.[51] Thus, many cadets and graduates condoned the practice provided it stayed within "reasonable limits."

Yet such limits were hard to define when tradition was the only guide, and dangerous practices such as forcing plebes to do splits over unsheathed bayonets persisted. MacArthur therefore decided to codify these limits. One of his first acts was to meet with a selected group of First Classmen. He charmed this group of cadets by treating them in a friendly, informal manner. He shook hands with each one instead of saluting, patted them on the arm, and offered them cigarettes, which were against regulations. MacArthur asked them to study the Fourth Class orientation system, and instructed Danford to establish a committee to prepare a pamphlet codifying the upperclassmen's relations with plebes.

For several weeks the First Class Committee debated, and finally codified, Fourth Class customs. The finished product, forwarded to MacArthur for his approval in early August, put an emphasis on positive leadership. MacArthur praised the cadets for lifting the "haze of uncertainty which has befogged the relationship of the classes" and for accepting "the responsibility for rectifying this condition."[52] He gathered the Academy's entire senior class to explain the committee's purpose and to enlist their support. Although Blaik noted that "bitter feelings arose as the presentation of changes to the Class was vigorously resisted by the traditionalists," another cadet recalled that MacArthur's "personal prestige carried the day and overcame the reluctance to cooperate on the part of those cadets who would have resisted an intrusion of authority into the traditions of the Corps of Cadets of which they felt themselves the guardians."[53] The new code was adopted and implemented, although the upperclassmen refused to abandon hazing altogether.

MacArthur decided to build upon this achievement by having the cadets form an Honor Committee. An unofficial honor code that banned lying, cheating, and stealing had functioned at the Academy since its early days, but had been enforced by the company tactical officers. MacArthur formed another committee of First Class cadets to articulate the standards of honorable behavior and codify the procedures governing the unwritten honor code. He published their recommendations in a pamphlet entitled *Traditions and Customs of the Corps*, which describes the quest for honor as the "most cherished sentiment in the life of the Corps." The Corps of Cadets, "individually and collectively," would be the "guardian of its own honor" and cadets had to report their peers' transgressions when the offense was a breach of honor.[54]

A Cadet Honor Committee selected by the corps was made responsible for interpreting the honor system to incoming plebes and sitting as a jury on violations of the code, under the commandant's supervision. Although cadets may not have had legal authority over the honor system, MacArthur's reforms gave them extraordinary influence in administering it.

MacArthur sought other ways of giving cadets more responsibilities in order to develop character. In May 1919 the *New York Times* declared: "We need less 'pipeclay' and less seclusion at the Military Academy—in one word, more democracy. During their four years' term the cadets see about as little of the world as the inmates of a convent. When they graduate they know little of human nature, and the only men they have handled are themselves."[55] MacArthur agreed, and noted a paradox at the heart of West Point: "At one end, we boast about a cadet's truth and honesty; and at the other, we don't trust him to go out the gates of this medieval keep."[56] He recalled that cadets "had no opportunity to familiarize themselves with the mores and standards of people in the world without, so that when they graduated and mingled freely with their fellow, they had no common background of knowledge and awareness." Consequently, "they were thrust out into the world a man in age, but as experienced as a high school boy. They were cloistered almost to a monastic extent."[57]

MacArthur overhauled cadet regulations to allow cadets to receive packages as ordinary mail without inspection. Whereas cadets had previously never handled money while at the Academy, they were now given $5 of their monthly pay of $50 in cash to spend how they pleased and thereby "exercise within a limited scope economy and responsibility."[58] MacArthur decreed that cadets "were no longer to be walled up within the Academy limits, but were to be treated as responsible young men," and believed these privileges "would serve both as a relaxation from the rigid grind of study and training, and as a means of keeping touch with life outside the walls of the institution." First Classmen were permitted six-hour leaves on weekends, and during the summer cadets received two-day leaves providing enough freedom to go into New York City. MacArthur expanded hours at the First Class Club and gave seniors the status of junior officers in their social relations with the post's officers, meaning they could make calls, attend parties, and even play cards with the officers and their wives. During the spring term First Classmen could walk out of the gates at will.[59]

MacArthur also sought to instill responsibility in the cadets by reforming disciplinary actions to reflect command responsibilities in the Regular

Army. Traditionally, if tactical officers found a cadet in violation of a regulation, the offender's name would appear on a "skin" list requiring a formal written response explaining the infraction. One day Danford came to see the superintendent. "Every morning I find on my desk a big pile of cadet explanations," he said.

> *This might have been all right in our day when the chief object seemed to be to teach us how to write official letters, but today it is utterly absurd. I would like to give each company tactical officer a room on the ground floor of barracks, call it the Company Orderly Room, and there, at appropriate times, have him, face to face with the offending cadet, discuss the delinquency involved, and award such demerits or such punishment as seems fit. In this way a cadet will learn how a company commander in the service handles his men, and will teach him how the good captain, through firmness, kindness and justice, builds the pride and espirit of his company.*

MacArthur listened thoughtfully as Danford explained his proposal. Then, striking his desk, he cried "Do it!"[60] The skin list was abolished, and MacArthur subsequently expanded the official responsibilities of cadet NCOs, making them similar to the duties of Regular Army NCOs.

Believing character to be as important as classroom brilliance for future officers, MacArthur allowed cadets to rate one another on their leadership ability, an assessment that had been the exclusive province of the company tactical officers. These peer ratings counted heavily in the final class standings, and although the accumulation of demerits still counted in the general class rankings, factors such as leadership and personality, military bearing and efficiency, athletic performance, and extracurricular activities were now also tallied.[61]

These dramatic changes in cadet regulations and discipline were matched by an equally ambitious attempt to drag West Point's academics into the twentieth century. In order to produce officers who understood human motivations and were knowledgeable about national and foreign affairs, MacArthur pursued drastic curriculum reforms to deemphasize technical subjects. He urged the introduction of courses in psychology and sociology, and the creation of a Department of Economics, Government, and History. MacArthur persuaded the Academic Board to expand English instruction to improve the cadets' writing skills, and ordered the Department of English and History to organize a course in public speaking and debating so that each cadet could obtain a better degree of "self-assurance and poise not heretofore made possible." To make room for these new courses, the Academic Board made substantial reductions in mathematics and drawing.[62] MacArthur also revamped the curriculum in other areas, dropping courses in geology and mineralogy and using that time to extend the offering in electricity and to introduce instruction in internal combustion engines, radio communications, and aerodynamics.[63]

In 1920 MacArthur circulated the newly approved postwar curriculum to senior officers and civilians for review and comment. He brought leaders in higher education to West Point to appraise the current program and recommend changes. Of the ninety-one educators, forty-three gave unqualified praise, and forty-eight approved it with further suggestions. MacArthur was confident, therefore, that the curriculum was "set on correct lines."[64] A common criticism, however, was of the lack of coordination between West Point's academic departments—which Jacob Devers called "tight little, isolated islands." MacArthur directed a questionnaire on the subject to each department head, and when he did not get satisfactory responses, he shocked the professors by suddenly appearing in classrooms, taking a seat in the rear, and taking notes. Afterward he took the unprecedented step of visiting instructors in their offices to offer suggestions for improving their teaching methods.[65]

As a result of these inspections, MacArthur discovered that cadets suffered not only from the overload in mathematics and natural sciences, but also from the instructors' pedagogical backwardness. Rather than attending lectures by subject matter experts, at the end of every class period cadets would receive a slip of paper with a task to be performed in front of the class during the next session, which the cadet would present using predetermined fixed phrases. Even in important subjects like military history cadets merely parroted names and dates, and would be praised or critiqued by the teacher with no discussion to raise questions about the materials or synthesize ideas. Once, when a confused cadet tried to get clarification about a text, the instructor declared, "I'm not here to answer questions but to mark you." Indeed, several professors told Ganoe that the only drawback to the Academy was instructing cadets, and it showed in their indifferent teaching.[66]

One reason so many faculty were poor teachers was that instructors' ability was less important a consideration in filling a position than their class rank as cadets and their personal relationship with the department heads. For decades senior faculty members could hire and fire at their own discretion, and like Charles Eliot, MacArthur thought the Academy's inbreeding had gone too far. This problem was exacerbated in 1920 when a large influx of new instructors was added to accommodate the Corps of Cadets' return to its regular peacetime strength. Former cadets detailed to West Point as instructors several years after graduation often found themselves ordered to teach a subject in which they were not proficient, much less expert. Capt. Joseph Lawton Collins had studied three years of Latin and three years of French before graduating from West Point in 1917. While on occupation duty in Germany from 1919 to 1920 he visited France several times and "had brushed up on French pronunciation" and thus expected to teach one of those languages. Yet when he reported to West Point on August 25, 1921, he was assigned to the Chemistry Department even though he "had scarcely given a thought to chemistry since graduation."[67]

Capt. Matthew Ridgway, Class of 1917, considered himself able to teach English, law, and Spanish since these were subjects he had excelled in as a cadet. Instead, he was assigned to teach second-year French to a class already well underway. Ridgway went to see Col. Cornelis de Witt Willcox, the head of West Point's department of modern languages. "I bluntly told Professor Willcox I didn't know enough French to order a scrambled egg in a French restaurant. I hadn't spoken or read a word of French since my yearling year, and I hadn't been particularly good at it then. I couldn't possibly see how I could do a good job as a French instructor." Willcox listened to the young officer plead his case. Finally, he dryly replied, "Your classes start tomorrow," before turning away. It took Ridgway three weeks of all-nighters to catch up with, and pass, the class he would teach.[68] Similarly, when Maj. Omar Bradley joined the faculty as a math instructor in September 1920, he and other new instructors had to attend afternoon courses to stay ahead of the plebes they were teaching, and his evenings were spent cramming for the lessons he was expected to teach the next morning. The next year he was moved up to a more advanced course for sophomores and once again found himself spending his afternoons studying to stay ahead of his students.[69]

MacArthur resolved to improve the level of instruction. In his first year he announced that the "front-board recitation" was no longer mandatory "in subjects which don't lend themselves readily to it." He encouraged instructors to devote more time for lectures, class discussions, lab work in the physical sciences, and oral drills in foreign languages. To enhance the quality of instruction and diversify the faculty, MacArthur encouraged professors to hire non–West Point officers who possessed college degrees and teaching experience, even providing them lists of such officers. Most department heads, however, scoffed at having non-Academy graduates on the faculty, arguing that they could not learn West Point's policies and methods quickly enough to be productive.[70]

Given this intransigence, MacArthur vented to Ganoe: "The professors are so secure, they have become set and smug. They deliver the same schedule year after year with the blessed unction that they have reached the zenith in education."[71] MacArthur decided to send them to civilian institutions to see for themselves the strides being made in education, hoping that their observations would persuade them of the need for reform. He secured War Department funding for the plan, and wrote letters of introduction to the presidents of the schools the professors would visit. In 1920–1921 nine professors visited twenty-four colleges and universities, mostly in the East and the Midwest. Devers was impressed by their changed attitude: "When the new orders had been carried out, and the fresh breezes had carried off some of the old, stagnant air, the individuals involved in the changes began to see the wisdom and validity of the demands of the young Superintendent."[72] Ganoe found that "the young members expressed enthusiasm for the experience on their return, but the older members continued to protest that the practice was valueless."[73]

Nevertheless, MacArthur was winning some faculty members over to his cause. In 1921, he convinced a majority of the Academic Board to agree to recommend three changes. First, instructors should spend the first year of their three-year appointment to West Point at civilian universities attending courses in the subject they would teach. Second, each professor would visit three separate institutions of higher education as an observer each year. And finally, to relieve the Academy's isolation, MacArthur made West Point a mecca for visiting scholars, political leaders, and military experts. On January 20, 1920, Brig. Gen. William Mitchell enthralled the cadets with stories of the air war over France and predicted a marvelous future for airpower. Despite the difficulty in reaching the Academy, the superintendent brought such luminaries as the king of Belgium, the Prince of Wales, Marshal Foch, and President Warren Harding, in addition to a plethora of guest lecturers from other colleges. MacArthur further attacked the Academy's traditional isolation by having courtesy copies of the New York *Herald* and the New York *World* delivered to the cadet barracks daily. He then required discussion of current events for the first fifteen minutes of class in the new economics and government course.[74]

MacArthur's attempt to transform West Point's curriculum and instruction extended to the tactical realm as well. He ended the Academy's nostalgic obsession with the Civil War, substituting study of the World War in its place. Extensive changes were made in the tactical department to update the cadets' education in supply, procurement, and modern ordnance. Yet these innovations were dwarfed by MacArthur's attempt to revolutionize the cadets' military training by abolishing West Point's traditional summer encampment. For over a century, once classes ended at graduation the cadets abandoned the barracks for Fort Clinton, the area east of Trophy Point, to do some drilling in the morning, rest or gossip in the afternoon, and attend formal hops in the evening. It involved much formality—dress uniforms, white gloves, excellent meals served by civilian waiters in a "palace of a mess hall," band concerts, a lot of fife and drum music—punctuated by impish guard duty pranks. The Academy's social life revolved around summer camp, where "cadets became better acquainted and . . . led a carefree life after the long and stiff session with academics."[75]

As West Point historian Lance Betros notes, "For someone just returning from war, watching the summer encampment of 1919 must have been disorienting." Indeed, after watching the corps in action MacArthur asked his adjutant: "How long are we going on preparing for the War of 1812?"[76] Condemning the summer camp as "a ludicrous caricature of life in the field," beginning in 1920 the superintendent ordered the First and Third Classes to report for summer training at Camp Dix, New Jersey. There, instead of carefree gaieties, they encountered hardened sergeants from the Regular Army who were thrilled at the opportunity to put the cadets through a program of basic training. Cadets received training on the weapons, equipment, and tactics used in the war, taking advantage of a training area where artillery could be fired at normal ranges, observation balloons and airplanes could be used, and tactical operations could be conducted on a variety of terrain.[77]

At the end of the exhausting training, MacArthur required the cadets to road march the 120 miles back to West Point with full packs and no help from the enlisted men. This reform reinforced MacArthur's efforts to transform the Fourth-Class System, as it enabled him and Commandant Danford to place Beast Barracks—the seven-week indoctrination for newly arrived plebes before the start of the next academic year—under commissioned officers rather than upperclassmen so that plebes' first experience would be under those who had led real units. MacArthur subsequently concluded that "the most important single feature of the military training system has been the removal of cadets from West Point to a regular army encampment for the summer period."[78]

Finally, to better prepare cadets to lead in the Regular Army, MacArthur revamped West Point's already formidable physical fitness program. During the war he learned that "troops in poor physical condition are worthless," and observed how much better athletes among the officer corps performed than non-athletes, and how much enlisted men admired them.[79] Whereas his predecessor believed athletics were no substitute for military training or the "more important and higher preparation for which the Military Academy was established," MacArthur felt they were *central* to developing leaders. "Over there," he told Ganoe:

> *I became convinced that the men who had taken part in organized sports made the best soldiers. They were the most dependable, hardy, courageous officers I had. Men who had contended physically against other human beings under rules of a game were the readiest to accept and enforce discipline. They were outstanding in leading soldiers and facing the enemy. It is a type appropriate to West Point.*[80]

In his vision of the officer of the future, MacArthur saw a man possessing great physical stamina who could play and coach in a variety of athletic endeavors. He wrote: "Nothing more quickly than competitive athletics brings out the qualities of leadership, quickness of decision, promptness of action, mental and muscular coordination, aggressiveness, and courage. And nothing so readily and so firmly establishes that indefinable spirit of group interest and pride which we know as morale."[81]

MacArthur established a mandatory intramural athletics program for the whole corps. He composed a quatrain which he ordered carved on the stone portals over the entrance to the gymnasium: "On the fields of friendly strife / Are sown the seeds that / Upon other fields and other days / Will bear the fruits of victory." With the chaplain's support, he abandoned the Academy's century old Sabbath observance rule and turned Sunday afternoon exercise into a vigorous intramural athletic program. Every cadet had to participate in at least one sport, and each company was required to field a team in football, baseball, soccer, lacrosse, tennis, basketball, track, golf, and polo. Cadet competitiveness was stoked by Commandant Danford's decision to incorporate athletics into the cadet rating scheme. Henceforth, a cadet's athletic prowess would count for 15 percent of his leadership rating, a component of his overall order of merit. This added incentive proved unnecessary as the program was enthusiastically received by the cadets. Between 70 and 75 percent of cadets participated in intramural sports—Maxwell Taylor later recalled the program "rooted me out of my deep chair at the library"—with the remainder playing on varsity teams. "Every man an athlete" became a rallying cry, and the competition became so spirited and rough that it was soon nicknamed "intra-murder."[82]

In MacArthur's vision future officers "must learn, not only how to perform themselves, but how to teach others." Thus, junior officers assigned to the academic departments were recruited to coach in the intramural program. Although his days and evenings were already full, Omar Bradley was also expected to serve as a coach. Unfortunately, the coaching assignments were made as haphazardly as were teaching duties. Bradley had been a three-year starter on the varsity baseball team as a cadet, and that sport would have seemed the obvious coaching assignment. Instead, he was tapped to coach soccer, a sport he knew nothing about having grown up in poverty in rural Missouri. Another officer, Lehman Miller, had played neither football nor soccer. But "since I knew football," Bradley later recalled, "he suggested we trade coaching jobs so that the company would receive expertise in at least one sport." The trade worked out well—Bradley coached his team to the intramural football championship, and Miller's soccer squad also won the title.[83]

MacArthur's conviction regarding sports' value to cadet development also applied to intercollegiate athletics, which he believed further honed cadet competitiveness, established contacts with other institutions of higher learning, generated positive media attention, and attracted more applicants. As superintendent, he expanded the number of varsity teams from three (baseball, basketball, and football) to seventeen, including boxing, cross country, golf, hockey, lacrosse, polo, rifle, soccer, swimming, tennis, track, and wrestling.[84] Although MacArthur had lettered in baseball as a cadet, his true passion was football, which seemed to embody the chaos, violence, and physical contact characteristic of war. He resolved to promote football at the Academy through aggressive recruiting. West Point's coaches had always worked hard to get prospective players nominated, but were stymied by the Academy's efforts to raise academic standards. MacArthur unapologetically declared: "I will be bold and frank in seeking candidates with athletic reputation and background," and authorized officers to conduct recruiting trips across the country to pursue the most talented players.[85] MacArthur himself tried to recruit a young coach who had just been hired by Notre Dame, but to his disappointment the then-unknown Knute Rockne chose to remain in South Bend. MacArthur was similarly dejected when Congress turned down his request to build a 50,000-seat stadium on the Hudson.

MacArthur gave football players special privileges during the season. When Earl Blaik came down with influenza playing in a rain-soaked contest against Tufts, MacArthur spared no effort in speeding his recovery for the upcoming Army-Navy game. "He sent his car and his chauffeur to take me for health-restoring rides out to Central Valley and around the Hudson Highlands," Blaik recalled. "The post surgeon ordered me to report three times a day for a glass of sherry." Although Blaik was "weak as a tabby cat" the Monday before the game, he made it to the Polo Grounds on Saturday and played fifty-eight minutes in a drizzling rain as Army suffered a heartbreaking 6–0 loss to the Midshipmen.[86]

During the football season MacArthur joined the coaches watching practice, discussing plays and players with "such absorption that the rest of the world vanished."[87] Blaik recalled: "Never a practice period passed that did not see the Supe, carrying a riding crop, jauntily stride onto the practice field." Once during baseball season, remembering MacArthur "had been a pretty fair ballplayer in his time," Blaik asked his advice on how to hit a curveball. "I wasn't too surprised either when the General loosened his stiff collar, took off his Sam Browne belt and stepped into the batter's box. It must have been the only time that I ever saw him fail to accomplish something he set out to do. When it was my turn to hit again, I not only couldn't hit a curve, I couldn't even hit a straight ball."[88] When Army upset Navy in baseball in the spring of 1922, the cadets paraded around the Plain at midnight in their pajamas. As drums beat, they built a huge bonfire, bawled Academy fight songs, and yelled their class yells. Instead of breaking up the reverie, the tactical officers were conspicuous by their absence, except for Maj. C. H. Bonesteel, who joined the party and made a warm speech of approval. MacArthur summoned Commandant Danford to his office the following morning. A grim look on his face, MacArthur said, "Well, Com, that was quite a party you put on last night."

"Yes, it was, sir," Danford said. "*Quite* a party!"

"How many of them did you skin?"

Bracing for a scolding, Danford replied, "Not a damn one!"

MacArthur pounded his desk. "Good!" he said. "You know, Com, I could hardly resist the impulse to get out and join them!"[89]

Whatever contributions athletics made to character development, at heart, MacArthur was simply a sports fan.

As necessary as his ambitious reform agenda might have been, MacArthur still needed buy-in from several groups: the War Department, the alumni in the officer corps, West Point's faculty (especially the Academic Board), and the Corps of Cadets. With the exception of the Army's leadership in Washington, however, he failed to gain significant support from any of these critical constituencies. For example, MacArthur never truly won over the corps despite sharing many of their enthusiasms. One cadet remembered: "Neither I nor the vast majority of my class ever saw the general, except when he was walking across diagonal walk, apparently lost in thought, his nose in the air, gazing at distant horizons as his publicity photos always portrayed him throughout his career." Another cadet who attended the initial meeting in 1919 to discuss hazing reforms said later that "he thought MacArthur to be somewhat of a poseur and not very frank with the cadets."[90] When the pamphlet outlining "acceptable" and "unacceptable" hazing practices was presented, many cadets felt they were not trusted and were being minimized, and the upperclassmen simply would not abandon the tradition. Blaik noted in his memoirs that "most of our classmates supported the new order. But there were still some among our 300-plus who stubbornly resisted anything that eased the burden of the plebes, since it had not been eased in their own plebedom."[91]

Although Ganoe later wrote "The whole idea, workings and success of the Honor Committee, in building a fresh honor code without benefit of tradition, were MacArthur's," many cadets felt the superintendent was attempting to take credit where it was not due. In 1923, the cadets wrote in the yearbook: "The Honor Committee has evolved from what was formerly known as the Vigilance Committee. Practically the only changes have been in the name."[92]

Maxwell Taylor noted that although MacArthur had done much for the corps during his superintendency, he "never made an effort to impress his personality on the cadets through direct communications with them. I do not ever recall his having made a speech to us and only a few cadets were ever asked to his house." Despite MacArthur's deep affection for West Point and the corps, "the cadets saw very little of this during his superintendency."[93]

MacArthur's reforms were greeted with hostility from alumni who believed the Academy had attained perfection in its time-tested methods.

Word of MacArthur's innovations reached them primarily through faculty letters. The offensive against hazing brought grumbling and remonstrances—*Beast Barracks made a man out of me*, Ganoe paraphrased the critics' arguments, *A soldier should early learn to take hard knocks*—but nothing upset the alumni more than MacArthur's liberalization of regulations. Again, Ganoe summarized the "Disgruntled Old Graduates": *"The Supe was producing a soft, spineless discipline which would yield graduates incapable of meeting the rigors of a soldier"; Altogether the Supe was allowing the cadet to become a flabby caricature of those stalwarts of former times.*[94] Alumni began writing letters excoriating MacArthur and his policies, and the stream of irate graduate visitors to the superintendent's office began to grow.

The alumni on the faculty were especially disturbed with MacArthur's unannounced visits to classrooms. Once again, Ganoe summarized their complaints: *"Even if he is the Supe, he has no right to go over the heads of the professors and shove into the section rooms." "All he's doing is embarrassing the instructors and belittling the professors."*[95] When MacArthur announced that front-board recitation was no longer mandatory, the faculty called it "a dangerous innovation" which would upset "the thoroughness of study and recitation." Not only was the superintendent altering traditional training methods, by breaking up summer camp at Fort Clinton he was disrupting the social order at the staid little post. The officers, and especially their wives, would miss the pageantry and the gaiety of relaxed summers and the active social life that centered on the encampment's nightly balls.[96]

Omar Bradley's recollections illustrated much of the junior faculty's opposition to MacArthur's program. As a professor of mathematics, Bradley wholeheartedly believed the quantitative disciplines were the best tools for instilling the mental discipline officers required, arguing: "The study of math, basically a study of logic, stimulates one's thinking and greatly improves one's power of reasoning. In later years, when I was faced with infinitely complex problems, often requiring immediate life-or-death decisions, I am certain that this immersion in mathematics helped me think more clearly and logically." Yet he supported the revitalization and liberalizing of West Point's academics. He also applauded MacArthur's new emphasis on fitness and athletics. Reflecting on his own experience on West Point's baseball team, he noted: "It is almost too trite to observe that in organized sports one learns the important art of group cooperation in goal achievement. No extracurricular endeavor I know of could better prepare a soldier for the battlefield."[97]

Yet Bradley disapproved of the relaxation of cadet discipline and deplored the abolition of summer camp. Unlike other officers who lamented its demise for social reasons—he and his wife Mary were teetotalers who neither drank nor smoke and consequently avoided big parties—Bradley believed it provided the new first classmen with an opportunity to exercise command. Moreover, MacArthur favored Walter E. French—a standout football and baseball player—so much that he "let it be known" that French was not to fail any course. Bradley was "severely disappointed" by the superintendent's intervention, recalling: "This act of favoritism was a blatant, even outrageous, corruption of West Point tradition and honor."[98]

The strongest opposition to MacArthur's innovations came neither from the cadets nor the junior faculty, but rather from the Academic Board, which consisted of the superintendent, the commandant, and the heads of the departments of instruction. They met in a dim boardroom with a filigreed mantelpiece carved with figures of historic warriors and a large medieval table and leather chairs. Each member had one vote, with the adjutant serving as a non-voting secretary. The board's powers were sweeping in matters of the curriculum, examinations, instructional methods, textbooks, and the admission and graduation of cadets. It therefore represented the center of gravity in the battle over MacArthur's proposed reforms. Ganoe, who would later serve for nearly a decade in civilian universities, said he had never encountered another "group so powerful and deeply entrenched."[99]

MacArthur had only two firm allies on the board: Danford and the head of the English department, Col. Lucius Holt, the only faculty member with a PhD and by reputation the best teacher at the Academy. Whereas MacArthur, Danford, and Ganoe were new to the board, the department heads were middle-aged or old men who had tenure and, in most cases, long experience as professors at the Academy. Five had been professors when MacArthur was a plebe, and most had not left the Academy for any significant length of time and were oblivious to developments in the country at large, in civilian universities, or even in the Regular Army itself. The department heads felt they were the true guardians of the Academy's hallowed standards and traditions, and viewed superintendents in general—and MacArthur in particular—as passing phenomena. As Ganoe noted, this "Old Guard" combined "all the sensitiveness of a committee of Congress, the stiffness of the priests of the Sanhedrin, and the security of the judges of the Supreme Court."[100]

Given this attitude, the prospects for compromise or deep reform along the lines MacArthur sought faced, at best, an uphill battle. Danford noted that from the start there was "a feeling of resentment" and "a real but polite hostility" toward MacArthur on the part of perhaps six professors.[101] The Academic Board grudgingly gave MacArthur the few tidbits previously noted, but rejected his pleas for broader offerings in the humanities. Of the more than 2,600 classroom hours, there was a shift of less than 10 percent from the technical studies to the non-technical. Consequently, the postwar curriculum was a virtual restoration of the past when compared to contemporary trends in higher education. MacArthur's innovations were rejected because "The members recognized the value of the traditional emphasis upon the more technical branches of study in the formation of habits of precision and accuracy and rigid reasoning. . . . The Board desires to maintain those same standards of mental discipline for which the institution has so long been famous."[102] The board further stated its conviction that "the Military Academy is intended to impart a specialized training for a specialized purpose and this purpose is not the same as that of any civilian institution."[103]

While professors agreed to MacArthur's proposal that every instructor be designated sufficiently in advance to permit a year's study at a civilian college, they balked when he suggested at a board meeting that more teaching at the Academy, especially in English, be done by alumni of other institutions and produced a list of Army officers meeting this criteria. An awkward silence followed. Finally, one of the oldest board members, an elderly colonel, replied that soldiers should learn to use weapons, not words. The superintendent's plan, he said, was a step backward. An instructor from outside simply could not fit into the section room, could not handle the cadets, and could not appreciate the West Point system. It was bound to fail.

As the professor sat down, MacArthur quietly pointed out that non-graduates were already teaching in the departments of modern languages and physical education with great success. He continued to defend his proposal, but the professor began to interrupt with increasing frequency. Soon he was cutting in on the middle of MacArthur's sentences. MacArthur accepted the interruptions patiently for as long as he was able, then suddenly froze with indignation. His expression "changed electrically to that of a cornered animal." He banged his fist on the table and yelled: "*Sit down, sir. I am the Superintendent!*"

A stunned silence followed as MacArthur looked around the room. Finally, he added: "Even if I weren't, I should be treated in a gentlemanly manner."[104]

Board members treated him with more outward respect after the confrontation, but never relented in their opposition to his reforms. While helpless to prevent his liberalization of cadet regulations, they repeatedly vetoed his proposals for academic innovations. One embodiment of this resistance came from Professor of Mathematics Col. Charles P. Echols, who was so opposed to the cut in "the fundamental study" that he submitted a minority report with the proposed four-year curriculum sent to the War Department in July 1920. He argued that the development of the "scientific form of reasoning" was paramount in producing skilled officers and that it was therefore a mistake to "narrow the basic scientific subject" in the curriculum. Echols's one-man insurgency against MacArthur continued after the curriculum was approved by Washington, as over the next five months he reported ninety-five of 572 plebes deficient in his course.[105]

Despite the Academic Board's traditionalism and the structural obstacle its opposition posed to MacArthur's plans, the failure to enact his reforms was not pre-ordained. Only Echols and Professors Robinson (Chemistry) and Carter (Natural Philosophy) were implacably opposed to his attack on the traditional system. MacArthur received support from Colonels Danford and Holt, and perhaps from the non-tenured professors who sat on his special subcommittee on mathematics. He may also have been able to win the support of those professors who had served in France, for many of the officers with whom he worked closely became devoted acolytes. Danford maintained that MacArthur's "was a gifted leadership, a leadership that kept you at a respectful distance, yet at the same time took you in as an esteemed member of his team, and very quickly had you working harder than you had ever worked before in your life, just because of the loyalty, admiration and respect in which you held him."[106] Jacob Devers's experience with the superintendent was typical. When Devers was assigned to take over the artillery detachment at West Point in the summer of 1919, he reported to the superintendent. Devers entered MacArthur's office and saluted. MacArthur told him to sit down and offered a cigarette, which he promptly lit for Devers. MacArthur then began pacing back and forth, "thinking aloud" and "talking about problems" at West Point. He eventually stopped, asked a few questions, and picked up a large report on his desk. He handed it to Devers and said, "I give you ten days to clean this up." Devers saw it was an inspector general's report detailing the numerous deficiencies of his new detachment. MacArthur told Devers that if he ever needed to see him about anything, his door was open, just "walk right in." Devers recalled that he was inspired enough that "I went down and I cleaned it up," even if he had to cut corners to achieve MacArthur's vision in ten days.[107]

MacArthur's distinctly paradoxical personality, however—combining brilliance, egotism, and aloofness—compounded his difficulties. MacArthur dressed as unconventionally at West Point as he had in the trenches, once again removing the wire brace from his hat so that it sat on his head in a cocky and slouched manner. Like a Prussian staff officer, he was seldom seen without a riding crop in hand. His habit of returning salutes by lifting it to the bill of his cap created the impression that "he was not only unconventional but perhaps a law unto himself."[108] When the brisk autumn air swept across the Plain, MacArthur wore a short overcoat and faded puttees that were lashed to his lean frame by curling, war-weary leather straps. General Pershing had strictly forbidden this style, and when Inspector General Eli A. Helmick visited the Academy wearing an overcoat that nearly touched the parade ground, MacArthur's short coat quickly disappeared. While such eccentricities may seem insignificant, given the Academy's pride in uniformity and punctiliousness in matters of military courtesy, some officers felt MacArthur's disregard for regulations set a bad example for cadets.[109]

MacArthur felt a strong sense of mission and considered the necessity of his reform program so self-evident that he never fully explained it to the Academic Board or considered the source of their opposition. When Ganoe warned, "General, you will meet with a world of opposition" for altering traditions like summer camp, MacArthur's eyes lit up and he said: "Chief, we met more than that in France and won."[110] The same sense of invincibility that led him to declare during the war that "all of Germany cannot fabricate the shell that would kill me" made him believe his determination alone was all that was needed to carry through his reforms. Yet even this force of personality itself was partially the actualization of his own self-mythologizing. When MacArthur arrived at West Point he was determined to maintain his image as a field soldier. Although he was provided with a mansion, a large salary, and a staff of servants, he had an Army cot set up in the basement where he shivered some nights wrapped in blankets to remind him of the hardships he and his men had endured in France. One day he hosted a group of New York sportswriters for lunch. They were impressed by the gold plates they ate from, but were more impressed when he showed them the cot in the basement. A week later the cook reported a gold plate missing, and the superintendent's house was turned inside out in a futile search. As the sportswriters were the last guests at the mansion, MacArthur wrote them hoping someone could shed light on the mystery. One writer replied that if the general had actually slept in the basement as frequently as he claimed he would have already found the missing plate, for it was between the two blankets piled on the cot where the writer had hidden it.[111]

Because of MacArthur's self-perception, he found it difficult to show proper respect to the professors. Rather than adopting a deferential tone, he set forth his proposals to them in what seemed to be ultimatums. He insulted them by announcing his intentions without consulting them or asking their advice. When MacArthur told the Academic Board that summer camp was being canceled, Ganoe recalls:

> *Some faces went dead, masking steely silence. Tightly pressed lips showed they were beyond the state of disagreement, evidently realizing it was too late to argue. I could feel their inward fires of stubborn hostility. It was plain to me that more even than the ruthless riddance of the time-honored camp, was the crowning insult of being thoroughly ignored before action was taken on such a grave measure.*[112]

When the faculty reacted negatively to his plans, MacArthur's aide Capt. Louis Hibbs said, the superintendent sometimes set out to deliberately antagonize them. During the period of tension between MacArthur and the department heads over setting qualifications for instructors, Hibbs was preparing to announce a meeting of the Academic Board and asked the general if it should be set for the usual time.

"No!" MacArthur replied. "Call the meeting at 4:30 P.M. I want them to come here hungry—and I'll keep them here that way till I get what I want."[113]

On another occasion, a senior professor informed MacArthur that he wanted to replace two of his department's instructors. Given that the handling of junior instructors was traditionally seen as the department chair's prerogative, such requests were normally granted without question. Yet MacArthur denied the request, and whereas he may have saved two instructors from an unfair dismissal, he jeopardized his broader reform agenda by making an enemy of their senior professor. As his biographer Geoffrey Perret writes, MacArthur "put them down daily, indirectly insulted their intelligence and told everyone who was half willing to listen how much he despised them. In the small, closed world of a college setting, almost everything he said would have gotten back to them."[114] MacArthur simply could not conceive that much of the opposition was provoked by his methods as well as his ends.

This cognitive dissonance was compounded by MacArthur's reclusive nature. "When you get to be a general," he told his aide, "You haven't any friends." This was patently untrue, as countless other generals retained long-standing friendships from their days as junior officers. But MacArthur's only real confidante was his mother Pinky, who served as the Academy's official hostess. MacArthur had West Point's reveille moved up an hour, and although he awoke with the rest of the post, he worked at his mansion through most of the morning. Between 1000 and 1130 he came in and disposed of his mail in an hour. From 1200 to 1300 he kept appointments before returning home to spend time with his mother. He was in meetings again until 1630 or 1700, after which he watched the cadets at athletic practice, dined, and passed the evening in his study reading history, literature, and military science.[115]

MacArthur showed no inclination to mentor the younger officers on the faculty or to guide their development as leaders. This was a shame, because the officers who missed the war were eager to profit from others' experience. Ridgway got officers returning from overseas duty, like Courtney Hodges, to offer "little tactical classes" twice a week in the officers' quarters.[116] Yet as Bradley recalled, "Except for sporting events, or an occasional ceremony, I seldom saw [MacArthur], even from a distance. I cannot recall a single exchange with him. I was but a baby Captain in the math department, he was a legendary general."[117] Even his adjutant, Ganoe, whose memoir of MacArthur's superintendency sometimes borders on the hagiographic, conceded his boss's reclusiveness. MacArthur "did not attend the Post parties, hops or informal teas. He did not appear for a drink at the Club or hobnob with any group. . . . Small talk, banalities, front-teeth smiles and vain ritual were particularly harrowing" for him.[118] His avoidance of social contact with the faculty—especially the Academic Board members—was taken by many as a superiority complex, and made his differences with them sharper than they might otherwise have been and more difficult to surmount.

By the summer of 1921 MacArthur had so thoroughly drained the faculty and alumni of good will that he could no longer innovate. Instead, he was merely fighting to preserve the reforms already enacted. Whereas MacArthur had initially benefited from Baker and March's patronage, this ended when Weeks became secretary of war and Pershing took over as chief of staff. On November 22, 1921, Pershing wrote the superintendent: "It is important, I think, that you should be made aware of the decision of the War Department to make the regulation with reference to foreign service applicable to the entire official personnel of the Army. The roster shows you to be high up for this service, but, in considering your case, it was not thought advisable to make a change during the academic year." He continued: "I am writing now to advise you that at the end of the present school year you will be available for a tour of service beyond the limits of the United States. The selection of your successor will be made shortly in order that he may have time to study his new duties, and be prepared to take over the office immediately after graduation in June, 1922."[119] The order was a shock to MacArthur. Although there was no fixed term for a superintendent's tour of duty, his predecessors had usually served for about four years.

Almost immediately West Point, the Army, and to a certain extent the nation were alive with rumors. One that gained traction was that MacArthur's dismissal was retaliation for stealing a woman from Pershing. In September 1921 a party of Army officers drove up to West Point and brought some female friends from New York with them. One of the women was Louise Cromwell Brooks, the stepdaughter of a J.P. Morgan partner and one of the world's richest heiresses. Brooks was a thirty-one-year-old divorcee with a pretty, round face, "lustrous brown eyes," and a vivacious manner. When she was introduced to MacArthur, both felt a strong mutual attraction bordering on love at first sight. He invited her to return to West Point for the first football game of the season against Yale several weeks later. Army lost the game, but MacArthur won the girl. When the final whistle blew, he proposed marriage, and Louise instantly said yes.[120]

Like many wealthy Americans, the Brookses had used their apartment in Paris to entertain American officers of the proper class and rank during the war. There Pershing met Louise, whom gossip connected him with romantically. Upon returning to Washington she sometimes served as Pershing's hostess, and an impending marriage was whispered in some corners of society. Many therefore assumed that Pershing was "exiling" MacArthur for having stolen his paramour. Yet when asked about the rumor Pershing told reporters, "It's all damn poppycock." Arguably the world's most eligible bachelor, he stated, "If I were married to all the ladies to whom the gossips have engaged me I would be a regular Brigham Young." MacArthur, for his part, also vehemently denied the allegation.[121]

A more plausible theory that some historians have suggested is that after Pershing's return to the United States, he and Louise decided to be friends. To keep herself amused, however, she started dating Pershing's aide, Col.

John G. Quekemeyer, the dashing captain of the Army polo team. Quekemeyer hoped to marry her, and Louise apparently did nothing to discourage this hope. Pershing's note to MacArthur in November 1921 was sent only a few days after Louise told Quekemeyer of her engagement. If MacArthur went abroad, it would likely be to Panama or the Philippines, posts distinguished more for their tropical heat and diseases than the luxuries Louise was accustomed to in Paris and New York. What Pershing intended, MacArthur told his fiancé, was to make her feel "intimidated and frightened into regretting that you engaged to marry me."[122]

Neither theory, however, holds up upon close scrutiny. When World War I ended, Brooks gave Pershing an ultimatum: Marry her, or no more fun in the bedroom. "Louise," he told her, "marrying you would be like buying a book for somebody else to read," and thus ended their romantic relationship. When Louise and MacArthur were married on Valentine's Day 1922, Pershing sent his purported rival a portrait of Louise painted by a Hungarian artist along with a card that said "With my compliments."[123] It remains to be explained why, if Pershing had such significant doubts about her faithfulness, he would wish these troubles upon a beloved aide. Other than suspicious timing the only positive evidence supporting this theory is MacArthur's statement to Louise. But given MacArthur's demonstrated penchant for concocting self-serving conspiracy theories about Pershing's "Chaumont clique," it is unclear why this hearsay should be taken at face value, particularly when an equally plausible and more parsimonious explanation exists.

As D. Clayton James concludes: "The key to understanding MacArthur's dismissal is less sensational than the vengeance of a jealous lover, but far more significant."[124] Pershing was a notoriously strict disciplinarian while serving as a tactical officer at the Academy. He was so thoroughly convinced those measures were correct for the Regular Army as well that when he assumed command of the AEF he declared West Point's standards for discipline and attention to detail would be the American Army's standards. Moreover, whereas MacArthur had been disappointed by the performance of the Academy graduates he had seen in France, Pershing was convinced that the traditional standards had directly contributed to the Allied victory. Consequently, Pershing's rating of MacArthur's performance and knowledge was "above average," which in Army-speak means "mediocre." He called MacArthur "a very able young officer with a fine record for courage" but said he "has an exalted opinion of himself." Of the forty-six active brigadier generals in the Army, Pershing rated MacArthur no better than thirty-eight.[125]

Thus, Occam's Razor suggests that when Pershing replaced March as chief of staff, the howl of outrage rising from the faculty and alumni reached his ears. He took a long hard look at West Point and disapproved of the new permissiveness. The *New York Times* speculated: "Why is Gen. MacArthur being removed from West Point? This is a question asked not only by his friends, but by many other people who have been interested in the improvements he has made in West Point. . . . The answer . . . will be seen in the type of officer chosen by this department to succeed him."[126] In January 1922, Pershing announced Brig. Gen. Fred W. Sladen's appointment as MacArthur's successor. An 1890 West Point graduate who had served as a tactics instructor and company commander there when MacArthur was a cadet, Sladen had earned the Distinguished Service Cross in the Meuse-Argonne. More importantly, he was a noted disciplinarian aligned with the traditionalists and the Academic Board. One cadet who served under Sladen when he was commandant of West Point remembered him as "a martinet who had swallowed a ramrod."[127] Almost as if answering the *Times'* question, upon hearing of Sladen's appointment MacArthur told Ganoe: "I fancy it means a reversal of many of the progressive policies which we inaugurated."[128] Thus, MacArthur's placement on the foreign-duty list served as a convenient pretext for removing an individualist reformer who created unnecessary difficulties in dealing with West Point's conservative alumni.

In his first year as superintendent, Sladen did all he could to resurrect the old order, halting all reforms and eliminating many of MacArthur's successful initiatives. The faculty's resentment toward MacArthur was so great that shortly after his departure the first change made was the reestablishment of summer camp. Taking a swipe at his predecessor, Sladen concluded in his first annual report that "The experience of the summer has proved conclusively that the practice, prevailing for more than a century before 1920, of maintaining a summer camp at West Point for military instruction was based upon sound principles."[129] Sladen returned Beast Barracks to the upper class cadets and revoked cadet privileges such as weekend leaves and spending money. Of MacArthur's disciplinary reforms, only the Honor Committee and the expanded athletics programs remained.

Sladen's actions pleased the old-guard professors of the Academic Board, who within weeks of MacArthur's departure began discussions to erase the innovations that had reduced the dominance of technical education in the curriculum. The new curriculum that resulted went into effect in January 1924. It not only restored the technical/non-technical balance of subjects from 1916, but "reflected the balance that prevailed in America's technical institutes of the Civil War period."[130] Historian Robert Cowley observed, "It was almost as if MacArthur had never been Superintendent and the clock had been turned back to 1915."[131] Even MacArthur, who had a penchant for wildly inflating his accomplishments, would uncharacteristically admit: "The success obtained did not even approximate to what I had in mind."[132]

If MacArthur lost the battle of West Point, however, a strong case can be made for his winning the larger war. After Sladen's reactionary regime, the liberal forces MacArthur had helped to unleash gained strength over the next two decades. In 1926—the same year Congress approved the separation of English and History into two departments—Maj. Gen. Merch B. Stewart replaced Sladen as superintendent and reportedly said: "Everything MacArthur changed is coming back in full force. His principles and practices will be carried on and improved as time goes on." His successors, particularly Maj. Gen. William D. Connor—superintendent from 1932 to 1938—followed the same policy. Even Pershing eventually accepted MacArthur's philosophy that the Academy existed to produce leaders of citizen-soldiers. In the first issue of the new cadet magazine *The Pointer* in 1923, the chief of staff wrote: "Heretofore requirements of service have forced the army officer to spend a large portion of his career out of touch with the everyday life of the American citizen. Today, however, the officer finds his principle [*sic*] mission to be the instruction and guidance of those patriotic fellow citizens who volunteer their services for the national defense."[133] Over the long term, the Academic Board increasingly rejected the paternalistic attitudes that had shaped Academy culture and embraced the idea that cadets deserved to be treated more like developing leaders than children. In the end, MacArthur's innovations were restored, his ideas accepted. As Stephen Ambrose concluded: "If Sylvanus Thayer dominated West Point in the nineteenth century, Douglas MacArthur dominated it in the twentieth."[134]

But this historical vindication was unknowable to MacArthur as he, his new bride, and her two children moved out of the superintendent's mansion in late June 1922. For the time being, he was the classic Greek tragic hero. Handsome, heroic, and pursuing a noble goal, he had failed in his quest due to a combination of the power of natural forces (the Academic Board, in this case) and his own hubris. But whereas Icarus found himself plunging into the sea as a result of his ambition, MacArthur once again found himself on a boat on September 5, 1922, this time departing San Francisco for his new assignment in the Philippine Department.

CHAPTER THREE

The Innovator's Dilemma:
Ike, Patton, and Billy Mitchell
After the War

IF DOUGLAS MACARTHUR WAS DISAPPOINTED BY HIS HOMECOMING, OTHER officers were close to distraught by the fact that they never made it to France. After graduating from West Point in 1917, Matthew Ridgway served on the U.S.-Mexico border rather than deploying with the AEF. When he received orders to report to West Point for duty as an instructor in September 1918, he thought it signaled "the death knell" of his career. "Once the Hun was beaten, the world would live in peace throughout my lifetime," Ridgway recalled thinking. "And the soldier who had no share in this last great victory of good over evil would be ruined."[1] Joe Collins would eventually join Ridgway at West Point (and later as a fellow corps commander in World War II), and was similarly convinced there would be no more large-scale wars, "and not having served in action I felt there wasn't much of a future for me in the Army."[2] Consequently, before receiving orders to serve in the Army of Occupation, he applied to Columbia Law School.

Omar Bradley spent the war even farther removed from France's battlefields. His regiment—the 14th Infantry—was assigned to police the Anaconda copper mines in central Montana that were deemed vital to the war effort and threatened by labor unrest. Bradley was thrilled when the 14th Infantry received orders to assemble at Camp Dodge, Iowa, in September 1918, as it suggested deployment to France was finally at hand. But while Bradley and his wife Mary walked down the streets of Des Moines one afternoon in November, church bells began to ring and whistles blew. The streets quickly filled with people wildly celebrating. The Germans had surrendered! The war was over! "I was glad the carnage had stopped," Bradley later wrote, "but I was now absolutely convinced that, having missed the war, I was professionally ruined. I could only look forward to a career lifetime of dull routine assignments and would be lucky to retire after thirty years as a lieutenant colonel."[3]

More than 900 miles to the east, Bradley's West Point classmate Capt. Norman Randolph was sitting in his commander's office at the Tank Corps school at Camp Colt near Gettysburg, Pennsylvania, when news of the Armistice arrived. Rudolph's boss had recently been promoted to lieutenant colonel, and—more importantly—received orders to deploy to France on November 18 to take command of an armored unit. "I suppose we'll spend the rest of our lives explaining why we didn't get into this war," the twenty-eight-year-old lieutenant colonel said angrily upon hearing the news. He was 5'11", 180 pounds, with broad shoulders and large hands. His light-brown hair sat upon a round, symmetrical face accentuated by large, sparkling blue eyes and thick lips that expanded around a disarming grin. In his deep resonant voice, he declared: "By God, from now on I am cutting myself a swath and will make up for this!"[4]

A quarter-century later, Dwight D. Eisenhower would more than fulfill his promise to Randolph.

Just as it was critical to Superman's iconography as a distinctly American hero that Clark Kent be raised in "Smallville" rather than Boston or Chicago, Dwight David Eisenhower's upbringing in Abilene, Kansas, was central to both the leader and the legend he would become. Eisenhower was born in 1890, the third of David and Ida Eisenhower's six sons. David Eisenhower was a failed shopkeeper and chronic underachiever who earned $100 a month working seventy-two hours a week as a machinist at the Abilene Dairy Creamery. Eisenhower's older brother Edgar—who eventually became a prosperous banker—later wrote, "God himself is the only one who knows how our parents managed to feed five mouths on dad's salary."[5] As one of Eisenhower's biographers notes, "There is no question that poverty steeled young Dwight's ambition and his determination to excel, to succeed."[6]

More surprising given his eventual profession, Eisenhower came from a family of strict pacifists. His parents were members of the River Brethren Faith, an offshoot of the Mennonites, and Ida—the family's moral center—had personally witnessed the devastation of the Civil War's Shenandoah Valley campaigns as a young girl in Mount Sidney, Virginia. Ida grew up knowing only one thing about the military: that it was "of Satan."[7] Eisenhower recalled his mother as "the most honest and sincere pacifist I ever knew," and when she caught her sons playing "Remember the Maine" or the Rough Riders she was horrified and lectured them on the wickedness of war.[8] Eisenhower therefore grew up with little knowledge of or interest in a military career. It was only when a close friend obsessed with attending the Naval Academy persuaded him the service academies would enable the impoverished young man to get a free education and continue his promising athletic career that Eisenhower became interested. Although he finished first in the competitive exam for Kansas's appointment, at nineteen he was too old for entrance into Annapolis. Thus, it was only because West Point had a higher entering age that Eisenhower ended up a cadet rather than a midshipman.

If there was little in Eisenhower's ancestry or upbringing to suggest a military career, his performance as a cadet did little to suggest he would become a successful officer. Whereas Pershing and MacArthur had been captains of the Corps of Cadets at West Point, and Marshall attained the equivalent position at VMI, Eisenhower spent his first years as a cadet flaunting the academy's basic disciplines. He accumulated demerits for minor infractions and displayed a marked indifference to West Point's draconian disciplinary code. "My success in compiling a staggering catalogue of demerits," Eisenhower recalled, "was largely due to a lack of motivation in almost everything other than athletics, except for the simple and stark resolve to get a college education."[9] Although Eisenhower was one of the most popular cadets in the Class of 1915, he would eventually stand 125th out of 162 in discipline. (He did better academically, finishing 61st, but did not overly exert himself in the classroom either.) One tactical officer disdainfully wrote: "We saw in Eisenhower a not uncommon type, a man who would thoroughly enjoy his army life, giving both to duty and recreation their fair values, [but] we did not see in him a man who would throw himself into his job so completely that nothing else would matter."[10] During his senior year West Point's medical board unanimously voted *not* to commission Eisenhower because his knee was so badly damaged from a football injury. It was only because the board's chairman—West Point's post surgeon Col. Henry Shaw—saw Eisenhower's leadership potential and rejected the board's finding that Eisenhower was even commissioned.

Eisenhower may have glided through his cadet years because he sensed true leadership had little to do with demerits, or because West Point's curriculum of rote memorization failed to engage his intellect. Yet even his first years as a second lieutenant were more significant for the radical change they brought to his personal life than for any professional accomplishments. After graduation in 1915 he was assigned to the 19th Infantry Regiment in San Antonio, a unit that included five other lieutenants destined to attain the rank of four-star general: Jacob Devers, Walton Walker, Wade Haislip, Robert Eichelberger, and Leonard "Gee" Gerow. During Eisenhower's first stint as officer of the day on a Sunday that October, Gerow was sitting on the porch of Mrs. Lulu Harris (the wife of a major in the 19th Infantry) talking to a family of civilians visiting the post.

"Hey, Ike! Come over here!"

Gerow and Harris introduced Eisenhower to John and Elvira Doud of Denver and their three daughters, including eighteen-year-old "Mamie." "He's a bruiser," Mamie thought, later recalling that Eisenhower was "just about the handsomest male I had ever seen."[11] The attraction was mutual. "I was intrigued by her appearance," Eisenhower recalled. Mamie was a "vivacious and attractive girl, smaller than average, saucy in the look about her face and in her whole attitude."[12] Within moments of their first meeting Eisenhower impulsively asked her if she would accompany him as he inspected the regiment's guard posts. Thus began a courtship that resulted in Ike and Mamie's marriage on July 1, 1916.

When the United States entered World War I in April 1917, Eisenhower was one of a dozen officers from the 19th Infantry selected as the cadre for the new 57th Regiment. Whereas a year earlier his application for service with Pershing's Punitive Expedition had been rejected, Eisenhower assumed that when the 57th was trained and equipped it would deploy to France. Eisenhower possessed a talent for teaching, however, going back to his days as a coach of West Point's junior varsity football team after his knee injury ended his playing days. He had proven such a good instructor that when the 57th Regiment deployed he was promoted to captain and ordered to Camp Oglethorpe, Georgia, to instruct officer candidates. In December 1917 he was transferred to Fort Leavenworth, Kansas, to instruct provisional second lieutenants. Eisenhower pestered the War Department with requests for overseas duty until he was finally summoned by the post commandant and read a letter from the War Department denying his latest request for overseas duty and admonishing him for having the nerve to seek it repeatedly.

While at Leavenworth he took a course in the Army's first tank school and studied newspaper accounts of the November 1917 battle of Cambrai. In February 1918 he received orders to report to Camp Meade, Maryland, to lead the 301st Heavy Tank Battalion, which was slated to deploy in the spring. But once again the War Department changed his orders. His superior, Col. Ira C. Welborn, had seen him training officer candidates in Georgia and specifically requested his services. Welborn's praise of Eisenhower's organizational ability had been so superlative that the authorities decided to send him to Camp Colt to command the newly created Tank Corps' first stateside training facility. "My mood was black," Eisenhower confessed. Although this was an important duty, "Some of my class were already in France. Others were ready to depart. I seemed embedded in the monotony and unsought safety of the Zone of the Interior. I could see myself, years later, silent at class reunions while others reminisced of battle."[13]

It was at Camp Colt, however, that Eisenhower first demonstrated his full potential. Located inside the Gettysburg National Park, Camp Colt was established in 1917 and accommodated 4,000 men. Eisenhower arrived on March 24, 1918, with only a handful of cadre. "I was very much on my own," he recalled. "There were no precedents except in basic training and I was the only regular officer in command. Now I really began to learn about responsibility."[14] Camp Colt eventually became both a mobilization and training center, and by mid-July 1918 Eisenhower had 10,000 men and 600 officers under his command.

The one thing he did not have at the Tank Corps training center, however, was tanks. Eisenhower and his staff resorted to every means they could think of to sustain morale and improve training. Ingeniously working with whatever material he could find—including scouring books, magazines, and military manuals for ideas that might have application to tank training—Eisenhower transformed the old battlefield into a first-class training camp, even using the slope of Little Round Top as the backdrop for an impromptu firing range for machine guns mounted to the backs of moving trucks. The Army's inspector general noted Eisenhower's unorthodox training methods, but admitted that while the camp did not follow "prescribed" training doctrine, the officers appeared "well-qualified" and the enlisted men "excellent." The result was an "excellent" command.[15]

For his service at Camp Colt, Welborn would eventually recommend Eisenhower for the Distinguished Service Medal, the Army's highest peacetime decoration. Welborn wrote: "I regard this officer as one of the most efficient young officers I have known. He had the duties and responsibilities commensurate with the rank of a brigadier general and he performed those duties under trying conditions in a highly credible manner."[16] Eisenhower's performance also brought rapid promotions, first to temporary major in June 1918, and then to temporary lieutenant colonel on October 14, his twenty-eighth birthday. Only ten members of West Point's Class of 1915 were promoted to lieutenant colonel during World War I, of which Eisenhower was the second.

Despite his success at Camp Colt, Eisenhower chafed at the job and desperately wanted to test his mettle on the battlefield. Thus, even more welcome than his promotion were the accompanying orders he received to lead the November contingent of troops from Camp Colt to the embarkation depot at Fort Dix, New Jersey, and from there deploy to France to assume command of an armored regiment. Welborn summoned Eisenhower to Washington, DC, and offered to recommend his promotion to full colonel if he would remain at Gettysburg. Eisenhower respectfully declined, saying he would prefer demotion to major if that would get him overseas. Eisenhower returned to Camp Colt to ready the troops for departure on November 18.

On the eleventh hour of the eleventh day of the eleventh month of 1918, however, the guns along the Western Front fell silent after four years of unimaginable carnage. Instead of taking command of an armored unit in France, Eisenhower was ordered to disband his command at Camp Colt. Although Mamie felt a deep sense of relief, Eisenhower was depressed that he had missed out on the greatest war in history. Shortly after the Armistice was declared, another classmate, Maj. Philip K. McNair, ran into Eisenhower on a train. "He was greatly upset," McNair recalled. "He hadn't been sent overseas and now he never would be. He said he had been educated to be a soldier, and when a war came along, he had to sit it out without even getting close to the battle. He was so keenly disappointed.... I had the definite impression that he intended on resigning his commission. I was sure he and the Army were through."[17] Eisenhower remembered: "I was mad, disappointed, and resented the fact that the war had passed me by." The prospects for his professional career, he noted, "were none too bright. I saw myself in the years ahead putting on weight in a meaningless chair-bound assignment, shuffling papers and filling out forms."[18]

Despite her obvious relief that her husband was out of harm's way, Mamie shared his disappointment at not having gone overseas. "I felt so sorry for him," she said. "After all this career he'd worked so hard for, and he thought so much of, he just didn't think there was going to be any solution" after trying so hard and failing to see combat in France.[19] Eisenhower briefly considered an offer from an Indiana businessman who had served as a junior officer at Camp Colt to join his manufacturing firm in Muncie at double a lieutenant colonel's salary. But "Mamie had quite an influence on me," Eisenhower recalled. "I was fed up. After all the studying and hard work, I wouldn't get into the war. Mamie kidded me a little bit, and we decided to go on in the Army."[20]

Three weeks after the Armistice Eisenhower closed down Camp Colt, and by December the once bustling complex resembled a ghost town. "No human enterprise goes flat so instantly as an Army training camp when war ends," Eisenhower observed sadly. He was subsequently sent to Dix, Fort Benning, and finally back to Camp Meade, a sandy post halfway between Washington and Baltimore.

Shortly after he arrived at Meade, the War Department announced plans to send a truck convoy coast-to-coast across America. A cross-country march had never been attempted before, and given that there were no road maps—and in some parts of the country no roads—the Army was not sure it *could* be done. Officially, the convoy's mission was "to test various military vehicles, many developed too late for use in World War I, and to determine by actual experience the feasibility of moving an army across the continent."[21] However, the Army was also looking for a way to convince the public—and the legislators debating the service's future—that they still needed an Army by demonstrating that it was not an anachronism, but rather a modern organization looking to America's future. Eisenhower, not yet integrated into the routine at Camp Meade and thirsting for an adventure to compensate for missing the war, immediately volunteered to serve as one of the Tank Corps' two observers, "partly for a lark and partly to learn."

Overall the expedition consisted of twenty-four officers, 258 enlisted men, roughly two dozen official observers, as well as a motley assortment of reporters and representatives of auto and tire manufacturers. The convoy departed from the Ellipse in Washington, DC, on July 7, 1919, bound for San Francisco more than 3,000 miles away. In march column the nearly eighty vehicles stretched more than 2 miles. In the absence of accurate maps or road signs, a detachment of cavalry scouts mounted on motorcycles reconnoitered the convoy's route. The convoy averaged 58 miles per day at an average speed of 6 miles per hour over what Eisenhower described as "average to nonexistent" roads. The official report noted the expedition suffered 230 accidents, including breakdowns, delays, mud, and quicksand. By the time the convoy reached San Francisco on Labor Day, it had been seen by an estimated 3.25 million people, and awareness of the expedition reached an estimated thirty-three million Americans. The Army's image was enhanced, and lessons were learned that were incorporated into the future design of military vehicles.[22]

When Eisenhower returned to Camp Meade that fall, the AEF Tank Corps had returned from France and merged with their stateside counterparts, including the remnants of his command at Camp Colt. The reformed Tank Corps was placed under the command of Brig. Gen. Samuel D. Rockenbach, a cavalry officer who had led the AEF's tanks. Rockenbach formed two brigades: the 304th, a light brigade equipped with French Renaults; and the 305th, a heavy brigade comprised of American-made Mark VIIIs that had come off the assembly line too late for use in France. Eisenhower became the executive officer—and later assumed command—of the 305th, while the 304th was commanded by a 6-foot-1, blue-gray–eyed colonel Eisenhower remembered as "tall, straight, and soldierly looking," but whose military bearing was betrayed by "a high, squeaking voice" that seemed ill suited to such a martial figure. But Col. George S. Patton Jr. would quickly become a good friend to Eisenhower, and eventually one of the most important people to his life and career.[23]

In 1919 it would have been difficult to find two officers more different from one another than Lt. Col. Dwight D. Eisenhower and Col. George S. Patton Jr. Whereas Eisenhower grew up poor, Patton came from a wealthy, almost aristocratic family. The Pattons were southern gentry, while his maternal ancestors had been among the first American settlers to reach California. Patton was born on November 11, 1885, on his family's ranch, which itself was part of their vast Spanish land grant whose acreage was eventually donated to found the city of Pasadena. While Ida Eisenhower's sons labored every day at chores to maintain their shabby house on South East Fourth Street in Abilene, the Pattons had a housekeeper, a dozen Mexican servants, a European cook, and a governess. The Pattons raised purebred cattle and blooded horses, and owned a vacation house on luxurious Catalina Island. Furthermore, after graduating from West Point, Patton married his distant cousin Beatrice Ayres, heiress to an immense textile fortune.[24]

Whereas Eisenhower's family were committed pacifists, the Pattons boasted a rich military heritage. Like the character "Lieutenant Dan" in *Forrest Gump*, George Patton could boast of having ancestors killed in nearly every American war. James Patton was killed during Gen. Edward Braddock's unsuccessful campaign against Fort Duquesne in the French-Indian War. Patton's great-grandfather Hugh Mercer, a brigadier general in the Continental Army, was killed at the battle of Princeton in 1777. Col. George S. Patton was a Confederate cavalryman killed at the Third Battle of Winchester in 1864, and the saddle he fell from on that fateful day was prominently displayed in the Patton home. Patton's decision to become an Army officer was prompted by his unwavering belief that it was his obligation as heir to the family name.

Patton's house was populated with family friends who recounted their own martial exploits, including Col. John Singleton Mosby, the legendary rebel cavalry commander known as the "Gray Ghost." Patton's father, a VMI graduate, read Herodotus's history of the Persian Wars to him as a child, as well as Caesar's *Commentaries* and biographies of Napoleon and Alexander the Great. The toys young George received had a similarly martial theme, including a wooden doll dressed as a French general, a soldier suit, a bolt-action rifle, and a homemade cross-handled sword.[25] All of this engendered in Patton a sense that he was a reincarnation of soldiers who had fought in the great battles of history. When he formally asked for Beatrice's hand in marriage, her father asked Patton to explain why he chose the military as a career rather than a respectable profession such as business or the law. "It is hard to answer intelligently the question: 'Why I want to be a Soldier?'" Patton replied. "For my own satisfaction I have tried to give myself reasons but have never found any logical ones. I only feel it inside. It is as natural for me to be a soldier as it is to breathe and would be as hard to give up all thought of it as it would be to stop breathing."[26]

After a year at VMI, Patton fulfilled his childhood ambition by entering West Point in 1904. Whereas Eisenhower had been an undistinguished but popular cadet, Patton was the polar opposite. Although he failed mathematics and had to repeat his plebe year, by his junior year he was named adjutant of the Corps of Cadets, a position he obsessively pursued to match his father's accomplishment at VMI. Yet to his classmates Patton was known as "Quill," the derogatory nickname for a cadet unduly interested in achieving rank, and they caricatured his overweening ambition in two spoofs in their yearbook. Even the commandant warned Patton about being *too* military. Thus, despite five years at the Academy, by the time Patton graduated in 1909 he could claim none of his classmates as close friends.[27]

Whereas Eisenhower did little to distinguish himself during the years between his commissioning and World War I, Patton attained a measure of celebrity and appeared destined for high command. At the 1912 Stockholm Olympics Patton became the first Army officer to represent the United States, finishing fifth in the Modern Pentathlon. While serving with the 15th Cavalry at Fort Myer he learned where Secretary of War Henry L. Stimson—an avid horseman—rode and soon became Stimson's regular companion on his morning rides. In mid-December 1912 he was temporarily transferred to the chief of staff's office, where he acted as both an action officer for chief of staff Maj. Gen. Leonard Wood and as social aide to Secretary Stimson. In 1913 Patton took leave and travelled to Saumur, France, to study fencing (his weakest event in the Pentathlon) at L'Ecole de Cavalrie. Based upon his studies he designed a new cavalry saber that was adopted as the official U.S. Army saber. Patton was subsequently ordered to Fort Riley to attend the Mounted Service School. He was made instructor in fencing and became the first officer to hold the title "Master of the Sword."

Patton served as an aide to General Pershing during the 1916 Punitive Expedition in Mexico. On May 14, Patton and a handful of men set out in three cars to buy corn for the command's horses. Patton played a hunch about where Gen. Julio Cardenas—the commander of Pancho Villa's elite bodyguard—might be hiding and led an improvised raid on a hacienda near the town of Rubio. Cardenas was killed in the ensuing firefight, the highest ranking Villista killed or captured during the ten-month hunt for the elusive bandit. As the correspondents covering the campaign were desperate for stories, the Rubio exploit quickly appeared in the American press. Newspaper readers were thrilled to have an attractive, young hero with whom they could associate the Punitive Expedition.[28]

Finally, whereas Eisenhower was stuck stateside toiling in an unglamorous—albeit necessary—position, Patton was serving at the tip of the spear on the Western Front. When Pershing was ordered to organize a division to take to France, he submitted a list of officers whom he wanted on his staff. Remembering his outstanding work in Mexico, Pershing asked Patton if he would like to command his Headquarters troops. Patton arrived in France with Pershing on April 17, 1917, and served as a junior aide to the AEF commander while overseeing the headquarters company of about 250 men. Yet he increasingly saw this position as a dead-end assignment. Fox Conner advised him that if he wanted to advance in rank he must leave Pershing's headquarters and recommended a transfer to the infantry. Patton had nearly decided to seek assignment as an infantry major when Col. LeRoy Eltinge visited Chaumont to report that a tank school was about to open in Langres and "would I take it?"[29] Conner's advice notwithstanding, Patton was intrigued by Eltinge's offer.

Although Patton's name is now closely associated with armored warfare, the devoted cavalryman did not join the Tank Corps out of any innovative vision that tanks represented the future of war. In July 1917 a French tank officer had regaled him "with lurid tales of the value of his pet hobby as a certain means of winning the war." Patton was skeptical, however, saying, "The Frenchman was crazy and the Tank not worth a damn."[30] Instead, Patton wrote his father that while there were a hundred majors in the infantry, there were none in the Tank Corps yet. Patton recognized that the novelty would garner greater media attention than the Army's traditional branches. If the armored vehicles *did* work and Patton ran the school and commanded the tanks, he might eventually be placed in charge of a brigade and be promoted to brigadier general. Finally, commanding tanks would likely get him into combat sooner, a prospect that appealed to Patton's self-perception as a warrior.[31]

Early in September 1917, therefore, Patton went to Pershing and requested a transfer. Pershing approved, and on November 18, Patton left AEF headquarters at Chaumont to attend the French Light Tank Training Center at Chamlieu in the forest of Compiègne. After two weeks at the French school, Patton was promoted to major and made director of the new American tank school at Langres that would train and equip men in the new branch. The entire AEF Tank Corps at the time consisted only of Patton and a lieutenant, and did not include a single tank. Yet by March 1918 the American training center consisted of 400 tanks and 5,000 officers and enlisted men.

His initial skepticism regarding the tank's value in combat notwithstanding, Patton quickly became an ardent student of the nascent art of armored warfare. He visited the tank factory at Betancourt outside Paris for a week and fastidiously inspected the machine and its components. Whenever tanks were in action, he rushed to the scene afterward to interview the tankers to gain insight into armored tactics. Patton organized his observations and ideas into a fifty-eight-page memo to the chief of the Tank Service, titled *Light Tanks*, which subsequently became the basis for U.S. tank operations. Patton was promoted to lieutenant colonel when he organized and commanded the 1st Light Tank Battalion at the beginning of April 1918. The unit became the

1st Light Tank Brigade in June, and while Rockenbach managed the Tank Corps' organization and logistics from an office at Chaumont, Patton led the tanks in the field, commanding fifty officers, 900 men, and twenty-five tanks.[32]

On September 26, the first day of the Meuse-Argonne offensive, Patton was leading his tankers from the front during the advance near Cheppy. While rallying infantrymen in his area to sustain the attack's momentum, he advanced toward the German trenches carrying only a walking stick and a pistol. Thirty yards from the German lines, Patton was shot through the groin, the bullet exiting near his rectum. It felt like a slap on the thigh, he later said, and he walked several paces before realizing he had been hit and collapsing to the ground. Of the six soldiers accompanying Patton, only one other man was not killed in the machine-gun burst. Patton's orderly, Pvt. Joe Angelo of Camden, New Jersey, dragged his commander into a shell hole, cut his trousers, mopped away the pool of blood, and bandaged his wound. Although bleeding profusely, Patton continued to direct his tanks from the crater until the area was secured an hour later. He gave his billfold and pistol to Angelo for safekeeping, and was carried on a litter to the medical station 3 kilometers away. Patton recommended Angelo for the Medal of Honor, and later told reporters "that when he was shot he fell down on the field and would have been killed if it had not been for the bravery of Private Joseph Angelo."[33] Patton was awarded the Distinguished Service Cross (DSC) for bravery under fire, and Joe Angelo won the DSC for saving Patton's life.

Upon his brigade's return to New York on March 17, 1919, Patton once again became the darling of the press. He had left for France as a junior captain, but now returned wearing a full colonel's eagles with his DSC, four battle stars, and the French Croix de Guerre on his chest. As the leading battlefield commander and expert on armored warfare, reporters quoted Patton and featured him in stories chronicling the Tank Corps' exploits. The *New York Herald* devoted more than half its coverage to him personally, with his photograph appearing under the caption: TANK FIGHTERS OF NEW YORK AMONG 2,110 BACK HOME, COLONEL PATTON TELLS HOW BIG MACHINES BY HUNDREDS ATTACKED GERMANS. His hometown *Los Angeles Herald* reported: TANK VICTORY OF YANKS IS DESCRIBED BY PATTON, and in newspapers from the *New York Times* to the *Richmond Times-Dispatch* he was the man of the hour.[34] Patton's brigade was assigned to the Tank Corps' home at Camp Meade. Because of Patton's legendary status within the fledgling organization, however, he had barely arrived at Meade when in mid-April he was ordered to temporary duty in Washington to help the Tank Board formulate tank regulations and prepare a course of instruction for tankers.

Despite the different paths they took to get there, when Eisenhower and Patton finally met they quickly became close friends. Both had been athletes and still relished competition: Eisenhower coached the Camp Meade football team, while Patton led the equestrian and pistol teams. Both had tempers and could swear as elegantly as any sergeant. Although Eisenhower could not join Patton in his obsessive polo playing—both because of his bad knee and the cost of maintaining the ponies—he and Patton enjoyed casual riding and shooting together. "From the beginning," Eisenhower reminisced, "we got along famously."[35]

Patton and Eisenhower played in a twice-weekly poker game with their fellow officers, their playing styles matching their personalities and eventual command styles. Patton's wealth meant he could afford to lose, and he bet with an aggression bordering on reckless abandon. Conversely, as a young man in Abilene Eisenhower learned to play cards from a local outdoorsman who was a mathematical genius and taught Ike that poker was a game of percentages. Eisenhower quickly realized that most officers knew "nothing about probabilities," and that by avoiding emotional play and following the odds he was able to become a "regular winner" and augment his meager salary.[36]

Once, President Wilson and Secretary Baker were inspecting Camp Meade and decided to visit some Army wives. They happened to knock on the Eisenhowers' door, and after a few minutes of small talk, Baker asked Mamie: "And what does your husband do best?"

"He plays an awfully good game of poker," Mamie replied cheerfully. Eisenhower, who had been preparing his unit for the inspection, was livid and berated his wife for not telling the secretary of war that he was an excellent soldier. Mamie had simply assumed that was common knowledge.[37]

When cards failed to provide sufficient excitement, one dark night in late 1919 the two officers climbed into Patton's touring car and drove up and down the unlit, two-lane blacktop road leading into Camp Meade. The highway had been plagued by a series of robberies, and Patton and Eisenhower's boredom led them to form their own posse. Armed with a half-dozen pistols, they slowly cruised along the road hoping to draw the bandits out.

Eisenhower recalled the adventure years later, explaining that "We wanted to run into one so we could see the guy's face when he found himself looking down the barrels of two guns." To their disappointment, the highwayman never appeared.[38]

In May 1920 the Army allowed post commanders to assign wartime barracks as quarters for married officers and their families, provided all remodeling, renovation, and furnishing expenses were paid by the officers themselves. At Camp Meade, Patton and Eisenhower were assigned abandoned wooden barracks covered by tarpaper on adjacent sandlots. It took a significant amount of effort to transform the oversized bunkhouses into suitable homes for their families. They hired off-duty soldiers to knock out walls, reroute plumbing, and section off the buildings to create bedrooms. Patton requisitioned the only paint colors available from the quartermaster. Consequently, his daughter Ruth Ellen recalled, "the whole part of the barracks we lived in was painted blue, yellow, blue and yellow, yellow and blue." Beatrice Patton solved the problem of what to do with the male latrines by "planting wandering jew and trailing ivy in the urinals."[39]

Because the wooden barracks were a potential tinderbox, indoor cooking was forbidden. For a time the Pattons had to eat in a mess hall, where most courses came out of a can, and even the best meals could never live up to Beatrice's standards.* When Beatrice finally issued an ultimatum that she must have a kitchen, the next day Patton drove up to their house in a tank dragging behind him a small signal house he had found abandoned on a firing range. "Here's your Goddam kitchen," he bellowed.

It too was painted blue and yellow.[40]

Eisenhower and Mamie expended similar money and labor to renovate their barracks, although the nearly $800 cost cut much more deeply for them. The task of furnishing and decorating their home went to Mamie, who recalled: "We didn't have a stick of furniture. I took orange crates and made a dressing table.... I got some cretonne and little thumb tacks and covered up the orange crates." The same cretonne adorned with Japanese prints she

---

* This is not to say that Beatrice Patton was spoiled or a shrinking violet. Once, the Pattons were attending an elegant white-tie event in Washington. While George parked their car, Beatrice waited in the foyer. Just then, an older, overweight officer observed Patton enter, resplendent in his dress uniform and medals and muttered, "Just look at the little boys they are promoting to Colonel these days; look at that young chicken still wet behind the ears, wearing a Colonel's eagle." The next thing Beatrice remembered was sitting astride the officer's shoulders, banging his head on the black-and-white-marble floor tiles "while Georgie and several others were trying to pull her off."

purchased by the yard to make drapes was also used to cover the army cots they used for beds. Mamie found a beat-up chaise and a table for the living room in a former Red Cross building classified as a "dump pile."

"My God, Mamie, you're not going to keep that?" Eisenhower asked.

"Yes, I like it," Mamie said. "I got it off the dump heap."[41]

The process of transforming the barracks into homes drew Patton and Eisenhower's families together. Eisenhower's three-year old son, Doud Dwight ("Ikky") spent hours at the Pattons' playing with George's daughters, Bea and Ruth Ellen. Patton's daughters idolized Mamie, whom they found "the most glamorous creature that ever appeared in our lives." Ruth Ellen recalled, "She drank a lot of iced tea, which she stirred by swirling it around in her glass. We thought this the ultimate in sophistication, and tried to do the same with our milk, with bad results."[42]

Ignoring the Eighteenth Amendment mandating Prohibition—and disproving Churchill's lament during the London victory parade—Eisenhower and Patton avidly partook in the new American pastime of making their own bootleg alcohol. Eisenhower distilled gin in an unused bathtub, while Patton brewed beer, storing it in a shed outside the kitchen shack. One summer evening there was a sudden noise outside the Pattons' barracks that sounded like a machine gun, followed by a series of soft booms. As their cook began screaming, Patton instinctively dove for cover. When they realized it was merely the beer bottles exploding from the heat, he rose, sheepishly explaining how much it had sounded like hostile fire. Beatrice "laughed and laughed and called him 'her hero' and he got very red," but she stopped when she realized he had genuinely been terrified. Although it would not be recognized as a distinct condition by the American Psychiatric Association until 1980, it is possible that Patton was suffering from some form of post-traumatic stress disorder resulting from his combat experience in France.[43]

Most importantly for their friendship, perhaps, was their professional curiosity. "Both of us were students of current military doctrine," Eisenhower recalled. "Part of our passion was our belief in tanks—a belief derided at the time by others." Both men believed mobility and firepower held the key to success on future battlefields, and that therefore tanks would dominate the next war. Desiring to learn more about the machines, in the summer of 1920 Eisenhower and Patton completely disassembled one of their tanks down to its nuts and bolts. "I had doubts that we would ever restore the vehicle to running order," Eisenhower admitted. During their spare hours in the afternoon they began reassembling the tank, "and so carefully had we done the work, that no pieces were left over and the machine operated when we were finished."[44]

In addition to commanding their respective units, they spent much of their time experimenting with the light and heavy tanks. The Renaults, small and light, often bogged down, and Patton and Eisenhower began using the heavier Mark VIII to tow the Renaults over rough terrain. The two tank pioneers decided to conduct an experiment to see how many Renaults a heavy tank could tow using an 18- to 20-foot steel cable. "Everything began fairly well," Eisenhower later recalled. "We got the first big tank across the obstacle. We had hitched three light tanks to it." As the grunting Mark VIII strained forward, the cable stretched, twisted, and finally snapped. "As it broke, the front half whirled around like a striking black snake and the flying end, at machine gun speed, snapped past our faces, cutting off brush and saplings as if the ground had been shaved with a sharp razor." The cable passed "not more than five or six inches" from their heads, which would have meant instant death for anyone it struck.

Eisenhower later recalled: "We were too startled at the moment to realize what had happened. But then we looked at each other. I'm sure I was just as pale as George."

That night, after dinner, Patton likened the incident to his near-fatal wounding in the Meuse-Argonne. "Ike, were you as scared as I was?" he asked.

Eisenhower nodded. "I was afraid to bring the subject up."[45]

Another afternoon the two officers were at the firing range trying to decide which machine gun was best suited for arming tanks. Patton was test firing a .30-caliber Browning machine gun while Eisenhower observed the bullets' trajectory through field glasses. "After George had fired a long burst," Eisenhower remembered, "the bullets were beginning to act strangely. I told him we ought to have another look at the target." Patton and Eisenhower had not made it far downrange before they heard the Browning bark behind them. Without warning the weapon had "cooked off" and began spewing bullets everywhere. Both men dashed for cover before maneuvering around the fire back to the gun. Patton grabbed the ammunition belt and gave it a hard twist, and the jammed weapon fell silent. "After that, we looked up sheepishly. We had acted like a couple of recruits."

Once again, the two men destined to lead America's armies into World War II a quarter-century later had narrowly averted disaster.

Although they resolved to be more careful, Patton and Eisenhower continued their experiments and imagined what tanks could do with better engines, suspensions, and tracks, as well as with bigger guns. Both men studied New Jersey mechanic and racing driver J. Walter Christie's revolutionary designs for tank drives and suspensions. Patton paid for a trip to Christie's workshops in Hoboken out of his own pocket, and even loaned him money. A demonstration of Christie's M1919 tank was arranged at Camp Meade for several generals from the War Department. The tank used for the demonstration drove to Meade on its own, covering some 250 miles at an average speed of 30 miles per hour. By itself, this impressive feat demonstrated that tanks could be made independent of rail transportation and deploy to battle on their own.

At Meade, Patton invited the generals to take the tank on a trial run. "It is so simple to handle," Patton declared, "that even a child can drive it." When none of the generals volunteered, Patton repeated his offer. "Well, gentlemen, who would like to take the first ride?" Again, there were no takers. Finally, Patton turned to Beatrice, who had come out to the muddy proving ground to watch the demonstration, and said, "All right, Bea, you demonstrate it!" Beatrice's dress was soiled and she lost her hat on the subsequent ride. Although she handled the vehicle with perfect aplomb and skill, the Ordnance Department rejected the Christie tank on the grounds it was too difficult to maneuver.[46]

Just as MacArthur faced certain implacable institutional obstacles in his effort to reform West Point, Patton and Eisenhower faced two significant organizational roadblocks to their attempts at innovation. First, next to aircraft, armor represented the costliest line item in the postwar Army budget. Amidst constant preaching of economy and more economy, even Pershing began to talk about the "economic impossibility of building enough tanks to constitute a mechanical army."[47] Whereas in France Patton routinely used thousands of tons of gallons of fuel in his tanks, under the parsimonious peacetime appropriations the tanks at Camp Meade were restricted to 500 gallons a day. Patton and Eisenhower's tanks burned through this in a few hours, and even this meager quota was cut to the point where they could only operate their tanks for a few minutes each day. Patton commanded four battalions, divided into twelve companies with about 300 Renaults. Yet by the time his AEF veterans were discharged, the 304th only had enough men to fill one company. "The rest," Patton lamented, "are simple skeletons."[48] A May 14, 1920 training exercise at Camp Meade illustrated the difficulties the postwar army faced. The mock order of attack, which gave unit objectives and boundaries and provided the other information needed for the maneuver, observed: "NOTE: Due to lack of troops, only [the] first assault line will be indicated by infantry."[49]

Even more detrimental to the Tank Corps' development than budgetary austerity, perhaps, were the decisions regarding armored warfare enshrined in the 1920 National Defense Act. During the 1919 congressional hearings on Army reorganization, both Secretary of War Baker and Gen. Peyton March argued for retaining the Tank Corps' independence. Although Pershing told the committees that "there is a great future for tanks," he concluded that "the Tank Corps should not be a large organization" and ought to be placed "under the chief of Infantry as an adjunct of that arm."[50] As with the proposed 500,000-man army, Pershing's towering reputation and his opposition sounded the death knell of the Tank Corps. Although the 1920 NDA established separate branches for the air service, the chemical corps, and the finance department, the Tank Corps was abolished and all tank units and personnel were assigned to the Infantry.

The Army, with its reverence for infantry as "the queen of battle," based its operational art on linear tactics and the straightforward movement of masses of troops. Official doctrine held that the mission of tanks was to precede attacking infantry by 50 yards, destroying machine-gun nests as they crept along at 3 miles per hour, and clearing a path for the troops through the enemy's wire. Because of this conception of the tank as just another front-line infantry weapon, there was no official interest in developing machines that moved faster than infantry could walk, needed heavy armor or cannon, nor was its range of significant concern.

Yet as Eisenhower explained: "George and I and a group of young officers thought this was wrong. Tanks could have a more valuable and more spectacular role. We believed . . . they should attack by surprise and mass."[51] Anticipating their eventual attendance at the prestigious School of the Line at Fort Leavenworth (as the Command and General Staff School was then called) Patton acquired copies of old tactical problems used there and asked Eisenhower and others to analyze them with him. "We'd go over to his house or my house," Eisenhower recalled, "and the two of us would sit down, and while our wives talked for the evening, we would work the problems. Then I would open up another pamphlet, find the answer, and grade ourselves."[52] After solving the problem in the accepted manner, they added tanks to the scenario and solved them again. In every case, the troops supported by tanks won.

As one historian observes, "Such wargaming exercises inevitably led to detailed discussion about how best to employ tanks. These, in turn, helped the participants, especially Patton and Eisenhower, focus their thoughts."[53] Almost simultaneously with European thinkers such as J. F. C. Fuller in Britain and Heinz Guderian in Germany, they concluded the tank had a role in future wars beyond its traditional mission of supporting the infantry. By using tanks in mass instead of spread out among the infantry units, Eisenhower and Patton argued, "they could break into the enemy's defensive positions, cause confusion, and by taking the enemy front line in reverse, make possible not only an advance by infantry, but envelopments of, or actual breakthroughs in, whole defense positions." As Eisenhower later said of this period, "These were the beginnings of a comprehensive tank doctrine that in George Patton's case would make him a legend."[54]

Although Patton and Eisenhower shared a common vision of the tank's potential, they held widely differing beliefs about other issues, which sometimes led to what Eisenhower recalled as "heated, sometimes almost screaming, argument[s] over matters that more often than not were doctrinal and academic rather than personal or material."[55] As Stephen Ambrose observed:

> They began an argument that would last until Patton's death. Patton thought that the chief ingredient in modern war was inspired leadership on the battlefield. Eisenhower felt that leadership was just one factor. He believed that Patton was inclined to indulge his romantic nature, neglecting such matters as logistics, a proper world-wide strategy, and getting along with allies.[56]

They both, however, believed another war was inevitable. Eisenhower remembered that "George was not only a believer, he was a flaming apostle. In idle conversations and in the studies we jointly undertook, he never said 'if' war might break out, it was always 'when.' 'Ike,' he'd say, 'This war may happen just about twenty years from now. This is what we'll do. I'll be Jackson, you'll be Lee. I don't want to do the heavy thinking; you do that and I'll get loose among our #%&%$# enemies.' This thought was repeated time and time again."[57]

This was not merely idle talk by Patton, who genuinely held the younger officer in high esteem. His respect for Eisenhower was such that when his old colleague from Chaumont, Brig. Gen. Fox Conner, mentioned over coffee one day that he was slotted to take over Camp Gaillard in Panama and needed to find a capable young officer to serve as his executive officer, Patton recommended Eisenhower. At Conner's request, in October 1920 George and Beatrice hosted a Sunday dinner party for Conner, to which Ike and Mamie were invited. After a midday meal, Conner wasted little time before asking the two younger officers to show him their tank training site. This was the first—and only—encouragement they had received from a senior officer, and given Conner's position as Pershing's chief of staff in Washington while the general waited to succeed March, he was considered perhaps the most influential officer in the Army. Conner, Eisenhower, and Patton walked down to the tank shops, the two tankers eagerly explaining their ideas to him en route. Conner found himself a chair in one of the machine shops and began to ask questions about tanks. He directed most of them at Eisenhower, who remembered: "Some could be answered briefly, while others required long explanations. By the time he had finished, it was almost dark and he was ready to go home. He said little except that it was interesting. He thanked us, and that was that."[58]

Even if he did not show it outwardly, Conner was impressed with the tank brigades' efficiency, and with Eisenhower's vision, knowledge, and ability to express them.

Although the Tank Corps' commander Rockenbach was perfectly content with the status quo and peacetime hibernation, "as enthusiasts," Eisenhower recalled, he and Patton "tried to win converts." In the blush of their enthusiasm they both wrote provocative articles supporting their theories for the *Infantry Journal*, the Army's leading theoretical periodical. Patton's piece, "Tanks in Future Wars," was published in May 1920. Patton decried the lack of interest in tanks, which he argued was due to ignorance. "Only those of us who doctored and nursed the grotesque war babies of 1918 through innumerable inherent ills of premature birth," he wrote, "know how bad they really were and, by virtue of that same intimate association, are capable of judging how much better they are now, and how surely they will continue to improve." He observed that:

> [I]n several countries tanks now exist which are capable of speeds across country varying from twelve to fifteen miles per hour, and on the road, up to twenty miles per hour. They are impervious to small arms, bullets, and shell fragments. They can cross trenches up to twelve feet in width. They have fine interior visibility and all around fire from both cannon and machine gun, and finally, they have a radius of action of more than two

hundred miles, without resupply of any sort. Such machines exist, and others will surpass them. It is futile to ignore the dreadful killing capacity of such arms.

Patton was adamant about tanks' future role, brashly calling for armor to act independently on the battlefield. In future wars tanks would guard rears and flanks, defend positions, and be used as offensive weapons.

To achieve its potential, however, Patton argued that the Tank Corps should *not* be incorporated into the infantry. "The tank is new and for the fulfillment of its destiny, it must remain independent," he wrote. "Not desiring or attempting to supplant infantry, cavalry, or artillery, it has no appetite to be absorbed by them." Absorbed, "we become the stepchild of that arm and the incompetent assistant of either of the others." The Tank Corps, he argued, "should be kept, as was the case among all armies in the World War, a separate entity" and in battle should "be assigned by higher authority to that unit where their presence will add the most to the general good." He colorfully concluded his essay by stating that "the Tank Corps grafted on Infantry, cavalry, artillery, or engineers will be like the third leg to a duck, worthless for control, for combat impotent."[59]

In November, Eisenhower published his article, "A Tank Discussion." Although he took a more conservative approach than Patton—in line with both the differences in their temperaments and the fact that the 1920 NDA eliminating the Tank Corps had already been passed—Eisenhower's article was still radical for an infantryman. He argued that those who opposed tanks fell into two classes: those who viewed tanks as a "freak development of trench warfare which has already outlived its usefulness," and those who "never had an opportunity to take part in an action supported by these machines" whose "knowledge of the power and deficiencies of the tank is based on hearsay."

Although we take armor's capability for granted today, in 1920 the vast majority of Army officers had never seen a tank much less become familiar with them. Thus, Eisenhower began by elucidating the tank's merits as an instrument of war, stressing its mobility, its ability to smash through barbed wire, and the protection it offered its crew. He also candidly acknowledged the tank's limitations in battle—it could not cross unbridged bodies of water, could not hold ground taken, and suffered serious problems of mechanical reliability. But most of these faults, he argued, were those of an immature technology. "The tank of the present is not a product of years of development of the ideal article for each part of itself, but rather the emergency result of emergency methods" necessitated by the war. "Study, observation and correction of faults," Eisenhower claimed, "will easily place [future] tank[s] on a level of mechanical efficiency with the best of our motor trucks today."

As opposed to Patton's call for armor to operate independently, Eisenhower—again, writing after the 1920 NDA—said that "in future wars tanks will be a profitable adjunct to the Infantry." Eisenhower suggested that infantry divisions could be reorganized by replacing the machine-gun battalion with a company of sixteen tanks, which he argued would provide more firepower and mobility. In conclusion, he wrote that "The clumsy, awkward and snaillike progress of the old tanks must be forgotten, and in their place we must picture this speedy, reliable and efficient engine of destruction" that "will be called upon to use their ability of swift movement and great fire power."[60]

The articles, both of which challenged existing doctrine, brought down the wrath of the Army establishment. The Tank Corps was now at the mercy of the chief of infantry, Maj. Gen. Charles S. Farnsworth, a "portly" officer who had no affection for either tanks or the men who commanded them. What Patton and Eisenhower had concluded was heresy to the infantry's leaders, who possessed a nearly liturgical faith in massed infantry attacks. Farnsworth abruptly summoned Eisenhower to Washington. In a short but icy interview, Eisenhower recalled, "I was told my ideas were not only wrong but dangerous and that henceforth I would keep them to myself. Particularly, I was not to publish anything incompatible with solid infantry doctrine. If I did, I would be hauled before a court-martial." Eisenhower believed Patton "was given the same message. This was a blow."[61] Both Eisenhower and Patton were stunned by the Army's intellectual rigidity, but neither dared defy Farnsworth.

Now *persona non grata* in his own branch, Eisenhower went to Rockenbach to request what he thought would be a simple transfer to the Infantry School at Fort Benning. But Rockenbach refused to endorse his application. Eisenhower had produced winning football seasons in 1919 and 1920—something that mattered a great deal in the laconic peacetime Army—and Rockenbach was not going to relinquish a coach who produced results. Rockenbach finally agreed to send Eisenhower's application on to the War Department, but warned it would likely be rejected, which it subsequently was.

Patton responded to the reprimand by getting angry and simply deciding to hell with it. He concluded the future of the tank service was bleak, and that without funds and commitment it had become a dead-end career path.

He wrote a formal letter through channels to the adjutant general asking to be relieved from his assignment with tanks and returned to duty with the cavalry. Although he hoped the cavalry "might display more imagination and receptiveness to ideas," at worst he could play polo and participate in horse shows and fox hunts while waiting for the War Department to move into the twentieth century. Patton's request was approved. After three years with a corps he literally brought to life in France, he delivered an emotional farewell to his tankers and transferred to Fort Myer, Virginia, and the Third Cavalry.[62]

Patton and Eisenhower parted ways. They remained casual friends, but would not serve together again for another two decades when the war they had foreseen from their barracks at Camp Meade finally erupted in Europe. Just as MacArthur's innovations would eventually be adopted by West Point, Patton and Eisenhower's vision of future armored warfare would be realized in the Sherman tanks produced for World War II. As an Eisenhower biographer observes, World War II "would prove the two young officers had it exactly right, so right in fact that their conclusions seem common place today. But in 1920 they were two decades ahead of most military theorists.... Eisenhower and Patton were true pioneers, original and creative in their own thought."[63]

Although Patton and Eisenhower were not prepared to sacrifice their careers to promote their heterodox ideas about armored warfare, there were other innovators who seemed to actively court martyrdom. Like MacArthur, William Mitchell was the progeny of an influential Wisconsin family. Mitchell's grandfather was a millionaire banker and railroad king, and a Milwaukee crony of Judge MacArthur. His father served with Arthur MacArthur in the Civil War, before eventually serving as a United States senator. When the Spanish-American War broke out in 1898, eighteen-year-old "Billy" quit college and enlisted in the First Wisconsin volunteer regiment. Thanks to his father's influence, it took less than a month for Mitchell to receive a second lieutenant's commission in a volunteer signal company. In 1901, after service in Cuba and the Philippines, Mitchell accepted a Regular Army commission in the Signal Corps.[64]

Just as Patton had once been cool to the idea of tanks as an important instrument of war, Mitchell was initially among the skeptics who supported keeping aviation in the Signal Corps. As a captain on the General Staff, in May 1913 Mitchell told a congressional hearing that airplanes were at best a reconnaissance system. Although it could be useful for artillery spotting, he argued, "The offensive value of this thing has yet to be proved. It is being experimented with—bomb dropping and machines carrying guns are being experimented with—but there is nothing to it so far except in an experimental way."[65] After finishing his General Staff assignment in June 1916, however, he moved to the Aviation Section in the office of the chief signal officer. Proving the adage "where you stand is where you sit," he immediately threw himself into the job of building up army aviation. In January 1917 the War Department decided to send an officer to Europe as an aeronautical observer. Mitchell—now a major—did not get along with the lieutenant colonel supervising him, and consequently volunteered for the position. Mitchell got the job and set sail for France on March 19, 1917.[66]

The next month the United States entered World War I. When Pershing's command party arrived in Paris on June 13, Mitchell was one of the first officers to greet them at the railroad station. Because he was the senior flyer in France, Pershing made him the AEF's aviation officer and instructed Mitchell—in a role similar to that which Patton would later assume with the nascent Tank Corps—to produce a "complete aviation project for the U.S. Army in France."[67] Mitchell was promoted to colonel in September, and in January 1918 was made the chief of Air Service, First Army, the top combat position. During the St. Mihiel offensive Mitchell commanded 1,481 American, British, and French airplanes, the largest aviation force to date in the war. He also commanded the First Army Air Service during the climactic Meuse-Argonne offensive.[68]

Mitchell's flamboyance while commanding the AEF's combat aviation elements brought him fame similar to MacArthur's, and when he returned to America in March 1919 he was determined to capitalize on his celebrity to bring about a revolution in U.S. military power. As a result of his experiences in the war, Mitchell believed that airpower now ranked with naval and ground warfare in importance, and that future military operations could not proceed on land or sea without command of the air by an "air force." He wrote that "the principal mission of Aeronautics is to destroy the aeronautical force of the enemy, and, after this, to attack his formations, both tactical and strategical, on the ground or on the water. . . . The secondary employment of Aeronautics pertains to their use as an auxiliary to troops on the ground for enhancing their effect against hostile troops."[69] Although the prioritization of establishing air superiority before conducting close air support is generally taken for granted today, in 1919 it was a revolutionary idea and fundamentally at odds with the War Department's infantry-centric policies.

When now–Brigadier General Mitchell returned for duty in Washington as the third assistant executive and chief, Training and Operations Group, Maj. Gen. Charles Menoher—MacArthur's commander in the Rainbow Division—headed the Air Service organization. Since Menoher was not a flyer and openly acknowledged Mitchell's superior expertise, Mitchell had an opportunity to dominate the Air Service. For nearly two years Mitchell tried to sell his views within government. He plied every means—conversations with fellow officers, interviews with reporters, testimony before congressional committees, public speeches, and magazine articles—to publicize his ideas. During the Army reorganization hearings, Mitchell and other airmen advocated an independent air force. In May 1919, Assistant Secretary of War Benedict Crowell published a report recommending an independent air service, and Mitchell wrote to "Hap" Arnold: "I think things look better every day for the air service."[70]

If Mitchell was a visionary, he was a notoriously difficult and temperamental prophet. He was opposed by nearly all senior Army and Navy officers, who saw aviation in a supporting role to ground forces or the fleet. The postwar Superior Board ruled that independence for Army aviation was justifiable only if air weapons had demonstrated a capability for decisive action in war like that of the Army or Navy. Yet "nothing so far brought out in the war shows that Aerial activities can be carried on, independently of ground troops, to such an extent as to materially affect the conduct of the war as a whole."[71] Key leaders such as Secretary Baker, March, and even Menoher were convinced that Army aviation was an adjunct to the ground battle and therefore had to be controlled by the ground commander. For once, Pershing agreed with March, arguing that "aviation is not an independent arm and cannot be for a long time to come, if ever."[72] Menoher and others pointed out that creating a new service would exacerbate existing interservice rivalries. Assistant Secretary of the Navy Franklin Delano Roosevelt agreed, telling the Senate reorganization hearings: "Two is company, and three is a crowd."[73]

In the end, no independent air force was created by the 1920 NDA. Instead, the Signal Corps' tiny prewar aviation section became the Army Air Service, a combat arm of 1,516 officers and 16,000 enlisted men, making it roughly equivalent with the infantry, cavalry, and field artillery. Although this was not what Billy Mitchell had hoped for, it was certainly better than the Tank Corps' fate under the NDA.

Despite their failure to win congressional approval for an independent service, the air advocates were not discouraged. In August 1920, less than two months after the NDA's passage, Mitchell published an essay in the *Review of Reviews* on "Our Army's Air Service." "We are convinced," he wrote, "that aviation can only be put on its feet in this country through the unification of all air activities ... under persons who are actually familiar with flying and the things that go with it." In addition to this gratuitous swipe at Menoher, Mitchell renewed his campaign on Capitol Hill, arguing that aviation should supplant the Navy as the basis for national defense. In January 1921 he testified before the House Committee on Appropriations that "Our system of coast defense is wrong. The only way to really defend a coast is with aircraft and mobile troops and their accessories." He added, "We can either destroy or sink any ship in existence today." Mitchell formally challenged the Navy to test his claims. Public pressure intensified for a bombing test handled by the Air Service, and shortly thereafter the War and Navy Departments agreed to conduct bombing tests under Navy control.[74]

In May 1921 Mitchell took command of the 1st Provisional Brigade, the unit formed to conduct the tests, which climaxed on July 20-21 with the bombing of the ex-German battleship *Ostfriesland*. Secretary of War Weeks, Secretary of the Navy Edwin Denby, Generals Pershing and Menoher, senators and representatives, foreign observers, reporters, and other distinguished guests went aboard the transport USS *Henderson* to witness the operation. The second 2,000-pound bomb dropped by Mitchell's squadron hit the *Ostfriesland*'s side armor, glanced off, and exploded 20 to 25 feet from the port side. The stern quickly settled, and within twenty-one minutes the battleship had turned over and disappeared below the sea.[75]

Naval officials denied the test was conclusive. The experiment was not under service conditions, they argued, for the *Ostfriesland* had been stationary and the bombers were guided to their target by a row of destroyers in near perfect weather conditions. Moreover, the battleship had been unmanned, meaning there was no crew to fire antiaircraft guns at the low-flying planes or to repair damage and keep the ship afloat. But on August 18 the Joint Board, headed by Pershing, submitted its report on the tests to the secretaries of War and Navy. Despite the Navy's protests, the board acknowledged that "the ships so attacked, whether submarine, destroyer, light cruiser, or battleship, were eventually sunk and by airplanes with bombs alone." It recognized that "aircraft carrying high-capacity, high-explosives bombs of sufficient size have adequate offensive power to sink or seriously damage any naval vessel at present constructed, provided such projectiles can be placed in the water alongside the vessel." Finally, the board doubted that "any type of vessel of sufficient strength" could be built to withstand the destructive force inherent in bombs carried from "shore bases or sheltered harbors."

Yet the Joint Board failed to make the only recommendation that mattered to Mitchell—the establishment of an independent air force.

Mitchell was irrepressible. After the tests, on July 29 he sent the 1st Provisional Brigade on a mock raid of New York City. Seventeen Martin bombers, a Handley Page, and a Caproni flew northward over the city in a great "V." Returning to its base at Langley Field in Virginia, he subsequently "bombed" Philadelphia, Wilmington, Baltimore, and—adding insult to injury—the U.S. Naval Academy at Annapolis.[76]

On August 29 Mitchell sent his after-action report on the naval tests and the mock bombing runs to General Menoher. Echoing Patton's argument about tank development, Mitchell concluded that "aviation can only be developed to its fullest extent under its own direction and control."[77] Menoher read Mitchell's report, noted his disapproval, and forwarded it to Secretary Weeks. Yet before either had a chance to officially respond, someone leaked the report to the *New York Times*. It was published on September 14, with the *Times* calling it a "sensational chapter" in the "aircraft versus capital ships" story.[78] This was the straw that broke the camel's back for Menoher. For months Mitchell had been airing his opinions on airpower and aviation organization, and in securing publicity for himself and his ideas he had brought unfavorable publicity on his superiors. Menoher decided either he or Mitchell had to go, and on September 16 asked to be relieved as chief of the Air Service.

Although Secretary Weeks decided to keep Mitchell, the strain of duty in Washington had begun to wear on the airman. In addition to his publicity campaign, the bombing tests, and butting heads with Menoher, in July 1921—at the height of the *Ostfriesland* controversy—his marriage of sixteen years collapsed with his separation from his wife Caroline and their three children. Most observers expected Mitchell to be appointed chief of the Air Service, but instead, on September 21 the position went to Maj. Gen. Mason Patrick, the officer whom Pershing had relied upon to bring discipline and organization to the AEF Air Service in France when Mitchell clashed with other officers. Mitchell confronted Patrick almost immediately, insisting on certain prerogatives as the "senior flying officer in the service," and threatened to resign if Patrick failed to meet his demands. Patrick called his bluff, however, and offered to accept his resignation, but Mitchell folded and rescinded it.[79]

Mitchell was constrained by other means as well. Whereas Menoher had been resented as a despised "kiwi"—an officer in the Air Service who could not fly an airplane—Patrick took flying lessons and became a pilot himself. This not only bought him credibility amongst the close-knit fraternity of aviators, it relegated Mitchell to being the second senior flyer in the Service. In June 1922 Secretary Weeks issued a public statement that he would not allow any serving officer "to go around the country attacking the organization of which he is a part." He further determined that Mitchell must submit his articles for official clearance, which temporarily prevented the maverick from writing any controversial pieces.[80] Finally, Patrick gave Mitchell numerous special assignments, several of which kept him away from the capital for long periods of time and temporarily solved the "idle hands" problem.

In the years after the 1920 NDA, the Air Service suffered a fate similar to that of the Army at large. The obsession with economy in the government and the American public had grown until the aviation strength levels authorized in 1920 were but fond memories. Whereas the NDA had envisaged 1,576 officers and 16,000 enlisted men in Army aviation, this authorized strength soon dropped to 1,061 officers and 8,764 enlisted men. By March 1923 the Air Service only had 880 officers and 8,349 enlisted men. Although Patrick estimated the Air Service needed $26 million in appropriations to address its deficiencies in materiel, the War Department only offered it $13 million for fiscal year 1923, and Congress only appropriated $12.7 million. As a board under Maj. Gen. William Lassiter appointed by the War Department in early 1924 to study Patrick's budget proposals concluded, "our Air Service [is] in a very unfortunate and critical situation" because of the reduction of its personnel strength and the deterioration of its equipment left over from war stocks.[81]

Billy Mitchell got remarried in October 1923 and departed on a combined inspection tour of the Pacific and Far East and extended honeymoon. He returned home in June 1924 reinvigorated, and began a campaign to publicize the Air Service's condition and win acceptance for his theories on airpower. Although Patrick shared some of Mitchell's ideas about aviation, he judiciously decided to keep working within normal bureaucratic channels. Mitchell, however, strenuously believed that "changes in military systems are brought about only through the pressure of public opinion or disaster in war."[82] He consequently took it upon himself to initiate a one-man push to force a shift in defense policy. From December 1924 to March 1925 he published a series of articles that were a broadside at all who disagreed with him. As Mitchell's friend, the British military aviation pioneer Gen. Sir Hugh Trenchard, observed, Mitchell tried "to convert his opponents by killing them first."[83]

In March 1924 the House appointed a select committee chaired by Representative Florian Lampert of Wisconsin to investigate the Air Service. Mitchell made frequent appearances before the Lampert Committee, where he castigated the War Department's aviation policy. In February 1925 he claimed that the War and Navy Departments were suppressing testimony by aviation officers through indirect threats of retaliation, and that consequently the committee could not get the whole truth about the deplorable aviation situation. Worse, he asserted that witnesses for other viewpoints were "in some cases" responsible for "possibly a falsification of evidence, with the evident intent to confuse Congress."[84] Yet when pressed on these points by Weeks, Mitchell could only show that there had been inaccuracies or differences of opinion rather than deliberate falsehoods.

Although Mitchell's scorched earth tactics won him a large following, it also made a number of enemies, including Navy officers, the General Staff, Secretary Weeks, and even President Calvin Coolidge. Pershing thought Mitchell's conduct was symptomatic of a kind of "Bolshevik bug" at work in the Army which had to be stamped out. Bradford Chynoweth, a member of Patton and Eisenhower's circle of armor visionaries at the Infantry Tank School who seldom refrained from criticizing Army leadership, nevertheless recalled that "Billy Mitchell was a grandstander who never played teamwork with anybody . . . his exaggerated denunciation of the Navy was unjustifiable."[85] Eventually Mitchell's charges became so outrageous that even the press—which had never hesitated to publicize his previous assertions—took exception. "It is one thing to accuse our military officials of being too slow or too stupid," the *New York Times* declared. "But it is quite another to charge them with willingness to hazard the security of the nation for the sake of their own personal comfort."[86] Secretary Weeks wrote to the president that Mitchell's "whole course had been so lawless, so contrary to the building up of an efficient organization, so lacking in reasonable teamwork, so indicative of a personal desire for publicity at the expense of everyone with whom he associated that his actions render him unfit for a high administrative post such as he now occupies."[87] Weeks told Coolidge he could not recommend Mitchell's reappointment as assistant chief of the Air Service when his term expired, and at the end of March 1925 Mitchell reverted to his permanent grade of colonel and was transferred to Fort Sam Houston, San Antonio, Texas, as the aviation officer of the Eighth Corps Area.

Even in semi-exile, Mitchell seemed to solicit controversy. On August 31, 1925, a Navy PN-9 aircraft disappeared somewhere over the Pacific during the first flight from San Francisco to Hawaii. Three days later, on September 3, the Navy dirigible *Shenandoah* crashed after running into severe weather over Ohio. In San Antonio, Mitchell issued a nine-page statement he gave to reporters alleging the tragedies were the "direct result of incompetency, criminal negligence, and almost treasonable administration of the national defense."[88] Mitchell appeared to be daring the Coolidge Administration to court-martial him. Two weeks passed while the War Department went through the customary investigation before announcing the decision to prosecute Mitchell. President Coolidge personally preferred the charges that "Mitchell had made statements which were insubordinate, contemptuous, disrespectful, and prejudicial to good order and military discipline."[89]

The court-martial convened on October 28 in a dingy old warehouse near the Capitol that made it appear the Army sought to "dampen the popular excitement aroused by the court-martial."[90] There were only seats for about one hundred people, which were filled every day. Washington, DC, was still a sleepy southern town in 1925, a far cry from today's wealthy, cosmopolitan city. Mitchell's trial was the most exciting event in the capital since Pershing and the AEF's homecoming in 1919, and reporters filled half the available seats at the trial. The image of the handsome and colorful Mitchell in the new Air Service uniform of shirt, tie, and blouse appearing in front of a dozen older generals in their old-fashioned, stiff, high collars guaranteed the defendant would be viewed as an underdog. As the *New York Times* noted, "the Mitchell trial is a good show, and that's why it's 'S.R.O.' [Standing Room Only] every day."[91]

The court-martial was supposed to determine whether or not Mitchell was guilty of conduct prejudicial to "good order and military discipline and ... conduct of a nature to bring discredit upon the military service." Three of the jurors were removed when defense challenges accused them of prejudice against Mitchell, including Fred Sladen and future chief of staff Maj. Gen. Charles Summerall. Maj. Gen. Robert L. Howze, a cavalryman who had commanded an infantry division in France, was appointed court president. Mitchell's civilian defense counsel, Representative Frank Reid of Illinois, initially pleaded that his client had only been exercising his right to free speech. But when Reid was permitted to introduce testimony and other evidence in support of Mitchell's theories, the trial turned into a dramatic, highly publicized—but legally irrelevant—debate on airpower. Although the judges had expected the trial to be completed quickly, it wound up stretching into seven weeks. One judge, Brig. Gen. Frank McCoy, humorously wrote to Mrs. Leonard Wood that he had planned only a short stay with friends in Washington but that the trial dragged on until he had to find new accommodations. He thought Mitchell and Reid were handling the publicity aspects of the "case so well that to the public the War Department is on trial instead of the festive Bill."[92]

Yet under strong cross-examination on both the charges and unrelated matters such as the question of an independent air corps, Mitchell's case was steadily undermined. The assistant trial judge advocate, Maj. Allen W. Gullion, was relentless and forced Mitchell to admit that his September 5 statement was based solely on opinion and not on fact. He also got Mitchell to concede that as a leader of the Air Service for several years, he bore a share of the responsibility for the military aviation conditions he had so strenuously condemned. Even Mitchell's close friends and admirers knew he was guilty as charged. Hap Arnold, one of his strongest supporters and later chief of the Air Corps in World War II, recalled: "A good showing was the best that could come of it. . . . The thing for which Mitchell was being tried he was guilty of, and except for Billy, everybody knew it, and knew what it meant."[93]

Next to Mitchell himself, the proceedings were possibly most painful for the commander of the III Corps Area and youngest member of the court, now–Major General Douglas MacArthur. Mitchell had served in the Philippines under MacArthur's father, and due to their family connections had known the younger MacArthur all his life. MacArthur had even dated one of Mitchell's sisters for a time in 1905, and called the instructions to serve on his friend's court-martial "one of the most distasteful orders I ever received."[94] MacArthur expressed no opinions during the proceedings, made no motions, and questioned no witnesses. His name was raised only once, when Representative Fiorello La Guardia testified. The future mayor of New York City had been a pilot under Mitchell in World War I, and was a champion of airpower. The Army prosecutor examining the congressman asked: "Mr. La Guardia, the newspapers recently . . . quoted you as saying . . . 'Billy Mitchell isn't being tried by a jury of his peers, but by nine beribboned dogrobbers of the General Staff.' Were you correctly quoted?"

"I didn't say beribboned."

The laughter in the courtroom delayed the proceedings for several minutes. Howze said: "The court would like to have you explain what was meant by your characterization of this court."

La Guardia said, "From my experience as a member of Congress and from my contact with the General Staff, I'm convinced that the training, the background, the experience and the attitude of officers of high rank of the Army are conducive to carrying out the wishes and desires of the General Staff." La Guardia thought for a second, and added: "I want to say that at that time I didn't know General MacArthur was on this court."

Again, the spectators burst into laughter, joined this time by the "beribboned dogrobbers" themselves.[95]

Other than this moment of levity, MacArthur sat in the court with "his features as cold as carved stone," and during a break in the proceedings Mitchell was overheard telling a supporter that "MacArthur looks like he's been drawn through a knothole." One journalist noted that MacArthur was "especially inattentive" during the trial because he and Louise "were like newlyweds, exchanging meaningful glances—Mrs. MacArthur smiling over a bunch of violets which she carried each day; her husband could hardly keep his eyes off her."[96]

In the end, the disciplinary issue prevailed. On December 17 the court-martial panel found Mitchell guilty on all eight counts. The verdict only required a two-thirds majority, but there was only one dissenting vote, and the individual votes were never revealed. Mitchell was sentenced to a five-year suspension from duty with forfeiture of pay and allowances. President Coolidge approved the sentence on January 26, 1926, but granted Mitchell full subsistence and half pay. When Mitchell responded by offering his resignation effective February 1, 1926, the War Department quickly accepted.

Mitchell spent the rest of his life as a civilian, free to agitate for an independent air corps, strategic bombardment, and stronger defenses in the Pacific. Because Mitchell seemed wedded to an unyielding radicalism, he no longer enjoyed any public allies amongst airmen on active duty. This was partly because there were signs that American military aviation was making progress. In December, Gen. Patrick submitted a plan calling for the immediate implementation of the Lassiter Board's recommendations. In 1926 Congress passed two bills—the Air Commerce Act and the Air Corps Act, the latter of which established the creation of an Army Air Corps analogous to the Marine Corps in its semi-independent status within the Navy. The act authorized an increase in Air Corps officer strength from 900 to 1,514, expanded its enlisted force from 9,760 to 16,000, and authorized the Air Corps to maintain 1,800 serviceable planes. The legislation also provided for an assistant secretary of war to oversee the Air Corps; three brigadier general assistants to the chief of Air Corps; the inclusion of an air section in each War Department General Staff division; and the requirement that the chief, two of the three brigadier generals, and 90 percent of the officers at each grade be flying officers.[97] Although Mitchell would enjoy a latter day reputation as a martyr and a prophet, it was the more politically astute Patrick who was responsible for securing the Air Corps position in the interwar Army.

While Billy Mitchell paid a heavy price for his dissent, there are worse fates that can befall a man than professional setbacks. If Eisenhower's career had hit an apparent wall in November 1920, he could take comfort in a warm, happy family life. During the first few years of their marriage, Ike and Mamie spent most of their time apart as Eisenhower was transferred from one dusty post to another training troops for World War I. Eisenhower lived in bachelor quarters at Camp Meade until the autumn of 1919, when Mamie—who had not seen her husband since Camp Colt's dismantling in November 1918—declared "quarters or no quarters" she was going to join him at Meade "if I have to live in a tent."[98]

They rented a wretched single room in a Laurel, Maryland boarding house that was too small to accommodate Ikky, who stayed with the Douds in Denver. After less than a month Mamie's life had become so intolerable that she packed up and took the train back to Denver and the comfort of her family. Mamie did not return to Meade until May 1920 when the abandoned barracks were made available. While Eisenhower and Mamie completed the renovation work, Ikky was left with Mamie's aunt in Boone, Iowa.

The blond cherub was three years old when he finally joined his parents at Camp Meade. For a brief period, their painful separations behind them, the Eisenhowers spent perhaps the happiest months of their married life. In particular, they delighted in Ikky's presence. Eisenhower became completely devoted to the young boy. Whereas his father had rarely shown any emotion or affection, Eisenhower hugged and kissed Ikky without any trace of self-consciousness. When Ike came home at the end of the day, he would pick Ikky up and carry him on his shoulders. One friend remembered how Eisenhower would lie on the floor pretending to be a kitten, or growl like a bulldog, playing the jester to make him laugh. "Deafening noises of the tanks enthralled him. A football scrimmage was pure delight. And a parade with martial music set him aglow," Eisenhower recalled. He admitted he was "inclined to display Ikky and his talents at the slightest excuse, or without one, for that matter."[99]

If Ikky was completely devoted to the soldiers, his affection was reciprocated as he became a mascot for the Tank Corps. Eisenhower's junior officers had a little uniform made for Ikky, complete with an overcoat and overseas cap. To his chortling delight, he was taken for rides on the roaring, smoke-shrouded tanks and was fussed over like a little hero. As Geoffrey Perret observes: "In the innocent yet somehow wise way of small children, [Ikky] won the affection of the entire camp."[100]

Eisenhower had just passed his thirtieth birthday as Christmas 1920 approached. Finally out from under the debt incurred from renovating their quarters, the family splurged by hiring a part-time maid and spoiling Ikky with presents, including a small red tricycle placed beneath the tree Ike had erected. On December 23, Mamie returned from a shopping trip to Baltimore to discover that Ikky was running a fever. At first it seemed to be a simple flu, but on Christmas Day he was too sick to open his presents. When the temperature did not subside, Ikky was hospitalized. His condition failed to improve, and a physician from Johns Hopkins Medical School was summoned for a consultation. Ikky, he said, had scarlet fever. "We have no cure for this," he said. "Either they get well or you lose them."[101]

Ikky was quarantined. Eisenhower was not allowed into his room, and could only sit on a porch outside and wave through a window to his little boy. "I haunted the halls of the hospital," Eisenhower recalled. "Hour after hour, Mamie and I could only hope and pray."[102] Ikky's little body fought the illness for ten days, but the scarlet fever turned into meningitis. Eisenhower was permitted into the room to be with his deteriorating son, but in the early morning hours of January 2, 1921, Ikky died in his arms.

Eisenhower, who had just been reunited with his son a few months before, was shattered.

When he and Mamie returned home, the red tricycle they had bought for Ikky remained forlornly beside their Christmas tree, a visible reminder of the enormous void left by his sudden passing. The Tank Corps' soldiers provided an honor guard as Ikky's tiny coffin was conveyed to the Baltimore train station for the sad journey to Denver, where it was interred in the family plot. "For a long time, it was as if a shining light had gone out of Ike's life," Mamie said later. "Throughout all the years that followed, the memory of those bleak days was a deep inner pain that never seemed to diminish."[103] Eisenhower never spoke publicly about Ikky's death until the publication of his 1967 memoir, in which he wrote: "This was the greatest disappointment and disaster in my life, the one I have never been able to forget completely. Today, when I think of it, even now as I write about it, the keenness of our loss comes back to me as fresh and terrible as it was in that long dark day soon after Christmas 1920."[104]

CHAPTER FOUR

Guardians of Empire

ALTHOUGH NOTHING COULD COMPARE TO THE AGONY OF IKKY'S DEATH, THE new year only brought more trials for Eisenhower. In June 1921, he learned that another officer at Camp Meade was being investigated for receiving subsidies for more than one abode. Eisenhower realized he might also have drawn the same allowance, as he had received $250.67 in reimbursement for light and heating expenses for Ikky when the boy was living in Iowa with Mamie's aunt during the renovation of their quarters at Meade. Eisenhower wrote the adjutant general and requested "a decision as to whether I was entitled to commutation I drew under the above conditions. In case it is decided that I was not entitled to same, request that this letter be referred to the auditor of the Army for a statement of the amount of commutation I drew between the dates mentioned, in order that I may refund the government."[1] He was told the regulation specifically stated that a monthly allowance could only be drawn for a single abode, and that by claiming Ikky as a dependent entitled to the allowance while the child was in Iowa he was in violation of Army regulations.[2]

Eisenhower claimed he was unaware of the regulation. Yet by 1921 the Army was downsizing and economizing wherever possible, and thus took a zero tolerance approach toward any disciplinary infractions. On June 21 the Army's adjutant general weighed in: "The Certificate[s] which this officer filed with his pay vouchers for the months of May to August 1920, inclusive, were on their face false and untrue.... and the result of this investigation leads me to the conclusion that ... Major Dwight D. Eisenhower, Inf., be brought to trial upon charges based upon the facts developed."[3] The fact that Eisenhower had self-reported his infraction and tried to pay back the difference were "not thought to materially affect the issue." The matter was subsequently turned over to the Army's inspector general, Brig. Gen. Eli A. Helmick, for further action.

Colonel Rockenbach tried to save his subordinate by delivering an oral reprimand to Eisenhower on July 18, but Helmick was not appeased. He turned the matter over to the II Corps Area commander, Brig. Gen. H. F. Hodges, "for further investigation and appropriate disciplinary action." Once again, aware of Eisenhower's potential, Hodges only elected to deliver a verbal reprimand. He wrote to the adjutant general on October 24 suggesting the relevant papers be gathered *if* it should be ruled that a trial was *not* barred by the reprimand. But in his opinion, "whatever was said" was all that needed to be said and the matter should be laid to rest.[4]

Once again, Helmick was not satisfied. On November 1 he wrote the adjutant general: "Major Eisenhower is a graduate of the Military Academy, of six years' commissioned service. That he should have knowingly attempted to defraud the government in this matter or, as he contends, that he was ignorant of the provisions of the laws governing commutation for dependents are alike inexplicable."[5] Helmick ordered an investigation that confirmed his position and concluded that Eisenhower had no excuse for not recognizing he was not entitled to draw the allowance. He denounced Eisenhower as a liar who submitted "false" statements to the Army and took "illegal" payments.[6] His damning report recommended that Eisenhower not only repay the allowance but should also be court-martialed.

Years later, Eisenhower admitted he was "on the ragged edge of breakdown that year." If the case went to court-martial he would certainly lose. Less than a year after the death of his beloved three-year-old son, it appeared likely he would be drummed out of the Army, his promising career over before it ever really got started. Unbeknownst to him at the time, however, Eisenhower had a guardian angel looking out for him. Fox Conner took command of an infantry brigade in Panama later in 1921 and, remembering that afternoon in Camp Meade's motor pool, requested Eisenhower as his executive officer. The War Department rejected Conner's application because officers under investigation could not be transferred. By this time, however, General Pershing had succeeded Peyton March as chief of staff, so Conner contacted George Marshall to see what could be done. Although the chief of staff did not typically intervene in personnel matters concerning mere majors, Pershing's respect and affection for Conner was such that he had Marshall contact the adjutant general.

Brigadier General Helmick may have been zealous, but he was not stupid. He realized that continuing to hound Eisenhower and end his career over $250.67 would not be looked upon favorably by the new Army establishment.

Consequently, he did a complete 180. Whereas in his earlier reports he had stated Eisenhower's claim that he was ignorant of the regulation governing commutations for dependents was "inexplicable," Helmick now declared that lack of knowledge must be "weighed in his favor."[7] On December 14, 1921, he wrote the adjutant general that while Eisenhower's offenses were "of the gravest character for which he might not only be dismissed from the service but imprisoned," he did not recommend a court-martial. Instead, Helmick suggested a formal reprimand be placed in Eisenhower's 201 file. The reprimand—which amounted to little more than a slap on the wrist—was administered by Brig. Gen. J. H. McRae, the assistant chief of staff, and a close friend of Conner's.[8]

Thus, after six emotionally excruciating months, Eisenhower's career was saved by the narrowest of margins. In late December 1921 he received orders to report to Camp Gaillard, Panama, for his first tour of foreign military service.

As a result of President McKinley's opportunistic decision to seize the Philippines at the outset of a war with Spain over Cuba nearly 10,000 miles away, in 1898 America inadvertently acquired an empire in the Pacific. After defeating the Spanish forces in the archipelago, an insurrection by Filipino patriots, and a decade of local insurgencies, in 1912 the War Department recommended creating a distinct overseas force to administer the seven regiments comprised of 9,800 soldiers designated as the permanent garrison in the Philippines, thereby cutting costs and simplifying training and administration. In 1913 this "Colonial Army" was extended to include Hawaii and the Canal Zone in Panama. These garrisons—together with a regiment protecting foreign legations in Tsientsing, China, and forces stationed in Alaska and Puerto Rico—meant that during the 1920s and 1930s an average of 27 percent of the Army was on foreign service at any given time, and that Regular Army officers and their families could expect to serve at least one tour abroad between the world wars.[9]

World War I shifted the balance of power in the Pacific and clarified the potential threats to American interests in the region. Japan had seized German territories in China, dominated Manchuria, and invaded Siberia with 120,000 troops. Besides demonstrating that Japan's ability to project military forces into Asia far exceeded that of any Western power, American officers who served alongside the Japanese in Russia became convinced that Japan intended to conquer East Asia and that its military eagerly anticipated a clash with the United States. Thus, unlike the skeletonized organizations in the continental United States, the prospect of sudden invasion meant the overseas departments were supposed to be fully operational commands ready to fight at a moment's notice. Yet the size and composition of these forces became subsumed in the debates over the U.S. Army in 1919 and 1920. Recognizing the economizing mood of Congress and aware of the maxim that he who tries to protect everything protects nothing, Pershing decided the primary function of the Regular Army was to serve as a cadre for the mass army. Thus, in July 1922, he cut the authorized Regular garrisons in Hawaii and the Philippines almost in half despite the apparent urgency of building up troop strength in the Pacific.[10]

This reduction of forces also affected the Army in Panama. When now–Brigadier General John Palmer took over the 19th Infantry Brigade at the Gatun Lock on the canal's Atlantic side in September 1923, every one of its units was dangerously understrength. On the Pacific side, Conner theoretically commanded a brigade as well. But in reality his brigade consisted of a single regiment, the 42nd Infantry. Conner's job was to reorganize and modernize the defense of the Canal Zone, and in the event of hostilities to defend the Culebra Cut. Moreover, upon arriving at Camp Gaillard Conner faced a morale crisis due to the "eccentricity" of the previous commander.

Before Eisenhower could even address these challenges he and Mamie had to get to Camp Gaillard, a journey which proved an ordeal in itself. On January 16, 1922, the Eisenhowers sailed for Panama aboard the SS *St. Mihiel*. Due to the last-minute arrival of a general, they were downgraded from a suite to a cramped, airless cabin, with a small couch and two narrow bunks, one atop the other. Mamie, who was claustrophobic, later recalled "I wasn't about to get in a bunk, so I'd sleep on that small seat" curled up uncomfortably.[11] The ship was rocked by storms during its ten-day journey, compounding Mamie's morning sickness with seasickness. Even Eisenhower, who was not prone to complaining, noted that "The accommodations were miserable. The Army Transport Corps evidently based their model loading pattern on advice given by sardine packers."[12] Once ashore in Panama, the Eisenhowers traveled along the canal on an old-fashioned train. When it reached the point nearest Camp Gaillard, they disembarked and had to walk hundreds of yards in the tropical heat across one of the lock gates, clinging to a rope over the narrow catwalk connecting the two shores as the muddy water of the canal rushed below them.

Things did not improve when they arrived at Camp Gaillard. Built by the French at the end of the nineteenth century on the edge of the Culebra Cut during their failed attempt to dig a canal, Gaillard had once been a beautiful residential district. But the houses had been unoccupied for nearly a decade since the French abandoned construction and were in a state of decay and disrepair. The ruins of structures that had collapsed into the cut were visible. Conditions were so dismal that when the Conners arrived at Gaillard the post adjutant had not unpacked their household goods on the assumption "that as soon as the General knew where he had been ordered, he would do everything in his power to have his orders changed."[13] A steep, uncertain path led to the ramshackle, two-story wooden hut on stilts that would serve as the Eisenhowers' quarters, and Mamie initially refused to enter the structure for fear the steps would collapse beneath her. The sheet metal roof caught the sun and trapped heat in the house below, and during the frequent tropical downpours it reverberated like a steel drum and leaked like a sieve. The back porch opened directly onto the encroaching jungle, and snakes, lizards, and insects were a constant presence outside. Once inside, Mamie discovered that in addition to the mold and rot, the hut "was covered with cockroaches, bedbugs, bats." When a bat got into the bedroom that first night, Mamie shouted for Eisenhower to kill it. He grabbed a sword and heroically jumped on chairs, tables, and the bed, missing the creature each time he slashed at it. "Once a week," Mamie remembered, "you'd take your bed and put the legs in cans of kerosene, and . . . take paper and light it and go all over the springs to get the bedbugs."[14] Consequently, Fox Conner's wife Virginia recalled that Mamie "made no bones about how mad she was that they had been ordered to such a horrid post."[15]

Although the Eisenhowers eventually turned the dilapidated structure into a semblance of a livable home, their problems during their first months in Panama went deeper than substandard housing. They desperately needed a change of scenery after Ikky's death, as every corner at Camp Meade seemed to hold memories of their lost son. Although Panama offered a new beginning, Virginia Conner felt their marriage had "reached a turning point. . . . It was evident that there was a serious difficulty at the time, largely, I think, because of the death of their child. They were two people drifting apart. . . . It was my feeling that their marriage was in danger. . . . there was no warmth between them. They seemed like two people moving in different directions."[16] Julie Nixon Eisenhower wrote that Ikky's death "closed a chapter in the marriage. It could never again be unblemished first love. Ike was no longer the untried idealist, Mamie no longer the blithely romantic spirit."[17]

When Mamie's parents visited in the spring, they were so appalled at the primitive conditions they insisted she return with them to Denver for the birth of the baby. This separation could easily have been the breaking point for the Eisenhowers' marriage. John Sheldon Doud Eisenhower was born on August 3, 1922, after which Mamie decided to return to Panama. "John did much to fill the gap that we felt so poignantly and so deeply every day of our lives since the death of our first son," Eisenhower later recalled. "While his arrival did not, of course, eliminate the grief we still felt, he was precious in his own right and he did much to take our minds off the tragedy."[18] More importantly, perhaps, Mamie concluded she would have to accept her husband for who he was and to make peace with Army life. Mamie's transformation upon her return was apparent to those around her. "After Johnny was born and Mamie felt better," Virginia Conner remembered, "I had the delight of seeing a rather callow young woman turn into a person to whom everyone turned. I have seen her, with her gay laugh and personality, smooth out Ike's occasional irritability."[19] Thus, the Eisenhowers survived their first significant marital crisis.

Domestic difficulties aside, from a professional standpoint Panama proved to be a highly rewarding tour of duty for Eisenhower, who described it as "one of the most interesting and constructive of my life." The reason, he wrote, "was the presence of one man, General Fox Conner." Shortly after their arrival, the Eisenhowers climbed through the hedge to introduce themselves to their new neighbors. While Virginia Conner worked to reassure Mamie that her house would be more than comfortable with a little work, Eisenhower's gaze was drawn to General Conner's enormous library. Conner asked what Eisenhower called "a casual question" and found that "I had little or no interest left in military history." Although Eisenhower loved ancient history as a child—his mother had to lock the history books in a closet to get him to do his chores instead of reading about the Greeks and Romans—he had lost interest in the subject because of "its treatment at West Point as an out-and-out memory course"—precisely the pattern MacArthur had tried to break while superintendent.[20]

Conner sensed Eisenhower's intelligence and curiosity, and sought to put them to use in his subordinate's professional development. He started by recommending and lending Eisenhower three historical works: *The Long Roll* by Mary Johnston; *The Exploits of Brigadier Gerard* by Arthur Conan Doyle; and *The Crisis* by the American novelist Winston Churchill. When Eisenhower returned the books saying how much he liked them, Conner replied:

"Wouldn't you like to know something of what the armies were actually doing during the period of the novels you've just read?"[21] Eisenhower was hooked, and under Conner's tutelage became an avid student of military history.

Eisenhower began to expand his horizon beyond tactics to grand strategy. He read the memoirs of great soldiers such as Grant and Sherman, immersing himself in their campaigns as well as those of Frederick the Great and Napoleon. Conner introduced him to the works of Polybius, Xenophon, and Vegetius, encouraged him to delve deeply into the battles of Greek and Roman antiquity, and had Eisenhower read Clausewitz's *On War*—three times. "Those German sentences. I tell you, it's trouble," Eisenhower recalled. "He'd quiz me. You know Clausewitz has these maxims. He'd make me tell what each one meant."[22] Eisenhower would later say that outside of the Bible, *On War* had the greatest effect on him from a military point of view. Swede Hazlett, Eisenhower's friend from Abilene who first encouraged him to apply to the military academies, visited him in Panama and reported that to facilitate his studies Ike "had fitted up the second-story screened porch of his quarters as a rough study, and here, with drawing boards and texts, he put in his spare time re-fighting the campaigns of the old masters."[23]

Eisenhower's studies were made easier by the light nature of his and Conner's duties. During the dry season they spent eight hours a day on horseback reconnoitering terrain, inspecting the regiment's preparations for defending the Canal Zone against a possible enemy attack, and maintaining the network of jungle trails used by the troops and their pack animals. At night, Eisenhower remembered, they "sat around a small camp fire and talked about the Civil War or Napoleon's operations."[24] After studying a text, Eisenhower endured a flurry of probing questions from Conner. It was not enough merely to have read a book. Conner insisted Eisenhower study it thoroughly and discuss with him the various alternatives available to commanders such as Napoleon, Grant, or Lee. According to Fox Conner Jr., "My father's method of teaching was very Socratic." He would ask Eisenhower "What was on Lee's mind? What did he know? What did he think he had to do? Why did he think that? What do you think the outcome would have been if his decision had been just the opposite?"[25] Nor was it enough that Eisenhower internalize the lessons learned from these texts—Conner also had him teach classes on these topics to the post's officers.

Conner did not stop at military works. He expanded Eisenhower's intellectual awareness by assigning Shakespeare, the Federalist Papers, and philosophical writers such as Plato, Tacitus, and even Nietzsche. Mamie was astounded that her husband could spend a day in the field, come home, eat dinner, read until two in the morning, and then get up four hours later and do it all again. But Conner had lit an intellectual spark in Eisenhower, who fondly recalled: "Life with General Conner was sort of a graduate school in military affairs and the humanities."[26]

One of Conner's unstated goals was to prepare Eisenhower for the Command and General Staff College at Fort Leavenworth. He made Eisenhower write tactical orders using the five-paragraph field order format—situation, mission, execution, supply, and communications—taught at Leavenworth. "Everyday . . . he made me write the field orders," Eisenhower recalled. "I wrote the field orders every single day for three years for everything we did." Eisenhower became so well acquainted with the techniques of preparing and issuing orders that they became second nature to him.[27]

Throughout these lessons, Conner stressed two points. The first was that "in all military history only one thing never changes—human nature. Terrain may change; weather may change; weapons may change, etc., but never human nature."[28] Second, Conner was convinced that the Treaty of Versailles ending World War I virtually guaranteed another war. He thought it would happen within a quarter-century, and he presciently understood that, as was the case in the Great War, it would have to be fought alongside allies. Consequently, he urged Eisenhower to learn everything he could about fighting as an allied force:

> He laid great stress in his instruction to me on what he called "the art of persuasion." Since no foreigner could be given outright administrative command of troops of another nation, they would have to be coordinated very closely and this needed persuasion. He would get out a book of applied psychology and we would talk it over. How do you get allies of different nations to march and think as a nation?[29]

Conner also advised Eisenhower to try for an assignment under his former colleague, Col. George C. Marshall. Conner told Eisenhower that "George Marshall knows more about the techniques of arranging allied commands than any man I know. He is nothing short of a genius."[30] Indeed, the highest praise Conner would give his subordinate was to say, "Eisenhower, you handled that just the way Marshall would have."[31]

Although Conner's mentorship of Eisenhower has gained almost mythic status, not everyone at Gaillard was enamored with the duo. Conner's job was to reorganize and modernize the defense of the Canal Zone. Given the attractions of Panama City—which consisted of countless bars, tattoo parlors, gambling joints, and brothels—getting the troops of his command into some kind of order was not easy. And like his former boss General Pershing, Conner did it by the book, which some officers thought was too harsh. Col. Clarence Deems Jr. described Conner as being "of the hard-boiled type—a Prussian in spirit. He was always right in his own estimation and did not seem to realize that others had their good points, too. He engendered antagonism, and in it the underlying feeling of that kind of loyalty that was enforced only, and not given in the outpouring of comradely affection."[32]

Eisenhower's closeness to Conner inevitably led to resentment among other officers in the brigade, and some regarded him as the commander's pampered pet and a martinet who urged Conner to be tougher on the men. Bradford Chynoweth, who had been in Eisenhower and Patton's informal study group at Camp Meade, commanded one of the three infantry battalions at Camp Gaillard. "As a team," he wrote fifty years later, Conner and Eisenhower "were the most ineffective training command that I can remember. Our officers, mostly war product, were in great need of instruction. They got none from headquarters. Fox and Ike visited every unit on the training field every morning, looked sour, criticized and condemned. Then they returned to their office, where Fox gave Ike lectures on military history."[33] Although he liked both men personally, Chynoweth thought Eisenhower was showing disturbing signs of becoming a "yes-man."[*]

---

[*] Chynoweth claimed that once, after a meeting in which he had strenuously disagreed with Conner, he and Eisenhower walked home together. "Ike," Chynoweth said, "you *know* that we were right yet you stood there and said nothing!" Eisenhower replied, "Chen, it is my policy in every post to do just exactly what the Top man desires." Chenoweth asked, "Right or wrong?" Eisenhower said, "The Commanding Officer is *never* wrong with me." To Eisenhower's detractors, this exchange marks him as little more than a careerist suck-up along the lines of loathsome Courtney Massengale in the classic Army novel *Once an Eagle.*

Although Eisenhower acknowledged that he and Chynoweth had engaged in "very fine and hot arguments" while serving together in Panama, Chynoweth's depiction of Eisenhower is a stark outlier in contrast to the rest of his career. Rather than adopting a "go-along-to-get-along" philosophy as Chynoweth suggests, Eisenhower was more likely expressing his genuine admiration for Conner. As Geoffrey Perret argues, what the notoriously acerbic Chynoweth "elevated and embellished into an Ike 'philosophy' was the core, nonetheless, of Ike's relationship with Fox Conner: whatever Conner said was right. But that was because it came from Conner, not because Conner was his boss." See Chynoweth, 101; Dwight D. Eisenhower, *Mandate for Change* (Garden City, NY: 1963), 440–42; Miller, 208; and Perret, 88.

In August 1924, Eisenhower became a permanent major and received orders to return to the United States after almost three years of service in the Canal Zone. In his final efficiency report, Conner wrote that his subordinate was "one of the most capable, efficient, and loyal officers I have ever met."[34] Eisenhower would later write that "in a lifetime of association with great and good men, [Conner] is the one more or less invisible figure to whom I owe an incalculable debt."[35] As one biographer summarizes Conner's importance to Eisenhower: "It was Conner who taught him the operational art of command. It was Conner who taught him how to apply military theory and history to real life situations. It was Conner who saved Eisenhower from certain court martial." Indeed, Conner had become a father figure to Eisenhower, arguably becoming more important than even his real father.[36]

Although he did not have to deal with a seasick spouse—Beatrice remained in Boston recovering from the birth of their third child—George Patton's voyage to Hawaii in March 1925 was as trying as the Eisenhowers' journey to Panama three years earlier. The Army transport taking Patton—and, coincidentally, Bradford Chynoweth—to the islands, the *Grant*, was a rickety old tub, and as it left San Francisco someone yelled from the pier: "I hope you make it!" The steering gear broke just outside the Golden Gate Bridge, and for a while the ship circled aimlessly. Worse, perhaps, on the third day out a fire on board the *Grant* burnt or waterlogged much of the Pattons' belongings, and Patton lost one of his great treasures: his collection of military history books that "was burned all to pieces."[37]

Yet as they drew closer to their destination, Patton could smell Hawaii's fragrance from six miles off shore. As one of his future corps commanders during the Sicily campaign, Lucian Truscott, recalled about arriving in Hawaii:

> *There is one thrill that can come only once in a lifetime. It is the first view of Diamond Head against the blue Hawaiian sky, the entry of the ship into Honolulu Harbor . . . the gaiety and excitement on ship and shore as the ship is edged into her berth . . . Hawaiian boys diving from amazing heights in the rigging into the water for coins tossed overboard by passengers who line the rails and watch from every vantage point on shipboard . . . flowers and leis . . . all the confusion that accompanied the arrival of transports in Honolulu is an unforgettable memory.*[38]

The clannish Air Corps welcomed its arrivals by flying out to meet them as they approached the harbor. On docking, the ship was serenaded by a regimental band and, for the officers, a host of service friends descended with flower leis.[39]

Despite this spectacle, Hawaii initially did not impress Patton. Honolulu was "sort of a cross between Leavenworth and Kansas City," he wrote Beatrice, and "was not quite as good as El Paso when we were there." Patton detested the islands' intense heat and humidity: "The climate while seeming cool is very sweaty if you walk seven or eight blocks you are very wet like a melon in an ice box."[40] The first weekend after his arrival, however, Patton "drove around half the island," finding it "beautiful and most interesting. Being in scenery as sort of a combination between Mexico and Florida." He told Beatrice he had been "riding twice and it is fine with some of the best scenery you can imagine. The trails in the hills are wonderful in their tropical beauty," and that despite his initial misgivings, "[N]ow it seems to me like a swell place and I am sure we shall have a good time."[41]

Patton was especially impressed with Schofield Barracks, the Hawaii Division's headquarters. Schofield was situated amid pineapple and sugar cane fields on Oahu's Leilehua plain between the Koolau and Waianae mountain ranges. Functionally, it covered the western approach to Honolulu—which lay about 23 miles away via a concrete road—and the northern approach to Pearl Harbor, 5 miles to the south. With his love of military pomp and ceremony, Patton was inexorably drawn to the post's parade grounds, green lawns, neat barracks, and eight bands.[42]

Like the U.S. forces deployed to Panama's Canal Zone, the Hawaiian Department had a real-life mission to prepare for every day. Whereas the popular mythology surrounding World War II depicts the 1941 Pearl Harbor attack as a complete surprise, in reality the Army had been preparing to defend Hawaii from a Japanese attack since the end of World War I when Japan received several Pacific island groups as compensation for supporting the Allies. Fearing further Japanese expansion, U.S. officials devised War Plan Orange as a blueprint for defeating Japan if it ever moved against America in the Pacific. Pearl Harbor would serve as the critical staging point for the anticipated counterattack, and as one Army War College committee explained, "Hawaii remains at the forefront of our defense of the Pacific Coast and is vital to us."[43]

The "Pineapple Army"—as the Hawaiian Department was affectionately known—was comprised of a coastal defense command and an infantry division, as well as air, staff, and support services. The "Hawaiian Division" was comprised of two brigades, each with two regiments. Maj. Gen. Charles P. Summerall, who commanded the Hawaiian Department from 1921 to 1924, adopted "they shall not land" as a slogan and began developing the 1924 Project for the Defense of Oahu. Summerall planned for a complete and integrated defense incorporating aviation, coast artillery, and mobile forces to repel an attempt to seize the island's naval bases by invasion. His scheme would require 304 airplanes—including 152 pursuit planes and eighty bombers—to prevent the establishment of a Japanese airdrome in the islands and "to find the enemy air force and destroy it and carry out destructive attacks against sea or ground organizations." Summerall requested new guns for the coastal fortresses and $9 million for ordnance, roads, searchlights, and signal equipment. Immediately upon mobilization the garrison would be reinforced from the mainland to three divisions (72,000 men), and civilian labor would be used to lay mines, build field fortifications, and prepare Oahu's physical defenses.[44]

Summerall's elegant plan, however, contained one fatal flaw—it relied on nonexistent manpower. When he took command Summerall directed his G-3 operations officer, Maj. Lesley J. McNair, and the assistant G-3 to seclude themselves and devote their entire time to preparing war plans. Unfortunately, their study found that at least 100,000 troops would be required to protect the potential landing places around Oahu, and that the 15,000 troops actually available were woefully inadequate.[45] When War Department inspectors asked him how he would employ 20,000 men in case of war, Patton replied that he was only able "to squeeze 7000 infantry out of the ruck of air service, quartermasters, doctors, and other useless apendages [sic] we think we need." Patton wrote his father in 1926: "Every one thinks he can keep the enemy from landing by shooting him in the water. As a matter of fact I could land here any time I wanted to and then beat hell out of the skeleton battalions sent to counter attack me."[46] In addition to manpower shortages, the high turnover of personnel undermined unit effectiveness. In 1926 Hawaii's commander reported that 38 percent of his officers and 46 percent of his enlisted men had completed their tour of duty and left Oahu in the past year. Units typically saw schools, guard duty, and post and regimental assignments further cut into their training time, and in 1923 the division's infantry received no training whatsoever because it had to unload, repack, and store 50,000 tons of War Reserve materials, most of which quickly rotted away.[47]

The 1920 National Defense Act envisioned the Hawaiian Department's Regular Army troops being supported by local reserves in wartime. Yet the department showed little enthusiasm for the citizen soldiers intended as the bulwark of continental defense. In 1924 Summerall dismissed the islands' manpower pool as being "of very low quality, lacks homogeneity, community interests and unity of purpose, speaks no common language, and its loyalty is questionable."[48] Although racial bias toward native Hawaiians tended to dissipate as officers grew more familiar with Hawaiian society, of far greater significance were suspicions regarding the allegiance of Hawaii's large Japanese community, which comprised 43 percent of Hawaii's population in 1921. Japanese workers lived on post and were employed tending Schofield Barracks's gardens and providing labor for various post activities, while the women worked as maids, cooks, and laundresses. Upon arriving in Hawaii, Summerall's chief of staff assured him that "we would never lack for servants, as the best of spies would be supplied." Summerall suspected his cook was actually a high-ranking Japanese officer, "as he was too artistic and intelligent to be a servant. We were careful never to have any papers or to discuss official matters at the house."[49] According to Patton's daughter Ruth Ellen: "When Japanese warships came into Honolulu to refuel or repair, there would always be parties of uniformed Japanese officers visiting these little farms. The word was that the farmers were relatives of the officers." Consequently, her father "wondered if there were not trained saboteurs, or signalmen, changing places with their so-called 'cousins' which would have been easy."[50] The fear that local Japanese would keep the enemy informed of the department's condition and movements led to the development of plans to deal with insurrection in the event of an invasion.*

The gap between the Hawaiian Department's requirements and its capabilities extended beyond its lack of infantry. Although the department's Air

---

* Racial prejudice aside, there was plenty of circumstantial evidence to justify concerns that the Japanese retained their allegiance to their homeland. As Brian McAllister Linn notes, Japanese immigrants to Hawaii were imbued with a culture based on assumptions of racial superiority and military prowess. Local Japanese were more assertive of their rights than earlier immigrants, and did not abandon their culture for American ways. Rather, they maintained their culture through language schools, temples, and a widely read and confrontational press. Saluting the emperor and other displays of allegiance were common, and despite discouragement from the Japanese government and consulate, parents continued to register their children as Japanese citizens. See Linn, 159. On the ambivalent loyalties of Hawaii's Japanese population, see also John J. Stephan, *Hawaii under the Rising Sun: Japan's Plans for Conquest after Pearl Harbor* (Honolulu: University of Hawaii Press, 1984), 14–15, 23–40.

Service boasted in 1925 that it could protect Oahu so that "the only ground troops necessary to defend Pearl Harbor would be those needed to handle the large alien population," in 1926 the 23rd Bombing Squadron reported it had only seven planes in commission and that many of these were unsafe due to the lack of spare parts. The 4th Observation Squadron possessed just six airplanes, all obsolete and dangerous DH-4s.[51] Similarly, the "Regimental Notes" in the July 1920 *Cavalry Journal* noted that during the 17th Cavalry's field exercise "With the exception of the sector in and around the city of Honolulu and Pearl Harbor, covered by the coast defense guns, the entire coastline of the island [approximately 100 miles] . . . was left to the sole regiment of line troops now in this department," and that "the number of horses was insufficient for the men at hand."[52] The minuscule interwar budgets and inadequate materiel meant that fuel was so restricted that the only time the Hawaiian Division's tanks moved was when they drove to and from their designated places in line during inspections. Whereas in Panama marksmanship was practiced fanatically, in Hawaii training at firing ranges was limited by both the cost and due to tourist complaints. Given these deficiencies in materiel and personnel, it is not surprising that the 1926 diary of at least one officer serving in Hawaii details luaus, swimming, fishing, golf, and hikes, with military duties only rarely intruding.[53]

Although some officers reveled in Hawaii's leisurely pace, for Patton it was a desperate letdown from his dreams of martial glory. Worse, upon arriving in the islands, Patton was assigned as the Hawaii Division's G-1, responsible for personnel and administration matters. As one of his first efficiency reports in Hawaii noted, Patton was "a man of energy and action . . . better qualified for active duty than the routine of office work."[54] Patton nevertheless tried to make the best of his situation. "The present indications are that I shall be kept on this down town job for another three months which is a great nusance [*sic*]," he wrote to his Aunt Nannie, "but there is no help for it." To General Pershing, he wrote: "I can imagine no more pleasant and instructive place to serve. While I am on the Staff—a place for which God never intended me—I can with the Hawaiian Division still see quite a lot of the troops."[55]

Although the work was dull, the relaxed tempo of an office job in a demobilized army left Patton ample time for his professional reading and socializing. The Pattons' wealth and connections provided entrée into Honolulu society, and before long they knew everyone in the islands who mattered socially. Patton devoted a significant amount of time to polo, which held the status of a distinct subculture among overseas officers, so much so that officers received an extra $10 a month subsistence for each horse—but nothing for their wives until after five years of service.[56] In the 1920s Schofield Barracks boasted the best polo field in the Army, and its officers—mounted on locally raised ponies—played year-round. Patton's Army team defeated two civilian teams to capture the Island championship in 1926, and Patton's ferocious play—likely the sublimation of his frustration as a desk-bound staff officer—became legendary. Following the matches, of course, the Pattons frequently entertained Oahu's sailing and horse set.[57]

Indeed, sports were pervasive in Hawaii. As Truscott noted, "Isolation on an island far from home and fireside and familiar surroundings posed some morale problems among young soldiers when the initial glamour of the romantic island adventure faded."[58] The Army's answer to such morale problems was activity, most notably in its emphasis on sports. Riding, baseball, swimming, boxing, and other athletic activities were available at Schofield Barracks, which was widely known as the biggest "jock strap post" in the Army. One veteran recalled that first class athletes "were given special privileges, such as very easy assignments. Most of their time was spent in practice of their sport."[59] Summerall candidly boasts: "I had our boxers do nothing but train so that, when they entered the ring, they could take care of themselves."[60] Schofield's teams dominated interpost and interservice boxing competitions, routinely humiliating the Navy contingent from Pearl Harbor. Other commands followed suit, fielding their own semipro boxing, baseball, football, and basketball teams. Thus, by 1926 the Hawaiian Department's commanding general reported: "All competitors in these sports are carefully trained and selected so they attain remarkably high efficiency, while the enthusiasm aroused in their competition is unbounded."[61]

Even Omar Bradley, who commanded an infantry battalion in the 27th Infantry Regiment, had ample time for recreation in Hawaii. He became an avid golfer, hitting the links four to five afternoons a week until he lowered his handicap down to four strokes. At the end of one round, the thirty-three-year-old teetotaler drank his first glass of whiskey, which he liked enough to make "a habit of having a bourbon and water or two (but never more) before dinner" for the rest of his life.[62] Bradley was also invited to try out for a trap-shooting team by a fellow major who lived across the street, but with whom the homey Bradleys were not close socially. After missing his first two shots, Bradley proceeded to hit the next twenty-three in a row. His neighbor, Patton, did not smile or congratulate Bradley. Instead, he simply muttered, "You'll do."

"I was not certain I wanted to be on the team," Bradley recalled years later. "Patton's style did not at all appeal to me. But I signed on for the sport of it."[63]

Not everybody was able to look past Patton's brusqueness so easily, however, and his direct manner got him into trouble with his superiors once again. In November 1926 Patton was appointed as the Hawaii Division's G-3 just in time to serve as an official observer for the 22nd Brigade's maneuvers. Patton was displeased by what he saw, and he severely criticized the unit's performance in his written report to the brigade commander, a brigadier general. As the G-3 Patton was certainly free to make comments, and he was likely right with regard to his assessment. Yet for a major to "correct" a general was at best imprudent, at worst tactless. As his biographer Carlo D'Este notes: "However true his remarks, the paper was highly indiscreet and should never have been delivered without the concurrence of the commanding general."[64] As with MacArthur's attempts at curriculum reform, the need for which appeared self-evident to the superintendent, Patton's abundant self-confidence verged on arrogance and blinded him as to how his actions might be perceived by others. And just like MacArthur, Patton's critiques generated significant resentment toward him.

Six months later the 3rd Battalion, 35th Infantry, and several planes of the 18th Pursuit Group held an exercise to test Patton's theory that troops under air attack should not seek concealment. Patton observed the demonstration and once again wrote a scathing critique, although this time he at least submitted his comments to the division commander—Maj. Gen. William R. Smith—for review. According to Patton the battalion's leaders had failed on numerous points and had missed the point of the proposed regulations. Once again, the strong language and denunciation of errors by a relatively young staff officer ruffled feathers. As the senior officers' complaints against Patton grew, Major General Smith reassigned him from the G-3 position to the G-2 (intelligence) billet, charging him with being "too positive in his thinking and too outspoken."[65]

Although Patton's new appointment was portrayed as a routine reassignment, the division chief of staff, Col. Francis W. Cooke, rated him merely "average" in all categories as G-3, and Patton was embittered by his removal. In January 1928 Major General Smith was abruptly recalled stateside to become West Point's superintendent. Army regulations dictated that he prepare efficiency reports on the officers he was leaving behind, and for those receiving negative reviews he was required to counsel them in person. Hence he called Major Patton to his office in Schofield Barracks, and in a booming voice rendered his judgment that: "This man would be invaluable in time of war but is a disturbing element in time of peace." Patton listened stiffly before snapping to attention and replying: "Thank you, sir. I regard your opinion as a great compliment."[66]

Despite George's professional frustrations, the Pattons genuinely loved the Hawaiian islands and found Honolulu society very much to their liking. Even before they arrived in the islands, Beatrice had immersed herself in Hawaiian history, and while George was playing polo, sailing, and fishing, she made numerous Hawaiian friends and became an expert on the islands' culture. "It was as if she had been waiting for Hawaii all her life," her daughter Ruth Ellen later wrote. Beatrice began writing a book of Hawaiian legends translated into French that was later published in Paris, and her study of Polynesian culture eventually resulted in a historical novel, *The Blood of the Shark*, published in 1936.[67] "The longer we stay here," Patton wrote his father, "the more we like it and hate the thought of leaving."[68] Patton requested a year's extension of his assignment in Hawaii, but was denied by the War Department.

Patton was given a chance at professional redemption when his old friend Fox Conner—now a major general—succeeded Smith as commander of the Hawaiian Division. Patton's final months in Hawaii were spent working on amphibious operations and studying supporting weapons for assault troops. In a series of training exercises on repelling an amphibious assault on Hawaii, he commanded the invading force, presaging his future commands during Operation *Torch* in Morocco and the invasion of Sicily. The final efficiency report for his Hawaiian tour of duty rated Patton "above average" and "superior." According to the acting chief of staff, Lt. Col. S. T. Mackall, Patton was "an outstanding officer; a student of military affairs, well above the average; intensely interested in his profession; he has taken full advantage of serving in Hawaii to become familiar with the military problem in the islands."[69] Conner added: "I have known him for fifteen years in both peace and war. I know of no one whom I would prefer as a subordinate officer."[70]

Thus, although his difficulties at working with those who disagreed with him had once again gotten him into trouble, Patton appeared to have emerged unscathed before departing the islands in 1928.

While sailing to the Philippines in the summer of 1922, Douglas MacArthur and his new family endured none of the trials that the Eisenhowers or Patton experienced on their voyages. Instead, the MacArthurs were the *cause* of the misery for the other one hundred Army officers and forty Army wives traveling with them on the transport *Logan*. As the highest-ranking officer on board, MacArthur's luggage was loaded first on the ship in San Francisco. Louise was accustomed to traveling in a certain style, and consequently filled the baggage hold with so many trunks, suitcases, and hatboxes that the other passengers were limited to one trunk each. The MacArthurs also put several automobiles aboard ship, leaving no room in the cargo hold for any other officers' cars. Thus, Louise managed to alienate nearly all the other officers and wives before the *Logan* even set sail, making MacArthur the most unpopular American officer in the Philippines before even starting his tour of duty.[71]

"The Philippines charmed me" at first sight, MacArthur recalled of his arrival for his first tour in 1903. "The amazingly attractive result of a mixture of Spanish culture and American industry, the languorous laze that seemed to glamorize even the most routine chores of life, the fun-loving men, the moonbeam delicacy of its lovely women, fastened me with a grip that has never relaxed."[72] When the *Logan* sailed into Manila harbor, MacArthur discovered profound changes had occurred in the islands over the subsequent two decades. Although "the massive bluff of Bataan and the lean grey grimness of Corregidor" remained the same, he marveled at "the progress that had been made" since 1904. American servicemen were still greeted by scores of beribboned officers and the Philippine Constabulary band, along with an assortment of Filipino laundrymen, mango and papaya vendors, and colorful taxis jostling for customers. But MacArthur recalled that beyond the lines of carabao-pulled carts sitting quayside, "new roads, new docks, new buildings were everywhere."[73] He was greeted by a familiar face, however. MacArthur's former boss, Gen. Leonard Wood, was now governor-general of the Philippines. Wood greeted his former subordinate warmly, and as the pair sat in Wood's office, the electric fan whirring above temporarily keeping the islands' oppressive humidity at bay, he waxed eloquent on the progress the Philippines had made since MacArthur's tour of duty.

During his tenure as military commander in the Philippines from 1906 to 1908, Wood had consolidated the scattered U.S. forces in two locations: at Fort William McKinley, an 8,000-acre post 6 miles outside Manila in Rizal Province that protected the capital and guarded against invasion from the south; and at Fort Stotsenburg 65 miles north of Manila in the Central Luzon Valley, from which troops could either counter a landing at Lingayen

Gulf or withdraw into the Bataan Peninsula. After World War I Stotsenburg became primarily a Filipino post with the exception of a small Air Corps base at Clark Field. The Americans now occupied only the harbor fortification, with a battalion of the 15th Infantry stationed at Fort McKinley and the 31st Infantry in Manila itself.[74]

Although the last Filipino *insurrectos* were subdued with the defeat of the Moro Rebellion in 1913, as in Hawaii, Japan posed the likeliest threat to the Philippines. In the autumn of 1922 a panel of generals and admirals representing the Joint Army and Navy Board drafted a strategic response to a hypothetical Japanese surprise invasion of the archipelago. The Joint Board's planners estimated it would take at least six months before reinforcements could arrive from the United States. In this scenario, the Philippine Department's mission would be to withdraw into Bataan, holding out there and on Corregidor for six months to prevent the Japanese from using Manila Harbor until naval reinforcements could arrive. A subsequent study in 1923 determined that mobile forces would conduct an "active defense by offensive and defensive operations," retiring to Bataan and Corregidor "to save the bulk of the Mobile Forces from annihilation or capture," and then "defend to the last the islands at the entrance to Manila Bay."[75] Although the planners recognized the difficulties defending the Philippines from a Japanese attack entailed, they believed losing the islands would "seriously affect American prestige and make offensive operations in the western Pacific extremely difficult."[76]

Yet as was the case in Hawaii, commanders in the Philippines struggled with the minuscule interwar budgets. Due to Congress's continued funding cuts, the authorized enlisted strength of the Philippines garrison was reduced with the rest of the Army, from 15,800 in 1921 to 12,115 in 1925. The Philippine Division lacked trucks, communications equipment, chemical warfare supplies, and firepower, as one of its two artillery battalions was equipped with the same light mountain guns and mules used during the Moro Rebellion. In 1921 the Philippine Department's air officer informed one board that in case of war he could muster ten airplanes, but if the enemy had "a single squadron of modern pursuit planes, the whole Air Force of the Philippines, would, of course, last only a few days."[77] Both departmental commanders during MacArthur's tour—Maj. Gen. William M. Wright and Maj. Gen. George W. Read—were convinced that the Philippine Department was seriously deficient in men and equipment for the mission assigned in War Plan Orange. And as one later department commander bluntly stated: "The Mission and the Force assigned to carry out the Mission are not harmonized," and that it was "impracticable to make up any War Plan worthy of the name based on the present garrison and its organization."[78]

Adding to the Army's struggles with personnel reductions were the restrictions created by the 1922 Washington Naval Treaty. Also known as the Five Power Treaty, it was a noble if misguided effort in diplomacy intended to avoid a naval arms race similar to that which was mistakenly believed to have caused World War I. In exchange for granting American and British superiority over Japan in battleships and cruisers at a fixed ratio of 5:5:3, the treaty prohibited the United States from establishing new fortified naval bases farther west than Oahu or improving the defenses in Manila Bay, Guam, or the Aleutian Islands. In practice, this construction ban effectively conceded regional dominance to Japan.

Yet even if Congress had been willing to fully fund the Army, and the Harding Administration had not turned to arms control as the solution to its strategic problems, many U.S. policymakers and officers questioned both the practicality and strategic value of defending the Philippines. Given that Japan was capable of throwing 300,000 troops into an invasion with little-to-no-warning and that the entire U.S. Army in 1922 was 160,000 men, it is doubtful the United States could *ever* deploy enough forces to adequately defend the islands. W. Cameron Forbes, a former governor-general, stated that the Philippines "are indefensible and from a military point of view are not worth defending." Forbes conceded, however, "The main thing is to make any interference with them as costly as possible."[79] The idea of defending the island as a cost-imposing strategy was echoed by members of the Joint Army Navy Planning Committee, who in 1922 argued that although Manila Bay would probably fall to Japan before the American fleet arrived, "the sacrifice of all our forces, both naval and military, would be justified by the damage done to our enemy."[80] Other defenders of the Army's mission in the Philippines cited moral justifications. Francis J. Kernan, who commanded the Philippine Department from 1919 to 1922, argued: "It would manifestly be a crime against humanity to withdraw our protecting supervision and leave these simple people a prey to a small oligarchy now in power and certain to perpetuate its power indefinitely."[81] The Army's chief planner baldly stated: "Our withdrawal would be encouragement to the pan-Asiatic movement . . . and [leave] our friends of the European nations to bear the white man's burden alone."[82]

Beyond his personal affection for the Philippines, MacArthur was a staunch defender of America's mission there. He inherited much of his unique attachment to the Philippines—both from a strategic and personal perspective—from his father. In 1902 Arthur MacArthur had testified before the Senate Committee on the Philippines that the islands' "strategical position is unexcelled by that of any other position in the world."[83] He even asserted that the American occupation of the Philippines was the most important "event recorded in the annals of mankind since the discovery" of the Americas.[84] Similarly, Douglas would later declare: "It was crystal clear to me that the future and, indeed, the very existence of America, were irrevocably entwined with Asia and its island outposts," especially the Philippines.[85]

If MacArthur's vision of the Philippines was romantic and grandiose, his duties upon returning to the islands in 1922 were disappointingly mundane. There was no open position in the islands for a one-star general, so the Philippine Department created one for him by establishing an artificial command called the Military District of Manila. The principal unit under MacArthur was the 31st Infantry, of whom Inspector General Helmick reported: "The men appeared to me to be an excellent body of men, but their training was not up to the standard of other organizations in the department." MacArthur had barely 500 men under his command, and his duties were ridiculously trivial, such as running the departmental rifle competition, a task that could just as easily have been performed by a lieutenant.[86]

MacArthur's assignment was not without its compensations. His friends arranged for his family to move into No. 1 Calle Victoria, or as it was known to Filipinos, the "House on the Wall." It was a lovely eighteenth-century building perched on the towering 350-year-old stone wall around the old city of Manila, with exquisite gardens, and wonderful views of the city on one side and the blue waters of Manila Bay on the other. Louise delighted in decorating the villa with Spanish colonial furniture and Chinese rugs. With virtually unlimited funds at her disposal, she had matching blue naval uniforms made for the servants, with the letters "MacA" stitched on the breast pocket. With the duty day typically ending at noon, MacArthur was able to renew his acquaintance with Manuel Quezon, whom he had been introduced to over dinner at Manila's Army and Navy Club in 1904. Quezon had since risen to become one of the most influential figures in Philippine politics as president of the Philippine Senate. MacArthur's attitudes were relatively enlightened for an Army officer of his generation, and he scorned the color line and regularly met with Quezon and other Filipino friends.[87]

MacArthur confided his dissatisfaction with his official duties to Wood. In early 1923 MacArthur briefly returned to the United States to look after his ailing mother, and shortly after returning to Manila in June he was assigned to command a brigade in the recently established Philippine Division, which was comprised of the 31st Infantry and two regiments of Filipino Scouts. With only 7,000 men, the Division was roughly one-quarter the size of a full-strength American infantry division. It was organized into two brigades, with MacArthur given command of the 23rd Brigade, at Fort McKinley, which consisted of the 45th and 57th Philippine Scout Regiments.

Although the Philippine Scouts had existed as the elite corps of Filipino volunteers since the units were created during the 1899–1902 insurrection, their integration into an organization under American command was a desperate effort to offset the lack of American troops. During the Philippine Division's inaugural maneuvers at Fort Stotsenburg in February 1923, however, the Scouts consistently outperformed their American counterparts. Major General Read reported to the War Department that "all companies of the 57th Infantry (PS) qualified 100% in rifle and machine gun marksmanship."[88] MacArthur developed a strong respect for the Filipinos under his command, later recalling that "they were excellent troops, completely professional, loyal, and devoted."[89]

For MacArthur, the assignment meant a welcome return to the routine of commanding an infantry unit, which during peacetime involved a greater variety of responsibilities than it had in France. The 23rd Brigade's various missions would be immediately recognizable to modern advisory and civil affairs units: administering livestock vaccinations during rinderpest and anthrax epidemics; organizing and training a ROTC unit at the University of the Philippines; and assisting the Philippine Constabulary to suppress outbreaks of banditry. In September 1923 MacArthur's troops even aided the Philippine Department's efforts to send 16,000 tons of relief supplies to the Tokyo-Yokohama area after it had been devastated by an earthquake, a precursor to modern humanitarian assistance missions.[90]

In addition to commanding the 23rd Brigade, MacArthur was placed in charge of a survey of the Bataan Peninsula. MacArthur was tasked to map out a defensive perimeter of the mountainous, wooded peninsula, possession of which—along with Corregidor, the small island off its southern tip—determined control of Manila Bay. Leading a party of surveyors and engineers, MacArthur recalled, "I covered every foot of rugged terrain, over its trails, up and down its steep mountainous slopes, and through its bamboo thickets."[91] Overcoming both the terrain and a malaria epidemic among the 14th Engineers' troops, MacArthur was able to map 40 square miles in 1923 and 1924.

MacArthur's tour was not without drama, however. On the morning of July 7, 1924, officers came rushing into his office with news that a mutiny had broken out in the Scout regiments. Though intended to symbolize a joint commitment to the defense of the islands, the Philippine Division was not immune to the undercurrents of tension that existed in nearly every American-Filipino interaction. For a year Governor-General Wood and Philippine leaders such as Quezon had clashed over the question of Philippine independence and self-rule. Extensive press coverage surrounding these disputes encouraged other groups in the islands to seek more equitable status, including the Scouts. Despite being vital to Philippine defense, the Scouts had traditionally received less than half the pay given American soldiers. They also did not get the professional recognition they deserved, and Maj. Vicente Lim, a Philippine Scout officer who graduated from West Point, admitted that he and other Filipino officers had often considered resigning their commissions because of the prejudice they endured.[92] This discontent was met with complacency by American commanders. Although aware of the discontent and of contacts between some Scouts and secret political societies, Philippine Department headquarters failed to pass this information on to field commanders. Fort McKinley's provost marshal had specifically been warned on June 27 of ongoing meetings between disgruntled Scouts in the barracks and in homes outside the post, yet failed to act until July 6 when he broke up one such meeting at the post hospital.

The next morning nearly 400 members of the 57th Infantry refused to fall in for routine drill or obey any orders. They were joined the next day by members of the 12th Medical Regiment, and only the quick action of their superiors—one officer drove his troops out of their barracks with a baseball bat—prevented more Scouts from participating. As soon as word reached MacArthur, he quickly called the military police to quell the scene. In all, 602 men mutinied. There was no violence, no attacks against American officers or on the facilities. The Scouts themselves called their disobedience a "strike" rather than a mutiny, and almost 400 of them returned to duty after the serious nature of their action was explained. The MPs rounded up the 222 Scouts who continued their rebellion and marched them off to the post guardhouse.[93]

Although the mutiny ended almost as quickly as it had begun, the story caused a national sensation. The mutineers were brought before a general court-martial board headed by MacArthur and charged with violating the 66th Article of War. They were dishonorably discharged and sentenced to five years of hard labor. A separate court-martial of the mutiny's leaders led to fifteen more convictions, with sentences ranging from five to twenty years of hard labor. American officers were divided over the mutiny's implications. Some believed it had been little more than a "peaceful strike" over pay, while others claimed it brought the Scouts' reliability into question. While the majority of the Scouts had not participated in the mutiny, given War Plan Orange's dependence upon their continuing loyalty the numbers involved worried the American military establishment. Massive investigations ensued to forestall further dissatisfaction. William E. Carraway, a Scout officer who interviewed many of the participants, concluded the soldiers' grievances were primarily a result of their inequitable pay, but was disturbed to find other signs of deep dissatisfaction. Major General Read stated: "It is clear that the grievance these men allege as a basis for their mutinous action is discrimination against the Philippine Scout soldier in pay, allowances, and benefits."[94]

Several officers participating in the investigations recognized the essential justice of the Scouts' demands. The War Department suggested that pay increases be implemented, that officers assigned to the Scouts be trained in the Filipinos' language and cultural values, and that channels of communications between the Scouts and their American commanders be strengthened. Some efforts to adjust the Filipinos' salaries and allowances more equitably were made, but given the War Department's economic retrenchment during this period and the Philippine Department's demonstrably tight budget, not much could be done.[95] One step the department could take, however, was a change in leadership. After the mutiny MacArthur was promoted to full command of the Philippine Division, likely because he was known to support equal status with white soldiers for his Filipino soldiers.

While MacArthur was dealing with the consequences of the Scout mutiny in the summer of 1924, Pinky MacArthur was writing obsequious letters to General Pershing beseeching him to promote her son before retiring as chief of staff. "Your own life is so full to overflowing with joy and happiness—and deserving success," she wrote Pershing, "that it may be hard for you to understand the heartache and disappointments in the lives of others. Won't you be real good and sweet—The 'Dear Old Jack' of long ago—and give me some assurance that you will give my Boy his well earned promotion before you leave the Army?"[96] What Pershing thought of these entreaties is not recorded. Yet when one considers that Pershing's wife Helen and his three young daughters were killed in a terrible house fire at the Presidio in 1915, one can only shudder at the narcissism required for Pinky to suggest he might not understand "the heartaches and disappointments" of others, especially in regard to something as comparatively trivial as a promotion.

Nevertheless, on MacArthur's efficiency report, Major General Read rated him first out of the thirty-five brigadier generals he knew personally. Consequently, on September 23, 1924, less than two months after taking over the Philippine Division, the War Department announced MacArthur's promotion to major general. When he pinned on his second star on January 1925, he became overqualified for any position in the islands except commander of the Philippine Department itself, and hence he was transferred stateside once again.

Arriving in Manila in 1922, MacArthur's career appeared to be in limbo after his removal as superintendent of West Point. Now, as he sailed away he was the youngest major general on active duty in the Army. The *New York Times* remarked that he "is considered one of the ablest and brightest of the younger officers of the regular army," and "with good health he stands a splendid chance of some day becoming head of the army."[97]

Yet if his professional fortunes had been reversed during his tour in the Philippines, so too had his personal life, albeit in the opposite direction. His marital troubles likely started early when Pinky refused to attend his and Louise's wedding. On the voyage to the Philippines Louise's children treated their new stepfather with a distant coolness that he more than reciprocated. Whereas Mamie Eisenhower was able to make peace with her husband's career and adjust to the terrible conditions in Panama, and Beatrice Patton positively thrived in Hawaii, Louise did neither. For a woman accustomed to Paris café society, Manila seemed hopelessly provincial and, as she wrote to her friends, "extremely dull." She involved herself in charitable activities, and even became a voluntary sheriff, but these did not provide much satisfaction. Although Manila's Army and Navy Club was famous throughout the Orient and the Army, combining "the qualities of a hotel, casino, library, and assembly hall" while serving as the center of Manila's social life, as at West Point MacArthur did little socializing. Their one frequent dinner guest was Leonard Wood, to whom Louise would bitterly and futilely complain about MacArthur's perceived exile.[98]

MacArthur's return to the United States should have saved the marriage as he and Louise moved into her mansion outside Baltimore and she resumed her familiar routine in high society. MacArthur tried to mingle with her clique, but their talk of charity balls and fox hunting bored him. Despite their romantic displays at Billy Mitchell's court-martial, the relationship continued to deteriorate. At Louise's suggestion J.P. Morgan and Company approached MacArthur, but he was not interested in their job offer. Louise became increasingly disillusioned with a husband stuck in what she perceived to be a pointless profession.

MacArthur's patronage of athletics at West Point led to a stint as president of the American Olympic Committee in 1928. After a triumphant U.S. performance at the Amsterdam games that summer, MacArthur received orders to return to Manila to assume command of the Philippine Department. "No assignment could have pleased me more," he remarked, and he found Manila to be "as bright and lively as ever."[99] This time, however, he traveled alone. Louise and her children remained in the States, and in June 1929 their divorce was finalized. MacArthur never mentions Louise's name in his memoirs, simply saying: "In February 1922 I entered into matrimony, but it was not successful, and ended in divorce years later for mutual incompatibility."[100]

As MacArthur had told his aide at West Point, "When you get to be a general you haven't any friends." For the time being the general's loneliness extended to matrimony as well.

On September 7, 1924, Lt. Col. George C. Marshall, his wife Lily, and his mother-in-law arrived at the Chinese port of Chingwantao aboard the Army transport *Thomas*. Their trip was uneventful, but only because of fortunate timing. "The port at which I landed ten days ago . . . was bombed yesterday," Marshall noted in a letter to General Pershing, "and eight miles to the north at Shan kai huan fighting is reported to have started this morning." Similarly, he told the new chief of staff, Maj. Gen. John L. Hines, that: "If we had docked at Ching wan tao five days later we would have been unable to make the trip up to Tientsin, as the railroad has been literally blocked with Chinese troop movements. . . . More than 50,000 troops have passed through here headed for Shan kai huan."[101] Once again, fortune smiled upon George C. Marshall.

Following the Boxer Rebellion of 1900, the imperial powers in China had demanded and received the right to station troops near Peking to safeguard their nationals and commercial interests. The United States forswore its own territorial concession for a decade, but when the nationalist revolution led by Dr. Sun Yat-sen that toppled the Manchu dynasty in 1911 proved unable to consolidate power and provide security throughout China, the United States deployed two battalions of the 15th Infantry Regiment to join the other foreign contingents in Tientsin, an industrial city of nearly one million inhabitants on the Peking-Mukden railway that was the main port and commercial center of northern China.[102] Even then the United States fastidiously paid rent until it inherited Germany's vacated concession after World War I. Consequently, the 15th Infantry settled its approximately fifty officers and 800 men into the brick barracks on Woodrow Wilson Street, formerly Kaiser Wilhemstrasse. The regiment also maintained a subpost manned by one rifle company at Tongshon 85 miles to the southeast to guard the Peking-Mukden Railway's stops, and a summer training camp near Shankaihuan on the coast.

The 15th Infantry's motto was "Can Do," taken from the pidgin phrase used by the Chinese to express the "ability to carry out the mission," and it was indeed considered one of the best regiments in the Army. Many of the 15th Infantry's privates had been regimental sergeant majors during the war, and its ranking noncommissioned officers were former captains and majors who had accepted the reduction in rank to remain on active duty until they qualified for retirement. One study of U.S forces in China finds that at least 18 percent of the men had either purchased their discharges to enlist for duty in China or had voluntarily taken a reduction in rank to serve with the 15th Infantry. "In the interwar army when promotions were glacially slow," the study notes, "for men to give up their rank seems to be an excellent indicator that the China Station was perceived as good duty."[103] After acclimating himself as the 15th's executive officer, Marshall wrote a friend: "This particular regiment has the most remarkably efficient personnel I have ever seen gathered in one group."[104] Inspector General Helmick concurred, noting in his 1925 report that "the 15th Infantry in China is a fine, well-trained body of soldiers, upholding the best traditions of our Army and a credit to our country."[105] Of the fifty-seven officers serving in the 15th Infantry in 1927, twenty-four eventually made general officer.[106]

The 15th Infantry was considered the prize of foreign assignments by both officers and soldiers for reasons beyond its sterling reputation. The handpicked officers lived in lavish style. A ten-room house with servants' quarters rented for $15 American, and the requisite staff of four to five servants, *amahs*, and handymen cost an additional $35–$50 per month. The enlisted troops enjoyed high morale, wore tailored uniforms, and were better fed than at perhaps any other post in the Army. The exchange rate made even American enlisted men seem wealthy, and a 1926 essay in the *Infantry*

Journal on the "Conditions of Service in China" noted that wives invariably accumulated "a rather impressive store of rugs, silver, linen, lingerie, embroideries, and other impediments" that would be utterly beyond their means "if priced on Fifth Avenue."[107]

Beyond these perks, China held another important attraction for ambitious officers—the possibility of seeing action. Following President Yuan Shi kai's death in 1916, China fell into anarchy and civil war. By the time Marshall arrived in China the central government was nothing but a convenient fiction. Sun Yat-sen's revolution had splintered, and while Sun's successor—Chiang Kai-shek—consolidated the Nationalist movement's power in the south, power in the north devolved to a rogues' gallery of warlords constantly fighting one another. Marshall wrote to Pershing that even after two years in country, "Conditions in China are too confused to admit of a reasonably accurate estimate as to what it is all about," and that "fighting is continuous."[108]

Although Chiang's Koumintang would eventually cement its control of the southern provinces and drive northward in 1926 promising to expel all foreigners from China, this danger remained remote in 1924. Instead the 15th Infantry's immediate concern was the violent struggle between the northern warlords, for whom the area around Tientsin became a focal point in the fighting. Marshal Chang Tso-lin, who in addition to banditry was the dominant military figure in Manchuria, had marched against Marshal Wu Pei-fu, who held Peking and therefore theoretical control of the government. The balance of power between the two rivals lay with Feng Yu-hsiang, the "Christian General" favored by Westerners because of his religion, at least those willing to overlook his practice of baptizing his recruits en masse with a fire hose. (As Marshall biographer Ed Cray wryly notes, "It was the thought that counts.")[109] With its railroads and nearby seaports—rich with food, clothing, and other supplies—and completely lacking any natural defensive barriers, Tientsin made an attractive target for the soldiers of both the victors and the vanquished. Most of the city's Western residents were on edge as the troop movements began, desperately counting on the 15th Infantry and four other foreign contingents for protection. Marshall arrived just as the 15th stood guard, ready to keep the warring factions out of Tientsin, hold the railroad, and defend themselves.

To meet the anticipated invasion, the international forces established a series of posts around Tientsin. Their orders were to prevent armed soldiers from entering the city. The 15th Infantry's area of responsibility stretched seven miles across canals, dikes, a branch of the rail line, and various bridges and roads. Whereas the manpower deficits in Panama, Hawaii, and the Philippines applied to notional future conflicts with Japan, the 15th Infantry had to try to defend U.S. interests in Tientsin with forces clearly insufficient to the task. In 1926 the commander of U.S. forces in China informed the War Department that a force of 25,000 would be needed just to keep the Peking-Mukden Railway open. In September–October 1924 Marshall had only 1,000 men at his disposal to face potentially 100,000 Chinese forces. Moreover, one inventory of American heavy weapons in all of China—including Marines stationed in Peking—indicated that U.S. forces possessed only sixty-five machine guns, six 37mm mortars, fifteen 3-inch Stokes mortars, fifty-two automatic rifles, and six 3-inch landing guns.[110] In the face of such overwhelming odds, the regiment worried that someone might become over-excited and fire without orders, thereby plunging U.S. forces into a full-scale battle with the warlords. One former 15th Infantry officer recalled the fear of such an incident was so great "that we were even required to disarm our train guards so there wouldn't be any danger of shooting," although given that the guards only consisted of a first lieutenant and twelve enlisted men, any determined attempt by Chinese forces would easily overwhelm the detachment. Instead, the 15th "put the regimental boxing team on as train guards," feeling confident "that they could take care of themselves."[111]

As the destitute and disorganized units of Wu's army streamed toward Tientsin, the 15th Infantry appeared to be caught between Scylla and the Charybdis: if they attempted to fight they would be annihilated; if they stood aside the United States would suffer a loss of prestige as Americans fled in desperation while Tientsin was sacked and pillaged. Marshall chose a third option: the 15th Infantry's troops were to employ a combination of bluff and bribery to divert the Chinese forces. The regiment established five outposts in its sector and stocked them with caches of rice, cabbage, and tea. The plan was to interdict the warlord's troops and warn them they could not enter Tientsin armed. In exchange for surrendering their weapons, they would be given food and allowed to proceed. They also would be given food if they chose to circumvent the city altogether. As with modern peacekeeping forces, all Marshall could do was hope "that sufficient tact and wisdom will be displayed" in order "to avoid violent phases during the trying period that is approaching."[112]

As with modern counterinsurgency, much of the responsibility for executing these delicate missions fell to the 15th Infantry's junior officers and noncommissioned officers armed with little more than a persuasive tongue, and as Marshall noted, were frequently "carried out ... with guns or knives pointed at their stomachs."[113] In the winter of 1925–1926, when Chang Tso-lin's troops were reported marching toward the restricted zone outside Tientsin, Marshall ordered the commander of the 15th's headquarters company to take as many men as necessary to go out and divert them. Matthew Ridgway had just completed the Army's Infantry School before requesting duty with the 15th Infantry, but nothing he learned at Fort Benning was applicable to the tactical situation now confronting him. Since not even the combined forces of the 15th Infantry and the nearby British regiment could have done much about "diverting" the 12,000 Chinese soldiers if they chose to enter Tientsin, Ridgway picked just two men to accompany him. "This was sufficient, I felt, to carry out my instructions," he later recalled, "which were to use 'bluff, expostulation, or entreaty,' but under no circumstances to fire unless I was fired upon."[114]

It was a clear, bitterly cold day. Bundled in furs and mounted on shaggy Manchurian ponies "of the breed that had carried the cavalrymen of Genghis Khan," Ridgway and his companions rode out, their feet freezing in the steel stirrups. Soon, across the plain they saw the dust of Chang's troops on the march. "To my considerable relief," Ridgway writes, "I saw it was skirting the restricted zone. We shadowed the force all day, staying well away on the flanks but keeping the column in view. We were not molested, nor did we make any attempt to molest them." When the "tan snake" of the warlord's column was safely past Tientsin, Captain Ridgway reported to Marshall. "He merely nodded. It was a routine contact."[115]

Indeed, in a similar incident Capt. William B. Tuttle and nine enlisted men confronted 5,000 armed Chinese who had entered the American defensive zone. Ordering his soldiers to remain in their truck, Tuttle confronted the warlord's troops alone as they advanced with fixed bayonets. After a tense standoff with a Chinese officer, the Chinese forces agreed to withdraw and Tuttle became a legend in the 15th Infantry's lore.[116]

The presence of American troops undoubtedly prevented killing and looting, and—in the modern vernacular—won "the hearts and minds" of the local population. The United States had sought no special privileges in China and had even used half of its $25 million in Boxer Rebellion reparations to educate Chinese students. This benevolence earned respect and moral authority amongst the Chinese intelligentsia and middle class. Moreover, the villages around Tientsin were so grateful for the protection the 15th Infantry provided from the warlords in 1924 that the next spring they presented the regiment with a white marble memorial gate for their compound.[117]

As with modern counterinsurgency, one key to the 15th Infantry's success was its officers' and NCO's proficiency in the local population's language. Marshall wrote to Brig. Gen. William C. Cocke: "We have had many contacts with the Chinese troops, some of them fraught with frightful possibilities, but so far we have been able to carry out our mission without provoking the fatal first shot. I think that the ability of every officer to speak Chinese has saved us."[118] Although Chinese is not easy for Westerners to learn, the 15th Infantry made its troops learn at least the rudiments of the language. In 1923, the commander of U.S. forces in China, Brig. Gen. William D. Connor, requested $400 from the adjutant general from contingency funds to hire teachers to teach "colloquial Chinese." The funding was approved, and all officers were required to attend the course. As Charles L. Bolte recalled, officers took lessons for at least "an hour a day," five days a week, for one year, and were examined to determine if they were qualified to be awarded the distinctive patch of interpreter.[119]

Perhaps no officer of the 15th Infantry undertook these studies more seriously than Marshall. Despite his indifferent record studying French during the war, Marshall plunged into his study of Chinese, determined to learn the language as quickly as anybody else. By April 1925 he was able to translate testimony in court and discuss treaty rights "with a fair degree of fluency." He completed the regiment's two-and-a-half-year course in eleven months, after which he informed former Pershing aide John Hughes: "Now I can carry on a casual conversation in Chinese with far, far less difficulty than I ever could manage in French. And I can even understand the wranglings and squabbles of the rickshaw men."[120]

Marshall had reported for duty just after the previous regimental commander had left and prior to the arrival of Col. William K. Naylor. Hence, from September 8 to November 21, 1924, he served as acting commander of the 15th Infantry. Marshall received a commendation from Brigadier General Connor on November 22 for his performance during that fall's civil uprising that read:

1. I desire to express to you my gratification at the prompt and efficient manner in which you took the necessary measures to meet the varied and changing situations confronting your Command during these past six weeks of Chinese Civil War.

2. The handling of your Command was especially commendable in that you had but recently arrived at this station and had had only a short time in which to familiarize yourself with the local plans and problems, which, by their peculiar nature, required unusual tact, patience, and foresight in bringing about their successful solution.[121]

With Naylor's arrival, Marshall reverted to executive officer and settled into the garrison routine. He enjoyed his new duties, particularly the opportunity to be with troops rather than in a staff position. He was hands-on in instructing sergeants and corporals, and the scattering of the outposts kept Marshall constantly in the saddle. Despite the paperwork his position entailed, he found time to train a Mongolian pony and rode 8–12 miles each morning, ending with a lap of the 1-mile Tientsin race course at full speed. He tried to organize an informal cavalry troop mounted on the small ponies and staged mounted hunting parties. In December 1925 he wrote to Brigadier General Palmer that he was riding about 25 miles a day on his rounds, which "was good fun and instructive."[122]

That month Colonel Naylor was relieved of command and the 15th Infantry's new commander—Col. Isaac Newell—was near the end of his career and content to leave the details of running the regiment to Marshall. As such, Marshall faced at least two command challenges unique to the 15th Infantry. First, as he had previously noted in a letter to Chief of Staff Hines: "The officers out here work harder than any other group with troops I have ever seen, yet we can only with difficulty find time for brief periods of training."[123] The exception was during the hot summer months, when companies were rotated to the regiment's firing range at Chingwantao, about 150 miles from Tientsin on the coast. The location was near a sandy beach and the resort area of Pei-hao. Most of the regiment's wives spent the entire summer there, and Marshall wrote that "bathing, riding, and shooting occupies the time."[124] When the shooting season ended in August, however, the regiment's scheduled field exercises were severely limited due to the highly cultivated fields around Tientsin. The troops could do little more than practice manning the defensive positions around the city, hence Marshall's assessment to Pershing in 1924 that despite the generally high quality of the regiment's officers, "when it comes to simple tactical problems . . . they all fall far below the standards they set in other matters."[125]

Marshall faced a different sort of problem with the regiment's enlisted men. While the 15th Infantry's officers attended to regimental matters and the various social affairs at the American Club and the foreign concessions, the enlisted men sought different entertainments that led to a dangerously high venereal disease rate. According to one study, in 1920 the regiment's rate of infection reached 43 percent, more than six-and-a-half times the rate of the stateside Army. One veteran of the regiment recalled that immediately outside the American barracks in Tientsin the "signs saying 'Bar' seemed to stretch into infinity."[126] Marshall summed up the problem in a letter to Pershing, lamenting: "Today is 'pay day' and we are up against the problem of cheap liquor and cheaper women."[127] To combat this scourge, Marshall ordered the building of an ice rink, encouraged athletics, developed amateur theatricals—anything to keep the men occupied.

These challenges notwithstanding, Marshall enjoyed his life in China. "I am more and more pleased with my choice of station and duty," he wrote in mid-1925. "It suits me perfectly, and the most disagreeable duty here is preferable to desk duty." He played squash in the afternoons and tennis at the American Club. Despite his staid personality, he admitted he found the dances, parties, amateur theatricals, and other social activities "very attractive." Moreover, he noted that Lily and her mother had also grown "very fond of China."[128] Lily wrote to another former Pershing aide: "We quite adore it over here and find life so easy. Many servants and much liquor make things *so* simple. We are actually accumulating some lovely things for our house—rugs—old mellow lacquer—some good screens and brocades—linen, etc. Viewed merely as a three-year shopping trip, our tour here would be well worthwhile."[129]

Marshall also developed lasting friendships in China, particularly with Majors E. Forrest Harding and Joseph Stilwell. Marshall and Stilwell made perhaps as mismatched a pair as Eisenhower and Patton. The hawk-nosed Stilwell possessed "a hard, lined, decisive face" atop a "lean and bony" frame that gave him "a deceptive air of fragility." He slumped and barely bothered with his uniform, whereas Marshall was perpetually upright and rigorous in the maintenance of his appearance so that one soldier described Marshall as "the most military looking man in the entire army."[130] Stilwell was profane and had a caustic tongue, earning the nickname "Vinegar Joe," whereas Marshall was circumspect and confined himself to the infrequent angry "damn." Marshall was an inveterate rider, whereas Stilwell deemed horses "all prance and fart and no sense."[131]

Yet they both shared a pragmatic approach to problems. During the war Stilwell had served in the 1st Division with Marshall—eventually rising to become chief intelligence officer for the IV Corps—and came away from the conflict having absorbed the same lessons: battlefield conditions demanded leaders who were flexible rather than officers unable to think beyond outdated field manuals. In Stilwell, Marshall also saw an officer who shared the privations of his troops. If Stilwell's battalion had to perform a 20-mile training march, Vinegar Joe would be there walking at the head of the column the entire way. Ridgway described Stilwell as a "crusty genius," and Jacob Devers recalled that Stilwell was "sarcastic but in a way that made you want to perform. I would have done anything for him."[132]

Stilwell was beginning his second tour in China when he joined the 15th Infantry as a battalion commander in September 1926. After rising to colonel in World War I—during which he was awarded the Distinguished Service Medal for his part in preparing the St. Mihiel offensive—in September 1919 he was reduced back to his prewar rank of captain. He subsequently asked the War Department: "How about sending me as far away from home as possible?" He had demonstrated a proficiency in languages at West Point, and had visited China in 1911 as a twenty-eight-year-old lieutenant while serving in the Philippines. Consequently, Stilwell was appointed to represent the Army as its first language officer for China. After a year of studying Chinese at the University of California, he was promoted to major in July 1920 and sailed with his family for China that August. He spent five hours a day in immersion language training, and attended seminars and lectures on Chinese history, religion, economics, and current affairs. Between classes he enjoyed wandering through Peking's markets. Within a month Stilwell was so enamored that he told the War Department that "Military Attache to China" was his only preferred assignment.

From April to June 1921 Stilwell served as the chief engineer for the Red Cross's road building program in Shansi province, enabling him to escape from Legation life and become acquainted with China on a working level. He worked daily with Chinese officials, village magistrates, contractors, construction bosses and laborers, learning Chinese habits, characteristics, and interrelations. As military attaché he studied China's soldiery and spent several days with Feng Yu-hsiang in 1922. As his biographer Barbara Tuchman notes: "On the roadbeds of Shansi and Shensi, in the villages and squalid inns of his one-man travels, he had come to know men and places far outside the foreigner's usual circle of Treaty Port, Legation Quarter and missionary compound. He had functioned with Chinese under Chinese conditions."[133]

Stilwell declined an offer to attend the Ecole de Guerre—France's staff college—when he learned of the opening for a battalion commander in the 15th Infantry. Thus, in August 1926 the Stilwells once again boarded an Army transport for China. "We all felt we were going home," his wife Winifred recalled. The 15th Infantry took advantage of Major Stilwell's knowledge of China and the Chinese. The regimental newspaper, *The Sentinel*, ran a column by him on current events in the Middle Kingdom. When Senator Hiram Bingham visited China and wanted to meet the deposed boy-emperor Henry Pu-Yi, Marshall arranged the interview and assigned Stilwell to serve as inter-preter.* Because of his record of adventurous journeys throughout China, in 1926 he was given the dangerous mission of obtaining at first hand a reliable estimate of Chiang Kai-shek's armies as they slowly marched toward Tien-tsin. Stilwell's three-week scouting mission earned a special commendation for "the highest type of efficiency, military intelligence, splendid determina-tion and courageous conduct" from the commander of U.S. forces in China, Brig. Gen. Joseph Castner. "Courage in battle when accompanied by com-rades is often seen," Castner wrote, "but a much higher courage is required by any individual who attempts what Major Stilwell accomplished—the close contact alone and unaided, with hundreds of ignorant, hostile anti-foreign Chinese troops of two contending armies." As Tuchman notes, Stilwell "was probably the only man with the necessary combination of military knowl-edge, Chinese knowledge and that 'higher courage' who could have carried out the mission to Hsuchow and returned."[134]

In December 1926, Marshall summarized his tour of duty in China, writing a friend: "My service in China has been delightful, interesting and several times, exciting. Politically it is the most interesting problem in the world today, and the most dangerous. From a military point of view, the ser-vice here has been more instructive than any where else in the army these days."[135] Although not the sentimental sort, he could have added that the eight months he and Stilwell served together in China had forged a lasting professional and personal bond between the two. Despite remaining aloof

---

* Future Chairman of the Joint Chiefs of Staff Maxwell Taylor relates an account of how he was sent to assist now-Colonel Joseph Stilwell in 1937. Taylor recalled that Stilwell "had a deep affection for the Chinese, an admiration for their achievements of the past, and a faith in the promise of their future." Stilwell openly flaunted the health codes established by Western doctors and loved to walk through Chinese markets and pick up fruit to eat after merely brushing off the dust with a sweaty sleeve. "Though I knew it was folly," Taylor writes, "I could do no less and soon became an ambulant case of chronic diarrhea while Stilwell seemed to flourish on our regime." See Taylor, 35.

with most adults, Marshall became friendly with Stilwell's children, and Stilwell was one of the only people close enough to Marshall to call him by his first name. This bond endured well after the Marshalls finally set sail for home in May 1927.

The 2013 publication *Army Leadership Development Strategy* posits a leadership development model comprised of three "domains": an *Institutional Domain* comprised of training, education, and experience gained in Army schools; a *Self-Development Domain* representing the influence of mentors, peers, and an officer or NCO's own program of self-development; and the *Operational Domain*, comprised of training and experience while assigned to organizations. Given that a quarter of the Army was stationed overseas during the interwar period, and Regular Army officers could expect to serve at least one tour abroad between the world wars, foreign service would appear likely to offer an important foundation for future army and corps commanders' development. This would appear especially likely given the presence of a real-world adversary (Japan), and the threat of sudden invasion meant the overseas departments were intended to be fully operational commands ready to fight at a moment's notice.

Yet the reality is much more opaque. Few if any officers served abroad in the theater in which they would eventually command an army, corps, or even a division in World War II. MacArthur and Stilwell's service in the Philippines and China, respectively, are notable exceptions to this rule, although in the former's case the strong personal affinity he developed with the Filipinos arguably skewed his strategic judgment in a counterproductive manner. Two other possible exceptions are Eisenhower, whose service with the American Battle Monuments Commission in France familiarized him with what would become the European Theater of Operations a decade later, and Robert Eichelberger, who served as chief intelligence officer for the American Expeditionary Forces in Siberia, and consequently was able to observe Japanese forces up close.[136] Yet these were unique assignments that stood entirely apart from the framework of the Army's overseas departments.

Moreover, although the units of America's Colonial Army were supposed to maintain a higher readiness than their stateside counterparts, the interwar era's budgetary shortfalls meant that the Hawaiian and Philippine Departments not only lacked sufficient forces to execute their assigned tasks, but also were unable to conduct large-scale maneuvers. The type of large-scale exercises needed to maintain tactical and operational proficiency, much less develop future strategic leaders, was further inhibited by geographic limitations: live-fire exercises in Hawaii were discouraged due to their adverse effects on the tourist trade, and the 15th Infantry was constrained by the local population's agricultural needs. Thus, overseas service was just as likely to contribute to the atrophy of an officer's tactical proficiency as its development.

This is not to say that these tours of duty did not have a significant influence on key officers' leadership development. Clearly, Eisenhower would not have developed into the strategic leader he became absent Fox Conner's tutelage. Similarly, Patton's study of amphibious operations during his time in the Hawaiian Department helped prepare him to lead the landings in North Africa and Sicily during the war. But again, both these examples could just as easily have been replicated in a stateside assignment, and were as much the result of these officers' commitment to self-development as the product of any leadership development variables attributable to the "Operational Domain" of service abroad.

CHAPTER FIVE

"It Was Our Schools That Saved the Army"

IN SEPTEMBER 1924, THREE MONTHS BEFORE HIS TOUR OF DUTY IN PANAMA ended, Eisenhower's heart sank as he was ordered back to Camp Meade to serve as assistant coach for the III Corps Area football team. Someone in Washington had decided the Army needed to beat the Marines, so the best coaches in the service were being assembled at Meade to produce a winning team. Consequently, Ike and Mamie were forced to return to the scene of their heartbreak, the post where Eisenhower's career was nearly ended. Worse, they were assigned to the same converted barracks they had lived in three years before, meaning they would be surrounded by reminders of their loss.

At least the assignment was only temporary. After the last game of the season, Eisenhower was ordered to take command of the 15th Light Tank Battalion at Fort Benning, which he noted were "the same old tanks I had commanded several years earlier."[1] To advance in the Army, Eisenhower somehow had to find his way back into the infantry mainstream. He worked up his courage to request an interview with Maj. Gen. Charles Farnsworth, the same chief of infantry who had threatened to court-martial him over his heretical ideas regarding tanks. Eisenhower pled his case to attend one of the service schools, but Farnsworth would not listen to his appeals.

By this time, Fox Conner had also returned from Panama, and was serving as deputy chief of staff to General Hines. Given that Conner's office was down the hall from Farnsworth's in the old State, War, and Navy Building, it is likely that Eisenhower visited his mentor. Although there is no record of their conversation, a few days later Eisenhower received a cryptic telegram:

NO MATTER WHAT ORDERS YOU RECEIVE FROM THE WAR DEPARTMENT, MAKE NO PROTEST, ACCEPT THEM WITHOUT QUESTION, SIGNED CONNER

Shortly thereafter, Eisenhower received orders transferring him from the Infantry to the Adjutant General's Corps and assigning him to Fort Logan, Colorado, for recruiting duty. For a talented young officer such as Eisenhower the assignment was an insult, and likely a career-killer as recruiting duty was normally a dead-end appointment for officers who had been repeatedly passed over for promotion. "Had anyone else suggested [such a move] I would have been outraged," Eisenhower recalled, "but with my solid belief in Fox Conner I kept my temper."[2]

Conner explained his plan in a letter that arrived a few days later. In order to outflank Farnsworth, Eisenhower would be temporarily transferred to the adjutant general's office and then be selected by the adjutant general—a friend of Conner's—to attend the Command and General Staff School (CGSS) at Fort Leavenworth as part of the adjutant general's quota of officers.[*] Consequently, Eisenhower went through the motions as an Army recruiter, and in April 1925 orders arrived notifying him of his selection to CGSS with the class entering in August 1925. "I was ready to fly," Eisenhower said, "and needed no airplane."[3]

Fort Leavenworth was a pleasant post occupying the bluffs overlooking the Missouri River near the Kansas-Missouri border, about 30 miles northwest of Kansas City. Situated near the eastern terminus of the Oregon and Santa Fe Trails, the roughly 12-square-mile fort was established by Col. Henry Leavenworth, commander of the 3rd Infantry Regiment, in 1827. In 1881

---

[*] Although a charming tale and a vivid example of the value of having a mentor to an officer's career, modern historians have uncovered evidence suggesting Conner's machinations were likely unnecessary. In August 1924, before receiving his orders for Camp Meade, Eisenhower wrote a letter—with Conner's endorsement—to the adjutant general requesting assignment to the CGSS. The letter ended up in the chief of infantry's office, where a staff officer appended a handwritten note on behalf of Farnsworth stating that Eisenhower was eligible to attend and his name "has been placed on the tentative list of those officers who will be considered to attend the 1925-26 course." In January 1925 the chief of infantry submitted a list of forty-seven infantry officers recommended to attend the 1925-26 course, of whom Eisenhower was number twenty-eight. Given that the branch chiefs had near total discretion over who attended CGSS, this recommendation meant an appointment was nearly a foregone conclusion. Thus, although neither Conner nor Eisenhower was apparently aware that the transfer was unnecessary, Carlo D'Este concludes: "There is nothing in the official record to suggest that in 1924–1925 Eisenhower was in disfavor or would not be selected to attend Leavenworth." See D'Este, *Eisenhower*, 176–78; Mark C. Bender, *Watershed at Leavenworth: Dwight D. Eisenhower and the Command and General Staff School* (Leavenworth, KS, 1990, CGSC Monograph), 37; and Peter J. Schifferle, *America's School for War: Fort Leavenworth, Officer Education, and Victory in World War II* (University Press of Kansas, 2010), 130.

the commanding general of the U.S. Army, William Tecumseh Sherman, established Leavenworth as the site of what would become the Army's most important school, the School of Application for Infantry and Cavalry. By the eve of World War I this had evolved into the School of the Line and the Army Staff College—the latter of which became the General Staff School until 1922, when both schools' designation was changed to the Command and General Staff School.

Beyond name changes, Leavenworth went through several distinct periods of development during the interwar years. From 1919 to 1923 there were two separate courses, with only the top half of the School of the Line's graduates continuing on to a second year at the General Staff School. Starting in 1923, however, to accommodate the large "hump" of officers who had entered the service during the war and had received no schooling in general staff procedures or higher command duties, the War Department reduced the course to a single year. From 1923 to 1929 the size of the one-year classes increased to about 235 officers, before CGSS returned to a two-year course in 1929.[4]

Whatever the length of the course, its purpose remained constant, following Secretary of War Baker's postwar call to modify "the pre-war system where the lessons learned in war indicated changes were necessary to make the system meet more modern requirements."[5] Despite the American public's postwar triumphalism, the Army's senior leadership realized the slaughter of the Meuse-Argonne campaign had revealed serious deficiencies in the essential tasks of modern war: planning, logistics, organization, and the "handling of large formations." Since the depleted postwar Army possessed few tactical formations or command opportunities, the CGSS concentrated its instruction on preparing officers for command and general staff duty at the division and corps levels. Although the specific course content evolved over the next two decades, the fundamental learning objectives of competence in handling large formations, problem-solving and decision-making skills, and confidence in these skills never changed. Graduates were expected to be able to perform in either command or staff billets two to three grades above their present ranks, a likely scenario if the Army expanded during a mobilization.[6]

The typical school day at CGSS was long and highly structured. For eight hours a day, five days a week, students attended class to absorb as much as could be taught in lectures, conferences, and practical problems about the tactics and combined arms operations of divisions and corps. Individual instructors typically specialized in one aspect of the course, lecturing, leading conferences, and preparing map exercises and problems relating to a single tactical problem. Consequently, one student wrote to a friend in 1926, his class had been taught by sixty different instructors. As a result, "We are not imbued with the personality of individual instructors, but rather left with the impression of a *composite* of the whole faculty; instruction by mass, rather than individual performers . . . There is the impression of a system of instruction paramount to any individual."[7]

Although large lectures, big and small conferences, and committee discussions were critical tools, the practical work—including map exercises, maneuvers, and problems—comprised 70 percent of total instruction. The heart of the "Leavenworth system" was tactical problem solving involving division and corps operations using a case method similar to that of law schools.[8] Students were assigned problems containing information on an enemy force of a variable size attacking or defending a position. The officers commanded the Blue Force, were given a mission, and had to decide upon a course of action. After the student had submitted his answer, the approved "school solution" was distributed, and the officers then determined the combat units' movements and the required logistical support. Individual student performances in these problems were graded two or three times per week, and were their predominant experience at Leavenworth.

The toughest assignments had strict time limits—sometimes two days, sometimes twenty-four hours, sometimes twelve hours. The stress created by these deadlines, the overall workload, and the schedule—which was much more demanding than the garrison routine of the interwar army—were compounded by intense competition for class standing. Graduates were rank-ordered by academic grades upon graduation, and as Lucian Truscott recalled, "Officers were made to feel their entire future careers depended on their class standings."[9] Some officers cracked under the strain, and nervous breakdowns, depression, and divorces were unexceptional, and there were even at least two suicides.* Some officers approached this challenge with macabre humor. Bradford Chynoweth later joked: "My class made a joint resolve that if anyone contemplated suicide, he would first kill an instructor."[10] But others such as Ernest Harmon admitted that "The two years I spent at Leavenworth

---

* Although multiple historians suggest the suicides were merely urban legends, Timothy K. Nenninger researched the deaths of every officer at Fort Leavenworth in the period. Eight student officers died; two were suicides. Maj. Frank A. Turner died on June 15, 1924, and Lt. Col. Emery T. Smith on December 3, 1924. Both officers were geographic bachelors separated from their families and were suffering stress from their grades, according to the Line of Duty investigations. See Schifferle, 237, fn8.

were the most difficult years of my training," and that "my disposition at home became as mean as that of a starving prairie wolf."[11] Although the commandant, Brig. Gen. Harry Smith, urged students in 1923 to get plenty of exercise and to maintain social contacts with their classmates and instructors, the CGSS course was *intended* to test the mettle of its students by exhausting them, placing them under great stress, and forcing them to think and react under extreme pressure similar to the conditions they would face in wartime.[12]

One officer who thrived under the pressure of CGSS was Troy C. Middleton. A graduate of Mississippi A&M, where he commanded the corps of cadets, Middleton enlisted in the Army in 1910 and passed a written exam to win a direct commission in 1912. In October 1918, during the Meuse-Argonne offensive, he was placed in command of the 39th Infantry Regiment. Three days later, at age twenty-nine, he became the youngest colonel in the American Expeditionary Force, and would receive the Distinguished Service Medal for his actions in combat. He graduated first out of his class of ninety-five officers at the Infantry School's advanced course, and in June 1924 finished eighth out of 248 officers at CGSS. Middleton was invited to stay on at Leavenworth as an instructor, although he later admitted, "I didn't even know I was under consideration and I certainly wouldn't have sought an appointment to the faculty." He taught at CGSS from 1924 to 1928, his students including almost every American division commander in Europe during World War II. Indeed, at one point every corps commander in the ETO had been a student under Middleton at Leavenworth.[13]

While a student at Leavenworth, Middleton made a habit of going on regular walks with a cavalryman in his class. One day, as they walked in a prairie snowstorm, his friend declared: "Troy, I'm going to be an honor graduate in this class."[14] This officer's drive to succeed epitomized how much stock ambitious officers placed on success at Leavenworth, for Middleton's friend, George S. Patton, had held a poor opinion of Leavenworth ever since he visited the post for a West Point dinner there a year earlier while he was at the Cavalry School at Fort Riley. "I don't think much of the place," Patton wrote his father.

All the men have a haunted look and all lie heavily about 75% claiming to have good marks and having bad and 25% claiming to be getting zeros and are realy [sic] at the top. To add to the joys of the prospect there are

three large penitentiaries in view at all times also a lunatic assilum [sic].
Still as one must go and as many fools have survived I suppose I will.[15]

Nevertheless, Patton threw himself into his studies with his usual intensity. Although he cultivated the impression that he did not take the course that seriously, Patton wrote to Bea that on a weekend when most of his classmates were relaxing, "I certainly busted all rules about studying today. I studied from 2:30 P.M. to 6 P.M. and from 7:15 to 11:45." Summarizing his performance thus far, he noted that "I have done better than I have expected on almost all the problems though I doubt if I stand as high relatively as I did at Riley. Still I hope to improve and I think some of the others will crack—I hope so."[16]

Patton redoubled his efforts, frequently studying deep into the night. This led to his being summoned before an academic board for allegedly employing an unauthorized study aid when a classmate "noticed [him] studying under a strange blue light and reported him."[17] Under questioning, Patton embarrassingly confessed that he had purchased and used the light because it supposedly restored his receding hairline. True to his vow to Middleton, Patton graduated twenty-fifth in their class and was cited as an honor graduate. Yet he remained skeptical about the school. Years later, he wrote to a young officer who had served on his staff in Hawaii and was about to attend CGSS that "high marks at Leavenworth depend more on TECHNIQUE than on INTELLIGENCE."[18]

Whereas Patton's confidence never wavered, Eisenhower's elation at being selected for CGSS quickly gave way to anxiety. The officers assigned to CGSS were not just the Army's intellectual elite, but like Middleton, most had graduated at or near the top of their class from one or more of the Army's other schools. Conversely, Eisenhower had not even *attended* the Infantry School, which was generally considered a prerequisite for CGSS. Most of his classmates would be older than him and possess more experience with Army staff work. Finally, an aide to the chief of infantry wrote warning him to avoid CGSS because "you will probably fail," and thereafter be useless as an infantry officer.[19]

Eisenhower shared these doubts in a letter to Conner and asked the general what he should study to prepare himself. Conner responded quickly and with encouragement.

You may not know it, but because of your three years' work in Panama,
you are far better trained and ready for Leavenworth than anybody I

know. You will recall that during your entire service there I required that
you write a field order for the operation of the post every day. . . . You
became so well acquainted with the techniques and routine of preparing
plans and orders for operations that included their logistics, that they will
be second nature to you. You will feel no sense of inferiority.[20]

Indeed, just as West Point was uniquely suited to MacArthur's intellectual gifts, Eisenhower enjoyed several advantages over his Leavenworth classmates. First, whether necessary or not, Eisenhower's transfer to the adjutant general's corps was beneficial, as recruiting duties took practically no time and allowed him ample opportunity to prepare for CGSS. He obtained copies of the Leavenworth problems from previous years, and as he had with Patton at Camp Meade, worked through them and checked his answers against the approved solutions. "It was by no means a chore," Eisenhower said. "I loved to do that kind of work . . . practical problems have always been my equivalent to crossword puzzles."[21]

Second, although CGSS students were encouraged to form study groups, Eisenhower declined an invitation to join a committee. Instead, he invited the friend who had introduced him to Mamie back at Fort Sam Houston a decade ago, Maj. Leonard "Gee" Gerow, to be his study partner. Gerow had graduated first from the Infantry School a few years prior, thereby enabling Eisenhower to gain the benefit of whatever Gee had learned at Benning. Eisenhower and Gerow both complemented and challenged each other, and together they converted the third floor of Eisenhower's quarters into what Ike called "a model command post." Maps were pinned up everywhere, and books, notes, pens, and pencils were strewn across a makeshift table on which the two officers studied war and prepared for upcoming classes and field problems. While the two men were working, no intrusions were allowed. John Eisenhower, who was three at the time, recalled his earliest memories as including "a new tricycle at Fort Leavenworth . . . an impressive pile of lumber stacked on the second floor of Otis Hall. . . . Mother singing to me in the car." But most vividly of all, he remembered:

the night I invaded Dad's attic study, normally off limits. He and his
friend Gee . . . were poring intensely over a large table, eyeshades protect-
ing them from the glare of a brilliant, low-hung lamp. I was too small
to see what was on the table but stared in wonderment at the huge maps
tacked on the wall. The two young officers were going over the next day's

tactical problem. Dad and Gee welcomed me with a laugh and shoved me out the door in the course of perhaps half a minute.[22]

As Ike recalled years later, "We learned far more in quiet concentration than in the lecture room."[23]

Eisenhower also benefited from another friendship while at CGSS. He had stayed in touch with Patton, and when he told his friend of his selection to CGSS, Patton sent him one hundred pages of detailed notes and observations on all aspects of the course, including the best way to tackle the 126 problems that were the course's core. Eisenhower brought Patton's notes with him to Leavenworth, and according to Mamie, "He studied them to tatters." Another way in which Eisenhower's previous experiences had uniquely prepared him for CGSS was that the battle of Gettysburg was often the subject of graded exercises. Eisenhower knew the terrain there intimately from his Camp Colt days, so "it never took me more than five minutes to stake out my problems where the others had to look up where the location of Seven Stars, Tawneytown, New Oxford and all the rest were. It would take the average fellow forty minutes and I'd take five."[24]

Finally, Eisenhower's natural gregariousness helped him immensely at CGSS. Whereas many students were reluctant to engage the faculty outside of class, Middleton recalled that "Ike used to come up to my office . . . He would sit on a corner of my desk and pump me for information. He always asked the most practical questions. And he wasn't after information about tests; he wanted to know what a commander should do in combat situations—knowing that I had led a regiment in hard fighting in France."[25] In a paper written for the adjutant general after the course (and subsequently published anonymously in several service journals), Eisenhower advised prospective students that "in addition to the instruction you receive in the conference room, during your study periods, and in the working of problems, you will gain a great deal by a method I call absorption." Eisenhower advised engaging the instructors outside the classroom, as "the little talks you will have with these officers who have been through the mill, and are now intimately connected with the school will prove invaluable to you."[26]

Most importantly, however, Eisenhower worked harder than he had ever worked before. Although in his memoirs he claimed to have only studied from 7:00 p.m. to 9:30 p.m. to maintain a fresh mind each day, with Mamie keeping time, Mamie remembered it differently. She told her biographer and friend, Dorothy Brandon, that Eisenhower followed "a driving routine—a snatched early breakfast and a hurried dinner after day-long classes. Rarely did he wait for Major Gerow to arrive, so anxious was he to begin his evening grind. . . . around midnight he would put in an appearance en route to a foray on the refrigerator." Alden Hatch, a friend of the Eisenhowers, wrote that "Often Mamie woke at one or two in the morning to find her husband still fighting his theoretical battles, while the mounds of cigarette stubs littered every ashtray. Frequently he worked all night."[27] The rare exception to this industriousness came on the weekends, when students were encouraged to "play hard." It was at Fort Leavenworth in 1926 that Eisenhower began what became a lifelong love affair with the sport of golf on the post's newly built course.

When the final rankings were posted, Eisenhower stood first in his class, two-tenths of a point ahead of Gerow. As a steady stream of well-wishers descended on the Eisenhowers' quarters, Mamie was giddy with delight. "I knew, every hour of every month at Leavenworth, that Ike would come out Number One," she said. "But when he made it, I was so tumbled inside with gladness, it was days before I could eat properly."[28] Eisenhower wrote Patton to tell him the good news and to thank him for the use of his notes. Patton replied:

Dear Ike:

Your letter delights me more than I can say. As soon as I saw the list I wrote you congratulating you on being honor, but I had no idea that in addition your [sic] were no. ONE. That certainly is fine.

It shows that Leavenworth is a good school if a HE man can come out one.

You are very kind to think that my notes helped you though I feel sure that you have done as well with out them. If a man thinks war long enough it is bound to effect him in a good way.[29]

Privately, Patton was less magnanimous, and was certain his papers were the secret of Eisenhower's success.[30] The commandant at Leavenworth, Brig. Gen. Edward King, wanted Eisenhower to remain at the CGSS as an instructor, but he had already been ordered back to Fort Benning for what he hoped would be an infantry command.

"I found the school itself to be exhilarating," Eisenhower recalled years later, and described his year at Leavenworth as the "watershed" moment in his career.[31] Yet the question of whether the CGSS made a positive contribution to leadership development in the interwar era remains a hotly debated topic amongst military historians and analysts. Many agree with Stephen Ambrose's assessment of CGSS that "the school did not encourage imagination, independent thought, or genius."[32] Historian Jorg Muth argues that at CGSS "ineffective courses were led by instructors who sometimes lacked knowledge of their fields and usually failed in didactics and pedagogics."[33] Other critics cite the "inadequacies" of the tactical doctrine at CGSS, arguing that Leavenworth ignored technological innovations such as aviation and tanks. Consequently, Boyd Dastrup concludes that "Leavenworth was not a seedbed of new thinking but a repository of old tactics based upon a bygone era."[34]

Patton was not the only CGSS graduate critical of the course. Charles Bolte thought that some of the requirements were "pretty far fetched," and Omar Bradley judged the problems and solutions presented in school lectures to be "trite, predictable, and often unrealistic."[35] Unsurprisingly, Chynoweth was harsh in his condemnation of CGSS. "The Instructor Staff were a hierarchy to whom the School doctrine was sacred," he remembered. "They were not teaching War. They were teaching Dogma."[36]

Perhaps no aspect of CGSS is as pilloried as the use of the "school solution" in the instruction and grading of practical exercises. Critics argue that officers were presented with only one right way to handle tactical problems and that success at Leavenworth required mostly conforming to prescribed doctrine and school methods. Innovation was discouraged and students who departed from "the system" were penalized. Joseph Lawton Collins recalls that when he attended CGSS, even the commandant—Brig. Gen. Stuart Heintzelman—worried about the rigid adherence to approved solutions:

> *Several times while I was a student, General Heintzelman, who had been listening in the back of the lecture room to an instructor's exposition of a type-solution to some tactical problem, would storm up to the platform to disagree with the patterned, school solution. He would apologize to the instructor, and would caution us to follow the instructor's guidance in any subsequent test problem. Then he would tell us what he would do under the conditions presented. He would add, "But you do what the instructor suggests, not what I say, or you will probably get a U [unsatisfactory] on the graded test."*

"Most of us students followed his advice," Collins says, "and played the instructor's game, often with tongue in cheek."[37] Most critics argue that this overreliance on a school solution produced a homogenized graduate incapable of bold, imaginative tactical decisions. Or as Muth concludes, "Such a teaching methodology has no place in a professional officer's education and it cannot be defended."[38]

Leavenworth's defenders readily concede CGSS was imperfect, but note that it was not intended to breed tactical geniuses, but rather competent staff officers. Indeed, the U.S. Army during this period scoffed at the very notion that military genius was something teachable rather than an innate quality that some men possessed and others simply lacked. The first commandant of the Army War College—and later chief of staff of the Army—Brig. Gen. Tasker Bliss wrote in 1903: "Those things that differentiate a Napoleon from other generals cannot be acquired in any school ... else Napoleons would be as thick in history as apple blossoms in a New England spring."[39] Later, perhaps the most influential U.S. military intellectual of the interwar era, John M. Palmer, wrote that "a good general staff officer is primarily a product of education. ... The gift of command is not. All history proves ... rugged moral qualities" made great commanders, not education.[40] Critical tasks such as preparing a movement order or a fire plan did not require creative thinking much less military genius, and the Army required officers who could perform tasks to standard, follow procedures, and harmonize their actions. The objective was to achieve uniformity in the *approach* to solving tactical problems, not in coming to identical solutions. Consequently, CGSS's purpose was to prepare an officer corps with a "high general average" of ability and knowledge capable of adjusting to evolving situations.[41]

Moreover, CGSS's defenders point to other positive effects of the Leavenworth experience. Except in rare cases, the course at Leavenworth was an officer's only experience with large-formation operations. Of equal importance, in the badly stove-piped interwar force, attending CGSS brought together promising officers from all the Army's branches. Leavenworth inculcated in an entire generation of officers a common language and a uniform problem-solving methodology they could not possibly obtain in their regular duties. For officers such as Middleton, Walter Bedell Smith, and others without a West Point ring—or an officer whose reputation at the military academy was less than stellar, such as Eisenhower—CGSS provided the single best chance for establishing (or recouping) his standing and reputation, which was critical in as incestuous an organization as the interwar Army.

Indeed, many of the officers frequently cited as critics of CGSS also recorded its benefits as well. Bradley recalled that he "profited from my years at Ft. Leavenworth. It was a good intellectual experience, good mental discipline." He further noted that "When the 'conventional' solution to a complex military problem is already well known by rote, unconventional—and often better—solutions are more likely to occur."[42] Years later Collins bluntly declared "it was our schools that saved the Army," and stated in his memoirs that "the courses at the Command and General Staff School were probably the most important in the entire system of military education, and were to prove invaluable during World War II."[43]

In fact, even the tyranny of the school solution may have been somewhat overstated. In 1926, for example, the school advised its instructors: "In marking problems, the school solution should not be followed rigidly. Where the student shows a logical, reasonable, sensible line of reasoning, he should receive full credit."[44] Instructors were warned that "the greatest care must be used to give proper value to a workable solution although it may differ from the solution issued by the school . . . Great care must be exercised to avoid injuring the initiative of officers." Instructors were specifically required to "bear in mind that each problem is susceptible of several sound solutions. Strict adherence to the school solution is a mistake and will be avoided."[45] Although Collins's anecdote regarding Brigadier General Heintzelman suggests this guidance was not strictly adhered to, other officers recalled the use of school solutions differently, as Forrest Harding's biographer records: "To his relief, Forrest learned that 'school solutions' followed no iron-clad orthodoxies. . . . It seldom took students long to realize that Leavenworth valued the logical mind over the brain full of miscellaneous facts."[46]

In the end, as Walter Bedell Smith's biographer D. K. R. Crosswell concludes, "As in most things, the truth rests somewhere in the middle" between Leavenworth's critics and its defenders. Historian Peter Schifferle concedes that "the story of Leavenworth as the educational institution for field-force effectiveness in WWII was hardly an unmitigated success," particularly in the lack of focus on mobilization duties, logistics, and airpower. Yet he ultimately concludes that "The explicit study of general staff principles and procedures at division and corps, the implied acquisition of confidence in staff skills, and the uneducated aspects of leadership . . . were the foundations for battlefield success in World War II."[47] The potential for widely divergent interpretations of CGSS value is perhaps best illustrated by an anecdote related by Ernest Harmon. While planning the 2nd Armored Division's crossing of the Albert

Canal in September 1944, Harmon recalled: "Indelibly fixed in my mind was a problem I had wrestled with years earlier at the Army's Command and General Staff School at Fort Leavenworth." During one map problem, Harmon proposed flanking an enemy holding the opposite shore by having cavalry ford 25 miles away and launch a surprise attack. His instructor, however, seemed intent on imposing his desired solution and claimed that Harmon had evaded the purpose of the problem: to demonstrate knowledge of how to properly conduct a river crossing in the face of the enemy. Harmon protested the instructor's ruling, but lost. In combat, however, Harmon seized the initiative, found a bridge outside the 2nd Armor Division's sector, crossed over another combat command, and rapidly outflanked the Germans holding the opposite bank.[48] To critics, this anecdote demonstrates the pointless inflexibility of the instructors at CGSS. On the other hand, it also demonstrates that such rigidity in the schoolhouse did not actually cripple the ingenuity and initiatives of officers when in combat.

As Crosswell notes, the truth of CGSS lies somewhere in the middle.

After Leavenworth, Eisenhower was appointed executive officer of the 24th Infantry Regiment at Fort Benning. The 24th was an all-black regiment—commanded by white officers—used as support troops for the Infantry School at Benning. Although black units had a proud heritage in combat during the Civil War and various Indian campaigns, in the segregated interwar Army they were regarded as second-class units, and assigning a CGSS honor graduate to a unit of support troops made little sense.[49]

Once again, Fox Conner came to Eisenhower's rescue.

In 1923 Congress had created the American Battle Monuments Commission to establish and maintain cemeteries and erect monuments to the nearly 120,000 Americans killed during the Great War and interred in Europe. The commission, headed by General Pershing, was also charged with preparing a guide for Americans visiting the burial and battle sites. Pershing needed somebody to complete the daunting task of writing the guide within six months. Conner recommended Eisenhower for the assignment. The work was challenging, as Eisenhower had to sort through unit histories and the AEF's official records and draft a narrative of the American effort in France. Pershing was delighted when Eisenhower submitted the guidebook—*A Guide to the American Battle Fields in Europe*—on time and wrote a lavish letter of commendation. Eisenhower, he said, "has shown superior ability not only in visualizing his work as a whole but in executing its many details in an efficient and timely manner. What he has done was accomplished only by the exercise of unusual intelligence and constant devotion to duty."[50] More importantly, perhaps, by the time the project was complete Eisenhower was arguably the best-informed officer in the Army on the AEF's strategy and operations other than Pershing and Conner. Shortly before finishing his assignment, Eisenhower learned he had been selected for the Army War College's next class. "To graduate from the War College had long been the ambition of almost every officer," he later wrote, "and I was anxious to take the assignment."[51]

Founded in 1903, the Army War College was the pinnacle of the inter-war Army education system, the gateway to high command and staff positions. The War College was located at Fort Humphreys (now McNair) along the Potomac River on land that had been set aside for military purposes in Pierre L'Enfant's original plan for the capital. The site had housed Army installations since 1791, making it second only to West Point as America's oldest Army post. It was also one of the most beautiful posts in the interwar Army, with two long, immaculately groomed quadrangles leading up to the ornate, Stanford White–designed Beaux-Arts academic building, "giving it the look and feel of a real university."[52]

Whereas the CGSS's purpose was to prepare field-grade officers for the general staff, the War College curriculum was designed to provide future generals with an overview of war, including: how armies were mobilized, supplied, and deployed; relations with allies; and grand strategy. From its inception, however, the college was closely affiliated with the Army General Staff, and before World War I tended to function less as a school than as a planning appendage of the War Plans Division. After the war Secretary Baker concluded:

> It has been made specially apparent that General Staff officers for duty with the War Department and for larger expeditionary forces should have broader knowledge, not only of their purely military duties, but also a full comprehension of all agencies, governmental as well as industrial, necessarily involved in a nation at war, to the end that coordinated effort may be secured . . . both in the preparation for and during the war.[53]

Thus, when Maj. Gen. James W. McAndrew became commandant in 1919, he sought to change the college's image as simply an adjunct to the General

Staff. Preparation for war was expanded to not only include military training, but also the study of relations between world powers. Consequently, Capt. Ridley McLean, the Navy liaison officer to the Army War College in 1921–1922, reported to the secretary of the navy that:

> *The course here covers war in its broadest aspect, the studies are national in character, all problems involve combined operations, the world rather than a limited area on land, is the theatre. . . . The course embraces a comprehensive series of lectures by men of preeminence, which is unrivalled in the United States. By access of the student body to the various Departments of the Government in this city, facilities are offered and training is afforded in the utilization in war plans of the vast amount of information available in their archives.*[54]

Leavenworth's adoption of a one-year curriculum led to a stricter bifurcation in which the CGSS prepared officers for command, training, and staff duties at the division and corps level, whereas the War College concentrated on producing officers suited for future command and staff functions in the corps areas and the War Department itself.

When Maj. Gen. William D. Connor took over the War College in 1927, he divided the course into two distinct phases: "Preparation for War" and "Conduct of War." Each class was divided into committees, each of which was responsible for examining a significant contemporary military problem. After a month of study and research, each committee prepared a "staff study" that it presented to the entire class, answering questions and defending their conclusions. The faculty offered critiques and commented upon the staff studies, but, unlike Leavenworth, did not offer "approved" solutions. While the committees researched and deliberated, the officers also attended lectures by nationally recognized experts from government and academia in subjects such as economics, political science, psychology, international law, foreign affairs, and history.[55]

The year at the War College produced none of the anxiety upon which Leavenworth prided itself. Whereas Leavenworth was about training, the War College focused on education. Assistant commandant Col. H. B. Crosby articulated the fundamental difference in the school's approach in his orientation lecture to the 1924–1925 class:

> *I believe I speak the truth when I say that no one helps his rating by blindly accepting the views of the faculty on any subject. This is distinctly*

a college—where we learn from an exchange of ideas and not by accepting unquestioned either the views of the faculty or the views of the student. At Leavenworth we accepted and should have accepted the principles and doctrines laid down by the faculty of that school. Here we reach our own conclusions, faculty and student, following a full and free discussion of the subject.[56]

Unlike the CGSS, which was a graded and competitive experience, the War College was closer to a civilian graduate school. General Connor clearly expressed his philosophy regarding the War College in his welcome remarks in September 1928:

In a very large measure the period of your self-development begins right now for in this institution there are no marks applied to your daily work and there are no periodic tests or final examinations that you must undergo to show the faculty what progress you have made or what advantages you have accumulated during the year's work. From now on you become, more than ever before, subject only to the critical judgment of your fellow officers.[57]

Consequently, one Eisenhower biographer notes, "To anyone subjected to the pressures at Leavenworth, the War College seemed by contrast to be pleasurably contrived for leisurely respite."[58]

In addition to their committee work, students focused on producing a paper on a self-selected topic. The papers were to be "broad enough to require General Staff actions in that it is of interest to the Army or Navy . . . should be of a live nature . . . treating questions that now need attention or will need it in the near future," and "should contribute something of value to the betterment of national defense."[59] Eisenhower chose the timely topic "An Enlisted Reserve for the Regular Army" for his staff memorandum. Although the isolationist sentiment in the 1920s made U.S. military intervention abroad an almost-taboo subject, he approached it without hesitation. Eisenhower argued that despite the increasingly pacifistic national mood, America's military should be structured to meet a possible foreign crisis. To do so, he advocated relying on an enlisted reserve rather than the National Guard, partly because "experience has shown that the cost of maintaining a soldier in the reserve is only a small fraction of that necessary to maintain him in the active force," and also because the former active duty enlisted men comprising such a reserve would be better trained than the Guardsmen.[60]

General Connor carefully evaluated his paper and wrote to Eisenhower: "The examination of your individual staff memorandum shows it to be of exceptional merit," noting that the chief of staff had directed it be circulated within the War Department.[61] Although Eisenhower was the youngest member of his class—and one of the youngest ever admitted to the War College—Connor rated him superior in eight of ten categories on his efficiency report. In short, Connor concluded, he was "a young officer of great promise" at thirty-seven years old.[62]

Conversely, Patton was somewhat older than his fellow students when he entered the War College in the fall of 1931. His relatively late selection for the course suggested his career progress had slowed, as most of his classmates had graduated from West Point several years after him. This only served to spur Patton's ambition and energy, however. Constantly laboring under the fear that he would fail to live up to the lofty destiny he imagined for himself, he pushed himself to make good and outwork his peers. As one classmate recalled, "Committee output was the work of the few who enjoyed working on military problems. . . . The outstanding worker in the class was George Patton . . . In every War College assignment, whether as chairman or subordinate, he went all-out."[63]

Patton submitted his research paper on "The Probable Characteristics of the Next War and the Organization, Tactics and Equipment Necessary to Meet Them." At fifty-six pages, with fourteen additional tables and photographs, it was an ambitious project. His inquiry started in 2500 BC, when "one of the earliest wars of which there is authoritative records occurred between Egypt and Syria during the Sixth Dynasty." Patton proceeded in this manner through more than forty case studies, seventeen of which were in the period of antiquity before the birth of Christ. Displaying the breadth and scope of his knowledge of military history, Patton made casual references to Sargon II, Cyrus and Cambyses, Philip and Alexander, Hannibal and Scipio, as well as numerous others. In the end, he concluded that in every instance the professional army proved superior to mass armies.[64]

As was the case with Eisenhower's paper, General Connor commended Patton "for work of exceptional merit." Yet when compared side-by-side, perhaps no other documents so perfectly illustrate the differences between Eisenhower and Patton. Whereas Patton's paper was fascinating and almost romantic in its assertion of certain continuities throughout history, the next decade's events ultimately disproved his thesis as America's mass mobilized citizen-army defeated the more professional *Wehrmacht*. Conversely, Eisenhower's writing was dry and functional, yet his policy proposals proved more practicable when finally enacted, albeit *after* World War II.

In addition to preparing his individual thesis, Patton was chairman of a student committee that presented a report on mechanized units. This seemed a natural fit for the officer who had done more than anybody else to develop American tank doctrine in the last war, as well as an opportunity for Patton to make the case for his innovative ideas about mechanized warfare that had been stifled at Camp Meade a decade earlier. Yet the committee's final report—which clearly bore Patton's imprint—endorsed the notion that there was no place in the Army for a major armored force operating independently. The mechanized units' proper function, they concluded, was to assist the existing arms: infantry and cavalry. In other words, there was no room in the Army for the mechanizationists. This represented a status-quo attitude, and was no advance over the doctrine of 1918 Patton had previously excoriated as inadequate. Patton had perhaps been chastised by his reprimands at Meade and in Hawaii and his belated attendance of the War College and decided that brilliant dissent was not worth the price. Regardless, Connor praised Patton's performance at the War College, noting that he was "an aggressive and capable officer of strong convictions. An untiring student, Proficiency in theoretical training for High Command: Superior. For War Department General Staff: Superior. Special aptitude for any particular class of duty: Command. Qualified for duty with any civilian component. Academic rating: Superior."[65]

Without the pressure of contending for grades, officers enjoyed numerous opportunities for leisure, socializing, and spending time with their families. Patton, for example, dressed for polo every day at noon and left for the stables as soon as class ended. One year the War College's softball team included Omar Bradley, Ernest Harmon, Bull Halsey, and Jonathan Wainwright. Middleton, who had played quarterback on several post teams as a young officer, similarly took up softball during his year at the War College. On an officer's salary, most attendees could not afford to participate in Washington, DC's social scene, and most lived cloistered together in apartments within walking distance of the school. Consequently, officers and their families socialized amongst themselves. Eisenhower's classmates included Gerow—Mamie and Katie Gerow had grown to be close friends—Walton Walker, and Wade Haislip. His brother Milton was in the capital as well, working as an aide to the secretary of agriculture, and to most of Washington at the time Major Eisenhower was known as "Milton's brother." The Eisenhowers threw frequent parties at their apartment at the Wyoming, often enlivened by the bathtub gin Ike concocted.[66]

Although its graduates of the late 1920s and the 1930s filled practically all of the Army and Army Air Force's high command and staff positions during World War II, the War College never occupied a position remotely comparable to Leavenworth's in the memoirs, oral histories, and letters of the World War II generals. As an institution, the War College's faculty and students rarely challenged established military policy, and was unimpressive in its treatment of topics such as coalition warfare. As one historian notes, "The Army War College failed to produce a Clausewitz, Mahan, Liddell Hart, or Quincy Wright," and it contributed only marginally to advancing any theory on the phenomenon of war. Yet as with the CGSS, the War College's aim was more utilitarian. It sought to produce competent, if not necessarily brilliant, leaders who could prepare the Army for war and to fight successfully when the next conflagration came. The school's committee problem-solving method further broke down the service-branch parochialism of the interwar Army and gave officers who would never have interacted otherwise an opportunity to work together and assess the strengths and weaknesses of their future colleagues.[67]

Arguably the most important—and most innovative—instruction during the interwar era took place at the branch service schools despite the fact they theoretically occupied the lowest rung in the Army's educational system. For example, after his stint commanding West Point's artillery detachment under MacArthur and finishing as a Distinguished Graduate (forty-second out of 258 officers) in Eisenhower and Gerow's CGSS class, in 1926 Maj. Jacob Devers reported to the Field Artillery School at Fort Sill, Oklahoma, to lead the gunnery department. There, in order to get fire on targets more quickly, Devers began experimenting with letting forward observers control artillery fire from their positions since they possessed the most current and accurate picture of the battlefield. He also initiated an effort to make fire direction procedures simpler yet more effective, an effort carried on with particular energy by Maj. Orlando Ward when he took over the gunnery department in 1931. Building on the previous years' experimentation, soon after Ward's arrival his instructors developed a new fire adjustment method that allowed fires from Battalion A to be called in by observers for Battalion B so the fires from both units could be massed on a target. Under Ward's guidance, the gunnery department could place accurate fires on a target of opportunity in ten minutes, a process previously requiring hours.[68]

Yet as Stephen P. Rosen notes in his seminal work on military innovation *Winning the Next War*, tactical and strategic reforms are often stillborn without a supportive senior officer capable of providing top cover for younger officers' experiments. In the case of the gunnery department's innovators, this support was provided by Lt. Col. Lesley J. McNair, who became assistant commandant of the Field Artillery School in 1929. The traditionalists within the Field Artillery believed battery commanders should retain full control over their batteries, including the execution of fire missions. Yet McNair quickly realized the potential of the gunnery department's new techniques and their importance to future artillery commanders. As assistant commandant, he was able to shield the gunnery department from the resistance of traditional-minded senior artillery officers similar to those in the infantry and cavalry who successfully suppressed Patton and Eisenhower's experiments with tanks. Consequently, Victor Davis Hanson notes that "the United States entered the war with the best system of synchronized artillery fire in the world," and that America's inexperienced soldiers were "covered by artillery barrages more accurate and numerous than those of their enemies."[69]

Perhaps an even more significant revolution in leadership development was transpiring concurrently at the Infantry School. The renaissance at Fort Benning, however, epitomized Gibbon's observation about the role accidents and fate play in the "fortune of nations."

Upon completing his tour at Tientsin, George Marshall was assigned to the Army War College as an instructor, an assignment he had previously turned down five times. Although Lily was overjoyed by this assignment and looked forward to decorating her new home at the Washington Barracks with the vases, rugs, screens, and wall hangings they had accumulated in China, Marshall dreaded exchanging duty with troops for a desk job in the city. Adding to his concerns was Lily's deteriorating health. She had never been robust, and by August 1927 the heart condition that had plagued her throughout her life had worsened alarmingly.

The doctors at Walter Reed Hospital determined that a goitrous thyroid was aggravating her condition and required a "long and extremely serious" operation on August 22. Pershing sent her flowers in the hospital as she slowly recovered. "The heart is a slow thing to improve," she wrote to the general, "but I pray I may be back in my own house at the War College before long."[70] Although Marshall called their quarters at the War College "the pleasantest house we have had in the Army," he had done little to unpack their belongings.[71] Marshall spent his days teaching from 0900–1630 each day, then racing across town to be with Lily from 6:00 P.M. on. "George is so *wonderful* and helps me so," Lily wrote her aunt. "He puts heart and strength in me."[72] Her doctors were optimistic and expected a full recovery. Lily agreed, and told Marshall she felt stronger and healthier than she had in many years. Finally, early on the morning of September 15, the doctor told Lily she could go home the next day. Delighted at the news of her impending discharge, she started a letter to tell her mother the good news.

Marshall had just begun his lecture at 9:00 A.M. when a guard entered the hall to call him to the telephone. Marshall "spoke for a moment over the phone, then put his head on his arms in deep grief," the guard recalled. "I asked him if I could do anything for him, and he replied, 'No, Mr. Throckmorton. I just had word my wife, who was to join me here today, has just died.'"[73]

Lily Marshall never finished the letter to her mother. A nurse found her dead, slumped over her desk. The last word she wrote was "George."[74]

The War College's adjutant, Capt. Frank B. Hayne, had served under Marshall in Tientsin. When he heard the news, he tried to call his former commander at Walter Reed, but was unable to reach him. "Quite unexpectedly," Hayne recalled:

> Marshall called me at my office and asked me to meet him at his quarters. Colonel Hjalmar Erickson, who was also a close friend of the general's, joined me; and we went together to his quarters. While we were waiting in his sitting room, he came in, obviously under great emotional strain and as white as a sheet; he sat down at his desk and wrote on a piece of paper, "Make all arrangements for the funeral. Don't ask me any questions."[75]

Marshall went to his room and remained there the rest of the day.

Marshall was stricken. Lily had been the center of his life and virtually his only emotional release. Now she was gone and he was alone. At forty-seven, an age by which most men's destinies are fully shaped, Marshall's life was suddenly cast adrift. Pershing, who as a widower himself could come closest to understanding his protégé's grief, wrote from Paris: "My dear Marshall . . . No one knows better than I what such a bereavement means, and my heart goes out to you very fully at this crisis in your life. It is at such moments that we realize that our reliance must be placed in the Father who rules over us all."[76] Marshall replied:

> *My dear General: Your telegram was deeply appreciated and your letter even more so . . . The truth is, the thought of all you had endured gave me heart and hope. But twenty six years of most intimate companionship, something I have known ever since I was a mere boy, leaves me lost in my best efforts to adjust myself to future prospects in life. If I had been given to club life or other intimacies with men outside of athletic diversions, or if there was a campaign on or other pressing duty demanding a concentrated effort, then I think I could do better. However, I will find a way.*[77]

For Marshall, that "way" was inevitably through mental and physical exertion. Yet in the void left by Lily's death, Marshall suddenly found his surroundings at the War College unbearable. "At a War College desk," he confided to a friend, "I thought I would explode."[78] As was true for Eisenhower at Camp Meade in the wake of Ikky's death, memories pressed hard upon Marshall. What he needed, he told Rose Page, was a change of assignment.

Fortunately, the Army rallied to its own. Chief of Staff Charles P. Summerall, under whom Marshall had served in the closing days of World War I, offered him a choice: He could remain at the War College, transfer to Governor's Island, New York, to serve as chief of staff for a corps area, or fill the recently vacated post of assistant commandant of the Infantry School. Marshall selected Fort Benning, and by early November had left Washington, DC.[79]

"Benning was a horrible place," Troy Middleton recalled, having served there in the early 1920s. The military reservation covered nearly 100,000 acres—or 150 square miles—on the eastern shore of the Chattahoochee River. The post's size forced the Army to lay down 27 miles of narrow gauge railroad in 1924 to facilitate travel between the barracks and the various training areas and ranges. The ground was so sandy that marching troops had to take three steps to gain two, and after an hour in the oppressive Georgia heat they looked "as if they had been stuccoed" as sweat bonded sand to their uniforms.[80] There were nearly 6,000 troops stationed at Benning: the 29th Infantry, which was used primarily for demonstrations and tests; the 24th Infantry, which was used for labor and construction; various special units such as artillery, armor, engineers, and signal companies attached to the Infantry School; the small Department of Experimentation; and the Academic Department. Throughout the 1920s Benning resembled a construction site more than a permanent Army post. In 1929 the inspector general noted the Academic Department's poor location and "unattractive housing" and the fact that almost 200 student officers could not find accommodations on base and were forced to pay the prohibitively high rents in nearby Columbus.[81]

The sparse amenities notwithstanding, Fort Benning was the heart and brains of the American infantry. When Marshall became assistant commandant on November 10, 1927, the Infantry School was only nine years old—an amalgamation of the small arms, machine-gun, and old Fort Sill infantry schools—created to address the deficiencies in U.S. infantry tactics exposed by the war. The school was responsible for training infantry lieutenants and captains in small unit tactics and with providing refresher courses for more senior officers, as well as for officers in the National Guard and the Organized Reserves.

The commandant, Brig. Gen. Campbell King, was responsible for the entire post. Because he knew and trusted Marshall, he gave him virtual carte blanche in designing the Infantry School's academic course. Marshall fully understood the importance of his assignment and embraced his authority. While with the 15th Infantry in Tientsin, he had participated in a regimental field exercise in which a young officer who was supposed to envelop the flank of an enemy became paralyzed because he could not draft a written order for seventy men on the basis of the incomplete terrain data given to him. "I learnt that he had stood first at Benning," Marshall recalled. "I then and there formed an intense desire to get my hands on Benning. The man was no fool, but he had been taught an absurd system."[82] Marshall was determined to rectify these inadequacies in doctrine and training, and he now had the authority and scope to make a difference. He enthusiastically plunged into his new assignment, and his subsequent five-year tenure at the Infantry School has come to be known as the "Benning Renaissance."

Marshall wanted to disseminate the ideas Pershing had developed during the war, particularly the concept of combat built upon firepower and maneuverability. Although he had never studied the classics of military thought or engaged in academic debates over military theory, Marshall *had* devoted considerable thought to the nature of the next war. "Picture the opening campaign of a war," he said in a lecture:

> *It is a cloud of uncertainties, haste, rapid movements, congestion on the roads, strange terrain, lack of ammunition and supplies at the right place at the right moment, failures of communications, terrific tests of endurance, and misunderstandings in direct proportion to the inexperience of the officers and the aggressive action of the enemy. Add to this a minimum of preliminary information on the enemy and of his dispositions, poor maps, and a speed of movement or an alteration of the situation, resulting from fast flying planes, fast moving tanks, armored cars, and motor transportation in general. There you have warfare of movement such as swept over Belgium or Northern France in 1914, but at far greater speed. That, gentlemen, is what you are supposed to be preparing for.*[83]

Under the previous system at Benning the officer was trained to solve a book situation on the basis of information about the enemy and terrain far more complete than was available on a real battlefield. Conversely, Marshall wrote, the leader "must be prepared to take prompt and decisive action in spite of the scarcity or total absence of reliable information. He must learn that in war, the abnormal is normal and that uncertainty is certain."[84]

Marshall was therefore constantly trying to toss the unexpected at the student officers. One class was dismayed when one morning Marshall required each of them to draw a sketch map of the route they had followed to the classroom, locating both natural and man-made terrain features. The point Marshall hoped to drive home was that a well-trained troop leader's mind was constantly attuned to the relevant military details of any situation in which he may suddenly be required to make a command decision. Marshall further believed that the Army's "equipment, administrative procedure and training requirements" were too complicated for anyone but professionals. Instead, he believed, "We must develop a technique and methods so simple and so brief that the citizen officer of good common sense can readily grasp the idea."[85] He deemphasized paperwork and detailed orders from higher headquarters so that battalions or smaller units could seize opportunities as they arose, and he insisted that orders and intelligence assessments not exceed one page. Moreover, Marshall stressed what in today's vernacular is often called the "90 percent solution," namely that a workable decision arrived at quickly was superior to the perfect tactic discovered after the opportunity to use it had passed. Indeed, "the real problem," he said, "is usually *when* to make a decision and not *what* the decision should be."[86]

Marshall's thinking was embodied in the manual of small-unit tactical lessons produced by the Infantry School's Tactical Section. Marshall had directed the officers in the Advanced Course to undertake a study of the AEF's operations in France to determine lessons learned—and those not learned—and to distill new tactics for infantry combat. These lessons were eventually published as *Infantry in Battle*. In the introduction, Marshall wrote: "By the use of numerous historical examples which tell of the absence of information, the lack of time, and the confusion of battle the reader is acquainted with the realities of war and the extremely difficult conditions under which tactical problems must be solved in the face of the enemy."[87] The book was a critical success. Basil Liddell Hart called it "the most valuable instructional military textbook. . . . published in many years," and *Infantry in Battle* was translated into German, Spanish, and Russian.[88]

To enact these reforms, however, Marshall first had to indoctrinate his staff of eighty instructors in his vision. Unfortunately, the Infantry School's faculty "had become unconscious creatures of technique," and Marshall had to undertake "an almost complete revamping of the instruction."[89] Striving to simplify, he demanded that his instructors "expunge the bunk."[90] He recalled to his biographer Forrest Pogue: "I had a terrible time getting instructors to simplify these things, because they'd had this elaborate Leavenworth training."[91] Marshall moved quickly to break the mold. One of his first directives was that "Any student's solution to a problem that ran radically counter to the approved school solution, and yet showed independent creative thinking, would be published to the class." When he took over the Infantry School's tactical section, Joseph Stilwell put it more bluntly, declaring himself open to any "screwball idea."[92] Once Marshall sat in on a tactics class when a young maverick—1st Lt. Charles T. "Buck" Lanham—disagreed with the school solution and offered his own. When the instructor disparaged Lanham's approach, Marshall stepped forward, "briskly demolished the instructor's solution, and praised Lanham's version." Collins noted that Marshall's edict, not to mention his example, helped to create "the spirit at Benning, which was a marvelous thing, because if anybody had any new ideas he was willing to try them instead of saying, 'Why don't you let the thing alone instead of stirring things up.'"[93]

Prior to Marshall's arrival, instructors read canned lectures that had been screened by the Editorial Section to guarantee conformity with approved doctrine. To combat such blind reliance on the book, Marshall recalled:

> *I finally forbade any reading and allowed them to have a card to note down the principal factors, but when I heard an instructor say one morning, "I am required this morning to discuss"—and then look down at his card to see what to discuss—it was merely a nervous gesture—I suppressed the card too, because I found it was many times more effective when a man talked off the cuff.*[94]

This was not an easy adjustment for even the most talented instructors. Although Omar Bradley was a natural teacher, he was not a gifted orator. When he joined the faculty in 1929, for his first lecture he drew up several cards with subject matter headings in large letters and placed them on the floor at his feet. That was the first and last time he cheated, however. Bradley soon realized he knew his material well enough that he did not need the crib sheets.[95]

Marshall stressed that "junior officers don't fight at their desks," so consequently 80 percent of learning was done in the field. He ended rehearsed tactical demonstrations and replaced them with unscripted field maneuvers. Matthew Ridgway, who returned for the Advanced Course under Marshall, remembered: "Many a time, in Infantry School, I had been given such a problem. A map would be thrust before me. 'You are here,' I was told. 'The enemy is here. The tactical situation is thus and so (it was always bad). Your battalion commander has been killed. You are now in command. What do you do?'"[96] Courtney Hodges recalled that "Marshall was extremely active. He was present at most of the field exercises."[97] Stilwell also left classroom lecturing largely to subordinates, but supervised every tactical exercise personally. They often provided poor maps or no maps for problems and maneuvers to simulate the confusion of a real battlefield, and constantly emphasized thoughtful and original responses to the unexpected. Once, after a 17-mile cross-country ride, Marshall ordered the student officers to dismount and draw a map of the terrain covered to help them "think on their feet."[98] Ridgway later recalled that such exercises created a "mental conditioning more important to a combat officer than any number of learned techniques."[99]

While some instructors eagerly embraced these reforms, many were reluctant to change. Those who would not—or could not—adapt were quickly replaced. Marshall needed men on his staff willing to experiment, to accept new solutions, and to encourage the unorthodox if it showed the student was thinking for himself. Yet if Marshall earned a reputation for ruthlessness with regard to personnel, he also made a significant effort to identify talented young officers and groom them for the highest levels of command. He assembled a four-man academic team to carry out his reforms: Stilwell headed the First Section, Tactics; Lt. Col. Morrison C. Stayer was in charge of Second Section, Logistics; Lt. Col. Ralph W. Kingman headed the Third Section, Weapons; and his friend Maj. E. Forrest Harding oversaw Fourth Section, History and Publications. Bradley noted that these men shared Marshall's "keen analytic intelligence, outspokenness, ingenuity. In sum, they were, like Marshall, highly creative."[100]

This was especially true of Stilwell, whom Marshall wanted so badly as head of the Tactical Section that he held the position open for a year until Stilwell was available. Marshall described Stilwell as possessing "a genius for instruction" and called him "one of the exceptionally brilliant and cultured men of the army" who was "ahead of his period in tactics and techniques."[101] At the same time, however, Bradley—who served under Stilwell for a year in the tactical section before succeeding Kingman—added that his superior was "one of the most challenging, difficult, and interesting personalities I ever encountered."[102] When he encountered stupidity or incompetence, Stilwell was unforgiving. Once, after a particularly caustic critique of a field exercise, a student officer drew a caricature of Stilwell with an unkind expression rising from a vinegar bottle with three Xs on the label. It was pinned on a bulletin board at the Infantry School, where it was widely appreciated. His occasionally acidic demeanor notwithstanding, Stilwell was both self-aware and had a sense of humor. He asked if he could keep the original and had photographs made of it which he sent to all his friends, hence the moniker "Vinegar" Joe.[103] On three separate occasions Marshall had to convince Brigadier General King not to relieve his difficult friend, who Bradley further described as "brilliant, professional, visionary, ingenious, aesthetic, athletic."[104]

Marshall continued his search for talented subordinates even in his final year at the Infantry School. In December 1931, Capt. Walter Bedell "Beetle" Smith, a veteran of combat in France who had been commissioned through the National Guard, was delivering a briefing on his experiences in the

Aisne-Marne offensive, which he said typified "the partially trained American Army of 1918 ... and the troops which American officers may expect to command in the early stages of any future war." In the twenty minutes allotted he provided a cogent and gripping narrative of events, from which he drew two clear lessons: the unexpected is the rule in war, and "success utterly depended" on small-unit initiative. Marshall happened to slip into the classroom as Smith began his talk, and the captain's presentation—to include tactical questions he asked his audience—and conclusions perfectly echoed his views. Marshall returned to his office and told another officer: "There is a man who would make a wonderful instructor and I'll bet no one has asked for him."[105]

In fact, Bradley had already gotten to know Smith quite well on the trapshooting range. He found the young captain to be "brittle, like Stilwell, a bit of a Prussian, and brutally frank." Yet the more time he spent with Smith the more strongly he felt the advance course student officer would make an excellent instructor. Thus, unbeknownst to Marshall when he inquired about Smith joining the faculty, Bradley's official request for Smith to serve as an instructor in his weapons section was already on the assistant commandant's desk. "No words were exchanged between us," Bradley recalled over three decades later, "but I was elated. I had 'discovered' Smith before he had."[106]

Marshall's recruitment efforts were not always so successful. In 1930, Pershing asked him to review the manuscript of his World War I memoirs, which were to be published the next year. The memoirs were little more than an expanded version of Pershing's daily diary, which made it impossible to tell the stories of the longer battles in a clear, coherent fashion. A young major on Pershing's staff at the Battle Monuments Commission, whose writing abilities the general respected, suggested Pershing substitute a narrative style for the accounts of the St. Mihiel and Meuse-Argonne battles. Pershing thought this was a good idea and, subsequently, asked the officer to write a draft of the chapters along those lines. Pershing liked the major's revisions, but said that "in such matters ... he always looked to one man to give him final advice. That man was Colonel George C. Marshall."[107]

Marshall went to Washington and read the revised manuscript. After conferring with Pershing in the general's office, Marshall went to the major's office. He declined the younger officer's invitation to sit down. "I think they're interesting," he said of the rewritten chapters. "Nevertheless, I've advised General Pershing to stick with his original idea. I think to break up the format right at the climax of the war would be a mistake."

The major nodded and said he understood that continuity was important, but added, "I still think that each of the two battles ought to be treated as a single narrative with the proper annotations to give it authenticity."

Marshall replied that this was a good idea, but brought the discussion to an end by stating that "Pershing would be happier if he stayed with the original scheme."[108]

Despite their disagreement, Marshall was impressed by the major, and upon returning to Benning sent the officer an offer to join the Infantry School's faculty. Yet because he already had orders for a coveted assignment with the General Staff, Dwight D. Eisenhower politely declined Marshall's invitation.

Marshall did more than just identify talented officers, however. He took his role as a mentor charged with developing his subordinates' leadership potential seriously. Much as Fox Conner had done with Eisenhower in Panama, Bradley, Stilwell, Collins, Bolte, and Chynoweth were amongst the instructors Marshall would summon to his quarters for discussions on the art of leading men in battle. Marshall or Maj. Gilbert Cook (who would command a corps in Europe under Patton during World War II) would assign a book or study—frequently on a non-military subject such as psychology, sociology, or economics, but sometimes on military history—and one or two of the group would deliver a report on the work's relevance to contemporary military problems. As Collins noted, "A lively discussion always followed."[109]

Although, as Bradley noted, Marshall outwardly "was austere, cold, aloof, succinct, prudish," off-duty he "had a discernible warmth and moderate sense of fun."[110] Collins said he "always felt at ease" with Marshall, who despite his "seemingly formidable appearance . . . was always accessible."[111] Courtney Hodges, whom the assistant commandant recruited to teach in the tactical section under Stilwell, recalled Marshall as "very sociable," and together with Bradley frequently went hunting with the assistant commandant.[112] Indeed, in his memoirs, Bradley described Marshall as "the most impressive man I ever knew," and stated that "no man had a greater influence on me personally or professionally."[113]

Although Marshall noted the move to Benning "was magical" and gave him "hundreds of interests, an unlimited field of activity, delightful associates, and all outdoors to play in," some hurts cannot be escaped so easily.[114] Shortly after Lily's death, even as strong-willed a soul as Marshall let his guard down and confessed to sixteen-year-old Rose Page: "Rose, I'm so lonely, so lonely." This loneliness stayed with him at Benning, where the nights and weekends hung heavy on him. Despite the presence of friends like Stilwell and Harding, Marshall remained mired in the grip of personal tragedy. One instructor at the Infantry School recalled that Marshall "seemed to live under a cloud of sorrow at Fort Benning."[115] Every room in his house was filled with pictures of Lily, constantly reminding him of his loss. He strove not to be alone, and in his letters he was persistently imploring friends to visit him at Benning.* Under the strain of constant work and his loneliness during his first years at Benning, Marshall lost weight, and his lean, bony face became more drawn and plain than ever.[116]

Sometime in the spring or early summer of 1929, Marshall received an invitation to a dinner party with his friends Mr. and Mrs. Tom Hudson who lived in Columbus. There Marshall was introduced to Katherine Boyce Tupper Brown, a forty-seven-year-old former actress and widow visiting from Baltimore. Marshall was standing by the fireplace when Mrs. Brown entered the room. "My first impression was of a tall, slender man with sandy hair and deep-set eyes," she later recalled. They immediately fell into an easy, bantering conversation that lasted the rest of the evening. Mrs. Brown was taken with the officer, with his imposing stature and his "way of looking right straight through you."[117]

At the end of the evening Marshall offered to drive Mrs. Brown home. She was staying with the mother of a college friend, and Marshall assured her he knew where the Blanchard residence was. The pair chatted as Marshall drove through the small town's darkened streets. Finally, after an hour, Mrs. Brown asked, "How long have you been at Fort Benning?"

"Two years," Marshall replied.

"Well, after two years, haven't you learned your way around Columbus?"

---

* Some examples of this pleading include:
  • To John M. Palmer, in December, 1927: "If you feel the need of going into retire for rest or writing, I think my house is just the place for you. You can fish, shoot, find lovely walks, or hunt wildcats."
  • To Brig. Gen. William H. Cocke, in January, 1929: "P.S. Is there any chance of your visiting me this spring?"
  • To Brig. Gen. Frank McCoy, in April 1929: "I wish you could stop here en route to San Antonio."
  • To Pershing in June 1929: "Please try and arrange to make me a visit this winter when the climate is most unfavorable in the north and delightful here."
See Bland, *The Papers of George Catlett Marshall*, Vol. I, 321, 341, 343.

"Extremely well," Marshall said, "or I could not have stayed off the block where Mrs. Blanchard lives!"[118]

The next day Marshall invited her to a reception on post, and when she demurred he sent a soldier in a car to get her. She came, and Marshall once again monopolized her at the reception. By the end of the day, with Mrs. Brown set to return to Baltimore, they had agreed to exchange letters.

They corresponded throughout the summer, and Marshall arranged another invitation for Mrs. Brown to visit Columbus. When she returned in the spring of 1930, Marshall cleared his schedule and devoted himself to her. By the end of the visit, Katherine considered them to be "tentatively engaged" pending the approval of her children, which she insisted upon. She had three children—Molly, sixteen; Clifton, fifteen; and Allen, twelve—whose father was a lawyer in Baltimore murdered in June 1928 by an irate client, and Katherine was understandably unsure of their acceptance of a stepfather. Indeed, Allen was initially dismayed, telling his mother, "I don't know about that, we are happy as we are." He reconsidered, however, and subsequently wrote to Marshall that "I hope you will come to Fire Island. Don't be nervous, it is okay with me." It was signed, "A friend in need is a friend indeed. Allen Brown."[119] Marshall spent five weeks with the Browns on Fire Island. On August 1, he wrote to Pershing to tell him he would be getting married in October, the first person he told of his impending nuptials after his sister.

Pershing stood as best man at the October 15 wedding in Baltimore. In fact, despite Marshall's many friends in the War Department and at the War College, Pershing was the only Washington, DC, friend invited to the small ceremony. Unfortunately, Pershing was spotted disembarking at Baltimore's train station, and what was supposed to be a quiet affair ended up drawing reporters and a large, unruly crowd. The unintended spectacle of their wedding day aside, Katherine Marshall would provide her husband with the emotional stability he needed, as well as with a ready-made family. Previously childless because of Lily's frail health, Marshall had always possessed a soft spot for children, whether it was the young Rose Page in Washington during the War Department years, Stilwell's children in China, or James Van Fleet's son Jimmy, whom Marshall allowed to chase golf balls when he was chipping shots in his yard at Benning. Unlike MacArthur, who was disinclined toward bonding with his stepchildren, Marshall fit easily and comfortably in his role as stepfather to Katherine's children, and achieved a significant degree of emotional fulfillment from them.[120]

Still, some things about Marshall remained unchanged by matrimony. "We hoped," Bradley recalled, that the assistant commandant's second marriage "would mellow and 'humanize'" him. "Katherine was charming and gracious," he said, and "it was obvious that they were deeply in love." Yet the hoped for mellowing did not occur. Marshall, Bradley wrote, "remained his same, formal, aloof self."[121]

Even if he remained aloof, Marshall's contemporaries nevertheless gave him full credit for the Benning Renaissance. Joseph D. Patch, an instructor during GCM's first year, later wrote: "In my opinion Col. Marshall did more for The Infantry School than anyone who ever served there. We were in a 'slump' and he pulled us out and ran the instruction on a realistic and practical basis. His tactical problems were based on real occurrences."[122] Although Marshall refused to take credit, Harding concurred that the initiative at Benning was Marshall's: "He would tell you what he wanted and then you would do it. There was something about him that made you do it, and of course you wanted to do it the way he wanted—which is the trait of a commanding officer."[123] Brigadier General King certainly agreed with these assessments. Because army regulations required that officers below the general officer rank had to serve in troop leading positions at least one in every five years, the Infantry School commandant issued a special order on April 25, 1931, assigning Marshall as the 24th Infantry's executive officer "for duty with troops, in addition to his other duties." This was, of course, the same position that Eisenhower had been rescued from in 1925. But this time the assignment was on paper only, a bureaucratic evasion intended to retain Marshall's services at the Infantry School beyond June 30, 1931.[124]

With the end of the school year in June 1932, however, Marshall was reassigned to Fort Screven, Georgia, "an unimportant station in the Army's scheme of things," he wrote to Pershing. But his impact had been made. One hundred and fifty future generals attended the Infantry School during Marshall's tenure, and another fifty served on the faculty. "Equally important," Bradley thought, "was the imaginative training Marshall imparted to the countless hundreds of junior officers who passed through the school during his time and who would lead—often brilliantly—the regiments and battalions under the command of those generals."[125] Even Muth, who is extremely critical of professional military education and leadership development in the interwar Army, concludes: "The only highlight of the U.S. Army's educational system in the first decades of the twentieth century was the Infantry School and then only when George C. Marshall was the assistant commander."[126]

The extended consequences of the education of these officers who would occupy senior command and staff positions in World War II had a greater impact than any of the manuals, supply techniques, or tactics that emerged from the Infantry School during these years.

This was Marshall's doing, to be sure, but it only came about due to the tragic accident of Lily's death that necessitated his transfer away from the War College.

The fortune of nations was indeed dependent upon accidents and fate.

CHAPTER SIX

The Army in the Great Depression

WHILE COMMANDING THE PHILIPPINE DEPARTMENT, DOUGLAS MACARTHUR kept one eye north across the Philippine Sea on Japan, and another halfway across the world on Washington, DC, where Army chief of staff Gen. Charles Summerall was due to reach the mandatory retirement age in March 1931. In July 1929 Summerall had cabled MacArthur that President Herbert Hoover wanted to appoint him as chief of Engineers, his original service branch. Despite the position's prestige, MacArthur turned the president down. In his memoirs he claimed he did not merit the position because he was not a talented enough engineer to ever gain the Corps of Engineers' confidence. But his correspondent friend Frazier Hunt was probably closer to the truth when he concluded MacArthur desperately hoped to succeed Summerall and was aware that "if he accepted the appointment, he would set a road block against his chances of ever being made Chief of Staff."[1]

Although he risked antagonizing Hoover, MacArthur's decision to accept West Point's superintendency a decade earlier—which allowed him to maintain his rank of brigadier general while his peers reverted to their prewar ranks—gave him the inside track to succeed Summerall. By 1930 MacArthur ranked seventh in seniority amongst the Army's major generals, but none of the six generals ahead of him had more than two years remaining before reaching the compulsory retirement age of sixty-four. This seniority did not guarantee MacArthur's appointment, however, especially given his previous slight of President Hoover. MacArthur needed allies to influence Hoover's decision, and particularly the support of the secretary of war, Patrick J. Hurley. Hurley was a "colorful, handsome, rich" young lawyer from Oklahoma with political ambitions of his own. He was skeptical, however, when Summerall proposed MacArthur as his possible successor. "A man who couldn't hold his woman shouldn't be Chief of Staff," Hurley said.[2] When Johnson

Hagood, now commander of the VII Corps Area, sang MacArthur's praises to him, Hurley replied: "Isn't he vain? Isn't he pompous? Intolerant of his superiors' wishes and overbearing towards civilians?"[3]

MacArthur *was* all those things. But he was also shrewd enough not to let his massive ego get in the way of his limitless ambition. When Hurley sent a routine communication on the Philippines to the Senate in 1930, MacArthur sent the secretary of war a congratulatory letter:

> *I have just read in the local papers your letter . . . and I cannot refrain from expressing to you the unbounded admiration it has caused me. It is the most comprehensive and statesmanlike paper that has ever been presented with reference to this complex and perplexing problem. At one stroke it has clarified issues which have perplexed and embarrassed statesmen for the last thirty years. If nothing else had ever been written upon the subject, your treatise would be complete and absolute. It leaves nothing to be said and has brought confidence and hope out of the morass of chaos and confusion which has existed in the minds of millions of people. It is the most statesmanlike utterance that has emanated from the American Government in many decades and renews in the hearts of many of us our confirmed faith in American principles and ideals. You have done a great and courageous piece of work and I am sure that the United States intends even greater things for you in the future. Please accept my heartiest congratulations not only for yourself personally but the great nation to which we both belong.*[4]

The letter's overbearing sycophancy worked on the vain secretary, who was suddenly convinced of MacArthur's wisdom and insight.

In addition to Hurley's conversion and Summerall's recommendation, Peyton March personally lobbied President Hoover for MacArthur's appointment. Consequently, the acting chief of staff sent a radiogram to Manila on August 5, 1930: "President has just announced your detail as Chief of Staff to succeed General Summerall. My heartiest congratulations."[5] His previous doubts notwithstanding, Hoover stated he had "searched the army for younger blood" and "finally determined upon General Douglas MacArthur. His brilliant abilities and a sterling character need no exposition from me."[6] Despite attaining the one honor to elude his father, MacArthur admitted: "I did not want to return to Washington, even though it meant the four stars of a general, and my first inclination was to try and beg off." He shared his doubts with his mother via telegram. Pinky MacArthur told her son to accept the position. He recalled, "She said my father would be ashamed if I showed timidity."[7]

Thus, on November 21, 1930, MacArthur was sworn in as the youngest chief of staff in the Army's history.

"I knew the dreadful ordeal that faced the new Chief of Staff," MacArthur would later write of his momentary indecision, "and shrank from it."[8] MacArthur's trepidation was justified. Although the 1920 NDA had envisioned a 280,000-man force, by 1930 the Army had fallen in strength to just 132,069 men, making it the sixteenth largest army in the world, less than Portugal or Greece. The Army was still living on World War I stocks. It employed trench mortars, worn-out French 75mm field guns, and used its .50-caliber machine guns as both an antitank and antiaircraft weapon. Only twelve postwar tanks were in service, and new rifles had not gone into production because the Army's warehouses were still overstocked with outdated 1903 Springfields. Moreover, MacArthur was taking command just as pacifism and isolationism were gaining ascendency with the American public. The 1928 Kellogg-Briand Pact had supposedly outlawed war, an illusion the American people willed themselves into believing, and the late 1920s and early 1930s saw the heyday of popular antiwar literature. Thus, as one historian notes, the Army MacArthur inherited was "understrength and underfunded, outdated in its doctrine and equipment, stagnant in promotions, untrained at division and higher levels, and largely without purpose, hope, or new ideas."[9]

Although the Great Depression would further erode the already diminished support for military spending, the Army's budget difficulties started before Black Tuesday and the October 1929 stock market crash. Throughout the 1920s the services' professional journals reflected concerns over seemingly trivial financial issues. Resources were so scarce that the chief of infantry took to the pages of the *Infantry Journal* in June 1923 to ask infantrymen to try to properly maintain typewriters and wring as much use out of their parts as possible. ("Think of what it means when all the orderly rooms in the Infantry want a new ribbon.")[10] Both the Democratic and Republican presidential candidates in 1928 had promised to reduce taxes, and although the Hoover Administration did not face any budget deficits until after Fiscal Year (FY) 1930 (June 30, 1930), Hoover had been tightening the government's fiscal belt even before the crash.

In the summer of 1929 President Hoover called his military advisers together and ordered a thorough survey of all military activities in order to reduce expenditures. The Army's leadership accepted the need for reduced spending to balance the federal budget, and the War Department General Staff prepared a report offering the Hoover Administration three options. The Hoover Administration chose the golden mean of the Army's "Plan II," and eventually $367 million was appropriated for FY 1931.[11] In July 1930, however, the president notified Secretary Hurley that he wanted to reduce the spending of funds already appropriated for FY 1931. Faced with the prospect of the bottom dropping out of the U.S. economy, Hoover said it was of the "utmost importance that government outlays for procurement be reduced in every possible way," and the War Department was admonished that—in addition to minor administrative savings—it was desirable to defer expenditure on major programs until "such time as government revenues have recovered."[12] The assistant secretary of war, Frederick H. Payne, replied on September 15 that the Army could withhold $20 million from total military and non-military expenditures for FY 1931. Yet Hoover's limiting figure of $444 million for both military and non-military funds* meant that War Department spending for FY 1931 would be about $65 million less than the appropriated figure of $509 million.[13]

This budgetary downward spiral continued after MacArthur succeeded Summerall. In May 1931 President Hoover summoned the new chief of staff and Secretary Hurley to his retreat in Rapidan, Virginia. By now the economy was in freefall, and with an impending budget deficit for FY 1931, the desperate president asked Hurley and MacArthur to find ways to immediately reduce military spending. Before the ascent of Keynesian economics and its acceptance of deficit spending, balanced budgets were considered the soundest way to restore the economy in a recession. Hoover therefore suggested imposing a round of forced retirements to reduce personnel costs and urged closing as many semi-active installations as possible. Despite MacArthur's misgivings, later that month the War Department announced the shuttering of fifty-three posts, most of which had garrisons below company size. Although personnel reductions were a sensitive subject for the Army, the General Staff also directed sweeping cutbacks in the personnel assigned to

---

* In addition to the Army's specific military activities, the War Department was charged with numerous non-military activities during the interwar years, including the improvement of rivers and harbors and flood control activities under the Corps of Engineers' direction. Hence, the total War Department appropriations were greater than Army's appropriations.

various corps areas and department headquarters in order to alleviate some of the pressure from the White House. This reduced the Army's end strength by 6,000 officers and enlisted men.[14]

Hoover's austerity measures were only the beginning, however. MacArthur arrived back in Washington just as a battle was brewing in Congress over the budget and the military's priorities that would quickly overshadow the Hoover Administration's cutbacks. Democrats had won forty House seats in the 1930 mid-term elections and gained control of the House when several Republican legislators died in early 1931. The Democrats knew the issue of the budget deficit and reduced military expenditures provided them with political ammunition to use against Hoover heading into the 1932 elections. Consequently, when the military appropriations bill came before Congress in December 1931, Democratic critics of the president were determined to reduce government expenditures through major cuts to the Army's budget. The House Subcommittee on Military Appropriations budget hearings began in late 1931, with MacArthur advocating for the War Department's position.[15]

MacArthur's primary antagonist in these showdowns was Representative Ross A. Collins of Mississippi, the subcommittee's chairman. Collins was "a quiet-mannered man who speaks softly and with a slow drawl," one reporter noted, but added that the Democrat was also a "master of political satire."[16] Collins refused to be awed by MacArthur's fame or service record, warning the chief of staff: "The day has passed when a General Staff can overawe legislators or browbeat the common man by presuming to have inside information or superior knowledge of existing military conditions in other countries."[17] MacArthur found himself fighting an uphill battle in Congress, and even his immaculate appearance and strict military bearing were held against him. Before one appropriations subcommittee hearing, then–Lieutenant Colonel George Kenney (who as a lieutenant general in World War II commanded MacArthur's air forces in the Pacific theater) overheard one congressman remark to another, "Well, it's about time to go over and hear what the Dude has to say."[18]

Representative Collins argued that given an expected deficit of $2 billion for FY 1933, it was necessary to reduce spending in order to keep the budget balanced and preserve "national integrity." MacArthur's testimony reaffirmed the General Staff's intention to reduce costs. He further noted that savings had been made by limiting all maintenance and repair projects and by postponing critical augmentation and improvement of equipment. He added that the increased pay and allowances appearing in the War Department's FY 1933 budget estimates were non-discretionary and specified by law. This led the subcommittee to conclude that if reductions were to be made, they would have to come from cutting down on personnel, both officers and enlisted.[19]

This set the stage for what the publisher of the *Army Navy Journal* called "one of the most serious crises since the Civil War."[20] The Hoover Administration's Budget Bureau had already slashed the War Department's request for $331 million by $15 million. Yet when Representative Collins's bill was reported out of committee to the House on May 5, 1932, the Army's appropriations were cut again to $281 million. Worse, from the Army's point-of-view, Collins inserted a clause into the budget that would impose a reduction of 2,000 officers. To MacArthur, it seemed as if the Army's very survival was at stake.[21]

In desperation, on May 9 MacArthur released a letter he sent to the House minority leader—Representative Bertrand D. Snell—reviewing the proposed officer reductions. "As the military adviser of the Government," MacArthur justified this unprecedented correspondence, writing:

> *I am ... taking the liberty of presenting to you the views of the General Staff on this important matter, with the hope that you will lay them before the House.*
>
> *Skilled officers, like all other professional men, are products of continuous and laborious study, training and experience. There is no short cut to the peculiar type of knowledge and ability they must possess. Trained officers constitute the most vitally essential element in modern war, and the only one that under no circumstances can be improvised or extemporized.*
>
> *An army can live on short rations, it can be insufficiently clothed and housed, it can even be poorly armed and equipped, but in action it is doomed to destruction without the trained and adequate leadership of officers. An efficient and sufficient corps of officers means the difference between victory and defeat.*

MacArthur urged that no reductions be made, as this would bring the country close to a condition "not conducive to security at home nor respect abroad."[22] Despite MacArthur's plea, the Democratic leadership of the House supported the bill, which passed 201–182.

MacArthur was not about to surrender, however. He repeatedly trekked to Capitol Hill to charm and cajole individual congressmen. As a result of his lobbying effort, on June 9 the Senate defeated the House bill. On July 12 Representative Collins sought to override the Senate vote and have the House reject the Senate amendment, but was defeated. It was a somewhat bittersweet victory, as the final appropriation for FY 1933 of $305 million was the Army's lowest since 1923. Nevertheless, MacArthur viewed Collins's attempt to reduce the officer corps as a vital threat aimed at the military's essential efficiency. In his annual report, he wrote: "No other attack aimed exclusively at the Army was so severely calculated to accomplish the disastrous emasculation of our defensive system as this one."[23]

Collins's proposal for reducing the Army's size did not stem from emotional pacifism or anti-militarism, however. Instead, he was an adherent of British military theorist B. H. Liddell Hart, an advocate of airpower and mechanization. Collins worried that the Army was not moving forward fast enough in policy and plans toward modernization of doctrine and organization. On May 10, 1932, he delivered a three-hour rebuttal on the House floor to MacArthur's open letter. He proclaimed that while other nations were moving toward modernization, the American Army and General Staff were "utterly unable to lift ourselves out of the rut and apply new principles to military science in the United States." Collins declared that widespread mechanization of the Army was needed and that money should be spent on tanks, modern guns, and planes, not on the wasteful civilian components and the "transient training of schoolboys." Denying the continued relevance or value of the mass "citizen" army, he championed the concept that the "defense of this country lies in the utilization of science and warfare by a comparatively small army of trained experts." Thus, he urged Congress to forget the expensive training of the masses and to shift the military's already anorexic budget to scientific advancement and mechanized means of defense.[24]

His ardent defense of the officer corps and the role of the Regular Army in training the civilian components notwithstanding, MacArthur was aware of airpower and armor's potential role in future wars. The chief of staff attended the French army maneuvers in 1931 near Thiems, where he had fought in 1918. "The next war is certain to be one of maneuver and movement," he reported to Secretary Hurley. "The nation that does not command the air will face deadly odds."[25] Yet technological advancement was difficult without consistent funding, and the obsolescence rate for military equipment in rapidly evolving fields such as air and armored warfare meant materiel scheduled in FY 1932 for procurement in FY 1934 might be obsolete by the time it was fielded in combat units. Under present conditions, MacArthur told the House Military Affairs Committee, "any attempt to maintain large units equipped with the latest and most efficient models of combat vehicles would entail the replacements of great amounts of equipment every few years. Manifestly the expense of such a procedure would be enormous."[26] Hence, with the limited funds available, MacArthur hesitated to rush toward mechanization and motorization.

This caution culminated in MacArthur's decision in May 1931 to disband Maj. Adna R. Chaffee's experimental Mechanized Force after just three years of existence. Given the extreme expenses involved, adequate funds to equip and organize an independent armored force would seemingly never be forthcoming, leading MacArthur to conclude it would be more economical to allow each traditional branch—infantry, cavalry, and field artillery—to develop its armored vehicles separately. Unfortunately, this decentralization retarded the development of modern tanks and caused the U.S. Army to fall far behind equally impoverished future adversaries in the development of armored tactics.[27]

Thus, when Collins excoriated MacArthur during the November 1932 hearings on the 1934 budget for failing to procure more tanks, the criticism was not strictly personal, but rather the passionate expression of an important philosophical divide on strategy. MacArthur, however, took any opposition to his views personally. In the glow of his legislative triumph over Collins earlier that year, he gloated in a cable to Assistant Secretary Payne: "Just hogtied a Mississippi cracker. House voted our way one seventy-five to fifty-four. Happy times are here again. /s/MacArthur."[28]

In reality, "happy times" had not arrived, nor was there even a glimpse of the proverbial light at the end of the tunnel. Any hope that the Hoover Administration would increase military estimates for FY 1934 were shattered in September 1932 when the president once again asked the War Department for further reductions. In December the Hoover Administration delivered its final budget to Congress, providing $277.7 million for military activities, $43.2 million less than the War Department's request, and a sharp reduction from the $305.7 million the Army had received for FY 1933. The reduction especially hurt the civilian components, with the CMTC (Citizens' Military Training Camps) and ROTC severely curtailed, and the National Guard's drill schedule cut in half. With the Army's authorized strength falling to

130,000 enlisted men and 12,000 officers, MacArthur said flatly that this was "below the point of safety."[29]

The Army's budget woes went from bad to worse with Franklin Delano Roosevelt's election in 1932. Throughout the campaign, Roosevelt had shrewdly avoided any discussion of international affairs and national defense, thereby keeping the electorate's focus on the Depression and making the election a referendum on Hoover's stewardship of the economy. Although MacArthur—filling in for an ailing General Pershing—led Roosevelt's inaugural parade, he knew his Republican friends were leaving town and that the new administration would soon target military appropriations. The New Deal's "liberal reform" faction opposed the "peace through strength" theory that underpinned U.S. national security strategy, and instead subscribed to the misguided belief that increased military expenditures led to arms races which subsequently led to escalated international tensions and inexorably to war. To serve as secretary of war, Roosevelt appointed Utah governor George Dern. A large, affable man, Dern's background was in mining, and he had no prior experience or interest in military affairs. As Geoffrey Perret notes, "The fact that someone like Dern got this appointment indicated how little importance Roosevelt attached to the military at the start of his administration."[30]

Roosevelt's staff held MacArthur in particular disdain, describing the chief of staff as a "martinet," "polished popinjay," "bellicose swashbuckler," and "warmonger."[31] The president had himself called MacArthur "one of the two most dangerous men in the country." (The other was Louisiana's demagogic senator Huey Long.) Roosevelt had worked with MacArthur while serving as assistant secretary of the navy in the Wilson Administration, and acknowledged his intelligence and brilliant service record. "I've known Doug for years," he explained to Rexford G. Tugwell, the head of his brain trust. "You've never heard him talk, but I have. He has the most portentous style of anyone I know. He talks in a voice that might come from an oracle's cave. He never doubts and never argues or suggests; he makes pronouncements. What he thinks is final."[32] Or, as Harold Ickes, head of the New Deal's Public Works Administration wrote: "MacArthur is the type of man who thinks that when he gets to Heaven, God will step down from the great white throne and bow him into His vacated seat."[33]

The new administration inherited Hoover's FY 1934 budget. In late March, soon after the inauguration and without any prior consultation with the War Department, Lewis Douglas, Roosevelt's new director of the Budget Bureau, directed that the Army's budget for FY 1934 be reduced a further

$90 million. A month later, Roosevelt announced he was considering a plan to furlough between 3,000 and 4,000 officers. MacArthur was incensed. He demanded an appointment with the president but was denied. "Unless I have word that I can talk with President Roosevelt by one this afternoon," he replied, "I shall hand in my resignation as Chief of Staff at two and shall explain my reasons in full to the press associations at three."[34]

Roosevelt agreed to see MacArthur.

Secretary Dern accompanied the chief of staff to the meeting, and initially took the lead in the discussion. In his quiet, deliberate manner, the secretary of war explained why it would be "a fatal error" to balance the budget on the back of the Army and National Guard, especially when Germany was rearming under its new chancellor and Japan was becoming more aggressive in the Pacific. Roosevelt grew impatient, and responded to Dern's dissertation with scorn until, as MacArthur later recalled, "the Secretary grew white and silent." MacArthur interjected, bluntly stating that America's security was at stake, but Roosevelt responded with sarcasm. Then, MacArthur remembered, "The tension began to boil over."

His voice trembling with outrage, MacArthur said: "When we lose the next war, and an American boy lying in the mud with an enemy bayonet through his belly and an enemy foot on his dying throat spits out his last curse, I want the name not to be MacArthur, but Roosevelt."

Roosevelt was livid. "You must not talk that way to the President," he roared.

MacArthur quickly apologized, but "felt that my Army career was at an end." He offered his resignation and got up to leave. As he reached the door, Roosevelt's voice came "with that cool detachment which was so reflected in his extraordinary self-control," MacArthur recalled.

"Don't be foolish, Douglas," Roosevelt said. "You and the budget must get together on this."

Secretary Dern caught up to MacArthur outside and jubilantly said, "You've saved the Army."

MacArthur did not respond. Instead, having seen his career, his *destiny* pass before his eyes, he vomited on the steps of the White House.[35]

In the end, Roosevelt directed the Budget Bureau to reconsider military expenditures for FY 1934. Military appropriations were eventually raised from the original White House figure of around $196 million to $225 million. More importantly from MacArthur's perspective, the plan to furlough Regular Army officers was dropped. Nevertheless, the budget was a devastating blow to the Army's training programs and service schools, leaving the Army less prepared to fight—and to teach other men how to fight—than ever. Addressing West Point's commencement in June 1933, MacArthur warned that "As the necessity of national defense is sacrificed in the name of economy, the United States presents a tempting spectacle."[36] Later that summer, MacArthur wrote in his annual report: "It is my conviction that at this moment the Army's strength in personnel and materiel and its readiness for employment are below the danger line."[37]

Moreover, the White House subsequently took deliberate steps to isolate MacArthur. In the summer of 1933 officials from the National Guard Association and the Reserve Officers Association met with President Roosevelt and persuaded him to reinstate the full schedule of National Guard armory drills and provide additional funds for field training of reserve officers. By taking these actions without consulting the chief of staff, Roosevelt weakened the General Staff's authority over the civilian components and their representatives. MacArthur attempted to circumvent the White House and the Budget Bureau by goading Congress into fulfilling its constitutional responsibilities of raising and overseeing the Army. In response, Roosevelt curtailed the Army's independence in its relations with Congress by instructing the War Department that all contemplated legislation requiring appropriations must first be submitted to the Budget Bureau for approval.[38]

The degree to which the Roosevelt Administration sought to work around MacArthur was perhaps most evident in February 1934, when the president sent his aide James Farley to ask the Army Air Corps chief Benjamin Foulois whether the Army's planes could carry the nation's airmail. In January, Senate investigators had found widespread corruption in the awarding of federal airmail contracts. Roosevelt angrily canceled the existing contracts, and when Foulois said the Air Corps was up to the task, gave the Army the job without consulting the chief of staff. Yet the president would soon discover that the glamorous Air Corps, seemingly the only part of the military that Congress liked, was in as desperate shape as the rest of the Army. It lacked instruments to fly in bad weather, its planes were not suited to carrying mail, and during a period of unusually poor weather twelve pilots were killed in crashes in the operation's first few weeks. Although the arrival of spring weather saw a significant drop in the accident rates, the War Department was criticized for the poorly equipped and trained Air Corps.[39]

The Air Corps was not the only Army branch suffering under the Depression era's freefalling budgets. In his annual report prepared in mid-1934,

MacArthur pointed out that the Army's materiel was "inadequate even for limited forces, and, such as they are, comprise principally World War equivalent, manifestly obsolescent." He stated that:

> *The prepatory mission devolving upon the Military Establishment in time of peace cannot in some respects be efficiently performed; while the grave responsibilities that would fall to it in emergency would require frantic improvisations and wasteful and possibly ineffective sacrifice of the Nation's manhood and material resources. This blunt expression of War Department conviction divulges the secret of our weakness, which if known only to professional soldiers had probably best remain concealed ... [but] are fully known to qualified military observers abroad."*[40]

For his troubles preaching military preparedness, MacArthur's critics called him an "insatiable pillager of the public purse," "thief," and "warmonger."[41] Once during a hearing, a congressman noted the Army's budget for toilet paper and asked MacArthur: "General, do you expect a serious epidemic of dysentery in the U.S. Army?"

Perhaps no longer able to stoically bear the burden of his dream job having turned into a nightmare, or perhaps simply venting the frustration innumerable executive branch officials have felt testifying before Congress, MacArthur bitterly replied: "I have humiliated myself. I have almost licked the boots of some gentlemen to get funds for the motorization and mechanization of the Army. Now, gentlemen, you have insulted me. I am as high in my profession as you are in yours. When you are ready to apologize, I shall be back."

Before he could leave the hearing room, the committee members expressed their regrets.[42]

It was a temporary and symbolic concession, however. During MacArthur's tenure as chief of staff, the Army's budget declined from $374 million to $284 million. The best MacArthur could do for the institution both he and his father had devoted their lives to was to assign priorities and fight a rearguard action against the inevitable budget ax.

The Great Depression not only devastated the Army's budget and any hopes for modernization, but also caused significant hardship on the men serving their country. On June 30, 1932, President Hoover signed the Omnibus

Economy Bill, which amongst other provisions required all officers to take unpaid furloughs totaling thirty days during FY 1933, equaling a pay cut of almost 10 percent. All paid leaves were prohibited, and after July 1 salary increases resulting from promotion or length of service were also banned. A system of compulsory leave was adopted, and individuals were required to take a proportion of their leave each month. As Lucian Truscott recalled, "There was never very much that officers and families could do with these fractional periods, even if they could have afforded it—which few could!"[43] These measures were unwelcome but manageable for officers above the rank of major. But for junior officers and enlisted men it brought a severe cut in their already modest living standards.

On March 10, 1933, the recently inaugurated Roosevelt sent his second emergency measure to Congress, requesting authority to cut some $500 million from the federal budget. What became known as the Economy Act included a 15 percent cut in Army pay. This meant that a second lieutenant's pay was reduced to $119 a month, almost 20 percent less than what he would have earned twenty-five years earlier. The enlisted ranks were even harder hit. Sergeants suffered reductions in pay from 20 to 23 percent, and privates as high as 44.7 percent, as their salaries fell to a poverty-level $17.85 a month.[44]

Although George and Katherine Marshall were not seriously impacted by these reductions, he saw how much it affected the lives of the soldiers under his command. In his first months at Fort Screven, he worked to alleviate the straitened circumstances of his 400-man regiment. Fearful that his men would not be able to feed their families, Marshall personally supervised the building of chicken coops and hog pens, and the planting of vegetable gardens. He ordered the mess officer to prepare larger portions of the midday meal, then permitted his men to buy the hot meals at cost for fifteen cents a day to take home to their families in a steaming pail. In order to discourage any prideful resistance to "taking charity," Katherine recalled, "We ate this mid-day dinner ourselves until the custom was well-established."[45] As one of Fort Screven's officers recalled, it was "A little thing, perhaps, but what a heart."[46]

Despite these deprivations, officer resignations and enlisted desertions declined dramatically during the Depression. Military employment was preferable to no employment, and the Army still enjoyed housing, discounted groceries, and medical and dental care. Conversely, as Arthur Schlesinger wrote, outside the Army's cloistered posts "The fog of despair hung over the land. One out of every four American workers lacked a job. Factories that had once darkened the skies with smoke stood ghostly and silent, like extinct volcanoes. Families slept in tarpaper shacks and tin-lined caves and scavenged like dogs for food in the city dump."[47] The American economy's implosion had overwhelmed millions of people who had done nothing to merit the hardships they now endured. After Black Tuesday, by mid-November 1929 some $26 billion had disappeared, roughly a third of the value of stocks recorded in September. By 1933 stockholders had seen three-quarters of their assets' value evaporate. Gross Domestic Product fell from $84.6 billion in 1929 to $41.7 billion in 1932. More than 5,000 banks failed between the Crash and Roosevelt's inauguration, wiping out some $7 billion in depositors' money. Unable to pay their mortgages, foreclosures accelerated and 150,000 homeowners lost their property in 1930, 200,000 in 1931, and 250,000 in 1932, thereby stripping millions of people of both their life savings and their shelter in a single blow.[48]

As the economic slump deepened, millions of Americans were thrown out of work, and by early 1932 over ten million people—nearly 20 percent of the labor force—were unemployed. War Department visits to factories to obtain statistics necessary for mobilization planning turned into "mournful walks through empty shops and past halted belt lines."[49] In big cities like Chicago and Detroit that were home to capital-goods industries like steelmaking and automobile manufacturing, the unemployment rate approached 50 percent. Lucius Clay, whose work for the Corps of Engineers in 1931 took him all over the Pittsburgh area (and who would later oversee the postwar reconstruction of West Germany), recalled: "It was a scene of shocking desolation. The mines were closed. People were out of work. And they were out of money. There was a shantytown in Pittsburgh where thousands of miners came looking for jobs. And there were no jobs."[50] In New York City entire families received an average of $2.39 a week in relief, and they were the lucky ones, as only one-quarter of the unemployed actually received any assistance. Even those workers who managed to stay on the payroll went on shorter hours, with as many as one-third of all employed persons working only part-time.[51]

Nowhere was the Depression more deeply felt, perhaps, than in rural America. Income from America's farms plummeted from the already lean $6 billion in 1929 to $2 billion in 1932. Unmarketable crops rotted in fields and unsellable livestock died on the hoof for lack of feed, while the Federal Farm Board's price stabilization mechanisms had exhausted their funds. In the countryside unrest erupted into violence. "Farmers stopped milk trucks along Iowa roads and poured the milk into the ditch. Mobs halted mortgage sales, ran the men from the banks and insurance companies out of town, intimidating courts and judges, demanded a moratorium on debts." The situation appeared so precarious that in 1931 the Hoover Administration quietly urged Congress not to further cut Army ground forces for fear that it would "lessen our means of maintaining domestic peace and order."[52]

Of all the groups seeking government assistance during the Depression, World War I veterans were the most vocal and the best organized. The war's end had discharged more than two million men from the military, creating the largest pool of veterans—and consequently the largest political lobby—since the Civil War. Many veterans still deeply resented that while they were barely subsisting on military pay and risking their lives, civilian workers who remained safely at home saw their salaries increase by an average of 200 to 300 percent. To appease them, in 1924 Congress passed a law issuing veterans "adjusted compensation certificates"—commonly called "bonuses"—whose value was based on the time each man spent in service during the war. Over three million veterans were issued certificates with a total face value of $3.5 billion—averaging a payout of about $1,000 per man—redeemable in 1945 or by their survivors in the event of their death.

In 1924, however, nobody could have anticipated the Great Depression and the onset of mass unemployment in 1930–1931. Countless veterans were now jobless, and by 1932 few could imagine even making it to 1945. For most of these men, their bonus certificates were the only thing they owned of any value. Although Congress passed a bill allowing half of the bonus to be cashed immediately, many veterans were not satisfied and demanded payment of the full balance. Consequently, in late 1931 Representative Wright Patman of Texas introduced a bill that would authorize payment of the rest of the bonus by issuing $2.4 billion in fiat money. This bill was controversial from the outset, and floor debates and voting on the Patman Bill were expected in late spring 1932.[53]

In May 1932, a band of 300 unemployed veterans in Portland, Oregon, decided to bring their plight home to the country and show support for the Bonus Bill by marching on Washington, DC. They chose Walter W. Waters, an unemployed cannery worker, as their leader. A tall, handsome man and eloquent orator, Waters had participated in many battles as a sergeant in the field artillery in MacArthur's Rainbow Division. The veterans traveled via railway boxcars across the western United States, raising money for food by holding impromptu military parades in whatever towns the freights deposited them. On May 21 they reached East Saint Louis, where railroad officials prevented them from boarding a Baltimore and Ohio freight train east. The veterans vowed that no trains would leave the yard without them aboard, and surreptitiously decoupled cars and soaped the rails in the marshalling yards. When they were finally dispersed by Illinois National Guard units and sent out of the state—and toward Washington, DC—on trucks, the "Battle of the B&O" became a front page story and triggered a mass migration of ex-servicemen. By the time Waters and his Oregon veterans arrived in Washington in late May, their group had more than tripled to 1,000 men.[54]

Veterans from across the country trekked to the capital, the marching and renewed comradeship temporarily removing the shame of unemployment. What started as a trickle soon became a flood, with as many as 25,000 men converging on Washington to make the "Bonus March" the largest protest in the capital's history to that point. The veterans, embracing the name from news reports of Waters's Oregon marchers, called themselves the Bonus Expeditionary Force (BEF). Waters was elected as the BEF's commander, and he organized their encampments along military lines. He announced there would be "no panhandling, no drinking, no radicalism," and the veterans' demeanor and orderliness earned them positive press.[55]

Bonus Marchers took up residence in half a dozen condemned buildings downtown on Pennsylvania Avenue, and set up camps on whatever unoccupied wasteland they could find. The largest camp was on a swampy stretch of mud flats on the Anacostia River's east bank, known as Anacostia Flats. There, the veterans erected a profusion of temporary shelters—tents, shacks, and hovels constructed from scrap lumber, packing cases, tin—anything that could conceivably be used to build a dwelling was hauled from nearby dumps by roaming bands of veterans on "requisition" duty. In the blink of an eye, a sprawling shantytown with about 15,000 occupants had arisen by the riverside, including 1,100 women and children accompanying their husbands and fathers. Life settled into a kind of order at Anacostia Flats. Falling back on the habits instilled during basic training fifteen years earlier, the veterans rose to the daily bugle call, held formations, waited in chow lines, performed various duties—lobbying, procuring supplies, camp maintenance, digging latrines (known as "Hoover villas")—and set down for the night at the bugle's call of retreat. The Bonus Army even had its own newspaper, the *B.E.F. News*, which debuted on June 25.[56]

Relations between the veterans and the authorities remained peaceful, largely due to one man's efforts. The District of Columbia's commissioners turned the job of controlling the BEF over to Police Superintendent Pelham D. Glassford. Six-foot-three inches tall with "a lithe, straight-carriage," Glassford was an extraordinarily handsome man who "exuded vitality." His innate good humor and sunny disposition earned him the nickname "Happy."[57] Glassford had graduated from West Point two years after MacArthur, and during the war had commanded the 103rd Field Artillery. His unit's outstanding combat record quickly won him promotion and at age thirty-four the distinction of being the AEF's youngest brigadier general. An intelligent, charming, and "aesthetically sensitive" man who did not act like a general or a police chief, Glassford openly sympathized with the Bonus Marchers. "Why some of those boys soldiered for me," he said. "They're my boys."[58] He believed the BEF was comprised of proud, impoverished men who should be respected and treated kindly while simultaneously encouraged to return home.

Glassford paid daily visits to the BEF, riding his big blue motorcycle into their midst. He directed his policemen to provide first aid for the veterans and their dependents, secured baseball equipment for them, and even arranged for the Marine Corps band to perform for them. Glassford enlisted the aid of the Salvation Army and other charitable groups to provide food and bedding, and was successful in prompting wealthy Washingtonians to contribute money for the veterans' care. One benefactor was Evalyn Walsh McLean, whose husband owned the *Washington Post* and editorialized against the marchers. One night, with Glassford by her side, she showed up at an all-night diner at 1:00 A.M. and purchased 1,000 sandwiches and 1,000 packs of cigarettes, which she personally distributed to the veterans until the sun rose. Glassford himself bought 1,000 cups of coffee, and would eventually spend more than $1,000 of his own money to buy provisions for the destitute veterans. Consequently, even though he represented the official establishment whom they were civilly disobeying, the veterans respected Glassford, and Waters called him "our friendly enemy."[59]

Wandering veterans looking for food and shelter had started appearing at Fort Myer's enlisted barracks—directly across the Potomac from the Capitol—in the winter of 1931–1932. Truscott, who was serving with the 3rd Cavalry at Myer at the time, remembered: "The soldiers were very sympathetic to these unfortunate men." Each month soldiers chipped in a dollar a piece toward wages for veterans willing to work in mess halls or stables. "They felt they were helping unfortunate comrades," said Truscott.[60]

Yet many in the Army's senior leadership sensed something sinister in the restless throng gathering within sight of the Capitol. Although the 1920s' Red Scare had dissipated, some members of the conservative General Staff viewed all protests during the Depression through red-tinted glasses. Communists *had* led demonstrations in New York, Philadelphia, Pittsburgh, Akron, Cleveland, Chicago, and Los Angeles—amongst other cities—that had triggered violent confrontations with the police. Similar protests in Dearborn, Michigan, produced fatalities, and rioters in Saint Louis seized and held city hall for several hours. To some, the Bonus March appeared a continuation of these increasingly violent protests. In early June 1932, Congress sought to make Army cots, blankets, tents, surplus clothing, and medical and mess facilities available to the BEF. The War Department opposed the plan, however, claiming that using Army stocks would violate "basic principles" of the military establishment and "require replacement with additional appropriations."[61] Deputy Chief of Staff George Van Horn Moseley was especially convinced the Bonus Army posed a threat and urged MacArthur that the Army should be ready to meet any emergency that might arise.*

Initially, MacArthur did not believe the BEF posed an imminent threat. Yet he recognized the possibility that the concentration of desperate and unemployed people in Washington, petitioning Congress *en masse*, was a potential source of unrest. On June 8, speaking at the University of Pittsburgh's commencement, he inveighed against the threat of "pacifism and its bed-fellow, Communism." MacArthur identified all demonstrators against the established order as either communists or their puppets, who were "organizing the forces of unrest and undermining the morals of the working man." Tolerance of such radicalism, he warned, would lead America to "dust and ashes," for "day by day this canker eats deeper into the body politic."[62] Two

---

* Even in an organization notorious for its social conservativism, Moseley was exceptional in his racism, xenophobia, and anti-Semitism. In a letter to a friend, Moseley enumerated his fears: "We pay great attention to the breeding of our hogs, our dogs, our horses, and our cattle, but we are just beginning to realize the . . . effects of absorbing objectionable blood in our breed of human beings. The pages of history give us the tragic stories of many one-time leading nations which . . . imported manpower of an inferior kind and then . . . intermarried with this inferior stock." After retiring in 1938 he became a bitter critic of FDR and the New Deal, saw the possibility of war with Germany as a Jewish conspiracy launched by the great investment banks (which in his view were controlled by Jews), and ultimately came to believe that the Jews of Europe "were receiving their just punishment for the crucifixion of Christ." See Gen. George Van Horn Moseley to Herbert Corey, May 24, 1932, Moseley Papers; and Moseley, "One Soldier's Journey," Vol. 4, 215–19.

days later, upon returning to Washington, MacArthur ordered the nine corps area commanders to inform him of any communist groups that passed through their areas posing as Bonus Marchers. The corps area commanders were directed to "report in secret code" the presence of communist elements and the names of the leaders of the Bonus Marchers with "known communist leanings."[63] MacArthur then instructed the G-2 Division to investigate the leadership of the marchers already in the District.

MacArthur eventually came around to Moseley's view regarding the BEF's threat and took precautionary action to prepare the Army for any eventuality. He directed the War Department's "White Plan"—which dealt with the Army's employment in the event of an uprising in Washington, DC—to be revised and updated. He ordered tanks brought down from Aberdeen Proving Ground, and had the 3rd Cavalry undergo anti-riot training and practice in dispersing large crowds.

While this training was underway in early July, the 3rd Cavalry's new executive officer reported for duty. Like MacArthur and Moseley, George Patton believed that communists had infiltrated the Bonus Marchers' rank. Patton denounced the veterans as "revolutionists," pampered by Hoover, then-Governor Roosevelt, and Speaker of the House John Nance Garner. Yearning for action against "the mob," Patton wrote his sister Nita: "This B.E.F. is a disgrace. This morning a number of them rushed into the capitol and forced their way into the west wing. In which instead of breaking their damned heads that heroic standard bearer of the Democrats—Mr. Garner had a conference with them . . . Just recall how every successful revolution has started by temporising [sic] the mob."[64]

Although MacArthur believed "the Communists hoped to incite revolutionary action" through the Bonus March, of the nine reports responding to his June 10th cable, only one suggested the presence of any troublemakers, and even then did not indicate that they were communists.[65] Instead, Gen. Edward L. King reported from Atlanta that communists and troublemakers were "making little effect on southern bonus marchers."[66] Gen. Malin Craig cabled from the Presidio that the veterans departing the West Coast for Washington had announced they would not tolerate any communist elements and that to his knowledge there was no evidence of communist influence. He added that the Bonus Marchers' "discipline" and "conduct were excellent."[67] The G-2 reported to MacArthur that of the twenty-six "so-called" leaders of the Bonus Army already in the capital, only three were reported to be communist or affiliated with communist organizations.

In reality, the BEF was a bastion of anti-communism. There *was* a band of less than 200 communists posing as veterans camped on the edge of the BEF's encampments. Rather than following Waters, these men recognized a bankrupt Detroit contractor and recent communist convert named John T. Pace as their leader. Though the communists repeatedly tried to score propaganda points by claiming undeserved credit for the Bonus March, the BEF's leaders tirelessly denounced communist activity, destroyed their leaflets, and expelled their leaders from the camps. Waters boasted of the BEF's attacks on communists, and on several occasions only prompt intervention by Glassford and his police prevented Pace and his comrades from being mobbed by BEF members enraged at their propagandizing. Col. Edward W. Starling, supervisor of presidential security for the Secret Service, had undercover agents and informers in the camps. "Generally speaking there were few Communists," he reported, "and they had little effect on the men's thinking. The veterans were Americans, down on their luck, but by no means ready to overthrow their government."[68]

Officially, the Hoover Administration treated the Bonus Army as a local problem and refused to meet with the BEF's leaders. In private, however, the president was moved by the veterans' plight. Hoover had first gained public attention by leading the effort to provide relief supplies to occupied Belgium during the war, and his leadership of the postwar Allied relief effort earned him the nickname "The Great Humanitarian." According to White House butler Alonzo Fields, who heard the breakfast discussions between Hoover and his Cabinet, Secretary Hurley protested that providing army kitchens for the marchers would be "accommodating" them "and we would just get more and more and more and more."[69] Hoover ignored Hurley's objections and secretly provided food, tents, equipment, and an army field hospital while consistently refusing calls to evict them from the District.

His personal feelings aside, the BEF posed a thorny political problem for Hoover. Although the bonus was popular, its payment would be terrible policy. The cost estimates for bonus legislation ranged up to $4 billion, a sum equal to the total annual federal income at the time. This would require a tax increase, the last thing America needed as the Depression deepened. Bankers testifying before the House Ways and Means Committee explained that full payment of the bonus would depress the bond market by absorbing funds needed for municipal, state, and industrial construction, dangerously affect the solvency of already hard-pressed banks by draining off deposits for investment in safer government bonds, and thereby retard recovery. Henry T. Rainey, the Democratic floor leader of the House, evoked the widespread fear that the fiat in Patman's bill would erode the dollar's value and risk the inflation that had plagued the mark in Weimar Germany. Supporters of other large-scale relief proposals—including the liberal *New Republic* and left-wing *The Nation*—agreed with the bankers, and opposed the bonus for fear it would obviate more general measures, a pertinent concern given that veterans' benefits already constituted 16 percent of federal spending even though veterans comprised less than 4 percent of the population. Thus, even World War I veterans in Congress such as Fiorello La Guardia and Hamilton Fish Jr. were amongst those opposing the bonus.[70]

As the White House, the War Department, and the District commissioners deliberated on what to do with the BEF, each day veterans turned up on Capitol Hill and lobbied Congress. On June 15, the House passed the bonus bill by a vote of 211 to 176, with forty representatives not voting. It was a victory for the Bonus Marchers, but a tougher fight lay ahead in the Senate, which was scheduled to vote on Patman's bill on the 17th. More than 6,000 veterans thronged Capitol Hill to maintain a vigil that day. As the debate continued into the evening hours, thousands more marchers streamed into the Capitol Plaza from Anacostia Flats and other camps. The number of people in the plaza soon rose to over 12,000, but instead of becoming disorderly, the crowd remained well behaved. The veterans lay in shirtsleeves on the green grass talking, napping in silence, or singing songs from the war, their harmonies audible inside the Senate chamber.[71]

Finally, well after the summer sun had set, Waters walked to the top of the Capitol steps and waved his arms. It took several minutes for the crowd to grow silent. His voice low and tired, Waters began, "Comrades!" There were shouts from the crowd, followed by a heavy, anticipatory silence. "Comrades, I have bad news." The Senate had rejected the Bonus Bill by a 62–18 margin, a crushing defeat. There was a scattering of boos, and the men in the plaza rustled with uncertainty. Yet despite their frustration and dire straits, the men began to sing:

> Oh beautiful, for spacious skies,
> For amber waves of grain . . .

When the rendition of "America" was finished, military shouts began to ring out across the Plaza: "California—over here," "New Yorkers—fall in here." Quietly, the 12,000 men formed into platoons and marched back to their grimy dwellings. In thirty minutes the square was empty and still.[72]

In the days following the Bonus Bill's defeat, some veterans and their families left Washington. On July 7, with some prodding from President Hoover, Congress passed a bill appropriating $100,000 in transportation funds for the veterans to return home, the train fares to be deducted from their bonus payments in 1945. About 6,000 Bonus Marchers accepted the fares, but many others stayed, either having no other place to go, or recognizing that no matter where they went they would still be jobless, hungry, and altogether without hope. For the roughly 15,000 who remained, "Stay till 1945" became their motto. Patience within the BEF began to wane, however, and tempers increasingly flared. Dissidents complained about a new system of regimentation instituted by Waters in late June, and after a series of factional quarrels, Waters would only agree to remain as leader on the condition he be granted dictatorial powers. On the eve of Congress's adjournment on July 16, Waters formally announced a new veterans' organization that would ensure law and order and eliminate subversives, christened the "Khaki Shirts." The *B.E.F. News* published his plans in a front-page article headlined: "Khaki Shirts—W.W. Waters Imagines One Million—Waters Outlines Road Ahead for New Organization." The article declared:

> *Inevitably such an organization brings up comparisons with the Facisti of Italy and the NAZI of Germany. . . . For five years Hitler was lampooned and derided, but today he controls Germany. Mussolini, before the war was a tramp printer driven from Italy because of his political views. But today he is a world figure. . . . The Khaki Shirts, however, would be essentially American.*[73]

As Waters became more dictatorial and grandiose in his plans, however, the veterans became increasingly indifferent to his directives.

As tensions within the BEF increased, the District commissioners began to sharply criticize Glassford's "softness." The 15,000 people jammed against the filthy Anacostia River under primitive conditions were increasingly viewed as a potential public health threat. Heat and moisture bred disease out of half-incinerated trash; flies swarmed in the tents and shacks; and the Anacostia bathed the western edge of the camp with the District's sewage. As the summer heat rose in the capital, the rancid odor of decaying food, sweat, urine, and chloride began to settle over the camp, and there was growing concern that an epidemic could spread from the shantytowns.[74]

By July 20, therefore, officialdom felt the veterans had had their day. Congress had adjourned—canceling the formal closing ceremonies for the session and sneaking out through the tunnels under the Capitol in order to avoid having to face the Bonus Marchers—and the members had returned to their districts. The authorities consequently saw the bonus issue as settled, and further petitioning as futile. Moreover, public support for the BEF waned. Ever since the first veterans had begun arriving in Washington, many had been occupying dilapidated buildings on Pennsylvania Avenue in what was, during better days, the city's central shopping district. Located three blocks west of Capitol Hill and a half-mile east of the White House, the partially demolished structures "stood like grotesque skeletons against the sky." The blighted area was due to be renovated under the Hoover Administration's widely approved expansion of government buildings along Pennsylvania Avenue. Ironically, this gave the District commissioners the pretext they sought, as erecting new, modern structures would create hundreds of jobs and ease unemployment in the District.[75]

On July 21 Glassford was ordered to evacuate the buildings on Pennsylvania Avenue that had been slated for demolition. With hundreds of marchers departing the city each day, however, the police superintendent argued that forcible eviction would risk bloodshed, whereas with time the problem would likely solve itself. The commissioners reluctantly granted a delay, but were clearly growing anxious. Finally, on July 27 President Hoover agreed to a request by the Treasury Department (who technically owned the properties) for the limited evacuation of the veterans from the condemned buildings. Glassford was ordered to provide protection for the Treasury agents and demolition workers who would go to the disputed structures at 10:00 A.M. the next day.[76]

It was already hot on the morning of the 28th as the police arrived at Pennsylvania between 3rd and 4th Streets to begin clearing the buildings, starting with the old armory. Although the 1,100 veterans there voted to stay in the structure until the government provided other shelter, by the time the Treasury agents and demolition crews arrived at 10:40 the police were already completing the evacuation. They had been met with a great deal of cursing from the veterans, but little physical resistance. Suddenly, a small group of Bonus Marchers carrying an American flag began pushing through the crowd of onlookers that had gathered to watch the eviction. Glassford realized they intended to reoccupy the armory, and quickly gathered his forces and rushed to intercept them.

"Give the cops hell!" someone shouted. The veterans charged the police line and a scuffle erupted.

Glassford stood in the center of the melee, pleading for an end to the fighting, when he was struck by a flying brick and collapsed. One of his men, Edward G. Scott, who had been awarded the Medal of Honor in the war, moved to protect his fallen commander. As he stood over Glassford, however, a brick struck him in the head. He spun around at the blow, and another brick to the temple rendered him unconscious, his skull fractured. Although the fracas had only lasted five minutes, six policemen were hospitalized, two with serious injuries.[77]

Glassford tried to reassure the District commissioners that the police remained in control of the situation, but to his subordinates and most reporters who had witnessed the encounter it had clearly been a riot. Shortly after 1:00 P.M. a second incident occurred. A squad of policemen had pushed their way into a partially demolished building near 4th and Pennsylvania when a crowd of veterans shouting, "Get Glassford! Get the Major!" forced their way into the structure and assaulted the police with a barrage of bricks and stones. One officer struggled with an assailant who was beating him with his own club while another veteran choked him. Slipping loose long enough to draw his revolver, the officer saw another attacker descending upon him with a brick in hand. He fired, and in an instant William Huska—a thirty-five-year-old veteran from Chicago who had served in France—dropped dead with a bullet in his heart. The panicked officer continued to fire wildly, fatally wounding another veteran. Again, although this assault was over as quickly as it had begun, three of the besieged policemen were hospitalized.[78]

The District's police officers now agreed that the crowd was far more dangerous than Glassford had believed. With only 600 policemen confronting thousands of potential rioters, senior officers now advised the District commissioners that the situation risked getting completely out of control, and demanded that federal troops be summoned. Upon hearing this recommendation, the commissioners immediately telephoned the White House to request federal support and then notified Chief of Staff MacArthur. President Hoover insisted they put their request in writing. They promptly sent a formal letter declaring that the police could no longer maintain law and order "except by the free use of firearms . . . however, the presence of Federal troops in some number will obviate the seriousness of the situation and result in far less violence and bloodshed."[79]

While the commissioners were drafting their request, at 1340 MacArthur issued orders to Brig. Gen. Perry L. Miles, commander of the 16th Infantry Brigade, to assemble his units at the Ellipse south of the White House. The 16th Brigade numbered about 600 troops from the 3rd Cavalry, the 1st Tank Regiment, and the 12th Infantry Regiment. At about 2:00 P.M., Patton telephoned the 3rd Cavalry's troop commanders, notifying them the squadron had been ordered into Washington to quell riots and that the troops were being alerted by the sergeant major. Secretary Hurley and MacArthur went to the Oval Office to urge the president to issue a proclamation of martial law, which Hoover refused to do. In fact, according to one account of the meeting, Hoover was so reluctant to commit troops that he suggested having the soldiers carry police batons rather than firearms. Hoover finally ordered the troops to clear the downtown area near the riot site at 3rd and Pennsylvania and then to herd the rioters back to their camps where an investigation into the day's violence would be conducted.[80]

MacArthur then made a surprising decision that would do much to shape the historical perceptions not only of subsequent events, but of him personally. He informed Brigadier General Miles that he would personally accompany the troops against the Bonus Marchers. Dismayed by the image of a four-star general commanding a minor operation with the potential to turn ugly, MacArthur's assistant tried to talk him out of it. "I told him that the matter could easily become a riot," Dwight Eisenhower later recalled, "and I thought it highly inappropriate for the Chief of Staff of the Army to be involved in anything like a local or street-corner embroilment." MacArthur summarily dismissed Eisenhower's objections. To him, "it was a question of Federal authority in the District of Columbia," Eisenhower wrote, "and because of his belief that there was 'incipient revolution in the air' he paid no attention to my dissent."*

---

* Although some historians doubt Eisenhower would have directly contradicted the chief of staff, photographs from that day show MacArthur delighted by the Army's actions to suppress the BEF, whereas Eisenhower appears almost visibly pained at the events unfolding before them. This is not to say Eisenhower was wholly sympathetic with the Bonus Marchers. In his memoir he writes: "Despite the fact that this was a national calamity affecting almost all citizens, some veterans seemed to feel that they should be regarded as a special class entitled to special privileges" (Eisenhower, *At Ease*, 215, 216). For accounts of the Bonus March that cast doubt upon Eisenhower's claim of confronting MacArthur, see Perret, *Eisenhower*, 112; D'Este, *Eisenhower*, 223–24; and Smith, *Eisenhower in War and Peace*, 111.

Instead, MacArthur ordered Eisenhower into uniform. Back then, in peacetime Washington officers wore civilian suits. MacArthur was wearing his summer whites that morning, and sent his Filipino valet back to Fort Myer to retrieve him a uniform. The orderly came back with MacArthur's most ornate uniform bearing the rows of ribbons and the medals he had won during the war. Unintentionally, this made it seem as if MacArthur were dressing for a parade rather than to suppress a riot.[81]

Meanwhile, as executive officer, Patton did not exercise direct command of any element of the 3rd Cavalry and was not required to participate in the operation. But like MacArthur, he considered the Bonus Marchers to be Bolsheviks in disguise; and like MacArthur, he simply could not resist an opportunity for action. Thus, when the squadron marched out through Arlington National Cemetery, pounded over the recently completed Memorial Bridge, and halted on the green expanse of the Ellipse at about 1430, Patton was at the head of the formation. There was a long delay while the squadron waited for the infantry battalion—which was being transported by steamer up the Potomac from Fort Washington—to arrive. Patton decided to use the time to reconnoiter the situation. Alone, he trotted stonily along Pennsylvania Avenue, where several thousand veterans had congregated. He was greeted by a mix of cheers and jeers.[82]

By 1630, almost three hours after MacArthur's assembly order, the Army was ready to march against its brothers-in-arms. The 200 cavalrymen spread across Pennsylvania Avenue in a column of platoons, trotting from the Treasury Building at 15th Street toward the Capitol. Trucks carrying tanks rolled slowly behind them, followed by about 400 infantrymen. Patton recalled that "As we passed the occupied buildings the Marchers cheered us and called, 'Here come our buddies.' The civilians in the crowd hissed us in a mild way."[83] Truscott wrote: "Simultaneously, so it seemed, every office building and business establishment in downtown Washington discharged its occupants onto the streets."[84] Another officer described the scene as "a fantastic mixture of rioters, spectators, shoppers, streetcars, baby carriages, police, infantry, and officers from the War and Navy Department in civilian clothes."[85] The cavalrymen wore steel helmets, carried gas masks and carbines at the sling, and held drawn sabers. The waiting veterans and the huge crowd of spectators initially seemed spellbound by the procession, and many sightseers greeted what looked like a parade with cheers and applause.

They were soon disabused of this misconception.

The cavalry quickly cleared the street in front of the disputed buildings. The infantry then fanned out to empty the buildings one by one. At about 1730, 200 soldiers rushed in to evacuate a building at 3rd and Pennsylvania when a group of veterans, shouting defiantly, let loose a hail of bricks. The troops retreated, and an officer gave the order to don gas masks. They threw tear gas grenades "by the hundreds," according to one eyewitness, through doors and windows. An infantry squad with fixed bayonets quickly pushed its way into the building. Bypassing the rioters they went at the double up the stairs to the roof. One witness reported that "the doors and windows belched forth veterans, who were running before their feet touched the ground."[86]

In minutes, "black smoke and orange flame rose from the shacks constructed between buildings." General Miles commented, "When the fires sprang up so quickly after the arrival of the troops, they were a distinct surprise to me . . . No orders for firing the shacks . . . were given."[87] Most of the veterans broke and ran, but some remained. Forced out into the streets, the veterans—and some of the spectators—began hurling tear gas canisters back at the soldiers. Recognizing NCOs they had served with during the war, they began taunting the troops. "But the soldiers sat like statues and answered back not a word," Truscott recalled. "Theirs was a magnificent illustration of Regular Army discipline."[88]

"Growing hate and defiance was evident," one officer reported, "from the 'boos', barrage of profanity, the throwing of rocks and the return of tear gas grenades."[89] The Army drove the Bonus Marchers off Capitol Hill. Hooting and boing, they retreated across Pennsylvania Avenue toward the Anacostia Flats. According to the *New York Times*, this is when the real battle occurred: "Down toward Anacostia the troops went, in a bruising affair all the way, with persons in the street swinging blows at the soldiers as they swept past, the cavalry wielding sabers and the infantry prodding with bayonets."[90] Patton recalled:

> *Bricks flew, sabers rose and fell with a comforting smack, and the mob ran. We moved on after them, occasionally meeting serious resistance. Once six men in a truck threw a regular barrage of bricks, and several men and horses were hit. Two of us charged at a gallop, and had some nice work at close range with the occupants of the truck, most of whom could not sit down for some days.*[91]

Lt. Col. Louis A. Kunzig noted that "as the troops proceeded through the area south of Four and One-half Street and Maryland Avenue, occupied by colored people, it was apparent that residents of that area were in sympathy with the Bonus Marchers."[92] Despite the stiffening resistance along the streets southeast of the Capitol, by nightfall the majority of veterans had retreated southward across the 11th Street Bridge into the Anacostia Flats. With tears streaming down his cheeks from the tear gas, MacArthur declared to a reporter: "It was a good job, quickly done, with no one injured." Yet in reality, the running battle from the Capitol to the river had resulted in the gassing of hundreds. At least forty people were injured by bricks, clubs, bayonets, and sabers, including one veteran whose ear was sliced off by a cavalryman.[93]

MacArthur halted his forces at 1830 for over two and a half hours to rest and feed them. While his troops relaxed, MacArthur had Glassford inform the Anacostia camp's inhabitants to evacuate immediately. At 2110, the advance toward the BEF's last stronghold resumed. Shortly after 2200, one of Waters's deputies approached an Army staff car carrying a white flag. He begged for an hour's truce to evacuate the camp, and MacArthur granted the request. At 2315, however, Miles's troops marched across the bridge and into the camp. A large searchlight provided by the District's fire department swept its beam across the pitch black camp, picking up scenes of panic—men frantically trying to start jalopies, mothers desperately calling for children, men and women running with children in their arms toward the far hills of the camp.[94]

The infantry had barely advanced 200 yards into the encampment when the darkness suddenly came alive with bursts of yellow, orange, and red. "The whole encampment of shacks and huts just ahead began burning," Eisenhower remembered.[95] The fires spread quickly amongst the tents, huts, and lean-tos, causing a conflagration amidst the more than 2,000 improvised dwellings on the river flats.* The infantry moved forward through this hellscape in a

---

* Who, or what, started the fires remains unknown. Three plausible scenarios have been put forward by witnesses and historians. According to multiple witnesses cited in contemporary newspapers, the troops set fires for illumination, and when the veterans saw this they thought the soldiers were going to set the whole camp afire and decided to finish the job. Conversely, all unit commanders denied their troops started the fires, and some officers believed the veterans acted out of spite, firing the tents which the government had loaned them. Eisenhower recalled "these ragged, discouraged people burning their own little things," and conjectured that setting fire to their own huts was a last desperate gesture of defiance. Consequently, the troops who were photographed with torches were mistakenly finishing what the veterans had started. A third possibility offered by General Miles after subsequent

long skirmish line. Except for a few intoxicated men, they initially met little resistance. Around midnight, however, when the troops reached the heights on the camp's southern edge, their right flank was greeted with a shower of rocks. Approximately 2,000 veterans had massed there in hopes of making a final stand. Yet before they could organize and charge the infantry's lines, they were dispersed by tear gas grenades. Consequently, while countless fires illuminated the low ground, the veterans and their families fled into the night. At 0200, "Assembly" was blown on the bugle, and the troops bivouacked for the night. Where thousands of impoverished men, women, and children had called the riverside camp home the night before, now only smoking embers and seared piles of rubble remained.[96]

Whether the clearing operation was necessary, or even authorized, remains controversial. As the operation downtown proceeded, the president told Secretary Hurley to forbid the troops from crossing the 11th Street Bridge and force the camp's evacuation. Hurley twice sent messengers to tell MacArthur and Miles that Hoover did not want the Army to pursue the veterans across the Anacostia River. What happened next remains as contentious as the question of who started the fires. Eisenhower, who was with MacArthur, confirmed that orders arrived, but that MacArthur snapped that he was "too busy" and did "not want either himself or his staff bothered by people coming down and pretending to bring orders."[97] General Moseley, who Secretary Hurley had dispatched to deliver the first of the two presidential messages, claimed, "As we walked away alone from the others, I delivered that message to [MacArthur] and discussed it with him. He was very much annoyed in having his plans interfered with in any way until they were executed completely."[98] For many years, these recollections shaped historical perceptions of these events, and particularly how it reflected upon MacArthur's character. His biographer William Manchester wrote that "MacArthur scorned orders from Hoover," while another biographer concluded: "Blatant insubordination was already a MacArthur hallmark."[99]

Yet as Geoffrey Perret has pointed out, Moseley's claim that he delivered Hurley's message to MacArthur is contradicted by multiple witnesses. The morning after the rout, Assistant Secretary of War for Air F. Trubee Davison encountered Assistant Secretary Payne and General Moseley talking at the

---

testing is that defective tear gas grenades and candles had ignited refuse in the camp and that soldiers had lit subsequent fires thinking an order to burn the huts had been issued. For examples of each of these explanations, see Dickson and Allen, 188; Eisenhower, *At Ease*, 218; and James, 402, 405–6.

War Department. "Payne and Moseley were patting themselves on the back about the wonderful job they had done, and I said, 'What in the world have you fellows done that's so terrific?'

"They said, 'Well, the President wrote an order to MacArthur to stop at the Anacostia bridge.'" They proudly told Davison they had ensured MacArthur never received the message, "with the result that MacArthur and the whole force went across the bridge."[100] Davison's story was seemingly corroborated by Eisenhower's recollection that "The President's message just didn't get to" MacArthur. Miles also insisted that MacArthur received no such order.[101]

Moseley's apparent insubordination, however, does not fully exonerate MacArthur. For as the evening progressed, Hoover heard almost nothing of what was happening in the streets and began to wonder if the chief of staff had received his order. He had Hurley send another officer to MacArthur to repeat his earlier order. The message was carried by Col. Edmund White of the General Staff, but Moseley again interceded and told him to literally "get lost." Consequently, the colonel took three hours to travel less than 3 miles. Both Eisenhower and Miles recalled that *this time* Hurley's verbal message was delivered to MacArthur. In his memoirs, MacArthur admitted, "I received words from the Secretary of War as we were in the midst of crossing the river, to suspend the operation at my discretion."[102] According to Miles, "General MacArthur sent back word that it was too late to abandon the operation. The troops were committed . . . and some had crossed the bridge already."[103] Thus, although he was not strictly guilty of "blatant insubordination," MacArthur had clearly, and on his own volition, exceeded the commander-in-chief's intent for the operation as conveyed personally at the Oval Office and in the subsequent message delivered by White.

MacArthur's reasons for doing so were quickly made clear. At 11:00 P.M. he summoned a staff car to take him back to the War Department. Eisenhower warned him that there would be reporters waiting to question him. "It might be the better part of wisdom, if not of valor, to avoid meeting them," Eisenhower said. Given that the evacuation "had not been a military idea, really, but a political order," let Secretary Hurley and the other civilian officials deal with the press.[104] MacArthur was supremely confident in his ability to handle reporters, however, and triumphantly hurried to the White House. He was met there by Secretary Hurley, and together they reported to the president. According to Assistant Secretary Davison, Hoover told him that he had been furious with MacArthur, and not knowing about Moseley's interference, had "upbraided" him for disobeying orders.[105]

Yet standing before a crowd of reporters at the War Department, MacArthur and Hurley greeted the press in the role of victors rather than as humbled men. MacArthur told the reporters:

> *That mob down there was a bad-looking mob. It was animated by the essence of revolution. The gentleness, the consideration with which they had been treated had been mistaken for weakness, and they had come to the conclusion, beyond the shadow of a doubt, that they were about to take over in some arbitrary way either the direct control of the Government or else to control it by indirect methods. It is my opinion that had the President not acted today, had he permitted this thing to go on for twenty-four hours more, he would have been faced with a grave situation which would have caused a real battle. Had he let it go on another week, I believe that the institutions of our Government would have been very severely threatened. I think it can be safely said that he had not only reached the end of an extraordinary patience but that he had gone to the very limit of his desire to avoid friction and trouble before he used force. . . . had he not acted with the force and vigor that he did, it would have been a very sad day for the country tomorrow.*[106]

Ignoring the fact that the BEF had rigorously checked protestors' discharge papers before they were admitted to the encampments, MacArthur said, "There were, in my opinion, few veteran soldiers in the group that we cleared out today; few indeed. . . . if there was one man in ten in that group today who is a veteran, it would surprise me." Later, the Veterans Bureau would conduct an extensive check of the Bonus Army's membership and concluded that 94 percent of its members were bona fide veterans.[107]

Despite the onlookers' obvious sympathy for the Bonus Marchers, MacArthur declared, "I have never seen greater relief on the part of the distressed populace than I saw today. I have released in my day more than one community which had been held in the grip of a foreign enemy. . . . At least a dozen people told me, especially in the Negro section, that a regular system of tribute was being levied on them by this insurrectionist group." MacArthur went on to proclaim: "I have been in many riots, but I think this is the first riot I ever was in or ever saw in which there was no real bloodshed. So far as I know, there is no man on either side who has been seriously injured."

In fact, twelve soldiers were injured—four from bricks, eight from tear gas—and press reports of civilian injuries ranged from fifty-three to sixty. Worst of all, Bernard Myers, a seven-week-old baby delivered in the camp, died in the hospital from a pulmonary condition exacerbated by exposure to tear gas.[108] Secretary Hurley enthusiastically supported the chief of staff's justifications, exclaiming: "It was a great victory. MacArthur did a great job. He is the man of the hour."[109]

In the end, even if Perret is correct that MacArthur did not directly disobey orders, given his deeply inaccurate and blatantly self-serving rationalization for evicting the BEF from Anacostia Flats, it is not a stretch to imagine that he *might have* done so had Moseley not been insubordinate first. As his biographer D. Clayton James concludes, MacArthur "acted with overzealous determination and reckless impulsiveness," and "These remarks were destined to sear [MacArthur's] reputation for years to come."[110]

MacArthur's press conference continued past midnight. As he spoke, thousands of veterans and hundreds of their wives and children wandered the streets of the capital in ragged, confused groups, seeking whatever shelter they could find, or at least a place to rest. As the sun rose over Anacostia Flats, the charred remains of hovels, the stench of open latrines, and withered poplar trees were all that remained of the once teeming camp. Pathetic remnants of camp life were strewn everywhere—scorched pots and pans, broken pieces of furniture, a baby's crib, a rocking horse, and little piles of vegetable scraps.[111] Amidst this wreckage, Patton and several 3rd Cavalry officers sat on hay bales, drinking coffee from an army field kitchen. They were recounting the previous day and night's action and discussing what the next move would be when a tall sergeant from the 12th Infantry approached. He had a small civilian in tow, and asked for Major Patton, saying that the man claimed to be a friend of the major's. When Patton saw them, his face flushed with anger. "Sergeant, I do not know this man. Take him away, and under no circumstances permit him to return!"

The sergeant led a dejected Joe Angelo away.

Patton told the other officers:

That man was my orderly during the war. When I was wounded, he dragged me from a shell hole under fire. I got him a decoration for it. Since the war, my mother and I have more than supported him. We have given him money. We have set him up in business several times. Can you imagine the headlines if the papers got wind of our meeting here this morning? Of course, we'll take care of him anyway.[112]

Nevertheless, the next day the *New York Times* printed a story on the incident under the headline: "A Cavalry Major Evicts Veteran Who Saved His Life in Battle."[113] The *Philadelphia Public Ledger*, the *Washington Daily News*, and other papers also ran stories recounting Joe Angelo's eviction by the man whose life he had saved in the Great War.

The veterans who—unlike Angelo—were able to escape further sweeps by the troops organized impromptu military formations. A motorcycle policeman led one procession of veterans—many carrying American flags— up Wisconsin Avenue to the Maryland border, where trucks were waiting to take them to Pennsylvania. Impressed by the orderly, dignified exodus, people lined the streets to cheer the men as they marched past.

The bedraggled mass of hungry men, women, and children begging for redress had come to symbolize the country's downtrodden millions, and despite a lack of support for the Bonus Bill itself, had inspired nationwide sympathy. The *Washington News* perhaps captured the nation's zeitgeist best when it wrote: "What a pitiful spectacle is that of the great American Government, mightiest in the world, chasing unarmed men, women, and children with Army tanks. If the Army must be called out to make war on unarmed citizens, this is no longer America."[114] In New York, glancing at the morning papers, the Democratic presidential nominee Franklin Roosevelt observed to future Supreme Court justice Felix Frankfurter, "Well, Felix, this elects me."[115] Hoover, exhibiting admirable personal loyalty but extremely poor political judgment, eventually endorsed MacArthur's dubious interpretation of the BEF. The episode thus came to symbolize the president's purported insensitivity to the plight of America's unemployed. Given that it was an election year, the Democrats mercilessly exploited the issue.

Finally, the use of Regular Army troops against unarmed civilians was an unmitigated public relations disaster for the Army. Although the troops had performed an unpleasant task in as efficient a manner as possible, the public viewed the use of military force itself as heavy-handed. The incident played directly into the hands of the anti-militarists and pacifist groups throughout the country, and in movie theaters all across America the U.S. Army and MacArthur were jeered. MacArthur in particular would be saddled with the public perception of the dashing, brilliant World War I hero and chief of staff as a right-wing "man on horseback" who hated the poor and downtrodden as much as he did radicals and communists.[116]

In the spring of 1933 the U.S. Army was at perhaps the lowest point in its history, its reputation bruised by the Bonus Army's eviction, facing a rising tide of isolationism, and slowly losing what it perceived to be an existential battle over its budget. It is ironic, then, that the institution's redemption arguably lay in an initiative that its senior leadership originally opposed.

In an effort to provide temporary relief, on March 21, 1933, President Roosevelt asked Congress "to create a civilian conservation corps to be used in simple work, not interfering with normal employment and confining itself to forestry, the prevention of soil erosion, flood control and similar projects."[117] Of all the New Deal's emergency measures, the Civilian Conservation Corps (CCC) was closest to Roosevelt's heart. He had done something similar as governor of New York, and sought to enroll 250,000 young men by July 1. Congress took only ten days to pass the bill establishing the CCC, leaving most of the details for the executive branch to determine. The plan for the CCC's creation, therefore, was paradoxically both improvised and complex: the Labor Department would recruit the volunteers; the Army would enroll them, put them through a two-week conditioning course, and transport them to work camps; and the Agriculture and Interior Departments would supervise the actual work. Thus, according to the regulations forwarded to all corps area commanders and published as an Army General Order on April 16, 1933, once the units were turned over to these departments at the work camps "the mission and responsibility of the United States Army would cease."[118]

The War Department had strongly and successfully opposed several congressional proposals in 1930–1931 to organize a special enlisted reserve corps that would employ jobless men on public works under Army supervision. MacArthur and Hurley both maintained that involvement in work relief or public construction projects to alleviate unemployment would cripple the Army's already precarious readiness. Nevertheless, a proposed Senate resolution of June 4, 1932, would have authorized the secretary of war to make available Army personnel and equipment to assist in an organized program for unemployment relief. The General Staff's G-3 section studied the facilities available for such a task and concluded the Army should only be used if Congress insisted, and only to the extent of caring for the 68,000 men who could be housed in existing facilities on Army posts. Citing this report, Hurley wrote to the Senate Military Affairs Committee's chairman, stressing the War Department's limited capacity for implementing the proposal. Consequently, the committee reported the bill unfavorably.[119]

Yet those arguments were unconvincing to Roosevelt, whose immediate concern was fighting the Depression at home, not a still notional enemy on foreign shores. He directed MacArthur to mobilize the CCC despite the chief of staff's strenuous objections that it would degrade Army readiness. The Regular Army answered the call, albeit reluctantly. As Omar Bradley later recalled, "The Army was not happy at being saddled with the CCC."[120] According to John S. D. Eisenhower, his father felt that "the Army was tapped enough without having to take on the CCC chore."[121] Indeed, most Army officers saw their support of the program as a diversion of an already skeleton force away from its primary mission of national defense.

In Roosevelt's original conception, tying the CCC closely to the military was neither necessary nor advisable. Indeed, if the emergency had not been so pressing, and if the president had not set July 1 as the deadline for all enrollees to be at work, the Agriculture and Interior Departments could have trained enough men and stockpiled enough equipment to have successfully run both the work camps and the work projects themselves. But given the president's parameters, Chief Forester R. Y. Stuart quickly realized that he and his agency could not handle the number of enrollees Roosevelt had mandated be in place by July 1. Reluctantly, the White House acknowledged it would be impossible to administer the work camps and ensure the CCC's success unless the Army took over and operated the work camps in addition to the conditioning camps.[122]

Consequently, on Saturday night, April 8, the War Department's representative on the CCC Advisory Council, Col. Duncan Major, was summoned to the White House. It was proposed to him that the Army expand its participation to include control over all matters of work camp activity except the actual technical supervision of the work itself. On April 12 the War Department informed all corps area commanders that the Army would be "responsible for all matters incident to command of the camps and their supply, administration, sanitation, medical care, hospitalization, and welfare."[123] On May 10, the CCC was placed under the War Department's control, and President Roosevelt ordered the Army to enroll and assign to the work camps the entire CCC complement of 274,000 within fifty days. The severe timeline created a sense of urgency that had been lacking in the laconic inter-war War Department, and work began immediately. Colonel Major wrote:

> *It was a momentous day. In a few hours more had been accomplished than in the previous month. A clear cut decision on a definite plan to fulfill a task the complete definition of which was positively ordered electrified the whole effort. The old order had changed. That afternoon all Assistant Chiefs of Staff and Chiefs of Services met. . . . The new mission was given, stirring everyone. Plans and actions for the field were required by the next morning. That night instead of a stray light here and there the War Department's windows were ablaze. The big machine was rolling in a war effort. The Army was under a test, but what a grand opportunity the task offered.*[124]

The General Staff achieved more in terms of planning in forty hours than the other departments had accomplished in forty days. On May 12, the War Department's plan was approved, and Secretary Hurley and MacArthur gave the CCC mobilization their full support.[125]

Before July 1 the Army created 1,315 work camps across the country and settled 250,000 young men—and 25,000 foresters—in them. The huge operation involved over 200 trains and 3,600 Army vehicles. The quarter-master general awarded contracts for 2.5 million yards of denim, one million jumpers, one-half million pairs of shoes, 3,000 trucks, one-quarter million cots, and 1.25 million pairs of trousers. A typical camp consisted of at least a dozen barracks, officers' quarters, a mess hall, recreation center, post exchange, classroom, dispensary, garage, blacksmith shop, bathhouse, supply room, and storage buildings. Each camp numbered about 200 enrollees under the control of two officers and several enlisted men, with the company divided into sections and subsections akin to platoons and squads under the supervision of leaders and assistant leaders analogous to platoon sergeants and squad leaders. "Camp formations" began at 0600 with reveille followed by raising the American flag. Calisthenics were held for fifteen minutes before breakfast at 0700. Forty-five minutes later "a work call" ensured that the camp and personal areas were cleaned. The enrollees—who received $30 a month while in the CCC—then departed for work, their tasks including planting 200 million trees, cutting fire breaks and constructing fire towers, cleaning streams and beaches, building small dams and bridges, and refurbishing roads and trails in national parks. Work crews usually returned to camp at 1600 and stood formation for the flag's lowering at retreat. Evening classes were held on vocational and personal development subjects, and a bugle played "Taps" at 2300 sounding "lights out."[126]

Despite the Roosevelt Administration's initial trepidation about its participation, the Army's efforts were indisputably the key to the CCC's success. MacArthur was ecstatic and sent a personal Army-wide congratulatory message. Reviewing the task and its accomplishment, the chief of staff declared that the CCC's mobilization "represented the greatest peacetime demand ever made upon the Army and constituted a task of character and preparations equivalent to emergencies of war." "Such splendid results," he explained, could only have been achieved because of the Army's "high morale," and "devotion to duty."[127] Moreover, MacArthur saw the operation as a means of demonstrating the officer corps' value to the public and Congress. "Particularly has it served to emphasize again the vital need for a strong corps of professional officers and for an efficient body of commissioned Reserves."[128]

Although he was quick to jump aboard the CCC's bandwagon once it proved successful and popular, MacArthur's most important contribution to the effort was to decentralize the Army's effort. As one historian of the CCC notes: "The problems of establishing work camps in the High Sierras, the deserts of New Mexico, the Florida swamps, and the Kentucky hills were so different that any rigid control of the procedures from the center would have created more difficulties than it would have solved."[129] In light of such widely varying conditions, MacArthur gave the nine corps area commanders the widest powers to establish and operate the camps in their corps area. The General Staff further directed the organization of subordinate district headquarters under the corps area headquarters to further delegate the numerous administrative and command problems. The district and company commanders were charged with "complete responsibility" for the camps, personnel administration, and welfare of the men.[130]

This decentralization gave a broad swath of officers leadership opportunities they might not have otherwise gained in the skeletal interwar Army. Maj. Mark Clark was the 7th Corps Area's assistant chief of staff G-2 for intelligence and assistant chief of staff G-3 for plans and training in March 1933. When the Army was placed in charge of the CCC, he assumed the additional position of deputy chief of staff for the CCC and oversaw the camps in the corps area. The corps area commander's published orders gave Clark the authority to "make all decisions and to take all necessary action in Civilian

Conservation Corps matters that would normally be submitted to the Commanding General." Given this increased responsibility, Clark traveled extensively to check on the state of morale, the quality of food, the conditions of cleanliness, and the progress of public works performed.[131] Charles Corlett was commanding the 317th Infantry at Vancouver Barracks, Washington, when he was ordered to scout locations for ten CCC camps. He was subsequently given command of the CCC's Eugene Division, overseeing 5,000 men in twenty-two camps.[132]

One of the Army's most effective officers in achieving the CCC's success was George Marshall. In June 1933, Marshall was made the commanding officer of the IV Corps Area's "District F," in charge of establishing nineteen camps in the 450 miles between Hinesville, Georgia, and southern Florida. He would later write to a friend that the CCC was "the most interesting problem of my Army career," and one of his assistants at Fort Screven recalled, Marshall "ate, breathed and digested the many CCC problems."[133] According to Katherine Marshall, Marshall was "fascinated by the opportunities he felt it afforded to build up the minds and bodies of the youth of this country and also to lessen the hardship of the depression."[134] Marshall stripped Screven of virtually all its officers in order to man the hastily organized receiving stations, and on a four-day trip from June 14 to 18 he visited all nineteen camps. To make the experiment succeed, he admitted, he could be "pretty ruthless about getting rid of the poor fish" among the officers. "I made it unmistakably clear to the captains," he wrote a friend, "that their continuance on this duty would depend entirely on the efficiency of their companies, the administration of the camps, excellence of the mess, morale of the men and work done in the woods" and that "I would be compelled to protect the interests of 200 boys, rather than one" officer.[135]

Marshall was so invested in his CCC responsibilities that when he received orders reassigning him from Screven to Fort Moultrie, South Carolina, to assume command of the entire 8th Infantry Brigade, he wrote to the 4th Corps Area commander, Maj. Gen. Edward L. King, to request that his transfer be delayed a month "as I am deep in the complicated business of building Camps in the Florida-Georgia swamp areas." For Marshall, overseeing the start of the new camps was more important than finally commanding a brigade.[136] When he did take command at Moultrie on June 29, District I had a total of eleven CCC camps and 1,915 men. In the ensuing months he set up fifteen additional camps in South Carolina, staffed them, and supervised the mobilization of the volunteers to fill those camps.

Not all Army officers were as enthusiastic about participating in the CCC, however, which entailed significant costs to the Army. Even before Congress passed the enacting legislation, Marshall wrote to an acquaintance, "We were enroute to Fort Benning for the annual Corps Areas Maneuvers when the concentration was called off because of the President's emergency employment proposal."[137] To handle the CCC mobilization, nearly all normal garrison duties were temporarily suspended. All but two Army schools were closed, and most of their faculties and all the student officers in attendance were ordered to CCC duty. Omar Bradley, for example, was pulled from his teaching duties at the Infantry School and placed in command of six all-black CCC companies at Benning. Officers were similarly recalled from training positions with the National Guard, the Organized Reserve Corps, and the Citizens' Military Training Camps and assigned to duty with the CCC. In several corps areas, the CCC utilized all the Regular Army officers available. By early September 1933, the inspector general reported to MacArthur that the Army's involvement with the CCC meant that combat units could not undertake any mission that would involve troop movements. He believed that if these conditions continued for one year, the Army would be virtually untrained and unable to meet an enemy. Indeed, MacArthur wanted his officers back even before the CCC had really gotten off the ground, and as early as April 11 the War Department contemplated the prompt relief of its Regular officers by reservists.[138]

But while the War Department was bemoaning the disruption to its training activities, it was becoming abundantly clear that the Army's participation in the CCC was worth the short-term costs. First, as one historian notes, "it exercised and refined mobilization systems to prepare a citizen army to fight and win a global war."[139] From May 12 to July 1, 1933, the Army placed 275,000 men in CCC camps. Colonel Major reported that "the mobilization of the C.C.C. with time as the essential element in the execution of the task has been the most valuable experience the Army has had since World War I."[140] In fact, this was more men processed than during a similar timeframe with America's entry into World War I, when 181,000 men were mobilized between April 7 and July 1, 1917. Marshall, who would oversee the next great mobilization, wrote to General Pershing that he considered the CCC "a major mobilization exercise and a splendid experience for the War Department and the Army."[141]

Second, unbeknownst at the time, the CCC provided the pretrained manpower to fill the Army's ranks upon mobilization for World War II with

Gen. John J. Pershing (center) and his staff aboard the USS *Leviathan*, returning from France in September 1919. Col. George C. Marshall is in the second row behind Pershing's right (viewer's left) shoulder. Col. Fox Conner is in the front row, two down from Pershing, looking at his commander rather than the camera. (PHOTO COURTESY OF GEORGE C. MARSHALL FOUNDATION)

General Pershing decorates Douglas MacArthur with the Distinguished Service Cross, October 15, 1918. Throughout the remainder of his career, however, MacArthur believed Pershing and his "Chaumont Gang" had conspired to deny him a Medal of Honor and harbored resentment toward them, including toward Marshall. (PHOTO COURTESY OF MACARTHUR MEMORIAL ARCHIVE)

MacArthur during his tenure as superintendent of the United States Military Academy at West Point. His educational and training innovations were both necessary and ahead of their times, but were undermined by West Point's traditionalist faculty and alumni. (PHOTO COURTESY OF MACARTHUR MEMORIAL ARCHIVE)

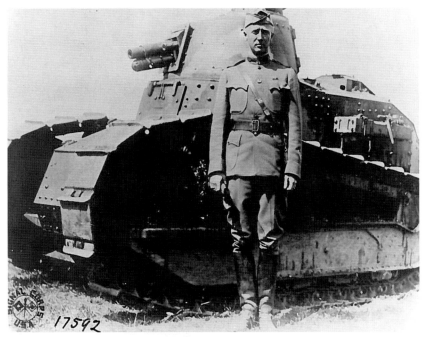

George S. Patton in front of a Renault tank, July 1918. Two months later, he would be seriously wounded while leading his tanks into battle on the first day of the Meuse-Argonne offensive. (PHOTO COURTESY OF THE PATTON MUSEUM)

Dwight D. Eisenhower posing beside a tank at Camp Meade, Maryland. His ingenuity at training American tankers made him too valuable to deploy to the Western Front in France. (PHOTO COURTESY OF THE DWIGHT D. EISENHOWER LIBRARY)

Patton (second row, fifth from the right) and Eisenhower (second row, fourth from the right) and the officers of America's Tank Corps at Camp Meade. (PHOTO COURTESY OF LIBRARY OF CONGRESS)

Doud Dwight "Ikky" Eisenhower (PHOTO COURTESY OF THE DWIGHT D. EISENHOWER LIBRARY)

Lily Coles Marshall in Tientsin, China. Her death shortly after returning to the United States would have profound effects on both George Marshall's career and, indirectly, on the U.S. Army. (PHOTO COURTESY OF GEORGE C. MARSHALL FOUNDATION)

Marshall and his senior instructors at the Infantry School, Fort Benning, Georgia. Joseph Stilwell is seated to Marshall's right (viewer's left); Omar Bradley is standing second from the left. (PHOTO COURTESY OF GEORGE C. MARSHALL FOUNDATION)

The partially demolished building at Pennsylvania Avenue and 4th Street where two Bonus Marchers were killed rioting against DC police attempting to evict them. (PHOTO COURTESY OF PANORAMIC IMAGES)

MacArthur and Eisenhower (left, partially obscured) during the Army's controversial suppression of the Bonus Riots on July 28, 1932. Although Eisenhower did not support the marchers, he advised the chief of staff to stay away from the military action lest he risk damaging the prestige of his office. MacArthur believed the risk to the republic was sufficient to warrant his presence. (PHOTO COURTESY OF MACARTHUR MEMORIAL ARCHIVE)

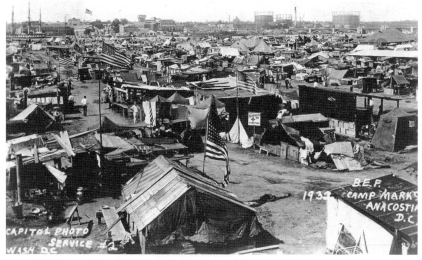

"Camp Marks" beside the Anacostia River—as seen before and after the Army's suppression of the riots on July 28, 1932—was the largest encampment during the 1932 Bonus March, serving as the temporary home to 15,000 destitute veterans and their families. (PHOTO COURTESY OF PANORAMIC IMAGES)

MacArthur arrives in Manila on October 26, 1935, to assume his duties as military adviser to the Commonwealth of the Philippine Islands with the mission of creating a Philippine army from scratch. Eisenhower, chief of staff for the advisory mission, stands behind him (third from the left) in mufti. (PHOTO COURTESY OF MACARTHUR MEMORIAL ARCHIVE)

MacArthur, Eisenhower (right), and Maj. T. J. Davis, at a formal occasion in Manila. Despite their smiles here, MacArthur's increasingly toxic leadership in the face of the advisory mission's difficulties helped to provoke a permanent split between himself and Eisenhower. (PHOTO COURTESY OF MACARTHUR MEMORIAL ARCHIVE)

Marshall's swearing in as U.S. Army chief of staff, September 1, 1939. Half a world away, German tanks and troops were pouring across the Polish border as the *Luftwaffe* terrorized Polish cities, killing thousands of civilians in a portent of the impending global conflict. (PHOTO COURTESY OF GEORGE C. MARSHALL FOUNDATION)

Patton and his family, Christmas 1939. Whereas the rest of his family is smiling and celebrating the occasion, Patton appears distant and depressed. (PATTON PAPERS, LIBRARY OF CONGRESS)

"The whole art of war consist[s] in catching the enemy by the nose and kicking him in the pants!" Patton in his element, addressing the troops of the 2nd Armored Division before the June 1941 Tennessee Maneuvers. (NATIONAL ARCHIVES)

Colonel Eisenhower outlines 3rd Army operations for Lt. Gen. Lesley McNair of Army General Headquarters, with Maj. Gen. H. A. Dargue looking on, at the 1941 Louisiana Maneuvers. (NATIONAL ARCHIVES)

Major General Patton overseeing construction of a pontoon bridge over the Red River by 2nd Armored Division engineers at the Louisiana Maneuvers, September 1941 (NATIONAL ARCHIVES)

Light tanks of the 68th Armored Regiment, 2nd Armored Division, advancing during the Louisiana Maneuvers, September 1941 (NATIONAL ARCHIVES)

Λ machine gunner of the 158th Infantry draws a bead on a 2nd Armored Division tank during the battle for Peason Ridge, September 17, 1941. (NATIONAL ARCHIVES)

Lieutenant Generals Walter Krueger (left) and Ben Lear (right) shake hands at the post–Louisiana Maneuvers critique. Krueger's Third Army soundly defeated Lear's Second Army in both phases of the maneuvers, and whereas Krueger would command the Sixth Army in the Philippines under MacArthur during the war, Lear would be relegated to stateside commands.
(NATIONAL ARCHIVES)

Brig. Gen. Mark Clark and Eisenhower, September 30, 1941, shortly after Clark played a practical joke on his friend by delaying the announcement of Ike's long-awaited promotion to brigadier general.
(NATIONAL ARCHIVES)

men who readily assumed the role of NCOs. By the time the CCC expired in 1942, it had not only put more than 2.5 million idle young men to work, it taught them how to live in the company of 200 other men from diverse backgrounds and geographic areas. As one enrollee summarized the experience, "Unlettered mountaineers from the West mingle with high-school graduates and college men from the centers of culture. Different races and nationalities look each other in the face, work and eat together for the first time."[142] The enrollees learned to take directions, and were taught the rudiments of sanitation, first aid, and personal hygiene, basically the same experience many would face again in an expanding wartime army. Thus, there was a measure of truth to Colonel Major's claim in December 1933 that "the personnel of the CCC constitutes today a group of potential military strength to the Nation, which with comparatively little training could be made ready for front-line duty."[143] Or as Mark Clark summarized the experience: "Though we did not realize it at the time, we were training Non-Commissioned Officers."[144]

In fact, the Army was training more than future senior enlisted men through the CCC. By February 1934, only 537 Regular officers remained on full-time duty with the CCC, down from a peak of 5,239, or roughly half the Regular Army's officer corps. Over 5,000 reserve officers were activated to take the place of the regulars, and enrollees eventually relieved almost all of the enlisted men in supervising the camps. In the 1930s the lack of an organized reserve meant that ROTC graduates received little-or-no military training after receiving their reserve commissions. Consequently, the CCC gave these officers the chance to hold leadership positions that would have been unavailable otherwise. Colonel Major observed that the CCC constituted an "excellent means for training the Reserves," and that "No better opportunity is presented in time of peace for practical leadership in command, administration, and supply, and the development of leadership and initiative."[145] Clark recalled that reserve officers "were being subtly trained in leadership and he believed the ability of the Regular Army to observe and evaluate them while they were on active duty was important in the selection of officers for higher command."[146] Even MacArthur told a Senate Committee in February 1935 that these men were now receiving training in administration and leadership in the camps and that, although it was not strictly military training, it was of inestimable value to them and to the Army.

The CCC offered opportunities for leadership development not only to Reserve officers, but to junior officers in the Regular Army as well. Since the enrollees were civilians and therefore outside the traditional military chain of command, "military discipline" was softened. Instead of commanding with the Articles of War's heavy sanctions behind them, they had to lead with understanding, sympathy, and the force of personality. These officers developed a leadership style based more on psychology than military discipline, a style better suited to training and organizing a citizen army of draftees than volunteers for the small Regular Army. For example, in July 1933 Maj. James Van Fleet was assigned as commanding officer of the 2nd Battalion, 5th Infantry Regiment, at Fort Williams, Maine. He was assigned concurrently as executive officer of the 1st District of the CCC. In this capacity, he supervised twenty-five companies of youths in camps throughout Maine and New Hampshire. He later noted that encouraging the young men in the CCC to perform meaningful work, to operate under military control, and to accept discipline was a matter of persuasion and example rather than enforced obedience to orders. Thus, although MacArthur had initially opposed the Army's participation in the CCC, it proved to be an ideal training ground in the very style of leadership he had hoped to encourage while trying to reform West Point more than a decade earlier.[147]

Finally, the Army's participation in the CCC restored some of the luster lost during the BEF's eviction from Anacostia Flats. MacArthur's report to the secretary of war in 1933—while pleading for the prompt return to the Regular Army's usual duties—noted the favorable attention the public was giving the Army for its CCC efforts. MacArthur's assistant noted in his diary in June 1933 that "We will lose no officers or men (at least at this time) and this concession was won because of the great numbers we are using on the Civilian Conservation Corps work."[148] Thus, despite Russell Weigley's contention that "the disruption of the Army's already feeble formations and its diversion from military tasks probably more than erased any advantage" gained from its involvement in the CCC, it is abundantly clear that the Army's long-term preparedness and effectiveness was greatly aided by participation in the CCC. As the acting chief of infantry wrote to Marshall in May 1933, although the CCC "work is onerous and probably distasteful to the Army as it is not exactly military work . . . it is the salvation of the Army."[149]

Army Chiefs of Staff traditionally served for four years, yet even before MacArthur's term was due to expire, throughout 1934 Roosevelt's advisers urged the president to relieve MacArthur. Conversely, Secretary Dern,

Democratic House Majority Leader Joseph W. Burns, and the Democrats on the House and Senate Military Affairs Committees advised Roosevelt to retain MacArthur at least through the passage of the military appropriations bill for FY 1936. Earlier that year Japan formally annexed Manchuria and renounced its obligations under the 1922 Washington Naval Treaties. Together with the growing menace of Nazi Germany, the international scene was becoming increasingly unstable. With the worst of the Depression over and the CCC having restored the Army's reputation, a new mood was sweeping over Congress and public opinion. Despite his previous battles with Congress, Dern and the congressional Democrats argued that MacArthur's knowledge of the complex legislation before the Congress was vital to the success of the Army's reorganization and national defense. Consequently, on December 12, 1934, Roosevelt took the unusual step of extending MacArthur's tenure beyond the normal four years. While making it clear that MacArthur would not serve another four-year term, the president announced that MacArthur would remain chief of staff until a successor could be appointed. In reality, Roosevelt was employing a tactic he would repeat on the eve of World War II. He wanted the Army chief of staff to serve as the stalking horse for the upcoming budget fight, which if the push for increased military appropriations proved unpopular, would also conveniently make MacArthur the fall guy.[150]

With international tensions rising and with the White House's apparent support, MacArthur felt confident enough to request an increase in appropriations for FY 1936, raising the War Department's budget to $361 million. This was MacArthur's largest request since becoming chief of staff, and the Budget Bureau slashed it to $331 million before submitting it to Congress. Yet instead of playing defense to cut the Army's losses, MacArthur was prepared to go on the offensive for once. In January 1935 he sat in full dress uniform with brightly polished boots before the House Subcommittee on Military Appropriations. He urged the subcommittee to repudiate the bureau's decision, to provide money to buy new equipment, to increase the officers corps from 12,000 to 14,000, and that the number of enlisted personnel be raised from 125,000 to the 165,000 the General Staff considered the bare minimum.[151]

MacArthur had prepared his ground better than before, and while Congress debated the budget, the chief of staff was running a behind-the-scenes lobbying campaign. The House gave the War Department $378 million for FY 1936, of which $318.7 million was strictly for military appropriations, an increase of around $38 million from the previous fiscal year. The final bill passed by the Senate in late March 1935 approved total FY 1936 Army appropriations of around $400 million, with the funds for military activities almost identical to the Army's original estimate submitted to the Budget Bureau of $361 million. Although the request for more officers was rejected, the bill provided for an increase in the Regular Army's enlisted strength to 165,000, the General Staff's long-sought goal. To many officers, MacArthur had wrought a miracle and saved the Army from virtual destruction. As the War Department rejoiced, MacArthur expressed his gratitude to congressmen and exultantly declared: "The change has come not too soon. The turn has at last been reached."[152]

In his final annual report that summer, MacArthur wrote:

For the first time since 1922, the Army enters a new fiscal year with a reasonable prospect of developing itself into a defense establishment commensurate in size and efficiency to the country's minimum needs. Obstacles, which for 13 years have impeded, if not inhibited, progress toward this goal, have only recently been either swept aside by Congress or materially reduced in importance. The present year definitely marks the beginning of a long-deferred resumption of military preparation on a scale demanded by the most casual regard for the Nation's safety and security.[153]

It was a stunning culmination of MacArthur's five-year campaign, one largely marked by frustrating setbacks and defeats. Although the growing talk of war in both Europe and Asia helped make the turnaround possible, much of the credit belonged to the chief of staff's persistence. General Pershing sent MacArthur a photograph of himself, beneath which was a handwritten tribute that began: "I have only praise for General MacArthur as Chief of Staff. He has fully measured up to that high position."[154] The *Washington Herald* correspondent wrote:

Brilliant and magnetic General Douglas MacArthur is going out as Chief of Staff in a blaze of splendid glory, the idol of the entire Army. His work in Washington is finished. A year ago the Army was on the rocks, demoralized, discouraged, and out of date. General MacArthur has saved it by putting through Congress the most constructive program for the land defenses since the World War.[155]

Or as D. Clayton James concludes, "MacArthur fought hard for the Army's needs and deserves a large portion of the credit for the upward swing of military appropriations that began in 1935."[156]

If, as he believed, MacArthur was destined to serve as Army chief of staff, fate had a cruel sense of irony. Arguably the most intellectually gifted officer of his generation, MacArthur attained his profession's pinnacle during a distinctly unheroic period in the Army's history. The Depression and America's turn inward ensured that whoever succeeded Summerall as chief of staff would be forced to expend most of his energy not on grand strategic designs or brilliant visions of military innovation, but rather on bureaucratic battles over a drastically shrinking pool of appropriations. Yet successful tactical retreats are sometimes necessary in war, and can significantly contribute to the final victory symbolized by the more glorious offensives. It was MacArthur's fate to be consigned to such an unglamorous role upon the apparent fulfillment of his lifelong ambition. Although Russell Weigley is technically correct in derisively observing that "The Army's equipment as well as its manpower and appropriations reached a nadir while Douglas MacArthur was chief of staff," historian Arthur Herman is closer to the mark in concluding, "In the end, it's hard to avoid the conclusion that MacArthur had saved the United States Army from dwindling to impotence."[157]

CHAPTER SEVEN

MacArthur and Eisenhower in the Shadow of the Rising Sun

EVEN BEFORE PRESIDENT ROOSEVELT EXTENDED HIS TENURE AS CHIEF OF staff, Douglas MacArthur was pondering his future. He was close to despondent at the thought of relinquishing his temporary four-star rank in the autumn of 1934 when he received a welcome visitor from the Philippines. Manuel Quezon was on his second trip to Washington in two years, having previously visited the capital to lobby for Philippine independence. The Great Depression had led U.S. policymakers to reconsider America's relationship to its Pacific colony and made Americans as eager to cut ties as Filipinos. Starting in 1932 a variety of independence bills were introduced in Congress until the Tydings-McDuffie Act was passed in 1934, granting the Philippines commonwealth status as a precursor to full independence in 1946.[1]

As president of the Philippine Senate, Quezon hoped to discuss the Commonwealth's defense with U.S. political and military leaders. While the Japanese navy had announced plans to break the Washington Naval Treaties and resume battleship construction, Japan's army completed its conquest of Manchuria. Many Philippine leaders believed they were Japan's next target. Expecting to preside over the new Commonwealth, Quezon reached out to the one person he believed would care about the Philippines' fate, his old friend MacArthur. As soon as the cordial greetings were dispensed with, Quezon cut to the chase. "General," he asked, "do you think that the Philippines, once independent, can defend itself?"

"I don't *think* the Philippines can defend themselves," MacArthur quickly replied, "I *know* they can."[2]

Reassured, Quezon asked MacArthur to come to Manila as his military adviser and to oversee the creation of a Philippine army. Again, MacArthur did not hesitate. "Yes, I will," he said, and the two men shook hands. Two months after Quezon's visit, MacArthur raised the subject with President Roosevelt and Secretary Dern. "Both of them were not only in complete sympathy but were enthusiastic," he wrote to Quezon.[3]

Indeed, it appeared to be an arrangement that benefited everyone involved. From Quezon's perspective, MacArthur was the obvious choice for the position. In addition to MacArthur's familiarity with the islands and his popularity with the Filipinos, Quezon believed a former chief of staff would possess considerable influence with the War Department. Quezon felt that entrusting MacArthur with the Philippines' security would bind America to his country's defense. For MacArthur, it would spare him the painful choice between retiring at age fifty-five or remaining on active duty subordinate to another chief of staff. It would also allow him to serve a people he loved deeply and to fulfill his father's mission of fostering the Philippines' freedom. Finally, sending MacArthur to Manila enabled Roosevelt to effectively exile, with honor, an ideological opponent before he could impact the 1936 election. Indeed, Roosevelt had seriously considered appointing MacArthur high commissioner to the Philippines, but when the Army's lawyers informed MacArthur that accepting the commissionership meant he would have to retire from the Army, he was unable to cut ties with the institution that had shaped his life literally since his birth.[4]

"I am prepared to devote the remainder of my life if necessary to securing a proper defense of the Philippine Nation," MacArthur wrote to Quezon. "No question that confronts it in ultimate analysis is of such importance. Some day it will mean the difference between life and death for your people."[5] Yet as they formalized a contract for the position, MacArthur imposed stiff terms. In addition to his Regular Army salary of $18,000 a year, he demanded $33,000 a year from the Philippine government—the same salary and allowances paid to the U.S. governor-general of the Philippines—and was to be provided with a seven-room, fully air-conditioned penthouse suite atop the luxurious Manila Hotel. MacArthur also obtained a letter from the adjutant general enabling him to make extra financial arrangements with the Commonwealth government without having to gain War Department approval in advance. MacArthur was thus able to secretly negotiate a commission of 46/100 of 1 percent on Philippine military spending through 1942 if the Philippine government accepted his defense budgets. Given that he and Quezon were discussing annual defense budgets of approximately $5 million a year, MacArthur stood to receive a performance bonus of roughly $250,000, a sum it would require fourteen years of service as chief of staff in the U.S. Army to obtain.[6]

On September 18, 1935, Secretary Dern issued Special Order Number 22 appointing MacArthur as military adviser to the Commonwealth of the Philippine Islands.[7] With his appointment as military adviser officially announced and his lucrative deal finalized, MacArthur turned his attention to deciding who would accompany him to Manila to staff the mission. Capt. Thomas Jefferson Davis, his personal aide of several years, would obviously accompany him. He also persuaded his physician, Maj. Howard J. Hutter, to go, although rather than advising on medical issues facing the nascent Philippine army his primary duty would be to attend to MacArthur's ailing mother. But above all others, from the time it became clear that he was returning to the Philippines, MacArthur insisted that Maj. Dwight D. Eisenhower accompany him.

Upon returning from France, where he served a second, more relaxed stint with the American Battlefield Monuments Commission, in November 1929 Eisenhower was assigned to Assistant Secretary of War Frederick Payne's office as executive assistant to Maj. Gen. George Van Horn Moseley, then Payne's principal military adviser. At Moseley's direction the Assistant Secretary's office began preparing plans for mobilizing American industry and manpower in the next war, with Eisenhower responsible for planning plant expansion. Although the resulting 180-page mobilization plan went largely unread, Eisenhower's efforts impressed Payne and Moseley. Moseley called Eisenhower "my brainy assistant" and recorded his appreciation in his subordinate's efficiency reports. He later wrote to Eisenhower: "You possess one of those exceptional minds which enables you to assemble and to analyze a set of facts, always drawing sound conclusions and, equally important, you have the ability to express those conclusions in clear and convincing form. Many officers can take the first two steps of a problem, but few have your ability of expression."[8]

After completing the mobilization study, Payne and Moseley relied on him for every writing task that came their way. Eisenhower drafted memos and letters, wrote speeches for Payne and Secretary Hurley, and authored their annual reports as well. In 1930 pacifist sentiments led Congress to pass a joint resolution establishing a War Policies Commission "to study and consider amending the Constitution, so that, should there be a war, its burden would fall equally on everyone and it would be profitable for no one."[9] The commission held hearings through May 1931. Eisenhower prepared witnesses before their testimony, and drafted MacArthur's official statement to the commission. Payne was so impressed with Eisenhower's work on the War Policies Commission and the industrial mobilization plan that he recommended him for immediate promotion from major to brigadier general.

Although MacArthur blocked this attempt to circumvent the Army's rigid seniority system, he too was impressed. He began utilizing Eisenhower's talents, asking him to draft some of his official letters and speeches, as well as having him draft the chief of staff's annual report for 1931. MacArthur put a commendation into the major's personnel file to thank him for accepting a special assignment and for his performance. "I write you this special commendation," Mac concluded, "so that you may fully realize that your outstanding talents and your ability to perform these highly important missions are fully appreciated."[10] Eisenhower was flattered, and Mamie had the letter framed. Eisenhower was soon installed in an office between Moseley and MacArthur, with direct access to both generals. In 1932 MacArthur endorsed Eisenhower's superlative efficiency report, declaring him "one of the most outstanding officers of his time and service . . . he has no superior in his grade."[11]

MacArthur was not alone in recognizing Eisenhower's abilities. As was the case after the Armistice, Ike received numerous job offers while serving in Washington. In early 1932 he received two offers within the Army. When Gen. William D. Connor—who as commandant of the War College had extensively praised Eisenhower in 1928—became West Point's superintendent in 1932, he asked Eisenhower to join him as the Academy's athletic director, an important position in the interwar Army, in part due to MacArthur's emphasis on athletics during *his* tenure a decade earlier. Similarly, Gen. Stuart Heintzelman wanted Eisenhower to return to Fort Leavenworth to serve as both a CGSS instructor and as commander of the infantry battalion stationed there. Eisenhower was ambivalent about returning to either West Point or Leavenworth. Yet before he could decide, MacArthur and Moseley denied both requests. In June 1933 Eisenhower was offered the position of executive manager of the Public Works Administration. Yet Eisenhower noted at the time that when he informed MacArthur, "He emphatically refused—so that's that! Probably it would have been a marvelous opportunity in some ways—but—I'm glad I'm staying with the General."[12]

Eisenhower's reputation as a writer also drew interest from the private sector. Publishing magnate William Randolph Hearst offered him a job as military editor for his newspaper chain. Hearst offered a salary of between $15,000 and $20,000 a year, a fortune compared to his annual Army salary of $3,000. Although the prospect of being financially self-sufficient for the first time in his life was tempting, after consulting Mamie and Milton he declined Hearst's offer. He remembered Fox Conner's prophecy regarding the inevitability of another conflict, and as Stephen Ambrose observes, "He did not want to report on that war—he wanted to fight it."[13]

Evaluating Eisenhower's performance, MacArthur acknowledged how much Eisenhower's talents were in demand: "The numbers of personal requests for your services brought to me by heads of many of the Army's principal activities during the past few years furnish convincing proof of the reputation you have established as an outstanding soldier."[14] Yet part of the reason Eisenhower refused these offers was his admiration for MacArthur, whom he called "essentially a romantic figure." MacArthur had assured him that "as long he stays in the Army I am one of the people earmarked for his 'gang.'" Eisenhower wrote that MacArthur was "decisive, personable," and "Very appreciative of good work, positive in his convictions—a genius in giving concise and clear instructions."[15] He was impressed by MacArthur's courage in fighting for greater Army appropriations in Congress despite the risk to his own standing. But what especially captivated Eisenhower was MacArthur's intellect. "He did have a hell of an intellect! My God, but he was smart. He had a *brain!*"[16] In his memoirs, Eisenhower remembered, "On any subject he chose to discuss, his knowledge, always amazingly comprehensive, and largely accurate, poured out in a torrent of words." Of course, Eisenhower also notes that "'Discuss' is hardly the correct word; discussion suggests dialogue and the General's conversations were usually monologues."[17]

Eisenhower formally remained in the Assistant Secretary's office until February 1933 when, with Roosevelt's inauguration approaching, Payne resigned and returned home to Massachusetts. MacArthur promptly had Eisenhower transferred to the General Staff. Eisenhower was never given an official job title, and his efficiency reports simply identified him as "on duty in Office Chief of Staff."[18] "I wasn't really an aide," he later recalled. "The job really didn't have a name. I called myself his good man Friday."[19] MacArthur installed Eisenhower in a broom closet–sized alcove adjacent to the chief of staff's large office. Their work spaces were separated only by a slatted door that did not reach the floor, and when MacArthur wanted Eisenhower he simply called by raising his voice. Yet as was the case for Marshall under Pershing a decade earlier, being MacArthur's assistant placed Eisenhower in a unique position for a mere major. Eisenhower worked for MacArthur on analyses, memos, and speeches, and wrote many of the letters and reports the chief of staff used to plead the Army's case before Congress. Thus, all of the Army's business—war plans, intelligence reports, promotion lists, and procurement plans—passed across his desk before it reached MacArthur.[20]

Eisenhower's duties were often complicated by the eccentric hours MacArthur kept, occasionally taking long breaks for lunch lasting hours at a time, and then keeping his staff at the office late into the night. MacArthur's lengthy absences from his office were frequently due to his secret visits to Isabel Rosario Cooper, the beautiful Eurasian mistress he brought back from the Philippines when she was sixteen, and whom he had set up in a suite at the Hotel Chastleton ten blocks north of the State, Navy, and War Building. When MacArthur brought a libel suit against columnists Drew Pearson and Robert S. Allen, claiming they had wrongly portrayed his treatment of the Bonus Army as "unwarranted, unnecessary, arbitrary, harsh, and brutal," Representative Collins made Pearson aware of Isabel's existence. Although he had already ended the relationship by this point, MacArthur dispatched Eisenhower to find Cooper. Ike could not locate her, however, because Pearson had found her first and hidden her away with his brother in a Baltimore apartment. When Pearson threatened to expose MacArthur's tryst, the general abruptly dropped the suit. MacArthur gave Isabel $15,000—nearly a year's salary—for his letters to her, and paid a similar sum to defray Pearson's legal costs. MacArthur's friend Adm. William Leahy believed MacArthur would have beaten Pearson in court. "He was a bachelor," Leahy remarked, "All he had to do was look everybody in the face and say: 'So what?'" But more than anything else, MacArthur feared his mother's disapproval. "Cunt can make you look awfully silly at times," Leahy concluded.[21]

MacArthur's biographer Frazier Hunt noted that Eisenhower "had the rare faculty of being able to put down on paper the exact shade of meaning that his superior desired. 'Ike got so he could write more like MacArthur than the General did himself,' was the way one officer who served on the General Staff at the time explained it. His mind was sharp and keen, and he had been perfectly trained in staff work."[22] Yet Eisenhower's prowess as MacArthur's amanuensis exacted a high price. Eisenhower's relentless intensity and perfectionism, combined with long hours spent reading dense position papers, chain smoking, and eating poorly took their toll on his health. He attempted to compensate for the stress through an active social life centered around the Eisenhower's home at the Wyoming Apartments, which included the Pattons, Gerows, and others. But he was plagued by gastrointestinal ailments and bursitis, and by the summer of 1934 his back problems had become so persistent and painful that he could barely function. Finally, that July he was admitted to Walter Reed for arthritis of the lumbar region, although he was also obviously suffering from exhaustion, and he spent forty days on his back in the Army hospital.[23]

Surprisingly, his health problems were not why Eisenhower was reluctant to accompany MacArthur to the Philippines. Although he had sought service in the islands in 1915 and 1919, by 1935 he desperately wanted a troop command. He thought he "deserved after years of staff work, a chance to serve again with troops."[24] With MacArthur leaving his position as chief of staff, Eisenhower believed he would finally get the line assignment he had long sought. Additionally, Mamie was nearly distraught by the news of the Philippines assignment. Understandably, she felt she had already served her time in the tropics with her three years in Panama. The Eisenhowers were also devastated by the untimely and horrifically painful death of Mamie's best friend, Gee Gerow's wife Katie, in the summer of 1935. Katie was believed to have contracted a mysterious illness while the Gerows were stationed in the Philippines, and Mamie was terrified of contracting the same disease. Consequently, she refused to join her husband in Manila, using the decision to permit John to finish the 1935–1936 school year in Washington as a convenient excuse.[25]

Despite Eisenhower's misgivings, he acquiesced to MacArthur's request. "General MacArthur lowered the boom on me," Eisenhower wrote. The chief of staff "said that he and I had worked together for a long time and he didn't want to bring in somebody new." Eisenhower was impressed, perhaps even touched, by the apparent sincerity with which MacArthur admitted his reliance upon him. Yet Eisenhower also acknowledged that "whatever might have been going on inside me, I was in no position to argue with the Chief of Staff."[26] According to John Eisenhower, his father feared MacArthur might be petty enough to ruin Eisenhower's career if spurned.

Of course, there *were* compensations to staying with MacArthur. The mission of creating an army from scratch would be a challenging assignment and a valuable experience. In addition to their Regular Army salaries, the members of the advisory group would draw an additional salary from the Philippine government. Finally, in the interwar Army's shrunken bureaucracy, there were few paths to advancement for an ambitious officer like Eisenhower. Following MacArthur to Manila meant continued close proximity to one of the Army's most dynamic leaders, and at worst, MacArthur assured him the staff detail would only be "for a year or so."[27]

As further inducement, MacArthur allowed Eisenhower to select any officer he wanted to help him create the defense plan and accompany them to the Philippines. Eisenhower chose his West Point classmate Maj. James B. Ord "because of his quickness of mind and ability as a staff officer."[28] Ord came from a distinguished military family, his grandfather having commanded a corps under Ulysses S. Grant during the Civil War. "Jimmy" had been born and raised in Mexico and spoke fluent Spanish, the Philippines' language of business and politics. Although the jovial, portly Ord "looked like central casting's idea of a small-town bank manager" in his thick, horn-rimmed glasses, he was the first officer from the Class of 1915 to win an award for valor.[29] He was recommended for the Medal of Honor during the Punitive Expedition to Mexico in 1916, and was eventually awarded the Army's second-highest decoration for bravery, the Distinguished Service Cross. Ord graduated from the Ecole de Guerre in Paris before attending CGSS with Eisenhower, and taught at both West Point and the Army War College. When recommending officers to serve as General Moseley's assistant in 1934, Eisenhower wrote that Ord "is a superior type in every respect. There is nothing too good to say about him, and if you ever get a hold of him you will never willingly let go."[30]

His staff assembled, MacArthur and his entourage left Washington on October 1, heading by train to San Francisco. Secretary Dern had issued orders for MacArthur to travel to Manila while still serving as Army chief of staff, and MacArthur believed that President Roosevelt had promised to delay naming his successor so that he could arrive in Manila still wearing four stars on his uniform, which he believed would enhance his prestige. Yet when the train arrived in Cheyenne, Wyoming, on October 2, a telegram from the War Department notified MacArthur that Roosevelt had just appointed Malin Craig as chief of staff, effective immediately. MacArthur instantaneously reverted from four stars to the two stars denoting his permanent rank of major general, and would now arrive in Manila as the *former* head of the U.S. Army. MacArthur lost his composure and launched into a tirade that Eisenhower described as "an explosive denunciation of politics, bad manners, bad judgment, broken promises, arrogance, unconstitutionality, insensitivity, and the way the world had gone to hell."[31]

MacArthur's wounded pride was temporarily forgotten during the voyage aboard the *President Harding* to Manila. At a cocktail party hosted by the ship's captain to honor Boston mayor James B. Curley, MacArthur met Jean Marie Faircloth, a vibrant, petite thirty-seven-year-old spinster. The daughter of an affluent Nashville banker, she possibly reminded him of the southern belle his mother had been. Jean was proud of her Confederate forebears, one of whom had fought against Arthur MacArthur in the Civil War. She was also captivated by soldiers, and was drawn to MacArthur. They struck up an immediate friendship, which blossomed into a quiet romance as the ship steamed across the Pacific. Jean was traveling to Shanghai to stay with friends, but remained on board at MacArthur's pleading and took up residence in Manila instead, where MacArthur and her were often seen together.[32]

The *President Harding* docked in Manila on October 26, arriving in time to attend Quezon's inauguration on November 15. The president-elect, the entire leadership of the new Philippine government, and much of the American expatriate community were at the dock to greet MacArthur. MacArthur immediately settled in to the air-conditioned penthouse at the Manila Hotel, allowing him to escape the city's pervasive and oppressive humidity. The views from the suite's two balconies were spectacular, with one affording a panoramic perspective on Manila Bay, and the other overlooking the walled heart of old Manila, the Intramuros. MacArthur liked to pace back and forth in deep thought across the terrace for about an hour each day. Yet the heart of the apartment was the library, where MacArthur housed he and his father's nearly 2,000-volume book collection and display cases preserving both MacArthurs' medals.[33]

The Philippines Defense Mission's headquarters were a short walk away in the Intramuros, housed in his former residence, 1 Calle Victoria, the large and picturesque building known as the House on the Wall. MacArthur's office was in the large, handsome room that had been his bedroom when he commanded the Military District of Manila. It was spacious, with a high ceiling, and offered stunning views of the bay and the city.

Initially, however, MacArthur could not fully enjoy these amenities. Shortly after boarding the *President Harding*, eighty-four-year-old Pinky became ill. Although MacArthur radioed ahead to Manila to ensure she would receive the best care possible, she died on December 3, 1935. In his memoirs, MacArthur credited her as the pillar of the MacArthur family, and lamented her departure as marking the passing of a generation: "Of the four of us who had started from the plains of New Mexico, three were now gone, leaving me in my loneliness only a memory of the household we had shared, so filled with graciousness and old-fashioned living."[34] Eisenhower observed that Pinky's death had a "deeply personal effect" on MacArthur and "affected the General's spirit for many months."[35] To his friend Charlie O'Laughlin, MacArthur wrote: "Mother's death has been a tremendous blow to me and I am finding the greatest difficulty in recoordinating myself to the changed conditions ... My loss has partially stunned me and I find myself groping desperately but futilely ... For the first [time] in my life, I need all the help I can get."[36]

MacArthur's grief added to the already daunting challenges that lay ahead. Most outside observers considered MacArthur's optimism regarding the Philippines' defenses unjustified. As early as 1907, the man who did the most to bring the archipelago into the American empire, Theodore Roosevelt, privately described the islands as an "Achilles heel" threatened by Japan. In the 1930s, Roosevelt's secretary of state Elihu Root estimated that the Japanese could take the islands within a week. And Henry Stimson, a former secretary of war and governor-general of the Philippines, told Quezon in March 1935 that "the American garrison and any garrison he could raise would be merely a pawn to fall into the hands of the Japanese."[37]

The American military establishment was almost uniformly negative about the possibility of defending the Philippines. War Plan Orange, formulated in 1923, had hoped the U.S. garrison could hold out for six months until naval reinforcements arrived. Yet Brig. Gen. Hugh Drum, chief of the War Plans Division, maintained in 1924 that in any war with Japan "the Philippines would in all probability be lost."[38] In the late 1920s, Maj. Gen. Johnson Hagood, then commanding the Philippines Division, told President Hoover that it was "not within the wildest possibility to maintain or to raise in the Philippine Islands a sufficient force to defend it against any probable foe." Hagood said that Corregidor, with its fortifications, and well-stocked with food, *might* hold out for six months or more, but that all other U.S. troops in the Philippines would be captured or killed in any war.[39] Yet Corregidor's commander, Brig. Gen. Stanley D. Embick, wrote in 1933 that "To carry out the present Orange plan, with the provisions for the early dispatch

---

* MacArthur's older brother, Arthur MacArthur III, was a U.S. Navy officer who served in World War I and died suddenly of appendicitis in 1923.

of our fleet to the Philippine waters, would be literally an act of madness."[40] Two years later, as head of the War Plans Division, Embick characterized the Philippines as a "military liability of incalculable magnitude."[41] Thus, during the interdepartmental negotiations in the autumn of 1935, the Army advocated concentrating U.S. forces on the triangle formed by Alaska, Hawaii, and Panama.

MacArthur nevertheless believed the new commonwealth comprised "the most important section of the great and vaguely defined region known as the Far East" which was poised to have a "universal influence upon the prosperity and welfare" of the world for centuries to come.[42] To MacArthur, therefore, the defense of the Philippines and U.S. national security were synonymous. When asked by Secretary Hurley whether the islands were an asset or a liability, MacArthur contended that they provided an essential naval base in the Western Pacific and that their possession allowed the Navy to protect U.S. Far Eastern interests. MacArthur argued passionately that not only were the Philippines the key to defending the Pacific, but that America had a higher moral obligation. Finally, the Philippines were personally important to MacArthur. His father had begun arming Filipinos to defend their country, and MacArthur felt obligated to bring his family's work to completion.[43]

When he became chief of staff in 1930, MacArthur threw out nearly a decade's worth of planning. He decided he would be "wasting time" trying to convince his subordinates in the General Staff of the Philippines' strategic value, and thus he "short-circuited" the process by going directly to President Hoover to inform him that in the event of war he would immediately dispatch two of America's stateside divisions to Manila even though as chief of staff he surely knew that outside of Hawaii there was not a single combat division in the country and that the reserves were in desperate condition. War Plan Orange was rewritten in 1933 to reflect MacArthur's views, calling for the immediate dispatch of six divisions—a force roughly equivalent to the entire Regular Army in the continental United States—just when these experienced troops would be needed to train the reserves and draftees.[44] Unsurprisingly, almost as soon as MacArthur left Washington in 1935, military planners reverted to the previous iteration of War Plan Orange with its emphasis on hemispheric defense.

The General Staff's pessimism notwithstanding, when MacArthur looked at the Philippines, he saw Switzerland—a small nation that had guarded its independence for four centuries by training and arming every able-bodied male. He told Secretary Hurley that "the Philippines can be successfully defended by the employment of native manpower against any probable attack."[45] MacArthur envisioned building a defense patterned after Switzerland's citizen-soldier system of conscription in which a core of 11,000 Filipino regulars would train 400,000 native troops to be mobilized at the outbreak of war. This program would be established over the course of a decade, with 40,000 reserve members trained annually and assigned to a "particular geographical area in which its individual members ordinarily reside."[46] Buttressed by a fleet of fifty patrol boats and 200 aircraft, these reservists would fight in small, mobile squads from their assorted home areas to defend the beaches against attack. The islands' terrain, much of which was covered by mountain and jungle, would further aid the defenders and frustrate potential invaders. Consequently, extrapolating from his father's war in which it took 100,000 American soldiers three years to suppress 20,000 Filipino insurgents, MacArthur estimated that conquering the Philippines would require "a half million men, ten billion dollars, tremendous casualties and three years' time," more than any potential adversary would want to endure.[47]

Prior to departing Washington, MacArthur asked the War College's commandant to create a special committee to work out the details of a defense plan based on his militia concept. Ord—then serving as an instructor at the War College—served as the committee's chairman, and the group began working in November 1934. Ord was instructed to prepare a plan based solely on military considerations, taking into consideration only elements such as population and local geographic and climatic conditions to determine the optimal force strength and organization. After Eisenhower reviewed the committee's findings, he and Ord presented the plan to MacArthur. The two majors proposed to build up the Philippine army gradually. The first year would be used to transition the Constabulary into a 20,000-man standing army. Once a network of training sites was established and a corps of trained NCOs to serve as instructors was developed, each year 40,000 recruits would be trained as reservists responsible for thirty years of military service. After a decade the Philippine army would boast ten reserve divisions, with the small standing army serving as its spearhead.[48]

Chief of Staff Craig and the War Plans Division were skeptical of MacArthur's concept, and in December 1935 nearly the entire General Staff endorsed a report debunking his assumptions. First, the War Plans Division dismissed the Swiss analogy, noting the vast geographic, social, and economic differences between the Philippines and Switzerland. Naval planners noted the Philippines had more coastline to defend than the United States, and that MacArthur's "mosquito fleet" of torpedo boats would scarcely slow the Japanese navy, which could match destroyers two-for-one against MacArthur's flimsy 65-footers. MacArthur's proposed air force would be overwhelmed by Japanese planes based on Formosa, less than 200 miles from Luzon, or Japan's aircraft carriers. Unlike Switzerland, the Philippines was not a "compact land unit," and rather than gaining a defender's typical advantage of secure interior lines, MacArthur's army would be scattered across a series of unconnected islands vulnerable to enemy blockade. Japan could easily overrun these small, isolated elements piecemeal through its vastly superior firepower and mobility. Instead, the War Plans Division proposed gradually expanding the Philippine Constabulary rather than building a large, expensive army.[49]

Although the Army recommended the United States withdraw entirely from the Philippines in 1946, America's political leaders feared that forsaking the Philippines in the event of war would undermine U.S. prestige. Hoover summarized this dilemma to MacArthur, saying the United States "had a definite moral responsibility in regard to the Philippine people but at the same time they were a great liability."[50] U.S. policymakers therefore chose to pursue a policy of calculated hypocrisy in which America would not abandon the Philippines, yet neither would it provide the U.S. military nor the Filipinos with the resources necessary to ensure the islands' defense.

Ord and Eisenhower encountered more immediate problems than Washington's skepticism. Their initial plan for the defense program suggested that an annual budget of fifty million pesos ($25 million) was the bare minimum acceptable to ensure the Commonwealth's security. MacArthur, however, declared that it was too expensive and ordered them to reduce the cost by half. With serious misgivings, Eisenhower and Ord went back to the drawing board. They made various revisions, such as equipping the Philippine army with obsolete American rifles and paying conscripts "little more than cigarette money." Eisenhower thought that "such a makeshift force would be rejected out of hand as worthless for defense."[51]

Instead, MacArthur finally revealed that the Philippine defense budget could not exceed $8 million and demanded still more cuts. Eisenhower and Ord subsequently trimmed the proposed training schedule for each recruit from twelve to six months. They stretched the munitions procurement program from ten to twenty years. Although any plausible defense of the archipelago would require naval and air forces to preempt or counter beach landings, Eisenhower recalled, "We could no longer think of a Navy of any size whatsoever and for the moment we abandoned the possibility of developing a small air force."[52] Whereas MacArthur had spent the last five years lecturing Congress on how critical officers were to an army, the projected professional force of 1,500 officers and 19,000 enlisted reserves was cut to 930 officers and 7,000 enlisted men in a single division that would act as a training cadre for ten reserve divisions developed through the annual conscription and training of 20,000 reservists each year. Eisenhower felt the contingent of officers was cut "to the point where this would be dangerously close to an army of recruits only." In his diary, he noted that "Ord and I expressed the conviction that with this kind of organization it would be difficult to sustain efficiency because of the lack of professional personnel."[53] Later, he recalled: "All Jimmy Ord and I could do was to assemble our proposals for a skeleton force that some day might have flesh put on its bones."[54] MacArthur presented their planning in April 1936 as the "Report on National Defense in the Philippines," which was quickly accepted by President Quezon and the Commonwealth legislature.

Despite the budgetary obstacles and the War Department's skepticism, MacArthur projected unwavering optimism in his first formal report to Quezon. Although not a single conscript had reported for duty yet, no training camps had been built, and no weapons had been procured, MacArthur declared that the "general progress in the development of the army has exceeded original anticipation." Regarding the army's costs, he assured that "directly and indirectly the defense plan makes every possible concession to economy consistent with efficiency. The result is that in the world today there is no other defensive system that provides an equal security at remotely comparable cost to the people maintaining it."[55] In a speech to Filipino officers at Baguio that August, MacArthur said "when the Philippine Defense Plan had reached fruition, it will represent a defensive strength that will give hesitation to the strongest and most ruthless nation in the world."[56] Similarly, in September *Collier's* quoted him as saying: "We're going to make it so very expensive for any nation to attack these islands that no nation will try it."[57]

MacArthur's misplaced confidence stemmed partly from a Napoleonic ego that convinced him his mere presence would assure success. It also derived from his romanticized view of Filipinos. Most American officers who served with the Scouts shared J. Lawton Collins's assessment that the Philippine Scouts were "fine, well-disciplined, loyal troops."[58] MacArthur never doubted that such excellent human material could be replicated on a larger scale to create the foundation of the Philippine army, and claimed that "without exception," American advisers "report remarkable progress on the part of every officer of the new Army with whom they habitually come in contact."[59]

Yet while Eisenhower initially had high expectations for the Philippine army and found there were some capable men in the Constabulary, "they seem, with few exceptions, unaccustomed to the requirements of administrative and executive procedure." He noted that in conference they seemed to understand well enough what was required and promised to deliver shortly. "But thereafter it is quite likely that nothing whatsoever will be done." Consequently, both he and Ord had "learned to expect from the Filipinos with whom we deal, a minimum of performance from a maximum of promise."[60] Moreover, Eisenhower complained, Quezon would make decisions and "we know nothing of them."[61]

In addition to these coordination problems, MacArthur's temperament was increasingly becoming an issue. Eisenhower urged the general to meet weekly with President Quezon to secure agreement on the numerous details the Mission faced, but MacArthur refused. He saw himself as an elder statesman and, Eisenhower observed, "He apparently thinks it would not be keeping with his rank and position for him to do so do."[62] Consequently, the task of liaising with Quezon devolved to Eisenhower, so much that Quezon gave him a private office in Malacanan Palace next to his own. Eisenhower believed MacArthur's ego was hurting the Mission, and recorded in his diary in January 1936: "The general is more and more indulging in the habit of damning everybody who disagrees with him over any detail, in extravagant, sometimes almost hysterical fashion." Moreover, "he seems to consider that the combined use of his rank, a stream of generalizations that are studded with malapropos, and a refusal to permit the presentation of opposing opinion will, by silencing his subordinates, establish the validity of his contentions."[63]

One day in the summer of 1936 MacArthur strode into the Mission's offices beaming. He announced that Quezon, pleased with their initial progress report, wanted to give the American officers high ranks in the new Philippine army. Eisenhower and Ord would be made generals and MacArthur would become a field marshal. Convinced that titles impressed Asians, and eager to hold a rank no other American officer had ever attained, MacArthur accepted the offer.

Eisenhower was aghast. He persuaded Ord and T. J. Davis that accepting these promotions would undermine the Mission's work by making them look ridiculous to their fellow American officers. Furthermore, holding these ranks would thereafter cast their advice to the Filipinos in terms of rank rather than the merit of their proposals. Eisenhower tried to convince MacArthur to refuse the title since it was rather ridiculous to be the field marshal of a virtually nonexistent army. He said: "General, you have been a four-star general. This is a *proud* thing. There's only been a few who had it. Why in the *hell* do you want a *banana* country giving you a field marshal-ship? This . . . this looks like you're trying for some kind of. . . ." MacArthur stopped him there. "Oh, Jesus," Eisenhower recalled. "He just gave me hell!"[64] Although MacArthur told Eisenhower he could not decline the promotion without offending Quezon, Eisenhower noted MacArthur "is tickled pink" with the rank.[65]

Thus, on August 24, 1936, MacArthur was formally presented with a gold baton symbolizing his new rank at an opulent ceremony at Malacanan Palace. Eisenhower watched in disbelief, calling the whole occasion "rather fantastic."[66] Half a world away, Pershing shared Eisenhower's opinion and felt all the field marshal silliness was just another manifestation of MacArthur's worst traits. He wrote to their mutual friend O'Laughlin that MacArthur's "appointment as Field Marshal of a State and an army, neither of which has, as yet, an independent existence, was more or less ridiculous."[67]

MacArthur delivered a stirring speech after the ceremony—for which he wore a specially designed sharkskin uniform consisting of black trousers and a white coat bedecked with braid, stars, and unique lapel designs—on the nobility of soldiers' sacrifices. American critics derided the remarks and mocked MacArthur as "the Napoleon of Luzon" and "the dandy of the Philippines."[68] Conversely, Filipino commentators praised his remarks, and MacArthur became a figure of awe amongst the Filipinos. As Quezon's wife Aurora once explained to U.S. High Commissioner Frank Murphy: "Frank, you don't seem to understand. Douglas is our brother."[69] Indeed, MacArthur initially had the new president's complete trust and virtual carte blanche in his program to create the Philippine army. Yet although MacArthur kept an office in the presidential palace, he rarely met or spoke with Quezon. Relations between them began to deteriorate until their old friendship had been replaced by what MacArthur called "a thinly veiled hostility."[70] MacArthur's advice was typically expressed as demands, and when he proved unable to produce supplies or equipment for the fledgling Philippine army, Quezon came to distrust his field marshal.

The fault was not entirely MacArthur's. What were vital priorities for the Mission and the Philippine army were treated with indifference and a lack of funding by the War Department. The Philippine Department commander, Maj. Gen. Lucius Holbrook, actually believed a Philippine army would serve as "an ever increasing potential Reserve for the American forces in the Philippines." He instituted a double assignment system so that each recruit was attached to a unit of both the Philippine army and a U.S. Army Organized Reserve, and he revised the Philippine Department's plans to include "the role the Philippine Army will play in the defense of the Philippines from now on."[71] He presented these views in "forceful fashion" to the War Department, and Eisenhower noted, "General Holbrook sees the entire problem exactly as we do and is doing everything possible to assist us."[72] Despite this support, Holbrook had no resources to spare, and could not help the Mission in any material way.

Worse, rather than alleviating the U.S. military's burden, the Philippine army continually required more equipment and money. With the international situation deteriorating, Chief of Staff Craig was determined to improve the Army's short-term readiness and was reluctant to commit precious men or materiel to what many deemed a peripheral region of dubious strategic value. MacArthur's incessant demands were particularly irritating given that he never bothered to consult the War Department about his policies, and that as a recent chief of staff he knew how resource starved the Army was.[73] By mid-1937, even Holbrook was fed up with MacArthur's raids on his staff to build up the Mission. He complained to Washington, and the War Department issued an order to MacArthur requiring him to obtain Washington's approval before transferring further personnel from the Philippine Department to his own staff.

Given that MacArthur's vision for Philippine defense required Washington's backing, Eisenhower urged MacArthur to return to the States to lobby for support. "It is becoming more and more evident," Eisenhower wrote in February 1936, "that there is no basic appreciation in the War Department of the local defense problem, at least as we see it." He wanted MacArthur to speak to Craig and Secretary Dern. "Jimmy and I believe that if this whole matter were clearly explained to the American Chief of Staff and Secretary of War, that very substantial and effective assistance would be forthcoming."[74] Once again, MacArthur refused Eisenhower's advice. Instead, he ordered him to prepare a paper explaining the "efficiency and soundness of the Philippine Defense Plan, and the idea that the American War Department should cooperate efficiently toward its development."[75]

MacArthur delayed traveling to Washington because he had convinced himself that Roosevelt was going to lose the November election, and all he had to do was wait until a more pliable Republican administration was in power. On the strength of a dubious *Literary Digest* poll, he proclaimed to Eisenhower and Davis that "[Alf] Landon is to be elected, probably by a landslide." When Eisenhower showed him letters from an Abilene friend predicting Landon would not even carry his home state of Kansas, MacArthur "got perfectly furious" and condemned Eisenhower's "stupidity." When Davis sided with Eisenhower, MacArthur denounced them both as "fearful and small-minded people who are afraid to express judgments that are obvious from the evidence at hand." After Roosevelt's overwhelming victory—he received 523 electoral votes to Landon's 8, as the challenger only carried Maine and Vermont—MacArthur backpedaled rapidly. He accused the *Literary Digest* of crookedness, but Eisenhower noted, "he's never expressed to TJ or to me any regret for his awful bawling out."[76]

While Eisenhower was dealing with MacArthur's erratic behavior, back in Washington Mamie acknowledged the reality that her husband would not be reassigned anytime soon, and that "if she wanted to stay married to Ike" she would have to move to Manila.[77] After John's graduation from the eighth grade, she and John sailed for the Philippines in the summer of 1936. Eisenhower met them at the pier, and she was shocked to see him completely bald, having shaved his head to keep cool in the sweltering heat. For the first year, Manila seemed to justify her trepidation. Although most of the Mission's staff lived in the Manila Hotel, only MacArthur's suite was air-conditioned. In contrast, the Eisenhowers' apartment was like a sauna, exacerbating an undiagnosed stomach disorder that kept Mamie in bed most days. The windows were shuttered during the day and opened during the cooler nights, and the large mosquito net that had to be let down each night triggered Mamie's claustrophobia. In April 1937, Mamie went to Baguio to visit John at the Episcopalian school he was attending. En route, she suffered a stomach hemorrhage and fell into a coma. She nearly died, and her weight fell below 100 pounds as she spent a month recuperating in the hospital.[78]

When Mamie returned to Manila, she was relieved to discover that a new wing of the Manila Hotel had been finished and the Eisenhowers were given an air-conditioned apartment. The cool air meant the windows could be closed and the netting eliminated, and soon the vibrant Mamie of Washington returned. She overcame her initial dislike of the Philippines, as virtually every day there was some social event, ranging from mah-jongg and bridge to polo matches and elaborate dinners at the Army-Navy club. "Oh, the social life was terrific," Mamie remembered, as she befriended Mildred Hodges (wife of then–Lieutenant Colonel Courtney Hodges) and Margo Clay (wife of then-Captain Lucius Clay), amongst others.[79]

Amidst the various setbacks and frustrations, 1936 provided some positive news for Eisenhower and Ord regarding the Philippine army. In April the first registration of twenty-year-old Filipino men was conducted, and an unexpectedly high total of 150,000 Filipinos responded. Although Eisenhower and Ord were suspicious of some recruits' legitimacy, they were pleasantly surprised at the number of young men who volunteered.

And then MacArthur threw them a curveball.

Because of the large registration, MacArthur told them to drastically change the training plan for 1937. Starting pretty much from scratch, Ord and Eisenhower's original plan called for training only 6,000 recruits in 1937. Yet MacArthur informed Eisenhower that Quezon had decided that 40,000—the target number not envisioned until 1941—be enrolled in 1937, half in January, half in July.[80]

Eisenhower was incredulous. First, it would not be possible to select and build the 125 training camps needed for the new recruits by January. "We cannot select each site carefully and provide proper technical supervision for each construction project," he wrote.[81] Even the camps that had already been selected were not ready, as most lacked adequate water, roads, and light. Additionally, equipment of nearly every type—rifles, tents, shoes—was lacking. Second, even if the infrastructure *could* be established in time, there were few officers coming from the Constabulary with previous military experience. This meant there were not enough competent officers to train the reservists or to properly maintain the small stock of available equipment. "We have no officer corps to supervise organization on such a scale," Eisenhower lamented, "and officers cannot be produced out of thin air."[82]

Above all else, Eisenhower and Ord warned MacArthur that there was no funding to support an expanded mobilization. "On June 15, 1936," Eisenhower wrote, "I presented to the General what was intended to be a protest against the 30 Division program, a memorandum in which the certain minimum costs were estimated."[83] The details were daunting. Eisenhower estimated the overall cost of the additional men to the ten-year plan at ten million pesos. The 1936 defense budget was already expended, and the expansion required borrowing against the next year's funding in order to complete the current year's program. "Jim and I undertook to get the general to modify his order," Eisenhower wrote. "We insisted further than the general thought we should, and he gave us one of his regular shouting tirades."[84] Eisenhower and Ord "urged a budgetary basis for all planning," and MacArthur "grew furious, accusing us of 'arguing technicalities' to defeat the conceptions of the high command!" MacArthur lectured his assistants on "adequacy of security" as represented by numbers of divisions trained and ready and "made some prophecies that additional money would be forthcoming." In the end, Eisenhower was forced to proceed on the new thirty-division plan "at the specific and unequivocal order of the Field Marshal."[85]

The first tranche of inductees arrived at the start of 1937, and over 19,000 trainees graduated in May. MacArthur told a journalist:

> *In every respect the first series of training camps has demonstrated the soundness of the plan ... The capacity of the Filipino officer and soldier, whether Regular, Reserve or trainee, to overcome difficulties, to absorb fundamentals of the military profession and to sustain a high morale and esprit while doing so, encourages a confidence in the successful outcome to the country's effort to prepare a respectable national defense."[86]*

But Eisenhower and Ord knew the program was a disaster. In order to meet MacArthur's demands to save money they had cut corners by shortening training time, reducing equipment, and discharging former Scout officers and NCOs who comprised the training cadre. The draftees reflected the diversity of the Philippines, but not necessarily in a good way—they spoke eight languages and eighty-seven different dialects, and much of the brief time for training was spent simply devising ways to communicate amongst themselves. Over 20 percent were illiterate, and more time was consumed teaching rudimentary principles of hygiene, barracks living, and the military structure necessary for a modern army. Consequently, the actual *military* training imparted during the five-and-a-half-month program was pathetically shallow, and almost none of the graduates could perform even the most basic tasks the program was supposed to impart.[87]

One observer of the trainees wrote:

> *General MacArthur, must have his tongue in his cheek when he sounds off about them or else he does not visit the training camps. I have visited a few here in the provinces. The state of affairs is indescribable. They put a poor miserable third lieutenant, with at the most six months training,*

237

in charge of several hundred of these savages who have never known a moment's restraint nor discipline in their lives ... they have no common language, it was quite impossible.[88]

After an inspection trip to southern Luzon three weeks into the second training period in July 1937, Eisenhower found that "with regard to the cadres the early inspections have been disappointing.... [the] conditions were found ... to be very unsatisfactory." He continued, "The constant rains are, of course, partially responsible for this but many other defects were traceable to neglect on the part of cadre officers."[89] Ord wrote his wife saying MacArthur's plans "might have been done by Jules Verne in his more imaginative moods."[90]

MacArthur was not actually present to witness the training himself. Just as the first wave of recruits arrived in January 1937, he and Quezon were finally traveling to Washington to attend the swearing-in of the new high commissioner, Paul V. McNutt. Their trip was nearly as disastrous as the training in the Philippines. Quezon alienated U.S. policymakers almost immediately upon their arrival in San Francisco by telling reporters he wanted Philippine independence not in 1946, but by the end of 1938. He reiterated this demand at a luncheon with President Roosevelt, who did not appreciate Quezon's announcement and rejected his plea. MacArthur did not fare any better in his lobbying efforts. He went to the War Department to acquire munitions for the Philippine army through loans or sales, but remembered "My request for supplies and equipment went unheeded."[91] Worse, perhaps, while stateside MacArthur was being honored at a dinner when the lead speaker, a retired army general, teased him by noting his Philippine field marshal uniform resembled that of a washroom attendant. MacArthur had to sit stonefaced, staring into space, as the audience around him laughed.[92]

When MacArthur returned from the United States he sent Ord to Washington to try to persuade the War Department to lend or sell munitions to the Philippines. The jovial, personable Ord had more success, writing Eisenhower: "I haven't yet figured out why there should be so much skepticism—and some hostility—concerning our plan—I think it must be because nobody knows a darned thing about it.—and every time I sit down and talk—answer questions about methods, organization, training, equipment and so on, they come around."[93]

While Ord was in Washington, Eisenhower inherited responsibility for the Philippine army's budget. When he warned MacArthur that it only provided one million pesos for mobilization equipment such as tents and mess kits, MacArthur ordered him to add 3.5 million pesos. Failure to supply recruits with this equipment, MacArthur declared, would "defeat his whole plan."[94] Eisenhower strenuously objected to MacArthur's impetuous demand to increase expenditures without commensurate savings. Eisenhower revised the budget to save 1.5 million pesos, but despite these deductions the 1937 budget totaled more than $12 million, 50 percent higher than planned.[95]

The budget crisis finally came to a head in October 1937. With Ord still in the United States, Eisenhower began to draft the 1938 budget to fund MacArthur's defense plan. His final figure was twenty-five million pesos, nine million more than the annual amount MacArthur had promised Quezon in 1935. MacArthur assured Eisenhower that world conditions, the Filipino desire for early independence, or perhaps money from the United States would produce the funds necessary to cover the gaping deficit. Yet when Ord returned to the Philippines in the fall and briefed Quezon that the budget was 50 percent higher than planned, the president was "astounded and furious."[96]

Quezon demanded an explanation from MacArthur on October 7, and the field marshal promptly threw his staff under the bus. MacArthur told Quezon that the over-budget expenditures were Eisenhower and Ord's fault and had been done without his approval. The next day MacArthur called a conference of his aides and claimed he had never authorized a budget over sixteen million pesos, and that the new budget made him look like "a fool or a knave."[97] Although MacArthur attempted to play off the situation as a "miscommunication," Eisenhower seethed at MacArthur's dishonesty and vented in his diary:

> *I've got to decide soon whether I can go much further with a person who, either consciously or unconsciously, deceives his boss, his subordinates and himself (probably) so incessantly as he does. I wonder whether he believes there is one atom of truth in his statements of this morning. . . . For some months, I've remained on this job, not because of the General, but in spite of him. . . . If the Marshal is to persist in his arbitrary methods, and is going to make things as unpleasant, if not impossible as today's homily indicated, then I'm for home."[98]*

Sensing his assistant's dissatisfaction, and keenly aware of his indispensability to the Mission's efforts, MacArthur tried to mollify Eisenhower by promoting him from senior adviser to chief of staff of the Defense Mission. Eisenhower shrewdly insisted that MacArthur delineate his responsibilities and clarify the Mission's organizational chart. He then wrote his own duties and asked MacArthur to sign off on the list, which he did. On Eisenhower's efficiency report, MacArthur described him as "a brilliant officer [who] in time of war should be promoted to general officer rank immediately."[99]

Eisenhower subsequently worked to convince the Philippine legislature to increase the defense budget. He wrote a speech for Quezon emphasizing the rising Japanese threat, the Filipino desire for early independence, and the escalating costs of raw materials. He also noted that more of the defense budget was being spent on sanitation education, literacy, and vocational training. Although the budget increase was approved, MacArthur's vision of thirty reserve divisions was scrapped for a more realistic fifteen-division plan. Nevertheless, Eisenhower feared that relying on accounting tricks and temporary funding to obscure the ongoing financial problems would inevitably come to a head. "We're like a bunch of skaters on thin ice, going faster and faster to keep from falling through, and always desperately looking for some lucky break that will carry us to firm footing. . . . Sooner or later there must be a day of reckoning."[100]

MacArthur's trip to the United States was not entirely unsuccessful. While in Washington that spring he reinterred his mother's remains next to his father in Arlington National Cemetery. With Pinky buried and Quezon continuing on to Europe, MacArthur slipped away to New York City on April 30. On that Friday morning, with only Majors Hutter and Davis accompanying him, he borrowed a car and driver from the local army commander and drove to the New York Municipal Building. Despite his flair for the dramatic, he wore a conservative brown suit as he married Jean Marie Faircloth in a quiet civil ceremony. As D. Clayton James notes, Jean "was a rare and remarkable woman who became an ideal mate" for MacArthur.[101] She understood and loved Army life, devoted herself to making a home for her general, and unlike Louise never competed with the Army for his affection. She and Mamie liked each other at once and often went shopping together in Manila's Philippine and Chinese markets. MacArthur would write that his marriage to Jean "was perhaps the smartest thing I have ever done. She has been my constant friend, sweetheart, and devoted supporter ever since. How she managed to put up with my eccentricities and crotchets all these years is quite beyond my comprehension."[102]

Upon returning to Manila, MacArthur had barely settled into his marital routine when in August 1937 General Craig informed him that his appointment in the Philippines would end after two years, and that he was to return to the United States for a new assignment no later than December 31. MacArthur launched into one of his diatribes castigating his enemies in Washington. Eisenhower recorded: "Gradually it percolated in to the Gen's head that the theory lending the greatest hopes for a successful outcome (from his standpoint) was one that held the C. of S. solely and exclusively responsible for the action. The motivation was, under this theory, jealousy; fear of the growing stature of Gen. MacA as a world figure; egotism; revenge by the 'Chaumont crowd.'" Eisenhower tried to keep MacArthur from reacting impetuously without knowing who was behind the decision. "The defense that T.J. and I put up was simply that we should give credit to the Chief of Staff for being an honorable person," Eisenhower wrote.[103] Indeed, MacArthur's friends in Washington and the War Department wrote to assure him that Craig was not behind the maneuvers to remove him from Manila, and Craig tried to mollify MacArthur by offering him any command he wanted in the United States. MacArthur nevertheless responded with outraged pride and petulance. "Your letter has amazed me," he cabled Craig. "The action suggested would constitute my summary relief. . . . Considering rank and position it can only be interpreted as constituting disciplinary action . . . my good name and professional reputation are threatened by the proposed action."[104]

MacArthur considered his options before applying for retirement on September 16. He disingenuously claimed his health was failing and that it was time to make way for younger, more deserving officers. But MacArthur's ego was such that he could not hide his true motivation. Whereas previous former chiefs of staff—including his mentor Leonard Wood—had gone on to other assignments, he wrote to Craig: "I find the thought repugnant of resuming to a subordinate command after having been military head of the Army . . . It would be as though President Roosevelt were required to go back to his functions as Assistant Secretary of the Navy."[105] MacArthur's request was approved, effective December 31, 1937. The War Department announced that he would retire with the rank of full general, a rare honor.

MacArthur had decided that he wanted to remain in the Philippines after his retirement and lobbied Quezon to retain him. The president came through by asking him to remain as military adviser employed directly by the Commonwealth and issuing an executive proclamation to that effect. Yet MacArthur's decision to retire ultimately hurt the Mission, as his newly retired status no longer permitted him to draw from the Philippine Department. As an active duty officer MacArthur had been Quezon's conduit to the corridors of power in Washington. Now he was merely field marshal of the Philippine army, and as just another official on the Commonwealth's payroll Quezon treated MacArthur with diminishing respect.[106]

More importantly, Quezon's enthusiasm for MacArthur's defense plan was waning. The primary stumbling block was the budget overruns, and as Geoffrey Perret concludes, "Whenever MacArthur tried to talk to him about Philippine defense, Don Manuel talked about Philippine poverty."[107] MacArthur came to believe that if Filipinos could actually see what their money was buying, "the morale of the whole population would be enhanced" and the necessary funds would be forthcoming. Consequently, in January 1938 MacArthur ordered Eisenhower and Ord to begin preparations for a massive mobilization of the 40,000 reservists to the outskirts of Manila where they would camp for three or four days, to be followed by a grand parade through downtown Manila. "Jimmy and I estimated the cost," Eisenhower recalled. "We told the General that it was impossible to do the thing within our budget." Eisenhower and Ord protested that the demonstration would divert "money that was desperately needed for more important purposes."[108] But always enamored with theater and prestige, MacArthur insisted on proceeding.

When Quezon learned about the preparations, however, he was furious and called MacArthur to express his displeasure and told him to cancel the plan immediately. Rather than anger Quezon, MacArthur once again laid the blame on Eisenhower and Ord, telling the president he had merely *suggested* a study be conducted on the idea. Eisenhower and Ord felt betrayed, as this "was certainly news to us."[109] Eisenhower spoke up: "General, all you're saying is that I'm a liar, and I am *not* a liar, and so I'd like to go back to the United States right away."

Knowing how invaluable Eisenhower was to the Mission, MacArthur tried to placate his chief of staff. He threw an arm around Eisenhower's shoulder and said, "It's fun to see that Dutch temper take you over. It's just a misunderstanding, and let's let it go at that."[110]

But Eisenhower never forgot MacArthur's refusal to accept responsibility, nor his patronizing manner. Three decades later he recalled, "That misunderstanding caused considerable resentment—and never again were we on the same warm and cordial terms."[111]

The only things keeping Eisenhower in Manila were his stubborn refusal to leave a project unfinished and his friendship with Ord. Eisenhower respected and enjoyed working with Jimmy. The pair collaborated so closely that they shared a joint cable address, "JIMIKE." In April 1937 they went to the Army hospital in Manila together to visit an old friend from Fort Leavenworth, Lt. Col. Troy Middleton, who was undergoing testing for an irregular heartbeat. When they arrived in Middleton's room, he handed Ord a cablegram he had received from the president of Louisiana State University, where Middleton had served as a well-respected ROTC instructor for six years. President Smith was asking Middleton to retire from the Army and become LSU's dean of administration at $5,400 a year. Middleton asked Ord how he would respond if he were in his place, and Ord quickly replied, "Take it. Here we are, all lieutenant colonels. We might get to be colonels before retirement. That $5,400 is good money." He handed the cable to Eisenhower, who took longer to study it. Finally, Eisenhower said, "No, Troy, I'd pass it up. A war is coming. With your record you ought to become a general. I'd turn it down."[112]

Middleton weighed his brothers in arms' advice. After a twenty-seven-year career in which he had been awarded the Distinguished Service Medal in World War I, finished eighth in his class at CGSS, and served for four years as a highly regarded instructor there, the low pay and dearth of opportunities for advancement based on merit led him to side with Ord. He filed for retirement, taking up his post at LSU in January 1938.

By that time Eisenhower had returned to the hospital, only this time as a patient. On January 28, 1938, he was admitted for an intestinal obstruction so acute that his abdomen was distended like that of a "dying frog."[113] This symptom was likely once again a manifestation of the strain of working for MacArthur. As a friend in the United States who spent time with Eisenhower in 1938 recalled: "He did look awful.... I'd seen him three years before, but I thought he looked ten years older in 1938, at least ten years older."[114] Eisenhower's hospitalization kept him from one of his favorite pastimes in the Philippines. Once his ambition had been to be a pilot, but in 1915 he abandoned that dream at John Doud's insistence as a precondition for marrying his daughter. But with Mamie still in Washington and thus unaware, in 1936 at the age of forty-six Eisenhower began taking flying lessons. The lessons were thrilling and provided welcome respite from his office routine. Even after Mamie arrived in Manila, he awoke before dawn and left the hotel at 0630 each day to fly with the two American airmen—Lieutenants Hugh Parker and William Lee—assigned to the Mission as advisers to the Philippine Army Air Corps before reporting for duty at 1 Calle Victoria. Although Mamie learned of these lessons once she relocated to Manila, she never found out that Lee and her husband had nearly been killed taking off from the Baguio airport. Their plane had failed to muster sufficient power during takeoff to clear a hill at the end of the runway. "We ain't going to make it," Lee announced. At the last possible moment Lee managed to clear the hill by a few inches. Eisenhower eventually logged more than 300 hours of flying time in the Philippines, and after passing his flight physical was certified as a qualified private pilot on July 1, 1939.[115]

Despite his near fatal experience with Lee—or perhaps because of it—Eisenhower was fastidious in ensuring his instructors were American. While Eisenhower was in the hospital, Ord had to make a trip to Baguio. He entered Ike's room on the morning of January 30 to tell him and mentioned that one of the Filipino trainees would serve as his pilot. "Get one of the American flight instructors," Eisenhower advised. "They'll be glad to do it."

Ord laughed and said, "Our Filipino boys are doing really well. I'll use one of them. I won't be gone more than a few hours. See you later this afternoon."[116]

That evening, Mamie came to the hospital. She told Eisenhower that Jimmy was dead.

As his plane neared Baguio's airstrip, Ord decided to drop a rock with a note attached at a friend's house to notify him of his arrival. He told the pilot to circle the house, and in doing so the student pilot misjudged his speed. The engine stalled, and the plane crash-landed on a hillside. Neither the pilot nor the plane was badly damaged. But Ord, who was leaning out the backseat, was whipped around violently upon impact and died from internal injuries two hours later.[117]

Ord's death devastated Eisenhower. He admitted to Ord's wife Emily that he was in a state of "bewilderment, loss and grief."[118] To Ord's sister he said he regarded Jimmy as "the most brilliant officer, of his time, in the American Army," and that he "felt as close to him as even to my own brothers."[119] A large crowd that included Quezon and other government officials attended Ord's funeral. Conspicuous by his absence was MacArthur, who had a life-long aversion to funerals. Quezon lamented that he was "grieved beyond measure over the tragic death of Colonel Ord," whom he described as one of the best friends the Philippine Commonwealth had ever had.[120] Eisenhower wrote: "Many, many people have lost a close companion and an intimate friend. I've lost this, also my right hand, and my partner on a tough job, who furnished most of the inspiration needed to keep me plugging away. With him gone much of the zest has departed from a job that we always tackled as a team, never as two individuals."[121] In 1950, in a message to their Class of 1915 classmates, Eisenhower said that Ord's "untimely death I shall always believe robbed our country of one of its most brilliant minds and potential leaders."[122] But more immediately, for months he simply missed hearing Ord walk into their office and greet him with his cheery, "Top of the morning, Comra-a-ade!"[123]

With Ord's death, MacArthur relied even more heavily on Eisenhower. He adopted a conciliatory attitude toward his top aide, listening to Eisenhower's views and actually following some of his advice for once. "It is difficult to believe that Jimmy's loss should have occasioned this change," Eisenhower noted, "but the fact is, that ever since then he has progressively grown more mellow, less arbitrary and less ready to allege sinister motive for every mere difference of opinion." He added, "The atmosphere has cleared to such an extent that this job, at long last, has become personally agreeable as well as professionally interesting."[124]

MacArthur urged Eisenhower to apply for a one-year extension, although it was Quezon who persuaded him to stay. By now, MacArthur's relations with Quezon had deteriorated to the point that the president more often turned to Eisenhower for advice. They held weekly meetings to keep Quezon abreast of military matters, and the conversation often turned to broader problems of governance. These talks frequently put Eisenhower in a difficult spot, as Quezon often spent most of the time complaining about MacArthur. Although Eisenhower always gave Quezon honest answers, he avoided criticizing his boss. Eisenhower and Mamie were frequently invited to elaborate formal dinners at Malacanan Palace, and he and Quezon became regular bridge partners with the president often inviting Eisenhower to spend weekends aboard the presidential yacht. When Quezon heard that Eisenhower was thinking of leaving, he applied all of his charm and pleaded with Ike not to jeopardize all the Defense Mission's accomplishments. Reluctantly, Eisenhower agreed to another year in the Philippines. When he requested three months leave in the United States in exchange for extending, MacArthur agreed.[125]

When the Eisenhowers sailed for America in the summer of 1938, Ord's replacement—Maj. Richard K. Sutherland, who had recently arrived from China, where he was serving with the 15th Infantry—filled in for him. The son of a U.S. senator from West Virginia, Sutherland had graduated from Yale in 1916, been commissioned as a second lieutenant in the infantry, and served in World War I. Eisenhower knew him when both officers were serving in the War Department and living in the Wyoming Apartments. He described Sutherland as "an able, conscientious man, with plenty of sense."[126] Others were not so kind in their assessments. Sutherland was almost universally disliked by both civilians and military personnel, and AP correspondent Clark Lee said Sutherland was "brusque, short-tempered, autocratic, and of a generally antagonizing nature."[127] One MacArthur biographer more bluntly describes Sutherland as an "unpleasant son of a bitch."[128] Nevertheless, Eisenhower wrote in his diary in April 1938 that Sutherland "is an excellent officer and I expect him to take a huge burden off my shoulders."[129]

While in the United States, Eisenhower spent more time retracing MacArthur and Ord's attempts to procure arms and munitions than on vacation. He found the War Department's complacency toward the Philippines astonishing. "They were unsympathetic," Eisenhower noted. "As long as the Philippines insisted on being independent, the War Department's attitude was that they could jolly well look out after their own defenses. To end the interminable frustrations at lower levels I went to the top."[130] Eisenhower met with General Craig, who agreed that a friendly Philippines capable of fighting a delaying action was a vital interest. Craig was impressed by Eisenhower, and he made calls to those subordinates who had been unwilling to discuss Eisenhower's shopping list. Eisenhower recalled: "Doors that had been tightly closed began to open and we secured a number of concessions and much assistance." Eisenhower convinced the War Department to consider the Philippine army as part of the U.S. Army Reserve, meaning equipment could be transferred without cost. Thanks to Craig, Eisenhower managed to: obtain a large quantity of Enfield .30'06 caliber rifles; scrounge what he could from the Signal, Quartermaster, Ordnance, and Medical corps; and travel to Wichita to purchase planes. The only items on his list he could not acquire were infantry mortars, which the U.S. Army itself was lacking. "The American Army itself was starved for appropriations. . . . There wasn't much the Army could do for the Philippines without cutting the ground from under U.S. preparedness," Eisenhower recalled. "With what I had 'liberated' and bought, I went back to Manila."[131]

En route, Eisenhower stopped briefly at Fort Lewis, Washington, to visit Maj. Mark Clark. Wayne, as Clark's friends called him, was a member of the West Point Class of 1917, where he was assigned to Eisenhower's company as a cadet. Although close relationships between members of different classes were discouraged to maintain the cadet chain of command, Eisenhower and Clark hit it off and formed what would become a deep and lasting friendship.

Clark had served as an acting infantry battalion commander in the 5th Division in June 1918 when he was seriously wounded the first time his unit came under German artillery fire. Although he recovered from his injuries, he was not able to return to combat duty. After the war he established a reputation as a training officer and by 1938 was considered one of the Army's rising stars. Eisenhower confided to his friend his desire to leave Manila and return to troop duty in the United States.[132]

Eisenhower was confident his trip to Washington had been a success when he and his family returned to the Philippines on November 5. Yet when they arrived in Manila, he was shocked to find "a vastly different situation, so far as it affects me and my work." While Eisenhower was away, MacArthur had reorganized the office, removing him as chief of staff and replacing him with Sutherland. Despite his prior lament to Craig that any reassignment would appear to be a reprimand, MacArthur stripped Eisenhower of any role in running the Mission and relegated him to overseeing plans and training.

MacArthur's motivations for making this change despite having highly praised Eisenhower were revealed by his dictate ending Eisenhower's liaison role with Quezon. Lucius Clay, at the time a captain detailed to the Mission, claimed the break was completely due to a misunderstanding by General MacArthur. He said:

> A group in the Philippine legislature decided that General Eisenhower was doing all the work and that he was being paid only $10,000 a year, whereas MacArthur was being given a beautiful penthouse apartment in the Manila Hotel and being paid a much more substantial sum. This little group of Filipino congressmen prepared to introduce a bill that would abolish the top job—MacArthur's job—and leave Eisenhower in charge. When Eisenhower heard about it, he went to them and told them that if they ever introduced that bill he would immediately ask to be returned to the United States. That under no circumstances would he be a party to it. But General MacArthur found out about it. And he simply couldn't believe that anybody in the Philippines would do that to him unless it were planned and manipulated. From that moment he had no more use for Eisenhower. And it was absolutely unfounded, although I'm sure that there were people who deliberately tried to convince MacArthur that Eisenhower was trying to knife him in the back.[133]

Indeed, Sutherland had ingratiated himself to MacArthur during Eisenhower's absence and poisoned his mind against Ike. Sutherland would later brag to Robert Eichelberger that he had "gotten rid of Eisenhower."[134]

Despite these humiliations, Eisenhower maintained his outward composure. "On the surface all is lovely," he wrote. "I will not give him the satisfaction of showing any resentment." Internally, however, he seethed. "I must say it is almost incomprehensible that after eight years of working for him, writing every word he publishes, keeping his secrets . . . he should suddenly turn on me, as he has all others who have ever been around him. He'd like to occupy a throne room surrounded by experts in flattery." Eisenhower wrote to Clark reaffirming his desire to leave the Philippines, and asked if he could be assigned to the 3rd Division at Fort Lewis. In his diary, he concluded: "My usefulness is so curtailed as to rob the job of much of its interest, so I'm going at the earliest possible moment."[135]

Following the upheaval created by MacArthur's reorganization, Eisenhower observed: "In the office itself the work's so uncoordinated that operation is difficult . . . since there is no head of this office—except the General."[136] On top of this internal turmoil, Quezon began working at cross purposes with his American advisers. The optimistic reports on the Philippine army's progress he received from MacArthur were contradicted by Filipino officers' pessimistic accounts. Now-Brig. Gen. Vicente Lim, for example, reported that the Philippine army had 100,000 enlisted men, but only 1,000 "half-baked trained officers." Consequently, Quezon grumbled that MacArthur had "hoodwinked" him.[137]

Japan's advances in China horrified Quezon, who began to contemplate the possibility of neutrality as a wave of defeatism swept over the Philippine leadership in 1938–1939. When Eisenhower traveled to Washington in the summer of 1938 to present MacArthur's case for more resources, Quezon headed to Tokyo for secret talks with Japan. Upon returning to Manila, Quezon told an audience in Rizal Stadium that "it's good to hear men say that the Philippines can repel an invasion, but it's not true and the people should know it isn't," adding that the islands "could not be defended even if every last Filipino were armed with modern weapons."[138] In 1939 he told the National Assembly that "developments in the European war have convinced me of the futility of spending money to carry on our program of defending the Philippines from foreign aggression, and this objective cannot be attained with the limited resources of the country for many years to come."[139] Even the soft-spoken vice president, Sergio Osmena, complained that MacArthur's program could not succeed and that "if pursued long enough it might well create conditions of false security against Japan."[140]

Quezon subsequently took steps to curb MacArthur's freedom of action. At his request the National Assembly established a Department of National Defense. Thereafter, MacArthur was required to clear his orders through the new department, limiting his authority to procure weapons, construct facilities, or enroll recruits without Quezon's approval. Quezon encouraged the Assembly to cut defense spending from 25 percent to 14 percent of the Commonwealth budget. Finally, in late 1939 Quezon proposed to High Commissioner Francis B. Sayre that President Roosevelt recall MacArthur. Although he eventually retreated from dismissing MacArthur, Quezon insisted that all further communications between them pass through his secretary.[141]

Despite MacArthur's attempts to restrict their contact, Eisenhower's talks and bridge games with the president continued. On the evening of March 28, 1939, during a conversation at Malacanan Palace, Quezon asked Eisenhower whether an inadequate officer corps was one of the Philippine army's main problems. When Eisenhower answered affirmatively, Quezon asked: "[I]f that is so, why did we plunge into the mass training of enlisted reservists *before* we had the officers, at a time when we *knew* we did not have them, to do the job with reasonable efficiency?"

"Because you directed it, in the spring of 1936," Eisenhower replied. "The original plan contemplated the calling of only 3,000 trainees in January, 1937, and, so Colonel Ord and I were informed, you decided to raise this to 20,000."

Quezon said that he had never made that decision, and had been *opposed* to the idea of rushing into the training of enlisted reservists. He also revealed that he bitterly opposed appointing MacArthur as field marshal, which he thought made his government look ridiculous, but was afraid to contradict MacArthur when he proposed the rank.[142]

Of course, at the time MacArthur had claimed both these decisions were Quezon's ideas. Now it was clear to Eisenhower that MacArthur had not only been lying to the president, but had repeatedly lied and refused to take responsibility for his actions to his staff as well.

In 1939, the consequences of these early missteps became clearer. The annual training mobilization was limited to ten days, and even then about half the reserve officers said they could not report for this abbreviated training. The

Philippine officer corps could not be maintained by the minimal number of schools established for that purpose. As Eisenhower noted, "We continue to suffer from the great error made in 1936 when it was decided to abandon a gradual process of development, beginning with officers, NCOs, and overhead, in favor of training hordes of draftees."[143]

The planned development of a Philippine navy consisting of fifty torpedo boats, which MacArthur imagined swarming out to sink enemy troop transports, was similarly disappointing. The U.S. Navy did not support this plan, and the only boats available were British. When Eisenhower learned they would cost $250,000 per boat, he was "staggered." Fifty boats would cost $12.5 million, the entire Philippine defense budget for a year and a half. In the end, only two PT boats were purchased from Norway.[144]

Efforts to build an air force of 250 planes, mainly fighters and trainers, also floundered. When William Lee pointed out that modern fighters cost $50,000–$60,000 each, and were more effective than PT boats against an invading force, Eisenhower said "Let's go see the old man." While MacArthur paced back and forth, Lee pressed his case. "Of course," Lee recalled, "you didn't get to talk much when you went to see MacArthur. He did the talking." Lee added that MacArthur "called me 'Commodore' for some damned reason or other."[145] But pilot training posed significant challenges in a country where few people owned or drove automobiles. Hugh Parker recalled that MacArthur was expecting to "get them off a carabao and into an airplane [but] they had very poor appreciation of speed, distance, or anything mechanical."[146] Consequently the Philippine Air Corps' first squadron was not organized until early 1939.

Despite these setbacks, MacArthur continued to make public statements that the defense plan was proceeding successfully and that the Philippines would be a match for any invading enemy. On November 2, 1938, he wrote in the *Christian Science Monitor* that Luzon had "only two coastal regions in which a hostile army of any size could land. Each of these is broken by strong defensive positions, which, if properly manned and prepared would present to any attacking force a practically impossible problem of penetration."[147] The following summer MacArthur again touted his plan's deterrent value to a group of reporters. "It would cost the enemy, in my opinion, at least a half million of men as casualties and upwards of five billions of dollars in money to pursue such an adventure with any hope of success." Besides, he said, "no rational reason exists why Japan or any other nation should covet the sovereignty of this country."[148]

Eisenhower listened in astonishment to these comments. It was as if MacArthur had not even read the newspapers. Yet Eisenhower *knew* his boss read the papers, for in his diary he complained, "The barest mention of [MacArthur]'s name in the gossip column of the poorest of [Manila's] universally poor daily periodicals sends him into hysterical delight or deepest despair, depending upon its note of praise or condemnation."[149] The problem was that MacArthur was dangerously disconnected from the Mission's day-to-day operations. He had left Eisenhower and Ord to administer the creation of the Philippine army, and had little interaction with the Filipinos who led the Philippine forces and in whom he expressed full confidence. As at West Point, MacArthur went to the office late in the morning, worked until about 1:00 P.M., then took a lunch break and a nap before returning to the office for another hour or two late in the afternoon. Once he was officially retired from the Army, his schedule was "more befitting a gentleman of leisure than a military adviser," and by 1938, Lucius Clay recalled, "General MacArthur never came to the office but about an hour a day. He would come down about one o'clock and stay until about two."[150] John Eisenhower, a future general himself, was less charitable: "MacArthur was in very bad shape in those days. . . . He was living in a dream world. It sounded almost like the last days of Hitler."[151]

MacArthur's detachment from reality in part stemmed from his newfound domesticity. On February 21, 1938, Jean gave birth to a baby boy, Arthur MacArthur IV. MacArthur was ecstatic, and anyone who visited their penthouse saw the imperious-looking military man transformed into a gentle, sympathetic father whose heart was overflowing with love for his son. Indeed, when Jean and their *amah* tried to let the baby cry out at night, it was MacArthur who broke first and tenderly picked Arthur up and walked him until he quieted.[152]

In May 1939, Clark delivered for Eisenhower, whose new orders directed him to the 15th Infantry at Fort Lewis, effective that November. Eisenhower wrote to Clark: "I can not tell you how anxiously we are looking forward to our return to the States and to service with a Regular Army officer. I feel like a boy who has been promised an electric train for Christmas."[153] His extended year was almost over when war erupted in Europe. On September 3, the Eisenhowers went to the apartment of a friend whose short-wave radio picked up signals from Europe and heard British prime minister

Neville Chamberlain declare war with Germany. "It's a sad day for Europe and for the whole civilized world," Eisenhower wrote. "If the war, which now seems upon us, is as long drawn out and disastrous, as bloody and as costly as was the so-called World War, then I believe that the remnants of nations emerging from it will be scarcely recognizable as the ones that entered it."[154]

Eisenhower received one final offer to return to civilian life. Manila was home to a large Jewish community, whose numbers were swelled by German Jews who had fled Hitler's repression and made their way east. Eisenhower had many friends amongst them, and his virulent anti-Nazi and anti-Hitler views were well known. Consequently, the Jewish Relief Committee of Manila approached Eisenhower and offered him a job resettling German Jews in Asia. They offered Eisenhower $60,000-a-year—six times his current salary, and roughly $2 million in today's dollars—for a minimum of five years. "The offer was, of course, appealing for several reasons," Eisenhower recalled. "By this time, I had become so committed to my profession that I declined."[155] With Fox Conner's premonitions about the next war on the cusp of fruition, Eisenhower felt compelled to remain in the Army.

MacArthur tried to talk Eisenhower into staying, saying the work he was doing in the Philippines far exceeded what a mere lieutenant colonel would be assigned back in the United States. Eisenhower did not take him seriously, however, and even if he had, by now service with MacArthur had lost its luster. Quezon was even more emphatic in insisting Eisenhower stay. He handed Eisenhower a blank contract for his services and said, "We'll tear up the old contract. I've already signed this one and it is filled in—except what you want as your emoluments for remaining. You will write that in."

Eisenhower thanked him but declined. He told Quezon "no amount of money can make me change my mind. My entire life has been given to this one thing, my country and my profession. I want to be there if what I fear is going to come about actually happens."[156] Eisenhower booked passages to San Francisco on the *President Cleveland*, sailing on December 13. "Mamie is counting the days," Eisenhower wrote to Gerow in October. "She really wants to come home . . . as the day draws near, I must say I begin to share her impatience."[157]

On December 12, at a farewell luncheon in Malacanan Palace, the Philippine army's officers presented Eisenhower with a Hamilton watch in "appreciation for your efforts in assisting and putting the Philippines Army to a high state of organization and efficiency during the last four years."[158] Quezon awarded him the Philippine Distinguished Service Star, the citation lauding Eisenhower's "exceptional talents . . . his professional attainments, his breadth of understanding, his zeal and magnetic leadership."[159] In his presentation, Quezon specifically praised Eisenhower's candor. "Whenever I asked Ike for an opinion," he said, "I got an answer. It may not have been what I wanted to hear, it may have displeased me, but it was always a straightforward and honest answer."[160]

MacArthur had written Eisenhower a warm letter on December 9. "I cannot tell you how deeply I regret your leaving," he said. "Your distinguished service has been characterized at all times by superior professional ability, unswerving loyalty and unselfish devotion to duty." MacArthur said he would miss Eisenhower, but would "follow with keen interest the brilliant career which unquestionably lies ahead for you."[161]

On the 13th, as the Eisenhowers boarded the *Cleveland*, it seemed as if Manila's entire American population had come to bid them farewell. To Eisenhower's surprise, General and Mrs. MacArthur came down to the docks to say goodbye. MacArthur gave Eisenhower a bottle of whiskey as a going away present. John felt the gift must have been Jean MacArthur's idea, but conceded the fact that the general was there at all "was uncommon for this normally thoughtless and egocentric man."[162] Theirs had been a stormy relationship, but that day, Eisenhower recalled, "We talked of the gloominess of world prospects . . . our forebodings turned toward Europe—not Asia."[163]

Finally, as the band played dockside, the army transport slipped its moorings and steamed out to sea. Overhead flew two aircraft piloted by Eisenhower's Army Air Corps friends. "It was a swell goodbye," Mamie remembered.[164]

MacArthur and Eisenhower would not see each other again until after World War II, long after they had made indelible marks upon world history on opposite sides of the globe from one another.

CHAPTER EIGHT

The Right Man in the
Right Place at the Right Time

At 3:00 a.m., September 1, 1939, the telephone beside George Marshall's bedside rang. A staff duty officer from the War Department was calling. Marshall listened quietly, then hung up the phone and turned to his sleepy wife. "Well, it's come," he told Katherine, and began dressing.[1] As befitted a nation at peace, he wore a white Palm Beach suit rather than a military uniform. Before leaving for his office he called his chief aide Orlando Ward at 3:50, and calmly told him to notify the Overseas Departments and the corps areas' headquarters that German divebombers were attacking Poland.

It was already supposed to be an eventful day. Later that morning in Secretary of War Harry Woodring's office, Marshall raised his right hand and took the oath of office as chief of staff of the Army. Yet instead of a celebratory reception, as German tanks and troops poured across the Polish border and the *Luftwaffe* terrorized Polish cities killing thousands of civilians, Marshall hurried off to an emergency conference at the White House to discuss the European crisis. A few days later, with his characteristic understatement, he noted to a friend: "My day of induction into office was momentous, with the starting of what appears to be a World War."[2]

Looking back through the lens of time, it almost seems that Marshall was destined to occupy this vital post at such a critical moment in history. Yet just four years earlier Marshall's ascension to chief of staff appeared to be at best a longshot, if not an outright impossibility. In October 1933 Marshall was deeply engrossed in refurbishing Fort Moultrie and overseeing the region's CCC work when he received orders relieving him of command and transferring him to Chicago to be senior instructor with the Illinois National Guard's 33rd Division. This was a ridiculously rudimentary assignment for

an officer who had led the Army's Infantry School, and marked a significant setback to his career. As Marshall vented to Pershing, "I have had the
discouraging experience of seeing the man I relieved in France as G-3 of
the army promoted years ago, and my assistant as G-3 of the army similarly
advanced six years ago."[3] In despair, for the first time in his career Marshall
asked to have his posting changed, and Pershing also appealed to the chief of
staff. But MacArthur, still bearing a grudge against "the Chaumont clique,"
had personally recommended Marshall for the backwater position. He told
Robert Eichelberger, who was serving as secretary to the General Staff, that
Marshall "will never be a brigadier general as long as I am Chief of Staff," and
replied to Pershing with a curt, "All requests refused."[4]

Marshall wrote resignedly to Pershing: "I can but wait, grow older, and
hope for a more favorable situation in Washington."[5] Katherine remembered that during those first months of exile in Chicago, "George had a
grey, drawn look which I had never seen before, and have seldom seen
since."[6] His disappointment notwithstanding, Marshall continued mentoring his former subordinates. In October 1934 he advised Buck Lanham not
to allow low rank and infrequent promotion to ruin his morale. "Keep your
wits about you and your eyes open; keep on working hard; sooner or later
the opportunity will present itself."[7] While serving as the operations officer
for VI Corps, and later as Second Army chief of staff based in Chicago,
Matthew Ridgway often sought out Marshall's advice. In the summer of
1936, Ridgway planned maneuvers in rural Illinois that proved a brilliant
success. Yet Ridgway had worked so intensely that at the operations' end
he collapsed in a bathroom from exhaustion and gashed his head. After
the incident, Marshall congratulated Ridgway but cautioned him about
overwork: "There is no need for you to demonstrate any further you are an
energetic, able workman," and advised the young major to "cultivate the art
of playing and loafing" and "to establish the reputation of being something
of a dilettante."[8]

Marshall practiced what he preached, and approached his duty with his
usual professionalism. In the summer of 1934 federal inspectors found every
unit of the 33rd at least satisfactory, the first time in years the division had
passed muster. In the 1936 Illinois maneuvers, Marshall borrowed two hundred trucks from General Motors to enable his "army" to execute a rapid
flanking envelopment that quickly won the war game. After observing Colonel Marshall for several months, the 33rd's commander, Brig. Gen. Roy D.
Keehn, went to see MacArthur in Washington and told him that Marshall

was too gifted to be wasted in a Guard position. Keehn insisted Marshall be promoted to brigadier general and given a challenge worthy of his talents.[9]

Finally, by 1936, Marshall was high enough on the seniority list—and MacArthur was no longer chief of staff—to receive what almost everyone realized was a long overdue promotion. Within a few days of pinning on his first star, he received orders to take command of the 5th Infantry Brigade at Vancouver Barracks, Washington. Back in command of troops, Marshall thrived. During joint Regular Army/National Guard maneuvers, Marshall was given command of the numerically inferior opposition force assigned the role of loser in the script. The operation began at night, and in compliance with his instructions Marshall moved his men after sundown into the designated assault positions. Yet whereas most commanders would not have attacked until morning in order to control the operation in daylight, Marshall initiated his assault at 2:00 A.M. His fellow commanders assumed he would be criticized in the post-maneuver critiques. Yet when Marshall explained that because his men had to cross open ground in the mock battle they would suffer fewer casualties from the enemy under the cover of darkness, the 3rd Division's operations officer praised his approach for its creativity.[10]

Marshall's energy and humanity kept the 5th Brigade's morale high, and during his command Vancouver Barracks's units had the highest reenlistment rate in the corps area. He was once again able to mentor talented subordinates. One officer who came to his attention at Vancouver Barracks was Maj. Mark Clark, the division G-3 who had bucked Leavenworth doctrine and praised Marshall's imagination on maneuvers. Clark's responsibilities put him in frequent contact with Marshall. Knowing the general had been First Army's chief of operations in France, when Clark discussed his plans with the division commander and chief of staff at Fort Lewis he asked, "Do you mind if I fly down and show them to General Marshall?"

"No, he would love it," they replied. Sure enough, Marshall was happy to review Clark's projects and to offer advice. Even when he was eventually transferred across the country to the War Department, Marshall encouraged Clark to send him his plans and offered advice.[11]

Marshall was also able to resume his work with the CCC, as he was responsible for overseeing thirty-five camps scattered throughout Oregon and southeastern Washington. Marshall was as fascinated as ever by the possibilities the CCC offered for developing solid, useful men. He often combined his inspections of camps in idyllic surroundings with fishing for steelhead salmon. Back at Vancouver Barracks he hunted pheasants and fished for dinner in the Columbia River bordering the airfield. When Marshall received orders in May 1938 transferring him to the War Plans Division, Katherine said it ended "two of the happiest years of our life."[12]

Chief of Staff Malin Craig had said as early as 1936 that he would bring Marshall to the War Department, and now Craig confided to his friend that War Plans was only a temporary assignment. Marshall was being groomed to succeed Stanley Embick as deputy chief of staff. Thus, on July 7, 1938, he reported for duty at the War Department in a wilted suit and straw boater. He quickly began reviewing war plans as the situation in Europe deteriorated. Marshall possessed little detailed knowledge of Air Corps' problems, and consequently embarked on a crash course in Air Corps' matters, including a week-long, 8,000-mile flying tour of Air Corps installations and aircraft facilities. After only three months with the War Plans Division, Marshall was elevated to deputy chief of staff on October 15, 1938.[13]

Craig was scheduled to retire as chief of staff on September 1, 1939, and Marshall's name quickly emerged as a possible replacement. Although Omar Bradley, then serving in the War Department's G-1, noted: "Among the officers of my rank and age . . . there was universal agreement that Marshall was by far the best possible man for the job," he was far from assured of attaining the position.[14] Since the post was created in 1921, only one of the previous eleven deputies had been promoted to chief of staff. At age fifty-seven, Craig's retirement represented Marshall's last chance, after which he would lack the required four years to serve before he reached his own mandatory retirement. Marshall was outranked by all twenty of the Army's major generals, as well as by eleven brigadier generals, although only four of those men had the requisite four years until mandatory retirement themselves. Consequently, Marshall ranked fifth in seniority behind Major Generals Hugh Drum, John L. DeWitt, Frank Rowell, and Walter Krueger. Of these five, Marshall's friend Drum was the clear frontrunner. Drum had been Pershing's First Army chief of staff in France, and was a major general by 1930 when Marshall was still a lieutenant colonel. Drum was a serious candidate for chief of staff when MacArthur was selected to the post in 1930 and again when Craig was appointed in 1935. He had served as MacArthur's deputy chief of staff, commander of the Hawaiian Department, and was currently commanding the First Army in New York.[15]

Worse, Marshall appeared to have fatally undermined his chances of succeeding Craig during a meeting with President Roosevelt in November 1938. Spurred to action by British and French appeasement at the

Munich Conference and by intelligence reports that exaggerated German air superiority, the president called a meeting on November 14 to lay out his program for addressing the rising threat to U.S. national security. Marshall accompanied General Craig to the White House, and sat on the outer edges of a meeting that included the president, Secretary of the Treasury Henry Morgenthau, WPA administrator and Roosevelt confidante Harry Hopkins, Assistant Secretary of War Louis Johnson, Chief of the Air Corps General "Hap" Arnold, and other presidential aides and advisers. Marshall listened with the others as Roosevelt "did the major portion of the talking."[16] Pausing only to place another cigarette in the holder, the president proposed an air force of 20,000 planes and production capacity of 24,000-per-year. Because Congress was sure to cut that enormous figure, Roosevelt ordered Craig to begin planning a $500 million program for 10,000 planes. "Had we had this summer 5,000 planes and the capacity immediately to produce 10,000 per year," he said, "Hitler would not have dared to take the stand he did."[17] His plan, however, did not include requests for the pilots, crews, organization, ground service, and maintenance facilities necessary for an actual, functional air force.

When the president finished, he went around the room asking each man for his opinion. "Most of them agreed with him entirely," Marshall remembered, and "had very little to say and were very soothing." Finally, Roosevelt came to Marshall and said, "Don't you think so, George?"

Marshall was not opposed to enlarging American airpower or the president's emphasis on rapid development. He recognized, however, that without the enlistment and training of aircrews and money for bases and other facilities the president's plan was wholly unbalanced and made little military sense. Marshall also bristled at Roosevelt's "misrepresentation of our intimacy," by using his first name.

"I am sorry, Mr. President," he replied, "but I don't agree with that at all."[18]

Roosevelt gave Marshall a startled look and abruptly dismissed the meeting.

Just as with his confrontation with General Pershing at Gondrecourt two decades earlier, as Marshall filed out of the room, "they all bade me good-bye and said that my tour in Washington was over."

But once again the more timid souls had misjudged Marshall's fate. Roosevelt realized Marshall "would tell him what was what, straight from the shoulder."[19] Additionally, Drum desperately wanted the Army's highest rank, and aggressively campaigned for the appointment. Yet his publicity campaign backfired by alienating President Roosevelt. "Drum, Drum," one magazine quoted Roosevelt as saying. "I wish he would stop beating his own drum."[20] Although Marshall hoped his record would be enough to recommend him for the position, he had influential supporters in Harry Hopkins, Malin Craig, and of course, General Pershing. Thus, on Sunday, April 23, 1939, the president summoned Marshall to his second-floor study in the White House to tell him he had decided in his favor.

Their conversation, held amidst Roosevelt's vast stamp collection, was brief. Marshall told the president that he wanted the right to say what he thought. "Is that all right?" he asked.

"Yes," Roosevelt replied from behind his stamp albums.

"You said 'yes' pleasantly, but it may be unpleasant," Marshall warned.[21]

Roosevelt smiled as Marshall rose. "I feel deeply honored, sir, and I will give you the best I have," Marshall promised.[22] On April 27 the appointment was made public. Marshall would become acting chief of staff on July 1, when Craig went on terminal leave, and would officially take over on September 1.

Marshall would have been justified in feeling trepidation similar to that expressed by MacArthur a decade earlier upon becoming chief of staff. Although MacArthur's Rearmament and Re-equipment Program had produced moderate but steady increases in appropriations and corresponding progress in equipping the Army—strides that continued under Malin Craig's leadership—the Army Marshall was inheriting was still in bad shape. The Army's total strength approached 190,000 officers and men, ranking seventeenth globally in manpower, sandwiched between Portugal and Bulgaria. Of the Army's nine infantry divisions, only four could muster even half the troops called for in their tables of organization, while the others were merely understrength brigades.[23]

In addition to being undermanned, the Army's equipment was aging or outdated. The bolt-action 1903 Springfield that served as the basic infantry rifle was obsolete. The infantry still used the inaccurate 3-inch Stokes mortar from World War I, the .50-caliber machine gun was still the primary antitank weapon, and the basic field artillery weapon remained the 75mm gun from the war. Army Ordnance had designed or approved newer weapons, but Congress had not appropriated procurement funds. Thus, *Life* noted that the U.S. Army was "the smallest, worst-equipped armed force of any major power."[24]

Marshall faced numerous other obstacles as he contemplated how to mobilize and modernize the Army. By the mid-1930s Americans had been inundated with revisionist histories claiming World War I had not been fought to make the world safe for democracy, but rather for the profit of Wall Street financiers and arms manufacturers. Historians William Langer and S. Everett Gleason observed: "Americans, having once believed erroneously, that war would settle everything, were now disposed to endorse the reverse fallacy that war could settle nothing."[25] While most Americans found Axis aggression and Nazism repugnant, a clear majority insisted the United States had no business getting involved in the European war. Between 1935 and 1937 Congress passed a series of neutrality acts designed to prevent the president from gradually dragging the country into war by aiding any of the belligerents. Indiana Democratic representative Louis Ludlow proposed a constitutional amendment requiring a national referendum for a declaration of war. Although the Ludlow Amendment was narrowly defeated by a vote of 209 to 188 on January 10, 1938, isolationists still viewed any rearmament as handing the president the means by which to involve America in another unnecessary war.[26]

Before his proposals for expanding the Army could face scrutiny from the American public and Congress, however, Marshall was handicapped by the War Department's dysfunctional civilian leadership. When George Dern died in 1936, his deputy, Harry Woodring, became secretary of war. Columnist Joseph Alsop called Woodring "a sleazy third-rater" and "a peanut-sized . . . politician distinguished only by the meanness of his nature."[27] Besides being incompetent, Woodring was an isolationist unwilling to push for significant military increases. Although the assistant secretary, Louis Johnson, was a committed internationalist, he was also an obstinate brawler who was conducting a campaign of anonymous press leaks to undercut Woodring and hopefully supplant him as secretary. By the time Marshall arrived in Washington, the two men were no longer speaking to each other. President Roosevelt tolerated this debilitating rivalry because, as Arthur Schlesinger Jr. notes, he "deliberately organized—or disorganized—his system of command to insure that important decisions were passed on to the top."[28] Yet the virtual state of war between Woodring and Johnson politicized every issue, prevented the War Department from speaking with a single voice at a critical juncture, and forced Marshall to walk an impossible political tightrope.

Even if the War Department were not, to use Bradley's description, "a minefield of political intrigue," Marshall's greatest challenge in preparing the Army for the coming conflict arguably lay with the man who appointed him chief of staff.[29] During his first term, President Roosevelt understandably subordinated foreign policy to his efforts to enact domestic economic reforms and stimulate recovery from the Depression. The president encouraged isolationist-inspired revisionist efforts such as the Nye Committee because it sought to discredit the same corporate titans and bankers who fiercely opposed the New Deal. Although Roosevelt entirely ignored foreign policy in his Second Inaugural Address on January 20, 1937, he was an internationalist at heart, and Axis aggression gradually became impossible to ignore. On October 5, 1937, Roosevelt delivered what became known as "the Quarantine Speech," in which he declared "The epidemic of world lawlessness is spreading," and must be contained by the international community, including the United States. He warned Americans that "the very foundations of civilization" were threatened, and the United States could not escape if the rest of the world were plunged into war. When the speech drew heavy criticism for its "war mongering" message, Roosevelt lamented: "It's a terrible thing to look over your shoulder when you are trying to lead—and find no one there."[30]

"Roosevelt's leadership in this case was neither valiant nor consistent," David Kennedy observes. "He had shown no stomach for the kind of prolonged confrontation with [the isolationists] that might change the course of American foreign policy."[31] Indeed, after the Munich agreement, Roosevelt had little doubt appeasement would fail or that war would soon follow. Yet he shrank from the task of educating the American public on these threats. He was intimidated by congressional isolationists, who had humiliated his political idol Woodrow Wilson in the fight over ratifying the Treaty of Versailles two decades earlier, and was loath to challenge them.[32]

Given the lack of presidential guidance and the seemingly aimless leadership during the last summer of uneasy peace, Marshall decided not to press for full-scale mobilization despite Hitler's invasion of Poland. Instead he set his sights on reequipping the existing authorized forces and preparing for further expansion. Doubting that he would get the Army expansion to the 280,000 Roosevelt had authorized, on September 7 Marshall drafted a letter to the president warning that "Essential Corps troops are essentially nonexistent," and that the National Guard was at half its authorized peacetime strength. In order to maintain "peace and neutrality in the midst of our troubled world," he argued for an immediate increase to 250,000 Regular Army and 320,000 National Guard.

Marshall received less than this from the president. Larger appropriations for ground forces suggested the president intended to send American forces to fight in Europe, and on September 8 Roosevelt stated: "There is no thought in any shape, manner or form, of putting the Nation, either in its defenses or in its internal economy, on a war basis."[33] Instead, Roosevelt declared a limited national emergency and increased the Regular Army by 17,000 men to 227,000 and authorized a National Guard of 235,000. The president's executive order also permitted expansion of the officer corps by assigning reserve officers to active duty. The administration's request was barely more than half the amount the War Department originally proposed, as Roosevelt claimed it "was all the public would be ready to accept without undue excitement."[34]

Even these modest increases were soon challenged. The *Blitzkrieg* that conquered Poland in three weeks gave way to six months of "*Sitzkrieg.*" The uneasy quiet of the so-called Phony War—during which Hitler consolidated his gains but launched no new military campaigns—sapped the initial zeal to rebuild America's defenses. Marshall met with sharp congressional opposition when he requested funds to equip the additional forces Roosevelt had authorized. Many leaders expressed the hope that Great Britain and France could contain Germany by themselves, permitting the United States to remain on the sidelines of the looming conflict. Questioned at a November 1939 hearing about America's defense buildup, Marshall explained that we were not building up but trying to *catch up* to the level authorized in the 1920 NDA. Although some senators privately urged him to openly declare that the nation's security depended on more military appropriations than Roosevelt was willing to grant, Marshall demurred. He wanted to avoid creating the impression that he was trying to push the country into war, and he recognized that no matter how tempting it might be to plead his case directly to the public, in the long run the Army would be best served by his working "within the team of which the president was the head."[35]

Although Marshall was impatient to bring the existing troops "to a full state of efficiency as quickly as possible," he counseled patience to his congressional liaison officer.[36] It was out of their hands, he said. "Events in Europe will develop in such a way as to affect congressional action."[37] Marshall therefore prioritized preparing industry for military production. As early as 1938 he had cautioned: "No matter how many billions of dollars placed at our disposal on the day war is declared, they will not buy ten cents worth of materiel for delivery under twelve months, and a great deal of it requires a year and a half to manufacture."[38] Marshall desperately wanted to avoid the "almost criminal lack of proper preparation" in the last war, when American troops "went into the line . . . [with] everything begged, borrowed, or stolen—certainly not manufactured in America."[39] This time, he told Congress, "We must be prepared to stand on our own feet from the outset."[40]

While waiting for world events to bring Congress around, Marshall focused on reforming—where possible—the Army. Besides establishing the army and corps headquarters enabled by the first tentative expansion in personnel, Marshall also approved Malin Craig's long-delayed plans to reorganize World War I's cumbersome four-regiment "square" division into the small, three-regiment "triangular" division to provide greater maneuverability and flexibility. Marshall arranged for the officer with whom he had shared a stateroom on the voyage to France in 1917, now–Brigadier General Lesley McNair, to be a reform-oriented commandant of the CGSS, and instructed him to immediately revise the outmoded tactical training. Finally, as deputy chief of staff, Marshall had observed that air officers were underrepresented on the General Staff and that most General Staff officers either had little interest in air-related issues or held a strong anti-air bias. Marshall found this situation deplorable, and took steps to more closely integrate the Air Corps into General Staff decision-making by moving more air officers onto the General Staff and by establishing a particularly close relationship with Hap Arnold.[41]

Closer to home, Marshall's tenure as deputy and acting chief of staff enabled him to observe the War Department bureaucracy up close, and he did not like what he saw. Virtually every staff section head had direct access to the chief of staff. In addition to the sixty-one officers with direct access, thirty other major and 350 smaller commands fell under his immediate control. Since most problems involved issues affecting two or more staff sections, virtually every issue was elevated to the chief of staff personally for decision. Moreover, decades of penurious appropriations had paralyzed initiative so that future general Anthony McAuliffe observed, "no one was willing to take a chance."[42] Marshall understandably felt this process was badly inefficient, as it overwhelmed him with unnecessary minutiae at a time when he needed to focus on larger, weightier matters.

Marshall therefore sought to establish a command and staff structure that centralized decision-making at the top while decentralizing the *execution* of policy to subordinates. He recognized, however, that any restructuring of the General Staff required legislative approval and risked sparking a "palace coup" by disgruntled senior officers. The legislative process of open testimony before parochial committee members would devolve into a prolonged and rancorous battle, Marshall said, so that even if he got his way, "I would be stirring up a most unfortunate morale situation at a critical moment and also would be defeating my purpose."[43] Unlike MacArthur at West Point, therefore, Marshall proceeded cautiously and strategically in implementing his envisioned bureaucratic reforms.

Willing to bide his time, Marshall exercised his command prerogative and fashioned his own inner headquarters. A week after taking over as acting chief of staff in July 1939, Marshall strode down the hall to see the assistant chief of staff for personnel, Brig. Gen. Lorenzo Gasser. "I'm sorry," Marshall said to Gasser, "but you've got one man in your section I want."

Gasser looked at Marshall and said, "I suppose you mean Bradley?"

"Yes," Marshall replied.[44]

Omar Bradley cleaned out his desk and joined Marshall's small inner staff, dubbed "The Secretariat," headed by now-Colonel Orlando Ward. A 1914 West Point graduate who—prior to helping lead the Field Artillery's gunnery revolution—had served in both the Punitive Expedition and in the Great War, Ward was "a quiet, studious type, who resembled a teacher more than a future armored division commander."[45] In addition to Bradley, Ward was assisted by Lt. Col. Stanley R. Mickelson, who combined expertise in antiaircraft artillery and statistics. Within Marshall's small inner office, the Secretariat collected the massive flow of staff studies and papers, decided which should go to Marshall or his deputy chief of staff, and then distilled papers for Marshall into one-page summaries to be presented each day for decision. The three men functioned as a team, with Ward sharing an unusual amount of responsibility with his nominal assistants. Bradley and Mickelson drafted about two-thirds of the outgoing messages, but neither proved especially adept at it. They agreed they needed an officer more skilled with the English language, and Bradley suggested Walter Bedell Smith. When he put Smith's name forward, Marshall replied, "Smith, do I know him?" Bradley tactfully reminded Marshall of the episode years earlier at Benning, and Smith was brought aboard.[46]

Smith was the first of several young officers—including J. Lawton Collins and Maxwell D. Taylor—destined to become high-ranking generals whom Marshall brought into the Secretariat during the prewar mobilization. Yet again in contrast to MacArthur, who prevented Eisenhower from returning to troop duty as long as he remained useful to the general, Marshall rewarded talented subordinates for their toil on the General Staff. Although he did not tolerate jockeying for field assignments, and often told his staff to relinquish any thought of escaping their desk jobs, outstanding performance in the secretariat served as a springboard to a command position. Marshall wanted to make Collins a permanent member of his staff, but Collins said: "General, do you remember the time down at Benning when you told Captain Bolte and me, 'If there is ever another war in the offing, don't let them stick you on a staff job as was done with me?'"

Marshall laughed aloud. "All right, Collins," he replied, "I will let you go."[47]

Collins subsequently became chief of staff for VII Corps en route to division and corps commands in the war. Similarly, when Bradley expressed his desire to leave the War Department, Marshall had him reassigned as the Infantry School's commandant. When Ward's tour with the General Staff ended, Marshall ensured he received his preferred assignment as commander of an armored regiment.

While they served under Marshall, however, the Secretariat had to prove themselves each and every day under tremendous pressure. Taylor recalled seeing "many a general officer in [Marshall's] outer office betraying a most unmilitary agitation while awaiting his turn to pass through the door to his office."[48] Despite having worked closely with the chief of staff at Benning, Bradley admitted he "was still in awe and some fear of the man." Anyone who came to see Marshall entered his office without knocking and took a seat across from him. They were to begin speaking when he looked up from his desk. Marshall then listened intently, allowing the presenting officer to state his business with briefings expected to be short and to the point. Marshall always asked sharply penetrating questions. "No matter how well I knew my subject," Bradley recalled, "he was apt to ask pertinent questions on something I didn't know. I was almost certain to be tripped up every time."[49]

Early in his tenure Marshall summoned the Secretariat into his office. "I'm disappointed in all of you."

An ashen-faced Ward managed to utter, "*Why*, sir?"

"You have not disagreed with anything I've done all week," Marshall replied.

Bradley assured the chief of staff that nothing had come through the office that week with which they disagreed. He assured Marshall they would surely have pointed it out to him. Nevertheless, Marshall still seemed "vaguely dissatisfied."

Several days later a staff study arrived that Ward, Bradley, and Mickleson agreed was deeply flawed. During their presentation to the boss they pointed out its glaring weaknesses. Marshall almost smiled as he declared, "Now, *that's* what I want. Unless I hear all the arguments for or against an action I am about to take, I don't know whether or not I'm right. If I hear all the arguments against some action and still find in favor of it, I'm *sure* I'm right."[50]

As they grew accustomed to their jobs, they found that Marshall wanted his staff to take the initiative whenever it could to resolve problems at the lowest level possible. They also discovered that rank did not equal wisdom in Marshall's eyes. As head of research and development for the supply component, McAuliffe recommended the Army stop producing the 37mm anti-aircraft gun in favor of a foreign-made 40mm gun. McAuliffe soon found himself in front of the chief of staff with the furious chief of ordnance, Maj. Gen. "Bull" Wesson, defending his recommendations. "A major argued with this major general the merits of the case," McAuliffe recalled, "and General Marshall supported me."[51]

Although he was generally able to control his fierce temper, his staff knew from experience that Marshall could convey almost as much disapproval through an icy stare. Indeed, Marshall's management style was not without its drawbacks. As Taylor notes, "His strong personality had such an unnerving effect on officers around him that it adversely affected the quality of their work."[52] Another shortcoming was Marshall's chronic inability to remember the names of people around him no matter how long they served with him. In addition to being unable to recall "Beedle" Smith from Benning, the names of other favorite subordinates frequently eluded him. Maj. Albert Wedemeyer became "that long-legged major in War Plans"; McAuliffe was "that blue-eyed major in G-4." He called his own secretary "Miss Mason" even though her name was actually *Nason*, and he confused Maxwell Taylor and another assistant secretary, Bob Young, "for no apparent reason."[53] As Marshall's biographer Ed Cray notes, however, "The foible softened the hard edge of a man who first appeared to younger men as very severe, a cold sort."[54]

Marshall's brusqueness with his staff and subordinates was partly an extension of his own rigid self-discipline. Marshall had little tolerance for mistakes, tardiness, or untidiness. Even Ward's cowlick seemed to offend the chief of staff's sense of order. He often interrupted his work to say, "Ward, make that hair lie down."[55] He managed to get through each day's meetings and the never-ending reports that crossed his desk only by adhering to a strict schedule. He rose at 6:30 A.M., was at the breakfast table by seven, and

arrived at his office in the Munitions Building sharply at 7:30. He immediately reviewed the logbook and summary of communications that had
arrived overnight. Afterward, he buzzed for Brigadier General Gasser (now
deputy chief of staff) and Ward who—accompanied by whichever assistant
was responsible for that day's briefings—entered the chief of staff's office
and awaited the signal to begin the presentation. After handling the day's
correspondence, dictating replies, or editing letters drafted for his signature,
by 10:00 A.M. Marshall turned to his appointment calendar and the line of
deputies waiting outside his office. At noon he returned to Quarters Number
1 at Fort Myer for a light lunch with Katherine, followed by a power nap and
a return to his office. Often saying that nobody ever had an original thought
after 3:00 P.M., he would try to depart the office by 4:00 or 5:00 P.M.—
although never before his inbox had been emptied—and thereafter "completely detach myself from Army affairs" to clear his mind to repeat the cycle
the next day. Evenings sometimes included a walk with Katherine, a movie
on post, or a social event, but he was almost always in bed by 9:00 P.M.

On January 3, 1940, President Roosevelt declared: "I am asking the Congress
for Army and navy increases which are based not on panic but on common sense. They are not as great as enthusiastic alarmists seek. They are not
as small as unrealistic persons claiming superior private information would
demand."[56] Roosevelt asked Congress for a small increase to $1.8 billion
for Fiscal Year 1941, which included an Army budget of $853 million. This
amount was over twice the budgets of the mid-1930s and $2 million more
than the expanded FY40 budget, but was still only a fraction of the possible requirements for war and the estimates Marshall and the General Staff
did not dare to offer publicly. In February, Marshall defended the proposal
against threats of congressional cutbacks, warning the House Appropriations
Committee: "As to the existing crisis abroad, we must face the facts. Any
major developments there should be paralleled by added precautions in this
country. If the situation grows more desperate, we should add to the numbers
of seasoned troops. . . . If Europe blazes in late spring or summer, we must
put our house in order before the sparks reach the Western Hemisphere."[57]
Pointing to the lack of fighting in Europe and focused on the June primary
elections, members of Congress paid little heed to Marshall's warning that
time was running out. The committee did not act upon the president's request
until April, when it imposed cuts totaling 10 percent. Where Roosevelt asked

for 496 new airplanes, the committee approved only fifty-seven, while a Senate committee cut already approved funding for two vital projects.

These cuts left Marshall discouraged, and in his frustration he turned to an old friend for help. Bernard Baruch, an influential financier and head of Wilson's War Industries Board during World War I, had served as confidant to several presidents, including Roosevelt. Marshall had met Baruch in the early 1920s while an aide to Pershing and had wisely maintained a cordial relationship ever since. Baruch frequently visited the chief of staff and "stood ready to do something for me the minute I wanted it done."[58] Marshall asked Baruch to set up a meeting with influential congressmen, and Baruch quickly arranged a dinner with key senators so Marshall could plead the Army's case. On the night of April 10, 1940, with Denmark's surrender to Germany dominating the afternoon headlines, Marshall explained the Army's needs until two or three in the morning. He spoke eloquently and passionately about the shortages, the lack of weapons and transportation, even of such basic items as blankets. Looking at the senators' stern faces, Marshall felt he had failed to persuade anyone. Exhausted, he confessed, "I feel culpable. My job as Chief of Staff is to convince you of our needs, and I have utterly failed. I don't know what to do."[59]

Senator Alva Adams sat silently for a long moment. Then he nodded and, speaking for most of his colleagues, told Marshall: "You came before the committee without even a piece of paper and you [just] got every damned thing you asked for."[60] Of course, Marshall did not get *everything* that evening, but he had deeply impressed the powerful senators and established new channels of communications with them. Consequently Baruch, who had pressed both Roosevelt and Congress for larger appropriations, considered the meeting "a turning point in convincing such critics . . . of the urgent need for speeding the rebuilding of our defenses."[61]

Five days later, on April 15, Marshall warned Secretary Woodring that the deteriorating international situation required him to advise an increase in the state of military preparations. President Roosevelt soon approved, in principle, the request for additional critical items for existing Regular Army and National Guard units, but subsequently cut the request from $35 million to $18 million. In addition to his fear of challenging congressional isolationists, Roosevelt's reversal may have been influenced by Treasury Secretary Morgenthau's warnings regarding the need for fiscal prudence and concern about exceeding U.S. debt limits. These priorities changed, however, on May 10, when the *Luftwaffe* began bombing French air bases, German paratroopers descended upon Rotterdam, and the *Wehrmacht*'s armored columns poured across the Luxembourg border into the Ardennes Forest. Morgenthau asked Marshall to brief him on the Army's needs with a proposal he could take to Roosevelt and Congress. "Just remember," he warned the chief of staff, "it is all new to me."[62]

On May 11 Marshall visited the Treasury Secretary. He was brutally frank in presenting a program calling for the creation of a balanced force of 1.25 million men by the end of 1941. Marshall's shopping list included enough planes to build a modern air force; munitions plants and all types of ammunition; reserve equipment; better pay, shelter, rations, and clothing for the troops; and more rifles, artillery, and antiaircraft guns. The immediate cost, Marshall estimated, was an additional $650 million, almost twice the Army appropriations the president requested in January. "It makes me dizzy," Marshall admitted.

"It makes me dizzy if we don't get it," Morgenthau replied.[63]

Marshall's arguments persuaded Morgenthau, who agreed to serve as the chief of staff's advocate when they met with the president two days later. But he also urged Marshall to speak out himself. "Stand right up and tell him what you think," Morgenthau advised. "There are too few people who do it and he likes it."[64]

On May 13, Marshall and Morgenthau took their case to the White House. Morgenthau opened the meeting, but as Marshall recalled, "he was getting very little chance to state his case."[65] As he had done with Secretary Dern during the 1933 meeting with MacArthur, the president joked and teased his old friend for being a harbinger of gloom. (Unlike Dern, Secretary Woodring, who was present at the meeting, said nothing in support of his chief of staff.) Roosevelt resorted to his usual technique of dominating the conversation to avoid dealing with the issue. He proposed building 50,000 planes a year and expanding the Navy, but he saw no pressing need to expand or develop ground forces. When he signaled an end to the meeting without a decision, Morgenthau asked: "Mr. President, will you hear out General Marshall?"

"I know exactly what he would say," Roosevelt replied. "There is no necessity for me hearing him at all."

Marshall walked over to the president and, standing over him, asked for three minutes of his time.

"Of course, General Marshall," Roosevelt said.[66]

In blunt terms, Marshall explained the Army's crucial requirements, his presentation growing more vehement as he progressed. "If you don't do something," he concluded, "and do it right away . . . I don't know what is going to happen to this country. *You have got to do something and you've got to do it today.*"[67] There was a long silence, as the president was visibly stunned by the normally reserved chief of staff's impassioned plea. Finally, Roosevelt asked the general to return the next day with a detailed list of his requirements.

Marshall returned with a proposed supplemental Army appropriation of $657 million. "I just sent a message to Congress just three weeks ago," Roosevelt protested. "What will they think of me?"

"Well, Mr. President, the world has changed since three weeks ago," Marshall replied. "I know you can get them to accept it; they can't evade it." Marshall later characterized this encounter as the breaking of a log jam, and personally drafted the president's message to Congress that would accompany the request.[68]

Following Hitler's invasion of France, even isolationist newspapers were now calling for increased defense spending, and Congress abruptly opened the public purse to defend the continental United States. With public opinion now solidly behind him, on May 16 the president went before a joint session of Congress to request $1.18 billion in new military appropriations, of which $732 million was earmarked for a 280,000-man Army. Within two weeks, Congress voted $1.5 billion more for defense, $320 million above what Roosevelt had requested.

As the *Wehrmacht* swept toward the Channel coast and disaster loomed, Marshall and others convinced Roosevelt to forward a second supplemental appropriations bill to Congress on May 31. Of this amount, $709 million was for Army needs. The president stated that "the almost incredible events of the past two weeks in the European conflict, particularly as a result of the use of aviation and mechanized equipment . . . necessitate another enlargement of our military program."[69] Congress not only approved the proposal, but also appropriated money to raise the authorized Regular Army enlisted strength from 230,000 to 375,000 and granted presidential power to call the National Guard into active service. The legislation raised total War Department appropriations to nearly $3 billion, thereby allowing the Army to stockpile critical, long-lead items for a force of two million, as well as to build an industrial base capable of supplying a total force of four million. The funds at the War Department's disposal dwarfed Marshall's requests of just two months earlier, and equaled the total Army budget for the previous five years.[70]

Marshall cautioned that the recent appropriations "would bear no fruit for at least a year, and for the majority of items, a year and a half to two years."[71] In the near-term, however, Marshall's biggest problem was not the lack of modern equipment, but rather keeping what he had. By the end of May 1940 the British were evacuating their army from the beaches of Dunkirk. Although most of its soldiers were saved in that extraordinary display of fortitude and heroism, it came at the cost of abandoning most of their army's weapons. The British were now pleading for warships to combat German U-boats and armaments to defend the home islands. The Nazi victories and the advent of airpower suddenly called into question the isolationist strategy of relying on the European balance of power and the Atlantic Ocean for defense. In one poll taken after Churchill's defiant June 4 address to the House of Commons ("We shall fight on the fields and in the streets . . . we shall never surrender") more than 80 percent of Americans favored sending as many arms as possible to the British, and President Roosevelt pledged to use all "the material resources of this nation" to support the British.[72]

Focused on transforming an emaciated Army into a modern force, Marshall initially opposed sharing the few modern military resources America possessed. The General Staff and several of Roosevelt's diplomatic advisers believed their ultimate responsibility was recruiting, training, and fielding an *American* fighting force, which at the time barely existed and could not be created without arms and equipment. Hence they argued that American soldiers, sailors, and airmen should have priority on American production. Moreover, most senior officers—partly informed by Ambassador Joseph Kennedy's defeatist reports—believed Great Britain could not possibly endure the Blitz. Walter Bedell Smith warned the chief of staff: "If we were required to mobilize after having released guns necessary for this mobilization and were found to be short . . . everyone who was a party to the deal might hope to be hanging from a lamp post."[73]

Marshall did not oppose aid in principle, but rather preferred to help the British after the United States had addressed its own critical needs. Marshall was particularly worried that shipping aircraft to England would cripple the Army's pilot training program. In a heated discussion with Morgenthau on May 22, Marshall asked Hap Arnold what it would mean to release one hundred of his newest aircraft to the British. At the time, the United States had just 260 pilots qualified to fly its 160 combat-worthy fighters and fifty-two bombers. Arnold estimated that one hundred planes would only replace three days of combat losses while setting the Air Corps training program back six months. As the Dunkirk evacuation began, a May 29 cable from London requesting pistols and submachine guns "to meet parachute attacks expected in the early future" led Marshall to relent somewhat.[74] President Roosevelt ordered every spare rifle and field piece and as much ammunition as possible sent immediately to Great Britain. Marshall declared the weapons to be surplus at a time when none existed, and the War Department released a million Springfield rifles, some automatic weapons and machine guns, and 75mm guns to help arm the Home Guard. "This distribution of World War weapons didn't hurt our training program," Marshall noted after the war, "Because there were enough left of the World War weapons for such training as we might want to use them for, and we were beginning to get deliveries on the modern weapons."[75]

When Churchill sought new B-17 bombers, however, Marshall drew the line, fearing such a transfer would seriously hamper North American defense. He was able to veto the request because Congress had voted on June 28 that no Army or Navy munitions could be transferred to foreign nations unless the chief of staff—or chief of naval operations—certified they were not essential to the United States' defense. Consequently, Marshall demanded evidence of British ability to survive before he would approve the president's proposal to send scarce bombers to England. If Great Britain were defeated after America sent supplies desperately needed at home, Marshall declared, "The Army and the Administration could never justify to the American people the risk they had taken."[76] When Roosevelt raised the issue again in September, Marshall bluntly informed him that there were only forty-nine bombers fit for duty in the continental United States. According to Morgenthau, the President's head shot back "as if someone had hit him in the chest."[77]

Ironically, the dispute over bomber transfers had a second-order effect that made Marshall's life much easier. In the wake of France's collapse, President Roosevelt finally recognized he could no longer endure the Woodring-Johnson feud that had rendered the War Department ineffective. When Woodring refused to sign off on a June 18 presidential order to sell seventeen new bombers to Britain, Roosevelt used his insubordination as a pretext to clean house among the War Department's civilian leadership. The next morning Roosevelt requested and received Woodring's resignation, and by the end of the day had replaced him with Republican stalwart Henry Stimson.

As one Marshall biographer notes, "Henry Stimson was all Woodring was not."[78] Stimson was an ardent and outspoken internationalist who the day before his appointment had delivered a radio address calling for compulsory military service, repeal of the Neutrality Act, and increased aid to Britain even if it required Navy convoys. Although seventy-two years old, Stimson was still intellectually sharp and brought unmatched prestige and experience to the office. After serving as William Howard Taft's secretary of war (and George Patton's riding partner), when America entered World War I Stimson—at the age of fifty—volunteered and served as a field artillery colonel in France. He subsequently served as governor-general of the Philippines under President Coolidge and as Herbert Hoover's secretary of state. Stimson not only revitalized the War Department's civilian leadership, he also provided Marshall with an effective intermediary and buffer between him and President Roosevelt that the chief of staff had heretofore lacked.

With Stimson on board and protecting his flank politically, on July 10 the president issued his third defense message to Congress calling for "total defense" and requesting the largest sum yet, more than $4.8 billion. Roosevelt called for funds to supply an army of 1.2 million men with another 800,000 in reserve. The money would procure tanks, guns, artillery, ammunition, and other equipment; help underwrite manufacturing plants needed to produce ordnance, equipment, and other critical items; and buy 15,000 more planes for the Army. Congress debated these requests for eight weeks before approving slightly over $4 billion along with $1.1 billion for the Navy.[79]

The previously parsimonious Congress was now willing to appropriate billions of dollars for defense with no clear idea of how to spend the funds. Although the weapons purchased with the money would be important, they raised the question of expanding the Army. At best, the 255,000-man Army could put five or six fully equipped divisions into battle. By comparison, however, Hitler already had 136 divisions in action and was believed to have around 200 in total. As the Nazis and their Soviet allies devoured Europe in the summer/fall of 1940, pressure mounted to call up the National Guard and Reserves. Given that recruiting alone could not provide the two million men needed, the obvious-yet-problematic solution was conscription. Conscription had been imposed on Americans only twice before—during the Civil War and World War I—and both times it had proved controversial. There had never been a *peacetime* draft in the nation's history, and in a presidential election year it was political dynamite.[80]

Grenville Clark, an influential New York lawyer and an old Republican friend of President Roosevelt's, took up the cause of introducing selective service in the spring of 1940 as "the only fair, efficient and democratic way to raise an army."[81] He put together a bipartisan movement to lobby congressmen, generals, the press, and other influential elites. Although Roosevelt favored conscription and tried to get it written into the Democratic platform, when Clark's group sought his support in May he refused. Marshall also initially declined to lend Clark's movement his official support despite having supported the notion of selective service since the debates over universal military training in the early 1920s. The chief of staff understood how explosive the draft issue would become, and again wanted to avoid creating the impression that the *Army* was pushing the country toward involvement in a new world war overseas. Beyond the political danger, Marshall questioned whether the Army could handle such a large buildup in a short time. There were no organized basic training camps, and draftees would require clothing, vehicles, and weapons that did not yet exist. Marshall would be forced to strip National Guard units across the country just as increased training was measurably improving their combat efficiency. Even if the facilities were available, an immediate draft would force him to strip his five partially mobilized Regular divisions of men to train the inductees. Unlike MacArthur's rush to increase the Philippine army's ranks, Marshall decided "We didn't have the instructors. . . . We had nobody to train these men if we got them in, and we just couldn't risk going into this thing in a slipshod manner."[82] Thus, in his meeting with Clark and his associates, Marshall was courteous but blunt in turning them down.

Marshall changed his mind, however, and a month later decided to support conscription. The fall of France and seemingly inevitable fall of Britain influenced his reversal, as had Secretary Stimson's determined arguments. Yet his support remained clandestine for fear of getting ahead of the president on the issue. There were two reasons for Marshall's reluctance: First, he believed strongly in civilian control of the military and that America's elected officials should be the ones to set defense policy, not its generals. More practically, however, he felt that any short-term gains from pleading his case directly to the public would be negated by the risk of losing President Roosevelt's trust and confidence. As a formal, austere man in an administration that ran on improvisation, good humor, and political cunning, the chief of staff stood outside the president's inner circle. Marshall understood Roosevelt's way of suborning people by misrepresenting their intimacy, and deliberately observed a formality with the president "so that he wouldn't be manipulated as 'one of the boys.'"[83] He insisted the president call him "General Marshall," not "George," and he refused to laugh at Roosevelt's jokes. Roosevelt was an avid sailor and still retained a strong affection for the service from his days as assistant secretary of the Navy, so much so that on one occasion Marshall remonstrated: "At least, Mr. President, stop speaking of the Army as 'they' and the Navy as 'we.'" Marshall's concerns over—and disagreements with—Roosevelt notwithstanding, he refused to make public statements contrary to presidential policies.[84]

While waiting for the president to signal his intent regarding the draft, Marshall again tended to matters on which he could exert control, this time focusing on the state of the Army's officer corps. As historian Stephen R. Taaffe notes, "Marshall had countless responsibilities—but he believed that his most significant and difficult task was recommending officers for the President to nominate as generals and assigning them to their posts."[85] In April 1940 Marshall told the House Military Affairs Committee (HMAC) that in the World War he had seen twenty-seven of the twenty-nine divisions sent into combat, "and there were more reliefs of field officers, those above the grade of captain, due to physical reasons than for any other cause."[86] Marshall once wrote to Edwin Harding that he regretted not occupying a position of power where he could promote younger officers of "brilliancy and talent damned by lack of rank to obscurity. There are so many junior officers of tremendous ability whose quality the service is losing all advantage of that is really tragic."[87]

Now, as chief of staff he had his chance. "I do not propose to send our young citizen soldiers into action," he told a reporter in 1939, "under commanders whose minds are no longer adaptable to the making of split-second decisions in the fast-moving war of today, nor whose bodies are no longer capable of standing up under the demands of field service."[88] Consequently, during a recess in a Senate appropriations hearing on August 7, 1940, Marshall spoke privately with Senator James Byrnes about this problem. Four months earlier he had appeared before the HMAC seeking a bill that would permit the War Department to promote younger officers. The committee had been unmoved by Marshall's request, however, and its chairman kept the measure from advancing to a floor vote. Byrnes promised to place the amendment before the Senate, and by September 9 it became law and paved the way for those officers stuck behind "the Hump" to earn high commands.[89]

Marshall created a "plucking committee" of six retired officers led by former Chief of Staff Craig and tasked them with reviewing the efficiency ratings of older officers. In its first six months, the panel removed 195 captains, majors, lieutenant colonels, and colonels, and over the next five years would designate 500 more colonels for immediate retirement. Marshall could be ruthless when it came to removing generals who did not measure up to his standards. When the CGSS superintendent preceding McNair estimated it would take eighteen months to produce new manuals, Marshall told him it had to be done in four. "He said it couldn't be done," Marshall recalled. "And I said, 'You be very careful about that, to tell me ... that a thing can or cannot be done.' He said, 'No, it can't be done.' I said. 'I'm sorry then, you are relieved.'" Similarly, when an officer Marshall described as "an intimate friend of mine" refused an emergency assignment to France because his wife was away and unable to pack his household goods, Marshall replied: "'[M]y god, man, we are at war and you are a general.' He said, 'Well, I'm sorry.' And I said, 'I'm sorry, too, but you will be retired tomorrow.' And I just moved him out. He was a very dear friend of mine."[90] Marshall's creation of the plucking board caused more bitterness than perhaps any other action he took as chief of staff, and cost him many friendships.

Marshall recognized the importance of living up to the standards he demanded of others, and as he was about to turn sixty, the age he had established for mandatory retirement of older officers no longer able to handle the rigors of command, he submitted his own resignation to President Roosevelt. After two weeks without receiving a reply, he called Harry Hopkins. "The President just laughs at you," he told Marshall. "He says no politician ever resigns a job and that's just talk." Marshall responded by marching to the White House to offer his resignation a second time, this time offering to train his successor for two or three months prior to stepping down. Once again, it was left to Hopkins to convey the news that the president had simply ignored his offer.[91]

After their lobbying efforts failed to sway the president or the War Department, Grenville Clark and the leaders of the Civilian Military Training Camps Association shifted their attention to Congress. They persuaded Senator Edward R. Burke (D-NE) to sponsor a selective service bill in the Senate, and James W. Wadsworth (R-NY) to do the same in the House. Marshall secretly sent three members of his staff to help draft the legislation, while Clark's committee launched a publicity campaign to educate Americans about why it was necessary. It was introduced in Congress in June, two days before France's capitulation to Germany, and hearings began on July 3. As reporters filed into the House committee room, copies of a letter from General Pershing endorsing the legislation were distributed.[92]

Once the bill was introduced and he could not be accused by antimilitarists of being its progenitor, Marshall went "all out in the arguments for its passage."[93] Together with Secretary Stimson, the chief of staff began a series of pilgrimages to Capitol Hill to testify and to court undecided congressmen. With President Roosevelt's approval, Marshall endorsed the Selective Service bill in the strongest terms. On July 30, he told the Senate Military Affairs Committee that there was "no conceivable way" to secure "trained, seasoned men in adequate numbers" to defend the country except through the draft.[94] When the isolationist senator Gerald Nye deemed the bill hasty and asked, "of course, General, we can entertain a hope that developments abroad in the next few months will be such that we can abandon a considerable part of this program, can we not?", Marshall just shook his head. "Senator," he said, "I am sorry that I cannot entertain any such hope at present. My fear is not that I am recommending too much but rather that I may find at some time in the future that I recommended too little. In fact, if I could feel now that I might expect some day to face an investigation for having recommended too much, my mind would be more at rest than it is at present." Marshall refused to sugarcoat the problem. A planned force composed of twenty-seven infantry divisions, two armored divisions, six cavalry divisions, and an Air Corps of 11,000 planes would still "be inadequate to wage a successful war with a fully prepared foreign power."[95] Indeed, Marshall was such an effective advocate that Morgenthau advised the president not to send anyone else to the Hill to speak on the bill's behalf.

Marshall's effectiveness notwithstanding, the isolationists in Congress and their supporters in the America First movement were confident of victory. Longtime antiwar senator Burton K. Wheeler of Montana denounced the bill as "a step toward totalitarianism."[96] Labor leader John L. Lewis similarly identified conscription with dictatorship, and the American Communist Party opposed the bill as well. A "mother's movement" started by a coalition of right-wing women's groups mobilized thousands of supporters who descended upon the Capitol dressed in black, many with mourning veils covering their faces. The women stalked and harassed members of Congress who were not avowedly isolationist, screaming and spitting at them and holding wailing vigils outside their offices. These demonstrations cowed enough legislators that the Burke-Wadsworth bill appeared headed for defeat in committee.[97]

With the *Luftwaffe* swarming the skies over England, President Roosevelt finally announced administration support of the draft bill on July 31. Yet after this declaration he did nothing to help secure the bill's passage until Wendell Wilkie, the Republican presidential nominee, defied his party's isolationists and came out in favor of the draft on August 17. Speaking to a crowd of 200,000 people in his home state of Indiana, Wilkie voiced support for "some form of selective service," saying it was "the only democratic way to secure the trained and competent manpower we need for national defense." Wilkie's acceptance of conscription neutralized the draft as a campaign issue, and finally convinced Roosevelt to make an unequivocal statement urging the Burke-Wadsworth bill's immediate passage. During an August 23 press conference, therefore, the president declared that he was "absolutely opposed" to any delay in enactment of the draft bill.[98]

Several weeks earlier, Roosevelt had asked Congress for authority to call out the National Guard if an emergency arose when it was not in session. On July 29, he further asked for power to place the Guard into active service for a year to provide immediate training. Marshall supported federalizing the Guard, and as with the Selective Service Act, couched the request in terms of hemispheric defense. On August 27, Congress authorized the Guard's induction into federal service and the activation of the Organized Reserves to fill the Army's ranks. National Guard units, the Enlisted Reserve Corps, and the reserve officers necessary to train them were brought onto active service as quickly as the Army could find or build them housing.[99]

By this time, the Selective Service Act had gained momentum. Marshall and Stimson's testimony—combined with the Clark committee's publicity campaign and France's shocking surrender—caused a shift in public opinion. Further, now that President Roosevelt explicitly endorsed the bill, Democratic congressional leaders united behind it. The measure's supporters were also helped by reporting and images from London depicting Germany's aerial assault on Great Britain. As one officer close to Marshall observed: "Every time Hitler bombed, we got another couple of votes."[100]

After defeating several amendments intended to cripple the bill, Congress passed the Selective Service Act (SSA) on September 10, and President Roosevelt signed it into law two days later. The law initiated a mandatory national registration beginning in October 1940 for a draft lottery involving all American males between the ages of twenty-one and thirty-five, and authorized a Regular Army of 500,000 men, a 270,000-man National Guard, and an inductee population of 630,000 men for an aggregate strength of 1.4 million. Defying Marshall and Chief of Naval Operations Adm. Harold Stark's call for "complete mobilization," however, the law limited draftees' service to one year and forbade their deployment outside the Western Hemisphere. Nevertheless, in what a *New York Times* reporter called "an historic muster," on Wednesday, October 16, more than sixteen million American men lined up at schools, public buildings, and churches to enroll. "For the first time in our history," Marshall said during a radio address, "we are beginning in time of peace to prepare against the possibility of war."[101] According to Marshall's biographer, Forrest Pogue, "It was the Selective Service Act of 1940 . . . that made possible the huge United States Army and Air Force that fought World War II."[102]

On paper, George Marshall finally had his army. Now he had to train it. Whether this was actually possible was unclear. "For almost twenty years," he lamented, "we had all of the time and almost none of the money. Today we have all of the money and no time."[103]

Increasingly overwhelmed by details despite his efforts to reform the General Staff bureaucracy, in July 1940 Marshall decided to activate a new organization, the General Headquarters (GHQ), which was to be the analogue of Pershing's AEF headquarters in France during World War I. Before it became an operational headquarters, however, its initial duty would be to train the Army's tactical units and prepare them for commitment to the theater of operations. Recognizing the difficulty of serving as both chief of staff and GHQ commander, Marshall chose his old friend Lesley McNair to serve as GHQ's chief of staff with responsibility for creating and training the Army's new divisions. Short, sandy haired, and a man of few words, McNair was plagued by the bane of career artillerymen since the first cannons were invented—damaged hearing. Deafness aside, he was intelligent, dynamic, and an experienced trainer, so much so that while Marshall retained nominal command of GHQ, he freely delegated authority over training to General McNair.

To assist McNair, Marshall summoned his protégé from the 3rd Infantry—newly promoted Lt. Col. Mark Clark—to Washington, DC. Clark arrived in the capital only to learn that McNair had already departed to observe units conducting field training. Clark flew out to join the general, and quickly learned that McNair "was a man who always wanted to see at first hand how things were working out, and there was never a time when he even considered the possibility of sitting back and getting information at second hand."[104] After three days together reviewing Regular Army and National Guard units, McNair had seen enough of the younger officer to entrust him with the job of overseeing operations and training.

McNair and Clark's first major task was to plan the new divisions' organization and training. The plan was to select the senior commanders and staff officers. Clark reviewed the lists of colonels and generals, selected the division commander and his two brigadier assistants for each infantry division, and took his choices to McNair and then to Marshall for approval. A cadre of several hundred noncommissioned officers was assembled, and they and the officers were all sent to appropriate schools. Several weeks before the new division was scheduled to be activated the officers and NCOs were reconvened at their new camp and given a brief period in which to learn to work as a team before the division's troops would arrive. This method allowed GHQ to create up to four new divisions each month.[105]

Once consolidated, the divisions immediately plunged into a fifty-two-week training program, the details of which GHQ had developed in advance for infantry, cavalry, and armored divisions. McNair instituted what he called "progressive training," a cycle moving through a well-understood sequence allowing individual and small unit training to occur in a distributed fashion, building to corps maneuvers as the final phase of independent unit training. All soldiers and units followed the same schedules without variation or exception. As the divisions took shape, McNair and Clark spent much of their time flying from camp to camp to monitor progress. Clark estimated that they flew 80,000 miles in one year, and throughout this period his admiration for his boss grew. He later wrote: "I found McNair one of the most brilliant, selfless and devoted soldiers I ever knew."[106]

GHQ's training program faced significant obstacles from the start, however. Of the first million men drafted into the Army, almost 40 percent were found unfit for general military service, and another 10 percent failed to measure up to fourth-grade educational standards. Although Army planners had assumed there were sufficient numbers of qualified junior officers in the National Guard and Reserves to meet the requirements of large-scale mobilization, too many were inadequately trained or otherwise unfit. Additionally, many educated reservists were snatched up by the Air Corps or other non-infantry divisions, creating a severe shortage of junior officers in the infantry. McNair came away from a visit to one division in September 1940 with the impression of the "blind leading the blind, and officers generally elsewhere."[107]

In addition to the dearth of quality officers and inductees, the Army had nowhere near enough housing for the personnel influx created by the Selective Service Act. Before the war the Army had maintained quarters for about 225,000 troops at its 320 posts. Now it had to accommodate a force of 1.4 million men. Congress did not provide funds for new camps before approving the draft, and bad weather, construction problems, and the task's sheer magnitude overwhelmed the Quartermaster Corps' small Construction Division and delayed construction. The requirement for camps thus slowed the calling up of both National Guardsmen and draftees.[108]

When troops were inducted, equipment for them remained desperately short throughout 1941. Despite half-a-year of notional rearmament, industrial output at the close of 1940 included no medium tanks, none of the new 105mm howitzers, no heavy-caliber antiaircraft guns, and virtually no heavy artillery. In training exercises, trucks with the word TANK painted on their sides substituted for real tanks, pieces of drain pipe represented antitank guns, and wooden tripods served as 60mm mortars. In the spring of 1941, the Army only possessed enough weapons and equipment for less than a tenth of the troops authorized by the Selective Service Act, and a War Department report that summer concluded: "Only a small portion of the field army is at present equipped for extended active operations under conditions of modern warfare."[109]

Part of the supply problem lay in the diversion of scant supplies overseas. In late 1940 Prime Minister Churchill informed President Roosevelt that British funds for purchasing U.S. war materiel were almost depleted. Elected to an unprecedented third term and freed from the constraints of the campaign, on December 29, 1940, President Roosevelt used a Fireside Chat to justify and encourage support for all aid to England short of war. "Never before since Jamestown and Plymouth Rock has our American civilization been in such danger as now," he said gravely. He explained the depth and extent of the threat posed by Germany, Italy, and Japan. "If Great Britain goes down," the president warned, "the Axis powers will control the continents of Europe, Asia, Africa, Australasia, and the high seas—and they will be in a position to bring enormous military and naval resources against this hemisphere. It is no exaggeration to say that all of us, in all the Americas, would be living at the point of a gun."

Roosevelt assured the American people "that there is far less chance of the United States getting into war, if we do all we can now to support the nations defending themselves against attack by the Axis than if we acquiesce in their defeat, submit tamely to an Axis victory, and wait our turn to be the object of attack in another war later on." Although the administration did not plan on sending an American expeditionary force outside its borders, "we must have more ships, more guns, more planes—more of everything. . . . We must be the great arsenal of democracy."[110]

By one estimate, one hundred million people across America and around the world heard Roosevelt's speech, one of the most successful he ever delivered. White House messages ran 100-to-1 in favor, while an opinion poll showed that 80 percent of those who heard or read the talk expressed approval against 12 percent opposed.[111]

On January 3, 1941, the President submitted his annual budget message to Congress requesting nearly $28.5 billion for defense. In his annual message to Congress three days later, Roosevelt announced he was sending the Lend-Lease Bill to Congress. Skirting the neutrality laws, Lend-Lease would permit the sale, transfer, exchange, or loan of war materiel to any nation's defense effort the president deemed vital to American security. Roosevelt sold the measure as a means of keeping the United States out of the war. Conversely, isolationists argued that it practically ensured American intervention. Senator Wheeler declared: "The lend-lease-five program is the New Deal's triple A foreign policy; it will plow under every fourth American boy." Among the key witnesses testifying against the bill were Roosevelt's own ambassador to Great Britain, Joseph P. Kennedy, and national hero aviator Charles Lindbergh, who declared that airpower made it impossible for Germany to conquer the United States or for it to be pushed out of France and the Low Countries. Nevertheless, the bill passed both houses in March by large majorities.[112]

Marshall welcomed and supported the Lend-Lease bill. In addition to aiding Great Britain, it would enable the United States to expand its industrial plant capacity, provide additional weapons and munitions for the defense of the United States and the Western Hemisphere, and allow him to create a long-range plan for military procurement. The logistics necessary to arm, equip, uniform, and house the growing Army, however, were complicated by the demands to send arms to the British. In 1940 President Roosevelt had ordered production of bombers to be divided "fifty-fifty" with England. Yet as Orlando Ward wrote in his diary, "The fifty-fifty deal is working with thirty-three planes for the U.S. and four hundred and nine for the foreigners, a fifty-fifty deal like one horse for them, one rabbit for us."[113] When Hitler shifted his attention to the east by launching a massive attack against the Soviet Union on June 22, 1941, it was agreed that Russia had to be given aid as long as its forces fought the Nazis. This meant yet another competitor for the still-scarce American war materials and a further dispersion of the American mobilization effort.[114]

Yet even if the U.S. Army did not face competition for arms and equipment from its future allies, it would still have faced significant materiel shortages in the spring of 1941. Throughout the debate over Lend-Lease, little attention was paid to the fact that America had a painfully long way to go before it could actually become the "arsenal of democracy." Few companies were eager to convert to defense production. Munitions firms and the nascent American aircraft industry had been burned in World War I when the government sued them to recover funds advanced for plant expansion. They had been unfairly vilified over the past two decades, and feared being stuck with excess capacity once again when the crisis ended. As *Life* magazine noted, "This spring, after one year of total verbal defense, we are producing mechanical luxuries that compete with defense not merely in normal but in boom quantities."[115]

The problems went well beyond competition with civilian demand, however. Procurement officers had to deal with a hopelessly dense tangle of laws, regulations, court decisions, and other rulings intended to prevent "blood profits," labor abuse, and other problems. Organized labor was exploiting its newfound clout so that in 1940 a total of 2,500 strikes had created 6.7 million idle labor days. In 1941 the number soared to 4,300 strikes, 23.1 million idle labor days, and by year's end one out of every twelve American workers had gone on strike. Even if organized labor were cooperative, by 1941 there were serious materiel shortages in items such as aluminum, and machine tools were limited. Thus, whereas by June 30, 1941, Congress had authorized $46.9 billion for defense programs, contracts had been let for only $21 billion of that amount, and only $7 billion had actually been dispersed for goods delivered. The editors at *Fortune* reported that summer that America was "not merely falling short" in becoming the arsenal of democracy President Roosevelt had envisaged, it was "failing spectacularly."[116]

Efforts to mobilize American industry to match the steeply escalating risk of war were further hampered by Roosevelt's uncertain leadership. Although most Americans expressed a desire to stay out of the fighting, by May 1941 68 percent of the public believed it was more important to help Great Britain than to keep out of war. Roosevelt had apparently concluded that the United States would ultimately have to enter the war, yet still had no strategy for how to proceed. Even in the administration's top councils, feeling was growing that the president was not supplying clear, sustained, or purposeful leadership. According to historian Kenneth S. Davis, during the crucial weeks and months following Lend-Lease's passage, "a strange, prolonged, exceedingly dangerous pause in presidential leadership" set in.[117] "My own feeling," Harold Ickes wrote in his diary, "is that the President has not aroused the country; has not really sounded the bell ... does not furnish the motive power that is required."[118] Felix Frankfurter told Ickes he was at a loss to understand the president's failure to take the initiative, and Ickes met secretly with Stimson, Secretary of the Navy Frank Knox, and Attorney General Robert Jackson to discuss ways of putting pressure on Roosevelt.[119]

Marshall and the Navy's leadership could not be as noncommittal as the president. They had to plan across a longer time span, for the decisions they made about construction supplies, equipment, and training posts would affect operational decisions for years. Yet as James MacGregor Burns notes, "Not only did Roosevelt evade strategic decision but he refused to let his military chiefs commit themselves on the most compelling matters."[120] The president's reluctance to issue clear-cut directives—along with his habit of changing his mind about production priorities—drove his service chiefs crazy. Marshall complained: "First the President wants 500 bombers a month and that dislocates the program. Then he says he wants so many tanks and that dislocates the program. The President will never sit down and talk about a complete program and have the whole thing move forward at the same time."[121] Indeed, although they would make a formidable team during the coming war, Marshall later remarked that from 1939 to 1941 he doubted the president's ability to lead America in a national emergency. "He wasn't always clear cut in his decisions," Marshall noted. "He could be swayed."[122] *Life* noted: "If the U.S. political leaders have set any military objectives, they have not made it clear to the Army. This is reflected in the training, which is not geared to any real military situation."[123] The military was not sure who or what it was preparing for, and industrialists had only a general notion of what was required from them, the urgency for producing, or how long the emergency would last.

Stimson finally confronted the president and persuaded him to act. On July 9 Roosevelt instructed Stimson and Knox to undertake a systemic survey of the "overall production requirements required to defeat our political enemies.... From your report we should be able to establish a munitions objective indicating the industrial capacity which this nation will require."[124] The task of preparing the study for the Army fell to Major Wedemeyer, who had only joined the General Staff in April. Although one of the Army's new generation of intellectuals who had studied for two years at the German War College, Wedemeyer was in many ways an unlikely choice for the assignment. He was a staunch isolationist, anti-Semitic, and was considered by some War Department officers to actually be sympathetic to Nazism.[125] Yet Wedemeyer's professional reading and studies gave him a broader strategic view than almost any of his contemporaries, and his sense of duty ultimately outweighed his personal convictions regarding U.S. entry into the war. Over the next three months he compiled and digested "mountains of data," conferred with the relevant staff sections, and met daily with the chief of staff, who told him: "Don't you ever fail to give me the benefit of your thinking or experience."[126]

In September Wedemeyer produced a fourteen-page report that provided "data and estimates" of the men, supplies, munitions, and transport required to win a possible two-front war. What became known as the "Victory Program" bluntly stated that U.S. security could only be achieved by defeating the Axis, and that in addition to arming and supplying allied forces this would require U.S. entry into the war. Wedemeyer's final plan concluded that "naval and air forces seldom, if ever, win important wars," and thus "It should be recognized as an almost invariable rule that only land armies can finally win wars."[127] To accomplish its objective, the Victory Program concluded the U.S. Army would eventually have to field 215 divisions, totaling roughly 8.7 million men. Wedemeyer subsequently used these figures to determine the Army's logistical requirements, and although he significantly overestimated the number of divisions, he came close to the total manpower that was needed. The formation of such large armies—and navies—depended entirely upon the conversion of industry to war production. Equipping that force and supplying the Allies in the interim, Wedemeyer concluded, would require at least doubling current production plans at the previously inconceivable cost of about $150 billion. Although the war's eventual cost approached $300 billion, Wedemeyer's report served as a bracing wake-up call for America's lackadaisical mobilization program and proved a remarkably prescient analysis that ended up serving as the basic blueprint for U.S. military planning and mobilization throughout the war.[128]

Even as logistical concerns occupied the General Staff's attention, the shadow of a catastrophic manpower crisis loomed just over the horizon. The Army had used draftees to fill out National Guard and most Regular Army units. Only two Regular divisions consisted entirely of volunteers and, on average, inductees comprised 25–50 percent of a division's manpower across most of the Army. Moreover, between 75 and 90 percent of each Regular division's officers were reservists activated when the Selective Service Act was implemented. Their terms of service were legislatively tied to those of the National Guardsmen. Consequently, with war drawing closer, some 987,000 draftees, National Guardsmen, and Reserve officers—70 percent of the Army—would be eligible to demobilize in the early fall of 1941.[129]

Throughout the first half of 1941, Marshall attempted to lay the groundwork with the president and Congress for extending the National Guard and draftees' terms of service. By late June, however, he recognized "his efforts had utterly failed."[130] Congress did not want to touch the subject, and Roosevelt—who had been warned by Speaker of the House Sam Rayburn that there were insufficient Democratic votes in the House to pass an extension bill—did not want to expend his limited political capital on the issue. Marshall knew that letting these trainees go home would result in "the complete destruction of the fabric of the army that we had built up. We would be in a worse predicament than we were a year before." Faced with what he feared would be "the greatest of tragedies," Marshall decided this time he could not afford to wait for Roosevelt. This time he decided to force the issue himself.[131]

In late June Marshall suggested to Stimson that the War Department issue a statement that, pending presidential and congressional approval, it intended to extend the length of service. The president reluctantly consented, but would not publicly endorse the idea. By pushing his staff even harder than usual, Marshall managed to complete his first biennial report as chief of staff in five days. The forty-page report described the Army's achievements over the previous two years before making a strong plea for the service extension lest the existing active force disintegrate. The report concluded: "The materiel phase of our task is generally understood. The personnel phase is not, and it is here that legal limitations, acceptable at the time of their passage, now hamstring the development of the Army into a force immediately available for whatever defensive measures may be necessary."[132]

The report was candid and sober. Yet when Marshall released it to the press on July 3, it was immediately mired in controversy. In a rare slip, Marshall had neglected to issue a press release with the report underscoring his major points in order to drive coverage and shape public opinion. Consequently, the press not only reported his argument, but also focused on his use of the term "task forces," which isolationists interpreted as a euphemism for the Army's intent to form expeditionary forces to fight overseas. This oversight caused even congressional moderates to back away from the report. President Roosevelt was forced to convene a secret meeting of congressional leaders from both parties at the White House on July 14, at which Marshall disavowed any thought of another expeditionary force.[133]

Marshall's efforts to win support for extending the Selective Service Act were complicated by a growing crisis within the Army. By the summer of 1941, morale in the ranks had sunk to rock bottom. In part, morale suffered from the uncertainty surrounding the draft extension, creating a circular problem. But more basically, the recruits simply chafed under the unfamiliar military discipline while digging latrines, peeling potatoes, and endlessly drilling for a pitiful $30 a month while undrafted friends back home earned six-to-seven times as much in defense factory jobs. A *Life* reporter interviewed 400 privates from five different regiments at Fort McClellan, Alabama, and reported half said they would desert in October when their one-year call-up was ended. The initials "OHIO," which stood for "Over the Hill In October," were found grafittied across the camps.[134] *New York Times* publisher Arthur Sulzberger dispatched his military correspondent to investigate, only to discover *Life* had actually *underestimated* the severity of the Army's morale problem. Yet whereas today's media would not hesitate to report and heavily promote such shocking findings, Sulzberger personally delivered copies of his correspondent's findings to Roosevelt and Marshall, assuring them that "I, for one, did not propose to make Hitler a present of the fact that there was bad morale in the armed forces."[135]

The morale crisis hit Marshall particularly hard given the priority he placed on troop welfare. The chief of staff constantly stressed to commanders that one of their primary responsibilities was to build and sustain morale. In 1940, he wrote to the commandant of the Infantry School: "We must effect a decided change in the state of mind of all staff officers ... to the end that anything that concerns troops in the field will be considered as of more importance than any other matter to be handled at the moment."[136] A reported shortage of recreation facilities led him to make an unannounced visit in civilian clothes to a small southern town overflowing with idle troops from a nearby Army post. His findings led him to establish a committee to plan recreational activities for the Army that led to the creation of the United Services Organization (USO). Despite these efforts, soldiers watching a newsreel at a camp in Mississippi booed loudly when images of President Roosevelt and Marshall appeared on the screen. The morale crisis reverberated on Capitol Hill, as congressional offices were flooded with letters and telegrams from resentful draftees and their angry parents, making the already uphill battle to extend the Selective Service Act even steeper.[137]

Few legislators would openly support extension, and one congressional aide told Marshall that "In forty years on the Hill he had never seen such fear of a bill."[138] Pressured by Marshall and Stimson, President Roosevelt finally agreed to explain to the public and Congress why the extension was so desperately needed. In a radio broadcast on July 21, Roosevelt stated that the danger to the country was "infinitely greater today" than the year before when the Selective Service Act was passed. "It is true that in modern war men without machines are of little value. It is equally true that machines without men are of no value at all. . . . Within two months disintegration, which would follow failure to take Congressional action, will commence in the armies of the United States. Time counts. The responsibility rests solely with the Congress."[139] Yet much of the opposition to extending the SSA derived from resentment of Roosevelt himself. In light of this opposition, Speaker Rayburn convinced the president and Secretary Stimson that *Marshall* should personally lead the fight. Rayburn said, "Of all the men who ever testified before any committee on which I served there is not one of them who has the influence with a committee of the House that General Marshall has."[140] Thus, in publicly advocating a service extension, Marshall found himself virtually alone.

The chief of staff testified repeatedly before committees of both houses of Congress that summer. Before the Senate Military Affairs Committee, Marshall nimbly distanced himself from the White House while taking full responsibility for the controversy his report had generated. "It may clarify the atmosphere," he said,

> *for me to explain that I made the specific recommendations regarding the extension of the twelve-month period of service . . . purely on the basis of a military necessity for the security of the country. The commander-in-chief, that is, the president, had no knowledge that I was going to make them. My report was submitted to the secretary of war and at the same time was released to the press. The recommendations were dictated by military necessity.[141]*

Speaking before the House Military Affairs Committee, Marshall asked the representatives to declare the existence of a national emergency. "The declaration of an emergency does not create it," Marshall said, his voice intense. "An emergency exists whether or not the Congress declares it. I am asking you to recognize the fact—the fact that the national interest is imperiled and that an emergency exists."[142] Given the realities of a world at war, Marshall argued, building up the Army was America's best chance to avoid war. He reminded the committee members that he was not seeking the Army's expansion, but rather that he wanted to focus on improving the quality of the existing divisions, something that could only be done if the service terms were extended. "It has been our determination to bring the Army to such a state of efficiency that nobody would dare to interfere with our freedom of action," he said.[143]

Although Marshall deliberately avoided discussion of any political issue that could be considered partisan, one subordinate described the chief of staff as "a consummate Army politician" who possessed "an uncanny eye for the political angle of every problem."[144] As he had done during his tour of American occupation forces in 1919 and insisted of his instructors at the Infantry School, Marshall routinely spoke without any notes "because I found that the minute you began to read you lost your audience."[145] As one biographer concludes, "In congressional hearings, Marshall was able to project an effective image of cool professionalism, thorough mastery of the facts, truthfulness, and nonpartisanship."[146] Or as Rayburn remembered, "He would tell the truth even if it hurt his cause. Congress always respected him" for this and "would give him things they would no one else."[147] One by one Marshall won over the Senate committee members, and following their recommendation, on August 7 the Senate voted 54–30 to proclaim a national emergency.

The House proved more difficult. By design the more short-sighted of the two bodies, anti-Roosevelt feeling ran stronger there, and isolationist Republicans who had repeatedly voted against preparedness bills in the past held a larger bloc of votes than in the Senate. Marshall turned to his ally Representative Wadsworth, who convened a meeting of forty Republicans he believed could be persuaded to vote "yes" in the Army and Navy Club's private dining room. "I talked to them from seven o'clock at night until two in the morning, struggling with them," Marshall recalled.[148] After hearing the chief of staff's pleas, one congressman retorted, "That's all very well. You put the case very well, but I'll be damned if I am going to go along with Mr. Roosevelt."

Infuriated, Marshall shot back: "You're going to let plain hatred of the personality dictate to you to do something that you realize is very harmful to the interests of the country!"

Marshall offered to personally do everything he could to support them in their next campaign if they voted for the extension. "They said it would have no effect," he recalled. "They'd just be defeated." Nevertheless, about a dozen congressmen were clearly moved to declare support for the measure even if it cost them the next election.[149]

While Marshall lobbied Congress, the isolationist America First movement mobilized against preparedness. The ubiquitous mothers' groups returned to Washington. Once again dressed in black and wearing veils, they wailed through candlelight vigils outside the homes of the extension's congressional supporters. The House called the question on August 12 amidst a flurry of last-minute lobbying and reports that forty-five Democrats stood opposed and another thirty-five were uncertain. As Rayburn took the Speaker's chair, he had no idea whether he and Wadsworth had enough votes to pass the bill. Before a tense gallery crowded with America Firsters and Mothers for America, the measure's supporters and opponents traded fiery exchanges of rhetoric. As the clerk called the roll, in a scene reminiscent of the Thirteenth Amendment vote in the movie *Lincoln*, the vote seesawed back and forth. As reporters compared tallies in the press gallery, some had the extension winning, others had it losing. In the end, the vote stood at 203–202 . . . in favor of the bill.[150]

By a single vote, the U.S. Army had been saved, the razor-thin margin possible only because of Marshall's patience and skill in presenting the Army's case to Congress.

While he remained chief of staff through to the final victories of 1945, George Marshall would later maintain that 1940 and 1941 were his hardest years in the position. As one military historian notes, while the achievements of those critical days are impressive in retrospect, "They appear truly monumental looking forward from the perspective of 1939."[151] That summer Marshall assumed command of an Army comprised of only about 170,000 inadequately armed and equipped men in three half-organized divisions, fifty-six air squadrons, and two small mechanized regiments. In the Capitol and around the country, any measures that smacked of involvement in another European war were greeted with ambivalence if not outright hostility. Yet over the next two years Marshall oversaw the passage of the first peacetime draft in American history, the federalization of the National Guard, the establishment of solid relations with the Navy and Congress, the distribution of war materiel to potential allies around the globe, the creation of detailed manpower and industrial mobilization plans, and the effective integration of the Army Air Corps into General Staff planning and improved combined-arms operations between air and ground forces. By the end of November 1941, there were 1.6 million officers and men in twenty-nine infantry, five armored, and two cavalry divisions, and almost 200 air squadrons, thereby enabling the Army to enter World War II "in infinitely better condition than in 1917."[152]

None of this would have been possible without George Marshall. As *Time* magazine later observed in naming the general its "Man of the Year" for 1943, "Never in U.S. history has a military man enjoyed such respect on Capitol Hill."[153] The Army's officer corps was reinvigorated by Marshall's determination to advance a whole new leadership generation into the general officer ranks. As D. K. Crosswell concluded, "Had Drum or some other officer become Chief of Staff instead of Marshall, the roster of World War II generals would have looked very different."[154] A confidant of Churchill's told Philip Graham, owner of the *Washington Post*, "I often saw the President and Marshall together and was left with the impression that Roosevelt held Marshall in something like awe."[155] Indeed, as Russell Weigley concludes, during this period Marshall became "the principal military architect of the Western democracies' ultimate victories over the Axis powers."[156]

CHAPTER NINE

Patton, Eisenhower, and the Largest Battle on U.S. Soil

"WE TALK A HELL OF A LOT ABOUT TACTICS," GEORGE PATTON WROTE TO A friend in 1926, "and we never get to brass tacks. Namely what is it that makes the Poor S.O.B. who constitutes the casualty list fight."[1] Patton believed the key to motivating men to fight, to risk their lives, and to kill for their country was through leadership. Thus, before every major operation he personally addressed his troops to make his expectations of them clear. "An armored division is the most powerful organization ever devised," he told the assembled 2nd Armored Division. "Years ago I wrote, and I see no reason to change it now, that the whole art of war consisted in catching the enemy by the nose and kicking him in the pants.... Make it a fixed principle, to find out where the enemy is, hold him in front by fire, and get around him." He exhorted his men: "Do not sit down, do not say 'I have done enough,' keep on, see what else you can do to raise the devil with the enemy.... You must have a desperate determination to go forward."[2]

Sometimes his speeches were more visceral than tactical: "War is a killing business," he told his tankers. "You've got to spill their blood, or they'll spill yours. Rip 'em up the belly, or shoot 'em in the guts."[3] Discipline was critical because a soldier's subconscious took over in the heat of battle amidst "the whistling of a questing bullet, the crash of a bursting shell, the gasp of a wounded friend, or the [gooey] mess of his brains which you wipe from your face."[4] Yet in September 1941, on the eve of the 2nd Armored's largest operation to date, Patton put the upcoming engagement in starkly personal terms in regard to both the objective and the incentive. "I will give anyone a $50 prize," the general declared, for the capture of "a certain S.O.B. named Eisenhower!"[5]

By 1940 the Army's problem was no longer a shortage of troops, but rather that those available were either poorly trained or not trained at all. George Marshall had seen firsthand how ill prepared American officers were for World War I. They had been unfamiliar with commanding large troop formations, and coordination between different branches and services had been lacking so that the AEF's initial operations were amateurish. The periodic Regular Army–National Guard maneuvers conducted in the interwar years did not improve these shortcomings, as they were little more than play-acting between notional forces. Moreover, in 1939 neither the Regular Army nor the National Guard even possessed any tactical corps or field army headquarters. Marshall therefore concluded that what America's burgeoning force needed were a series of complex training exercises conducted in an environment as close as possible to the battlefield's exacting realities. He regarded such maneuvers as "a great college of leadership for the higher officers" and a "wonderful practical schooling" for younger leaders and their men, and on January 28, 1941, he announced the four field armies would be tested in the largest maneuvers in U.S. military history.[6]

Only a few years earlier, however, it seemed unlikely that either Patton, or his quarry Eisenhower, would be among the commanders tested in these maneuvers.

In November 1931, upon his beloved Aunt Nannie's death, Patton wrote an emotional letter to his mother who had died three years earlier. "Forgive me," he wrote, "I had always prayed to show my love by doing something famous for you, to justify what you called me when I got back from France, 'My hero son.' Perhaps I still may but time grows short."[7] His dread of failing to fulfill his self-appointed destiny grew over the next decade, plunging Patton into a spiral of despair and self-destructive behavior. Ruth Ellen noted that "he looked stricken to the heart" when he walked his oldest daughter Bee down the aisle for her wedding in June 1934. "All his determination to remain forever young was being undermined by having a daughter get married. He was forty-nine years old, and he still had not won a war or kept his part of the bargain with Grandfather Ayer about winning the glory."[8] One night Beatrice and his son George IV found Patton weeping over J. F. C. Fuller's *Generalship: Its Diseases and Their Cure.* The volume lay open to an appendix of history's greatest generals and their ages when they won their greatest victories. At forty-nine, Patton was already older than almost all of them.[9]

In 1935 Patton received orders back to Hawaii. Although the Pattons had enjoyed their previous tour there, this time he was miserable. He was once again assigned to a staff position at Fort Shafter as the Hawaii Department's intelligence officer, which felt like a career dead end. Worse, in retribution for an incident in which Patton had spewed profanity and shown him up during a polo tournament, the department commander, General Drum, devastated him in his efficiency report. Angry and bitter over his professional frustrations, Patton seriously considered resigning his commission.[10]

Patton began showing signs of a serious midlife crisis. On November 11, the morning of his fiftieth birthday, he turned toward the wall and refused to get out of bed. He began drinking recklessly at social functions, a proclivity whose consequences were exacerbated after he was concussed from a fall during a polo match that left him with symptoms of what would now be recognized as traumatic brain injury (TBI). Ruth Ellen was horrified when he began hanging out with her circle of friends among Fort Shafter's young officers and ladies, often getting falling down drunk in their company. "He did not appear well when he got tight," she remembered. "He got tearful and sentimental; recited poetry out of place and context and picked on Ma. . . . It was horrible to see feet of clay where the winged heels once were." Beatrice bought a book entitled *Change of Life in Men*, which Ruth Ellen recalled "simply infuriated him . . . he burned it."[11]

Worse indignities were still to come when Beatrice's niece Jean Gordon visited the family. Described as "a lovely young woman of great charm, intelligence, and sensitivity," Jean was the same age—twenty-one—as Ruth Ellen, and one of her closest friends. Yet Jean nevertheless made a play for Patton, who was flattered that a beautiful young woman would find a balding, middle-aged man attractive. He was powerless to resist, and neither he nor Jean attempted to conceal their mutual attraction. Beatrice fell ill just before a family trip to the big island, and she naively permitted her husband and Jean to go on alone together. When the pair returned from their sojourn neither Beatrice nor Ruth Ellen doubted they had become intimate. When Jean eventually departed Hawaii, Patton waved frantically to her ship from the end of the pier, "Making a damned fool of himself," thought Ruth Ellen. Beatrice had overlooked his previous flirtations with a younger social set interested in liquor and sex, but Jean was family, and Patton's affair with her was an altogether different and deeper humiliation. Standing on the pier that day, Beatrice turned to Ruth Ellen and said: "You know, it's lucky for us that I don't have a mother, because if I did, I'd pack up and go to her now;

and your father needs me. He doesn't know it, but he needs me. In fact," she hesitated for a moment, then continued, "right now he needs me more than I need him." She said, "I want you to remember that I didn't leave your father. I stuck with him because I am all that he really has."[12]

In the spring of 1937 Patton received orders returning him to Fort Riley. Before reporting to duty, the family took a vacation at their estate in Massachusetts hoping to leave the troubles of Hawaii behind them. One day while out riding, Beatrice's horse suddenly kicked at a butterfly, its hoof breaking Patton's leg with a sound "like a dry stick snapping."[13] Patton suffered a compound fracture and then phlebitis, a clot in his bloodstream that came within seconds of killing him. He was hospitalized for over three months, and then immobilized at home for three more. The Army investigated to determine whether alcohol had played any role in the accident. The inquiry exonerated him, but Patton was humiliated that it was ever deemed necessary. For Patton, this was a new low. Although he recovered fully, the injury was serious enough that it almost ended his military service just as international crises seemed to be bringing his long sought after war. Thus, Ruth Ellen wrote, "His frenetic tour under General Drum, his growing discouragement with lack of promotion, and his ever present worry that he would never have 'his war' piled up on him, and he was suicidally depressed."[14]

Patton fully regained his health by the summer of 1938, and finally regained his wartime rank on July 1 when he was promoted to colonel. With the promotion came command of the 5th Cavalry, a regiment of the 1st Cavalry Division under the command of Maj. Gen. Kenyon Joyce at Fort Clark, Texas. In the heart of southwest Texas's badlands, 138 miles due west of San Antonio, Fort Clark was the Army's ultimate backwater, a post where old cavalrymen were sent to quietly finish their careers. It was a monotonous and frustrating tour for Patton, as the troops at Clark did not share his martial fervor. But at least he was back with a line unit.[15]

He was distraught, therefore, when the Chief of Cavalry, Maj. Gen. John Herr, personally called Patton at home in December. Herr informed him he was being reassigned to Fort Myer to take command of the post and the 3rd Cavalry, relieving Jonathan Wainwright, who was going into debt from the social expenses that came with commanding Fort Myer. Beatrice and Ruth Ellen watched Patton's face fall as Herr conveyed the news. Although it had been exciting to serve there as a younger officer, the 3rd Cavalry's mission was largely ceremonial, parading for visiting dignitaries and providing color guards for state funerals and national holidays. Patton would thus be on the sidelines as operational units devoted themselves to training in response to the rumbles of war in Europe and Asia. Patton hung up the phone and immediately took out his frustration on Beatrice. "You and your money have ruined my career!" he cried, conveniently ignoring the fact he had never hesitated to flaunt their wealth when it seemed useful to advancing his career.[16]

While Patton was languishing professionally and teetering on the brink of self-destruction, the tank forces he had helped foster into existence were experiencing a renaissance. In 1922 the War Department had stated that tanks' primary mission was "to facilitate the uninterrupted advance of the rifleman in the attack," and in 1931 MacArthur had disbanded the experimental Mechanized Force. Consequently, from 1920 to 1935 only thirty-five tanks were built in the United States.[17] Although down, the advocates of mechanization were never out, and throughout the interwar period the *Cavalry Journal* "reflected a healthy exchange of ideas concerning mechanization."[18] Early in 1938 the War Department directed the Cavalry and Infantry to develop mechanized forces. The Cavalry formed two mechanized regiments at Fort Knox, and organized the 7th Cavalry Brigade (Mechanized), which Col. Adna R. Chaffee took command of that September. Under Chaffee's leadership, the brigade compiled an impressive record of accomplishments in field tests and maneuvers. At the same time, and perhaps more importantly, the shocking success of German panzers spearheading victories in Poland and France revealed the obsolescence of American tank doctrine and cast further doubt upon horse cavalry's relevance in modern warfare.

Despite his preeminent role in creating the AEF's tank corps, Patton stood squarely outside these developments. As one historian notes, "During the 1920s and early 1930s he was one of the most outspoken defenders of the traditionalist military outlook and one of the most caustic and popular critics of the concept of mechanization."[19] After departing Camp Meade in 1921 Patton reversed his previous positions and argued that there was no place for the tank in the cavalry, since "at present there is no tank . . . which can keep up with Cavalry."[20] Reviewing Maj. Basil C. Denning's *The Future of the British Army* in 1929, Patton wrote in the *Cavalry Journal*: "He fails to consider the historical fact that the initial appearance of every new weapon has invariably marked the zenith of its influence despite the fact that usually the weapon itself has become thereafter increasingly deadly."[21] In April 1930 Patton told the American Remount Association: "To me it seems that a person who says that since machines are faster than horses, horses should be scrapped and machines only secured is on a mental parity with the poor man who on seeing an overcoat of undoubted warmth in a second hand store sells his pants to purchase the coat only to find that in summer it is burdensome and not wholly satisfying even in December...."[22] In a 1933 article in the *Cavalry Journal* he warned his readers of historical examples of military innovations that were heralded as the key to victory only to fail the test of battle:

> *When Samson took the fresh jawbone of an ass and slew a thousand men therewith he probably started such a vogue for the weapon, especially among the Philistines, that for years no prudent donkey dared to bray.... History is replete with countless other instances of military implements each in its day heralded as ... the key to victory—yet each in its turn subsiding to its useful but inconspicuous niche.... Today machines hold the place formerly occupied by the jawbone.... They too shall pass.*[23]

Indeed, Patton concluded a lecture at the Marine Corps School at Quantico by declaring: "Let me say that the greatest ill-luck I can wish those who think cavalry is dead, is to be against us in the next war. They will be the corpses, not we."[24]

To be sure, Patton was a prolific enough writer that one can find statements from these years suggesting he had not completely abandoned his belief in mechanization. Together with Maj. C. C. Benson, Patton wrote "Mechanization and Cavalry" for the June 1930 *Cavalry Journal*. "The fighting machine is here to stay," they wrote, "and if our cavalry has not lost its traditional alertness and adaptability, we will frankly accept it at its true worth."[25] While publicly condemning mechanization he nevertheless developed an organizational table for a mechanized cavalry regiment that might be deployed with the traditional horse cavalry. Yet the farthest Patton was willing to venture was to agree that it was desirable to attach armored cars to a cavalry division.

Patton's defenders dismiss his more embarrassingly anachronistic pronouncements as the result of his need to appease his traditionalist superiors within the Cavalry branch. Carlo D'Este concludes: "He accepted that the cavalry of the future must be mechanized to replace the horse, but as a representative in high standing of the chief of cavalry, he could hardly recommend the demise of his own service."[26] Yet this argument is problematic for two reasons. First, some senior cavalrymen actually supported mechanization, such as Maj. Gen. Guy Henry, who served as chief of cavalry from 1930 to 1934 and as commandant of the Cavalry School from 1935 to 1938. Second, Patton did not just denigrate armor's potential in his published writings, but in his personal correspondence as well. In 1929, he wrote to his former Camp Meade colleague Bradford Chynoweth that "I have seldom found places where any machines could operate with out [*sic*] the assistance of infantry to fight for it and cavalry to see for it. . . . In other words an offensive reserve used to give the nock [*sic*] out punch after normal troops have fought the enemy sufficiently—several days probably—to determine his weak spot."[27] Even *if* Patton's anti-mechanization writings were merely professional self-preservation, it is not to his credit that he put his career above the Army's combat effectiveness, especially given that there were numerous other cavalry officers willing to risk theirs in order to advocate for the tank. As Patton's biographer Martin Blumenson concludes, "Whether [Patton] actually believed that the horse had a place in modern warfare, or as everyone was saying, in the next war, or whether he was forced into defending the horse against his convictions with respect to tanks and armored cars was probably something he himself could not have said with assurance."[28]

Patton's desperation and resulting willingness to put his ambition ahead of the Army's mission reached its apogee during the Third Army maneuvers in April/May 1940. He was selected to be an umpire for exercises pitting the 7th Cavalry Brigade and its recently formed infantry counterpart—the Provisional Tank Brigade—from Fort Benning against Patton's former division, the 1st Cavalry. In theory, one benefit of Patton's transfer to Fort Myer was that his proximity to the War Department would enable him to see just how advanced the push for total mechanization had become. Yet as the maneuver approached, Patton passed confidential information on to his former commander, Kenyon Joyce. Supposedly a neutral observer, Patton offered suggestions to Joyce such as advising the jamming of the tanks' radio frequencies, and ended his letter to Joyce with a handwritten postscript: "Please keep the dope I got from Col. Wood SECRET so I can get more."[29] Even with Patton's attempts to skew the maneuvers in the horse cavalry's favor, Chaffee's combined mechanized and tank forces thrashed Joyce's division.

Patton could no longer deny the tank's superiority on the battlefield. At the exercises' conclusion, he joined a group of officers led by Chaffee who met secretly in the basement of an Alexandria, Louisiana, high school to decide the time had come to break free from the powerful chiefs of Cavalry and Infantry's interference. Brig. Gen. Frank Andrews, the Army's assistant chief of staff for operations, was present as Chaffee drafted a proposal for an independent armored force. Andrews reviewed the draft and promised to present it to General Marshall. Upon reading the "basement conspirators" recommendations on June 6, Marshall took less than an hour to approve Chaffee's plan and inform the branch chiefs of his decision to create an autonomous armored force and order them to turn their tanks over to the new branch. The War Department officially activated the Armored Force on July 10, 1940, and appointed Chaffee commander. At Fort Knox, the 1st Armored Division was organized around the mechanized cavalry brigade under the command of Brig. Gen. Bruce Magruder. At Benning, the Provisional Tank Brigade became the nucleus for the 2nd Armored Division, with a cavalry-man who had led one of the mechanized regiments, Brig. Gen. Charles L. Scott, commanding.[30]

As soon as the maneuvers ended Patton sent Chaffee a congratulatory letter—and discreetly requested to be considered for a job in the soon-to-be-organized Armored Force. On June 28, Chafee replied: "I put you on my preferred list as a brigade commander for an armored brigade. I think it is a job which you could do to the queen's taste and I need just such a man of your experience . . . I shall always be happy to know that you are around close in any capacity when there is fighting to be done."[31] In July, while attending Ruth Ellen's wedding, Patton learned from a Boston newspaper that he had been chosen to command one of the newly created units, the 2nd Armored Division's 2nd Brigade. Brigadier General Scott had selected him from among those whom Chaffee considered qualified and eligible for the position. It took Patton several hours to restrain his joy and compose himself before writing letters of thanks to the generals whose influence he believed had brought him such a plum assignment.

The world's tragedy would be Patton's salvation. The 2nd Armored Brigade consisted of two light tank regiments, one medium tank regiment, a field artillery regiment, and a battalion of engineers—350 officers, 5,500 men, 383 tanks, 202 armored cars, and twenty-four 105mm howitzers. Soon after his arrival on July 27, Patton wrote Pershing: "The whole thing is most interesting as most of the tactics have yet to be worked out and there is a great chance for ingenuity and leadership."[32] Patton was reinvigorated, and attempted to replicate the methods by which he had achieved success in France. He believed in personal contact with his men, and began at Benning by energetically intervening in every detail of tank operations and training, and trying to do everything himself. Like most of the Army in 1940, the 2nd Armored Division was understrength and pitifully equipped, with most of its materiel either antiquated or nonexistent. Unable to obtain spare parts for the brigade's tanks, one of Patton's mechanics casually noted that most of them were ordinary parts he used to order from Sears Roebuck. Patton seized upon the remark and proceeded to order them from Sears Roebuck, paying the bill out of his own pocket. Although it is not known how much he spent to maintain the brigade's tanks, at least once he had to send an $800 check for a single order to keep his vehicles running.[33]

Within a few weeks Chaffee was replaced as the I Armored Corps' commander by Patton's superior, Brigadier General Scott. Although Chaffee had done more than anybody else to bring about the Armored Force, and was described by Robert W. Grow (who would command the 6th Armored Division in Europe) as "the finest tactician I ever knew," he was slowly withering away from cancer.[34] In September, therefore, Patton became the 2nd Armored Division's acting commander. At first, he found that the division's draftees lacked the enthusiasm of the men he had led into battle in 1918. As one sympathetic biographer notes, "Instead of whipping these men and vehicles into an efficient organization along the line of the plans he himself had drafted, he confused and disorganized everything with his constant intervention."[35] As his frustration mounted, however, Patton began to acknowledge and correct his mistakes. He made himself highly visible to his draftees and set rigorous standards in physical conditioning, handling vehicles, and skill in weapons. Once, a soldier was at the firing range when he looked up and saw the division commander by his side. When Patton asked what he was doing, the enlisted man replied, "Just trying to hit the target."

"You are like hell!" Patton cried in his high-pitched voice. "You are trying to kill some German son of a bitch before he can kill you!"[36]

When the 2nd Armored's troops were seen in Columbus in sloppy uniforms, some drunk and disorderly, Patton issued an edict enforcing the highest standards of dress and discipline. "If you can't get them to salute when they should salute, and wear the clothes you tell them to wear," he explained, "how are you going to get them to die for their country?"[37] Soldiers paid a hefty fine for ignoring Patton's rules, and soldierly pride and discipline became "one of the division's hallmarks."[38] Patton ordered an amphitheater built at Benning and assembled his troops for a series of exuberant motivational lectures, punctuated with the rawest profanities soldiers rarely heard from grizzled drill sergeants, much less division commanders. Yet as Maj. Isaac D. White—the reconnaissance battalion commander who eventually rose to command the division during the war—recalled: "General Patton was really the person who instilled the division with great pride in itself and developed a great esprit, as well as a great deal of the aggressiveness which characterized the division throughout the war."[39] In November 1940 Patton's old riding partner, Secretary of War Stimson, visited Benning and was deeply impressed by the 2nd Armored. "The progress which has been made . . . is astounding," he noted in his diary, "and reflects great credit upon" Scott and Patton.[40]

In December Patton led 6,500 troops in more than 1,000 tanks and vehicles on a 360-mile road march from Benning to Panama City, Florida, and back, testing their road discipline and ability to move. His stress on maintenance paid off, as only one tank broke down on the expedition and had to be towed back home. In April 1941 Patton was awarded his second star and made actual commander of the 2nd Armored. Two months later the division left Benning on another extended road march, this time to Manchester, Tennessee, to participate in Gen. Ben Lear's Second Army maneuvers. As the division historian notes, "Umpires with the tankers called the road march the most magnificent ever made by tanks."[41] At the Tennessee Maneuvers, the division was unimpressive at first, but as Patton developed his feel of control and sense of movements, it gained momentum. In the maneuvers' second exercise he used slashing and unorthodox tactics to cut behind the 5th Infantry Division's lines, decimate it, and capture its commander, Brig. Gen. Cortlandt Parker, and his staff. Similarly, although the maneuvers' next phase was expected to last an entire day, the 2nd Armored's aggressive attacks overwhelmed their opponents in just three hours.[42]

Journalists began to notice, and as the division's successes piled up, Patton rose to national prominence. The "squeak-voiced Major General George S. Patton, Jr. . . . hides much military culture behind the Army's best smoke-screen of profanity," *Time* magazine reported on February 14, 1941. Like God, his soldiers said, Patton "had the damndest way of showing up when things went wrong. Unlike God, he had been known to dash leg-long into a creek, get a stalled tank and its wretched crew out of the water and back into the line of march, practically by the power of his curses." The *Saturday Evening Post* reported on Patton and his division, and the general appeared on the cover of the July 7, 1941, issue of *Life* magazine standing in the turret of his tank, holding binoculars, wearing a tank helmet with chin strap and shoulder holster and pistol, and the scowling war face he had practiced since childhood. Inside, a lengthy article praised the leadership of "Patton of the Armored Force" and the 2nd Armored's realistic training.[43]

Whereas some senior leaders questioned Patton's suitability for high command, George Marshall had once presciently noted that "George will take a unit through hell and high water." But Marshall was also prescient in adding that one must "keep a tight rope round his neck" lest Patton go too far.[44] Indeed, Patton's rising profile served to reinforce his brash conduct to the point where it bordered on insubordination. When Chaffee finally died in August 1941, Marshall appointed Jacob Devers to succeed him as Armored Force commander. Although Devers had no direct experience with tanks, as an artilleryman he had grappled deeply with the implications of mechanization for his branch, and the chief of staff specifically wanted a commander who had not been involved in any of the cavalry and infantry infighting of the 1930s.

Patton was surprised by the appointment, and was initially a thorn in Devers's side. Although they were West Point classmates and polo team-mates at Fort Myer in the early 1930s, they were not close. More impor-tantly, whereas Patton stressed mobility and employed light tanks like cavalry, Devers believed the European battlefields had shown the need for increased armor protection and heavier guns, and that tanks' firepower mattered as much as their speed. Consequently, Patton, who felt *he* was the armor expert, sent Secretary Stimson notes through Undersecretary John McCloy chal-lenging Devers's armor expertise and hence his authority to command.[45]

Needing to demonstrate he could handle his defiant subordinate, Devers traveled to Fort Benning to confront Patton. Devers had dinner at the Pat-tons, after which Beatrice and the other guest ("an old cavalryman") rose to leave the generals to discuss business. Devers asked Beatrice to stay. "I need a judge in here," he said. "George and I are going to settle some things right here, and you know George and I know him."

Devers then turned to Patton. "Now, George, I have your recommenda-tions [and] we've given them all careful consideration," he said. "I don't give a damn who commands, but I'm the commanding officer right now, and I'm going to command, and I'm going to make the decisions, and here they are."

Devers outlined his plans regarding tank modifications that emphasized armor protection over speed, concluding: "These are the decisions. They've been made. I'm going to tell you right now. I went up and talked to General Marshall—just as I'm talking to you—and he has given me the go ahead.

Now are you going to fall in line and be on the team and work with me on this, or are you going to send these notes to Mr. Stimson?"

Patton rose to his feet, stood at attention, and saluted. "Jake," he said, "you are the boss and I'm one of your commanders, and I'll play ball."[46]

The air between them cleared, both men went about their respective duties with Patton understanding his place. In time, he grew to appreciate Devers's skills and knowledge of tanks, later writing his superior to admit he had "certainly made a convert of me."[47]

Almost as soon as Patton took command of the 2nd Armored Brigade, he wrote an old friend from his days with the Tank Corps at Camp Meade to ask if he would be interested in serving under Patton when he was given command of an armored division. "It would be great to be in the tanks once more," the officer replied, "and even better to be associated with you again. . . . [I]f there's a chance of that kind of an assignment, I'd be for it 100%." Indeed, given that he had missed out on deploying in World War I and had largely been stuck in a succession of desk jobs since their time together at Meade, the opportunity to command one of Patton's regiments seemed like a dream come true for Dwight D. Eisenhower.

Yet even as recently as eight months prior, Eisenhower's dream of commanding troops seemed destined to be thwarted once again. On January 4, 1940, the SS *President Coolidge* docked in San Francisco after a three-week voyage from Manila. As the Eisenhowers stood on the pier awaiting their luggage, Ike recalled, "a very military looking sergeant came down the line paging Colonel Eisenhower. . . . Upon acknowledging, unwillingly, my identity . . . I was handed an order" to report for temporary duty with Lt. Gen. John L. DeWitt's Fourth Army at the Presidio.[48] The Fourth Army's Regular Army and National Guard troops, spread from Minnesota to the West Coast, were scheduled to conduct a combined exercise in California. The problem of how to move thousands of troops from distances up to a thousand miles and arrive nearly simultaneously at the training area within three weeks had overwhelmed DeWitt's inexperienced staff, so much so that one division supply officer suffered a nervous breakdown. DeWitt had commanded the Philippine Department in 1936–1937, and also knew Eisenhower from his War Department days. Consequently, he appropriated Eisenhower and assigned him to help plan the maneuvers. He assured the anxious Eisenhower that the assignment was only temporary "pick and shovel work" drafting orders to assemble the dispersed units. By the end of January, he promised, Eisenhower could proceed to Fort Lewis.[49]

Eisenhower quickly solved this Gordian knot of assembling all troops at one point by simply creating a second assembly area. While walking along the designated invasion beach at Monterrey Bay a few days before his 3rd Division arrived, Eisenhower saw DeWitt's bald and bustling figure approaching. Walking beside him was the chief of staff, whom Eisenhower had not seen since that day thirteen years earlier outside General Pershing's office. Marshall greeted Eisenhower, but did not ask him about MacArthur, his experiences in the Philippines, or even his thoughts on the upcoming maneuvers. Instead, alluding to how cheap personal servants were in the archipelago and how little real work most officers had to perform, he drily asked: "Have you learned to tie your own shoes again since coming back, Eisenhower?"

Eisenhower grinned and said, "Yes, Sir, I am capable of that chore, anyhow."[50]

Although DeWitt was reluctant to let Eisenhower go, he was true to his word and released him. Instead of returning to Fort Lewis, however, Eisenhower joined the 3rd Division in the middle of its maneuvers at Camp Ord on the northern shore of Monterey Bay. At Ord (named in honor of Jimmy Ord's grandfather, Maj. Gen. E. O. C. Ord) Eisenhower was reunited with Mark Clark. In addition to his duties as the division's operations officer, Clark was responsible for lining up players for the division commander's nightly poker games. Although Maj. Gen. Walter C. Sweeney disliked having strangers in the game, Clark told him "that Eisenhower had got back from the Philippines with a pocket full of money."

"Have him here by seven o'clock," Sweeney said.

Although Eisenhower had long since traded poker for bridge to avoid the awkwardness of taking his subordinates' money, when the game ended at midnight he was $50 ahead, much of it Sweeney's. Clark remembered that "the General was furious," and insisted that Eisenhower return the next night. "I'm going to get back what I lost," Sweeney declared. Eisenhower continued to win, however, and was able to put aside enough money to buy Mamie an expensive gift for their twenty-fifth anniversary.[51]

When the 3rd Division returned to Fort Lewis, Eisenhower was assigned to the 15th Infantry, which had returned stateside after being withdrawn from China by President Roosevelt in 1938 following the Japanese attack on the USS *Panay*. Eisenhower was appointed as the 15th Infantry's executive officer—Marshall's former position—and, better still from his perspective, as commander of the regiment's 1st Battalion. Like virtually every other unit in 1940, however, the 15th Infantry was at about half-strength and underequipped. Eisenhower noted in his diary that "of an authorized strength of 2961, plus band, we are short:

About 1300 men
all 60mm mortars
all eight m.g.
all modified BAR (1918-A-2)
½ our 50 cals
½ our 81mm mortars
½ our 37mm guns"[52]

Worse, he found that "The officers and men lacked any sense of urgency. Athletics, recreation, and entertainment took precedence in most units over serious training. Some of the officers, in the long years of peace, had worn for themselves deep ruts of professional routine within which they are sheltered from vexing new ideas and troublesome problems."[53]

Yet just as Eisenhower's poker skills had not diminished despite nearly two decades away from the game, neither had his instincts as a commander dulled despite not having led troops since he commanded the 301st Heavy Tank Battalion at Camp Meade in 1921. One of the first things he did was to assemble the battalion's officers. "If any of you think we are not going to war, I don't want you in my battalion," he declared. "We're going to war. This country is going to war, and I want people who are prepared to fight that war." As this was before Germany's invasion of France, Eisenhower's impassioned warnings earned him the sobriquet "Alarmist Ike." "What Eisenhower said was scary," one subordinate recalled, "but nobody quit the battalion."[54]

As he had been at Camp Colt in 1918, Eisenhower was stern but fair, and insisted on military discipline. "He made an immediate impression on everybody," said Burton S. Barr, "and there was no room for nonsense. . . . He was pretty popular among the men, but he was no easy taskmaster."[55] The 15th Infantry's commander, Col. Jesse Ladd, called Eisenhower "an enthusiastic, aggressive officer of the highest type. One of the few Army officers whom I consider deserves a straight rating of superior."[56] Echoing Hap Arnold's assessment of then-Lieutenant Marshall nearly three decades earlier, in the fall of 1940 Maj. Edwin B. Howard wrote to his wife: "Janie, you've always wanted to see what a general looks like before he becomes a general. Well, just take a look at Colonel Eisenhower."[57]

For his part, Eisenhower was in heaven. "I've been with this regiment about five months, and am having the time of my life," he wrote to Omar Bradley. "Like everyone else in the army, we're up to our necks in work and in problems big and little. But this work is fun!"[58] That summer the division returned to California for maneuvers at the Hunter Liggett military reservation, 50 miles south of Monterey, where the 15th Infantry faced off against Col. Robert L. Eichelberger's 30th Infantry. Eisenhower led his battalion in one attack after another, and told "Gee" Gerow that "It was a lot of fun. I froze at night, never had, in any one stretch, more than 1&3/4 hours of sleep, and at times was really fagged out."[59] In the end, he wrote another friend, "I was fully repaid when . . . my youngsters . . . kept on going and delivering handsomely after five days of almost no sleep!" He concluded, "Nothing can kill my own enthusiasm for this job at hand. . . . So far I'm having a fine time!"[60]

Although he was more than content leading infantrymen, Eisenhower was excited when Patton wrote to gauge his interest in returning to tanks. "I suppose it's too much to hope that I could have a regiment in your division," Eisenhower replied on September 17, 1940. "I'm still almost three years away from my colonelcy. But I think I could do a damn good job of commanding a regiment."[61] Patton wrote back to say he expected to get command of one of the two armor divisions, and that although he would prefer to have Eisenhower as his chief of staff, he understood his desire for a command. "No matter how we get together we will go PLACES," Patton said, concluding that he hoped "we are together for a long and BLOODY war."[62] Patton wrote again on November 1, advising Eisenhower to hurry his application for a transfer. "If you have any pull . . . use it for there will be 10 new generals in this corps pretty damn soon."[63]

Indeed, upon receiving Patton's offer, Eisenhower immediately reached out to his friends in Washington, DC. At the end of October he confided to Clark—who by now was with GHQ—that his ambition was to command an armored regiment under Patton and asked him to relay this to the chief of infantry. "They will probably think me a conceited individual," he wrote, "but I see no objection to setting your sights high. Actually, I will be delighted to serve in the Armored Corps in almost any capacity, but I do hope to avoid Staff and to stay on troop duty for some time to come."[64] That same day he wrote a similar letter to T. J. Davis, his Manila compatriot who was now in the Adjutant General's office. "My ambition is to go, eventually, to the armored outfit," Eisenhower said.

Serving with Patton "would be a swell job and I only hope that the War Department won't consider me too junior in rank to get a regiment."[65]

Aware that his reputation throughout the Army was that of an outstanding staff officer, Eisenhower worried he might get assigned to another staff position that would preclude a post with the Armored Force. This nightmare appeared to come true in mid-November when he received a telegram from Gerow, now a brigadier general and the War Plans Division's deputy director. Gerow wrote: "I NEED YOU IN WAR PLANS DIVISION. DO YOU SERIOUSLY OBJECT TO BEING DETAILED ON THE WAR DEPT. GENERAL STAFF AND ASSIGNED HERE. PLEASE REPLY IMMEDIATELY."[66] Eisenhower was so stunned he suffered a severe, painful attack of shingles. From his bed, he wrote a three-page, single-spaced letter to his old friend. "Your telegram, arriving this morning, sent me into a tailspin," he began. "I want to make it clear that I am, and have always been, very serious in my belief that the individual's preferences and desires should have little, if any, weight in determining his assignment, when superior authority is making a decision in the matter." However, he bluntly told Gerow that if given a choice, he would rather stay with troops. He enjoyed "the fascinating work of handling soldiers" and his tour with the 15th had "completely reassured" him that "I am capable of handling command jobs" even if he still had to prove it to others. Eisenhower strongly recommended Clark to Gerow instead, but added, "I do not need to tell you whatever I am told to do will be done as well as I know how to do it." He concluded, "If war starts, I expect to see you raise the roof to get a command, and *I go along!*"[67]

Gerow understood his friend's reluctance to leave his post and telegraphed Eisenhower: "After careful consideration of contents of your letter . . . I have withdrawn my request for your detail to War Plans Divn. Will write details later. Regret our service together must be postponed."[68] Gerow and Patton were not the only officers vying for Eisenhower. Other commanders and staffs requested his services, but all were disapproved by the chief of infantry, thanks partly to Clark's intervention. In virtually every instance, however, Eisenhower was sought as a staff officer rather than a commander. By November 30, he finally lost his fight to stay with the troops and was appointed chief of staff of the 3rd Infantry Division, the 15th Infantry's parent unit. As Stephen Ambrose notes, "Eisenhower escaped staff duty in D.C., only to be put on a staff in Washington State." It was a small consolation that his designation was "General Staff *with* troops" in order to give Eisenhower credit for the command time needed for future promotions.[69]

Eisenhower only spent three months as Maj. Gen. Charles Thompson's chief of staff before he was relieved of duty on March 1, 1941, and assigned as chief of staff of the IX Army Corps commanded by Patton's former superior, Kenyon Joyce. In Eisenhower's efficiency report Thompson described his chief of staff as "affable, energetic, dynamic, zealous, original, loyal, capable, dependable, and outstanding." He added that Eisenhower was "superior in handling of officers and men, in performance of field duties, in administrative and executive duties, in training troops, in tactical handling of troops."[70] Eisenhower was subsequently appointed colonel (temporary) with rank from March 6. Despite once again being relegated to staff duty, Eisenhower noted in his diary that he was "finding this job most intriguing and interesting, with Gen J[oyce] a swell commander & fine person to work for."[71] Joyce was equally appreciative of his subordinate, writing that Eisenhower was "one of the ablest officers in the Army. *This officer is thoroughly qualified for division command at this time.*"[72]

In June 1941 Eisenhower was in the middle of IX Corps' maneuvers at Jolon, California, awaiting a report from one of the divisions when General Joyce was called away for a phone call. After he hung up several minutes later, Joyce called his chief of staff over to him. "Start packing," the general told Eisenhower. "Go to [Fort] Lewis for orders, which will direct you to go to San Antonio as Chief of Staff, Third Army."[73]

It is an understatement to say that Lt. Gen. Walter Krueger was unique amongst the interwar Army's officers. He was born in January 1881 in Flatow, Germany, the son of a prominent landowner who served as an army officer during the Franco-Prussian War. When he was eight years old his father died and his widowed mother immigrated to Saint Louis. Krueger dropped out of high school and enlisted in the Army when the Spanish-American War erupted, and from 1898 to 1941 he served with distinction in Cuba, fought in the Philippine Insurrection, participated in Pershing's Punitive Expedition into Mexico in 1916, and was awarded the Distinguished Service Medal for his service on tank and infantry staffs during World War I.* As he rose from private to three-star general, Krueger commanded every

---

* Krueger was actually shipped home for several months in 1918 due to French unease with his Prussian heritage. However, he was considered a valuable enough asset that the AEF quietly returned him to the Western Front with the 84th Infantry.

unit in the Army from a rifle squad to a division and a corps and was experienced at the highest staff level, having led the War Plans Division from 1936 to 1938. Marshall described Krueger to Stimson as "one of the intellectuals of the Army," for Krueger spoke three languages, translated the leading German military texts of the era into English as a young officer, and had attended *and* taught at both the Army and Naval War Colleges.[74] Yet he was highly regarded in the enlisted ranks as "a soldier's soldier," and at age sixty-two he was still in superb physical condition, possessing seemingly limitless stamina that frequently left younger men in his wake. He was a combat infantryman at heart, and explained to his men that "Weapons are no good unless there are guts at both sides of the bayonet."[75]

On May 16, 1941, Krueger was elevated from command of VIII Corps to command of Third Army. He immediately began preparing for the GHQ army-on-army maneuvers scheduled for that September, with perhaps his most pressing task being identifying and bringing qualified personnel to the Third Army. In particular, Krueger needed a first-rate chief of staff. He had recommended his students at the War College obtain the services of a strong and forceful chief of staff, who:

> is the chief adviser and personal representative of the commander. He assists the commander in the supervision and coordination of the command and should enjoy his complete confidence and a considerable degree of independence in the performance of his duties. He is responsible for the working of the whole staff, and, under the orders of his commander, for the control and coordination of the operations of the troops.[76]

In the autumn of 1940 he had placed Eisenhower first on his preference list for VIII Corps' chief of staff only to be told by the War Department that Ike was too junior for the position. This time Krueger knew better than to go through channels and wrote directly to his old friend George Marshall, with whom he had served as lieutenants in G Company, 30th Infantry, in the Philippines in 1901, and then from 1908 to 1910 as the only lieutenants on the CGSS faculty at Leavenworth. He told Marshall that he needed to replace his current chief of staff because "In my judgment, that position demands a younger man, one possessing broad vision, progressive ideas, a thorough grasp of the magnitude of the problem involved in handling an Army, and lots of initiative and resourcefulness. LTC Dwight D. Eisenhower, Infantry, is such a man."[77] Although regulations required an army chief of staff to be a general, Marshall waived the rule for Krueger and on June 24 cut the orders transferring Eisenhower to Fort Sam Houston as the new Third Army chief of staff.

The Eisenhowers arrived in San Antonio on July 1, their twenty-fifth wedding anniversary. Within two weeks of assuming his duties Krueger wrote to a friend in the War Department that Eisenhower "is going strong."[78] The array of tasks immediately confronting Krueger and Eisenhower was daunting. Together they oversaw command post exercises for the senior commanders and staffs across Third Army, as well as lower-level maneuvers. Eisenhower described the training as a "big job" made more difficult by many officers who were "not so hot" and had no experience with large operations. Concurrent with overseeing training Krueger and Eisenhower had to figure out how best to organize their headquarters. Eisenhower commented to Gerow that "since none of us has ever functioned on an Army Staff . . . we are having some difficulty in deciding just how many individuals are needed in each section. Moreover, since our only source of experienced officers is the troop units, every time we take a good man we hurt an organization."[79] Krueger and Eisenhower faced what the Army today calls a "wicked problem"— one in which every solution creates another equally pressing dilemma to be solved. "Luckily, I've spent most of my life in large headquarters," Eisenhower wrote George Van Horn Moseley, "so [I] am not overpowered by the mass of details."[80]

Nevertheless, Eisenhower wrote Wade Haislip, "My own hours are from 6:00 A.M. to 11:00 P.M., every day. . . . The General keeps worse hours than any of the rest of us. Darned if I know how he keeps up!"[81] Krueger was notoriously hard on his staff. One officer recalled "I have never served under an officer whom I dislike more, nor for whom I had greater admiration."[82] Eisenhower relieved much of the Third Army's burden simply by being available and willing to listen. "My office seems to provide the only 'cracker-barrel' in [Third] Army," he wrote Moseley. "Everyone comes in here to discuss his troubles, and I'm often astonished how much better they seem to work after they have had a chance to recite their woes."[83]

Krueger and Eisenhower's biggest challenge, however, was scrambling to prepare for the upcoming Louisiana Maneuvers. In addtition to testing the Army's new equipment and doctrine, in 1941 McNair and Clark were eager to see how effective their training programs had been. As Brig. Gen. Harry L.

Twaddle, Army G-3, explained to the House Appropriations Committee's military affairs subcommittee:

> *The great expansion of the Army, which has occurred since last fall, has produced numerous new headquarters from battalion to Army, staffed with officers who, as yet, have had little opportunity to acquire by first hand experience the knowledge necessary in moving, supplying, and controlling large concentrations of troops and maneuvering them in the field. Such knowledge cannot be gained by study alone. Actual experience is essential.*[84]

To provide this experience GHQ planned two large maneuvers in the eastern United States for the fall of 1941, with the first in Louisiana in September. Involving over 500,000 soldiers, more than double the troops who fought the Civil War's largest battle at Chancellorsville and nearly half of the Army's combat strength, the Louisiana Maneuvers would be the largest peacetime exercise in American history. "Our staff job in getting ready for the maneuvers is a big one," Eisenhower wrote a friend, as he was responsible for moving all ten of the Third Army's divisions—more than 240,000 soldiers stationed from California to Texas—to Louisiana.[85]

Opposing Krueger's "Blue" Third Army was Lt. Gen. Ben Lear's "Red" Second Army comprised of the VII Corps and the I Armored Corps. Sixty-two years old, Lear's forty-three-year career had been divided between infantry and cavalry commands and staff assignments. Lear was known more for his abrasive manner and his unpopularity with his troops than for his tactical brilliance. J. Lawton Collins, VII Corps chief of staff, recalled him as "a big, gruff cavalryman" more concerned with close order drill and proper saluting than the tactical training of VII Corps' National Guard units.[86] Lear got off to a bad start at the maneuvers when he gained publicity for disciplining soldiers who whistled at shorts-clad female golfers, earning the nickname "Yoo-Hoo Lear" from the press. Ernest Harmon, who served with Lear two decades earlier at the Cavalry School, concluded, "When the Army and Providence made Lear an officer they spoiled a good first sergeant."[87]

Yet Lear was a meticulous planner, had an eye for detail, and in Louisiana was surrounded by a cadre of talented and aggressive officers. Although Second Army had only 130,000 men, they were mostly regulars and they possessed a powerful mechanized force in the 1st and 2nd Armored Divisions. Indeed, following the 2nd Armored's successes in Tennessee, many thought George Patton was worth a division by himself. Conversely, although Krueger had 270,000 troops from the IV, V, and VIII Corps, they were mostly Guardsmen desperately short of training and serving in regiments led by older, untested officers.[88]

The theater of operations consisted of 30,000 square miles extending from Shreveport south to Lake Charles, and from Jasper, Texas, to the Mississippi River. The maneuver area was sparsely populated, broken up by rice fields, uncharted swamps, and thick forests scarred by dirt backroads that turned to muck with the slightest precipitation. The battleground's dominant terrain features were the Red River, running northwest-to-southeast from Shreveport to Alexandria, and Peason Ridge, an east-west range of high ground in the 604,000-acre wilderness of the Kisatchie National Forest.[89]

In addition to fighting Second Army's "Red" forces, Third Army would be battling the elements. American soldiers had long experience with the region's inhospitality. A century earlier, then-Lieutenant Ulysses S. Grant was stationed in the area, writing that "the troublesome insects of creation ... abound here. The swamps are full of alligators and the woods are full of redbugs and ticks."[90] Prior to the maneuvers, Eisenhower wrote to Gerow, "All the old-timers here say that we are going into a God awful spot, to live with mud, malaria, mosquitoes and misery."[91] Once he arrived in Louisiana, Eisenhower wrote a journalist friend that "If you're allergic to red bugs, ticks, heat and humidity, I advise against" coming to report on the maneuvers.[92] Years later, as they slogged through the jungles of the South Pacific or the frozen battlefields of Europe, many veterans still shuddered at the memory of how rough conditions in the Louisiana Maneuvers had been.

There would be no elaborate, scripted scenarios dictating the action in the Louisiana Maneuvers. When assigning Clark the task of drafting the basic directive for the battle, McNair cautioned him to keep it "as simple as possible." Clark took a Standard Oil road map, drew two large ovals to represent the armies, added a line to separate them, and then wrote up a mission for each. Lear's Second Army would cross the Red River and attack Krueger's Third Army; the Third Army would move east toward the Red River to block the Second Army's advance. Otherwise the maneuver would be free, allowing the commanders to do what they wanted within the designated geographic boundaries.[93]

The goal was to make the maneuvers as much like real war as possible in order to test and train under near-battle conditions, to include the handling of logistics. For August and September, Third Army received four million

.30-caliber blanks and 170,000 antitank rounds. To make the battle sound more realistic, the Army built seven loudspeaker-equipped trucks to roam the maneuver area and broadcast prerecorded battlefield noises. Other than proscribing mechanized combat after sundown for safety reasons, action would be continuous day and night until one side or another prevailed. Even with such precautions, the Army anticipated 136 deaths and 40,000 hospitalizations during the two weeks of maneuvers.[94]

Just as in real war, the success or failure of the battle rested upon the outcome of small-scale engagements. Since people could not really be killed, shells fired, bridges demolished, or tanks destroyed, an elaborate set of umpires' rules was established. Poor umpiring had contributed to the problems encountered in earlier maneuvers, so GHQ prepared a new Umpire's Manual for the Louisiana Maneuvers and increased the number of umpires trained. McNair had authored multiple reports and memos on umpiring maneuvers while at the Army War College, and his expertise on the subject was unmatched. This experience, plus the GHQ's lack of personnel (only twenty-nine officers and sixty-four enlisted men as of June 1941) led to McNair personally supervising the new manual's drafting. Firepower points (e.g., one point for a rifle, six for a .30-caliber machine gun) were assigned, and when opposing units met the umpires would determine who advanced and who was pushed back based on their comparative firepower scores. Artillery fire's impact area would be marked with flags, and "casualties" would be assessed against a unit caught in the area. There were casualty percentages for troops attacked by airplanes, and loss percentages for air units exposed to antiaircraft fire. Although GHQ considered it impractical to actually blow up bridges, umpires supervised the execution of "demolitions" to ensure such operations were carried out in detail, while bridge replacement involved the actual construction of a new structure beside the notionally destroyed bridge.[95]

The most controversial rules, however, were those established to adjudicate engagements between tanks and antitank guns. Many officers, including McNair, believed that finding a way to defeat armored operations was the Army's most urgent problem. McNair thought the German panzer's effectiveness was due to the absence or ineffectiveness of Polish and French defenses, and he adamantly argued that towed antitank guns, aggressively deployed, could eliminate the armor threat. On August 8 he ordered Lear to convert two artillery brigades into nine antitank battalions and give them to Third Army for use in the Louisiana Maneuvers. These battalions were subsequently organized into three antitank groups and were to be highly mobile, relatively self-sustaining, and to serve as an aggressive army-wide antitank reserve. Reflecting McNair's bias, the maneuvers' rules credited an antitank gun with knocking out up to one tank per minute and were given an unrealistically long range, while tanks could knock out antitank guns only by "overrunning" them. Moreover, weapons the Ordnance Department had already deemed ineffective against armor—such as the 37mm gun and .50-caliber machine gun—were designated as tank killers in Louisiana.[96]

Before the maneuvers' first phase, Lear's six divisions occupied the Red assembly area between Shreveport and Alexandria, north of the Red River. The Third Army assembled just north of Lake Charles. On September 12, Lear received orders to invade Blue territory by moving across the Red River at 0500 on September 15. His mission was to "destroy enemy now concentrated in vicinity of Lake Charles." Lear planned to cross the Red River and launch an armored attack from Peason Ridge's west end into Krueger's left flank and rear. Lear's plan was sound, but his powerful armored force was not to attack until VII Corps had also crossed the Red River and occupied a crescent-shaped line running from Fort Jesup to Colfax on the Red River.[97]

Krueger's instructions from GHQ actually played into Lear's hands, as he was told that enemy forces were moving toward the Red River and was ordered to advance northward and destroy the Red Army. Together with Eisenhower, Krueger formulated a straightforward plan of operations with the VIII Corps on the left, VI Corps in the center, and V Corps on the right, all moving vigorously to the northeast. Krueger placed the 1st Cavalry Division and the three antitank groups in reserve behind the Sabine River, and gave the 3rd Air Task Force commander, Gen. Herbert Dargue, the simplest order of all: find the Red armored force. Thus, Krueger hoped to trap the Second Army against the Red River between Natchitoches and Alexandria and annihilate them.[98]

The battle began before dawn on September 15 amidst torrential rain showers. Lear pushed his troops across the muddy Red River with the armored divisions leading the way. Patton's reconnaissance elements crossed north of Natchitoches and raced west, reaching their initial objective between Many and Fort Jesup before the last artillery and infantry units had crossed the Clarence–Grand Ecore highway bridge. Patton's tanks crossed between Shreveport and Natchitoches and lumbered toward their concealed assembly positions near Many.[99]

Yet Second Army's plans began to unravel almost immediately. Despite the heavy rains and dogfights with Second Army's pursuit planes—which produced the exercise's first real-life fatalities—Krueger's airmen located the Red armor's river crossings. The first planes appeared overhead at about 0820, and thereafter a continuous stream of Blue A-20A attack bombers and Navy divebombers harassed the 1st Armored Division and conducted air raids against key crossing points. This created bottlenecks at the bridges and severely restricted Lear's attempts to get the bulk of his forces into action.

As Lear struggled to bring VII Corps across the river and into the center and eastern wing of Second Army's line, Patton's reconnaissance battalion made contact with a strong detachment of Blue cavalry from VIII Corps at Many. Like John Buford's cavalrymen on the battle of Gettysburg's first day, the 113th Cavalry Regiment fought a steady covering action all day against a growing force of 2nd Armored tanks and infantry. Although the 2nd Armored's 41st Infantry Regiment pushed the Blue cavalry back, and by nightfall had established a vital foothold on Peason Ridge, Krueger's ground and air forces had accomplished their primary objective and located both Red armored divisions. It was clear to Krueger that the 2nd Armored had reached positions far to the west between Many and the Sabine River. "Operations this morning were quite productive," Eisenhower wrote to Kenyon Joyce, "both as to information and tactical effect. We've located at least a large part of the hostile mechanization, and if we can stymie it in the swamps and batter it to pieces with our [Antitank] Groups, those Reds are going to be on the run by day after tomorrow."[100]

On Tuesday, September 16, Red Second Army consolidated its positions and—as per Lear's original plan, brought up the remaining elements of the I Armored Corps and VII Corps. Yet Krueger had made two adjustments overnight that changed the equation on the battlefield. First, rather than continuing its original drive toward the Red River, Third Army completely reoriented its axis of advance to establish its lines parallel with those of the Second Army. Second, having determined that Patton's division was massed on his west flank, Krueger attached the 1st Antitank Group to VIII Corps. Thus, when the 2nd Armored attempted to push in the direction of Leesville to expand the jump-off positions on Peason Ridge for the next day's scheduled attack, the 45th Division halted them, seized the initiative, and by nightfall nearly pushed Patton off Peason Ridge altogether. Lear recognized that without secure footholds on Peason Ridge there would be no room to bring the 1st Armored Division into the line of battle, and consequently postponed the I Armored Corps' planned strike to September 18.[101]

Worse, whereas when night fell on the 16th Krueger had eight of his nine infantry divisions in line, Lear's order for September 17 kept five of Red's eight divisions idle. Lear's intent was to preserve the impact of the armor attack planned for the 18th, but it effectively ceded the initiative and allowed Third Army to complete its reorientation and threaten his east flank. Not only would the 2nd Armored and two other divisions have to withstand the Blue onslaught by themselves on the 17th, but Lear expected them to launch limited attacks as well.[102]

Early on Wednesday the 17th, Patton's 2nd Armored Brigade launched an assault aimed at shoving the Blue VIII Corps back in preparation for the next day's armored attack. The tankers made little headway, however, as the north-south roads were covered by Blue antitank guns. At the critical road juncture of Mount Carmel, a 2nd Armored Brigade column collided with infantry and antitank forces from the 45th Division. Tanks, scout cars, soldiers, and guns surged back and forth throughout the day in a seesaw affair while aircraft roared overhead and sound trucks blasted battle noises. By nightfall Blue forces had repelled the tanks and closed on Mount Carmel from three sides, gaining a tentative grip on the town. Meanwhile, Krueger ordered attacks on the Second Army's center and in the flat open ground on Lear's eastern flank that pushed the Red Army back.[103]

Despite these setbacks, Lear proceeded with the planned armor attack on the 18th. Most of I Armored Corps' forces had been scattered throughout the Second Army's lines in an attempt to stabilize Red positions against increasing Blue pressure. Hence the I Armored Corps' mission devolved primarily onto the 2nd Armored Division, which launched its two-pronged attack at 0600. After advancing a few miles on the western end of the line, the 2nd Armored Brigade collided with Blue antitank guns north of Florien, its lead battalion losing twenty of its twenty-three tanks before withdrawing. The brigade left Florien in Blue hands, and continued its southward advance by sidestepping west of the Many-Leesville highway. It advanced 10 miles but failed to secure any of its objectives before Blue antitank guns redeployed in its path and brought the column to a halt late in the day.[104]

At the same time, Patton's eastern column renewed the battle for Mount Carmel. The 69th Armor Regiment opened the battle north of the town by driving off a force of Blue infantry from the 45th Division. To avoid the long, wooded defiles leading toward Mount Carmel, the 68th Armor Regiment shifted the bulk of its forces about 3 miles to the east. This maneuver out-flanked the 45th Infantry in Mount Carmel, but brought the 68th against a formidable concentration of Blue antitank guns that served as the last Blue defense between the armor regiments and the open ground leading to Leesville. The 68th attacked the antitank cordon at noon. Without adequate artillery and infantry support, however, the Red tanks were forced to charge the antitank positions and attempt to overrun them. Although it forced the Blue guns to yield some ground, after two hours of intense fighting the 68th failed to achieve a breakthrough and sustained heavy casualties. The tanks withdrew and re-formed, and at roughly 1645 resumed their futile frontal assaults against the wall of antitank guns. In the end, the 68th Armored only overran nine antitank guns at a cost of thirty-one tanks. Meanwhile, the 67th Armor Regiment probed into the forest even farther to the east, desperately searching for a gap in the Blue line. The 67th's medium tanks drove a salient into the Blue line, but once again Blue antitank guns pushed them back and ended the Red threat to Peason Ridge.[105]

The battle for Mount Carmel on the 18th was the bitterest fighting of the maneuver. When the umpires halted action at 1830, Patton had lost ninety-eight light tanks, seventeen medium tanks, and ninety-eight other armored vehicles.

To the east, the 1st Armored Division struck the Blue line's center near the Kisatchie National Forest and met with even less success. Magruder's main force bogged down in swamps and densely wooded hills, and disintegrated as an effective fighting force. Confident that Lear's armor was pinned down, Krueger committed Third Army's reserves in an all-out attack. Blue forces seized 1st Armored's gasoline train, and adding insult to injury, airplanes dropped propaganda pamphlets over Second Army positions declaring:

> *Your commanders are withholding from you the terrible fact of your defeat. Your gasoline stores have been captured. From now on, if you move, you do it on the soles of your shoes. Your food stores have been captured. Your dinner tonight is going to be what was left over from yesterday. No one is going to bring up any of the steaks that the men of the Third Army will have tonight. Rout, disaster, hunger, sleepless nights in the forests and swamps are ahead of you—unless you surrender.*[106]

Indeed, Lear himself had to evacuate his command post on two separate occasions to avoid capture.

Krueger was also on the move throughout the maneuvers. Yet rather than evading capture, Krueger was conducting inspections, observing his men, and teaching tactics and other aspects of soldiering. Third Army units transmitted the informal code word "Meatsaw"—a reference to the general's insistence on strict hygiene standards during spot inspections of field kitchens—to indicate their commander was nearby. Indeed, many of the Third Army's enlisted men remembered Krueger's sincere interest in their welfare. Bill Mauldin, who would gain fame during the war as a cartoonist, was serving in the 45th Infantry in the maneuvers when he encountered Krueger. "It is an awesome experience," he recalled, "when a man with three stars on each shoulders steps out of the bushes and demands to see your bare feet because of his concerns over the performance of army boots."[107]

Krueger continued his attack on September 19. Overnight the 1st Cavalry Division crossed the Sabine River from Texas to get behind Patton's division. When elements of the retreating 2nd Armored reached Zwolle, they joined the Red 2nd Cavalry Division in a battle against the 1st Cavalry for possession of the town. Red cavalry and tanks became tangled, and Blue attack aircraft strafed the jumbled columns. As the confusion mounted, Blue cavalry infiltrated the Red lines and captured some mired tanks. In a panic to escape, Red soldiers raced to their vehicles and recklessly drove through marked artillery barrages. In the east, Krueger sent his 37th and 38th Infantry Divisions northward against Lear's left flank. The two divisions pushed through Red's VII Corps and threatened to cut off the Second Army from its crossing points over the Red River. With the battle's conclusion no longer in doubt, at 1530 McNair mercifully called the first phase of the exercise to a halt. "Had it been a real war," Hanson Baldwin of the *New York Times* reported, "Lear's force would have been annihilated."[108] Another journalist noted that armored troops who were "cocky and brave" on Monday were "silent and unhappy" on Friday.[109]

The conclusion of the "Battle of the Red River" brought only a brief respite to the Second and Third Armies' weary troops. GHQ had already set in motion the preliminaries for Phase Two, and there was only a five-day pause for logistical regrouping before the second maneuver began. The armies' roles were reversed for the second phase. The 2nd Armored Division was attached to Krueger's attacking Blue force, whose mission was to capture Shreveport and defeat Lear's Red force defending the city. In return Second Army received two of the three antitank groups as well as a company of paratroopers from the 502nd Parachute Battalion. Consequently, Third Army would outnumber Second Army four corps to one, eleven divisions to seven, and 219,346 men to 123,451, a nearly 1.8:1 ratio, in order to test a small army's ability to defend itself against an army possessing greater numbers of infantry and tanks and greater mobility.[110]

Although GHQ had deprived Second Army of much of its striking capability, it gave Lear the simpler mission. If the Red force could simply avoid destruction and keep the invaders out of Shreveport until notional "reinforcements" arrived on September 30, its mission would be fulfilled. Lear's strategy, therefore, was to delay by withdrawing to a succession of concentric defensive lines 10 to 15 miles apart, ranging out from Shreveport to a distance of 60 miles, while destroying every bridge and culvert left behind. This would wear his opponent down while denying the advancing Blue forces any opportunity to bring its superior numbers to bear. For his part, Krueger planned a three-corps advance northward between the Red and Sabine Rivers straight toward Shreveport. Once the Second Army was pinned down by his infantry divisions he would unleash his armor against a weak spot in the enemy lines.[111]

When the second phase began on September 24, the tail end of a category two hurricane swept over the maneuver area. Although the eye of the storm—with winds exceeding 100 miles per hour—passed over Houston, winds and rain grounded aircraft, flattened camps, and soaked the troops as they moved to their lines of departure. "The Army got a good drenching," Eisenhower wrote Gerow on September 25. "Yet when the problem started at noon yesterday, everybody was full of vim and ready to go."[112] At noon Third Army swarmed north toward Shreveport and the Red enemy. Instead of finding Red's main force that afternoon, they encountered the first of more than 900 demolitions that would frustrate them throughout the maneuver. In the deluge's wake, the streams became muddy torrents and the rivers raging floods. The bayous were swollen and mottled with dead branches, silt, and mud. As per Lear's orders, virtually every bridge and culvert in the main battle zone was posted as destroyed, slowing Third Army's advance to a crawl. At one bridge flagged as destroyed, Eisenhower recalled, a corporal brought his squad up, looked at the umpire's flag, and after a moment's hesitation began to march his men across it.

"Hey, don't you see that the bridge is destroyed?" the umpire yelled.

"Of course I can see it's destroyed," the corporal answered. "Can't you see we're swimming?"

Levity aside, it was a wise decision, as multiple soldiers had drowned attempting to swim swarming rivers during the maneuvers' first phase.[113]

Red forces further impeded the Third Army's advance by covering key demolitions with special delay task forces that repeatedly disrupted the Blue engineers' attempts to repair demolitions. The Blue troops were forced to deploy for battle each time, only for the Red raiders to slip away before they could be pinned down. As McNair noted, the struggle became "the Battle of the Bridges. If there is any one lesson which stands above all others, it is the decisive influence of destroyed bridges."[114]

Third Army advanced about 20 miles by nightfall of the first day. Under the cover of darkness, Second Army fell back in an orderly manner from the first to the intermediate delay position. At dawn on the 25th, 45 miles of muddy roads and hundreds of new demolitions separated the Red and Blue main forces. Throughout September 25 the Blue engineers struggled to clear routes while traffic backed up behind them, inviting punishing raids from Red's 2nd Air Task Force. By midnight Third Army's main body was still south of Lear's initial delaying position, which Second Army had abandoned the day before.[115]

When Lear declined to do battle, Kreuger abandoned his conventional frontal assault and embraced Eisenhower's plan for a bold flank attack with the I Armored Corps. The 2nd Armored Brigade, followed by the 2nd Infantry Division (motorized), would make an envelopment and recross the Sabine River near Logansport in order to cut the Red VII Corps' communications with Shreveport. Meanwhile, Patton would personally lead another column consisting of the 41st Infantry Regiment and other attached units on a wide circuit through Texas to attack Shreveport from the west.

Blue commanders and staff hurriedly completed the new plans and issued orders at 1730 on September 25. Patton's column made rapid progress throughout the 26th, aided by the division commander's ability to pay for the gasoline required to refuel his vehicles out of his own pocket at commercial filling stations. The advance nearly stalled at the rain-swollen Angelina River south of Nacogdoches, where the vital highway bridge was marked as demolished. Yet since rising water had covered the simulated charges and no other preparations were apparent, an umpire accompanying the Blue column declared the bridge to be improperly destroyed, allowing the armored column to cross. Patton brushed aside delaying actions by elements of the Red 2nd Cavalry Division and 4th Cavalry Regiment that evening, and by midnight his column was at Henderson having covered nearly 200 miles in twenty-four hours.[116]

In the absence of effective countermeasures,* on September 27 Patton roared into Second Army's western flank. His orders had called for him to turn east at Marshall, Texas, almost due west of Shreveport, which he would then attack. Yet upon hearing that the Red force at Greenwood, Louisiana—which lay astride his avenue of advance—had been reinforced by an antitank battalion, he decided not to launch a frontal attack there. Instead, he led his column even farther north on a route that took it around Caddo Lake and allowed him to attack Shreveport from the north, in effect taking the city from the rear. Lear hurriedly dispatched the 6th Division's antitank battalion into the path of Patton's advance and later reinforced it with the 1st Antitank Group. Reconnaissance and infantry elements of the Red antitank units finally intercepted Patton's column 15 miles north of Shreveport at day's end.[117]

While Patton completed his envelopment, the rest of Third Army continued its frustrating advance between the Sabine and Red Rivers. Faced with pressure from GHQ and his own staff to do something besides withdraw, however, Lear yielded and ordered Second Army to hold its positions until the evening of September 27. This allowed Third Army to finally bring the Second Army to bay on the morning of the 28th. When the Red VII Corps tried to pull the 27th Division off the line and replace it with the 33rd Division from the Corps' reserve, advancing Blue forces detected the passage of lines and succeeded in forcing a gap in the Red position. The VIII Corps drove through Red's defensive lines and into Mansfield, where heavy fighting ensued.[118]

North of Shreveport, Patton was at the end of a 300-mile supply line, isolated from the rest of Third Army, and commanding a force barely larger than a regiment. Naturally, he decided to attack. Emulating Robert E. Lee at Chancellorsville, Patton split his already small command, driving into the western edge of Shreveport with one column while the other ferried the Red River north of town. This column swung around to the east and captured Barksdale airfield, the main base of Red's 2nd Air Task Force.[119]

---

* As Christopher Gabel notes, Lear missed multiple opportunities to impede Patton's dash. Throughout the 26th Red cavalry and air reconnaissance maintained contact with the armored columns as they drove through Texas. By 1300 on the 26th, VII Corps' intelligence officer warned of the impending flanking attack, yet Lear remained indifferent and kept both his antitank groups in reserve. Moreover, rather than deploying his paratroopers to seize/destroy bridges along Patton's route or cut his communications line, Lear squandered them in a strategically irrelevant raid against Eunice, Louisiana, 100 miles behind Third Army's main body. See Gabel, 106–7.

Lear finally reacted to Patton's drive by sending elements of Magruder's 1st Armored to oppose him. Yet at 1655, with the climactic battle under way, GHQ abruptly terminated the exercise. Although the "Battle of Shreveport" was far from decided, McNair decided the maneuver had fulfilled its purpose and sought to avoid street fighting in Shreveport and Mansfield during rush hour on Monday the 29th. The battle was halted, McNair stated, "not by the tactical situation, but by the calendar."[120] Regardless, the 100,000 citizens of Shreveport broke out red decorations in honor of the forces that had defended them. They rang church bells to celebrate the deliverance of their city from the Blue invaders and chanted "We're for Lear."

Overall, the Louisiana Maneuvers were a success for the Army, albeit a qualified one. First, they gave American officers invaluable hands-on experience in moving large units on an unprecedented scale. The 2nd Armored Division, for example, had traveled over 600 miles from Fort Benning, utilizing a combination of road and rail, while the 1st Armored moved over 700 miles from Fort Knox. Years later, Mark Clark recalled: "When Pearl Harbor happened . . . there was [a] great clamor to get troops to the west coast, and I thought to myself at the time . . . how lucky we [were] that we just had maneuvers. We'd moved a corps. Two or three months before that you would say, 'How do you move a corps?'"[121] Whereas during the 1940 maneuvers administration of supply sometimes broke down so badly that the Guardsmen were left without food, the Louisiana Maneuvers were a logistical triumph. In Third Army alone, Eisenhower oversaw the preparation of over sixteen million meals consuming over 11.5 million pounds of bread, nine million pounds of potatoes, and 8.5 million pounds of meat. Indeed, General McNair remarked that the logistical planning was largely responsible for the Third Army's success.[122]

The 1941 maneuvers also helped prepare the Army and the nation psychologically for war. Whereas the Army's public image had hit rock bottom nine years earlier in the wake of the Bonus March, public perception of the Army changed for the better during the 1941 maneuvers. Although sixty-one soldiers died during the Louisiana and Carolina maneuvers, there was no public outcry. Meaningful training, even in mock battle, also reinvigorated the morale of citizen-soldiers who had cried "OHIO" only weeks before.[123]

The maneuvers were only partially successful, however, as a test of organization and doctrine. "These maneuvers," Krueger wrote a friend, "gave us the first chance we have ever had of coordinating infantry, artillery, armored forces, antitank forces, antiaircraft forces and air forces of magnitude."[124] Experience was gained in two of the most difficult military operations, withdrawals and river crossings, requiring coordination between engineers and ground troops. The maneuvers also helped persuade officers skeptical of close air support's potential as a force multiplier for maneuver operations. Moreover, Krueger and Eisenhower's actions clearly anticipated the operational art that would characterize U.S. operations in World War II, as Third Army fought on a broad front while retaining a high degree of responsiveness due to the skillful use of motor transport and the latitude Krueger gave to subordinate commanders.[125]

Yet if the broad outlines of infantry and fire support doctrines were validated in Louisiana, their execution left much to be desired. McNair, GHQ observers, and even civilian correspondents noted throughout the exercises that many small units showed little proficiency in the skills they were supposed to have mastered during their mobilization training programs. Indeed, Collins observed a deterioration in basic skills during the army-versus-army maneuvers. He noted that companies and battalions tended to get lost in the "big picture," leading to carelessness and the development of bad habits. "It is almost impossible to get American soldiers to take seriously attacks from planes that simply fly overhead," he later wrote. "Troops tend to stick to the roads instead of moving in deployed formations across country." Secure in the knowledge that only blanks were being fired, soldiers would "fail to take cover from theoretical bombardment, artillery or machine-gun fire."[126] Among the serious training deficiencies McNair noted were a reluctance to utilize entrenchments in defense, and especially poor reconnaissance and security, which he described as "one of the most serious faults observed during the maneuver." At a post-maneuvers critique, McNair stated that "In spite of the remarkable progress of the year just past, there must be no idea in anyone's mind that further training is unnecessary."[127] Yet as Marshall told a senator who criticized the maneuvers because of all the mistakes made: "My God, Senator, that's the reason I do it. I want the mistakes down in Louisiana, not over in Europe, and the only way to do this thing is to try it out, and if it doesn't work, find out what we need to make it work."[128]

The Louisiana Maneuvers' results reflected particularly poorly on the Armored Force, as the most obvious lesson from the first phase appeared to be the startling victory of antitank forces over tanks. For observers such as McNair, the maneuvers had settled the "outstanding question" of whether the tank could be stopped. Conversely, others such as Devers refused to give the antitank forces much credit, declaring after the Carolina Maneuvers: "We were licked by a set of umpire's rules."[129] While the umpiring rules for antitank engagements were clearly biased toward the guns, and unfavorable terrain and inclement weather further hampered the armored forces in Louisiana, the primary cause of their failure lay with their own doctrinal deficiencies. Like the British, the American armored divisions at that time separated tanks into a pure armor brigade and the infantry into its own regiment. Divisions tended to only deploy one arm at a time, and hence tank regiments, infantry regiments, and artillery batteries usually acted independently. Reconnaissance elements were poorly coordinated with the main body units moving to the attack, and infantry existed primarily to protect the lines of communication, secure captured objectives, and prepare the way for the strike echelon's decisive attacks. Thus, commanders found themselves futilely charging positions that would have fallen easily to foot soldiers.[130]

To their credit, Devers and other armor officers quickly realized the necessity of combined arms teams of tanks, infantry, and artillery. As Patton told the 2nd Armored Division's officers after the maneuvers: "We still fail to use every weapon every time.... Each time we fight with only one weapon when we could use several weapons, we are not winning a battle, we are making fools of ourselves."[131] Brig. Gen. Orlando Ward, now commanding the 1st Armored Division's 1st Armored Brigade, wrote his former boss Marshall after the maneuvers that "We should have teams consisting of infantry, artillery, and tanks working together all the time and then if it is necessary to augment one arm or the other it can be done without disruption."[132] Devers attributed the poor performance to undertrained junior officers and poor staff work at the regiment and divisional levels. Admirably, Patton took personal responsibility for his division's shortcomings in Louisiana: "Tactically I made mistakes, both in training and in operations, which I am now correcting through further education of myself and the officers of this division." He then reassured his officers: "We made a damned good try. I shall be delighted to lead you against any enemy, confident in the fact that your disciplined valor and high training will bring victory."[133] Regardless of the cause, the exaggerated notion of armor's invincibility was dissipated, and armor's failure to dominate the Louisiana Maneuvers was (incorrectly) interpreted by McNair and Marshall as validation of the emerging antitank program.

The shortcomings exposed during the mock battles were in some sense a blessing to Marshall, as they provided tangible evidence of the need to reinvigorate the officer corps with younger leaders. "One of the things that is causing the greatest troubles is that of eliminating unfit officers, at all grades and of all components," Eisenhower noted during the Louisiana Maneuvers. "It is a hard thing to do, and in many cases it is too hard for some of the people in charge. But it is a job that has got to be done."[134] McNair blamed inadequate troop training on the lack of discipline, which he attributed to poor officer leadership. "A commander who can not develop proper discipline must be replaced," he said. "Leadership and command can and must be improved."[135] At the highest levels, he found that orders were often too complex, obscure, and late, sometimes not reaching subordinate commands until after the hour they were to be executed. This was exactly what Marshall had been warning against for two decades, and on September 29—the day after the second phase had ended—the chief of staff wrote the field armies' commanding generals urging them to reexamine officer fitness in their commands. As word spread that wide-ranging officer "reclassifications" were imminent, Secretary Stimson asked reporters to tone down their references to a "purge," warning: "If you write a lot of stories about purging officers, that is not good for the morale either of officers or men."[136] Yet of the forty-two division, corps, and army commanders who took part in the 1941 GHQ maneuvers, thirty-one were relieved or shunted aside.

The maneuvers not only exposed the overage and unfit, but also helped to identify the Army's most promising leaders. Mark Clark, for example, wrote the maneuver scenarios and earned accolades as the Army's preeminent planner, with Collins describing him as "a man with a keen analytical mind, thorough military knowledge, great driving force, and organizing skill."[137] Whereas General Scott displayed a lack of command and control directing the I Armored Corps in Louisiana, Patton superbly managed coordination and control, and emerged as the star of the armored forces. Shortly thereafter, Marshall assigned Scott to serve as observer to the British forces fighting in the Middle East and appointed Patton commander of I Armored Corps.[138]

Yet perhaps the most noteworthy officer to emerge from the Louisiana Maneuvers was Eisenhower, who won praise for his performance as Third Army's chief of staff and received national attention from the press. Journalist Robert Sherrod reported that Eisenhower "looked like a soldier. He talked like an educated man. He was very forceful, altogether, as I've said, the most impressive man I'd seen."[139] Drew Pearson and Robert Allen—whom, ironically, Eisenhower had eviscerated in his diary when they were hounding his boss, Douglas MacArthur, a decade earlier—chronicled the war games in their "Washington Merry Go-Round" column, writing that chief among the

Army's "young aces" was "Colonel Dwight Eisenhower ... who conceived and directed the strategy that routed the Second Army. Eisenhower has a steel-trap mind plus unusual physical vigor."[140] Allen wrote Krueger personally to praise his chief of staff, "who took time out to give a group of us a very brilliant explanation of the tactical situation and was helpful in other ways. I don't have to tell you that in Colonel Eisenhouer [sic] you have one of the finest and ablest officers in the army."[141] Krueger agreed, and when General Marshall asked him at the maneuvers' conclusion what officer Krueger thought best suited to fill his former positions heading the War Plans Division, Krueger named Eisenhower "though I was loath to lose him."[142]

Eisenhower's role in Third Army's victory has been exaggerated with the clarity of hindsight and his subsequent achievements. In reality, Krueger and Eisenhower formulated the winning strategy together and were more flexible in making changes than the conservative Lear. Although Carlo D'Este notes that "Eisenhower's presence and his long experience served to add common sense and stability to the Third Army staff," command responsibility rested with Krueger.[143] To his credit, Eisenhower acknowledges in his memoirs that "I was given unsought publicity in a newspaper column whose author attributed credit to me that should have gone to General Krueger."[144] The reason the press gave Eisenhower much of the accolades for Krueger's success was that while the Third Army commander exercised hands-on command, he insisted his chief of staff remain close to headquarters.[145] Krueger shunned the limelight, and thus it fell upon Eisenhower to conduct the twice-daily press briefings. Eisenhower had learned the importance of cultivating and guiding the press—what the modern military calls "strategic communications"—from the debacle of the Bonus March. Like Marshall with Congress, his honesty was a pleasant surprise to the reporters used to covering leaders obsessed with obfuscating over any shortcomings in their organizations.

The Louisiana Maneuvers ended with a final moment of drama for Eisenhower. Mark Clark conducted the exercises' final "hot wash" with the senior leaders who had just finished the fight for Shreveport. After reviewing the lessons learned regarding organization, training, and equipment, Clark pulled out a piece of paper from the War Department. The following officers, he declared, had just been promoted to brigadier general. He announced the names of more than a dozen colonels, and at the end of the list said, "That's it."

Officers rose to leave. The new brigadiers, glowing with pride, were mobbed by their colleagues offering congratulations, shaking their hands and slapping their backs. Eisenhower was almost out the door when Clark's gavel slammed and silenced the celebration.

"I'm sorry, I beg your pardon, I have omitted one name," Clark said. His words hung in the air for a moment before he called the name: "Dwight D. Eisenhower."

Eisenhower came toward Clark laughing. "You son of a bitch," he said. "I'll get you."

Clark laughed and extended his hand to congratulate his friend.[146]

Eisenhower humbly noted to Gerow: "One thing is certain—when they get clear down to my place on the list, they are passing out stars with considerable abandon."[147] Yet when they returned to Fort Sam Houston, the 3rd Division's officers wanted to hold a parade in Eisenhower's honor. He refused a proposed gun salute, claiming it would be a waste of gunpowder. Despite his protestations, they gave him an honor guard. He told Clark: "I'm completely overcome . . . I've always been on the other end of such things, and I hope to heck I don't fall over my own feet! But durned if the prospect doesn't scare me more than would an order to go charge Hitler's legions!"[148]

After sitting out the war, after seeing his career threatened for his heterodoxy and by an overzealous inspector general at Camp Meade, after the repeated frustrations at being unable to gain a command position throughout the 1920s and 1930s and the increasing sense of isolation from his branch of service, and after enduring MacArthur's toxic leadership in the Philippines, Eisenhower appeared to finally have made good on his promise to "cut a swath" for himself in the U.S. Army.

CHAPTER TEN

Generals at War

EVEN DURING HIS MOST TRYING DAYS AS CHIEF OF STAFF, GEORGE MARshall tried to find time for roughly an hour of horseback riding in the early morning or late afternoon on the trails between Fort Myer and the Potomac, an area now occupied by the Pentagon and its surrounding highways. Marshall claimed this did him "a world of good" and enabled him to "keep things in focus and shed almost all worries."[1] Sunday, December 7, 1941, was no different. That morning, riding a sorrel named Prepared, he kept "a pretty lively gait" on the paths along the Virginia side of the Memorial Bridge. When he returned to Quarters Number One at Fort Myer, Katherine told him of frantic calls from the War Department, particularly from the Far Eastern Intelligence officer. He quickly showered and changed before having a car take him to the War Department.

Marshall's aides handed him a recently intercepted diplomatic cable from Tokyo instructing the Japanese ambassador to reject America's latest peace proposal and officially terminate negotiations with the United States. Given the deteriorating relations between the two nations, this was not a surprise. But what caught Marshall's eye was that Ambassador Nomura was ordered to deliver the message *specifically* at 1:00 P.M., Washington, DC, time. The chief of staff immediately drafted a cable to the army commanders in the Philippines, Panama, San Francisco, and Hawaii: "Japanese are presenting at 1PM Eastern Standard Time today what amounts to an ultimatum. . . . Just what significance the hour set may have we do not know but be on the alert accordingly. Inform naval authorities of this communication."[2] The warning was immediately encoded and dispatched by radio to all destinations. A series of technical problems necessitated the message be sent by commercial telegraph to Hawaii, however, which did not reach Gen. William Short at Schofield Barracks until it was too late.

Just before 8:00 A.M., Hawaii time, 190 Japanese divebombers, torpedo planes, and fighters attacked U.S. military installations in and around Pearl Harbor and Honolulu, followed by a second wave of 170 planes. Having achieved complete surprise, over the next two hours the Japanese destroyed 188 aircraft, sank or crippled eighteen warships—including the bulk of the American battle fleet—and killed 2,403 American servicemen.

Although Marshall's discipline kept him from appearing apprehensive or gloomy in front of his staff, the day's events shook him to the core. That night he returned home "grim and grey" and said nothing to Katherine "except that he was tired and was going to bed."[3] He quickly regained his equilibrium, and amongst a hundred other decisions made in Pearl Harbor's aftermath, on December 11 ordered the War Plan Division's chief of Pacific operations— Col. Charles W. Bundy—to travel to Hawaii to survey the destruction and begin to determine how such a disaster could have happened.

At Third Army headquarters, Dwight Eisenhower had no reason to suspect anything unusual when the direct line connecting Third Army to the War Department rang early on December 12. His phones had barely ceased ringing for the past five days, and as he picked up the receiver he expected yet another order for immediate execution in a seemingly endless stream of frenzied directives from Washington.

"Is that you, Ike?" the familiar, grizzled voice of Walter Bedell Smith asked.

"Yes."

"The Chief says for you to hop a plane and get up here right away. Tell your boss that formal orders will come through later."

Eisenhower, needing to know how to pack, asked how long he would be in Washington.

"I don't know," Smith replied. "Just come along."

Eisenhower asked what kind of duty he would be performing.

"The Chief said you get on a plane and get up here," Smith repeated, and that was it.[4]

The night before, Colonel Bundy's B-17 had flown into a storm front over the Rocky Mountains. Somewhere south of Denver, the plane crashed into a peak, killing Bundy and everyone else on board.

Once again, a tragedy would significantly alter America's course in the world war that was now upon them.

When one takes a step back to view America's participation in World War II in its totality, to include the two decades between the wars, it becomes clear how much of the Army's generalship was foreshadowed by their experiences during the interwar years. Yet this sense of inevitability was unknowable to Eisenhower in those first few dark weeks in Washington. To Ike it seemed as if his worst fear appeared to be coming true. Instead of the troop command he desperately wanted after missing combat in World War I, he appeared destined for another desk job. Upon arriving in the capital, Eisenhower's immediate superior in the War Plans Division was Gee Gerow. Gerow was not decisive enough to suit Marshall, however, and in mid-February he was sent back to the field to command the 29th Infantry Division. Marshall appointed Eisenhower to replace Gerow, making him the chief of staff's primary plans and operations officer. "Well," Gerow mordantly joked to his friend, "I got Pearl Harbor on the books; lost the [Philippines], Singapore, Sumatra, and all the [Dutch East Indies] north of the barrier. Let's see what you can do."[5]

Eisenhower once again distinguished himself for the thoroughness of his analyses and the lucidity of his reports, and quickly gained Marshall's confidence.[6] In June 1942 Eisenhower wrote a friend that the months in Washington had been a "tough, intensive grind."[7] Perhaps no issue created more headaches initially than the Philippines and his old boss, Douglas MacArthur. MacArthur's problems in early 1942 were a direct result of his failures during the interwar years, specifically his inability to be honest with those in his chain of command when real world conditions made it impossible for him to succeed at the level sufficient to justify his ego. When the truth and MacArthur's self-regard clashed, MacArthur reliably shaped reality to suit his arrogance.

The former chief of staff had reached a professional nadir in the year-and-a-half following Eisenhower's departure from Manila. In October 1940, the War Plans Division recommended withdrawing all U.S. forces in the Pacific to east of the 180-degree meridian, which meant sacrificing the Philippines to the rapacious Japanese empire. President Roosevelt appeared ready to abandon the Commonwealth's defense in a White House meeting with his secretaries of State, War, and the Navy in January 1941. Marshall's notes detailed the president's conclusion "that we would stand on the defensive in the Pacific with the fleet based in Hawaii" and "that there would be no naval reinforcement of the Philippines."[8] Worse, MacArthur had become increasingly detached from U.S. decision-making. Officers in the Philippines derided him as "the Napoleon of Luzon." When Theodore White of *Time* magazine visited Manila in December 1940, he was told MacArthur "cut no more ice in this U.S. Army than a corporal."[9]

MacArthur was desperate to get back in the game. In February 1941, he wrote a letter to Marshall intended to remind the chief of staff of his availability for active service. In March, amidst rumors that High Commissioner Francis Sayre would be recalled to the State Department, MacArthur once again sought the appointment. Attempting to replicate his successful flattery of Patrick Hurley a decade earlier, he wrote to Roosevelt's press aide Steven Early that the president "has proved himself not only our greatest statesmen but what to me is even more thrilling, our greatest military strategist." While such praise may have been merited *after* the war, there was certainly no justification for such obsequiousness in 1941.[10] When this attempt failed, he wrote again in April suggesting Early recommend that MacArthur be returned to active duty. Lacking any positive response, on May 29 he wrote Marshall to say he would be closing the Defense Mission and returning to the United States. Having MacArthur in the United States, where he could stir discord through his friends in the conservative press and amongst congressional Republicans, was a dangerous proposition. Consequently, on June 20, Marshall told MacArthur to stay in Manila. "Both the Secretary and I are much concerned about the situation in the Far East," Marshall wrote. "During our discussions about three months ago it was decided that your outstanding qualifications and vast experience in the Philippines makes you the logical selection for the Army Commander in the Far East should the situation approach a crisis."[11] On July 26, following Japanese troop movements into Southeast Asia, President Roosevelt placed the Philippine army under American control and appointed MacArthur as Commanding General, United States Army Forces in the Far East (USAFFE).

"I feel like a new dog in an old uniform," MacArthur ecstatically told his staff.[12] He informed the War Department that his strength totaled more than 100,000 American and Filipino troops. Although Japan had six million men under arms, many veterans of fighting in China, MacArthur wrote that he was "confident that we can successfully resist any effort that may be made against us."[13] Yet the Filipino forces MacArthur bragged about consisted primarily of names on an availability roster rather than trained troops. One American officer noted his recruits lacked everything from steel helmets to clothes, and wore sneakers "so deteriorated from age and use that most of the men were barefooted within a few days."[14] Bradford Chynoweth commented that MacArthur "did not have any army—they were a mob."[15] He noted that his Philippine army division, the 61st Infantry, had no basic training and "no officers or NCOs able to use initiative in a decentralized command."[16]

Although Chynoweth believed that "MacArthur was in a complete fog about his Army," the USAFFE commander actually had few illusions about how poorly the training program was going. MacArthur wrote to his former superior George Grunert, "In my inspections to date I have found large groups of trainees and their officers standing around and doing nothing ... there was a complete lack of decisiveness in instructional procedure. Some American officers were practically ignorant of what was going on, and a pall of inactivity was evident."[17] Nevertheless he gave glowing appraisals of his plan to defend the Philippines to journalists such as Clare Booth Luce.

Whereas spinning correspondents for purposes of morale and deterrence may be justifiable, there was no excuse for deceiving his chain of command. MacArthur assured Marshall that "The Philippine Army units that have been called are now mobilizing in a most satisfactory manner, and the whole program is progressing by leaps and bounds."[18] As D. Clayton James observes, MacArthur's "overconfidence and unjustified optimism as to the abilities of himself, his staff, and the untried Filipino soldiers unfortunately became a contagion which ultimately affected even the War Department and the Joint Army and Navy Board."[19] In February the General Staff had vetoed an Air Corps suggestion that Luzon be reinforced with heavy bombers. Now Marshall—who should have known better—ordered Hap Arnold to send four bomber groups of seventy planes each and 260 fighters to the Far East Air Force. By December 1, MacArthur's air arm included half of all heavy bombers and one-sixth of all fighters the Army had overseas. In September fourteen infantry companies arrived in the Philippines, to be followed by more than 450 officers to train the Filipino regiments, a tank battalion, and the redeployed 4th Marine Regiment from Shanghai. Thus, MacArthur's deceptive reports led Washington to rush precious men and materiel to the Philippines in a desperate attempt to accomplish a mission that for two decades the Army's planners had deemed impossible.[20]

On November 27, MacArthur and the commanders in Hawaii received a "final alert" from the War Department and a "war warning" from the Navy. Yet in a meeting that day with Adm. Thomas Hart and Commissioner Sayre, MacArthur paced the room, puffed on his cigar, and confidently proclaimed that the existing alignment and movement of Japanese troops convinced him that there would be no attack before the spring. He similarly told the commander of the North Luzon Force, Brig. Gen. Jonathan Wainwright, "You'll probably have until about April to train those troops."[21] Nevertheless, the next day MacArthur cabled Marshall, declaring "Everything is in readiness for the conduct of a successful defense."[22] As was the case with his optimism, MacArthur's nonchalance was contagious. The commander of MacArthur's air force recalled that when he arrived in Manila in November 1941, "work hours, training schedules, and operating procedures" of U.S. forces in the Philippines "were still based on the good old days of peace conditions in the tropics."[23] Similarly, Chynoweth felt that USAFFE headquarters—which was staffed by officers Eisenhower derided as "bootlickers"—put nightlife ahead of war.[24]

The strategic error of pouring scarce resources into the Philippines in 1941 was compounded by MacArthur's tactical and operational mistakes after Pearl Harbor. MacArthur was awakened shortly after 3:00 A.M. with news of the Japanese attack. For once, however, his famous confidence abandoned him, and MacArthur uncharacteristically hesitated to act without clear instructions from Washington. He declined to mount a counterattack against Japanese positions on Formosa, claiming that Japan had only attacked the United States rather than the allegedly sovereign Philippines—which was not scheduled to attain independence for another five years. He failed to even take the precautionary measure of dispersing his own aircraft. When Japanese bombers began their attack at 7:15 A.M., MacArthur's force of some three dozen B-17 bombers and more than 200 other aircraft was destroyed. Upon hearing this, Marshall fumed. "Four hours, and our aircraft were still on the ground in the open—perfect targets. I sweated blood to get planes to the Philippines. It is inexplicable."[25] Despite months of pleading for them, MacArthur now suddenly dismissed the bombers as "hardly more than a token force" which was "hopelessly outnumbered" and "never had a chance of winning."[26]

MacArthur had persuaded his superiors in Washington to alter his mission, so that rather than simply defending Manila Bay as per War Plan Orange he was now authorized to execute his preferred strategy of defending the entire archipelago. Yet MacArthur quickly abandoned his plan to repel the invaders on the beaches when Japanese forces landed at Lingayen Bay on December 22. Wainwright's forces withdrew across Luzon's central plan, covering the American and Filipino retreat into the Bataan peninsula. Pershing called the withdrawal "a masterpiece, one of the greatest moves in all military history" and the retreat into Bataan became a staple of postwar studies at the CGSS.[27] Upon arriving in Bataan, however, U.S. commanders found their supplies had been dispersed around the island in support of MacArthur's scheme rather than stockpiled for a protracted siege and defense of Bataan. Combined with the increase in U.S. forces throughout 1941, this meant they lacked food and medicine, and were soon plunged into misery as thousands fell victim to malnourishment and tropical diseases. MacArthur established a command post inside a railroad tunnel on the island fortress of Corregidor, and only visited the troops fighting on Bataan once even though they were just five minutes away by torpedo boat. Consequently, they derisively nicknamed him "Dugout Doug." This was unfair in a sense, for few dispute MacArthur's physical courage. Geoffrey Perret is closer to the mark in concluding that "it was moral courage that was in short supply." In the end, MacArthur could not bear to face the men he had led into such desperate straits.[28]

Due to MacArthur's self-promoting communiques, however, the press latched on to the general as the "Lion of Luzon," courageously and cunningly staving off the Japanese invaders. Although MacArthur suggested he was prepared to die on Corregidor, President Roosevelt decided he could not risk the former chief of staff falling into Japanese hands. Knowing the garrison was doomed, on February 23, 1942, Marshall notified MacArthur that "the President directs you to proceed to Mindanao . . . as quickly as possible. From Mindanao you will proceed to Australia where you will assume command of all United States troops."[29] On the night of March 12, MacArthur, his family, and his personal staff made a daring escape through the Japanese blockade in four PT boats. To counter Axis propaganda mocking MacArthur as a coward who had deserted his men, and to change the narrative of the Philippines' fall from one of humiliating defeat to heroic sacrifice, Marshall decided to award MacArthur his long sought after Medal of Honor, citing his "heroic conduct of defensive and offensive operations on the Bataan peninsula." Although MacArthur urged the troops now under Wainwright's command to break out of Bataan and take to the mountains as guerrillas, this was a ridiculous notion. They were weakened from subsisting on quarter-rations, and 80 percent of them were crippled by malaria and/or dysentery. Despite their valiant defense, the 76,000 troops on Bataan surrendered on April 9, followed by Corregidor's capitulation on May 6.[30]

Upon arriving in Adelaide, Australia, on the evening of March 21, 1942, MacArthur famously declared: "The President of the United States ordered me to break through the Japanese lines and proceed from Corregidor to Australia for the purpose, as I understand it, of organizing the American offensive against Japan, a primary object of which is the relief of the Philippines. I came through, and I shall return." Arguably, MacArthur should have been relieved after the Philippines fiasco. Instead, the Joint Chiefs of Staff placed him in charge of the newly created Southwest Pacific Area theater. Although he often equated his own interests with those of the United States—especially redeeming his personal reputation by prioritizing the liberation of the Philippines—he proceeded to lead one of the most brilliant campaigns of World War II. MacArthur's strategy leapfrogged and isolated Japanese strongpoints. With the help of his air commander, Gen. George Kenney, he mastered combined arms operations and struck deep into the Japanese flanks and rear in a series of movements from Australia to New Guinea and the Solomon Islands, culminating in the invasion and liberation of Luzon. One historian described MacArthur's eighty-seven amphibious landings that cut off Japanese escape routes and lines of communication as "ingenious and dazzling thrusts which never stopped until Japan was beaten down."[31]

As was the case with his career between the wars, however, MacArthur's brilliance in the Pacific was accompanied by his arrogance, pettiness, and dishonesty. During the New Guinea campaign, MacArthur never visited the front, but permitted press reports from his headquarters declaring that he was leading troops in battle. He routinely issued communiques exaggerating Japanese losses, denigrating the Navy's contributions, and totally ignoring his subordinate commanders fighting at the front. After Maj. Gen. Robert Eichelberger's skillful rescue of the stalled Papuan campaign at Buna in 1942, *Life* and the *Saturday Evening Post* ran stories about the corps commander. Jealous of his subordinate's publicity, MacArthur summoned him and said: "Do you realize I could reduce you to the grade of Colonel tomorrow and send you home?"[32] Thereafter he exiled Eichelberger to Australia, restricted him to training American units for other commanders to lead, and blocked his transfer to the European theater until finally giving Eichelberger command of Eighth Army in late 1944 for the invasion of the Philippines. Back in action, Eichelberger delivered what Stephen Taaffe describes as a "virtuoso performance in liberating the central and southern Philippines."[33]

Even as his victories piled up, MacArthur complained that "probably no commander in American history has been so poorly supported."[34] In reality, however, his strength relative to what the Japanese could bring to bear against him compared favorably to the force ratios with which Eisenhower would attempt to defeat Germany in Western Europe. In the end, MacArthur's

World War II service almost perfectly mirrored his career between the wars—
brilliant achievements in the service of his country and the Army mixed with
shocking egotism and arrogance.

While MacArthur was still organizing his command in May 1942, Marshall sent Eisenhower, Hap Arnold, and Mark Clark on an inspection trip to
England to check on early American preparations for Operation *Roundup*,
the proposed Allied invasion of France tentatively scheduled for the spring
of 1943. Eisenhower and his colleagues concluded the American commander
in London was out of touch and lacked sufficient drive. On June 8, at Marshall's request, Eisenhower presented a draft proposal to create a European
Theater of Operations (ETO) in London. Three days later, Marshall selected
Eisenhower over 355 senior officers to command all American forces in the
ETO.[35]

When *Roundup* was abandoned in favor of Operation *Torch* in North
Africa, French resentment toward the British stemming from the Royal Navy's
sinking of the French fleet at Mers-el-Kabir in July 1940 meant the commander had to be an American, even though the British contributed nearly
half the troops, almost all the naval strength, and possessed more combat
experience. Marshall's first choice for a North Africa command had not been
Eisenhower, but rather Joseph Stilwell. While commanding the 7th Infantry
Division in the May 1940 maneuvers, Stilwell had captured Jonathan Wainwright's 1st Cavalry Division's headquarters. His corps commander ranked
him first out of forty-seven major generals in the Army. In a subsequent
prewar GHQ survey of general officers, Joseph Stilwell was ranked first in
merit amongst the Army's nine corps commanders. On December 22, 1941,
Marshall summoned his old friend to Washington, where Stilwell learned
he had been chosen to command Plan Black, a proposed landing in French
West Africa to eliminate the Vichy French submarine base that threatened
South America. Two days later the Dakar operation was scratched, and Stilwell was put to work planning *Gymnast*—the precursor to *Torch*—expecting
that he would lead the invasion of North Africa.[36]

President Roosevelt, however, was growing increasingly nervous about
Japanese advances in China, fearing that if Chiang Kai-shek's government
surrendered all of Asia would fall. "If China goes under," he said to his son
Elliott, "how many divisions of Japanese troops do you think will be freed—to
do what?"[37] Marshall sought to help Chiang wage a more effective campaign

against the one million Japanese troops in China and Southeast Asia, and needed a high-ranking American officer to advise Chiang. He offered the position to Lt. Gen. Hugh Drum, who was reluctant to accept because *he* expected to command U.S. expeditionary forces in Europe. This hesitation disqualified Drum in Secretary Stimson's eyes, and given Stilwell's unparalleled expertise on China, there was nobody else remotely as qualified. On January 23, therefore, Marshall officially offered his friend the position.[38]

Stilwell wore multiple hats in China: commander of all U.S. forces in China, Burma, and India; Lend-Lease administrator; Roosevelt's personal military representative to Chiang; and, theoretically, Chiang's chief of staff. But soon after arriving in Chungking in mid-1942 Stilwell concluded that Chiang's government was "playing the USA for a sucker" by "looking for an Allied victory without making any further effort on its part to secure it," while expecting "to have piled up at the end of the war a supply of munitions" to be used in an eventual showdown with Mao Tse-tung's Communist forces.[39] Whereas the China post required enormous tact, diplomacy, and patience, it is an understatement to say these were not "Vinegar Joe"'s strengths. Stilwell cared more about defending China, perhaps, than the mercurial and corrupt Chiang. He quickly developed a personal contempt that he scarcely bothered to conceal, and took to calling Chiang, a compact man with a clean-shaven head, "the Peanut."[40] Stimson called Stilwell's "the most difficult task assigned to any American in the entire war."[41] Marshall recognized the impossible position he had put his friend into, and continually sent him messages of appreciation. Although Stilwell led American and Chinese forces in a successful campaign to reopen the Burma Road to China in the summer of 1944, Chiang successfully engineered his recall. In the end, the Army's best prewar commander was destined never to command an American army in battle because of the unique expertise he gained in the interwar years.

Command of the North Africa invasion therefore fell to Eisenhower. Yet in his first combat experience, Eisenhower was uncharacteristically hesitant and defensive in his tactics. Lucian Truscott, who led the 3rd Division's assault on Port Lyautey in Morocco, described the *Torch* landing as "a hit and miss affair that would have spelled disaster against a well-armed enemy intent on resistance."[42] Eisenhower himself wrote about the subsequent failed advance on Tunisia to his successor at the War Plans Division: "I think the best way to describe our operations to date is that they have violated every recognized principle of war, are in conflict with all operational and logistic methods laid down in textbooks, and will be condemned, in their entirety, by all Leavenworth and War College classes for the next twenty-five years."[43] Eisenhower's interwar experience as a staff officer led him to concentrate too much on administrative matters and politics, and to try to do too much himself. Rather than a bold advance, such as he helped design during the Louisiana maneuvers, he insisted on an orderly march. Although Eisenhower was not in tactical command of U.S. troops in their first real battle against Axis forces at Kasserine Pass, Stephen Ambrose notes, "his performance was miserable," and only Rommel's logistical difficulties saved the Allies from a humiliating defeat.[44] Although Allied forces eventually prevailed in Tunisia, capturing 275,000 Axis troops with their surrender on May 13, 1943, Omar Bradley later wrote that only the need to maintain an American face on the campaign saved Eisenhower's job. "Ike led an extraordinarily charmed life.... I felt certain that after Kasserine Pass he would have been fired."[45] Indeed, even Eisenhower wrote to his son John in February 1943 to warn, "It is possible that a necessity might arise for my relief and consequent demotion."[46]

Bradley's critique is fair, but somewhat overstated. Although Eisenhower's battlefield management in North Africa left much to be desired, he was commanding green troops armed with inferior weapons, led by an incompetent corps commander—Lloyd Fredendall—against what Rick Atkinson argues were "perhaps the most experienced desert fighters on earth."[47] The key question was whether Eisenhower could learn from his mistakes. As he wrote to a friend, "We are learning something every day, and in general do not make the same mistake twice."[48] Most importantly, unlike his more parochial subordinates, Eisenhower recognized that maintaining the Anglo-American alliance was vital to strategic success. A key to victory in the North Africa campaign was Eisenhower's ability to persuade the often fractious British and American generals to work together.

Retaining Eisenhower in command had important second-order effects throughout the war, perhaps affecting few officers as much as George Patton. In June 1942, when the British fortress at Tobruk fell to Rommel's *Afrikakorps*, Eisenhower recommended to Marshall that Patton—who at the time was commanding the Army's Desert Training Center—lead a one-division expeditionary force to support the British. Although this force was never deployed, Patton would lead Operation *Torch*'s amphibious assaults in Morocco. Before deploying, Patton visited General Pershing at his quarters in Walter Reed Hospital and kneeled by his bedside to receive his blessing.

The landings in Morocco were successful, and Patton was slated to get his third star and preparing to lead an army in the invasion of Sicily when he was instructed to take command of II Corps in March 1943 after the Kasserine Pass disaster. Patton rehabilitated the Corps' four divisions and infused a fighting spirit among them. He led them to a victory at El Guettar that was minor in operational terms, but significant in terms of improving American morale by showing they *could* defeat the *Wehrmacht* in battle, before ceding command of II Corps to Bradley for the final victory in Tunisia.[49]

Patton subsequently commanded the Seventh Army in the Sicilian campaign. Patton's forces sent the German and Italian opposition reeling across Sicily past Palermo. Yet although Patton had proved a master of pursuit, he was not as successful at fighting the excruciating set-piece battle he faced when his army turned east for the drive to Messina, during which one in eight of his inexperienced troops became a casualty. Worse, Sicily represented a missed opportunity, as nearly 250,000 German and Italian troops escaped to the Italian mainland. This strategic error was not Patton's responsibility, however, and following the capture of Messina in August 1943, Eisenhower wrote to Marshall that Patton "has conducted a campaign where the brilliant successes scored must be attributed directly to his energy, determination and unflagging aggressiveness. The operations of the Seventh Army are going to be classed as a model of swift conquest by future classes in the War College."[50]

Eisenhower also warned Marshall that "Patton continues to exhibit some of those unfortunate personal traits of which you and I have always known and which during this campaign caused me some uncomfortable days."[51] This was a reference to the two incidents on August 3 and 10 in which Patton verbally abused and physically struck soldiers recovering from battle fatigue in field hospitals. Although the slapping incidents warranted a formal investigation and charges of conduct unbecoming an officer, Eisenhower swept them under the rug. "If this thing ever gets out," he wrote, "they'll be howling for Patton's scalp, and that will be the end of Patton's services in this war. I simply cannot let that happen. Patton is indispensable to the war effort—one of the guarantors of our victory."[52] Eisenhower asked newspaper correspondents to withhold publication of the incidents lest they result in violent condemnation of Patton that might necessitate his friend's firing. Demaree Bess, of the *Saturday Evening Post*, speaking for the pool of forty-plus reporters, emphasized that they were Americans first and journalists second, and none of them filed a story on the incidents. On November 22, however, Drew Pearson broke the story on his syndicated radio show. Congressmen demanded Patton's recall and court-martial. Patton, frightened by his action's ramifications, wrote Eisenhower an apology. "I am at a loss to find words with which to express my chagrin and grief at having given you, a man to whom I owe everything, and for whom I would gladly lay down my life, cause to be displeased with me."[53] Eisenhower, strongly supported by Marshall and Stimson, waited out the protests and kept Patton in Europe.

Mark Clark similarly benefited from Eisenhower's rise and his survival after North Africa. Upon appointing him to command the ETO, Marshall allowed Eisenhower to select his immediate subordinates and staff. Eisenhower named two men, the first being Walter Bedell Smith, then secretary of the General Staff. "Beetle" would serve as Eisenhower's chief of staff for the war's duration, handling all administrative duties. Although he was known to some as "Eisenhower's son-of-a-bitch," the supreme commander told a friend, "I wish I had a dozen like him. If I did, I would simply buy a fishing-rod and write home every week about my wonderful accomplishments in winning the war."[54] The second officer Eisenhower requested was Clark, whom he described as "the best organizer, planner, and trainer of troops I have yet met."[55] Clark initially served as Eisenhower's deputy in North Africa before being given command of Fifth Army—the headquarters planning the future invasion of Italy—in January 1943. When Eisenhower asked Clark to take over II Corps from the hapless Fredendall after Kasserine Pass, however, Clark refused his friend's request. He perceived the move from commanding an army in the rear to a corps in active combat as a demotion rather than as his duty.

Worse, Clark's plan for Fifth Army's invasion of Italy nearly proved disastrous. His amphibious assault at Salerno consisted of three divisions—one American, the other two British—with a follow-up force of two more divisions. Yet Clark diluted its impact by attacking across a 36-mile front, with his beachhead split by the fast-flowing Sele River. He ignored the Pacific War's lessons about amphibious operations and chose to forego preparatory bombardment in the hope of achieving tactical surprise. When the Germans counterattacked on September 12, 1943, they seemed about to drive the Allies into the sea. Clark wavered, and informed Eisenhower that he was making plans to evacuate his headquarters back to the ships, ostensibly to control both sectors and continue the battle in whichever one offered the greater chance for success.[56]

The commander of the American 45th "Thunderbird" Division was appalled by the thought of withdrawal from Salerno and Clark's inconstancy. Troy Middleton had volunteered to return to active duty in July 1940. Although Marshall described him as "the outstanding infantry regimental commander on the battlefield in France," the chief of staff turned down his offer for the time being.[57] When Middleton volunteered again after Pearl Harbor, he was activated on January 23, 1942, as a lieutenant colonel until McNair gave him command of the 45th Infantry Division. At Salerno, Middleton confronted Clark: "Put food and ammunition behind the 45th," he shouted as shells screamed overhead. "We're staying."[58] By nightfall the situation was stabilized thanks to the warships off shore, who rained naval gunfire on the onrushing panzers.

Clark relieved his corps commander at Salerno, Maj. Gen. Ernest Dawley, but the amphibious assault was a harbinger of the Italian campaign's travails. In January 1944, Clark ordered a frontal assault across the Gari River that resulted in the destruction of two regiments of the 36th Infantry Division without any corresponding tactical gains.* Similarly, his attempt to flank the German defensive lines through an amphibious landing at Anzio quickly became bogged down and the Allied beachhead threatened. Clark once again scapegoated the corps commander, this time Maj. Gen. John Lucas. The operation was only salvaged by his replacement Truscott's inspired leadership.

In fairness, the Italian campaign was fought on unfavorable terrain in abominable weather against more experienced German troops led by a general—Albert Kesserling—who was a master of the tactical defense. Yet even when conditions were favorable, Clark underperformed. Once the stalemate at the Gustav Line was broken and Fifth Army forces were again moving north, rather than closing the noose around Kesselring's retreating forces Clark directed his corps at Anzio strike north for Rome. The Italian capital—which was politically prestigious but strategically irrelevant—fell on June 5, 1944. The next day Allied forces stormed the beaches at Normandy. Clark shook his head. "The sons-a-bitches," he said. "They didn't even let us have the newspaper headlines for the fall of Rome for one day."[59]

Despite his stellar prewar reputation as a planner and trainer, Clark's command was noteworthy more for his unhealthy craving of attention and fame than any strategic acumen. Clark made sure he was constantly followed by a photographer whom he instructed to capture his "facially best" left side.

---

* The action is more commonly known as the battle of Rapido River.

Eric Sevareid, a war correspondent in Italy, described Clark as vainglorious, self-seeking, and riven by vanity and pride, "the victim of the natural pressures of his position and fame."[60] One staff officer considered Clark "a goddamned study in arrogance," while another saw "conceit wrapped around him like a halo."[61] Lyman Lemnitzer, the deputy commander of 15th Army Group overseeing Fifth Army, thought Clark should be relieved. Fortunately for Clark, the outstanding reputation he had earned working with Eisenhower and Marshall in the interwar years enabled him—for better or worse—to survive the Italian campaign's repeated disasters.

Clark also likely benefited from the fact that the Italian campaign was generally considered peripheral to the war's main effort. Everybody's focus was on the opening of the Western Front against Germany, in particular the question of who would be Operation *Overlord*'s supreme commander. The position was originally supposed to go to British field marshal Alan Brooke. This decision was changed, however, when it became obvious the United States would contribute the preponderance of the invasion's materiel and manpower. The consensus was that President Roosevelt would appoint Marshall to lead *Overlord* and that Eisenhower would be recalled to act as chief of staff. Marshall had emerged as the first among equals in both the Joint Chiefs of Staff and the Allied Combined Chiefs of Staff. Churchill praised Marshall "as a rugged soldier and a magnificent organizer," and by 1943 made it a practice to have dinner with him at the outset of every Anglo-American conference.[62] In anticipation of her husband's new assignment, Katherine Marshall quietly began moving the family's belongings out of the chief of staff's quarters at Fort Myer to their Leesburg, Virginia, home.

When the news leaked that General Marshall was going to command the invasion, it created a furor in Washington. The ranking Republicans on the Senate Military Affairs Committee met confidentially with Secretary Stimson to express their concerns. Stimson recalled: "They told me how much they relied on him not only individually, but how they were able to carry controversial matters through with their colleagues if they could say that the measure in question had the approval of Marshall."[63] The president's military advisers also voiced strong reservations. Admirals Leahy and Ernest King, and General Arnold each privately approached Roosevelt to urge him to keep Marshall in Washington. Admiral King told the president: "We have the winning combination here in Washington, why break it up?"[64]

The most surprising opposition to Marshall's appointment, however, came from his mentor and friend, General Pershing. From his room at Walter Reed, Pershing wrote President Roosevelt urging that Marshall be retained as chief of staff. "I am so deeply disturbed by the repeated newspaper reports that General Marshall is to be transferred to a tactical command in England that I am writing to express my fervent hope that these reports are unfounded." Pershing argued that "to transfer him to a tactical command in a limited area, no matter how seemingly important, is to deprive ourselves of the benefit of his outstanding strategic ability and experience. I know of no one at all comparable to replace him as chief of staff."[65]

"You are absolutely right about George Marshall," Roosevelt replied, and yet "I think it is only a fair thing to give George a chance in the field. . . . I want George to be the Pershing of the Second World War—and he cannot be that if we keep him here."*

Roosevelt especially wanted to reward Marshall for all he had done to bring the Army, the nation, to this point. But the seed of doubt had been planted. Without Marshall, who could keep the abrasive and Anglophobic Admiral King cooperative, or deter MacArthur from insubordination in the Pacific? On December 4, Roosevelt sent Harry Hopkins to discuss the appointment with Marshall, hoping once again that the general would take the lead on a difficult decision. Marshall wanted the command of *Overlord*, a position his biographer Forrest Pogue noted would be "the climax to which all his career had been directed."[66] All Marshall had to do was say "yes" and the position was his. Yet as with his appointment to chief of staff four years earlier, Marshall believed the decision belonged to the commander-in-chief alone, and once again refused to lobby for it or even express a personal preference one way or another.

The next day President Roosevelt finally met with Marshall himself. Stopping in Cairo en route to the December 1943 Tehran Conference, he called Marshall to his villa, where they met alone. The president was uncharacteristically hesitant, raising a number of trivial issues before broaching the question:

---

* Roosevelt expressed a similar sentiment while discussing the appointment with Eisenhower: "Ike, you and I know who was the Chief of Staff during the last years of the Civil War but practically no one else knows, although the names of field generals—Grant, of course, and Lee, and Jackson, Sherman, Sheridan and the others—every schoolboy knows them. I hate to think that 50 years from now practically nobody will know who George Marshall was. That is one of the reasons I want George to have the big command—he is entitled to his place in history as a great General." Sherwood, *Roosevelt and Hopkins*, 770.

What post—supreme commander or chief of staff—would Marshall prefer? Marshall later recalled: "I made virtually the same reply I made to Hopkins. I recall saying I would not attempt to estimate my capabilities; the President would have to do that; I merely wished to make it clear that whatever the decision, I would go along with it . . . the issue was too great for any personal feelings to be considered."[67] Even with "the most coveted command in the history of warfare" at stake, Marshall still put duty above personal glory.[68]

Roosevelt made his decision.

He told Marshall, "I didn't feel I could sleep at ease if you were out of Washington."[69] He later explained that relieving Marshall as chief of staff would hurt congressional relations and the war effort as a whole because his replacement, no matter how capable, would lack Marshall's experience and depth. With Marshall eliminated from consideration, Eisenhower was the logical choice to lead *Overlord*. As Roosevelt dictated, Marshall wrote the historic cable that read: "From the President to Marshal Stalin. The immediate appointment of General Eisenhower to command of Overlord operation has been decided upon." Marshall remained stoic as the president signed the message, any private turmoil held tightly within himself.

Two days later, President Roosevelt stopped in Tunis on his way back to Washington. He was taken off his plane and placed in Eisenhower's car. As they began to drive, the president turned to Eisenhower and casually said, "Well, Ike, you are going to command Overlord."[70]

The story of Marshall's sacrifice comes with a tragic footnote. On May 31, 1944, six days before the Normandy invasion, Marshall arrived at his office at his usual early hour. Instead of the typical stack of cables and reports, on this day only a sealed, personal cable from General Clark lay upon his desk. Marshall opened the envelope and read Clark's news that 1st Lt. Allen Brown—who as a twelve-year-old boy had blessed Marshall's courtship of his mother with the words "a friend in need is a friend indeed"—had been killed in action in the Alban Hills south of Rome.

Marshall excused himself to his staff. He silently drove to Quarter Number 1 at Fort Myer to tell Katherine of her youngest son's death. Behind the closed doors of his wife's bedroom, he attempted to comfort Katherine. Marshall was stricken as well. With no children of his own, he had virtually adopted Allen as his own, and his aide Frank McCarthy remembered, "Allen was the apple of his eye."[71]

One can only speculate whether or how this tragedy might have affected preparations for D-Day had Marshall seized the opportunity to become supreme commander. In all probability Marshall would have mourned quietly while the vast machinery of the Allied invasion he had set in motion proceeded apace. In the real world, however, the Marshalls mourned in private, just one of hundreds of thousands of grieving American families whose sons made the ultimate sacrifice for their country.

Once appointed as supreme commander, Eisenhower began assembling his team. He needed more than fifty corps and division commanders, and insisted on selecting the American generals himself. His first choice, selecting an army group commander, was easy. When suggesting possible senior commanders for the cross-Channel attack to Marshall in August 1943, Eisenhower wrote that Omar Bradley "has brains, a fine capacity for leadership and a thorough understanding of the requirements of modern battle. He has never caused me one moment of worry."[72] Since becoming chief of staff, Marshall had systematically moved Bradley from one important post to another—commandant of the Infantry School, commanding general of the 82nd Airborne—to prepare him for the grand responsibilities he envisioned for him. Bradley ran II Corps much less flamboyantly than Patton, and had acquired a reputation as "the GI's general" thanks to the worshipful dispatches of war correspondent Ernest Pyle. Despite Patton's notoriety, it was Bradley who actually led II Corps to victory and emerged from the North African campaign with the best reputation within the U.S. Army. In June 1943, Eisenhower described Bradley as "about the best rounded, well-balanced senior officer that we have in the service. His judgements are always sound. . . . I feel there is no position in the Army that he could not fill with success."[73]

Eisenhower insisted on Gerow as one of his two corps commanders in *Overlord*. The other was Maj. Gen. J. Lawton Collins, who had performed superbly in the Pacific while gaining expertise on amphibious operations. During the Guadalcanal campaign he received the nickname "Lightning Joe" for his aggressiveness and dash. Eisenhower and Bradley agreed that Courtney Hodges would lead First Army when a beachhead was firmly established and Bradley ascended to the 12th Army Group command. For the first follow-on corps, Eisenhower picked another old friend, Troy Middleton, whose performances at Sicily, Salerno, and southern Italy had impressed him. Clark had reluctantly relieved Middleton from command of the 45th

Division because Middleton was exhausted and dispirited from an arthritic knee that kept him in constant pain. Although Marshall believed Middleton was head and shoulders above all other stateside corps commanders, he stressed the seriousness of a corps commander being able to physically fulfill his duties. Eisenhower responded: "I'd rather have Troy Middleton on crutches than most of these people."[74] Just to be safe, Marshall assigned a sergeant to Middleton who had been a physical therapist before the war, with orders to massage the general's knee twice a day.

The general Eisenhower wanted most, however, was unavailable. Lucian Truscott had led the U.S. Army Rangers in the ill-fated Canadian raid on Dieppe, fought well at Casablanca during Operation *Torch*, and whipped the Third Division into the best-trained division in theater. Yet he had just been given command of the corps at Anzio, was desperately fighting the Germans in Italy, and could not be spared.

The most difficult personnel decision for Eisenhower was what to do with George Patton. Although dismayed by his personal conduct on Sicily, Eisenhower remained fond of his old friend. When Eisenhower solicited Middleton's opinion, Patton's former Leavenworth walking partner replied, "Hell, I would have him up here. He is a fighter and that's what you pay an officer to do, is fight.... Get him up here Ike."[75] Yet because of Patton's character flaws—and his disdain for the importance of logistics and allies— Eisenhower would not elevate him above his current rank of army commander. Instead he assigned Patton command of Bradley's second American army, the Third Army, the flanking force that would go ashore once Hodges's First Army had cleared a buffer to allow an attack against Brittany. Bradley had grown increasingly disenchanted with Patton's leadership style in North Africa and Sicily, but reluctantly accepted Eisenhower's decision. Years later he wrote, "Had Eisenhower asked for my opinion I would have counseled against the selection."[76]

Eisenhower did not announce that Patton was commanding Third Army, but rather the "First United States Army Group" (FUSAG), a fictitious force headquartered at Dover as part of the war's most ambitious deception plan, Operation *Quicksilver*. The Allies sought to convince the Germans that the Normandy landings were merely a feint intended to make them shift their panzers away from the Pas de Calais, where Patton would lead an army group ashore. Patton was the perfect choice for this notional command, as the *Wehrmacht*'s senior leadership viewed him as America's most dangerous commander. The deception proved remarkably effective, with at least twenty-two

German divisions remaining in the Pas de Calais at the end of June, fixed there by the threat of Patton's FUSAG.

Yet Patton's lack of personal discipline nearly preempted both *Quicksilver's* success and his long-awaited shot at martial glory. On April 25, he visited Knutsford, England's Welcome Club, and in his brief remarks to the charitable women who had established the morale center he off-handedly declared that the British and Americans would rule the world together after the war, only adding their Russian allies as an afterthought. Although the speech was innocuous, it played into the narrative of Patton as a loose cannon. The American press sensationalized the remarks and opened a new round of criticism in Congress. On April 30, Eisenhower summoned him for a meeting, while informing Marshall: "I have grown so weary of the trouble he constantly causes you and the War Department . . . that I am seriously contemplating the most drastic action."[77] The next day he added that "I will relieve him from command and send him home unless some new and unforeseen information should be developed in this case," although he pledged not to do so until he had heard back from the chief of staff.[78]

Eisenhower acknowledged that Patton's "exact remarks on this occasion were incorrectly reported and somewhat misinterpreted in the press."[79] Yet perhaps more than the trouble Patton created for Marshall in Congress, Eisenhower was tired of Patton's scathing critiques of his leadership as supreme commander. Just as he had disparaged Eisenhower's accomplishment in graduating first at CGSS behind his friend's back, Patton sneeringly referred to Eisenhower as "Divine Destiny" in letters home, and called him "the best general the British have got."[80] Despite Eisenhower's role in saving him after the slapping incidents, in his diary Patton described him as "a Popinjay—a stuffed doll," "too weak a character to be worthy of us," and repeatedly compared him—unfavorably—to Benedict Arnold.[81] Whereas Bradley privately held similar, albeit much milder, sentiments, he *never* expressed such thoughts aloud. Yet just as in Hawaii in the 1920s, Patton was incapable of discretion, and Eisenhower surely would have been aware of such remarks.

Patton reported to Eisenhower on May 1. As his old friend stood at attention before his desk, Eisenhower scolded him mercilessly. Tears streamed down Patton's face as he assured Eisenhower of his loyalty and appreciation. Then, Eisenhower recalled, "In a gesture of almost little-boy contriteness, he put his head on my shoulder." Patton's steel helmet fell off and noisily bounced across the floor, increasing the moment's awkwardness. Indeed, the whole scene struck Eisenhower as "ridiculous."[82] The next day a cable arrived from Marshall. "The decision is entirely yours," the chief of staff told Eisenhower. "Do not consider the War Department position in this matter. Consider only Overlord. . . . Everything else is of minor importance."[83] In the end, Eisenhower decided Marshall was right and retained Patton.

Eisenhower's personnel decisions would pay dividends in the months ahead. The successful D-Day landings became bogged down in Normandy's bocage country. Bradley launched Operation *Fortitude* on July 3, but this effort to advance across a broad front gained only 7 miles of territory at the cost of 40,000 battle casualties. The British-led Operation *Goodwood* was even less successful. Bradley went back to the drawing board to plan Operation *Cobra*, which aimed to break the stalemate by more narrowly concentrating the attacking forces. As one historian notes, "Bradley's genius burned brightest in the creation of a complex operation, and he poured his heart and soul into the details of this breakout."[84] Beginning on the morning of July 25, 2,500 warplanes pounded the German defenses, followed by massed fire from over 1,000 artillery pieces. Bradley chose Collins's VII Corps to lead the ground assault because he thought Collins was "nervy and ambitious."[85] Collins justified his former Infantry School faculty colleague's confidence by holding nothing back and committing his entire reserve on the battle's second day. The carpet bombing had disoriented the Germans' tactical reserve and prevented any counterattack to seal the breech in the German lines. By July 27, Collins had reached Coutances, while Middleton's VIII Corps operating on VII Corps' right seized Granville and Avranches. The Germans attempted to withdraw from the closing trap, but ran into VII Corps on the night of July 29-30. One American officer described the carnage from Collins's attack and the tactical air support on the retreating Germans as "the most Godless sight I have ever witnessed on any battlefield."[86]

The *Cobra* breakout came at an unexpected cost. During the initial bombardments, some planes dropped their munitions short of the German lines, with "friendly fire" killing or wounding over 600 soldiers. Among the dead was Lt. Gen. Lesley McNair. Denied a combat command because of his deafness, McNair perhaps overcompensated by venturing as close to the front line as possible while on inspection trips to review the product of GHQ's training program. He had already been wounded while observing the fighting in North Africa, and this time his body was thrown 80 feet from the slit trench he occupied and was only identifiable by the three stars found on the shoulder of the shredded corpse. McNair was the highest-ranking U.S. officer killed in action in World War II.

With the gap created in the German lines, the situation was perfect for a former cavalryman like Patton. The Third Army exploited the *Cobra* breakthrough, driving across central France and clawing his way through Lorraine. After the war, Bradley wrote: "George soon caused me to repent" on his previous reservations about Patton, who

> *trooped for 12th Army Group with unbound loyalty and eagerness. . . . Before many more months had passed, the* new *Patton had totally obliterated my unwarranted apprehensions; we formed as amiable and contented a team as existed in the senior command. No longer the cocky martinet who had strutted through Sicily, Patton had now become a judicious, reasonable and likeable commander.*[87]

Initially, the only friction to Patton's advance was the tyranny of logistics. The original *Overlord* plan had envisioned an offensive consolidation along the Seine about ninety days after June 6. Patton blew past this phase line in late August, and by September 14 the Allies had advanced to where the logisticians expected to reach only in May 1945, putting Third Army beyond the reach of the Allies' principal supply points in Normandy. Although Jacob Devers's Sixth Army Group's invasion of southern France—which liberated the vital ports of Toulon and Marseille—would eventually alleviate these logistical difficulties, for the time being there simply was not enough fuel to support Patton's pursuit without shutting down all other operations in northwest Europe and creating a dangerously exposed salient. Unable to simply write a personal check to fuel his tanks as he had in Louisiana, Patton—ever disdainful of logistics—fumed at what he believed were missed opportunities.[*]

Patton's pursuit and the rest of the Allied offensive stalled along the West Wall of fortifications protecting the German frontier. As winter set in, the Allies prepared for the decisive push into Germany in the new year. On

---

[*] One object of Patton's ire was his superior, Omar Bradley, who prevented Patton's troops from closing a 15-mile gap in the Allied lines at Falaise in order to encircle nineteen German divisions. Bradley felt 12th Army Group's lines would be overextended and hence too brittle to withstand a concentrated German attack, thereby negating the purpose of the proposed encirclement. "I much preferred a solid shoulder at Argentan," he wrote later, "to the possibility of a broken neck at Falaise." Bradley, *A Soldier's Story*, 304–5.

December 16, however, 250,000 German troops organized into twenty-five divisions counterattacked through the Ardennes Forest, which was lightly defended by 83,000 tired or green U.S. troops. The German assault caught the American high command completely by surprise, falling heaviest upon Middleton's VIII Corps. Although gloom and confusion pervaded his headquarters, Middleton remained calm and drew upon the intellect that had marked his career. He concentrated on the road hubs of St. Vith and Bastogne, and instead of retreating chose to make his stand there, committing his remaining reserves and arriving reinforcements to their defense. This bold decision would set the terms of the battle to come.[88]

Matthew Ridgway's XVIII Corps, fresh from refitting after the failed Operation *Market Garden* offensive in Holland, was directed to help seal the 20-mile gap between V Corps and VIII Corps, with the 101st Airborne occupying Bastogne. Ridgway had served in Marshall's War Department in the War Plans Division, constantly badgering Walter Bedell Smith for a transfer until the chief of staff finally assigned him to be Bradley's deputy commander in the 82nd Airborne. He rose to the legendary division's command and led it with distinction in Sicily, Italy, and Normandy, where he personally parachuted into action the night before D-Day. As one observer later remembered, "The force that emanated from [Ridgway] was awesome. It reminded me of Superman. You had the impression he could knock over a building with a single blow, or stare a hole through a wall, if he wanted to. It was a powerful *presence*."[89] He was promoted to the corps command for Market Garden, and his determination trickled down to his subordinates. When the commander of the Panzer Corps surrounding Bastogne demanded the 101st's surrender on December 22, the division's assistant commander Anthony McAuliffe—who as a major had debated major generals in front of Chief of Staff Marshall before the war—famously responded with a single word: "Nuts."

Middleton and McAuliffe's performance at the Battle of the Bulge stands in particular contrast to that of Courtney Hodges. During the northwest Europe campaign, Hodges's First Army fought the hardest battles, inflicted and sustained the highest casualties, and gained more ground than any other American field army. Yet Hodges was so demoralized by the German attack's scale and suddenness that he took to his bed. He remained inexplicably unavailable for two more days, and his chief of staff, Maj. Gen. William B. Kean assumed de facto command. Kean later claimed Hodges had been "barely conscious with viral pneumonia." Another aide, however, remembered seeing Hodges at his desk, semiconscious, with his head cradled in his arms.[90]

The Battle of the Bulge also brought out the best in Middleton's friends and superiors, Eisenhower and Patton. Prior to the German offensive, Bradley, Patton, and Field Marshal Bernard Montgomery had filled their diaries, letters, and conversations with criticism belittling Eisenhower. Many war correspondents saw him as an amiable, chairman-of-the-board type, a military manager and diplomat rather than a battlefield commander. Yet despite the shock and pain of the initial Allied losses, Eisenhower was the first to realize that Hitler had handed them a tremendous opportunity. During the December 19 commanders' conference at Verdun, he seized the mantle of leadership and declared: "The present situation is to be regarded as an opportunity for us and not a disaster. There will be only cheerful faces at this conference table."[91]

Eisenhower turned to Patton and directed him to lead a counterattack against the Germans' southern flank. "When can you start?" he asked.

"As soon as you're through with me," Patton replied.

Eisenhower repeated his question. "When can you attack?"

"The morning of December 21," Patton said confidently, "with three divisions."[92]

Some officers gasped in disbelief at the notion that Third Army could disengage on its front, move three divisions 100 miles over icy roads and difficult terrain, and be prepared to conduct offensive operations within forty-eight hours. Yet Patton had anticipated this situation and had already begun the necessary preparations. He assured them they only had to give the word to put the selected units in motion. "This time the Kraut has stuck his head in a meat grinder," Patton crowed. "And this time I've got hold of the handle."[93]

"Don't be fatuous, George!" replied Eisenhower. "If you try to go that early you won't have all three divisions ready and you'll go piecemeal. You will start on the twenty-second and I want your initial blow to be a strong one."[94]

Patton's 4th Armored and 26th and 80th Infantry Divisions made a 90-degree left turn and attacked to the north. The counterattack was 35 miles broad and caught the Germans unaware along their salient's southern edge.[95] Few American generals would have had the audacity to have conceived Third Army's redeployment, much less the skill Patton demonstrated in executing it.

Patton's maneuver was not the only reason the *Wehrmacht's* thrust was defeated. Ignoring Montgomery's order to withdraw 30 miles, Collins's VII Corps launched an equally decisive attack from the salient's northern flank. Meanwhile, on December 26 Ernest Harmon threw his 2nd Armored Division straight at the oncoming Germans. Within twenty hours, the 2nd Panzer lost half its tanks and most of its self-propelled artillery. Finally, the weather cleared allowing Allied airpower to be brought to bear. In the end, the Bulge gave Eisenhower the battle he sought. In one month the equivalent of twenty full-strength German divisions was destroyed. More than 700 armored vehicles had been lost in the Ardennes, and German personnel losses ranged somewhere between 45,000 and 98,000.[96] In the House of Commons, Winston Churchill stated that the Bulge "is undoubtedly the greatest American battle of the war and will, I believe, be regarded as an ever famous American victory."[97]

There was still a great deal of hard fighting after the Battle of the Bulge: including the elimination of the Colmar Pocket in Alsace; Operations *Veritable* and *Grenade* over the flooded Roer; the crossing of the Rhine River (Operations *Varsity* and *Plunder*) in March 1945; and the final encirclement of the Ruhr in April. Yet after the Bulge, the war's outcome was no longer in doubt. Amongst other consequences, the diversion of supplies, armor, and reserves to the Western offensive left the *Wehrmacht* helpless to stave off the Red Army's advances in the east. When the Germans finally surrendered on May 7, 1945, Eisenhower foreswore any grandiloquent victory statement, and simply cabled the Combined Chiefs of Staff: "The mission of this Allied force was fulfilled at 0241, local time, May 7th, 1945." Normally sparse with his praise for even his most gifted subordinates, Marshall wrote to Eisenhower:

> *You have completed your mission with the greatest victory in the history of warfare. You have commanded with outstanding success the most powerful military force that has ever been assembled. . . . You have made history for the good of all mankind, and you have stood for all we hope for and admire in an officer of the United States Army. These are my tributes and my personal thanks.*[98]

For his part, Eisenhower reserved his greatest praise for his superior, writing to Marshall: "Our Army and people have never been so indebted to any soldier."[99] Similarly, Bradley wrote: "In the army we often scoff at the myth of the indispensable man. . . . General Marshall, however, was an exception, for if ever a man was indispensable in a time of national crisis, he was that man."[100]

The essence of Marshall and Eisenhower's key contributions to the Allied victory were perhaps best summarized by their British partners. In his memoirs, Montgomery wrote, "I would not class Ike as a great soldier in the true sense of the word," yet readily conceded that Eisenhower "was a great Supreme Commander.... I know of no other person who could have welded the Allied forces into such a fine fighting machine in the way he did, and keep the balance among the many conflicting and disturbing elements which threatened at times to wreck the ship."[101] Meanwhile, Churchill effused to Marshall: "It has not fallen to your lot to command the great armies. You have had to create them, organize them, and inspire them. Under your guiding hand the mighty and valiant formations which have swept across France and Germany were brought into being and perfected in an amazing space of time...."[102]

In the end, both Marshall and Eisenhower's key leadership contributions to the war stemmed directly from their unique experiences in the interwar years, especially their early service under General Pershing and Fox Conner. Marshall's work on the boards evaluating the AEF's lessons learned taught him the dangers of divided command; his service as recorder to the board investigating the Army's promotion system familiarized him with the career backgrounds of many men who would later lead America's armies, corps, and divisions in Europe and the Pacific. Pershing's nationwide inspection tour of Army camps and war plants in the winter of 1919–1920 gave Marshall unparalleled understanding of logistical issues that proved critical to the America's prewar mobilization; and his experiences preparing Pershing for numerous congressional hearings and his briefing of senior policymakers exposed him to Washington's inner workings and enabled him to reassure a skeptical Congress in the final, critical years before the war. Similarly, if Eisenhower was indispensable because he was the only officer with the amicability, patience, and diplomatic skills to manage the fractious Allied command, his success derived in large measure from those mentoring sessions in Panama two decades earlier when Fox Conner imparted the importance of coalition warfare to the young major. Serving in the Philippines under MacArthur, he learned how to deal with difficult personalities and a foreign head of state and government while organizing an army from scratch, an experience that prepared him well for dealing with our British allies. As Atkinson notes, Eisenhower was not a great battlefield commander, but his ability to compromise and coordinate "was precisely what this war—this total, global war—required."[103]

This conclusion holds true for the majority of the Army's senior commanders in World War II. The Pacific War course was largely shaped first by MacArthur's hubristic belief that he could defend the Philippines, and then by his Southwest Pacific campaign, which echoed both the brilliance of his plans to reform West Point and the dishonesty and pettiness of his toxic leadership in Manila in the 1930s. Patton's aggressive campaigns in Sicily and France echoed his early concepts for armored warfare expressed at Camp Meade and his belief that dramatic leadership would inspire men to fight and kill in battle. At the same time, his outspokenness and tendency toward emotional extremes—which had gotten him into trouble at Meade and in Hawaii, and cast him under the pall of depression for several years—resurfaced in the slapping incidents and his indiscreet critiques of Eisenhower that nearly ended his service before he could achieve the martial glory he had pursued his entire life. Omar Bradley conducted his campaigns with the careful precision of the former mathematics professor he was, and other "Marshall Men" such as J. Lawton Collins and Matthew Ridgway embodied the aggressive, improvisational spirit of the "Benning Renaissance." To the extent that other commanders such as Clark and Hodges failed to live up to their lofty prewar reputations, their failures stemmed from failures of temperament that were undetectable in the tranquility of the interwar years.

Returning to the question of whether men are born great or achieve greatness, the Army's experience in the interwar years and World War II suggests that the influence of the institutional and operational domains on leadership development was limited. Neither the pre–World War I U.S. Military Academy—which produced 70 percent of the Army's World War II army and corps commanders—nor the Army's interwar professional military education institutions appear to have been a significant positive or negative variable in terms of leadership development. Although they did not encourage creativity in officers, neither did they inhibit ingenuity to the degree their critics suggest. Moreover, the Army's promotions system during this period—which forced talented junior officers to languish at lower ranks—was the antithesis of leadership development, and was quickly discarded by Marshall upon becoming chief of staff.

Similarly, the correlation between variables in the operational domain and successful leadership development in the interwar Army appears weak at best. The major Army organizations in the continental United States had been skeletonized due to fiscal constraints in the 1920s and 1930s, with the supposedly fully operational commands in the Colonial Army not much better off. This made large-scale training exercises impractical, and denied young officers the experience of maneuvering large formations, and the Army in general the chance to experiment with doctrine and tactics. Conversely, overseeing the Civilian Conservation Corps camps gave officers such as Marshall, McNair, Bradley, Krueger, Charles Corlett, James Van Fleet, Ernest Harmon, and nearly 3,000 other Regular Army officers experience mobilizing large bodies of men and working with the civilians who would comprise America's World War II force. Although this experience provided an opportunity for leadership development, it was the accidental byproduct of a mission that the Army's senior leadership did not want in the first place.

In the end, variables that today would be classified as falling within the "self-development domain" appear to have been the most significant for America's World War II generals. The importance of having mentors to oversee their development appears to have been critical. Beyond Conner's mentorship of Eisenhower and Pershing's support for Marshall during the interwar years, Marshall himself played a significant role in developing the officers on the Infantry School's faculty, including Bradley, Collins, "Beetle" Smith, Ridgway, and Gilbert Cook. Equally important in cultivating talented subordinates was a commander's ability to appreciate and productively channel dissent. Marshall was fortunate to serve under such leadership not only under Pershing, but twenty years later when he dared to openly disagree with President Roosevelt's pronouncements on mobilization in the November 1938 Oval Office meeting. Marshall not only tolerated respectful dissent, but as assistant commandant of the Infantry School and as chief of staff actively encouraged his subordinates to challenge his viewpoints. This forbearance had effects when these future generals went to war. As Ridgway recalls, "I shall go to my grave humbly proud of the fact that on at least four occasions I have stood up at the risk of my career and denounced what I considered to be ill-considered tactical schemes which I was convinced would result in useless slaughter."[104]

Even those generals who did not identify a single senior officer as their mentor consistently strove to develop themselves as leaders on their own time. In his final *Annual Report* as chief of staff, MacArthur concluded:

> *More than most professions the military is forced to depend upon intelligent interpretation of the past of signposts charting the future. Devoid of opportunity in peace, for self-instruction through actual practice of his profession, the soldier makes maximum use of historical record in assuring*

the readiness of himself and his command to function efficiently in emer-
gency. The facts derived from historical analysis he applies to conditions
of the present and the proximate future, thus developing a synthesis of
appropriate method, organization, and doctrine.[105]

Consequently, historian Jorg Muth observes of the Army's WWII commanders: "From their book order lists, book inventories, discussion of various books in their correspondence, and existing former officers' libraries, a
direct connection between outstanding officership and avid readership can
be drawn."[106] Collins stated that one prepares for war "by reading military
history," while Ridgway said, "My advice to any young officer is Read-Read-
Read.... Learn from the successes of the great ones and their failures....
Then take these experiences and apply them to yourself."[107] Patton similarly
declared, "The officer must be so soaked in military lore that he does the military thing automatically," and that this "study must continue after entry into
the service and last until the day of retirement."[108] Finally, Marshall placed
such a great emphasis on reading that he gave the Infantry School's librarian
$10,000-per-year—at a time when funds were scarce—for the purchase of
books in order to build up the military library.[109]

Finally, almost all of the key American generals suffered some sort of personal tragedy during the two decades between the world wars. Some suffered
the sudden death of a spouse (Marshall, Gerow, and Corlett) or a child (Eisenhower and Bradley) or endured failed marriages (MacArthur and Ridgway,
twice); some saw their careers seemingly derailed by sudden reliefs of command (MacArthur), negative evaluations (Patton), potential court-martial
(Eisenhower), or stagnation due to personal spite (Marshall ... at the hands
of MacArthur); and some suffered from depression and other symptoms that
today would likely be classified as PTSD/TBI (Patton). This type of personal
resiliency is not something that can be taught in schools or trained into potential leaders, but rather derives from an internal strength and indomitable spirit.

In a sense, the lives of these and other future generals are illustrative
of their nation's travails during these years. For just as each officer demonstrated a resiliency to endure through professional and personal setbacks, all
across the country Americans found a way to persevere through the misery
of the Depression years. Like Marshall, Eisenhower, MacArthur, Patton, and
numerous other officers, the American people had the fortitude to endure
the tragedy of the interwar years and emerge with the strength necessary to
triumph over one of the greatest evils ever to threaten civilization.

EPILOGUE

THE LEADERSHIP TRAITS DEVELOPED IN THE INTERWAR YEARS SHAPED THE
Army—and America—for another two decades after World War II. A succession of "Marshall Men" followed their mentor as Army chief of staff:
Eisenhower, Bradley, Collins, Ridgway, and Maxwell Taylor. It was not until
1959, when Lyman Lemnitzer—who served on Eisenhower's staff in London
in the ETO's early days—was sworn in that the Army was led by an officer
who did not serve directly under George Marshall. Eisenhower would serve
as president of the United States from 1953 until 1961, and Taylor served as
Chairman of the Joint Chiefs of Staff (JCS) from 1962 to 1964, and then as
Lyndon Johnson's ambassador to South Vietnam during the critical year of
July 1964–July 1965.

While some officers prospered in the postwar era, others were doomed
by the war's end for reasons that were entirely predictable based on their
experiences in the interwar era. Soon "I will be out of a job," George Patton
wrote to Beatrice, warning that peacetime "is going to be hell on me. I will
probably be a great nuisance."[1] His words turned out to be prophetic, only
the headaches he caused were for Eisenhower, not his wife. During the early
occupation of Germany, Patton was made military governor of Bavaria, a post
for which Marshall and Eisenhower *should* have known he was temperamentally unsuited. On August 11, 1945, Patton wrote Eisenhower to complain
that "a great many inexperienced or inefficient people" were holding positions
in local government as a result of de-Nazification.[2] He publicly condemned
the policy and hired former Nazis to restore the railroads and public works.
He became almost delusional in his rantings against Jews and Communists,
and at one point his frustration over dealing with traumatized Holocaust
survivors led him to declare he was "thinking of building" his own concentration camps "for some of these goddamn Jews."[3] Eisenhower told him, "Shut
up, George," but then ordered him to hold a press conference to squelch
reports that he was anti-Semitic. Patton complied, and began by stating "I
despise and abhor Nazis and Hitlerism as much as anyone." He quickly went
off-message, however, and announced, "The way I see it, this Nazi thing is
very much like a Democratic and Republican election fight."[4]

357

Patton was summoned to Frankfurt, where on September 28 Eisenhower relieved him of command and reassigned him to take over the Fifteenth Army, the headquarters in charge of rounding up documents for the Army's official history of the war. On December 9, Patton was critically injured in a car accident outside Mannheim. Paralyzed from the neck down, he held on for nearly two weeks before succumbing to an embolism on December 21.

In the end, Major General Smith's assessment of Patton seventeen years earlier in Hawaii had proven correct: he was an invaluable combat leader when the nation needed him, but he was a disturbing element in the peace that followed.

Another officer whose postwar career closely echoed the highs and lows of the interwar years was Douglas MacArthur. On August 15, 1945, MacArthur was named supreme commander for the Allied Powers, and for the next six years his performance in this position resembled a sine wave alternating between his brilliance and his hubris. MacArthur's decision not to try Emperor Hirohito for war crimes helped maintain the Japanese people's dignity in defeat, and his aloofness and self-aggrandizement provided an imperious substitute for the emperor and helped ensure the occupation of Japan's success. Yet at the same time, as had been the case in the Philippines a decade prior, MacArthur completely disregarded his responsibility for training and maintaining standards amongst the large number of ground troops under his command. His neglect contributed significantly to the military disasters that followed the North Korean People's Army (NKPA) invasion of South Korea in June 1950.

MacArthur rebounded from this debacle with what Adm. Bull Halsey called "the most masterly and audacious strategic course in all history."[5] The Inchon landing on September 15 cut off the NKPA, relieved the U.S. troops besieged in Pusan, and within a few weeks routed the NKPA's remnants back across the 38th Parallel. Yet MacArthur's hubris once again took hold, and he ordered his commanders "to drive forward with all speed and . . . use any and all ground forces . . . to secure all of North Korea."[6] Refusing to believe that the Chinese would dare to intervene, MacArthur assured President Harry Truman and correspondents that American troops could begin returning home by Christmas.

When the Chinese launched a massive counterattack in November that threw the American and UN forces into a headlong retreat back below Seoul,

MacArthur once again refused to accept responsibility for his mistakes. He told reporters that all his problems dealing with the Chinese were due to the restrictions placed on him by Washington, which were "an enormous handicap without precedent in military history."[7] Although he claimed that the choice in Korea was between evacuation and escalation—to include the use of nuclear weapons—in December Matthew Ridgway assumed command of all UN ground forces* and launched a series of attacks that recaptured Seoul and drove the Chinese back to the 38th Parallel. This exposed the falsity of MacArthur's strategic assessment and suggested he was not indispensable. MacArthur responded by attempting to take credit for Ridgway's offensive.

As with the loss of the Philippines, MacArthur conflated his personal honor with U.S. strategic interests, and sought to redeem himself for the fiasco south of the Yalu River through another large-scale offensive. President Truman, however, wanted to exploit the recent battlefield gains to announce a peace initiative. MacArthur intentionally torpedoed negotiations by issuing his own ultimatum to Peking threatening its annihilation. Despite a blanket gag order on all military commanders and senior civil servants, MacArthur gave interviews to conservative publications in which he attacked the restrictions under which he had to operate. Finally, he attempted to repeat the tactic he had employed as chief of staff during the Army's budget battles two decades earlier. On April 5, House Minority Leader Joseph Martin publicly read a letter in which MacArthur criticized American foreign policy's Eurocentrism and called for escalating the war into China itself. "There is no substitute for victory," MacArthur declared. "If we are not in Korea to win then this Truman administration should be indicted for the murder of thousands of boys."[8] With a stroke of the pen, MacArthur was blatantly challenging the principle of the president's constitutional authority as commander-in-chief.

Truman was enraged. On the morning of April 6 he met with his advisers to solicit their views on MacArthur. The Joint Chiefs—including MacArthur's former West Point subordinates Bradley and Collins—voted unanimously for MacArthur's dismissal "because the military must be controlled by a civilian in this country."[9] Secretary of Defense George Marshall said that he reviewed "all those telegrams and communications . . . over the past two or three years" and had reluctantly "come to the conclusion that the general should have been relieved two or three years ago."[10] Consequently, on

---

* On December 23, Eighth Army commander Gen. Walton Walker, who had commanded a corps under Patton in World War II, was killed in a jeep accident.

April 10 President Truman fired MacArthur, relieving him of his commands in Korea, Japan, and of U.S. Army Forces in the Far East.

Half-a-million people lined the streets of San Francisco to greet MacArthur on his return to the United States, and the general was invited to address a joint session of Congress. For thirty-four minutes—including thirty interruptions for standing ovations—he delivered a virtuoso performance that held the senators, representatives, and a nationwide television and radio audience in thrall. With the romantic eloquence that had inspired so many subordinate officers, he concluded his remarks in a trembling voice:

> *I am closing my fifty-two years of military service. When I joined the Army even before the turn of the century, it was the fulfillment of all my boyish hopes and dreams. The world has turned over many times since I took the oath on the Plain at West Point, and the hopes and dreams have long since vanished. But I still remember the refrain of one of the most popular barrack ballads of that day which proclaimed most proudly that—"Old soldiers never die, they just fade away." And like the old soldier of that ballad, I now close my military career and just fade away— an old soldier who tried to do his duty as G-d gave him the light to see that duty. Goodbye.*[11]

Thirty-two years after his disappointing homecoming from France, New York City feted MacArthur with the largest ticker-tape parade in its history, the crowd numbering several million.

Of course, it was not in MacArthur's nature to simply "fade away." On May 3, two weeks after his address, Congress opened hearings on the Korean War. MacArthur was the first witness, and like Pershing three decades earlier, testified for three days. MacArthur reiterated his criticisms of the Truman Administration's foreign policy and its strategy in Korea, and claimed that all his recommendations on fighting the war had been accepted by the Joint Chiefs but were blocked by the White House and State Department. Even for MacArthur, this claim was remarkable in its brazenness, as he *had* to know there was an extensive documentary record to the contrary. MacArthur followed his Senate testimony by crossing the country giving talks and frequently heated political speeches—still wearing his full uniform and his many decorations—with an eye toward the 1952 presidential campaign.[12]

The Joint Chiefs followed MacArthur at the Korea hearings, their testimony directly contradicting him on numerous critical points. General Bradley,

Chairman of the Joint Chiefs of Staff, forcefully warned that MacArthur's policy would involve the United States "in the wrong war, at the wrong place, at the wrong time and with the wrong enemy."[13] The administration's star rebuttal witness, however, was George Marshall. The secretary of defense insisted that he and the Joint Chiefs did *not* support MacArthur's politico-military ideas, which risked all-out war in the Far East for uncertain gains, would alienate America's European allies and expose them to Soviet aggression, and subsequently leave the United States isolated. As he left the hearings, Senator Wayne Morse said to Richard Nixon, "I know which of those generals I trust."[14]

MacArthur's prestige was ultimately diminished by the hearings and his bitter publicity campaign. His presidential bomblet soon faded, and his keynote address at the 1952 Republican Convention was possibly the worst speech of his career, destroying his chances of becoming a dark horse candidate. C. L. Sulzberger wrote, "He said nothing but sheer baloney. One could feel the electricity gradually running out of the room. I think he cooked his own goose."[15]

After seeing another former general win the Republican nomination and the White House in 1952, MacArthur effectively retired from public life. In one final irony in a lifetime of paradoxes, he and Jean took up permanent residence in New York City's Waldorf-Astoria, the same hotel MacArthur had sworn he would never set foot in again back in 1919.

Dwight D. Eisenhower succeeded Marshall as chief of staff in November 1945, serving in that position until February 7, 1948, when he attended Bradley's swearing-in as his successor. He and Mamie moved to New York that June when Eisenhower became president of Columbia University. He attempted to bridge what is today sometimes called the "academic-policy gap," by having scholars mix with financiers, industrialists, and military officers at global seminars he convened. But then, as now, the professors were loath to come down from their ivory towers, and viewed Eisenhower's efforts as naïve.

When Germany surrendered, Field Marshal Alan Brooke told Eisenhower that if there were another war, "we would entrust our last man and our last shilling to your command."[16] When the North Atlantic Treaty Organization (NATO) was created to deter Soviet aggression in 1949, leaders on both sides of the Atlantic unanimously agreed that Eisenhower was the "only man" who could take command of the NATO forces. He held this position until he was drawn into Republican politics in order to block Senator Robert Taft's likely nomination, which threatened to return the party to its pre-war isolationism. Field Marshal Montgomery had observed that Eisenhower possessed "the power of drawing the hearts of men towards him as a magnet attracts the bits of metal. He merely has to smile at you, and you trust him at once."[17] The American people agreed with Monty, as Eisenhower won the nomination and easily defeated Governor Adlai Stevenson in the general election, 442–89 electoral votes.

Even before his inauguration, everybody underestimated President Eisenhower. In the Oval Office, Truman predicted to his staff: "He'll sit right here and he'll say do this, do that! And nothing will happen. Poor Ike—it won't be a bit like the Army. He'll find it very frustrating."[18] Conversely, the Republican Party's elders considered him a political neophyte to be manipulated. Both Democrats and Republicans saw what they wanted to see in Ike rather than taking stock of his actual experience. Eisenhower had spent six years from 1929 to 1935 serving under Generals Moseley and MacArthur in the War Department, plus two more years as chief of staff, and thus was better educated in Washington's ways than the establishment imagined. Although the media and the intelligentsia looked down upon him as an amicable, golf-playing mediocrity, Eisenhower perfected what has come to be called "the hidden-hand presidency." He provided his administration with firm policy direction, but allowed his subordinates to be the front men for these initiatives and thereby the "lightning rods" for criticism while he cast himself as an uncontroversial head of state.[19] The economy prospered during Eisenhower's two terms, while he deployed the 101st Airborne to support desegregation in Little Rock, Arkansas, and, based on his experience in the 1919 Trans-Continental Motor Convoy, built the interstate highway system that bears his name.

Unsurprisingly, Eisenhower took a hands-on approach to foreign and defense policy. His 1953 "Project Solarium" strategic-planning exercise is generally considered the model for intelligent national security policymaking process. Eisenhower ended the Korean War, avoided new military entanglements, and adroitly managed a series of foreign policy crises including Diem Bien Phu and Quemoy/Matsu in Asia; the Suez Crisis and Lebanon intervention in the Middle East; and various showdowns with the Soviet Union over Berlin and the shootdown of U-2 pilot Gary Powers. Throughout his two terms he provided steady, strategic leadership, while in the words of his biographer William I. Hitchcock, overseeing "the full mobilization of American society" to fight the Cold War.[20]

Overall, the Eisenhower presidency was viewed as a success at the time, and despite seeming lackluster compared to his more glamorous successor, has only grown in stature over the decades.

Arguably the biggest black mark on Eisenhower's postwar career, surprisingly, had to do with George Marshall. The "Organizer of Victory" had refused a million dollars for his war memoirs, and on November 27, 1945, after forty-three years and nine months in uniform, he went into a well-deserved retirement. That afternoon, however, he received a phone call from President Truman asking him to undertake a special diplomatic mission to help end China's civil war. As much as he looked forward to spending his days with his fishing rod or in his garden, his sense of duty was such that he could not refuse a request from his commander-in-chief. Marshall was a gifted negotiator, but the ideological differences and animosity between the Nationalists and Communists made any agreement impossible. As Barbara Tuchman concludes, "China was a problem for which there was no American solution."[21]

Although Marshall's mission ultimately failed, in January 1947 Truman appointed him secretary of state. On June 5, the secretary was scheduled to receive an honorary degree from Harvard—the other honorees included T. S. Eliot, J. Robert Oppenheimer, former senator James Wadsworth, and Omar Bradley—and deliver the commencement address. In a succinct 1,500-word speech that lasted only ten minutes, Marshall laid out the European Recovery Plan (ERP). With Europe still devastated from the war's destruction and threatened by Soviet subversion and aggression, Marshall proposed a massive economic aid program to rehabilitate the shattered continent. Much as Roosevelt had done with the Selective Service Act, President Truman recognized his secretary of state's prestige as the key to making the historic initiative palatable to a skeptical Congress, and began referring to the ERP as "the Marshall Plan." Although Marshall himself never called it that, the Marshall Plan eventually provided the ailing European economies with over $12 billion (almost $100 billion in today's dollars) in aid, succeeding beyond all expectations and earning its creator the 1953 Nobel Peace Prize, the first career military man ever to be so honored.

Marshall retired a second time when President Truman began his second term on January 20, 1949. He was once again unsuccessful at *staying* retired, however, for in September 1950, in the wake of the initial debacle of the

Korean War, Truman prevailed upon him to return to office once more as secretary of defense. Marshall agreed to accept the appointment, but on the condition that he would only serve for one year. As a career officer, Marshall was technically ineligible for the position under the 1947 National Security Act, but the House of Representatives quickly voted an exemption for him, 220–105.

Wisconsin senator Joseph McCarthy stirred up opposition to Marshall's appointment as secretary of defense, however, accusing Marshall's diplomatic mission of having "lost" China to Mao Tse-tung's Communists. Worse, under the guise of anti-Communism, McCarthy and other extremist senators shamelessly attacked Marshall's patriotism. McCarthy produced a 60,000-word account of Marshall's career that portrayed him as a Soviet agent, and someone who "would sell his own grandmother for any advantage."[22] In an unhinged diatribe on the Senate floor, William Jenner of Indiana condemned Marshall as "a front man for traitors" and declared "The truth is this is no new role for him, for General George C. Marshall is a living lie."[23]

At an impromptu press conference in Denver in August 1952, reporters confronted candidate Eisenhower about McCarthy's charges against Marshall. Eisenhower became angry and began to pace around the room. He called the general "one of the patriots of this country . . . the perfect example of patriotism and loyal servant of the United States." He flatly declared: "I have no patience with anyone who can find in his record of service for this country anything to criticize."[24] Four days later, Eisenhower was due to campaign in Milwaukee, with McCarthy scheduled to appear on the platform with him. Eisenhower asked his speechwriter to compose a tribute to Marshall for delivery "right in McCarthy's back yard." Republican Party leaders and Wisconsin's governor objected, and urged their nominee to say nothing. Before the event, in the privacy of a hotel suite, Eisenhower berated McCarthy for half an hour for his reckless accusations. One Eisenhower aide recalled that Ike "just took McCarthy apart. I never heard the General so cold-bloodedly skin a man."[25] Yet in public Eisenhower skipped the offending paragraphs and stood on the same stage as the senator. The media was astonished, interpreting Eisenhower's silence as an endorsement of McCarthy's views.

Although the episode haunted Eisenhower the rest of his life, the one public figure who never took umbrage to his appearance with McCarthy was Marshall himself, who dismissed the incident as part of the inherent nastiness of politics. "Eisenhower was forced into a compromise," Marshall told

Rose Page Wilson. "There is no more independence in politics than there is in jail."[26] Katherine Marshall later told her husband's biographer not to "attack President Eisenhower about the McCarthy thing; he did everything in the world to make it up to George and me."[27] Indeed, the Marshalls were invited to the inauguration as members of the official party with the general serving as the Inauguration Parade's grand marshal. They were frequently invited to White House dinners honoring visiting heads of state at which President Eisenhower placed Marshall in precedence immediately after the vice president and the secretary of state.

Perhaps the greatest honor Eisenhower bestowed upon Marshall came in 1953 when he appointed his former superior to lead the American delegation—which also included Omar Bradley and Chief Justice Earl Warren—to Queen Elizabeth II's coronation. Arriving in Westminster Abbey, Marshall walked toward his designated seat near the altar. Amongst the more than 8,000 guests packed into the abbey's transects and nave, Royal Gallery and staircases, were innumerable nobility and heads of state. As Marshall and the American delegation made their way forward from the west entrance, he noticed the dignitaries were rising to their feet as the Americans passed. Puzzled, he looked around to see who had come in the abbey.

"Who are they rising for?" he whispered to Bradley.

"You," Bradley replied.

Just before the ceremony began, first Churchill, then Alan Brooke and Bernard Montgomery, each wearing their robes as Lords of the Realm, entered the abbey. Each stepped out of the official procession to shake hands with Marshall. They were acknowledging the debt that not only the United Kingdom, but the entire free world owed the man Churchill called "the noblest Roman of them all."

Acknowledgments

It would be an understatement to say that this book has been a long time coming. The idea first percolated in my mind in the late 1990s when I was a young First Lieutenant in the 82nd Airborne, and while reading Henry Kissinger's *Diplomacy* learned the U.S. Army was only the seventeenth largest in the world when World War II started. It made me wonder how the legends I hoped to emulate back then—Eisenhower, Patton, Bradley, Ridgway, et al.—developed into the leaders they became in such a small force. This riddle seemed particularly relevant in the interregnum between the Cold War's end and the 9/11 attacks, when the belief that major wars were obsolete was as prevalent—and just as mistaken—as it had been during the interwar era.

This idea would never have been more than a personal obsession, however, if not for the help of numerous facilitators to whom I am deeply indebted: Nadia Schadlow, Marin Stremecki, Kathy Lavery, and everybody at the Smith Richardson Foundation, which provided generous funding for this book's research; Douglas Feith, Joel Scanlon, and Sean Kelly of the Hudson Institute for their research support; and Rich Davis, Juan Zarate, and Andrea Fatica of Artis International. Thank you to Dave Reisch, Stephanie Otto, and Meredith Dias at Rowman & Littlefield for seeing this book through to publication. And I'm especially grateful to my agent, E. J. McCarthy, for his patience and support as this project moved forward in fits and starts.

In turning the ideas in my head into something substantive, I was aided by a small battalion of archivists who helped guide my research: James Zobel of the MacArthur Memorial; Jeffrey S. Kozak of the George C. Marshall Library; the staff at the Dwight D. Eisenhower Library, especially Valoise Armstrong and Kathy Struss; Nathan Jones of the George S. Patton Museum; Michael E. Lynch, Adria P. Olmi, and Shannon S. Schwaller of the U.S. Army Heritage and Education Center; Lara Szypszak and the staff of both the Library of Congress's Manuscripts Division and Jefferson Reading Room; and Holly Reed and the numerous staffers of the National Archives' Still Picture Reference Team.

I would also like to thank the numerous subject matter experts, colleagues, and friends who generously provided advice on key research questions, read various drafts of the manuscript, or otherwise supported the research that eventually produced this book, to include: David Johnson, Daniel Holt, James Jay Carafano, Stephen P. Rosen, Gen. James Conway (USMC, Ret.), LTG Joseph Harrington (USA, Ret.), Col. Anthony Lugo, Col. Shane Morgan, Col. Christopher Hickey, Griff Norquist, Kevin T. Carroll, and Scott Hopkins. Your insights and advice were greatly appreciated, and any errors or oversights that remain are entirely mine.

Finally, I owe a special debt to my wife, Marya. It is hard to put into words how much I appreciate your support and your patience through the many challenges life threw at us during the researching and writing of this book. Although my name appears on the cover, this book is arguably as much the result of your hard work and sacrifices as it is mine, for which I am forever grateful.

This book is dedicated to our sons David and Ari. To paraphrase John Adams, *I study war so that they can study mathematics and philosophy . . . or painting, poetry, and music.* May they someday draw inspiration from how Marshall, Eisenhower, and many of the other leaders in this book overcame tragedy and hardships in order to serve their country, achieve greatness, and make the world a better place.

NOTES

Abbreviations
DDEL: Dwight D. Eisenhower Library, Abilene, Kansas
FDRL: Franklin Delano Roosevelt Library, Hyde Park, New York
GCML: George C. Marshall Foundation Research Library, Lexington, Virginia
LOC: Library of Congress, Washington, DC
MMA: Douglas A. MacArthur Memorial Archive, Norfolk, Virginia
USAMHI: United States Army Military History Institute, Carlisle, Pennslyvania

Introduction: Homecoming
1 On the pandemonium surrounding the *Leviathan*'s arrival and Pershing's homecoming, see Donald Smythe, *Pershing: General of the Armies* (Bloomington: Indiana University Press, 1986), 259; and Frank E. Vandiver, *Black Jack: The Life and Times of John J. Pershing*, 2 vols. (College Station: Texas A&M University Press, 1977), 1036.
2 Vandiver, *Black Jack*, 703, 1036.
3 Carlo D'Este, *Patton: A Genius for War* (New York: HarperCollins, 1995), 292, 294.
4 Quoted in Edward M. Coffman, *The Regulars: The American Army, 1898–1941* (Cambridge, MA: Harvard University Press, 2004), 239.
5 Douglas MacArthur, *Reminiscences* (New York: McGraw-Hill, 1964), 90.
6 Mark Landler and Allison Kopicki, "Skepticism Over U.S. Involvement in Foreign Conflicts," *New York Times*, June 6, 2013; and Susan Page, "USA Today Poll: Opposition to Syrian Airstrikes Surges," *USA Today*, September 9, 2013, available at http://www.usatoday.com/story/news/politics/2013/09/09/president-obama-syria-airstrikes-usa-today-pew-poll-opposition-surges/2785311/. When asked about the level of American engagement in April 2003, the *New York Times*/CBS Poll found 48 percent said the United States should take the lead, while 43 percent said it should not. In 2013, only 35 percent said the United States should take the lead, with 58 percent saying it should not.
7 Pew Research, *America's Place in the World 2013*, December 3, 2013, available at http://www.people-press.org/2013/12/03/public-sees-u-s-power-declining-as-support-for-global-engagement-slips/.
8 On the question of the Trump Administration's supposed isolationism, see Elliott Abrams, "Trump the Traditionalist: A Surprisingly Standard Foreign Policy," *Foreign Affairs* (July/August 2017); and Walter Russell Mead, "Trump Is No 'Isolationist'," *Wall Street Journal*, October 22, 2018.
9 *Quadrennial Defense Review, 2014*, iv; *War Department Annual Report, 1924*, 6–7, as quoted in David E. Johnson, *Fast Tanks and Heavy Bombers: Innovation in the U.S. Army, 1917–1945* (Ithaca, NY: Cornell University Press, 1998), 67.

10 "Assails Army Economy," *New York Times*, October 12, 1997, 23, as quoted in Johnson, *Fast Tanks and Heavy Bombers*, 68.

11 Odierno quoted in James Kitfield, "A Hollow Military Again?" *National Journal*, June 12, 2013. See also Paul McLeary, "New U.S. Army Memo Details 'Devastating' Effects of Cuts," DefenseNews.com, February 5, 2013.

12 *Quadrennial Defense Review, 2014*, iv; *War Department Annual Report, 1924*, 6–7, as quoted in Johnson, 67.

13 Mattis quoted in Sandra Erwin, "Mattis Is 'Shocked' by U.S. Military Readiness Crisis," *The National Interest*, June 13, 2017.

14 Lt. Col. Paul Yingling, "A Failure in Generalship," *Armed Forces Journal*, May 2007.

15 Thomas Ricks, "General Failure," *The Atlantic*, November 2012.

16 Daniel L. Davis, "Purge the Generals," *Armed Forces Journal*, August 2013.

17 See James Fallows, "The Tragedy of the American Military," *The Atlantic*, January/February 2015.

18 See Daniel Bolger, *Why We Lost: A General's Inside Account of the Iraq and Afghanistan Wars* (New York: Houghton Mifflin, 2014).

19 See Tim Kane, *Bleeding Talent: How the US Military Mismanages Great Leaders and Why It's Time for a Revolution* (New York: Palgrave Macmillan, 2012); Donald Vandergriff, *The Path to Victory: America's Army and the Revolution in Human Affairs* (Novato, CA: Presidio Press, 2002), but especially the independently published 2013 revised edition; David Barno and Nora Bensahel, *Building Better Generals* (Washington, DC: Center for a New American Security, 2013); and David Barno, "Military Brain Drain: The Pentagon's Top Brass Is Driving Away All the Smart People," ForeignPolicy.com, February 13, 2013.

20 See *2018 Army Strategy*, p. 2, available at https://www.army.mil/e2/downloads/rv7/the_army_strategy_2018.pdf, accessed January 9, 2019; and the Honorable Patrick J. Murphy and General Mark A. Milley, *2016 Army Posture Statement*, 2nd Session, 114th Congress, March-April 2016, pp. 6–7. The other three components are manning, training, and equipping the Army.

21 Winston Churchill, *Address to the General Staff*, U.S. Army, April 19, 1946, as quoted in George S. Pappas, *Prudens Futuri: The U.S. Army War College, 1901–1967* (Carlisle Barracks, PA: Walsworth Publishing Company, 1967), 137.

22 Letter from Henry L. Stimson to Harry S. Truman, September 1, 1950, as quoted in Peter J. Schifferle, *America's School for War: Fort Leavenworth, Officer Education, and Victory in World War II* (Lawrence, KS: University Press of Kansas, 2010), 194.

23 See U.S. Army, *Army Leadership Development Strategy 2013* (Washington, DC: Department of the Army, 2013).

Chapter One: The General's Apprentice: Marshall's Years with Pershing

1 MacArthur, *Reminiscences*, 46.

2 Donald Smythe, *Guerrilla Warrior: The Early Life of John J. Pershing* (New York: Charles Scribner's Sons, 1973), 262.

3 D'Este, *Patton*, 158; See also Smythe, *Pershing: General of the Armies*, 238, 239.

4 Smythe, *Pershing: General of the Armies*, 46.

5 Smythe, *Pershing: General of the Armies*, 54; Forrest C. Pogue, *George C. Marshall: The Education of a General, 1880–1939* (New York: Viking, 1964), 152.

6 Vandiver, *Black Jack*, 798; Mark Perry, *Partners in Command: George Marshall and Dwight Eisenhower in War and Peace* (New York: Penguin Press, 2007), 22; and Mark A. Stoler, *George C. Marshall: Soldier-Statesman of the American Century* (Boston: Twayne Publishers, 1989), 37.

7 Ed Cray, *General of the Army: George C. Marshall, Soldier and Statesman* (New York: W.W. Norton & Co., 1990), 57.

8 Perry, *Partners in Command*, 16.

9 Robert Payne, *The Marshall Story: A Biography of General George C. Marshall* (New York: Prentice Hall, 1951), 20.

10 Pogue, *Education of a General*, 55.

11 Ibid., 55–56; Cray, *General of the Army*, 28; and Stoler, *George C. Marshall*, 10.

12 Cray, *General of the Army*, 23, 29; Stoler, George C. Marshall, 10, 12.

13 Cray, *General of the Army*, 30.

14 George C. Marshall NA/201 File, Box 1, Folder 1A, GCML. See also H. H. Arnold, *Global Mission* (New York: Harper & Brothers, 1949), 44; and Stoler, *George C. Marshall*, 27.

15 Cray, *General of the Army*, 56.

16 Pogue, *Education of a General*, 170.

17 Edward M. Coffman, *The War to End All Wars: The American Military Experience in World War I* (London: Oxford University Press, 1968), 266–67.

18 Payne, *Marshall Story*, 74.

19 Stoler, *George C. Marshall*, 40.

20 John J. Pershing, *My Experiences in the World War*, Vol. 2 (New York: Frederick A. Stokes, 1931), 286.

21 Stanley Weintraub, *15 Stars: Eisenhower, MacArthur, Marshall: Three Generals Who Saved the American Century* (New York: Free Press, 2007), 123. See also Cray, *General of the Army*, 83.

22 Coffman, *The Regulars*, 219.

23 Smythe, *Pershing: General of the Armies*, 247.

24 Pogue, *Education of a General*, 196.

25 Smythe, *Pershing: General of the Armies*, 256.

26 Larry I. Bland, ed., *George C. Marshall Interviews and Reminiscences for Forrest C. Pogue* (Lexington, VA: George C. Marshall Foundation, 1991) [Hereafter cited as *Marshall Interviews*], 229; and Rose Page Wilson, *General Marshall Remembered* (Englewood Cliffs, NJ: Prentice Hall, Inc., 1968), 30.

27 Cray, *General of the Army*, 87.

28 George C. Marshall, *Memoirs of My Services in the World War* (Boston: Houghton Mifflin, 1976), 217.

29 On the NYC parade, see Vandiver, *Black Jack*, 1040.

30 Josephus Daniels, *The Wilson Era: Years of War and After, 1917–1923* (Chapel Hill, NC: The University of North Carolina Press, 1946), 174; Smythe, *Pershing: General of the Armies*, 261.

31 Bland, *Marshall Interviews*, 247.

32 *Congressional Record*, 65th Congress, 3rd session (1918–1919), Vol. 57, Part 4, 3301.

33 *Congressional Record*, 65th Congress, 3rd session (1918–1919), Vol. 57, Part 4, 3475.

34 Coffman, *The Regulars*, 228.

35 Edward M. Coffman, "Peyton C. March: Greatest Unsung American General of World War I," *Military History Quarterly*, June 2006.

36 *New York Times*, February 13, 1921, VII, 2.

37 Edward M. Coffman, *The Hilt of the Sword: The Career of Peyton C. March* (Madison, WI: The University of Wisconsin Press, 1966), 151. See also 114, 140, and 149.

38 U.S. Congress, House of Representatives, Committee on Military Affairs, *Hearings on Army Reorganization*, 65th Congress, 3rd session (1919), 42, 64.

39 Smythe, *Pershing: General of the Armies*, 261.

40 U.S. Senate, Subcommittee of the Committee on Military Affairs, *Hearings, Reorganization of the Army*, 66th Cong., 2nd session, 1919, 55.

41 New and Chamberlain quoted in Smythe, *Pershing: General of the Armies*, 261.

42 *Congressional Record*, 66th Congress, 1st session (1919), Vol. 58, Part 5, 4476, as quoted in Coffman, *Hilt of the Sword*, 188.

43 Peyton March to Marlborough Churchill, February 18, 1919, March Papers, Box 22, as quoted in Coffman, *Hilt of the Sword*, 190.

44 Coffman, *Hilt of the Sword*, 179, 197, 199; and Russell Weigley, *History of the United States Army* (New York: Macmillan and Company, 1967), 397.

45 Senate, *Reorganization Hearings*, 1177, as quoted in Coffman, *Hilt of the Sword*, 199.

46 Palmer quoted in Coffman, *The Regulars*, 228. See also Weigley, *History of the United States Army*, 397–98.

47 James Wadsworth, "The Reminiscences of James W. Wadsworth," as quoted in Coffman, *Hilt of the Sword*, 199.

48 See Coffman, *Hilt of the Sword*, 200; and Cray, *General of the Army*, 91.

49 George C. Marshall, *The Papers of George Catlett Marshall, Volume 1: The Soldierly Spirit, December 1880–June 1939*, Larry I. Bland, ed. (Baltimore: Johns Hopkins University Press, 1981) [Hereafter cited as Bland, *The Soldierly Spirit*], 200.

50 Baker quoted in Smythe, *Pershing: General of the Armies*, 91. See also Coffman, *Hilt of the Sword*, 115.

51 Smythe, *Pershing: General of the Armies*, 167.

52 Ibid., 89, 91; Cray, *General of the Army*, 91; and Coffman, *Hilt of the Sword*, 118.

53 I. B. Holley Jr., *General John M. Palmer, Citizen Soldiers, and the Army of a Democracy* (Westport, CT: Greenwood Press, 1986), 361. On the Sam Browne dispute, see also Donald Smythe, "The Pershing-March Conflict in World War I," *Parameters*, Vol. XI, no. 4 (1980), 56; and Brian Neumann, "A Question of Authority: Reassessing the March-Pershing Rivalry," *Journal of Military History* 73, no. 4 (October 2009), 1138–39.

54 John J. Pershing Diary, August 22, 1918, 637, Pershing Papers, LOC. See also Smythe, *Pershing: General of the Armies*, 167.

55 Smythe, *Pershing: General of the Armies*, 254.

56 Henry Gerard Phillips, *The Making of a Professional: Manton S. Eddy, USA* (Westport, CT: Greenwood Press, 2000), 36; and Harbord to Pershing, June 14, 1919, Harbord Papers, Personal War Letters.

57 Coffman, *Hilt of the Sword*, 194–95.

58 Virginia Conner, *What Father Forbad* (Philadelphia: Dorrance & Company, 1951), 89–91.

59 Bland, *Marshall Interviews*, 247.

60 Coffman, *Hilt of the Sword*, 200.

61 U.S. Congress, *Reorganization of the Army, Hearings before the Subcommittee of the Committee on Military Affairs on S. 2691, 2694 and 2715*. 66th Congress, 1st and 2nd session, 1919–1920, Vol. 2: 1572, 1782, as quoted in Smythe, *Pershing: General of the Armies*, 262.

62 Senate, *Reorganization Hearings*, 1605, as quoted in Coffman, *Hilt of the Sword*, 202.

63 *Stars and Stripes*, November 8, 1919.

64 Richard W. Stewart, ed., *American Military History, Volume II: The United States Army in a Global Era, 1917–2008* (Washington, DC: U.S. Army Center of Military History, 2010), 57.

65 On the NDA, see ibid., 57–58, and Weigley, *History of the United States Army*, 400, 403, 404.

66 Weigley, *History of the United States Army*, 400.

67 William A. Ganoe, *The History of the United States Army* (New York: D. Appleton-Century, 1924), 485.

68 Smythe, *Pershing: General of the Armies*, 266; Stoler, *George C. Marshall*, 46; and Coffman, *Hilt of the Sword*, 208–9.

69 Smythe, *Pershing: General of the Armies*, 267.

70 *Congressional Record*, 66th Congress, 3rd session (1920–1921), Vol. 60, Part 3, 2384.

71 "Address Before Headmasters Association—Boston," February 10, 1923, GCML, Marshall Papers [Pentagon Office—Speeches].

72 Weigley, *History of the United States Army*, 401; Coffman, *Hilt of the Sword*, 210.

73 D. Clayton James, *The Years of MacArthur*, Vol. I: *1880–1940* (Boston: Houghton Mifflin Company, 1970), 285.

74 William Farrington, ed., *Cowboy Pete: An Autobiography of Major General Charles H. Corlett* (Santa Fe, NM: Sleeping Fox Publishers, 1974), p. 50.

75 Bland, *Marshall Interviews*, 252–53.

76 Baker quoted in Coffman, *Hilt of the Sword*, 166. See also Smythe, *Pershing: General of the Armies*, 264.

77 Smythe, *Pershing: General of the Armies*, 265.

78 *Congressional Record*, 66th Congress, 1st session (1919), Vol. 58, Part 5, 4467.

79 Bland, *Marshall Interviews*, 251.

80 Smythe, *Pershing: General of the Armies*, 264, 268.

81 Weigley, *History of the United States Army*, 404–5; Smythe, *Pershing: General of the Armies*, 275.

82 *Congressional Record*, 67th Congress, 1st session (1921), Vol. 61, Part 3, 2150, as quoted in Coffman, *Hilt of the Sword*, 221.

83 Harbord to Pershing, June 26, 1921, LOC, Pershing Papers, Box 88.

84 William Wright to John Pershing, June 23, 1921, LOC, Pershing Papers, Box 217.

85 Smythe, *Pershing: General of the Armies*, 278, 279.

86 Bland, *Marshall Interviews*, 90.

87 Vandiver, *Black Jack*, 1058.

88 Bland, *Marshall Interviews*, 90.

89 Stoler, *George C. Marshall*, 44, 47; and Vandiver, *Black Jack*, 1064.

90 Wilson, *General Marshall Remembered*, 21–22.

91 George C. Marshall, "Profiting By War Experiences," *Infantry Journal* 18 (January 1921), 34–37. See also Payne, *Marshall Story*, 95–97.

92 Smythe, *Pershing: General of the Armies*, 247–48.

93 Pogue, *Education of a General*, 226.

94 Bland, *The Soldierly Spirit*, 202.

95 Ibid., 259.

96 Omar N. Bradley and Clay Blair, *A General's Life* (New York: Simon and Schuster, 1983), 63–64.

Chapter Two: MacArthur at West Point

1 MacArthur, *Reminiscences*, 72.

2 Faubian Bowers, "The Late General MacArthur," *Esquire*, January 1967, 93.

3 Geoffrey Perret, *Old Soldiers Never Die: The Life of Douglas MacArthur* (New York: Random House, 1996), 40.

4 Stephen E. Ambrose, *Duty, Honor, Country: A History of West Point* (Baltimore: The Johns Hopkins Press, 1999), 260; Perret, *Old Soldiers Never Die*, 114; William Manchester, *American Caesar: Douglas MacArthur, 1880–1964* (Boston: Little, Brown and Company, 1983), 116.

5 Coffman, *Hilt of the Sword*, 186.

6 *An Act Fixing the Military Peace Establishment of the United States*, March 16, 1802, *Statutes at Large*, 7th Congress, 1st session, 2: 137, as quoted in Lance Betros, *Carved from Granite: West Point Since 1902* (College Station: Texas A&M University Press, 2012), 4.

7 Ambrose, *Duty, Honor, Country*, 91, 122.

8 *Report of the Commission*, Senate Document, No. 3, 36th Congress, 2nd Session (Washington, DC: 1860), 56–57, as quoted in Ambrose, *Duty, Honor, Country*, 145–46. See also Ernest R. Dupuy, *Men of West Point: The First 150 Years of the United States Military Academy* (New York: William Sloane Associates, 1951), 25–53.

9 Ambrose, *Duty, Honor, Country*, 180.

10 U.S. Military Academy, *The Centennial of the United States Military Academy 1802–1902* (Washington, DC: Government Printing Office, 1904), Vol. 1, 20.

11 Quoted in Roger H. Nye, "The United States Military Academy in an Era of Educational Reform, 1900–1925," Unpublished doctoral dissertation, Columbia University, 1968, 285.

12 William A. Ganoe, *MacArthur Close Up: Much Then and Some Now* (New York: Vantage Press, 1962), 15.

13 Ambrose, *Duty, Honor, Country*, 259; Thomas J. Fleming, *West Point* (New York: William Morris & Co., 1969), 304; Nye, "The United States Military Academy," 288.

14 Robert Cowley, "The Great War and After," in Robert Cowley and Thomas Guinzberg, eds., *West Point: Two Centuries of Honor and Tradition* (New York: Warner, 2002), 170; Nye, "The United States Military Academy," 289.

15 Jacob L. Devers, "The Mark of the Man on USMA," *Assembly* XXIII (Spring, 1964), 17.

16 Ambrose, *Duty, Honor, Country*, 197; and Betros, *Carved from Granite*, 2.

17 Letter of General Committee to Superintendent, December 13, 1918, USMA AG Files, 351.051, Curriculum 1917–1920, item D-9, 2f, as quoted in Nye, "The United States Military Academy," 292.

18 James, *Years of MacArthur*, Vol. I, 74.

19 Maxwell Taylor, *Swords and Ploughshares* (New York: W. W. Norton, 1972), 25; See also Betros, *Carved from Granite*, 29.

20 Quoted in Ambrose, *Duty, Honor, Country*, 258.

21 Cowley, "The Great War and After," 149; Jorg Muth, *Command Culture: Officer Education in the U.S. Army and the German Armed Forces, 1901–1940, and the Consequences for World War II* (Denton: University of North Texas Press, 2011), 44.

22 Gen. Tasker Bliss to Col. John Biddle, March 1, 1917, USMA AG Files, 351.051, Curriculum-1917, 1, as quoted in Nye, "The United States Military Academy," 270.

23 Memorandum of Dr. C. R. Mann for Mr. F. P. Keppel, January 8, 1919, National Archives, 351.1, Box 25, Project Files, Army Schools, West Point, *passim*, as quoted in Nye, "The United States Military Academy," 295.

24 Quoted in T. Bentley Mott, "West Point: A Criticism," *Harper's*, March 1934, 478–79.

25 Quoted in Muth, *Command Culture*, 43.

26 Fleming, *West Point*, 305–6. See also *New York Times*, May 9, 1920.

27 Manchester, *American Caesar*, 50.

28 On Arthur MacArthur, see Kenneth Ray Young, *The General's General: The Life and Times of Arthur MacArthur* (Boulder, CO: Westview Press, 1994).

29 James, *Years of MacArthur*, Vol. I, 56; See also Manchester, *American Caesar*, 39.

30 Frazier Hunt, *The Untold Story of Douglas MacArthur* (Chicago: Devon-Adair Co., 1954), 18.

31 On MacArthur's cadet career, see Manchester, *American Caesar*, 49–54.

32 Perret, *Old Soldiers Never Die*, 76.

33 Manchester, *American Caesar*, 86, 88, 89.

34 Martin Blumenson, *The Patton Papers, Volume II, 1885–1940* (Boston: Houghton-Mifflin, 1972), 634.

35 Jules Archer, *Front-Line General: Douglas MacArthur* (New York: Julian Messner Inc., 1963), 57.

36 Cowley, "The Great War and After," 156; See also Perret, *Old Soldiers Never Die*, 99.

37 Manchester, *American Caesar*, 3.

38 William A. White, *The Autobiography of William Allen White* (New York: The MacMillan Company, 1946), 572.

39 Perret, *Old Soldiers Never Die*, 87.

40 Manchester, *American Caesar*, 84, 92, 110.

41 Quoted in Ganoe, *MacArthur Close Up*, 25.

42 See Earl Blaik, "A Cadet Under MacArthur," *Assembly* XXIII (Spring, 1964), 8; and Perret, *Old Soldiers Never Die*, 115.

43 See Taylor, *Swords and Ploughshares*, 26; Perret, *Old Soldiers Never Die*, 116–17; James, *Years of MacArthur*, Vol. I, 264–65.

44 *Annual Report of the Superintendent, 1920* (West Point, NY: United States Military Academy Press, 1920), 4. MacArthur was not the first to express this theory of leadership. In a January 1919 memo to Secretary Baker, Third Assistant Secretary of War Frank P. Kepel described the Army officer as "primarily a human engineer," and that as such he required that "the social sciences of humanity, and in particular the art of human relationships, should be a very fundamental part of his equipment." See Memorandum of Mr. F. P. Keppel to Secretary of War N. B. Baker, January 20, 1919, National Archives, 351.1, Project Files, Army Schools, West Point, 1, as quoted in Nye, "The United States Military Academy," 296.

45 MacArthur, *Reminiscences*, 77, 80.

46 See MacArthur to Herman Beukema, July 10, 1939, MMA, RG 1, Box 2; and Blaik, "A Cadet Under MacArthur," 8.

47 *Annual Report of the Superintendent, 1920*, 3.

48 Quoted in Ganoe, *MacArthur Close Up*, 105.

49 James, *Years of MacArthur*, Vol. I, 276; Blaik, "A Cadet Under MacArthur," 9.

50 Quoted in Morris Janowitz, *The Professional Soldier: A Social and Political Portrait* (Glencoe, IL: Free Press, 1960), 129–30.

51 Muth, *Command Culture*, 50; Jim DeFelice, *Omar Bradley: General at War* (New York: Regnery History, 2011), 20. Superintendent Tillman believed hazing trained cadets in "alertness and military bearing. . . . Each class knows that its predecessors have practiced it, the authorities and alumni all acknowledge its beneficial effects within reason." Tillman memoirs (unpublished), quoted in Betros, *Carved from Granite*, 244–45.

52 MacArthur to acting commandant, 2nd endorsement, August 6, 1919, to "Resolutions of the Class of 1920 to the Commandant," August 4, 1919.

53 Blaik, "A Cadet Under MacArthur," 9; Taylor, *Swords and Ploughshares*, 26.

54 United States Military Academy, Class of 1920, *Traditions and Customs of the Corps*, 5–6, as quoted in Betros, *Carved from Granite*, 267.

55 *New York Times*, May 21, 1919.

56 Ganoe, *MacArthur Close Up*, 113.

57 MacArthur, *Reminiscences*, 81.

58 *Annual Report of the Superintendent, 1921* (West Point, NY: United States Military Academy Press, 1921), 11–12.

59 See MacArthur, *Reminiscences*, 81; James, *Years of MacArthur*, Vol. I, 279; and Ambrose, *Duty, Honor, Country*, 272.

60 Robert M., Danford, "USMA's 31st Superintendent," *Assembly*, XXIII, no. 1 (Spring, 1964), 14.

61 See Ambrose, *Duty, Honor, Country*, 280.

62 *Annual Report of the Superintendent*, 1921, 14. See also Betros, *Carved from Granite*, 121–22.

63 See James, *Years of MacArthur*, Vol. I, 271.

64 *Annual Report of the Superintendent, 1921*, 6. See also Betros, *Carved from Granite*, 45.

65 See Devers, "The Mark of the Man on USMA," 18; Nye, "The United States Military Academy," 326; and James, *Years of MacArthur*, Vol. I, 273.

66 See Ganoe, *MacArthur Close Up*, 96, 97; and Muth, *Command Culture*, 67–69.

67 Joseph Lawton Collins, *Lightning Joe: An Autobiography* (Baton Rouge: Louisiana State University Press, 1979), 43.

68 Matthew B. Ridgway, *Soldier: The Memoirs of Matthew B. Ridgway*, Reprint (Westport, CT: Greenwood Press, 1974; originally published by Harper, 1956), 33.

69 DeFelice, *Omar Bradley*, 33–34.

70 See James, *Years of MacArthur*, Vol. I, 274; Betros, *Carved from Granite*, 122.

71 Ganoe, *MacArthur Close Up*, 88.

72 Devers, "The Mark of the Man on USMA," 19.

73 Ganoe, *MacArthur Close Up*, 92–93. See also Ambrose, *Duty, Honor, Country*, 269; Betros, *Carved from Granite*, 123; and Nye, "The United States Military Academy," 328.

74 See Ambrose, *Duty, Honor, Country*, 270; James, *Years of MacArthur*, Vol. I, 274–75; and Nye, "The United States Military Academy," 312.

75 Blaik, "A Cadet Under MacArthur," 11. See also Ambrose, *Duty, Honor, Country*, 271; and Ganoe, *MacArthur Close Up*, 307.

76 Quoted in Fleming, *West Point*, 307.

77 See also James, *Years of MacArthur*, Vol. I, 279.

78 *Annual Report of the Superintendent, 1922* (West Point, NY: United States Military Academy Press, 1922), 8.

79 MacArthur, *Reminiscences*, 81.

80 Ganoe, *MacArthur Close Up*, 76. Tillman quote in Memorandum No. 27, Headquarters USMA, April 4, 1918, West Point Archives, as quoted in Betros, *Carved from Granite*, 172.

81 *Annual Report of the Superintendent, 1922*, 11.

82 See Betros, *Carved from Granite*, 173; Fleming, *West Point*, 311; Manchester, *American Caesar*, 124; and Taylor, *Swords and Ploughshares*, 27.

83 See Bradley, *A General's Life*, 51; Alan Axelrod, *Bradley: A Biography* (New York: Palgrave MacMillan, 2008), 40; MacArthur, *Reminiscences*, 81–82.

84 Betros, *Carved from Granite*, 174.

85 MacArthur quoted in Ganoe, *MacArthur Close Up*, 76.

86 Earl Blaik, *The Red Blaik Story* (New Rochelle, NY: Arlington House, 1960), 46–48. See also Fleming, *West Point*, 312.

87 Ganoe, *MacArthur Close Up*, 75.

88 Blaik, "A Cadet Under MacArthur," 9–11.

89 Ganoe, *MacArthur Close Up*, 60–61.

90 Both quotes from W. S. Nye to Stephen Ambrose, December 3, 1964, as quoted in Ambrose, *Duty, Honor, Country*, 267, 277. In the latter quote Nye is citing his roommate's impression.

91 Blaik, *Red Blaik Story*, 32–33.

92 *Howitzer, 1923, The Yearbook of the Corps of Cadets* (West Point, NY: The Howitzer Board, 1923), 420. See also Ganoe, *MacArthur Close Up*, 112.

93 Taylor, *Swords and Ploughshares*, 28.

94 Ganoe, *MacArthur Close Up*, 107.

95 Ibid., 41.

96 James, *Years of MacArthur*, Vol. I, 274; Betros, 220.

97 Bradley, *A General's Life*, 34, 51.

98 Ibid., 52.

99 Ganoe, *MacArthur Close Up*, 35; See also James, *Years of MacArthur*, Vol. I, 267.

100 Ganoe, *MacArthur Close Up*, 36. See also Ambrose, *Duty, Honor, Country*, 202, 265; and James, *Years of MacArthur*, Vol. I, 267.

101 Danford, "USMA's 31st Superintendent," 13.

102 *Annual Report of the Superintendent, 1920*, 21. See also Nye, "The United States Military Academy," 309, 310.

103 *Annual Report of the Superintendent, 1920*, 6.

104 Ganoe, *MacArthur Close Up*, 97–99; Danford, 13.

105 See Minority Endorsement dated July 16, 1920, Charles P. Echols, USMA, AG Files, 351.05, Curriculum 1920, Item D-18, as quoted in Nye, "The United States Military Academy," 321.

106 Danford quoted in James, *Years of MacArthur*, Vol. I, 269.

107 Coffman, *The Regulars*, 226–27.

108 Ambrose, *Duty, Honor, Country*, 267.

109 James, *Years of MacArthur*, Vol. I, 270.

110 Ganoe, *MacArthur Close Up*, 33–34.

111 Douglas B. Kendrick, *Memoirs of a 20th Century Army Surgeon* (Manhattan, KS: Sunflower University Press, 1992), 198.

112 Ganoe, *MacArthur Close Up*, 151.

113 James, *Years of MacArthur*, Vol. I, 268.

114 Perret, *Old Soldiers Never Die*, 117. See also Arthur Herman, *Douglas MacArthur: American Warrior* (New York: Random House, 2016), 168.

115 Manchester, *American Caesar*, 120.

116 Matthew Ridgway Interview, November 24, 1971, 48, USAMHI, Ridgway Papers, Box 89.

117 Bradley, *A General's Life*, 51.

118 Ganoe, *MacArthur Close Up*, 141–42.

119 Pershing to MacArthur, November 22, 1921, LOC, Pershing Papers, Box 121.

120 Perret, *Old Soldiers Never Die*, 124–25.

121 Pershing quoted in *New York Times*, February 10, 1922, 3. See also Smythe, *Pershing: General of the Armies*, 277.

122 MacArthur quoted in Joseph M. Maddelena, ed., *Profiles in History: The Passionate and Poetic Pen of Douglas MacArthur* (Beverly Hills, CA: Profiles in History Auction House, 1991), 8. See also Perret, *Old Soldiers Never Die*, 125, 127.

123 Tyler Abell, ed., *Drew Pearson Diaries* (New York: Holt, Rinehart and Winston, 1974), 412–13.

124 In his letter ordering MacArthur's transfer, Pershing expressed his own dissatisfaction with MacArthur's actions as superintendent, especially his agreeing to testify on Capitol Hill about the West Point budget without notifying either Pershing or the secretary of war. See James, *Years of MacArthur*, Vol. I, 290, 292.

125 DM 201 File, MMA.

126 *New York Times*, February 5, 1922.

127 Bradford Grethen Chynoweth, *Bellamy Park: Memoirs* (Hicksville, NY: Exposition Press, 1975), 57.

128 Ganoe, *MacArthur Close Up*, 157.

129 *Annual Report of the Superintendent, 1923* (West Point, NY: United States Military Academy Press, 1923), 7.

130 Nye, "The United States Military Academy," 332–33.

131 Cowley, "The Great War and After," 174.

132 Fleming, *West Point*, 311.

133 Pershing, Stewart quoted in Fleming, *West Point*, 318–319.

134 Ambrose, *Duty, Honor, Country*, 283.

Chapter Three: The Innovator's Dilemma: Ike, Patton, and Billy Mitchell
After the War

1 Ridgway, *Soldier*, 32.

2 Collins, *Lightning Joe*, 32.

3 Bradley, *A General's Life*, 36, 46.

4 Norman Randolph to Dwight D. Eisenhower, June 20, 1945, Box 97, Pre-Presidential Papers, DDEL. See also Stephen E. Ambrose, *Eisenhower*, Vol. I: *Soldier, General of the Army, President-Elect, 1890–1952* (New York: Simon and Schuster, 1983), 41; and Matthew F. Holland, *Eisenhower Between the Wars: The Making of A General and Statesman* (Westport, CT: Praeger, 2001), 4.

5 John McCallum, *Six Roads from Abilene: Some Personal Recollections of Edgar Eisenhower* (Seattle: Wood & Reber, 1960), 20.

6 See Peter Lyon, *Eisenhower: Portrait of a Hero* (Boston: Little, Brown, 1974), 40.

7 Ray I. Witter Interview, DDEL.

8 Dwight D. Eisenhower, *At Ease: Stories I Tell to Friends* (New York: McGraw Hill, 1967), 106.

9 Ibid., 12.

10 Kenneth S. Davis, *Soldier of Democracy* (New York: Doubleday, Doran and Company, Inc., 1945), 146.

11 Steve Nash, *The Eisenhowers: Reluctant Dynasty* (Garden City, NY: Doubleday, 1978), 35.

12 Eisenhower, *At Ease*, 113.

13 Ibid., 136.

14 Ibid., 138.

15 Holland, *Eisenhower Between the Wars*, 40.

16 Dwight D. Eisenhower efficiency report, March 15, 1918, to November 15, 1918, DDEL.

17 "From Plebe to President," *Collier's*, June 10, 1955. See also Carlo D'Este, *Eisenhower: A Soldier's Life* (New York: John Macrae/Holt, 2002), 136–37.

18 Eisenhower, *At Ease*, 155.

19 D'Este, *Eisenhower*, 139.

20 Edgar F. Puryear, *Nineteen Stars: A Study in Military Character and Leadership* (Novato, CA: Presidio Press, 1971), 293.

21 Quoted in *Overview* (the official newsletter of the Eisenhower Foundation, Abilene, KS) 10, no. 3 (Fall 1984).

22 Eisenhower, *At Ease*, 157–58; D'Este, *Eisenhower*, 140–43; and Jean Edward Smith, *Eisenhower in War and Peace*, (New York: Random House, 2012), 50–51.

23 Eisenhower, *At Ease*, 169.

24 See Smith, *Eisenhower in War and Peace*, 53–55.

25 Robert H. Patton, *The Pattons: A Personal History of an American Family* (New York: Crown Publishers, 1994), 91, 93.

26 Ladislas Farago, *Patton: Ordeal and Triumph* (Yardley, PA: Westholme Publishing, 1964), 56.

27 Stanley P. Hirshson, *General Patton: A Soldier's Life* (New York: HarperCollins, 2002), 38; Coffman, *The Regulars*, 148.

28 On the Rubio firefight, see Benjamin Runkle, *Wanted Dead or Alive: Manhunts from Geronimo to bin Laden* (New York: Palgrave Macmillan, 2011), 95–97.

29 D'Este, *Eisenhower*, 126.

30 Patton, *The Pattons*, 170.

31 George Patton Jr., to George Patton Sr., n.p., November 6, 1917, LOC, Patton Papers, Box 20. See also Hirshson, *General Patton*, 101, and Patton, *The Pattons*, 170–71.

32 Martin Blumenson, *Patton: The Man Behind the Legend, 1885–1945* (New York: William Morrow and Company, 1985), 98–99, 105–6.

33 *New York Times*, March 18, 1919, and *New York Herald*, March 18, 1919. See also Blumenson, *Patton Papers*, Vol. II, 113–14; and Patton, *The Pattons*, 184–85.

34 See *New York Herald*, March 18, 1919; and D'Este, *Patton*, 281. All press clippings of Patton's homecoming are in Box 11, Patton Papers, LOC.

35 Eisenhower, *At Ease*, 169. See also Ambrose, *Eisenhower*, 70.

36 Eisenhower, *At Ease*, 88–90.

37 See Lester David and Irene David, *Ike and Mamie: The Story of the General and His Lady* (New York: Putnam, 1983), 73–74; and Susan Eisenhower, *Mrs. Ike: Memories and Reflections on the Life of Mamie Eisenhower* (New York: Farrar Straus & Giroux, 1996), 64.

38 John S.D. Eisenhower, *General Ike: A Personal Reminiscence* (New York: Free Press, 2003), 1–2.

39 D'Este, *Patton*, 286.

40 Ibid., 286–87.

41 Mamie Doud Eisenhower oral history, DDEL, 14.

42 D'Este, *Patton*, 291.

43 See Ruth Ellen Patton Totten, *The Button Box: A Daughter's Loving Memoir of Mrs. George S. Patton* (Columbia: University of Missouri Press, 2005), 124. On the history of

PTSD, see David J. Morris, *The Evil Hours: A Biography of Post-Traumatic Stress Disorder* (New York: Houghton Mifflin Harcourt, 2015).

44 Eisenhower, *At Ease*, 169–70.

45 Ibid., 171.

46 Farago, *Patton*, 100–101.

47 Ibid., 101.

48 Hirshson, *General Patton*, 199.

49 Blumenson, *Patton Papers*, Vol. II, 802.

50 George Hoffman, "The Demise of the U.S. Tank Corps and Medium Tank Development Program," *Military Affairs*, February 1973, 23. See also D'Este, *Patton*, 299.

51 Eisenhower, *At Ease*, 179.

52 Puryear, *Nineteen Stars*, 162.

53 Dale E. Wilson, "Patton, Eisenhower, and the Birth of American Armor," paper presented to the Society for Military History, May 1993, as quoted in D'Este, *Eisenhower*, 154.

54 Eisenhower, *At Ease*, 170, 173.

55 Eisenhower, *Crusade in Europe* (Garden City, NY: Doubleday & Company, Inc., 1948), 41.

56 Stephen Ambrose, "A Fateful Friendship," *American Heritage*, April 1969, 97.

57 Dwight D. Eisenhower, "Unpublished Assessments of World War II Personalities," Box 7, Post-Presidential Papers, A-WR series, DDEL.

58 Eisenhower, *At Ease*, 178.

59 See George S. Patton Jr. "Tanks in Future Wars," *Infantry Journal* 16 (May 1920), 958–62.

60 See Dwight D. Eisenhower, "A Tank Discussion," *Infantry Journal* 17 (November 1920), 454–58.

61 Eisenhower, *At Ease*, 173. Also see Chynoweth, *Bellamy Park*, 90.

62 Ambrose, *Eisenhower*, 72; Blumenson, *Patton Papers*, Vol. II, 805–6, 808.

63 Ambrose, *Eisenhower*, 71–72.

64 Alfred F. Hurley, *Billy Mitchell: Crusader for Air Power*, rev. ed. (Bloomington, IN: Indiana University Press, 1975), 2–3.

65 U.S. Congress, House Committee on Military Affairs, *Hearings in Connection with HR 5304*, 63rd Congress, 1st session, 1913, quoted in Johnson, *Fast Tanks and Heavy Bombers*, 41.

66 Hurley, *Billy Mitchell*, 21.

67 Ibid., 29.

68 Johnson, *Fast Tanks and Heavy Bombers*, 49.

69 Brig. Gen. William Mitchell, "Tactical Application of Military Aeronautics," 1, 167, 603–7 (1919), USAFHRA, as quoted in Johnson, *Fast Tanks and Heavy Bombers*, 82.

70 Mitchell to Arnold, July 25, 1919, William Mitchell Papers, LOC, Box 7.

71 "Report of the Superior Board," 81–82, as quoted in Johnson, *Fast Tanks and Heavy Bombers*, 50.

72 Senate, *Reorganization of the Army*, 2:1686, 279, 287, as quoted in Johnson, *Fast Tanks and Heavy Bombers*, 52–53.

73 Senate, *Reorganization Hearings*, 743, as quoted in Coffman, *The Hilt of the Sword*, 205.

74 Johnson, *Fast Tanks and Heavy Bombers*, 82–83.

75 Maurer Maurer, *Aviation in the U.S. Army, 1919–1939* (Washington, D.C: U.S. Air Force, 1987), 119–20.

76 Ibid., 121.

77 Ibid.

78 *New York Times*, September 14, 1921, 1.

79 Johnson, *Fast Tanks and Heavy Bombers*, 84.

80 "Says Army Officers Must Not Criticize," *New York Times*, June 25, 1922, 21, quoted in Johnson, *Fast Tanks and Heavy Bombers*, 66–67. See also *idem*, 84.

81 Hurley, *Billy Mitchell*, 83–85; Johnson, *Fast Tanks and Heavy Bombers*, 86.

82 Hurley, *Billy Mitchell*, 92. See also Maurer, *Aviation in the U.S. Army* 127.

83 Andrew Boyle, *Trenchard* (New York: W.W. Norton & Company, 1962), 472.

84 U.S. Congress, House, *Select Committee on Inquiry into Operation of the U.S. Air Services*, 69th Congress, 1st Session (1925), 1674–75, 1887, 3020–23, as quoted in Hurley, *Billy Mitchell*, 95–96. See also Johnson, *Fast Tanks and Heavy Bombers*, 86–87.

85 Chynoweth, *Bellamy Park*, 95. Pershing quoted in Hurley, 104.

86 "Intolerable Charges," *New York Times*, February 22, 1925, 4.

87 Hurley, *Billy Mitchell*, 98.

88 William Mitchell, "Statement of William Mitchell Concerning the Recent Air Accidents," September 5, 1925. See also "Mitchell Charges Force Davis to Act," *New York Times*, September 6, 1925, quoted in Johnson, 87.

89 Maurer, *Aviation in the U.S. Army*, 129.

90 Isaac Don Levine, *Mitchell, Pioneer of Air Power* (New York: Duell, Sloan and Pearce, 1943), 345.

91 "The Intense Drama of the Mitchell Trial," *New York Times*, November 15, 1925.

92 Hurley, *Billy Mitchell*, 105. See also *idem*, 104, and James, *Years of MacArthur*, Vol. I, 307–8.

93 H. H. Arnold, *Global Mission*, 120.

94 MacArthur, *Reminiscences*, 85.

95 Burke Davis, *The Billy Mitchell Affair* (New York: Random House, 1967), 295.

96 Ibid., 267, 327.

97 See Johnson, *Fast Tanks and Heavy Bombers*, 90.

98 Dorothy Barret Brandon, *Mamie: A Portrait of a First Lady* (New York: Scribner, 1954), 106–8.

99 Eisenhower, *At Ease*, 180. See also Merle Miller, *Ike the Soldier: As They Knew Him* (New York: G.P. Putnam's Sons, 1987), 191.

100 Geoffrey Perret, *Eisenhower* (New York: Random House, 1999), 78.

101 Susan Eisenhower, *Mrs. Ike*, 67.

102 Eisenhower, *At Ease*, 181.

103 Steve Neal, *The Eisenhowers: Reluctant Dynasty* (Garden City, NY: Doubleday and Co., 1978), 64–65.

104 Eisenhower, *At Ease*, 181.

Chapter Four: Guardians of Empire

1 Miller, *Ike the Soldier*, 198.

2 D'Este, *Eisenhower*, 161.

3 Miller, *Ike the Soldier*, 198.

4 Ibid., 200, 201.

5 Ibid., 202.

6 Holland, *Eisenhower Between the Wars*, 155.

7 Miller, *Ike the Soldier*, 203.

8 Smith, *Eisenhower in War and Peace*, 64.

9 Coffman, *The Regulars*, 326.

10 Brian McAllister Linn, *Guardians of Empire: The U.S. Army and the Pacific, 1920–1940* (Chapel Hill, NC: University of North Carolina Press, 1997), 62–63, 146–47, 165.

11 D'Este, *Eisenhower*, 164.

12 Eisenhower, *At Ease*, 183.

13 Conner, *What Father Forbad*, 113.

14 Mamie Doud Eisenhower Oral History, DDEL.

15 Conner, *What Father Forbad*, 120.

16 Miller, *Ike the Soldier*, 208.

17 Julie Nixon Eisenhower, *Special People* (New York: Simon and Schuster, 1977), 198.

18 Eisenhower, *At Ease*, 194.

19 Conner, *What Father Forbad*, 120–21.

20 Eisenhower, *At Ease*, 185. See also Perry, *Partners in Command*, 44; and Miller, *Ike the Soldier*, 85, 210.

21 Eisenhower, *At Ease*, 185.

22 Charles H. Brown, "Fox Conner: A General's General," John Ray Skates, ed., *Journal of Mississippi History* (August 1987), 205.

23 Ambrose, *Eisenhower*, 77. "Bible" quote from Miller, *Ike the Soldier*, 210–11.

24 Eisenhower, *At Ease*, 186.

25 Miller, *Ike the Soldier*, 210. See also D'Este, *Eisenhower*, 167, 168.

26 Eisenhower, *At Ease*, 187.

27 Puryear, *Nineteen Stars*, 162. See also Cole Kingseed, "Mentoring General Ike," *Military Review*, October 1990.

28 Miller, *Ike the Soldier*, 211.

29 Brown, "Fox Conner," 209. See also Edward Cox, *Grey Eminence: Fox Connor and the Art of Mentorship* (Stillwater, OK: New Forums Press, Inc., 2011), 90.

30 Eisenhower, *At Ease*, 195.

31 Davis, *Soldier of Democracy*, 196–97.

32 Miller, *Ike the Soldier*, 209.

33 Chynoweth, *Bellamy Park*, 100.

34 Ambrose, *Eisenhower*, 40.

35 Eisenhower, *At Ease*, 187.

36 Holland, *Eisenhower Between the Wars*, 96.

37 Hirshson, 176, 177.

38 Lucian K. Truscott Jr., *The Twilight of the U.S. Cavalry: Life in the Old Army, 1917–1942* (Lawrence: University of Kansas Press, 1989), 26.

39 Linn, 68.

40 Hirshson, 177.

41 Patton to Beatrice Ayer Patton, n.p., April 6, 1925, Patton Papers.

42 Brian McAllister Linn notes that Schofield Barracks was also cursed with dozens of shoddily constructed wartime structures. The 19th Infantry, for example, had to live in collapsing barracks with leaking roofs, no water, and malfunctioning sewers for over a decade. A decade after the war had ended, over half the posts' enlisted men still lived in "dilapidated shacks" that were practically uninhabitable. See Linn, *Guardians of Empire*, 71–72.

43 Report of Committee No. 5, The Region of the Pacific and the Region of the Caribbean, March 1, 1923, F 254-5, AWCCA, as quoted in Linn, *Guardians of Empire*, 194. See also Hirshson, 178.

44 Linn, *Guardians of Empire*, 195–96.

45 Charles Pelot Summerall, *The Way of Duty, Honor, Country: The Memoirs of General Charles Pelot Summerall* (Lexington: The University Press of Kentucky, 2010), 178. On McNair's role in the development of the plan, see Mark T. Calhoun, *General Lesley J. McNair: Unsung Architect of the U.S. Army* (Lawrence: University Press of Kansas, 2015), 64–70.

46 Quoted in Hirshson, 181.

47 For example, the 27th Infantry lost 93,635 of its 154,700 man-hours allotted for training to a variety of unrelated duties. See Linn, *Guardians of Empire*, 64, 201.

48 Charles P. Summerall to AG, May 20, 1924, E 6051, RG 395, as quoted in Linn, *Guardians of Empire*, 152.

49 Summerall, *The Way of Duty, Honor, Country*, 177.

50 D'Este, *Patton*, 338.

51 Linn, *Guardians of Empire*, 205–6.

52 Quoted in Truscott, *The Twilight of the U.S. Cavalry*, 39, 40.

53 See Linn, *Guardians of Empire*, 120, 200.

54 Patton Efficiency Report, October 30, 1925, Microfilm Reel 1, Patton Papers, LOC.

55 Blumenson, *Patton Papers*, Vol. II, 869, 883.

56 Linn, *Guardians of Empire*, 120. Even during the height of the Great Depression, the Army spent $1 million on polo ponies each year while allocating a mere $60,000 for tank development. See Constance Greene et al., *The Ordnance Department: Planning Munitions for War*, USAWWII (Washington, DC, 1955), 195.

57 Blumenson, *Patton Papers*, Vol. II, 875, 914.

58 Truscott, *The Twilight of the U.S. Cavalry*, 30.

59 Robert W. Keeney to Brian M. Linn, February 16, 1994, quoted in Linn, *Guardians of Empire*, 118. See also *idem*, 116.

60 Summerall, *The Way of Duty, Honor, Country*, 183.

61 Edward M. Lewis to AG, Sub: Annual Report, HD, FY 1926, June 30, 1926, AGO 319.12 HD (6-30-26), RG 407, as quoted in Linn, *Guardians of Empire*, 117.

62 Bradley, *A General's Life*, 58.

63 Ibid., 59.

64 See D'Este, *Patton*, 340, and Blumenson, *Patton Papers*, Vol. II, 884.

65 Blumenson, *Patton Papers*, Vol. II, 889.

66 Farago, *Patton*, 112. See also Blumenson, *Patton Papers*, Vol. II, 890.

67 Totten, *The Button Box*, 145.

68 Blumenson, *Patton Papers*, Vol. II, 882.

69 Ibid., 913.

70 Patton Efficiency Report, June 25, 1928, Microfilm Reel 1, Patton Papers, LOC.

71 Perret, *Old Soldiers Never Die*, 129–30; and Herman, *Douglas MacArthur*, 178–79.

72 MacArthur, *Reminiscences*, 29.

73 Ibid., 84; and Perret, *Old Soldiers Never Die*, 129.

74 Linn, *Guardians of Empire*, 70.

75 Ibid., 188. See also Manchester, *American Caesar*, 132.

76 Pershing to Sec. War, July 7, 1923, quoted in Louis Morton, *Strategy and Command: The First Two Years* (Washington, DC: Office of the Chief of Military History, 1962), 39.

77 Linn, *Guardians of Empire*, 205. See also James, *Years of MacArthur*, Vol. I, 297–98.

78 See William Lassiter to George S. Simonds, August 31, 1928, WPD 3251, RG 165; and Report on the Defense of the Philippine Islands by Maj. Gen. Wm. Lassiter, August 21, 1928, AGO 660.2 PD (8-21-28), RG 407, both quoted in Linn, 188.

79 Manchester, *American Caesar*, 142.

80 JANPC to JB, Sub: Defense of the Philippine Islands, April 13, 1922, F 179, Box 6, E 258, RG 165, as quoted in Linn, *Guardians of Empire*, 187.

81 Linn, *Guardians of Empire*, 186.

82 Herman, *Douglas MacArthur*, 180–81.

83 U.S. Congress, Senate, *Affairs in the Philippine Islands*, 867, quoted in Linn, *Guardians of Empire*, 20.

84 Carol Morris Petillo, *Douglas MacArthur: The Philippine Years* (Bloomington: Indiana University Press, 1981), 7.

85 MacArthur, *Reminiscences*, 32.

86 James, *Years of MacArthur*, Vol. I, 299; Perret, *Old Soldiers Never Die*, 130.

87 As Stanley Karnow notes, however, although MacArthur "disregarded color, he respected class. He confined his social circle of Filipinos to rich landlords, who gave him [a] biased perspective of the Philippines." See Stanley Karnow, *In Our Image: America's Empire in the Philippines* (New York: Random House, 1989), 258.

88 James, *Years of MacArthur*, Vol. I, 301.

89 Herman, *Douglas MacArthur*, 183.

90 James, *Years of MacArthur*, Vol. I, 301.

91 MacArthur, *Reminiscences*, 84.

92 Petillo, *Douglas MacArthur*, 132; and Linn, *Guardians of Empire*, 123.

93 Petillo, *Douglas MacArthur*, 132; Linn, *Guardians of Empire*, 148; and Herman, *Douglas MacArthur*, 184.

94 Read to TAG, September 6 and October 21, 1924, quoted in James, *Years of MacArthur*, Vol. I, 303. See also Petillo, 132–33; and Linn, *Guardians of Empire*, 148.

95 Petillo, *Douglas MacArthur*, 133.

96 Mary MacArthur to General Pershing, n.d., Pershing Papers, Box 121, LOC.

97 *New York Times*, September 23, 1924.

98 On the Army and Navy Club, see L. Mervin Maus, *An Army Officer on Leave in Japan* (Chicago: A.C. McClurg, 1911), 4. Louise quoted in Karnow, *In Our Image*, 263.

99 MacArthur, *Reminiscences*, 87, 88.

100 Ibid., 83.

101 Marshall to Gen. John J. Pershing, September 18, 1924; and Marshall to Maj. Gen. John L. Hines, September 21, 1924, in Bland, *The Soldierly Spirit*, 264, 266.

102 The regiment's third battalion remained stationed in the Philippines. See Stoler, *George C. Marshall*, 51–52.

103 Dennis L. Noble, *The Eagle and the Dragon: The United States Military in China, 1901–1937* (Westport, CT: 1990), 61.

104 Marshall to Brig. Gen. William H. Cocke, December 26, 1926, in Bland, *The Soldierly Spirit*, 299.

105 Helmick to the Chief of Staff, October 22, 1925, NA/RG 159 (Reports), as quoted in Bland, *The Soldierly Spirit*, 263.

106 Stoler, *George C. Marshall*, 52–53.

107 *Infantry Journal* 29 (August 1926), 171; See also Cray, *General of the Army*, 96.

108 Marshall to Gen. John J. Pershing, August 25, 1926, in Bland, *The Soldierly Spirit*, 293. See also Stoler, *George C. Marshall*, 52.

109 Cray, *General of the Army*, 97.

110 "Strength of Allied Forces in China on December 1, 1926," Box 628, RG 45, as quoted in Noble, *The Eagle and the Dragon*, 204. See also Noble, *The Eagle and the Dragon*, 194, and Barbara Tuchman, *Stilwell and the American Experience in China 1911–1945* (New York: Macmillan, 1970), 106.

111 Gen. Paul L. Freeman interview by Col. James N. Ellis, Senior Officer Debriefing Program (SODP), U.S. Army War College (AWC), November 29 and 30, 1973, 21, Paul L. Freeman Papers, A, USMHI.

112 Marshall to Gen. John J. Pershing, December 26, 1926, in Bland, *The Soldierly Spirit*, 294. See also Noble, *The Eagle and the Dragon*, 194.

113 Marshall to John C. Hughes, January 2, 1925, GCML, John C. Hughes Papers.

114 Ridgway, *Soldier*, 35.

115 Ibid., 35.

116 See Noble, *The Eagle and the Dragon*, 195–97.

117 Cray, *General of the Army*, 97; Pogue, *Education of a General*, 234.

118 Marshall to Cocke, December 26, 1926, 299.

119 Gen. Charles L. Bolte interview by Arthur Zoebelin, Senior Officer Debriefing Program, Army War College, 1971–1972, Archives, USMHI, Carlisle, PA.

120 Marshall to Maj. Gen. John L. Hines, June 6, 1925, in Bland, *The Soldierly Spirit*, 276–77. See also Cray, *General of the Army*, 88–89.

121 NA/201 File, GCML.

122 Marshall to Brig. Gen. John McA Palmer, December 31, 1925, in Bland, *The Soldierly Spirit*, 284. See also Cray, *General of the Army*, 99.

123 Marshall to Maj. Gen. John L. Hines, in Bland, *The Soldierly Spirit*, 278.

124 Marshall to Hughes, January 2, 1925. See also Noble, *The Eagle and the Dragon*, 89–90.

125 Marshall to Gen. John J. Pershing, January 30, 1925, in Bland, *The Soldierly Spirit*, 274.

126 Charles G. Finney, *The Old China Hands* (Garden City, NY: Doubleday, 1961; reprint, Westport, CT: Greenwood Press, 1977), 38; see also Coffman, *The Regulars*, 335. Barbara Tuchman put the 15th's VD rate at three times that of the U.S. Army. See Tuchman, *Stilwell and the American Experience in China*, 98.

127 Marshall to Pershing, January 30, 1925.

128 Marshall to John C. Hughes, July 18, 1925, GCML, John C. Hughes Papers. See also Bland, *The Soldierly Spirit*, 277, 291.

129 Cray, *General of the Army*, 97.

130 Tuchman,, *Stilwell and the American Experience in China*, 4, 102.

131 Cray, *General of the Army*, 100.

132 Devers quoted in Tuchman, 21; See also Cray, *General of the Army*, 100–101; and Ridgway, *Soldier*, 42.

133 Tuchman, *Stilwell and the American Experience in China*, 89. On Stilwell's experiences in China from 1920 to 1923, see *idem*, 65–89.

134 Tuchman, *Stilwell and the American Experience in China*, 114.

135 Marshall to Cocke, December 26, 1926.

136 On Eichelberger's early experience observing the Japanese army, see Robert L. Eichelberger, *Dear Miss Em: General Eichelberger's War in the Pacific, 1942–1945*, Jay Luvaas ed. (Westport, CT: Greenwood Press, 1972), 7–11.

Chapter Five: "It Was Our Schools That Saved the Army"

1 Eisenhower, *At Ease*, 198.

2 Ibid., 199.

3 Ibid., 200.

4 In 1935 the course reverted to a one-year schedule in order to produce more trained officers in anticipation of conflict arising from the growing international tensions. See Timothy K. Nenninger, "Leavenworth and Its Critics: The U.S. Army Command and General Staff School, 1920–1940," *Journal of Military History* 56 (April 1994), 201–2; and D'Este, *Patton*, 330.

5 U.S. War Department, *Annual Report of the Secretary of War, 1919*, 23, as quoted in Pappas, *Prudens Futuri*, 90.

6 Schifferle, *America's School for War*, 15, 65.

7 Maj. Stuart C. Godfrey, "Command and General Staff School," *Field Artillery Journal* (September-October 1926 and November-December 1926), 521, as quoted in Timothy K. Nenninger, "Creating Officers: The Leavenworth Experience, 1920–1940," *Military Review* 69 (November 1989), 63. See also Nenninger, "Creating Officers," 62–63.

8 Indeed, in his introductory remarks to the CGSS Class of 1924, the commandant, Brig. Gen. Harry Smith, explicitly compared the school's methods to those of Harvard and other law schools. See Hirshson, *General Patton*, 170.

9 Truscott, *The Twilight of the U.S. Cavalry*, 139. One exception was Capt. Terry Mesa De La Allen, who on his first day at CGSS brushed off a tactical problem. When asked what the enemy's intentions were, Allen wrote that he didn't know, "The enemy didn't tell me," and left to make a tennis date with the daughter of a senior officer. Allen would go on to command the 1st Infantry Division in North Africa and Sicily. See Gerald Astor, *Terrible Terry Allen: Combat General of World War II—The Life of an American Soldier* (New York: Ballantine Books, 2003), 72.

10 Chynoweth, *Bellamy Park*, 121.

11 Ernest N. Harmon, with Milton MacKaye and William Ross MacKaye, *Combat Commander: Autobiography of a Soldier* (Englewood Cliffs, NJ: Prentice-Hall, 1970), 50.

12 Schifferle, *America's School for War*, 125. In order to eliminate the "unhealthy" concern among students over grades, class standing, and competition, in 1927 the CGSS eliminated the designation of honors and distinguished graduates.

13 Frank James Price, *Troy H. Middleton: A Biography* (Baton Rouge: Louisiana State University Press, 1974), 67–69, 89–91.

14 Ibid., 89.

15 Quoted in Hirshson, *General Patton*, 168.

16 Quoted in D'Este, *Patton*, 330.

17 Charles E. Heller, "World War I and the Interwar Years, 1916–1939," in John W. Partin, ed., *A Brief History of Fort Leavenworth, 1827–1983* (Fort Leavenworth, KS: Combat Studies Institute, 1983), 52.

18 George S. Patton to Floyd L. Parks, January 26, 1933, Floyd L. Parks Papers, Box 8, DDEL. The CGSS commandant apparently nominated Patton to become a member of the faculty at Leavenworth, but he was one of the rare instances where the commandant's request was not granted. No reason was noted in the records except for two question marks penciled in next to Patton's name. See Schifferle, *America's School for War*, 90.

19 Eisenhower, *At Ease*, 201. See also Michael Korda, *Ike: An American Hero* (New York: HarperCollins, 2007), 170; and Ambrose, *Eisenhower*, 79.

20 Eisenhower, *At Ease*, 201.

21 Miller, *Ike the Soldier*, 225.

22 John S. D. Eisenhower, *Strictly Personal* (Garden City, NY: Doubleday, 1974), 2. See also Eisenhower, *At Ease*, 203.

23 Eisenhower, *At Ease*, 203.

24 Miller, *Ike the Soldier*, 225–26, 227.

25 Price, *Troy H. Middleton*, 91.

26 See A Young Graduate, "The Leavenworth Course," *Cavalry Journal* 30, no. 6 (1927), also in Daniel D. Holt and James W. Leyerzapf, eds., *Eisenhower: The Prewar Diaries and Selected Papers, 1905–1941* (Baltimore: Johns Hopkins University Press, 1988), 52. Other students noticed that Eisenhower spent a lot of time talking to instructors, which encouraged one of his West Point classmates who was at Leavenworth that year, Roscoe B. Woodruff, to suggest long afterward that Eisenhower improved his grades by brownnosing the staff. Yet as Geoffrey Perret notes, "The truth was, Eisenhower had discovered something that Woodruff and others had failed to put to the test: The instructors *wanted* students to talk to them about the problems." See Perret, *Eisenhower*, 94.

27 Miller, *Ike the Soldier*, 229.

28 Dorothy Barrett Brandon, *Mamie Doud Eisenhower: A Portrait of a First Lady* (New York: Charles Scribner's Sons, 1954), 158.

29 George S. Patton Jr. to Dwight D. Eisenhower, July 9, 1926, DDEL, Box 91, Pre-Presidential Papers.

30 Martin Blumenson, *Patton: The Man Behind the Legend, 1885–1945* (New York: William Morrow and Company, 1985), 126.

31 Eisenhower, *At Ease*, 198.

32 Ambrose, *Eisenhower*, 80.

33 Muth, *Command Culture*, 190.

34 Boyd L. Dastrup, *The U.S. Army Command and General Staff College: A Centennial History* (Manhattan, KS: Sunflower University Press, 1982), 74.

35 Coffman, *The Regulars*, 283; See also Bradley, *A General's Life*, 60.

36 Chynoweth, *Bellamy Park*, 121.

37 Collins, *Lightning Joe*, 56–57.

38 Muth, *Command Culture*, 177. For a useful summary of several prominent critiques of CGSS, see Nenninger, "Leavenworth and Its Critics," 208–13.

39 Report of Brigadier General Bliss, November 11, 1903, 90, as quoted in Harry P. Ball, *Of Responsible Command: A History of the U.S. Army War College* (Carlisle Barracks, PA: Alumni Association of the United States Army War College, 1983), 213.

40 John McAuley Palmer to George A. Lynch, May 21, 1938, quoted in Bland, *The Soldierly Spirit*, 599–600. Similarly, the director of the General Staff School, Col. Willey Howell, stated that the "ability to command" is based on three elements: the "physical, the psychological, and the professional. Some of these may be acquired in a school; some may not." See Director, General Staff School, *Annual Report, 1921–1922*, 49–50, as quoted in Schifferle, *America's School for War*, 73.

41 Nenninger, "Leavenworth and Its Critics," 226–27; and D. K. R. Crosswell, *Beetle: The Life of General Walter Bedell Smith* (Lexington: University of Kentucky Press, 2010), 188.

42 Bradley, *A General's Life*, 61.

43 Collins quoted in Coffman, *The Regulars*, 289; See also Collins, *Lightning Joe*, 57.

44 General Service Schools, *Memorandum No. 4*, September 13, 1926, Archives, Combined Arms Research Library, Fort Leavenworth, KS, as quoted in Nenninger, "Leavenworth and Its Critics," 227.

45 GSSP, *Instruction Circular No. 1* (GSSP, 1926–1927), 46–50, as quoted in Schifferle, *America's School for War*, 113.

46 Leslie Anders, *Gentle Knight: The Life and Times of Major General Edwin Forrest Harding* (Kent, OH: Kent State University Press, 1985), 117–18.

47 Crosswell, *Beetle*, 187; Schifferle, *America's School for War*, 186–87, 193.

48 Harmon, *Combat Commander*, 209–10.

49 Smith, *Eisenhower in War and Peace*, 74–75.

50 Pershing to Eisenhower, August 15, 1927, DDEL, Pre-Presidential Papers, Box 92.

51 Eisenhower, *At Ease*, 204.

52 Crosswell, *Beetle*, 194.

53 *Secretary of War Report, War Department Annual Reports, 1919*, I: 28, as quoted in Ball, *Of Responsible Command*, 151.

54 Ridley McLean, Letter to the Secretary of the Navy, January 3, 1922, as quoted in Pappas, *Prudens Futuri*, 116–17.

55 Ball, *Of Responsible Command*, 212–13; Schifferle, *America's School for War*, 34; and Holland, *Eisenhower Between the Wars*, 127, 141.

56 H. B. Crosby, "Orientation Lecture to the Army War College Class of 1924–1925," as quoted in Michael R. Matheny, *Carrying the War to the Enemy: American Operational Art to 1945* (Norman: University of Oklahoma Press, 2011), 57.

57 William D. Connor, *Address to the Class of 1929*, September 1, 1928, as quoted in Pappas, *Prudens Futuri*, 127.

58 Lyon, *Eisenhower*, 62.

59 Benjamin F. Cooling, "Dwight D. Eisenhower at the Army War College, 1927–1928," *Parameters* Vol. 5, no. 1, 1975, 27.

60 Dwight D. Eisenhower, "An Enlisted Reserve for the Regular Army," March 15, 1928, in Holt and Leyerzapf, *Eisenhower*, 62–78.

61 W. D. Connor to DDE, May 5, 1928, Connor folder, Box 23, Pre-Presidential Papers, DDEL.

62 Eisenhower efficiency report, June 30, 1928, DDEL.

63 Chynoweth, *Bellamy Park*, 133. See also Martin Blumenson, "George S. Patton's Student Days at the Army War College," *Parameters* Vol. V, no. 2, 25.

64 Blumenson, "George S. Patton's Student Days," 28–29.

65 Ibid., 31–32; and D'Este, *Patton*, 349.

66 Crosswell, *Beetle*, 197–98; Bradley, *A General's Life*, 75; and Miller, *Ike the Soldier*, 237–38.

67 Ball, *Of Responsible Command*, 246, 248, 253.

68 John A. Adams, *General Jacob Devers: World War II's Forgotten Four Star* (Bloomington: Indiana University Press, 2015), 25–26; and Mark T. Calhoun, *General Lesley J. McNair: Unsung Architect of the US Army* (Lawrence: University Press of Kansas, 2015), 127, 132, 136–37.

69 Victor Davis Hanson, *The Second World Wars: How the First Global Conflict Was Fought and Won* (New York: Basic Books, 2017), 387–88.

70 Pogue, *Education of a General*, 245.

71 Marshall to Mrs. Thomas B. Coles, August 20, 1927, in Bland, *The Soldierly Spirit*, 311.

72 Elizabeth C. Marshall to Mrs. Thomas B. Cole, September 5-6, 1927, GCML, Research File (GCM-Miscellaneous Family—Lily Coles Marshall).

73 Pogue, *Education of a General*, 246.

74 Cray, *General of the Army*, 103.

75 Puryear, *Nineteen Stars*, 53.

76 John J. Pershing to George C. Marshall, October 6, 1927, in Bland, *The Soldierly Spirit*, 315. See also Stoler, *George C. Marshall*, 54–55.

77 George C. Marshall to John J. Pershing, October 14, 1927, in Bland, *The Soldierly Spirit*, 315.

78 George C. Marshall to Maj. Gen. Stephen J. Fuqua, November 25, 1932, Marshall Papers (Fort Screven), Box 1, GCML.

79 Cray, *General of the Army*, 104.

80 Price, *Troy H. Middleton*, 78, 80.

81 Pogue, *Education of a General*, 247–48.

82 George C. Marshall to Brig. Gen. Stuart Heintzelman, December 18, 1933, Marshall Papers (Illinois National Guard), Box 1, GCML.

83 George C. Marshall, Lecture, "Development in Tactics," ca. 1927, Marshall Papers Box 110 (Pentagon Office-Speeches), GCML.

84 Payne, *Marshall Story*, 106. See also Crosswell, *Beetle*, 167, 169.

85 Bradley, *A General's Life*, 64.

86 Pogue, *Education of a General*, 251.

87 *Infantry in Battle*, ix. See also Paul F. Braim, *The Will to Win: The Life of General James A. Van Fleet* (Annapolis, MD: Naval Institute Press, 2001), 55.

88 Crosswell, *Beetle*, 174.

89 Ibid., 166; and Pogue, *Education of a General*, 249.

90 George C. Marshall to Maj. Gen. Stuart Heintzelman, December 4, 1933, Marshall Papers (Illinois National Guard), Box 1, GCML.

91 Bland, *Marshall Interviews*, 543.

92 Bradley, *A General's Life*, 66.

93 Pogue, *Education of a General*, 256. See also Coffman, *The Regulars*, 264.

94 Bland, *Marshall Interviews*, 544.

95 Bradley, *A General's Life*, 66.

96 Ridgway, *Soldier*, 199.

97 Stephan T. Wishnevsky, *Courtney Hicks Hodges: From Private to Four-Star General in the United States Army* (London: McFarland, 2006), 54.

98 Gen. George H. Decker to Forrest C. Pogue, November 5, 1964, Research File (Miscellaneous), GCML.

99 Bradley, *A General's Life*, 66.

100 Ibid., 65. See also Axelrod, *Bradley*, 51, 53.

101 Tuchman, *Stilwell and the American Experience in China*, 125, 130.

102 Bradley, *A General's Life*, 65.

103 Tuchman, *Stilwell and the American Experience in China*, 125.

104 Bradley, *A General's Life*, 65.

105 Crosswell, *Beetle*, 172–73.

106 Bradley, *A General's Life*, 69. See also Axelrod, *Bradley*, 54.

107 Eisenhower, *At Ease*, 207–8. See also Ambrose, *Eisenhower*, 84.

108 Eisenhower, *At Ease*, 208–9.

109 Collins, *Lightning Joe*, 51–52. See also Pogue, *Education of a General*, 260.

110 Bradley, *A General's Life*, 65.

111 Collins, *Lightning Joe*, 49, 50.

112 Wishnevsky, *Courtney Hicks Hodges*, 51, 54.

113 Bradley, *A General's Life*, 63.

114 Marshall to Fuqua, November 25, 1932.

115 Col. David Hardee, Air Instructor at the Infantry School from 1927 to 1929, Letter to Forrest C. Pogue, GCML, Miscellaneous Research File.

116 Pogue, *Education of a General*, 261–62.

117 Katherine Tupper Marshall, *Together: Annals of an Army Wife* (New York: Tupper & Love, 1946), 3. See also Pogue, *Education of a General*, 107–8.

118 Marshall, *Together*, 2–3.

119 Ibid., 3.

120 Bland, *The Soldierly Spirit*, 359, 360; Stoler, *George C. Marshall*, 58; and Braim, *Will to Win*, 54.

121 Bradley, *A General's Life*, 69–70.

122 Maj. Gen. Joseph D. Patch to Forrest Pogue, November 4, 1960, as quoted in Bland, *The Soldierly Spirit*, 320.

123 Pogue, *Education of a General*, 260.

124 Cray, *General of the Army*, 110–11.

125 Bradley, *A General's Life*, 73.

126 Muth, *Command Culture*, 193.

Chapter Six: The Army in the Great Depression

1 MacArthur, *Reminiscences*, 88–89; Hunt, *Untold Story of MacArthur*, 125.

2 James, *Years of MacArthur*, Vol. I, 344.

3 Herman, *Douglas MacArthur*, 200.

4 Manchester, *American Caesar*, 143.

5 Herman, *Douglas MacArthur*, 201.

6 Manchester, *American Caesar*, 144.

7 MacArthur, *Reminiscences*, 89.

8 Ibid., 89.

9 Thomas W. Collier, "The Army and the Great Depression," *Parameters*, September 1988, 102. See also Manchester, *American Caesar*, 146, 153.

10 Notes from the Chief of Infantry, *Infantry* 22, no. 6 (June 1923), 680–81, as quoted in Schifferle, *America's School for War*, 18.

11 On the War Department's three plans, see John W. Killigrew, "The Impact of the Great Depression on the Army, 1929–1936," PhD dissertation, Indiana University, 1960, 19–20, 40–41; and Michael J. Meese, "Defense Decision Making Under Budget Stringency: Explaining Downsizing in the United States Army," PhD dissertation, Princeton University, 2000, 63–64.

12 Hoover to Hurley, July 29, 1930, AG 111, RG 94, NA, as quoted in Killigrew, "Impact of the Great Depression," 54.

13 Killigrew, "Impact of the Great Depression," 54–55.

14 Herman, *Douglas MacArthur*, 209–10.

15 James, *Years of MacArthur*, Vol. I, 352, 355; Killigrew, "Impact of the Great Depression," 103–4.

16 James, *Years of MacArthur*, Vol. I, 356.

17 James, *Years of MacArthur*, Vol. I, 426–27.

18 George C. Kenney, *The MacArthur I Know* (New York: Duell, Sloan, and Pearce, 1952), 25.

19 Killigrew, "Impact of the Great Depression," 103, 104, 109.

20 John Callan O'Laughlin to MacArthur, July 21, 1932, John C. O'Laughlin Papers, Box 25, LOC.

21 Herman, *Douglas MacArthur*, 210.

22 Letter, Gen. Douglas MacArthur to the Honorable Bertrand D. Snell, May 9, 1932. AG 111, RG 94, NA.

23 *Annual Report of the Secretary of War, 1932* (Washington, DC: GPO, 1932), 60.

24 Killigrew, "Impact of the Great Depression," 125–26.

25 Manchester, *American Caesar*, 146.

26 Statement of Gen. Douglas MacArthur Before the House Committee of Military Affairs, April 26, 1933, 29, MMA RG 1, Box 3, Folder 1. See also Killigrew, "Impact of the Great Depression," 68, 258.

27 James, *Years of MacArthur*, Vol. I, 358; Killigrew, "Impact of the Great Depression," 85. Conversely, David Johnson argues that Army culture and bureaucracy bore greater responsibility than budgetary issues for the Army's failure to adequately develop armor doctrine during the interwar period. See Johnson, *Fast Tanks and Heavy Bombers*.

28 Telegraph, MacArthur to Payne, July 12, 1932, AG 111, RG 94, NA, as quoted in Killigrew, "Impact of the Great Depression," 122.

29 James, *Years of MacArthur*, Vol. I, 426; Killigrew, "Impact of the Great Depression," 199–200, 202; and Perret, *Old Soldiers Never Die*, 152.

30 Perret, *Old Soldiers Never Die*, 163. See also Killigrew, "Impact of the Great Depression," 221, 370.

31 Mark Perry, *The Most Dangerous Man in America: The Making of Douglas MacArthur* (New York: Basic Books, 2014), 3.

32 Rexford G. Tugwell, *The Brains Trust* (New York: Viking Press, 1968), 427–34.

33 Harold L. Ickes, *The Secret Diary of Harold L. Ickes: Volume I: The First Thousand Days, 1933–1936* (New York: Simon & Schuster, 1953–1954), 71.

34 John Hersey, *Men on Bataan* (New York: Alfred A. Knopf, 1942), 162. See also Perret, *Old Soldiers Never Die*, 172–73; and Killigrew, "Impact of the Great Depression," 225.

35 MacArthur, *Reminiscences*, 428–29.

36 James, *Years of MacArthur*, Vol. I, 431. See also Killigrew, "Impact of the Great Depression," 231.

37 *Annual Report of the Secretary of War, 1933* (Washington, DC: GPO, 1933), 49.

38 Killigrew, "Impact of the Great Depression," 240, 363.

39 James, *Years of MacArthur*, Vol. I, 437; Perret, *Old Soldiers Never Die*, 184.

40 *Report of the Secretary of War, 1934* (Washington, DC: GPO, 1934), 34.

41 Puryear, *Nineteen Stars*, 117.

42 Manchester, *American Caesar*, 153.

43 Truscott, *The Twilight of the U.S. Cavalry*, 133. See also Bland, *The Soldierly Spirit*, 390, fn2.

44 Perret, *Old Soldiers Never Die*, 150, 172; Cray, *General of the Army*, 113.

45 Marshall, *Together*, 12. See also Cray, *General of the Army*, 113.

46 Puryear, *Nineteen Stars*, 53.

47 Arthur M. Schlesinger Jr., *The Crisis of the Old Order: 1919–1933* (Boston: Houghton Mifflin Company, 1957), 3.

48 David M. Kennedy, *Freedom from Fear: The American People in Depression and War, 1929–1945* (New York: Oxford University Press, 1999), 38, 162–63.

49 Dulany Terrett, "The Technical Services—The Signal Corps: The Emergency," *United States Army in World War II* (Washington, DC: Office of the Chief of Military History, 1956), 67.

50 Jean Edward Smith, *Lucius D. Clay: An American Life* (New York: Henry Holt and Company, 1990), 56. See also Kennedy, *Freedom from Fear*, 86–87.

51 Schlesinger, *Crisis of the Old Order*, 74, 249.

52 Ibid., 3, 256; and Kennedy, *Freedom from Fear*, 85, 163.

53 James, *Years of MacArthur*, Vol. I, 384–85; Weintraub, *15 Stars*, 81.

54 Schlesinger, *Crisis of the Old Order*, 256–57; James, *Years of MacArthur*, Vol. I, 385, 387.

55 James, *Years of MacArthur*, Vol. I, 387. See also Paul Dickson and Thomas B. Allen, *The Bonus Army: An American Epic* (New York: Walker & Company, 2004), 77, 90.

56 Perret, *Old Soldiers Never Die*, 156; Schlesinger, *Crisis of the Old Order*, 258–59; and Donald J. Lisio, *The President and Protest: Hoover, MacArthur, and the Bonus Riot* (New York: Fordham University Press, 1994), 77, 79.

57 Member of Gardner Jackson, The Oral History Collection of Columbia University, 383–84, as quoted in Lisio, *The President and Protest*, 70. See also *idem*, 51.

58 Schlesinger, *Crisis of the Old Order*, 260.

59 James, *Years of MacArthur*, Vol. I, 389.

60 Truscott, *The Twilight of the U.S. Cavalry*, 121; Dickson and Allen, *Bonus Army*, 74.

61 Herman, *Douglas MacArthur*, 213–14; James, *Years of MacArthur*, Vol. I, 384–85; and Killigrew, "Impact of the Great Depression," 161.

62 James, *Years of MacArthur*, Vol. I, 390.

63 Memo, AC/S G-2 for the AG, June 10, 1932, for radiogram to all Corps Area Commanders, AG 240 Bonus (5-29-32) Section 1, RG 94, NA, as quoted in Killigrew, "Impact of the Great Depression."

64 Hirshson, *General Patton*, 206, 207.

65 James, *Years of MacArthur*, Vol. I, 386, 381.

66 Telegram, King, Fort McPherson to AG, June 11, 45-WVR, AG 240 Bonus (5-28-32) Section 1, RG 94, NA, as quoted in Killigrew, 164.

67 Telegram, Craig to AG, June 14, 1932. WAG 61, AG 240 Bonus (5-28-32) Section 1, RG 94, NA, quoted in Killigrew, "Impact of the Great Depression," 164.

68 Col. Edward W. Starling and Thomas Sugrue, *Starling of the White House: The Story of the Man Whose Secret Service Detail Guarded Five Presidents from Woodrow Wilson to Franklin D. Roosevelt* (New York: Simon & Schuster, 1946), 296. See also James, *Years of MacArthur*, Vol. I, 388, and Dickson and Allen, *Bonus Army*, 124.

69 Lisio, *The President and Protest*, xiii.

70 Dickson and Allen, *Bonus Army*, 35, 59; Lisio, *The President and Protest*, 26–27, 33, 37, 47–48, and 110–11.

71 See Lisio, *The President and Protest*, 111, 113; and Dickson and Allen, *Bonus Army*, 127.

72 Schlesinger, *Crisis of the Old Order*, 258.

73 *B.E.F. News*, July 23, 1932, as quoted in Dickson and Allen, *Bonus Army*, 152. See also James, *Years of MacArthur*, Vol. I, 391–93, and Lisio, *The President and Protest*, 121–22.

74 James, *Years of MacArthur*, Vol. I, 393; Schlesinger, 259.

75 Lisio, *The President and Protest*, 142, 171; Dickson and Allen, *Bonus Army*, 152, 156–57.

76 James, *Years of MacArthur*, Vol. I, 394–95.

77 Ibid., 396; Lisio, 177–79; and Perret, *Old Soldiers Never Die*, 157.

78 Lisio, *The President and Protest*, 185–86.

79 Perret, *Old Soldiers Never Die*, 157.

80 Theodore G. Joslin, *Hoover off the Record* (Garden City, NY: Doubleday, 1934), 268. The president's desire to keep the scope of operations limited is reflected in Secretary Hurley's first draft of the troop order: "After having cleared the area where the riot had just occurred, you will maintain contact with the rioters until they have crossed the Anacostia Bridge, order them into the veterans' camps in Anacostia. Surround all veterans camps in Anacostia and hold all campers, rioters and marchers until the names of all of them can be tabulated and their fingerprints taken." See Lisio, *The President and Protest*, 199.

81 Herman, *Douglas MacArthur*, 218.

82 D'Este, *Patton*, 352–53; Blumenson, *Patton Papers, Vol. II*, 134.

83 Blumenson, *Patton Papers*, Vol. II, 977–78.

84 Truscott, *The Twilight of the U.S. Cavalry*, 127.

85 H. W. Blakely, "When the Army Was Smeared," *Combat Forces Journal*, February 1952, 29.

86 James, *Years of MacArthur*, Vol. I, 400. See also Lisio, *The President and Protest*, 205; and Herman, *Douglas MacArthur*, 219.

87 James, *Years of MacArthur*, Vol. I, 400.

88 Truscott, *The Twilight of the U.S. Cavalry*, 128.

89 Lt. Col. Louis A. Kunzig, quoted in James, *Years of MacArthur*, Vol. I, 400–401.

90 Lisio, *The President and Protest*, 209.

91 Blumenson, *Patton Papers*, Vol. II, 978.

92 James, *Years of MacArthur*, Vol. I, 401.

93 Ibid.

94 Lisio, *The President and Protest*, 208; Dickson and Allen, *Bonus Army*, 180.

95 Eisenhower, *At Ease*, 217.

96 James, *Years of MacArthur*, Vol. I, 402.

97 Eisenhower, *At Ease*, 217–18.

98 George Van Horn Moseley, "One Soldier's Journey," Unpublished Memoir, Vol. II, 144–45, George Van Horn Moseley Papers, Box 13, LOC.

99 Manchester, *American Caesar*, 152; Weintraub, *15 Stars*, 83.

100 F. Trubee Davison (Henle Interview), 1–3, Herbert Hoover Library, as quoted in Perret, *Old Soldiers Never Die*, 159.

101 Perret, *Old Soldiers Never Die*, 159.

102 MacArthur, *Reminiscences*, 95. See also Perret, *Old Soldiers Never Die*, 160.

103 Perry L. Miles, *Fallen Leaves* (Berkeley, CA: Wuerth Publishing, 1964), 309.

104 Eisenhower, *At Ease*, 217–18.

105 F. Trubee Davison, Interview, Oral History Collection, HHPL. See also Lisio, *The President and Protest*, 214–15.

106 War Department transcript of MacArthur press conference, July 29, 1932, quoted in Dickson and Allen, *Bonus Army*, 181–82.

107 James, *Years of MacArthur*, Vol. I, 403, 407.

108 Ibid., 406; Lisio, *The President and Protest*, 239. Specifically, the *Washington Post* had reported that sixty persons were treated for injuries; *Time* cited fifty-six; and the *New York Herald Tribune* listed fifty-three.

109 Lisio, *The President and Protest*, 220.

110 James, *Years of MacArthur*, Vol. I, 403, 409.

111 Lisio, *The President and Protest*, 222.

112 Truscott, *The Twilight of the U.S. Cavalry*, 129.

113 See "A Cavalry Major Evicts Veteran Who Saved His Life in Battle," *New York Times*, July 30, 1932.

114 *Washington News* quoted in Schlesinger, 265. See also Lisio, *The President and Protest*, 81, 223; Dickson and Allen, *Bonus Army*, 190.

115 Lisio, *The President and Protest*, 285.

116 Killigrew, "Impact of the Great Depression," 174; Herman, *Douglas MacArthur*, 223.

117 Bland, *The Soldierly Spirit*, 392.

118 War Department Regulation (Provisional), April 5, 1933. By Order of the Secretary of War, Douglas MacArthur, Chief of Staff. AG 324.5 CCC (3-25-33) Section 1, RG 94, NA, as quoted in Killigrew, "Impact of the Great Depression," 295. See also Herman, *Douglas MacArthur*, 228.

119 James, 383; Charles W. Johnson, "The Civilian Conservation Corps: The Role of the Army," PhD dissertation, University of Michigan, 1968, 4.

120 Bradley, *A General's Life*, 72.

121 Miller, *Ike the Soldier*, 270.

122 C. W. Johnson, "The Civilian Conservation Corps," 8–9.

123 Killigrew, "Impact of the Great Depression," 297–98, 299.

124 Duncan K. Major to Robert Fechner, June 30, 1933, Official Files 268, FDRL, as quoted in Charles E. Heller, "The U.S. Army, the Civilian Conservation Corps, and Leadership for World War II, 1933–1942" *Armed Forces & Society* Vol. 36, no. 3, 443.

125 James, *Years of MacArthur*, Vol. I, 419–20.

126 Cray, *General of the Army*, 114; C. W. Johnson, "Civilian Conservation Corps," 14–15; and Heller, "The U.S. Army, the Civilian Conservation Corps, and Leadership for World War II, 1933–1942," 446–47.

127 MacArthur quoted in Heller, "U.S. Army," 444.

128 *Annual Report of the Secretary of War, 1933*, 8.

129 C. W. Johnson, "Civilian Conservation Corps," 12.

130 Killigrew, "Impact of the Great Depression," 299–300.

131 Martin Blumenson, *Mark Clark: The Last of the Great World War II Commanders* (New York: Congdon & Weed, Inc, 1984), 35.

132 William Farrington, ed., *Cowboy Pete: An Autobiography of Major General Charles H. Corlett* (Santa Fe, NM: Sleeping Fox Publishers, 1974), 54.

133 Marshall to Maj. Gen. George Van Horn Moseley, April 5, 1934, GCML, Marshall Papers, Box 1; Reuben E. Jenkins to Forrest C. Pogue, October 26, 1960, GCML/ Research File (Fort Screven).

134 Marshall, *Together*, 13.

135 Marshall to Maj. Gen. George Van Horn Moseley, April 5, 1934.

136 See Marshall to Col. Clyde R. Abraham, May 26, 1933; and Marshall to Maj. Gen. Edward L. King, May 26, 1933, both in GCML, Marshall Papers (Fort Screven) Box 1.

137 Marshall to Capt. Germain Seligman, March 29, 1933, GCML, Marshall Papers, Box 1 (Fort Screven).

138 C. W. Johnson, "Civilian Conservation Corps," 13–14, 59.

139 Heller, "U.S. Army," 440.

140 Duncan K. Major to Robert Fechner, June 30, 1933, Official Files 268, FDRL, as quoted in Heller, "U.S. Army," 449.

141 George C. Marshall to John J. Pershing, July 11, 1933, in Bland, *The Soldierly Spirit*, 398.

142 Leslie Alexander Lucy, *The Soil Soldiers: The Civilian Conservation Corps in the Great Depression* (Radnor, PA: Chilton Book Company, 1976), 115.

143 Memo, Major for Assistant Chief of Staff, G-3, December 22, 1933, RG 94 GA Files, as quoted in C. W. Johnson, "Civilian Conservation Corps," 227. See also *idem*, 226.

144 Heller, "U.S. Army," 448.

145 Letter, WD Rep on CCC Advisory Council for Chief of Staff, December 14, 1935. AG 324.5 CCC (3-25-33) Section 1, Part III, November 1935, RG 94, NA, as quoted in Killigrew, "Impact of the Great Depression," 342.

146 Heller, "U.S. Army," 445.

147 Braim, *Will to Win*, 57–58.

148 Dwight D. Eisenhower Chief of Staff Diary, June 18, 1933, in Holt and Leyerzapf, *Eisenhower*, 252.

149 Col. Lawrence Halstead to Marshall, May 26, 1933, GCML, Marshall Papers, Box 1; See also Weigley, *History of the United States Army*, 402.

150 James, *Years of MacArthur*, Vol. I, 443, 445–46; Lisio, *The President and Protest*, 289.

151 Herman, *Douglas MacArthur*, 242; Perret, *Old Soldiers Never Die*, 175.

152 MacArthur quoted in Elias Huzar, *The Purse and the Sword* (Ithaca, NY: Cornell University Press, 1950), 139. See also Killigrew, "Impact of the Great Depression," 382, 384–85.

153 *Report of the Chief of Staff, U.S. Army*, 1935 (Washington, DC: GPO, 1935), 1.

154 James, *Years of MacArthur*, Vol. I, 492.

155 *Washington Herald*, August 2, 1935, as quoted in James, *Years of MacArthur*, Vol. I, 454.

156 James, *Years of MacArthur*, Vol. I, 461.

157 Herman, *Douglas MacArthur*, 251; Weigley quoted in James, *Years of MacArthur*, Vol. I, 461.

Chapter Seven: MacArthur and Eisenhower in the Shadow of the Rising Sun

1 Michael Schaller, *Douglas MacArthur: The Far Eastern General* (Oxford: Oxford University Press, 1989), 21–25; and Herman, *Douglas MacArthur*, 245.

2 Manuel Quezon, *The Good Fight* (New York, 1946), 153–55.

3 MacArthur to Manuel Quezon, December 27, 1934, RG 18, MMA.

4 Brands, 165; J. S. D. Eisenhower, *General Ike*, 23; and Perret, *Old Soldiers Never Die*, 187.

5 MacArthur to Quezon, June 1, 1935, RG 18, MMA.

6 "Memorandum of the Terms of the Agreement Between the President of the Philippine Commonwealth and General MacArthur," n.d., RG1, Box 1, Folder 2, MMA.

7 "Orders to General MacArthur," September 18, 1935, RG 1, Box 3, Folder 1, MMA.

8 Moseley to Eisenhower, February 18, 1933, DDEL. See also Smith, *Eisenhower in War and Peace*, 92–93; and Ambrose, *Eisenhower*, 88, 90.

9 Public Resolution Number 98, 71st Congress, 2nd session, H.J. Res. 251, quoted in Smith, *Eisenhower in War and Peace*, 99.

10 MacArthur to Eisenhower, November 4, 1931, DDEL. See also Ambrose, *Eisenhower*, 92.

11 Second endorsement to Eisenhower efficiency report, July 1931–1932, DDEL, Personnel Records, Box 4.

12 Dwight D. Eisenhower, Chief of Staff diary, June 2, 1933, in Holt and Leyerzapf, *Eisenhower*, 252; See also D'Este, *Eisenhower*, 216; Holland, *Eisenhower Between the Wars*, 107, 169; and Smith, *Eisenhower in War and Peace*, 102.

13 Ambrose, *Eisenhower*, 101; See also D'Este, *Eisenhower*, 213.

14 Douglas MacArthur to Eisenhower, September 30, 1935, DDE Pre-Presidential Papers, 1916–1952, Misc. File, Box 24, 1935.

15 Eisenhower Diary, Chief of Staff Diary, June 15, 1932, in Holt and Leyerzapf, *Eisenhower*, 230. See also Eisenhower, *At Ease*, 214.

16 Lyon, *Eisenhower*, 71.

17 Eisenhower, *At Ease*, 214.

18 Smith, *Eisenhower in War and Peace*, 103; Perret, *Eisenhower*, 115.

19 Miller, *Ike the Soldier*, 268–69.

20 Perret, *Eisenhower*, 115, 116; Korda, *Ike*, 194.

21 Leahy quoted in Karnow, *In Our Image*, 269. See also Korda, *Ike*, 192; and Smith, *Eisenhower in War and Peace*, 116.

22 Hunt, *Untold Story of MacArthur*, 171.

23 Jonathan W. Jordan, *Brothers, Rivals, Victors: Eisenhower, Patton, Bradley, and the Partnership That Drove the Allied Conquest in Europe* (New York: New American Library, 2011), 125; D'Este, *Eisenhower*, 209, 229.

24 Eisenhower, *At Ease*, 219.

25 D'Este, *Eisenhower*, 229–30, 232.

26 Eisenhower, *At Ease*, 219–20.

27 Ibid., 219.

28 Ibid., 220.

29 Perret, *Eisenhower*, 119, 123.

30 Dwight D. Eisenhower to Gen. George V. H. Moseley, November 23, 1934, DDEL, Pre-Presidential Papers, Box 84. See also Holland, *Eisenhower Between the Wars*, 189.

31 Eisenhower, *At Ease*, 223. See also James, *Years of MacArthur*, Vol. I, 492–93; and Schaller, *Douglas MacArthur*, 27, 29.

32 James, *Years of MacArthur*, Vol. I, 495; Perry, *Most Dangerous Man*, 50; and Karnow, *In Our Image*, 270.

33 Herman, *Douglas MacArthur*, 255–56; Manchester, *American Caesar*, 164; and Perret, *Old Soldiers Never Die*, 193, 194.

34 MacArthur, *Reminiscences*, 103.

35 Eisenhower, *At Ease*, 224.

36 MacArthur to John Callan O'Laughlin, December 9, 1935, O'Laughlin Papers, LOC.

37 Stimson Diary, March 30, 1935, as quoted in Herman, *Douglas MacArthur*, 263. See also Schaller, *Douglas MacArthur*, 28; and Karnow, *In Our Image*, 272.

38 Hugh A. Drum to C/S, Sub: Missions of the Regular Army, February 15, 1924, WPD 1549, RG 165, as quoted in Linn, *Guardians of Empire*, 172.

39 Manchester, *American Caesar*, 170. See also Perret, *Old Soldiers Never Die*, 195.

40 Stanley D. Embick to CG, PD, Sub: Military Policy of U.S. in Philippine Islands, April 19, 1933, AGO 093.5 PD (10-2031), CF, RG 407, as quoted in Manchester, *American Caesar*, 170.

41 Louis Morton, "War Plan Orange: Evolution of a Strategy," *World Politics*, Vol. 11, no. 2 (January 1959), 242.

42 MacArthur quoted in Schaller, *Douglas MacArthur*, 32.

43 Perret, *Old Soldiers Never Die*, 196, 198; and Linn, *Guardians of Empire*, 174.

44 Douglas MacArthur to Bonner Fellers, June 1, 1939, RG 1, Box 2, Folder 10, MMA; Linn, *Guardians of Empire*, 176; and Smith, *Eisenhower in War and Peace*, 127.

45 Douglas MacArthur to SW, Sub: Military Value of the Philippine Islands to the United States, October 1931, AGO 093.5 PI (10-2-31), RG 407, as quoted in Linn, *Guardians of Empire*, 174.

46 Petillo, *Douglas MacArthur*, 179.

47 Karnow, *In Our Image*, 272.

48 Holt and Leyerzapf, *Eisenhower*, 289; Schaller, *Douglas MacArthur*, 28; and Perret, *Eisenhower*, 125.

49 General Embick to Chief of Staff, December 2, 1935, WPD 3389-29, RG 165. See also Schaller, *Douglas MacArthur*, 33, 34; and Brands, 176.

50 Moseley, "One Soldier's Journey," Vol. 2, 153. See also Herman, *Douglas MacArthur*, 263.

51 Eisenhower, *At Ease*, 221; Ambrose, *Eisenhower*, 105.

52 Eisenhower, *At Ease*, 222; Ambrose, *Eisenhower*, 105.

53 Robert H. Ferrell, ed., *The Eisenhower Diaries* (New York: Norton, 1981), 10. See also Holland, *Eisenhower Between the Wars*, 190.

54 Eisenhower, *At Ease*, 220.

55 "Report on National Defense in the Philippines" (Manila: Bureau of Printing, 1936), 30, 44, RG 1, Box 1, Folder 3, MMA.

56 Douglas MacArthur, *A Soldier Speaks: Public Papers and Speeches of General of the Army Douglas MacArthur*, Vorin E. Whan, ed. (New York: Frederick A. Praeger, 1965), 101.

57 *Collier's*, September 5, 1936.

58 Collins, *Lightning Joe*, 61.

59 "Report on National Defense in the Philippines," 50.

60 Eisenhower Diary, December 27, 1935, in Ferrell, *Eisenhower Diaries*, 11-12.

61 Ferrell, *Eisenhower Diaries*, 19–20.

62 Eisenhower diary, May 29, 1936 (Second Entry), in Ferrell, 20. See also Kerry Irish, "Dwight Eisenhower and Douglas MacArthur in the Philippines: There Must Be a Day of Reckoning," *Journal of Military History* 74 (April 2010), 454.

63 Eisenhower, Philippine Diary, January 20, 1936, in Holt and Leyerzapf, *Eisenhower*, 304.

64 Lyon, *Eisenhower*, 78.

65 Eisenhower Diary, July 1, 1936, in Holt and Leyerzapf, *Eisenhower*, 326.

66 MMA, RG 40, Eisenhower interview, 71.

67 Pershing to John Callan O'Laughlin, June 10, 1937, O'Laughlin Papers, LOC.

68 Manchester, *American Caesar*, 172.

69 Karnow, *In Our Image*, 271.

70 MacArthur, *Reminiscences*, 166. See also D'Este, *Eisenhower*, 239.

71 Linn, *Guardians of Empire*, 232.

72 Eisenhower Diary, July 1, 1935, in Holt and Leyerzapf, *Eisenhower*, 326.

73 Furthermore, key leaders in the War Department were suspicious of how the Filipinos would use the weapons provided them. Brig. Gen. Walter Krueger, chief of the War Plans Division from 1936 to 1938, believed that "arming the Filipinos constitutes a potential danger for the U.S." See James, *Years of MacArthur*, Vol. I, 544; and Linn, *Guardians of Empire*, 235, 242.

74 Eisenhower diary, February 15, 1936, in Ferrell, 17.

75 Eisenhower diary, March 1, 1936, in Ferrell, 17–18.

76 Eisenhower diary, September 26, 1936, and November 15, 1936, in Ferrell, 21–22.

77 Susan Eisenhower, *Mrs. Ike*, 136–37.

78 Ambrose, *Eisenhower*, 107–8; and Miller, *Ike the Soldier*, 282.

79 Mamie Doud Eisenhower Oral History, DDEL, 65. See also Ambrose, *Eisenhower*, 108–9.

80 See Irish, "Dwight Eisenhower and Douglas MacArthur in the Philippines," 447, 455.

81 Eisenhower Diary, May 29, 1936 (Second Entry), in Ferrell, 20.

82 Ibid. See also Perret, *Old Soldiers Never Die*, 216–17; and James, *Years of MacArthur*, Vol. I, 514.

83 Eisenhower Diary, December 25, 1936, in Holt and Leyerzapf, *Eisenhower*, 361.

84 Eisenhower Philippine Diary, May 29, 1936 (Second Entry), in Ferrell, 20. See also Irish, "Dwight Eisenhower and Douglas MacArthur in the Philippines," 455.

85 Eisenhower Diary, December 25, 1936, in Holt and Leyerzapf, *Eisenhower*, 361–62.

86 MacArthur Response to Vincent A. Pacis, July 26, 1937, RG 1, Box 3, Folder 3, MMA.

87 Herman, *Douglas MacArthur*, 268–69, 276.

88 Letter from a British manager of a sugar estate, August 25, 1937, File: Philippine Islands, Box 154, Pre-Presidential, 1916–1952, DDE Papers, DDEL.

89 Eisenhower Letter to James Ord, July 29, 1937, RG 1, Box 1, Folder 6A, MMA.

90 James Ord to Emily Ord, October 28, 1937, DDE Pre-Presidential Papers 1916–52, Misc. File, Box 24, 1936.

91 MacArthur, *Reminiscences*, 106.

92 Herman, *Douglas MacArthur*, 272.

93 Ord to Eisenhower, June 27, 1937, DDE Pre-Presidential Papers, 1916–52, Misc. files, Box 24, 1937 (1).

94 Eisenhower Diary, June 21, 1937, in Holt and Leyerzapf, *Eisenhower*, 335. See also Irish, "Dwight Eisenhower and Douglas MacArthur in the Philippines," 456.

95 Irish, "Dwight Eisenhower and Douglas MacArthur in the Philippines," 456.

96 Ibid., 457–58.

97 Eisenhower diary entry, October 8, 1937, in Holt and Leyerzapf, *Eisenhower*, 361.

98 Ibid., 363.

99 Efficiency Report, 12/31/37, Eisenhower 201 File, DDEL. See also Irish, "Dwight Eisenhower and Douglas MacArthur in the Philippines," 460–61.

100 Eisenhower diary entry, December 21, 1937, in Holt and Leyerzapf, *Eisenhower*, 371. See also Irish, "Dwight Eisenhower and Douglas MacArthur in the Philippines," 459–60, 462.

101 James, *Years of MacArthur*, Vol. I, 554.

102 MacArthur, *Reminiscences*, 106.

103 Eisenhower Diary, August 25, 1937, in Holt and Leyerzapf, *Eisenhower*, 335.

104 Cable, MacArthur to Craig, August 22, 1937, MMA.

105 MacArthur to Craig, September 16, 1937, as quoted in James, *Years of MacArthur*, Vol. I, 522.

106 Schaller, *Douglas MacArthur*, 38.

107 Perret, *Eisenhower*, 129.

108 Eisenhower, *At Ease*, 225.

109 Ibid., 226. See also Ambrose, *Eisenhower*, 112; and Irish, "Dwight Eisenhower and Douglas MacArthur in the Philippines," 463.

110 Eisenhower, *At Ease*, 226–27.

111 Ibid., 226.

112 Price, *Troy H. Middleton*, 121.

113 D'Este, *Eisenhower*, 247.

114 Aksel Nielsen, quoted in Miller, *Ike the Soldier*, 294.

115 D'Este, *Eisenhower*, 243–44; Holland, *Eisenhower Between the Wars*, 191–92.

116 Eisenhower, *At Ease*, 227.

117 Ibid., 227–28; D'Este, *Eisenhower*, 247.

118 Eisenhower to Emily Ord, January 31, 1938, in Holt and Leyerzapf, *Eisenhower*, 373.

119 Eisenhower to Mrs. E. T. Spencer, March 26, 1938, DDEL.

120 Quezon quoted in C. H. Tenney's tribute to Ord, USMA Archives, quoted in D'Este, *Eisenhower*, 247.

121 Eisenhower Diary, February 15, 1938, in Holt and Leyerzapf, *Eisenhower*, 376.

122 Miller, *Ike the Soldier*, 290.

123 Eisenhower Diary, February 15, 1938, in Holt and Leyerzapf, *Eisenhower*, 376.

124 Eisenhower Diary, June 18, 1938, in Holt and Leyerzapf, *Eisenhower*, 383, 384.

125 D'Este, *Eisenhower*, 239, 243; Holland, *Eisenhower Between the Wars*, 195, 197; and Perret, *Old Soldiers Never Die*, 215.

126 Eisenhower Diary, May 28, 1938, in Holt and Leyerzapf, *Eisenhower*, 381.

127 Miller, *Ike the Soldier*, 291.

128 Perret, *Old Soldiers Never Die*, 288.

129 Eisenhower Diary, April 14, 1938, in Holt and Leyerzapf, *Eisenhower*, 381.

130 Manchester, *American Caesar*, 183.

131 Eisenhower, *At Ease*, 224–25, 229.

132 D'Este, *Eisenhower*, 251–52; Blumenson, *Mark Clark*, 17.

133 Smith, *Lucius Clay*, 80–81.

134 Eichelberger, unpublished memoir, USAMHI. See also D'Este, *Eisenhower*, 248–49, 251.

135 Eisenhower Diary, November 10, 1938, in Holt and Leyerzapf, *Eisenhower*, 411.

136 Eisenhower Diary, March 9, 1939, in Holt and Leyerzapf, *Eisenhower*, 423.

137 Ricardo Trota Jose, *The Philippine Army, 1935–1942* (Manila: Ateneo De Manila University Press, 1992), 122. See also Perret, *Old Soldiers Never Die*, 221.

138 Manchester, *American Caesar*, 182.

139 Theodore Friend, *Between Two Empires: The Ordeal of the Philippines, 1929–1946* (New Haven, CT: Yale University Press, 1965), 192–93.

140 James, *Years of MacArthur*, Vol. I, 536.

141 Karnow, *In Our Image*, 276; Schaller, *Douglas MacArthur*, 40.

142 Eisenhower Diary, April 5, 1939, in Holt and Leyerzapf, *Eisenhower*, 430–31.

143 Eisenhower Diary, March 18, 1939, in Holt and Leyerzapf, *Eisenhower*, 424.

144 Perret, *Old Soldiers Never Die*, 218–19.

145 William Lee (Hasdorf Interview), 82, DDEL.

146 Hugh Parker, (Burg Interview), 12, 28, DDEL. See also Perret, *Old Soldiers Never Die*, 219–20.

147 *Christian Science Monitor*, November 2, 1938, as quoted in Manchester, *American Caesar*, 185.

148 James, *Years of MacArthur*, Vol. I, 537.

149 Eisenhower Diary, October 8, 1937, in Holt and Leyerzapf, *Eisenhower*, 363.

150 Smith, *Lucius Clay*, 78. See also Linn, *Guardians of Empire*, 240–41; and D'Este, *Eisenhower*, 240.

151 Miller, *Ike the Soldier*, 290.

152 James, *Years of MacArthur*, Vol. I, 555.

153 Eisenhower to Maj. Mark Clark, September 23, 1939, in Holt and Leyerzapf, *Eisenhower*, 447.

154 Eisenhower diary, September 3, 1939, in Holt and Leyerzapf, *Eisenhower*, 436.

155 Eisenhower, *At Ease*, 229. See also Holland, *Eisenhower Between the Wars*, 200.

156 Eisenhower, *At Ease*, 231.

157 Eisenhower, Letter to L. T. Gerow, October 11, 1939, DDEL, Pre-Presidential Papers, Box 46.

158 Holland, *Eisenhower Between the Wars*, 198.

159 Ambrose, *Eisenhower*, 117.

160 Karnow, *In Our Image*, 276.

161 MacArthur Letter to Eisenhower, December 9, 1939, DDEL, Pre-Presidential Papers, Box 74.

162 Miller, *Ike the Soldier*, 302; Ambrose, *Eisenhower*, 117.

163 MMA Interview with Eisenhower.

164 D'Este, *Eisenhower*, 255.

Chapter Eight: The Right Man in the Right Place at the Right Time

1 *Life*, January 3, 1944, 77.

2 Marshall to G. Edward MacGirvin, September 6, 1939, Marshall Papers, Box 31 (Pentagon Office-Correspondence), GCML.

3 Marshall to Gen. John J. Pershing, November 19, 1934, in Bland, *The Soldierly Spirit*, 446–47.

4 Robert L. Eichelberger Papers, Box 1, "Unpublished Memoirs," 197, USAMHI.

5 Weintraub, *15 Stars*, 88.

6 Katherine Marshall, *Together*, 18.

7 Marshall to Charles T. Lanham, October 29, 1934, in Bland, *The Soldierly Spirit*, 439.

8 Marshall to Maj. M. B. Ridgway, August 24, 1936, Ridgway Papers, Box 34D, USAMHI. See also Jonathan M. Soffer, *General Matthew B. Ridgway: From Progressivism to Reaganism, 1895–1993* (Westport, CT: Praeger, 1998), 22.

9 Puryear, *Nineteen Stars*, 61.

10 Pogue, *Education of a General*, 315–16; and Blumenson, *Mark Clark*, 41.

11 Blumenson, *Mark Clark*, 40–42.

12 Marshall, *Together*, 24. See also Cray, *General of the Army*, 121.

13 Pogue, *Education of a General*, 315, 319, 320; Cray, *General of the Army*, 124, 126, 130.

14 Bradley, *A General's Life*, 82.

15 Coffman, *The Regulars*, 373; Cray, *General of the Army*, 137.

16 Bland, *Marshall Interviews*, 87.

17 Quoted in Cray, *General of the Army*, 131.

18 Bland, *Marshall Interviews*, 86–87.

19 William W. Spencer Interview with Marshall, September 7, 1949, Marshall Papers, GCML.

20 Pogue, *Education of a General*, 326–29.

21 Ibid., 330; Cray, *General of the Army*, 139.

22 *Life*, January 3, 1944, 77.

23 Pogue, *Education of a General*, 332–33; Weigley, *History of the United States Army*, 419.

24 Richard M. Ketchum, *The Borrowed Years, 1938–1941: America on the Way to War* (New York: Random House, 1989), 540. See also Weigley, *History of the United States Army*, 419; and Cray, *General of the Army*, 146.

25 William S. Langer and S. Everett Gleason, *The Challenge to Isolation: 1937–1940* (New York: Harper, 1952), 14.

26 Stoler, *George C. Marshall*, 64, 69; Kennedy, *Freedom from Fear*, 402–3.

27 Joseph W. Alsop, *"I've Seen the Best of It": Memoirs* (New York: Norton, 1992), 139.

28 Robert Dallek, *Franklin D. Roosevelt and American Foreign Policy, 1932–1945* (Oxford: Oxford University Press, 1979), 29. See also Lynn Olson, *Those Angry Days: Roosevelt, Lindbergh, and America's Fight over World War II, 1939–1941* (New York: Random House, 2013), 202.

29 Bradley, *A General's Life*, 80.

30 Kennedy, *Freedom from Fear*, 406. See also Maury Klein, *A Call to Arms: Mobilizing America for World War II* (New York: Bloomsbury Press, 2013), 16.

31 Kennedy, *Freedom from Fear*, 406.

32 Olson, *Those Angry Days*, xx, 33.

33 Robert Sherwood, *Roosevelt and Hopkins: An Intimate History* (New York: Harper & Brothers, 1948), 134.

34 Mark S. Watson, *Chief of Staff—Prewar Plans and Preparations* (Washington, DC: U.S. Army Historical Division/GPO, 1950), 157. See also Weigley, *History of the United States Army*, 424.

35 Bland, *Marshall Interviews*, 297. See also John T. Nelsen II, *General George C. Marshall: Strategic Leadership and the Challenges of Reconstituting the Army, 1939–1941* (Carlisle Barracks, PA: Strategic Studies Institute, 1993), 21, 25.

36 Marshall, Speech to the Army Ordnance Association, October 11, 1939, 8, Marshall Papers, Box 110 (Pentagon Office-Speeches), GCML.

37 Watson, *Chief of Staff*, 164.

38 George C. Marshall, Address at Brunswick, MD, November 6, 1938, 6, Marshall Papers, Box 110 (Pentagon Office-Speeches), GCML.

39 Crosswell, *Beetle*, 215.

40 Marshall, Statement before the House of Representatives, Subcommittee on Appropriations, November 27, 1939, "Testimonies," 33–34, Marshall Papers, GCML.

41 Nelsen, 14, 64–65. One step Marshall declined to take was to establish an independent Air Force. "To my mind," he later explained, "it was utterly out of the question to organize a separate Air Corps in the course of the war. Arnold felt the same way I did. We just didn't have the trained staffs to function them." See Bland, *Marshall Interviews*, 315.

42 "The Reminiscences of General Anthony C. McAuliffe," Oral History Research Office, Columbia University, 1963, 49, as quoted in Cray, *General of the Army*, 195.

43 George C. Marshall to Brig. Gen. John McA Palmer, March 12, 1942, in Larry Bland, ed., *The Papers of George Catlett Marshall*, Vol. 3, *"The Right Man for the Job," December 7, 1941–May 31, 1943* (Baltimore: Johns Hopkins University Press, 1991), 129.

44 Bradley, *A General's Life*, 82–83.

45 Forrest C. Pogue, *George C. Marshall: Ordeal and Hope, 1939–1942* (New York: Viking, 1966), 8.

46 Crosswell, *Beetle*, 201.

47 Collins, *Lightning Joe*, 98.

48 Taylor, *Swords and Ploughshares*, 40.

49 Bradley, *A General's Life*, 83.

50 Ibid., 84.

51 "The Reminiscences of General Anthony C. McAuliffe," 47.

52 Taylor, *Swords and Ploughshares*, 40.

53 See Albert C. Wedemeyer, *Wedemeyer Reports!* (New York: Henry Holt, 1958), 62; "The Reminiscences of General Anthony McAuliffe," 67; and Taylor, *Swords and Ploughshares*, 40.

54 Cray, *General of the Army*, 194–95.

55 Russell A. Gugeler, *Major General Orlando Ward: Life of a Leader* (Oakland, OR: Red Anvil Press, 2009), 143.

56 Klein, *A Call to Arms*, 19.

57 William Frye, *Marshall, Citizen Soldier* (New York: Bubbs-Merrill, 1947), 273.

58 Bland, *Marshall Interviews*, 484.

59 Ibid., 574. See also Cray, *General of the Army*, 152.

60 Frederick Lewis Allen, "The Lesson of 1917," *Harper's*, September 1940, 344–46 , as quoted in Klein, *A Call to Arms*, 54.

61 Bernard Baruch, *The Public Years* (New York: Holt, Rinehart & Winston, 1960), 278.

62 Klein, *A Call to Arms*, 55. See also Nelsen, *General George C. Marshall*, 29–30.

63 John Morton Blum, *From the Morgenthau Diaries, Volume 2: Years of Urgency, 1938–1941* (Boston: Houghton Mifflin, 1965), 138–41. See also Nelsen, *General George C. Marshall*, 30.

64 Pogue, *Ordeal and Hope*, 30.

65 Bland, *Marshall Interviews*, 329.

66 Ibid., 329. See also Klein, *A Call to Arms*, 55.

67 Blum, *From the Morgenthau Diaries*, Vol. 2, 141–44.

68 Bland, *Marshall Interviews*, 331; Pogue, *Ordeal and Hope*, 32.

69 Samuel L. Rosenman, ed., *The Public Papers and Addresses of Franklin D. Roosevelt*, Vol. IX (New York: The Macmillan Company, 1941), no. 58.

70 Nelsen, *General George C. Marshall*, 32.

71 Ibid., 33.

72 Olson, *Those Angry Days*, 128, 160; and Stoler, *George C. Marshall*, 71.

73 Pogue, *Ordeal and Hope*, 53.

74 Hessel D. Hall, *North American Supply* (London: Her Majesty's Stationery Office, 1955), 132. See also Cray, *General of the Army*, 158.

75 Bland, *Marshall Interviews*, 317. See also Klein, *A Call to Arms*, 39.

76 Langer and Gleason, *The Challenge of Isolation*, 569.

77 Blum, *From the Morgenthau Diaries*, Vol. 2, 162–63. See also Stoler, *George C. Marshall*, 75.

78 Cray, *General of the Army*, 16.

79 The appropriations also funded 4,000 planes for the navy and the creation of a two-ocean navy. See Klein, *A Call to Arms*, 56, 81.

80 Ibid., 59, 81; Olson, *Those Angry Days*, 196–97.

81 Quoted in Nelsen, *General George C. Marshall*, 34.

82 Bland, *Marshall Interviews*, 299. See also Cray, *General of the Army*, 167; Nelsen, *General George C. Marshall*, 24, 35.

83 Gen. Thomas Handy Interview, 1974, U.S. Military History Institute, Carlisle, PA, section 4, 12.

84 Bland, *Marshall Interviews*, 610–11.

85 Stephen R. Taaffe, *Marshall and His Generals: U.S. Army Commanders in World War II* (Lawrence: University Press of Kansas, 2011), 4–5.

86 Cray, *General of the Army*, 174.

87 Marshall to Lt. Col. Edwin Harding, October 31, 1934, in Bland, *The Soldierly Spirit*, 440.

88 Eric Larabee, *Commander in Chief: Franklin Delano Roosevelt, His Lieutenants, and Their War* (New York: Harper & Row, 1987), 101.

89 Cray, *General of the Army*, 174.

90 Bland, *Marshall Interviews*, 306, 534. See also Cray, *General of the Army*, 174–75.

91 Pogue, *Ordeal and Hope*, 99.

92 Weigley, *History of the United States Army*, 426; Olson, *Those Angry Days*, 197, 210.

93 Bland, *Marshall Interviews*, 305.

94 Pogue, *Ordeal and Hope*, 60.

95 *Second Supplemental National Defense Appropriations Bill for 1941*, Hearings Before the Subcommittee of the Committee on Appropriations, United States Senate (Washington, DC: Government Printing Office, 1940), 22, 241.

96 *Newsweek*, August 5, 1940, 13–16, quoted in Klein, *A Call to Arms*, 82.

97 Olson, *Those Angry Days*, 213–14.

98 Ibid., 216–17.

99 Klein, *A Call to Arms*, 82–83; Stewart, *American Military History*, Vol. II, 71.

100 John G. Clifford, "Grenville Clark and the Origins of the Selective Service," *The Review of Politics*, January 1973, 31–32. See also Olson, *Those Angry Days*, 212.

101 Stoler, *George C. Marshall*, 76.

102 Pogue, *Ordeal and Hope*, 62.

103 Stoler, *George C. Marshall*, 76.

104 Mark W. Clark, *Calculated Risk* (New York: Harper & Brothers, 1950), 13.

105 Coffman, *The Regulars*, 380; Clark, 14.

106 Clark, 13. See also Blumenson, *Mark Clark*, 50–51.

107 McNair quoted in Weigley, *History of the United States Army*, 428.

108 Klein, *A Call to Arms*, 120, 250.

109 "Biennial Report of the Chief of Staff, July 1," in War Department, *Report of the Secretary of War to the President, 1941* (Washington, DC: GPO, 1941), 55. See also Weigley, *History of the United States Army*, 431–32; and Olson, *Those Angry Days*, 299–300, 357.

110 Russell D. Buhite and David W. Levy, eds., *FDR's Fireside Chats* (Norman: University of Oklahoma Press, 1992), 163–73.

111 Dallek, *Franklin D. Roosevelt*, 257.

112 James MacGregor Burns, *Roosevelt: The Soldier of Freedom, 1940–1945* (New York: Harcourt, Inc., 1970), 44–46. See also Crosswell, *Beetle*, 221.

113 Quoted in Gugeler, *Major General Orlando Ward*, 136.

114 Stoler, *George C. Marshall*, 81–82.

115 "LIFE on the Newsfronts of the World," *Life*, July 14, 1941, 20. See also Klein, *A Call to Arms*, 67, 98.

116 Quoted in Pogue, *Ordeal and Hope*, 157. See also Klein, *A Call to Arms*, 94, 141, 148, 215.

117 Kenneth S. Davis, *FDR: The War President, 1940–1943* (New York: Random House, 2000), 152. See also Dallek, *Franklin D. Roosevelt*, 267.

118 Ickes Diary, Vol. 3, 526–27, as quoted in Kennedy, *Freedom from Fear*, 494.

119 Burns, *Soldier of Freedom*, 65–66, 91.

120 Ibid., 84.

121 Blum, *From the Morgenthau Diaries*, Vol. 2, 275–76.

122 Pogue, *Ordeal and Hope*, 22–23.

123 Quoted in Olson, *Those Angry Days*, 341.

124 Watson, *Chief of Staff*, 338–39.

125 See Joseph Bendersky, *The "Jewish Threat": The Anti-Semitic Politics of the U.S. Army* (New York: Basic Books, 2000), 238; and Wedemeyer, *Wedemeyer Reports!*, 41.

126 Coffman, *The Regulars*, 377.

127 "Joint Board Estimates of United States Overall Production Requirements," September 11, 1941, as quoted in Cray, *General of the Army*, 201.

128 Kennedy, *Freedom from Fear*, 486; Coffman, *The Regulars*, 378; and Olson, *Those Angry Days*, 415.

129 Nelsen, *General George C. Marshall*, 39.

130 Marshall, *Together*, 91.

131 Bland, *Marshall Interviews*, 286.

132 "Biennial Report of the Chief of Staff of the United States Army, July 1, 1939 to June 30, 1941, to the Secretary of War," as quoted in Payne, *Marshall Story*, 128–29. See also Klein, *A Call to Arms*, 212–13.

133 Cray, *General of the Army*, 203–4; Nelsen, *General George C. Marshall*, 41.

134 *Life*, August 18, 1941, 17. See also Olson, *Those Angry Days*, 341.

135 See Stephen D. Westbrook, "The Railey Report and Army Morale, 1941," *Military Review*, June 1980.

136 Marshall to Brig. Gen. Asa L. Singleton, March 23, 1940, Marshall Papers (Pentagon Office, Selected), GCML.

137 Cray, *General of the Army*, 178; Olson, *Those Angry Days*, 341, 351.

138 Pogue, *Ordeal and Hope*, 148.

139 Davis, *FDR*, 252.

140 Nelsen, *General George C. Marshall*, 43.

141 *Retention of Reserve Components and Selectees in Military Service Beyond Twelve Months*, Hearings Before the Committee on Military Affairs, United States Senate, July 17, 1941 (Washington, DC: Government Printing Office, 1941), 3.

142 Cray, *General of the Army*, 209.

143 Ibid., 208.

144 Paul M. Robinett Diary, January 16 and 30, 1941, GCML.

145 Bland, *Marshall Interviews*, 355.

146 Stoler, *George C. Marshall*, 77.

147 Pogue, *George C. Marshall: Organizer of Victory, 1943–1945* (New York: Viking Press, 1973), 131.

148 Bland, *Marshall Interviews*, 303. See also Cray, *General of the Army*, 208.

149 Bland, *Marshall Interviews*, 303.

150 This result may have only stood thanks to Rayburn's mastery of arcane House procedure, through which he was able to prevent members from switching their votes. See Olson, *Those Angry Days*, 354–57; Cray, *General of the Army*, 210; and Klein, *A Call to Arms*, 214.

151 Nelsen, *General George C. Marshall*, 83.

152 Weigley, *History of the United States Army*, 436. See also Coffman, *The Regulars*, 373–74; Nelsen, *General George C. Marshall*, 81, 83.

153 "General: Man of the Year," *Time*, Vol. 43, January 3, 1944, 15–18.

154 Crosswell, *Beetle*, 206.

155 Andrew Roberts, *Masters and Commanders: How Four Titans Won the War in the West, 1941–1945* (New York: Harper, 2005), 30.

156 Weigley, *History of the United States Army*, 421.

Chapter Nine: Patton, Eisenhower, and the Largest Battle on U.S. Soil

1 Patton to Eisenhower, July 9, 1926, DDEL.

2 "Address to Officers and Men of the Second Armored Division," 4–5, May 17, 1941, Box 5, Patton Papers. See also Blumenson, *Patton*, 156.

3 Farago, Patton, 151.

4 "Address to Officers and Men of the Second Armored Division," 1.

5 Henry Cabot Lodge, *The Storm Has Many Eyes* (New York: W.W. Norton, 1973), 76.

6 George Marshall, Speech to the Army Ordnance Association, October 11, 1939, in Bland, Ritenour, and Wunderlin, eds., *"We Cannot Delay,"* 83.

7 Blumenson, *Patton Papers*, Vol. II, 970.

8 Totten, *The Button Box*, 240.

9 Patton, *The Pattons*, 229.

10 Ibid., 224–25.

11 Totten, *The Button Box*, 258. See also Jordan, *Brothers, Rivals, Victors*, 21, and Patton, *The Pattons*, 227–28.

12 Patton, *The Pattons*, 234. See also D'Este, *Patton*, 359.

13 D'Este, *Patton*, 362–63.

14 Totten, *The Button Box*, 286. See also Patton, *The Pattons*, 235–36, and Blumenson, *Patton*, 137–40.

15 D'Este, *Patton*, 366.

16 Patton, *The Pattons*, 243.

17 Blumenson, *Patton Papers*, Vol. II, 1048.

18 Dean A. Nowowiejski, "Adaption to Change: U.S. Army Cavalry Doctrine and Mechanization, 1938–1945" (Monograph, U.S. Army School of Advanced Military Studies, 1994), 13.

19 William J. Woolley, "Patton and the Concept of Mechanized Warfare," *Parameters*, Vol. 15, no. 3, 72.

20 George S. Patton Jr., "The Cavalry Man," 1921, GSP #49, Military Writings, 1921, as quoted in Woolley, "Patton and the Concept of Mechanized Warfare," 76.

21 George S. Patton Jr., "Book Review: The Future of the British Army," *Cavalry Journal* 38 (April 1929), 293. Patton was even more savage toward J. F. C. Fuller and B. H. Liddell-Hart, condemning the former for only having reached the rank of lieutenant colonel during the war, and simply dismissing the latter as a "hack." See Blumenson, *Patton Papers*, Vol. II, 938–39.

22 Blumenson, *Patton Papers*, Vol. II, 952.

23 George S. Patton Jr., "Mechanized Forces: A Lecture," *Cavalry Journal* 42 (Sept.-Oct. 1933), 8.

24 Blumenson, *Patton Papers*, Vol. II, 961.

25 George S. Patton Jr., and C .C. Benson, "Mechanization and Cavalry," *Cavalry Journal* 39 (April 1930), 234–40.

26 D'Este, *Patton*, 345–46.

27 Patton to Chynoweth, n.p., May 29, 1929, Box 1, Chynoweth Papers, USAMHI.

28 Blumenson, *Patton Papers*, Vol. II, 947.

29 Patton to Joyce, February 6, 1940, Kenyon A. Joyce Papers, USAMHI. See also Robert Bateman, "Was George S. Patton a Sleazy Suck-Up?" *Daily Beast*, May 1, 2016.

30 Christopher R. Gabel, *The U.S. Army GHQ Maneuvers of 1941* (Washington, DC: Center of Military History, 1991), 23–24; See also Coffman, *The Regulars*, 389.

31 Blumenson, *Patton Papers*, Vol. II, 1041.

32 Blumenson, *Patton Papers*, Vol. II, 1044.

33 Farago, *Patton*, 141, 145; D'Este, *Patton*, 381–82.

34 Robert W. Grow, "The Ten Lean Years: From the Mechanized Force (1930) to the Armored Force (1940)," *Armor* 96 (May-June 1987), 25.

35 Farago, *Patton*, 141, 142.

36 Coffman, *The Regulars*, 389–90.

37 Harry Semmes, *Portrait of Patton* (New York: Appleton-Century-Crofts, Inc., 1955), 8.

38 Donald E. Houston, *Hell on Wheels: The 2d Armored Division* (San Rafael, CA: Presidio Press, 1977), 43.

39 Isaac D. White, Oral History, October 29, 1977, White Papers, USAMHI.

40 Henry L. Stimson Diary, November 16, 1940, quoted in Hirshson, *General Patton*, 235.

41 Houston, *Hell on Wheels*, 64–65.

42 Blumenson, *Patton*, 156.

43 *Life*, July 7, 1941.

44 Leonard Mosley, *Marshall: Organizer of Victory* (London: Methuen, 1982), 189.

45 Adams, *General Jacob Devers*, 72.

46 Devers recounts this confrontation in two different sources: Reminiscences of General Jacob L. Devers, 96–98, November 18, 1974, DDEL; and Thomas Griess interview with Jacob Devers, tape 38, 19, Griess Research Collection, York County Heritage Trust, as quoted in Adams, *General Jacob Devers*, 73.

47 Adams, *General Jacob Devers*, 73.

48 Eisenhower to Hugh A. Parker, February 8, 1941, Miscellaneous Manuscripts, DDEL.

49 Eisenhower Philippine Diary, January 25, 1940, in Holt and Leyerzapf, *Eisenhower*, 460. See also Holland, *Eisenhower Between the Wars*, 209; D'Este, *Eisenhower*, 261; and Smith, *Eisenhower in War and Peace*, 151.

50 Eisenhower, *At Ease*, 236.

51 Miller, *Ike the Soldier*, 308–9. See also D'Este, *Eisenhower*, 262; and Maurine Clark, *Captain's Bride, General's Lady: The Memoirs of Mrs. Mark W. Clark* (New York, McGraw-Hill, 1956), 71–72.

52 Eisenhower, Fort Lewis Diary, September 26, 1940, in Holt and Leyerzapf, *Eisenhower*, 494.

53 Miller, *Ike the Soldier*, 309.

54 Ibid., 310.

55 Ibid.

56 Eisenhower Efficiency Report, June 30, 1940, DDEL.

57 Quoted in Eisenhower, *General Ike*, 35.

58 Eisenhower to Omar Bradley, July 1, 1940, in Holt and Leyerzapf, *Eisenhower*, 467.

59 Eisenhower to Leonard T. Gerow, August 25, 1940, DDEL. See also Perret, *Eisenhower*, 138.

60 Eisenhower to Everett Hughes, November 26, 1940, DDEL, in Holt and Leyerzapf, *Eisenhower*, 509–10.

61 Eisenhower to George S. Patton Jr., September 17, 1940, DDE papers, DDEL.

62 Patton to Eisenhower, October 1, 1940, DDE Papers, DDEL.

63 Patton to Eisenhower, November 1, 1940, DDEL.

64 Eisenhower to Mark Clark, October 31, 1940, DDEL.

65 Eisenhower to Maj. T. J. Davis, October 31, 1940, DDEL, in Holt and Leyerzapf, *Eisenhower*, 499.

66 Eisenhower, *At Ease*, 238.

67 Eisenhower to Leonard T. Gerow, November 18, 1940, Pre-Presidential Papers, DDEL. See also Ambrose, *Eisenhower*, 126.

68 Gerow to Eisenhower, November 18, 1940, Pre-Presidential Papers, DDEL.

69 Ambrose, *Eisenhower*, 126–27; D'Este, *Eisenhower*, p. 268.

70 Eisenhower Efficiency Report, March 5, 1941, DDEL.

71 Eisenhower Fort Lewis Diary, April 4, 1941, in Holt and Leyerzapf, *Eisenhower*, 516. See also Miller, *Ike the Soldier*, 318–19.

72 Eisenhower Efficiency Report, June 21, 1941, DDEL.

73 Eisenhower to Brig. Gen. Leonard T. Gerow, July 7, 1941, in Holt and Leyerzapf, *Eisenhower*, 529.

74 Marshall to Henry L. Stimson, May 3, 1941, in Bland, Ritenour, and Wunderlin, eds, *"We Cannot Delay,"* 492–93. See also Kevin C. Holzimmer, *General Walter Krueger: Unsung Hero of the Pacific War* (Lawrence: University Press of Kansas, 2007), 9–31; and Smith, *Eisenhower in War and Peace*, 164–65.

75 R. W. MacGregor to Krueger, August 31, 1964, Box 40, Krueger Papers, USMA Archives. See also D'Este, *Eisenhower*, 279.

76 Quoted in Holzimmer, *General Walter Krueger*, 44–45.

77 Krueger to Marshall, June 11, 1941, GCML, Marshall Papers (Pentagon Office, Selected).

78 Krueger to Maj. Gen. William S. Bryden, August 2, 1941, Box 3, Krueger Papers, USMA Archives.

79 Eisenhower to Brig. Gen. Leonard T. Gerow, July 18, 1941, in Holt and Leyerzapf, *Eisenhower*, 530.

80 Eisenhower to George Van Horn Moseley, August 28, 1941, Box 84, Pre-Presidential Papers, DDEL.

81 Eisenhower to Wade Haislip, August 1941, in Holt and Leyerzapf, *Eisenhower*, 537.

82 Lt. Col. Edwin T. Wheatley to Walter Krueger Jr., August 21, 1967, Box 3, Krueger Papers, as quoted in D'Este, *Eisenhower*, 275.

83 Eisenhower to George Van Horn Moseley, August 28, 1941, Box 84, Pre-Presidential Papers, DDEL.

84 U.S. Congress, House Subcommittee of the Committee for Appropriations, *War Department Military Establishment Bill FY 1942, Hearings*, 77th Congress, 1st session, 1941, 241, as quoted in Gabel, *U.S. Army GHQ Maneuvers*, 50–51.

85 Eisenhower to Gerow, July 18, 1941, in Holt and Leyerzapf, *Eisenhower*, 530. See also Holland, *Eisenhower Between the Wars*, 215–16.

86 Collins, *Lightning Joe*, 101.

87 Harmon, *Combat Commander*, 46.

88 Gabel, *U.S. Army GHQ Maneuvers*, 79–80; Perret, *Eisenhower*, 42.

89 Thaddeus Holt, "The Final Scrimmage," *MHQ—The Quarterly Journal of Military History* 4, no. 2 (Winter 1992), 36; and Mark Perry, "The Greatest War Games," *Military History* 25, no. 6 (February/March 2009), 52.

90 Quoted in Holt, "The Final Scrimmage," 36.

91 Eisenhower to Leonard Gerow, August 5, 1941, in Holt and Leyerzapf, *Eisenhower*, 538.

92 Eisenhower to Rupert Hughes, August 27, 1941, in Holt and Leyerzapf, *Eisenhower*, 540.

93 Coffman, *The Regulars*, 394.

94 Gabel, *U.S. Army GHQ Maneuvers*, 45–46, 49, 58.

95 Ibid., 45–47; Holt, "The Final Scrimmage," 33–34; and Calhoun, *General Lesley J. McNair*, 111–19, 229.

96 Gabel, *U.S. Army GHQ Maneuvers*, 48–49, 54.

97 Ibid., 64–67; Holzimmer, *General Walter Krueger*, 78, 80.

98 Gabel, *U.S. Army GHQ Maneuvers*, 67–68; Holzimmer, *General Walter Krueger*, 80.

99 Gabel, *U.S. Army GHQ Maneuvers*, 69–70.

100 Eisenhower to Maj. Gen. Kenyon Joyce, September 15, 1941, in Holt and Leyerzapf, *Eisenhower*, 543. See also Gabel, *U.S. Army GHQ Maneuvers*, 70–71; and Holzimmer, *General Walter Krueger*, 80.

101 Gabel, *U.S. Army GHQ Maneuvers*, 72–74; Holzimmer, *General Walter Krueger*, 82.

102 Gabel, *U.S. Army GHQ* Maneuvers, 74.

103 Ibid., 74–75; Holzimmer, *General Walter Krueger*, 82.

104 Holzimmer, 82; Gabel, *U.S. Army GHQ Maneuvers*, 79.

105 Gabel, *U.S. Army GHQ Maneuvers*, 79–80.

106 Miller, *Ike the Soldier*, 327. See also Gabel, *U.S. Army GHQ Maneuvers*, 84; and Holt, "The Final Scrimmage," 35.

107 Lee Kennett, *G.I. The American Soldier in World War II* (New York: Charles Scribner's Sons, 1987), 34. See also Holzimmer, *General Walter Krueger*, 93–94.

108 *New York Times*, September 17, 1941. See also Gabel, *U.S. Army GHQ Maneuvers*, 86; and Holzimmer, *General Walter Krueger*, 82, 84.

109 "Big Maneuvers Test U.S. Army," *Life*, October 6, 1941, 33–43.

110 Gabel, *U.S. Army GHQ Maneuvers*, 96; Holzimmer, *General Walter Krueger*, 85.

111 Gabel, *U.S. Army GHQ Maneuvers*, 97, 99; Holt, "The Final Scrimmage," 37–38; and Holzimmer, *General Walter Krueger*, 85.

112 Eisenhower to Gerow, September 25, 1941, in Holt and Leyerzapf, *Eisenhower*, 545.

113 Eisenhower, *At Ease*, 243–44. See also Gabel, *U.S. Army GHQ Maneuvers*, 100–101.

114 Hirshson, *General Patton*, 249–50. See also Gabel, *U.S. Army GHQ Maneuvers*, 101.

115 Gabel, *U.S. Army GHQ Maneuvers*, 101–2.

116 Ibid., 105.

117 Ibid., 107–8; Hirshson, *General Patton*, 250.

118 Gabel, *U.S. Army GHQ Maneuvers*, 108–10.

119 Ibid., 110.

120 Comments by Lt. Gen. L. J. McNair, 2nd Phase, GHQ-Directed Maneuvers, AG 353 (6-16-45) Sec 1-3, RG 407 NA, as quoted in Gabel, *U.S. Army GHQ Maneuvers*, 111.

121 Mark W. Clark, Oral History, Sec 1, 128, USAMHI.

122 Holland, *Eisenhower Between the Wars*, 220.

123 Gabel, *U.S. Army GHQ Maneuvers*, 193.

124 Walter Krueger to Edward F. McGlachlin Jr., November 7, 1941, Box 5, Krueger Papers, USMA, as quoted in Holzimmer, 93.

125 Gabel, *U.S. Army GHQ Maneuvers*, 119, 188.

126 Collins, *Lightning Joe*, 115.

127 Critique of 2nd Phase of GHQ-Maneuvers, "Clark's Copy," RG 337 57D, NA, as quoted in Gabel, *U.S. Army GHQ Maneuvers*, 166.

128 Pogue, *Ordeal and Hope*, 89.

129 "Second Battle of Carolinas," *Time*, December 8, 1941.

130 Adams, *General Jacob Devers*, 78; Gabel, *U.S. Army GHQ Maneuvers*, 25, 89–90, 120–21.

131 Adams, *General Jacob Devers*, 79.

132 Brig. Gen. Orlando Ward to Chief of Staff, December 2, 1941, Maneuvers memoranda, General Correspondence, RG 337 57, HQ AGF, NA, as quoted in Gabel, *U.S. Army GHQ Maneuvers*, 177.

133 D'Este, *Patton*, 401. Contemporary observers also argued that Lear badly mishandled the I Armored Corps in the Maneuvers' first phase. In a report delivered at the CGSS, it was suggested that had the I Armored Corps kept rolling on September 15 instead of waiting for the rest of Second Army, Leesville might have been captured and Third Army's flank turned. Additionally, this report questioned the use of the 2nd Armored Division to defend part of the line for three days when other reserve units were available. See Gabel, *U.S. Army GHQ Maneuvers*, 90.

134 Eisenhower to Brig. Gen. Leonard T. Gerow, September 25, 1941, in Holt and Leyerzapf, *Eisenhower*, 545.

135 Comments by Lt. Gen. L. J. McNair, 2nd Phase, GHQ-Directed Maneuvers, AG 353 (6-16-45) Sec 1-3, RG 407 NA, Army AG Decimal File 1940–45, NA, as quoted in Gabel, *U.S. Army GHQ Maneuvers*, 115.

136 Gabel, *U.S. Army GHQ Maneuvers*, 115.

137 Collins, *Lightning Joe*, 114. See also D'Este, *Eisenhower*, 280.

138 Holland, *Eisenhower Between the Wars*, 218; Blumenson, *Patton*, 156, 159.

139 Holland, *Eisenhower Between the Wars*, 219.

140 Drew Pearson and Robert S. Allen, "Its Stonewall Krueger," *Washington Post*, October 2, 1941.

141 Robert S. Allen to Walter Krueger, September 29, 1941, Eisenhower Pre-Presidential Papers, 1916–1952, Misc. File, Box 25, 1941 (Aug-Sep).

142 Walter Krueger, *From Down Under to Nippon: The Story of Sixth Army in World War II* (Washington, DC: Combat Forces Press, 1953), 4.

143 D'Este, *Eisenhower*, 280.

144 Eisenhower, *At Ease*, 244.

145 Krueger wrote: "I wanted a man there to look after things. I always felt that the commander of his [Chief of Staff] should always be at headquarters." See Holzimmer, *General Walter Krueger*, 77.

146 Blumenson, *Mark Clark*, 54; Perret, *Eisenhower*, 142–43.

147 Eisenhower to Leonard T. Gerow, October 4, 1941, in Holt and Leyerzapf, *Eisenhower*, 547.

148 Eisenhower to Mark Clark, October 7, 1941, in Holt and Leyerzapf, *Eisenhower*, 550.

Chapter 10: Generals at War

1 Marshall to General Malin Craig, September 19, 1939, in Bland, Ritenour, and Wunderlin, eds, *"We Cannot Delay,"* 59.

2 Quoted in Pogue, *Ordeal and Hope*, 229.

3 Marshall, *Together*, 99.

4 Eisenhower, *Crusade in Europe*, 13–14.

5 Eisenhower Diary, February 16, 1942, in *The Papers of Dwight David Eisenhower* (Baltimore: The Johns Hopkins Press, 1970) [Hereafter cited as *Eisenhower Papers*], Vol. I, 109.

6 Ambrose, *Eisenhower*, 134–36, 144.

7 Eisenhower to Brig. Gen. Spencer Akin, June 19, 1942, *Eisenhower Papers*, Vol. I, 343.

8 Watson, *Chief of Staff*, 124–25.

9 Theodore H. White, *In Search of History* (New York: HarperCollins, 1978), 108.

10 MacArthur to Steven Early, March 21, 1941, as quoted in Petillo, *Douglas MacArthur*, 196–97.

11 Marshall to Gen. Douglas MacArthur, June 20, 1941, MMA, Record Group 1.

12 Karnow, *In Our Image*, 383.

13 MacArthur to John Callahan O'Laughlin, October 6, 1941, O'Laughlin Papers, LOC.

14 Karnow, *In Our Image*, 284.

15 Bradley Chynoweth, Oral Reminiscences, 14, MMA, RG 49, Box 2.

16 Chynoweth, *Bellamy Park*, 197.

17 MacArthur to George Grunert, September 7, 1941, MMA.

18 MacArthur to George Marshall, September 9, 1941, MMA.

19 James, *Years of MacArthur*, Vol. I, 600.

20 Cray, *General of the Army*, 230, 231.

21 Jonathan Wainwright, with Robert Considine, *General Wainwright's Story* (Garden City, NY: Doubleday & Company, 1946), 13. See also Francis B. Sayre, *Glad Adventure* (New York: MacMillan, 1957), 221; and Schaller, *Douglas MacArthur*, 53–54.

22 Perret, *Old Soldiers Never Die*, 246.

23 Lewis H. Brereton, *The Brereton Diaries* (New York: William Morrow, 1946), 21.

24 Chynoweth, *Bellamy Park*, 193.

25 Wilson, *General Marshall Remembered*, 246.

26 Weintraub, *15 Stars*, 21.

27 Pershing quoted in Manchester, *American Caesar*, 218. See also Perret, *Old Soldiers Never Die*, 263.

28 Geoffrey Perret, *There's a War to Be Won: The United States Army in World War II* (New York: Random House, 1991), 54. See also Manchester, *American Caesar*, 235–36.

29 Marshall to Douglas MacArthur, February 23, 1942, MMA.

30 Herman, *Douglas MacArthur*, 423, 431; Cray, *General of the Army*, 297–99; Kennedy, *Freedom from Fear*, 259.

31 Mark S. Watson, *Saturday Review*, September 26, 1964. See also Stoler, *George C. Marshall*, 119.

32 Manchester, *American Caesar*, 322.

33 Taaffe, *Marshall and His Generals*, 328.

34 Perret, *Old Soldiers Never Die*, 355. See also Manchester, *American Caesar*, 322, 326, 327, 413.

35 Taaffe, *Marshall and His Generals*, 54; Perret, *Eisenhower*, 160.

36 Tuchman, *Stilwell and the American Experience in China*, 208, 225, 231–32.

37 Tuchman, *Stilwell and the American Experience in China*, 238.

38 Tuchman, *Stilwell and the American Experience in China*, 240, 243, 245.

39 Stilwell quoted in Pogue, *Ordeal and Hope*, 366. See also Kennedy, *Freedom from Fear*, 671–73.

40 Michael Schaller, *The U.S. Crusade in China, 1939–1945* (New York: Columbia University Press, 1979), 169.

41 Tuchman, *Stilwell and the American Experience in China*, 506.

42 D'Este, *Eisenhower*, 359.

43 Eisenhower to Thomas Handy, December 7, 1942, in *Eisenhower Papers*, Vol. 2, 811.

44 Ambrose, *Eisenhower*, 214, 231.

45 Bradley, *A General's Life*, 130.

46 Eisenhower to John S. D. Eisenhower, February 19, 1943, *Eisenhower Papers*, Vol. 2, 965–66.

47 Rick Atkinson, *An Army at Dawn: The War in North Africa, 1942–1943* (New York: Henry Holt, 2002), 346.

48 Eisenhower to Charles Moreau Harger, April 23, 1943, *Eisenhower Papers*, Vol. II, 1100.

49 Blumenson, *Patton*, 167, 181, 184, 188.

50 Eisenhower to Marshall, August 24, 1943, *Eisenhower Papers*, Vol. II, 1353.

51 Ibid.

52 Stephen Ambrose, *The Supreme Commander: The War Years of General Dwight D. Eisenhower* (Garden City, NY: Doubleday, 1970), 229.

53 Eisenhower, *Crusade in Europe*, 201.

54 Eisenhower to Charles Gailey, September 19, 1942, *Eisenhower Papers*, Vol. 1, 568; see also D'Este, *Eisenhower*, 317.

55 Ambrose, *Eisenhower*, 237.

56 Perret, *Eisenhower*, 236, 238.

57 Price, *Troy H. Middleton*, 135.

58 Perry, *Partners in Command*, 220.

59 Ibid., 304.

60 Quoted in Blumenson, *Mark Clark*, 3.

61 Rick Atkinson, *The Day of Battle: The War in Sicily and Italy, 1943–1944* (New York: Henry Holt, 2007), 184.

62 Winston S. Churchill, *The Second World War*, Vol. 4: *The Hinge of Fate* (Boston: Houghton Mifflin, 1950), 813. See also Puryear, *Nineteen Stars*, 173.

63 Stimson Diary, September 15, 1943.

64 Puryear, *Nineteen Stars*, 339–40.

65 John J. Pershing to Franklin D. Roosevelt, September 29, 1943, in Marshall Library File, GCML.

66 Forrest C. Pogue, *George C. Marshall: Organizer of Victory, 1943–1945* (New York: Viking, 1973), 320.

67 Weintraub, *15 Stars*, 209.

68 Ambrose, *Eisenhower*, 271.

69 Pogue, *Organizer of Victory*, 321.

70 Eisenhower, *Crusade in Europe*, 206–7.

71 Cray, *General of the Army*, 450; Perry, *Partners in Command*, 295.

72 Eisenhower to Marshall, August 24, 1943.

73 Eisenhower, "Memorandum for Personal File," August 11, 1943, in Butcher, 6/11/43, DDEL (Pre-Presidential Papers, Box 166); See also Taaffe, *Marshall and His Generals*, 76, 79, 81.

74 William M. Hoge, *Engineers Memoirs* (Washington, DC: Office of History, U.S. Army Corps of Engineers, 1993), 204. See also Ambrose, *Eisenhower*, 296; and Taaffe, *Marshall and His Generals*, 104, 172, 175.

75 Troy Middleton, interview by Orley B. Caudill, 1975, An Oral History with Troy H. Middleton, Mississippi Oral History Collection, University of Southern Mississippi, 37, as quoted in Taaffe, *Marshall and His Generals*, 179.

76 Omar N. Bradley, *A Soldier's Story*, (New York: Henry Holt and Company, 1951), 229. See also Jordan, *Brothers, Rivals, Victors*, 250.

77 Eisenhower to Marshall, April 29, 1944, in *Eisenhower Papers*, Vol. 3, 1837.

78 Eisenhower to Marshall, April 30, 1944, in *Eisenhower Papers*, Vol. 3, 1840.

79 Eisenhower to Marshall, April 29, 1944.

80 Perret, *Eisenhower*, 324–25.

81 Patton Diary, May 18, 1943; and April 26, 1944, Patton Papers, LOC, Boxes 2 & 3; See also Jordan, *Brothers, Rivals, Victors*, 160.

82 Eisenhower, *At Ease*, 270. See also Ambrose, *Eisenhower*, 298.

83 *Eisenhower Papers*, Vol. III, 1841, fn2.

84 Jordan, *Brothers, Rivals, Victors*, 354.

85 Ambrose, *Eisenhower*, 324.

86 Russell Weigley, *Eisenhower's Lieutenants: The Campaign of France and Germany, 1944–1945* (Bloomington: Indiana University Press, 1981), 160.

87 Bradley, *A Soldier's Story*, 355–56.

88 Taaffe, *Marshall and His Generals*, 262–64.

89 Quoted in Clay Blair, *The Forgotten War: America in Korea, 1950–1953* (New York: Times Books, 1987), 559.

90 Taaffe, *Marshall and His Generals*, 169, 264; Weintraub, *15 Stars*, 294.

91 Eisenhower, *Crusade in Europe*, 350. See also Ambrose, *Eisenhower*, 344, 366; Perret, *Eisenhower*, 324.

92 Perret, *Eisenhower*, 329.

93 William K. Goolrick and Ogden Tanner, *Battle of the Bulge* (Alexandria, VA: Time-Life Books, 1979), 111.

94 Perret, *Eisenhower*, 329.

95 Perry, *Partners in Command*, 342.

96 Rick Atkinson, *The Guns at Last Light: The War in Western Europe, 1944–1945* (New York: Henry Holt and Company, 2013), 489. Atkinson labels Bradley's claim of more than a quarter-million enemy casualties as "presposterous."

97 Forrest C. Pogue, *The Supreme Command: The United States Army in World War II* (Washington, DC: U.S. Army, 1989), 389.

98 Marshall to Eisenhower, May 8, 1945, *Eisenhower Papers*, Vol. 6, 14–15.

99 Eisenhower to Marshall, May 8, 1945, *Eisenhower Papers*, Vol. 6, 14.

100 Bradley, *A General's Life*, 205.

101 Bernard Law, Viscount Montgomery of Alamein, *The Memoirs of the Field-Marshal the Viscount Montgomery of Alamein, K.G.* (Cleveland: The World Publishing Company, 1958), 484.

102 Winston Churchill to George C. Marshall, May 17, 1945, GCML.

103 Rick Atkinson, *The Day of Battle: The War in Sicily and Italy, 1943–1944* (New York: Henry Holt and Company, 2007), 50.

104 Ridgway, *Soldier*, 29.

105 *Annual Report of the Secretary of War, 1935* (Washington, D.C.: GPO, 1935), 72.

106 Muth, *Command Culture*, 202.

107 "Conversations with General J. Lawton Collins," *Combat Studies Institute Report*, No. 5, 1983, 3; Matthew Ridgway Interview, August 29, 1969, 88, USAMHI, Ridgway Papers, Box 88.

108 Blumenson, *Patton Papers*, Vol. II, 734.

109 Truman Smith, Unpublished Memoirs, GCML.

Epilogue

1 Blumenson, *Patton*, 268.

2 Ambrose, *Eisenhower*, 423.

3 Perry, *Partners in Command*, 369.

4 Farago, *Patton*, 196–97.

5 Quoted in Manchester, *American Caesar*, 580.

6 James F. Schnabel and Robert J. Watson, *The History of the Joint Chiefs of Staff and National Policy: 1950–1951, The Korean War: Part One*, 274.

7 *U.S. News & World Report*, December 1, 1950.

8 MacArthur to Martin, March 20, 1951, MMA. See also Perret, *Old Soldiers Never Die*, 366–68.

9 Manchester, *American Caesar*, 401.

10 Weintraub, *15 Stars*, 457.

11 MacArthur, *Reminiscences*, 401–5.

12 Perret, *Old Soldiers Never Die*, 574.

13 Hearings before the Senate Committee on Armed Services and Committee on Foreign Relations, *Military Situation in the Far East*, 1951, 82nd Congress, 1st session, pt. 1, 323–724, 732.

14 Weintraub, *15 Stars*, 464; Stoler, *George C. Marshall*, 188–89.

15 C. L. Sulzberger, *A Long Row of Candles: Memories and Diaries, 1934–1954* (New York: MacMillan, 1969), 769; Manchester, *American Caesar*, 683, 686.

16 Ambrose, *Eisenhower*, 409.

17 Montgomery, *Memoirs*, 484.

18 David McCullough, *Truman* (New York: Simon & Schuster, 1992), 914.

19 Fred I. Greenstein, *The Hidden Hand Presidency: Eisenhower as Leader* (New York: Basic Books, 1982), 91.

20 William I. Hitchcock, *The Age of Eisenhower: American and the World in the 1950s* (New York: Simon & Schuster, 2018), 109.

21 Tuchman, *Stilwell and the American Experience in China*, 531. See also Weintraub, *15 Stars*, xiii, 368; and Stoler, *George C. Marshall*, 145, 147.

22 Joseph McCarthy, *America's Retreat from Victory* (New York: Devin-Adair Publishing Company, 1951), 143.

23 *Congressional Record*, September 15, 1950, 14913–14914.

24 Dwight D. Eisenhower, *The White House Years: Mandate for Change* (Garden City, NY: Doubleday, 1963), 318. See also Ambrose, *Eisenhower*, 548.

25 Kevin McCann quoted in Ambrose, *Eisenhower*, 563. See also Weintraub, *15 Stars*, 404.

26 John S. D. Eisenhower, *General Ike*, 109.

27 Forrest C. Pogue, *Marshall: Statesman, 1945–1959* (New York: Viking, 1987), 497–98.

Index